THE BUILDINGS OF ENGLAND
BERKSHIRE
NIKOLAUS PEVSNER

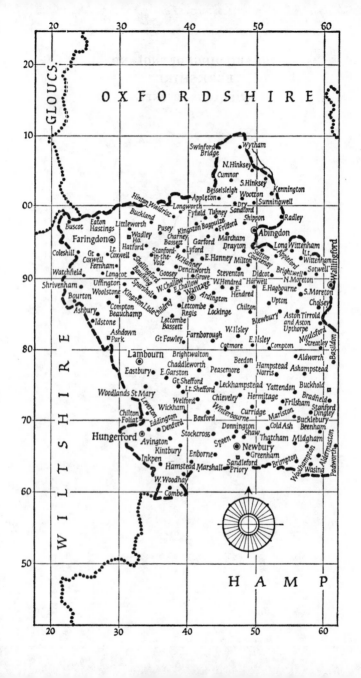

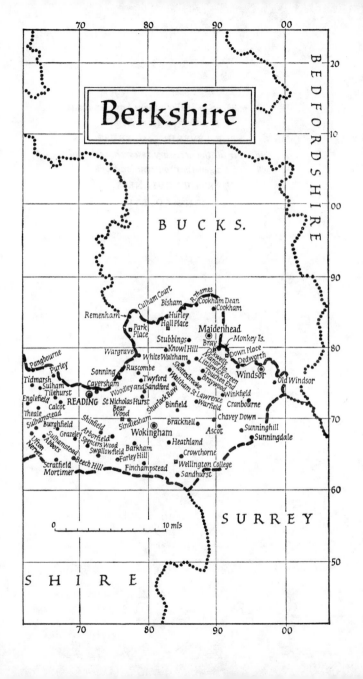

Berkshire

BEDFORDSHIRE

20

10

00

B U C K S.

90

Culham Court
Bisham
R. Thames
Cookham Dean
Cookham
Remenham
Hurley
Hall Place
Park
Place
Stubbings
Maidenhead
Bray
Monkey Is.
Wargrave
Knowl Hill
Down Place
Pangbourne
White Waltham
Elwells
Dedworth
Purley
Ruscombe
Manor Ho.
Littlewick Green
Windsor
Tidmarsh
Sonning
Twyford
Shottesbrooke
Touchen End
Old Windsor
Suhlam
Caversham
Woodley and
Sandford
Waltham St Lawrence
Braywood
Tilehurst
Englefield
St Nicholas Hurst
Shurlock Row
Winkfield
Calcot
Bear
Wood
Binfield
Warfield
Cranbourne
Theale
Sulhamstead
Shinfield
Sindlesham
Chavey Down
Burghfield
Arborfield
Bracknell
Grazeley
Wokingham
Ascot
Sunninghill
Ufton
Abbots
Spencers Wood
Heathland
Sunningdale
Nervet
Swallowfield
Barkham
Crowthorne
Stratfield
Mortimer
Beech Hill
Farley Hill
Wellington College
Finchampstead
Sandhurst

READING

0   10 mls

SURREY

60

50

S H I R E

70   80   90   00

70   80   90   00

The publication of this volume has been made
possible by a grant from
THE LEVERHULME TRUST
to cover all the necessary research work and
by a generous contribution from
ARTHUR GUINNESS,
SON & CO. LTD

THE BUILDINGS OF ENGLAND

Berkshire

BY

NIKOLAUS PEVSNER

★

PENGUIN BOOKS

PENGUIN BOOKS

Published by the Penguin Group
27 Wrights Lane, London W8 5TZ, England
Viking Penguin Inc., 40 West 23rd Street, New York, New York 10010, USA
Penguin Books Australia Ltd, Ringwood, Victoria, Australia
Penguin Books Canada Ltd, 2801 John Street, Markham, Ontario, Canada L3R 1B4
Penguin Books (NZ) Ltd, 182–190 Wairau Road, Auckland 10, New Zealand

Penguin Books Ltd, Registered Offices: Harmondsworth, Middlesex, England

—

First published 1966
Reprinted 1975, 1988

—

ISBN 0 14 0710.30 2

—

—

Made and printed in Great Britain
by Butler & Tanner Ltd, Frome and London
Set in Monotype Plantin

CHI NON FA, NON SBAGLIA

CONTENTS

★

Map References

★

The numbers printed in italic type in the margin against the place names in the gazetteer of the book indicate the position of the place in question on the index map (pages 2–3), which is divided into sections by the 10-kilometre reference lines of the National Grid. The reference given here omits the two initial letters (formerly numbers) which in a full grid reference refer to the 100-kilometre squares into which the country is divided. The first two numbers indicate the *western* boundary, and the last two the *southern* boundary, of the 10-kilometre square in which the place in question is situated. For example Abingdon (reference 4090) will be found in the 10-kilometre square bounded by grid lines 40 and 50 on the *west* and 90 and 00 on the *south*; Pangbourne (reference 6070) in the square bounded by grid lines 60 and 70 on the *west* and 70 and 80 on the *south*.

The map contains all those places, whether towns, villages, or isolated buildings, which are the subject of separate entries in the text.

FOREWORD

Berkshire is the first county I had to travel and describe after my wife had died. She had driven me through nearly all the preceding counties, had done all the day-to-day planning, and more and more also visited the buildings. Four eyes see more than two, and her eyes were quicker than mine. I fear this volume will have suffered from that private circumstance. The journey could not have the zest, the fun, the cursing in common which all belonged to so well tried a partnership. I am all the more grateful to those who offered their help and thus made the book possible. My son Dieter drove me for two weeks, my senior assistant Mrs Judy Nairn for one, and Mr John Newman for another. Where would I have been without them?

And where would I have been without Mrs Helen Braham (then Miss Helen Butterworth) and Mrs Sonya Wood (then Miss Sonya Hopkins), who shared the tedious job of extracting all the information which has to be available before I can take over? To them also I express my gratitude. Then there are those good friends Mrs Camilla Israel and Sir Allen Lane and Lady Lane who made it possible for us to exchange for more than a week the pub or hotel for a temporary home, The Old Kennels, Bucklebury Slade, and Priory Farm, Beech Hill.

But the number of those to whom I owe a debt of gratitude is much greater. The cases grow where recognition is needed so often that initials are used to indicate indebtedness. To the familiar NBR for the National Buildings Record, MHLG for the Ministry of Housing and Local Government, GR for the Goodhart-Rendel index of Victorian churches, TK for Sir Thomas Kendrick's lists of Victorian stained glass, PF for Mr Peter Ferriday's index of Victorian restorations, I have now to add GS for Mr Geoffrey Spain's invaluable and rapidly growing lists of tenders from the architectural magazines, and BC for the Rev. Basil Clarke's extracts from Berkshire ecclesiastical papers which he most kindly offered me for use.

Basil Clarke in addition examined the whole of the galleys for Victorian accuracy, Mr Neville Hadcock examined the Newbury galleys, and Messrs Maurice Bond, the Hon. Custodian of the Muniments of St George's Chapel, and Robert Mackworth-Young, the Windsor Castle Librarian, after having conducted me in the greatest detail over Windsor Castle and answered any number of tedious questions, finally read the galley proofs as well and commented on them. I also wish to thank Mr S. H. Horrocks, the Reading Borough Librarian, Mr W. J. Smith, the Berkshire County Archivist, Mr J. C. Powell, the Maidenhead Borough Librarian, and Mr M. Hocking, the Abingdon Librarian. Mr S. E. Rigold of the Ancient Monuments Department, Ministry of Public Building and Works, helped me on timber roofs, Denis Evinson on Catholic building in the C19, Stuart Smith on Alfred Waterhouse, John Hills on Bradfield College, the Rev. and Mrs H. F. D. Sparke on Wytham.

Mr Derek Simpson, in addition to the introduction on prehistory, did the gazetteer on prehistoric and Roman antiquities. Mr Terence Miller's notes on Berkshire geology will be found on p. 47.

After these I must thank more generally all those rectors and vicars who have helped me by answering letters about their churches and by examining proofs, and those owners or occupiers of houses who have allowed me entry and also replied to inquiries. I owe it to the latter to state here that description of a house in my gazetteer does not necessarily mean its being open to the public.

The principles on which the following gazetteer is founded are the same as in the twenty-nine volumes of the Buildings of England which precede it. I have myself seen everything that I describe. Where this is not the case the information obtained by other means is placed in brackets. Information ought to be as complete as the space of the volume permits for churches prior to c.1830 and all town houses, manor houses, and country houses of more than purely local interest. Movable furnishings are not included in secular buildings, though they are in churches. Exceptions to the latter rule are bells, hatchments, chests, chairs, plain fonts, and altar tables. Royal arms, coffin lids with foliate crosses, and brasses of post-Reformation date are mentioned occasionally, church plate of after 1830 only rarely. Village crosses are omitted where only a plain base or stump of the shaft survives. As for churches and chapels of after 1830, I had to make a selection, and this is dictated by architectural value or by significance otherwise in the light of architectural history. The same applies to secular buildings of the C19 and C20.

Finally, as in all previous volumes, it is necessary to end the foreword to this with an appeal to all users to draw my attention to errors and omissions.

INTRODUCTION

PREHISTORY AND ROMAN ANTIQUITIES
BY DEREK SIMPSON

The earliest evidence for human settlement in Berkshire is the numerous flint tools – hand axes – of the Old Stone Age (Palaeolithic), abundant both in public museums and private collections. Unfortunately many of them are unlocated, but the comparatively small number whose contexts are known all come from gravel deposits (e.g. Abingdon, Earley, Reading), indicating settlement in river valleys. Most of the axes are of Acheulean type and belong to the second of the three major periods which came between those of intense cold during the Ice Age. A few rare finds of implements and flakes of Mousterian type probably belong to the last interglacial phase and might indicate the presence of Neanderthal man, as this industry is associated with the physical type on the Continent, although no fossil human remains have been found in Berkshire.

The gradual retreat of the ice and increasingly warm conditions at the end of the last glaciation produced a considerable change in the environment in which prehistoric man lived, notably in the encroachment of forests, first of birch and pine and later of oak. To meet these changes technological improvements and a new pattern of settlement were evolved. The Mesolithic groups, like their Palaeolithic predecessors, were hunters, but now their quarry were the roe and red deer and wild pig, which they pursued through the forests with the aid of dogs, their only domesticated species. Evidence for these hunters comes from numerous sites in the county. Their flint axes, the so-called Thames Picks, are recorded, chiefly as surface finds, from the Thames Valley, with a particular concentration below the Goring Gap. These tools reflect the forested conditions in which their makers lived and represent a positive reaction to the spread of forests and the problem of forest clearance. The settlement sites so far discovered all lie in the tributaries of the Thames, possibly because in the main valley the sites have been covered by later alluvium. The most important group is in the Kennet Valley (e.g. Newbury, Thatcham, Speen). At Thatcham, on the shores of a small lake, Mesolithic hunters had cleared the pine and birch to provide living space. No structures other than hearths were found during the excavation of the site, and presumably the group lived in tents which have left no trace. The lakeside was first settled *c.* 8000 B.C. and was occupied intermittently by hunters over a period of about a thousand years.

The first farming communities settled in Britain in the middle of the fourth millennium. The primary areas of settlement were the lightly forested downs of Wessex and Sussex, and the Berkshire Downs, the N extension of the former province, appear to have been included in this primary area, although the characteristic monuments of this first farming culture – the Windmill Hill Culture – are not so numerous in the county as in the chalk lands to the S. These first farmers practised a mixed economy of cereal production and stock breeding, and it is with the latter activity that the causewayed camps are to be associated. The majority of these camps occupy hill-top situations on the chalk, but the only Berkshire example of the type, at Abingdon, is a low-lying site on the Thames gravels. The interrupted construction of its ditches with numerous causeways is typical, but here use has been made of the natural barriers of the two rivers, the ditches blocking access to the spur which they form. Occupation of causewayed camps appears to have been intermittent and primarily in the autumn, when herds would be rounded up within the confines of the camp for identification, barter, and slaughter. The camps contain little in their interiors to suggest use as permanent settlements, the most consistently recurring features being storage pits, as at Abingdon. The axes of stone from Great Langdale, Westmorland, found at Abingdon also indicate that these periodic gatherings within the camps provided opportunities for trade, and probably too for religious activities. Elsewhere in the county the former presence of these farming communities is attested by flint axes, ranging from roughly flaked, unfinished specimens to the carefully ground and polished final products. Most of these axes occur as stray finds, but in some cases they are associated with a considerable quantity of knapping debris and other flint tools (e.g. Uffington, West Woodhay).

Another category of monument characteristic of the culture is 3a the earthen long barrow, represented by the sites of Wayland's & 2 Smithy, Ashbury and Gallows Hill, Combe. The long barrow is an elongated earthen mound, generally wedge-shaped in plan, the material being obtained from flanking quarry ditches. Beneath the broader, generally E, end of the mound are found multiple inhumation burials. The thirteen partially articulated skeletons beneath the Wayland's Smithy barrow lay in a ridged-roofed mortuary enclosure of wood and stone and similar mortuary buildings have been noted under long barrows elsewhere in Britain. At this site too the relative chronological relationship between the earthen long barrow and the stone-built chambered tomb was established. After the construction of the long barrow the mound was enlarged by the digging of two new flanking ditches and a megalithic tomb and façade added to its s end. The material of this enlarged mound was revetted with a series of large sarsen slabs set along its flanks. This structure, and a probable second monument at Lambourn, are N outliers of a distinctive group of megalithic tombs centred on the Cotswold region and lands bordering the estuary of the Severn. The material from them suggests that they overlap chronologically with the causewayed camps and earthen long barrows and that many features of their material culture and economy are common to both groups.

Later Neolithic groups, characterized by coarse, poorly fired pottery richly ornamented with cord, bird-bone, and fingernail impressions and by a series of flint types which appear to owe much to Mesolithic flint-knapping traditions, have left no distinctive monuments in the county. Their economy appears to have been based on stock raising, perhaps supplemented by hunting, both dictating a semi-nomadic existence. Traces of their occupation have been found in the upper filling of the ditches of the Abingdon causewayed camp, and their characteristic flint equipment, including scrapers, knives, and arrowheads, was associated with flint-knapping debris in several parts of the county marking the sites of temporary encampments. The distribution of axes from the axe factories of Craig Llwyd in North Wales, Langdale in Westmorland, and from several outcrops in Cornwall is probably the work of these groups, whose nomadic existence would make them familiar with the natural routes across Britain along which these and less durable trade goods passed.

From c. 2000 B.C. the last stone-using peoples, the Beaker Folk, began to settle in Berkshire, penetrating the county by way of the Thames valley from landfalls in East Britain. A number of the earthen round barrows on the downs (e.g. The Seven Barrows, Lambourn) covered inhumation burials accompanied by their characteristic drinking cups. Two cultural groups are represented in the finds from the region: one is marked by Bell Beakers with smooth, S-shaped profile, the second by pots with tall necks separated from a globular body by a marked constriction.

Each group has its own characteristic ornaments and weapons, but the latter are largely represented as stray finds in the county, such as the stone battle-axes from Aston Upthorpe and North Hinksey. The battle-axes are part of the equipment of the Long-Necked-Beaker groups, which also includes beautifully flaked flint daggers (an example comes from one of the Lambourn Seven Barrows), copies of the rarer riveted bronze forms, and finely worked barb-and-tang arrowheads of flint. The distribution of finds shows a concentration on the chalk downs and valley gravels, and many of the ring ditches, representing the ditches of ploughed-out barrows, are probably to be attributed to these Late Neolithic settlers.

In the Early Bronze Age (*c.*1650–1400 B.C.), Berkshire marks the N limits of the brilliant Wessex Culture with its centre in South Wiltshire and Dorset. None of the many round barrows have so far produced examples of the exotic material which characterizes the culture, but the forms of the monuments themselves – bell, disc, and saucer barrows – indicate that the Berkshire Downs are to be included within its province. The finds from the few excavated sites suggest a more impoverished society than that at the heart of the culture in the S. Collared urns containing cremations embody, both in their form and in the rite itself, the continuing Neolithic ceramic and funerary traditions overlain by the foreign-derived culture of the Wessex chieftains. Graves provide almost all the material evidence although a small ditched enclosure on Rams Hill, Kingston Lisle, has produced collared-urn sherds. The site is probably a stock enclosure.

The later phases of the Bronze Age are even less well represented by structures and finds. Admittedly one can perceive the increasing proficiency of the bronze smith in the growing variety and complexity of his products, although these are largely represented in the county by stray finds. Occasional hoards like that from Yattendon Court indicate that the area benefited incidentally from the reorganization of the bronze industry in the Later Bronze Age. Most of the bronzes come from near the Thames, however, lost by merchants plying their trade along this great natural route. Some of the groups of small rectangular fields termed Celtic Fields which occur on the downs may be the work of Late Bronze Age groups, as has been demonstrated elsewhere, but most probably belong to the Early Iron Age, when evidence suggests a considerable increase in population.

In the middle of the C4 a village of small, circular, timber-built houses was constructed on Blewburton Hill (Aston Tirrold), with their associated grain storage pits defended by a palisade. Similar open village settlements are known from the area, e.g. Frilford (*see* Garford). These first iron-using peoples appear to have been peasants subsisting on mixed farming but capable of purchasing the fine haematite-coated pottery of the Wessex Iron Age A Culture. The threat of invasion from the s by more war-like Iron Age B groups must have prompted the construction of the first fortifications on hilltops *c.*300 B.C. (e.g. Blewburton Hill). The evidence from Blewburton points to the abandonment of these hilltop sites after their initial fortification, and the mixed A/B Culture must have lived in comparative security until the end of the c2, when a threat of invasion again produced a wave of hill-fort building. The relationship of these new forts – e.g. Grimsbury Tower (Hermitage), Bussock Wood (Winterbourne), Caesar's Camp (Bracknell) – is with the sw in Sussex and Kent and suggests a movement of peoples from that area reacting to the threat of Belgic, Iron Age C, invasion.

For the c1 the evidence of archaeology can be supplemented by that of the native coinage and classical references, and something of the politics and personalities of the period can now be discerned. About 50 B.C., after the great revolt in Gaul, one of the Belgic tribes, the Atrebates, under their leader Commius, fled to Britain, where their territory embraced the modern county of Berkshire. The material remains of these newcomers are scan-tily represented in the county. The Atrebates settled in Britain as a tribal unit, and, like other Belgic peoples in the sE, appear to have been better organized both socially and economically than the Iron Age groups to the N and W. The most striking economic change was the introduction of a native gold and silver coinage, although the economic unit appears still to be the isolated farm-stead defined by a rectilinear ditched enclosure, e.g. Robin Hood's Arbour, Maidenhead and Windmill Hill, Hinton Wal-drist. The most famous monument of the latter part of the pre-historic Iron Age in the region is the great chalk-cut figure of a stylized horse at Uffington, whose form can be matched on the3b contemporary coinage. Hillfort building was not a major aspect of Belgic culture, and the changing settlement pattern is marked by occupation of the heavier clay soils of the valleys which had previously been shunned. Tribal centres, too, tend to occur in low-lying areas associated with natural routes and rivers (a quirk of modern political geography has detached from the county the Atrebatic tribal centre at Silchester). The re-fortification of some of the Berkshire hillforts however (Blewburton) was probably in response to a new threat from their powerful neighbours to the N of the Thames, the Catuvellauni. The suzerainty of the Commian dynasty over Berkshire was brought to a close c. A.D. 25, when the Catuvellauni under their great king Cunobelin crossed the Thames to annex the N part of the kingdom. Their conquest was short-lived, and within two decades the area had been incorporated in the Roman Empire.

The impact of Roman life and Roman culture has left no outstanding monuments. There are no towns in the area, although lesser settlements existed at Thatcham and Reading, the latter probably serving as the river port of Silchester (Calleva Atrebatum), the cantonal capital. Villas – e.g. Hampstead Norris (*see* Hermitage) and Letcombe Regis (*see* Wantage) – are again few, in part perhaps because of the absence of any major population centres which would provide a market for their produce. The only modern excavation of one of these sites is that at Cox Green, Maidenhead, built in the C2 and subject to a number of structural alterations and additions which continued until the late C4. The commoner form of rural unit was the native farmstead, e.g. Uffington and Ashbury (*see* Ashdown Park), which differed little in form from its prehistoric antecedents and was romanized only to the extent that its inhabitants now used industrially produced pottery and metal tools and trinkets of Roman character. This same continuity from prehistoric to Roman times is also reflected in religious ideas. At Frilford (*see* Garford) a Romano-British temple was built on the site of an earlier Iron Age shrine, emphasizing the continuing sanctity of the site.

As elsewhere, the history of the last decades of Roman rule in Berkshire is obscure, but the Saxon penetration by way of the Thames must have been achieved early in the C5. Their presence is marked by a series of flat cemeteries (e.g. Frilford, Abingdon) and indirectly by the great linear earthworks known as Grim's Bank (*see* Aldermaston), built by the Britons, centred on Silchester, as a bulwark against Saxon incursions. Apart from cemeteries, the only contemporary sites of note are the villages at Radley and Sutton Courtenay. At the latter site over forty small rectangular huts were excavated. Some of these squalid buildings may have been dwellings, but others produced evidence of weaving and pottery manufacture.

THE BUILDINGS OF BERKSHIRE
BY NIKOLAUS PEVSNER

Berkshire is half home county, half West Country. Even the

way people speak leaves no doubt about that. The E as far as Reading is now commuters' or weekenders' territory. The W is what it is in its own right. The Downs link it to Wiltshire. The sense of remoteness which they create, of being alone with nature, is something one can never experience nearer London. And Berkshire landscape has more variety even than this; for there are also the sandy heath and pinewoods bordering on Bagshot Heath and the military areas, the well wooded hilly country between Newbury and the Thames, a country of commons and prep schools, and the Thames-side estates of the mansions of nobility and the rich and the villas of the affluent and more and more of bungalows and flats.

As varied as the landscape are the building materials. A note on Berkshire geology is appended on p. 47. Here it is enough to say that the county does not participate in the oolitic limestone, England's best stone. Instead stones had to be used qualitatively so indifferent as the chalk and the sarsen stones of the Downs, the ragstone available locally or near by, the rare, dark brown conglomerate from the Bagshot sands, and the ubiquitous flint.

Reading Abbey, by far the most important monastic establishment of Berkshire, is of flint. It was founded for Cluniacs – the most powerful and active order of the time – by Henry I in 1121 and was his favourite abbey. But Abingdon Abbey had the most venerable history, having been founded in the C7 and refounded by St Aethelwold. Of Abingdon we have only a gatehouse and a minor administrative range left, of Reading also a gatehouse and dramatic but uneloquent ruins.* Of other [34a] monastic houses no more survives. The county anyway was never rich in them. Besides Reading and Abingdon there were only three other Benedictine houses, Hurley, where the Norman nave of the church and the refectory range exist, Steventon, a cell of Bec-Hellouin, where a timber-framed hall range is supposed to have belonged to the guest quarters, and Wallingford, where nothing has remained. The house of Benedictine nuns at Broomhall also is completely gone. The Augustinian Canons had three houses: Bisham, Poughley, and Sandleford. At Bisham, taken over in 1337 from the Templars, whose great hall, porch, and solar can still be seen, the Augustinians added a cloister, highly irregular in site and appearance. At Poughley near Chaddleworth there is just a bit of walling, at Sandleford

* Fragments from Reading Abbey, or said to be from Reading Abbey, are at St James Reading, St Giles Reading, and Park Place.

one C14 roof. Otherwise nothing is left, except for a substantial part of the Greyfriars church of Reading. This was the only Franciscan house in the county, and the Dominicans did not have even one.

And if Berkshire is poor in major monastic remains (and has no cathedral), it is in the secular field as poor in major towns. Reading is the only one with more than 100,000 inhabitants (1961: 120,000), and Reading is a town for which one can safely predict fast growth. Otherwise there are Maidenhead with only 35,000, Windsor with 27,000, Newbury with 20,000, Abingdon with 14,000, and Wokingham with 11,000, and heaven preserve Berkshire from a 200,000 new town between Newbury and Hungerford.

For it will be seen that altogether Berkshire is a moderate county, a county which offers to the traveller, whether he looks at nature or buildings, plenty of enjoyment, but few great thrills – none in fact in architecture except for Windsor Castle.

These introductory pages are bound to reflect that situation. For ANGLO-SAXON art and architecture, to start with, there is hardly anything to summarize: the W tower of Wickham, the lower parts of the crossing tower of Cholsey, a doorway *ex situ* at Aston Tirrold, a large coffin lid inscribed to Aegelwardus who died in 1017 at Stratfield Mortimer, and – the only visually ₁₃rewarding item – a tympanum, also early C11, at Strattenborough Castle Farm Coleshill which is of the Viking style called by the archaeologists Ringerike.

Of NORMAN there is quantitatively of course more, but qualitatively also not much: the wide early C12 nave of Buckland, the rare plan of Cholsey with transepts provided with apsed E chapels and probably a major E apse as well, nave, aisles, and crossing at Lambourn, the rib-vaulted crossing and rib-vaulted chancel of Blewbury, the complete village church of Avington, including a formerly rib-vaulted chancel – the ribs carrying beakhead decoration – the splendid (if over-restored) apse arch and chancel arch of St Leonard Wallingford, a fragmentary W façade at St Nicholas Abingdon, and just one round tower at Great Shefford. Of doorways there are plenty, but really richly decorated ones are confined to Bucklebury, Lambourn, and Tidmarsh. The most interesting tympanum is that with a scene ₁₄ₐdoubtfully connected with the Alexander romance at Charney Bassett. Nearly all these are Late Norman jobs. PILLAR PISCINAS have been preserved oddly often. As for FONTS, one is used to finding Norman ones everywhere, many completely

plain (and in that case not even listed in my gazetteer), many
also decorated. Of these the majority have just blind arcading,
straightforward or intersecting; in some cases the space under
the arches is used for stylized leaf motifs or the space in the
spandrels. At Avington there are instead eleven figures. At 14b
Childrey is a Norman lead font of *c.*1200 with little figures of
bishops, at Long Wittenham another, with rosettes, wheels, and
also little bishops.* The standard Purbeck 'table-top' type with
shallow blank arches curiously enough is preserved only once,
in spite of the relative proximity of the Isle of Purbeck (Shrivenham). Of other church furnishings only a few Late Norman
DOORS with iron hinge-enrichments can be referred to (Buckland, Sparsholt, Kingston Lisle).

But the finest door is mid C13 and led into the galilee of 16b
Henry III's EARLY ENGLISH Royal Chapel at Windsor Castle.
It is covered in scroll-work all over.‡ Unfortunately nearly all
has been swept away of that major job, begun just a few years
before Westminster Abbey, about 1240. We have no more than
the doorway to which this door belongs, two blank arches l. and
r., and one range of blank arches with a sumptuous doorway of
the cloister adjoining the chapel to the N. On the walls of the
galilee and the cloister two exquisite painted heads have been
uncovered, mid C13, and as good as any C13 PAINTING anywhere in England. But of the SECULAR BUILDINGS of Henry
III at Windsor Castle we can see no more than one plain N
window of a N–S hall range in the Lower Ward. Windsor Castle
was built by William the Conqueror, but it was then a motte-
and-bailey castle of a standard type – lower bailey – motte –
upper bailey – and had no stone buildings. It was Henry II who
built the first stone walls, of which quite something can still be 35
recognized by the expert, in spite of a hundred and fifty years
of sweeping restorations, and he built the shell keep, i.e. the
Round Tower, as well. Of the royal dwelling in the Upper Ward
there are again only mute walls. Henry III's towers are recognizable by their semicircular or nearly semicircular form. Of
all he provided for the royal apartment in the Upper Ward we
have nothing telling. But this scanty evidence can be strengthened
by looking round the MANOR HOUSES. Looking round castles,
other than Windsor, would not pay. Only at Donnington is the
late C14 gatehouse of a once oblong castle with angle towers, 37

* Woolstone has a lead font as late as C14.
‡ Other scrolled iron door-hinges at Blewbury (C13 ?), Buckland, Faring- 16a
don (C13* of splendid quality), Frilsham, Lockinge, Uffington (C13).

licensed in 1386, and at Wallingford some fragments of towers
and of the collegiate church on the castle. Other castles need
not engage our attention at all. So to the manor houses. Norman
Hall at Sutton Courtenay has its main range with a doorway
and lancets of c.1200, Appleton Manor a sumptuous doorway
with stiff-leaf capitals of about the same date or a little later,
Bisham Abbey, then a preceptory of the Templars, a big, rib-
vaulted late C13 porch, the S wall of the substantial great hall,
and a solar window, the Chequer Room of Abingdon Abbey its
34b late C13 chimneystack with tiny lancet openings, and Charney
Bassett the solar wing with chapel of c.1280. Fyfield Manor with
hall, porch, and service wing takes us out of the C13 into the
early C14.

This is more of a harvest than the EARLY ENGLISH
CHURCHES can yield. Admittedly, if one includes minor things
in one's study, one can build up a nice sequence of transition
from Late Norman to mature Early English, watching how the
square abacus of round piers becomes octagonal and then
round, the round arch becomes pointed, the moulded or heavily
roll-moulded arch is replaced by the slightly and then the fully
chamfered or double-chamfered arch, and so on. However, one
must be careful. In Berkshire the square abacus still appears
with waterleaf capitals, i.e. capitals of c.1170–80, and even with
pointed arches (e.g. Appleton). Stiff-leaf is complete before
1200 – that is proved by the date 1196 at St Laurence Reading.
Early stiff-leaf is easily distinguished from mature stiff-leaf, the
former having much of the bell of the capital visible, the latter
rich and varied in directions. The time after 1250 is recognizable
by plate tracery and then bar tracery and finally by the arrival
of intersecting and Y-tracery and the pointed-trefoiled lights
and their grouping in three stepped ones under one arch, as
they liked it especially in Berkshire. All this belongs to the end
of the C13, and all this is general considerations. Individual
buildings worth including in a summary are few. The most
interesting church and one highly idiosyncratic is Uffington.* It
has a grand porch and a crossing tower, and the chancel was
meant to be vaulted. Uffington is of c.1250, Wantage, also cruciform, is a little later. Several villages have earlier C13 chancels
with lancet windows and groups of three in the E wall (e.g.
Chieveley, Cholsey). Tidmarsh has a polygonal apse which is a
great rarity in England, Abingdon a proud N tower, Little Cox-

8b   * Even if one assigns the windows of the transept chapels to the C17.

well a double bellcote, Baulking a very plain stone rood screen, Sparsholt – again something rare – an E.E. wooden rood screen, St George's Chapel Windsor a fragment of a beautiful Purbeck marble font with a head and stiff-leaf, and several churches have WALL PAINTING of the C13, some of it – e.g. the Virgin at Hampstead Norris – very beautiful, some – especially the scenes at Ashampstead – very interesting. Of masonry patterns and tendril patterns there are also examples. An initial examination of funerary monuments can still be delayed; for they link up with the Dec rather than the E.E. phase.

For the DECORATED we are a little better provided with dates. This is the story they tell. A chantry was founded at North Moreton in 1299. The E and W windows of the chapel have the characteristic motif of arches upon arches, the motif familiar from the Wells Lady Chapel, and not yet any ogees.*
Money was left to the building of the Greyfriars at Reading in 1311. What remains of the church has reticulated side by side with intersecting tracery. At Shottesbrooke in 1337 a college was established, and the (still cruciform) church has exuberant flowing tracery. The only tracery which can compare with this is that of the chancel of Warfield, which is very rich inside as 4a well. Another richly appointed chancel is that of Sparsholt. Stanford-in-the-Vale has Kentish tracery, Cumnor and North Hinksey wilful tracery of straight-sided lozenges under a straight-sided arch. Finally, to conclude with another date, the N chapel at East Hagbourne is entirely Dec, yet was founded by a husband and wife who died in 1403 and 1414. 1375 is the earliest date one would permit oneself to suggest, and that is a late date for Dec, especially since Perp had certainly entered the county by 1350.

Edward III created the Order of the Garter in 1348. In 1350–4 he built at Windsor the chapter house and possibly the chapel for his order, the latter as a replacement of Henry III's chapel. He also built a lavish porch from the NW into Henry 4b III's cloister, and nearly rebuilt the cloister. The porch with a lierne-vault and blank wall decoration is a demonstrative piece of the transition from Dec to Perp, but in the cloister with its tracery and the one remaining window of the chapter house the PERPENDICULAR style is complete, just about fifteen to twenty years after it had been introduced at St Paul's and Gloucester. Mr Harvey has recently made out a case for attributing the

* The same motif occurs at Chilton and Cholsey.

chapel (i.e. what is now the Albert Memorial Chapel), always assigned to Henry VII, also to Edward III, with the tracery of its tall windows and its polygonal apse inspired by Lichfield Cathedral.

If this chapel is the major monument of the Early Perp in Berkshire, St George's Chapel is the major monument of the Late Perp, and of course one of the major monuments of the style in all England. It is one of the four royal chapels of c.1440 to c.1520 which epitomize the best in late medieval English architecture. Henry VI started with Eton and King's in the 1440s. They were not continued while he was in eclipse. Only when he was firmly established did Edward IV return to them; but his own enterprise was St George's Chapel, begun in 1475. It was completed only by Henry VII towards the end of his reign, and he also probably completed or remodelled Edward III's chapel. St George's Chapel is visually as thrilling outside as inside. Outside what makes it unique is the position of the transept exactly halfway between W end and E end, a demonstration of balance which shows that England was getting ready for the Renaissance, and the polygonal closing of the transept, taken over perhaps from the polygonal apse of Edward III's chapel and done now with so much conviction that it was re-echoed in the E chapel and the W chapels. These features combine to make of St George's a building to be taken in at one go and broadwise and not in the W–E way of medieval progress. Internally St George's is emphatically Late Perp in its stress on depressed arches and a vault of the same depressed section. The vault is in fact almost a coved ceiling, with lierne stars in the *plafond* and palm-frond ribs up the coving. Fan-vaulting, which was to culminate in Bath Abbey and King's College Chapel, occurs only in the aisles. Vaulting in the aisles apparently started about 1480, but the main vaults are by *William Vertue* and belong only to 1506 etc.

Anything after St George's Chapel is of course an anti-climax, but the Newbury parish church is a substantial, prosperous building, all of a piece, which would hold its own among parish churches anywhere. No wonder, if one remembers Jack of Newbury (*see* p. 179). The church is of *c.*1500–32. Abingdon rebuilt its parish church too, very spacious, with double aisles, but architecturally unenterprising. The piers are octagonal throughout, with concave sides – a motif familiar from Campden and North Leach. Octagonal piers with straight sides and double-chamfered arches are the standard elements of Perp, and indeed

of Dec, arcades. In the gazetteer they will be called just that
and left alone. Another general remark may here come in. Roofs
are usually of the tie-beam and kingpost type, and they also are
often not mentioned in the gazetteer. Otherwise no generalization
can be made, except that village churches often have the timber
bell-turrets with shingled broach spires so frequent in Surrey
and Sussex too,* and that in large parts of the county the Victorian restorers had enough money available to replace most
external features which would have given interest to the buildings. After this a brief catalogue of worthwhile Perp items: the
complete Perp crossing tower of Shrivenham, the Waynflete
Chantry transported from Magdalen Chapel Oxford to Theale
(its arches are straight-sided, its tracery of the lozenge kind
which the Dec style had invented), the timber arcade of Radley,‡
and the two detached chapels with priest's house at East
Hendred and Fyfield.§

FURNISHINGS of course are more frequent now, and MONU-
MENTS must take their place with them. DECORATED first, i.e.
from the late C13 to the mid C14. As regards monuments, Berkshire has first and foremost the series of eight at Aldworth, six
of them under ornate (if drastically restored) canopies. One of 25a
the ladies is in the arrangement of the drapery still in the C13
cathedral tradition, one of the men is in a posture of which one 25b
might not have considered even the Dec style capable. Not only
are his legs crossed – this convention is universal in England,
even if wholly absent on the Continent – but his whole body
writhes and twists. Yet some stiff-leaf on the slab itself makes a
very early Dec date a necessity. At Childrey is a cross-legged
knight in a recess with ballflower, that characteristic early C14
motif, at Sparsholt are three oaken effigies (and others at Bark- 26a
ham and Burghfield). Cross-legged stone effigies also at Burghfield and Sparsholt. Didcot has a late C13 mitred abbot of
Purbeck marble, Long Wittenham an amazing late C13 miniature 17b
stone effigy built into a piscina. In Hampstead Norris church is
a mysterious relief, over 2 ft high, of a man on horseback, also 15
late C13, and very accomplished. What did it belong to? Of the
late C13 fragment at Ardington we also do not know what it
belonged to. Then PAINTING and the beautiful early C14
Annunciation at Enborne and some C14 figures at Aldermaston

---

* Stone spires are not lacking, but Berkshire is not a spire county. The
most prominent example is perhaps Abingdon.
‡ Another, of 1592, at Winkfield.
§ Detached Perp chapels also at Newbury and Thatcham.

and Kingston Lisle, and STAINED GLASS with the S chapel E
18a window of North Moreton of *c.*1300–10, and one of the two
fairly complete windows in the county. The other is the great W
21 window of St George's Chapel, and that of course is long past
the end of Dec.

So to the PERPENDICULAR in the matters of FURNISHINGS
and monuments. St George's Chapel has also interesting
heraldic GLASS of the late C15, and it has the finest WOODWORK
19 by far in the stalls with their misericords, made by *William
Berkeley* and others in 1478–85, and extremely skilfully restored
and supplemented by *Henry Emlyn* in 1787–90. The stalls have
high canopies, exceptional poppyheads with whole scenes carved
in relief, relief carvings in the tympana and spandrels of the
traceried desk fronts, and innumerable misericords. The carving
is naïve and not at all courtly. But set against the stall backs are
the Garter Plates, ENAMEL plaques with the arms of the
Knights of the Garter, a unique set stretching in time from the
C14 to the C20. The quality of some of them is exquisite. Stalls
with misericords, though minor ones, are also at Wantage. The
18b best of the Perp wooden screens is at Warfield, Perp stone
screens are in the transept chapels of St George's (with the hemp-
bray of Sir Reginald Bray), and a great part of the exquisite
iron screen of Edward IV's chantry (by the Cornish blacksmith
John Tresilian) is again in St George's Chapel. This is without
doubt the finest piece of C15 smith's work in England. Of iron
also the eminently curious almsbox in St George's with the
initial h repeated on it, a sign that it was meant for donations to
the cult of Henry VI, when this had established itself for a short
time after the king's body had been brought from Chertsey in
1484. The best late medieval GLASS is that of *c.*1460 at Ockwells
Manor, all armorial, the best late medieval PAINTING the ceiling
20a of one of the chancel chapels at Abingdon which dates from the
late C14. The two bishops from the Urswick Chantry at Windsor
are early C16 and good too, the paintings in the Hastings
Chantry of 1503 are thoroughly bad, those in the Oxenbridge
Chantry of 1522 are indifferent and certainly the work of a
Fleming.

Chantries really ought to be listed as MONUMENTS. St
George's Chapel has two more, the Beaufort Chapel being the
counterpart to the Urswick Chapel, i.e. early C16, and that odd
little excrescence in the angle between S transept and S chancel
aisle, Bishop King's Chantry of 1492–6. Why he, a canon like
others and apparently no special benefactor, should have been

allowed this one addition to the superb unity of the chapel
remains a mystery. The only effigies to go with any of these
chapels are those of the Earl of Worcester †1526 in the Beaufort
Chapel. They are of alabaster, and Berkshire has quite a good
series of alabaster monuments, from that at Wantage †1361 to
Sir Thomas Fettiplace †c.1442 at Little Shefford and Lord
Roos †1513 at Windsor and Sir George Forster (his wife died 27
in 1526) at Aldermaston, both the last-named ones with
mourners. But the most moving monument is that of Sir John
Golafre †1442 at Fyfield with the cadaver on a tier below the 26b
effigy, the type introduced in France c.1400 and established in
England by Bishop Fleming's Monument at Lincoln Cathedral
of c.1435.* BRASSES need no special mention in the county,
although there are about eighty-five effigies of before 1550.‡
But one other type of Perp monument may in conclusion be
referred to, although it is also a national rather than local type:
the tomb recess of Purbeck marble, made no doubt on the isle
and exported to whoever paid for them. They have a tomb-chest,
angle shafts, and a canopy with pendant arches or a plain, very
depressed and almost straight horizontal arch, vaulting inside,
and the effigies of brass on the lid of the tomb-chest or against
the back wall. Such monuments survive in Berkshire at Bisham,
Childrey, St Nicholas Hurst, Englefield (c.1500), Cookham
(†1517), Little Shefford (†1524), and also Faringdon (†1547),
St George's Chapel Windsor (†1551), and Cumnor (c.1572).
These are amazingly late dates, and they may be explained by
the pirating of an existing tomb or Easter Sepulchre. But it
remains a fact that Berkshire did not accept the Italian Renaissance with enthusiasm.

SECULAR BUILDINGS show that too. In that field we have
not looked round for anything yet after the C13. What is worth
recording? It is rather a *mixtum compositum*. First at Windsor
Castle more work on the fortifications by Edward III, including 35
the heightening of the Round Tower, and by Henry VIII,
including the Great Gate. The College meanwhile built a high
hall for the Vicars Choral in 1415–16, but otherwise nothing in
stone. Timber-framed are the Horseshoe Cloister w of the
chapel (which is now so thoroughly by *Sir George Gilbert Scott*)
and a canon's house now called Merbeck and which has a good

---

* Almost as moving in its own strange way is the Throkmorton Monument 28a
(†1535) at Shottesbrooke with the deceased appearing as if he were lying in
a stone coffin.

‡ Counting couples etc. as one.

hall roof. Both have the infilling of brick, but brick otherwise
did not establish itself in Berkshire as early as, say, in London
and at Hampton Court. Altogether timber-framing remained a
widespread technique, even occasionally for so major a house as
38 Ockwells Manor of 1446/66, a courtyard house of interesting
and unusual planning features and with a delightful (if also
much restored) façade. As a rule the interest of timber-framed
buildings does not show externally, and so my gazetteer may
not always do justice to the most deserving ones. The NBR for
instance has a list of cruck houses and cottages in Berkshire.
Only a few of them have been taken over here (e.g. two at Long
Wittenham). Some of the best roofs must however be listed:
the C14 roof of the hall at Middle Farm Harwell, the C15 roof of
the great hall of the so-called guest house of Steventon Priory,
and the C14 roof of the hall at The Abbey, Sutton Courtenay.
The Abbey is a C14 courtyard house and preserves e.g. one
major window with flowing tracery. Compton Beauchamp is a
courtyard house too, but has no more of our period now than
one early C16 window. Wytham Abbey is early C16 and had
originally two courtyards. Of the surviving details the best is an
oriel window. Hendred House East Hendred has a big C15
chimneypiece in the hall (apart from a C13 chapel, of which two
lancets are evidence).

36b   That leaves as a postscript Christ's Hospital Abingdon,
founded in 1446, with a wooden cloister in front of its one long
range, such as those of the Canons' Cloister and the Horseshoe
at Windsor and, even more similar, the courtyard of Ockwells
Manor of the same years as Christ's Hospital. A second postscript must be two BARNS, one internally perhaps the finest in
England – the Great Coxwell barn of the C14 – the other only a
36a shadow of its former self, the Cholsey barn which was built about
1200, pulled down in 1815, and later partly and not satisfactorily
re-erected. It was the largest barn in Europe, 303 ft long (Reading Abbey Church was 375 ft long), and had stone piers to divide
nave from aisles. The mighty roof went down from a height of 51
to a mere 8 ft.

     Where is the dividing line between Gothic and RENAISSANCE
in Berkshire? Its importance can be exaggerated. The Italian
Renaissance was introduced by the Court as a fashion of ornament rather than a new conception of art and architecture. When
that began to form, in the Elizabethan Age, it was more indebted
to the Perpendicular, to English tradition, and to the Nether-
lands, than to the Mediterranean. Even so, it is worth investi-

gating where and when the Italian Renaissance made its first appearance. For Berkshire the answer is clear. In the N transept of St George's Chapel remains a fragment of a decorative frame of a wall panel which is of coloured glazed maiolica or fayence, i.e. the della Robbia technique introduced in England by *Giovanni da Majano* in the roundels of Roman Emperors on the gateways of Hampton Court in 1521. He must have done this frame – one probably of several – as well, and so the date we are looking for is presumably about 1520–5.* The next monument is Henry VIII's oriel inside St George's Chapel with Gothic arches but Renaissance balusters, undated but probably of *c*.1530. The next actual date is 1533, the date of the death of Sir Thomas Unton, whose alabaster monument at Faringdon has colonnettes, wreaths, and shell-niches, i.e. typical Early Renaissance elements. But after that nothing followed immediately. In monuments the Essex Monument at Lambourn – date of death 1558 – is, if anything, less Renaissance than that at Faringdon. But from 1560 onwards the EARLY ELIZABETHAN style began to spread, and this included Quattrocento motifs on pilasters and friezes. The examples are the surviving frieze of the Perkyns Monument at Ufton Nervet – date of death 1560 – and a chimneypiece at Bisham Abbey of about 1560. The house, 39a converted from the Templars' preceptory and Augustinian abbey, has stepped brick gables, and windows with mullions and a transom or a mullion-and-transom cross and a shallow pediment.

Berkshire has little to offer of ELIZABETHAN AND JACO-BEAN ARCHITECTURE AND ART. Englefield House, much enlarged and internally completely changed in the C19, and Shaw House, completed in 1581, are really the only major houses. Shaw House is of brick, and designed on the E-plan. On 40a the same plan, but timber-framed, is the substantial Ufton Court of the same years. Of brick again, but smaller, are Hinton House of before 1589, Stanlake Park, Haines Hill,‡ and High Chimneys, all in the parish of St Nicholas Hurst, and all of Elizabethan type, though High Chimneys is dated as amazingly late as 1661.§ At Windsor Queen Elizabeth's Gallery dates 39b

* We must of course exclude from this chronology the North Italian Adoration of the Magi (Verona?) of the early C15 at Littlewick Green, a 20b panel, 10 ft long, because it was not made in or for Berkshire.

‡ Haines Hill, which I have not been able to enter, has, according to the VCH, an original long gallery.

§ The Almshouses at St Nicholas Hurst are still later and yet entirely pre-classical. They were founded in 1682.

probably from 1583, the date on the ornate chimneypiece. South
Fawley Manor House, Great Fawley, has a date 1614, the Jesus
Hospital at Bray, one of the largest almshouse foundations in
the county, a date 1627. Small's House, Mackney, Sotwell is undated, which is a pity, as it is an extremely interesting house on a
quite exceptional plan: two oblong ranges (of which one contained the hall), kept close together and connected by a square
link in which the staircase is placed.

This exhausts secular building qualifying for inclusion here.
Of CHURCH ARCHITECTURE no one would expect much. It was
a rare age for new church buildings, or even parts of buildings.
7 Foremost in Berkshire is Bishop Jewel's w porch of Sunningwell church of c.1560–70, polygonal with incorrectly shaped
columns and originally a steep-pitched polygonal roof. Equally
interesting is the internal remodelling of Winkfield church in
1592. The church, probably formerly of nave and aisles, was
made two-naved with a dividing timber arcade. The w tower of
Lockinge is dated 1564, but of no interest. Otherwise, where
towers were rebuilt, they were made of brick. There are no
fixed early dates, but those of Bradfield and Wargrave are
assigned to the c16. St Nicholas Hurst is of 1612, Purley of
8a 1626, Winkfield of 1629, and Ruscombe of 1638–9 – the latter
two with mullioned-and-transomed windows entirely of brick –
and the lower part of Easthampstead (Bracknell) looks Jacobean
too.*

In CHURCH FURNISHINGS also Berkshire simply follows the
national rule that little was done afresh in the late c16, and much
only in the Laudian period. Proof is an examination of Pulpits.
There may well be undated Elizabethan ones – e.g. the exceptionally fine one with Floris motifs at Aldworth – but as for
dates, this is the tally: Newbury 1607 (quite splendid), Waltham
St Lawrence 1619 (fragmentary), Binfield 1628, Easthampstead
(Bracknell) 1631, St Peter Didcot 1634, St Helen Abingdon
1636, Ruscombe c.1639, West Hanney 1649. The Font Case of
Long Wittenham (an unusual object) is undated; so is that of
22a Stanford-in-the-Vale, but the wrought-iron Hourglass Stand at
St Nicholas Hurst has a date 1636,‡ and the completely Perp Font
at Bray is, according to accounts, of 1647 (unless they refer to a
font which has disappeared). Only in MONUMENTS – and this

---

* Later dated Berkshire brick towers are as follows: Boxford c.1692,
Pangbourne 1718, Finchampstead 1720, Basildon 1734, Peasemore 1737,
Tilehurst 1737, Brimpton 1748, Winterbourne 1759.
22b ‡ Another hourglass stand is at Binfield.

is the national situation again – are quantity and quality higher. Indeed one is hard put to it to select for such a summary as this. The types are well known: the recumbent effigy on a tomb-chest remains from the Middle Ages, the kneeling figure or figures (two facing one another across a prayer desk) is the most usual new type, a Flemish type. Material is stone or preferably, and almost without exception with aesthetically better results, alabaster. Decoration is Flemish rather than Italian: strapwork often handled very successfully, columns of touch, coffered arches shallow or deeper. So here is a catalogue of major examples. Recumbent effigies of alabaster: Sir Philip and Sir Thomas Hoby, Bisham, †1558 and †1566, Earl of Lincoln, St George's Chapel, †1585, Appleton 1593, Speen †1597, Tilehurst †1627, Arborfield †1639, and Radley a few years before (†1631 and †1632). The last-named is by *Nicholas Stone*. The county has nothing typologically more interesting by him. Recumbent effigies of stone: Pangbourne †1625. Semi-reclining effigies, laid stiffly on one side: Little Wittenham †1611, Uffington †1638. Kneeling figures: Bisham †1609, Sonning †1630, St Nicholas Hurst †1631 (three groups framed by columns). That leaves the exceptions. There is an Early Elizabethan type without any figures, just with a framed inscription, ornament, and a decorative coat of arms. This in Berkshire is represented by a monument at Hurley (†1558 and †1579 – which date is valid?). Frontal demi-figures were usual for scholars and divines: John Blagrave, the mathematician, †1611 at St Laurence Reading (with Mannerist surrounding allegorical figures) and Giles Tomson, Bishop of Gloucester, †1612, at Windsor Chapel. Small brass plates appear in the county, not only with upright or kneeling figures, but also in a less standard way. They are often framed in stone, perhaps with a guilloche or an egg-and-dart motif. But the finest, most delightedly remembered Jacobean monument in Berkshire is that of Margaret Hoby at Bisham (†1605), which is an obelisk carried by four swans with a heart on top.*

In a history of art and architecture on a European scale, England in the fifty years between 1615 and 1665 would be represented by the work of Inigo Jones, Webb, Pratt, May, and so on to Wren, i.e. by the introduction and the spread of Palladianism and then the French and Dutch classical style of the C17, and by the work of Rubens and van Dyck in and for England and

---

* As an appendix a STATUE of Queen Elizabeth I must be recorded. It is now in Cumnor church, but is said to come from the Earl of Leicester's house, Dean Court. It is not a masterpiece.

their effect on the country. The fascinating thing about any
provincial survey is the mixture between the contribution of the
central, London, events to the region or county and the cross-
currents in opposition to them, or in misunderstanding or half-
understanding of them. As for Berkshire, Coleshill by *Pratt* of
the 1650s was central, London, stuff, but it has alas gone completely. Hamstead Marshall of the 1660s by *Gerbier*, completed
by *Winde*, looks in engravings of the same type as Coleshill, but
not so pure. It disappeared after only about fifty years. Aldermaston Court also is no longer in existence. If one can trust the
date 1636, the house was one of the very earliest of the brick-
box type which became so characteristic of the English smaller-
scale country house for two hundred years to come. The next
in date are Chevening in Kent, perhaps by Inigo Jones, and
built before 1638, and a house certainly by Jones of which we
have his drawing dated 1639.* Ashdown, that adorable doll's
40b house, five by five bays, with a hipped roof and a belvedere
cupola and two symmetrical detached ranges delineating the
forecourt, remains as the early representation of the type in
Berkshire. Its architect and its date are unrecorded. Its style is
decidedly Dutch. The 1660s are the most likely date.

   Sir John Summerson has christened the provincial version of
this style, with its quirks and its resistance to classicity, Artisan
Mannerism. It is interestingly and enjoyably represented in
Berkshire. Semi-classical is West Woodhay House, which carries
the date 1635 more than once. Can it be so early? It is the brick-
box type entirely, with hipped roof. Only its raised brick
window surrounds and raised brick quoins join it to the group
with which we are now dealing. Semi-classical also is one canon's
house inside Windsor Castle dated 1660. It has giant pilasters
along its front, and the Ionic capitals are made of cut brick.
Semi-classical again, and really only departing from the correct
line in a steep gable-like instead of a correct pediment, is the
44 Lucas Hospital at Wokingham, dated 1665. It is a big composition with projecting wings and a cupola. More Artisan Mannerism are Milton House, Welford Park, and Hall's Farmhouse
Farley Hill, all three undated, and all three of course of brick.

41   * The only surviving part of Aldermaston Court is the staircase, and this
is also of great importance as being one of the earliest where the balustrade
of banisters is replaced by a pierced parapet. The details are on the way
from strapwork to the gristle and the leaves of the second third of the
century. Other early examples of the pierced parapet are Radclive in
Buckinghamshire of 1621 and Cromwell House, Highgate, London, of
c.1637–40.

The first has giant pilasters with waistbands which turn out to be fleurs-de-lis and a typical sub-Inigo chimneypiece. It also has an Inigo plaster ceiling. The second has raised brick window surrounds like West Woodhay but a raised vertical strip to connect the windows vertically. The third has not only raised brick angle quoins but crazy brick quoins framing every bay of windows. At The Priory, Beech Hill, dated 1648 are two specially characteristic chimneypieces, and at Newbury is a house, dated 1669 (8 Northbrook Street), which, instead of giant pilasters, has superimposed short pilasters, a special fashion of the mid c17. Another fashionable motif, only a little later, say of *c*.1660–75, is the so-called Ipswich window, a three-light window with a wider centre light, a transom in each side light, and an arch instead in the middle light. The *locus classicus* is Sparrowe's House at Ipswich of *c*.1670. It occurs a number of times at Abingdon, and also at Sutton Courtenay, especially in the Manor House. The Manor House has also the charming and uncommon motif of a colonnade with Tuscan columns forming a loggia below one wing of the house. The gatepiers of the Manor House 42c are typical of the years *c*.1660, and Berkshire has indeed a fine collection of later c17 gatepiers, including one at Besselsleigh, several at Coleshill, and a whole minuet of them alone on 42a, a lawn where the mansion of Hamstead Marshall had once b, d, stood. One step forward from these and one has *Talman's* e, f former doorway (now garden gateway) of Swallowfield Park. 43 Talman worked here for the Earl of Clarendon in 1689–91, and his may indeed be the H-shaped house that now exists, even if devoid of other telling external features. But it has inside a spectacular if small oval vestibule with lush stucco. The outbuildings are interesting too, of brick, extensive, and with giant pilasters and heavy loggias or arcades, looking decidedly 1700 and Late Wren in character, i.e. Office of Works style of the turn of the century (Talman was Comptroller under Wren from 1689 to 1702). At Windsor Castle *Hugh May* did an extensive remodelling and rebuilding job from 1675 onwards. It included the most spectacular staircase in England and one of the most Baroque interiors, the chapel, but all of it was swept 12 away by Wyatville and we have nothing left but two round-arched giant windows in Henry III's Tower. May was Surveyor of Windsor from 1673 to his death in 1684, i.e. came under Wren as Surveyor General. Of all May's interior work only three rooms remain. The woodwork by *Grinling Gibbons* and *Henry* 46 *Phillips* is superb, the painting by *Verrio* pedestrian.

With these buildings the first PUBLIC BUILDINGS must be
45b named, and especially the splendid Town Hall of Abingdon of
1678–82, built and perhaps designed by *Christopher Kempster*,
one of Wren's City masons. It has the usual open ground floor,
long, slender giant pilasters above, a hipped roof, and a cupola.
45a The Windsor Town Hall of *c.*1687–90 was designed by *Sir
Thomas Fitch* and is less correct, with its giant pilasters on the
upper floor (above the open ground floor) set in, i.e. away from,
quoins. *Wren* supervised the completion of the building. The
late C17 Town Hall at Faringdon is smaller and more provincial.
The Town Hall at Wallingford with the date 1670 is the earliest
of the group. It has much sturdier, more Jacobean, columns,
but a Venetian window and a hipped roof.*

No interior decoration of these years needs recording apart
from Talman's stucco work at Swallowfield, nor any CHURCH
FURNISHINGS apart from the remains of *Grinling Gibbons*'s
gorgeous wooden railing round the former Royal Pew at
Windsor Castle now in the parish church and perhaps one or
the other brass Chandelier on the Dutch pattern. That at
Sonning is dated 1675, two at St Helen Abingdon are 1710 and
1713, that at Wantage 1711, and then the type continued un-
changed right into the C19.‡

In MONUMENTS the interesting development is the loosening
of the stiffness of Jacobean attitudes and also of Jacobean typo-
logical conventions. The former is illustrated in a recumbent
effigy at St Nicholas Hurst (†1651) and a semi-reclining effigy at
Coleshill (†1647), followed by the Bishop Brideoake at Windsor
Castle (†1678), also semi-reclining but now quite at ease, the
latter by Katherine Thomas at Waltham St Lawrence †1658,
which is just a short stubby column in a niche with an urn on
top of an oddly organic shape, and no figures at all. A few years
later the Rich monument at Sonning (†1667 and 1663) consists
of two white urns on a black slab held up by four white putti.
Of new motifs the bust in an oval recess appears at Sonning

* Yet earlier and a job out of the ordinary is the Cloth Hall (now Museum)
at Newbury of 1626–7, timber-framed and perhaps also originally open
below, and the longer attached range with an upper wooden balcony or
gallery which was a store house and lay close to the former wharf. It is
supposed to date from *c.*1660–80. The Cloth Hall was, it seems, an early
municipal weaving workshop. At Denchworth is a small house known as
the Wool Store. This is dated 1708 and still pre-classical, with mullioned-
and-transomed windows, even if they are now composed symmetrically.

‡ Little Coxwell 1729, Buckland given 1733, Caversham 1743, Harwell
1766, Aldermaston C18, Wootton C18 ?, Sutton Courtenay 1821 – a survival
or revival.

with a date of death 1653, thick compact garlands of the Inigo Jones kind (apart from the chimneypiece at Milton House) at St Mary Reading with a date of death 1635 and at Buckland c.1648, the open curly pediment at Buckland with a date of death 1658, and twisted columns at Sonning with a date of death 1665 (or 1656). Add to this the two frontal demi-figures perfectly at ease at Wantage (†1684) and the two lively kneelers with a third figure upright behind at St Nicholas Hurst (†1683), and we are ready for the C18. The former is by *William Bird* of Oxford, the latter by *William Stanton*.*

But our survey has so far omitted any reference to CHURCHES after 1600. There are few, and of what there is little need detain us. For the first half of the C17 there is just one major building: Shrivenham of 1638. It is large, and it is complete. It has a plain oblong plan built round the Perp crossing tower, a W porch and two symmetrically placed E entrances, and large, even, straight-headed Perp windows of three to five lights, but Tuscan columns inside – a general impression totally different from that 11b of any medieval church and curiously Protestant, in spite of its Laudian date. For the second half of the century only the riddle of Uffington and Buckland comes in here, that is, the date of the windows with mullions just pushing up without any compromise into the two-centred arch or (at Uffington) into a hard 8b triangular top. The VCH calls them C13. They can hardly be. At Uffington we know of repairs in 1677–9. This seems a more convincing date.‡ For the C18 there is pretty well nothing, that is of before the Gothic Revival. The church at Pusey, St Peter Wallingford, and the church at Kingston Bagpuize are the only ones to mention, the first of c.1745–50, the third of 1799–1800, the second of 1760–9. *Sir Robert Taylor*'s spire of St Peter belongs in 9a another context. The scarcity is the same in church furnishings.

MONUMENTS of value are more frequent and illustrate, as do the mansions, the growing acceptance of a Berkshire country place by Londoners or half-Londoners. At the beginning stand two types: White Waltham, †1723, by *W. Palmer*, large and competent and purely architectural with no figures,§ and

* By *Edward Stanton* a minor monument at Faringdon (†1706), and another, in partnership with *Horsnaile*, at St Mary Wallingford (†1722).

‡ Egglestone Abbey in the North Riding of Yorkshire has windows just like those of Uffington, and there it is admittedly more difficult to argue for a C17 date.

§ Of the same year, most elegantly done and anonymous, Theodore Randue in St George's Chapel Windsor, and of 1719, more Vanbrughian and also anonymous, a monument at Shellingford.

Kintbury, †1711, with two free-standing busts and an urn on a pedestal. *Peter Scheemakers* took this up for a monument also at Kintbury, †1754, and *Thomas Scheemakers* for yet another at Kintbury, †1767. A much better *Peter Scheemakers* is at Pusey church, †1742 and †1753 – a seated woman by a bust – a weak one again with busts in Windsor parish church, †1735. But the *nec plus ultra* of manipulating busts is *Hickey's chef d'œuvre* at St Helen Abingdon, 1782, with six busts ingeniously arranged. There is no Roubiliac in Berkshire, and the only *Rysbrack* (Coleshill †1751) is comparatively insignificant. In fact the most impressive monument of the mid-century is surprising by name
31a of sculptor and by style. It is *Thomas Carter's* Mrs Benyon †1777 at Englefield, a fully Berninesque relief.

When it comes to EIGHTEENTH-CENTURY HOUSES numbers and variety grow at once beyond what we have so far found in Berkshire. Yet, before the Victorian Age, the county had few really grand mansions. Only three of the C18 can be called grand, and even they more for reasons strictly architectural than for reasons of sheer size. They are Buckland House
50a by the younger *Wood* of Bath, Benham Park Speen by *Capability*
50b *Brown*, and Basildon Park by *John Carr* of York. The first is of 1757 etc. and was doubled in size at the beginning of the C20, the second is of 1772–5, the third of 1776. Buckland House has some splendid interiors too, especially the so-called chapel, all exposed stone, Basildon Park a curious recessed portico within which by two small staircases one reaches the *piano nobile*.

Of medium-size however there is a great deal. The first third of the century in particular is very rich, in the towns as well as the country. The series starts just before 1700 with the Old House Hotel at Windsor, connected hypothetically with *Wren*, a quiet, dignified brick house near the river. Also hypothetically connected with *Wren* and also at Windsor is the Masonic Hall, but this represents rather the style of Hawksmoor and in any case is as late as 1725–6. The typical early C18 or rather Early Georgian house in Berkshire is faced with blue vitrified or, in some areas, pale grey vitrified brick and has red-brick or rubbed-red-brick dressings. Often the blue brick is used as headers only. Windows are segment-headed, and roofs disappear behind parapets. Kirby House, Inkpen, of 1733 is a typical example. A group of such houses have the centre raised and also introduce some other means of dramatization. Vanbrugh inspiration is likely. To this group belong Kingston House
47b at Kingston Bagpuize, West Hanney House of 1727, a house in

Church Street Faringdon, Manor Farm at West Challow, Coxe's Hall at Stanford-in-the-Vale of 1733, and also the specially swagger Ardington House of 1721, where it is the side elevation rather than the front that exhibits Vanbrughian features. To the same group belong the very individual Brick Alley Alms- 47a houses at Abingdon of 1718 and their arched giant recesses, inside which the upper floors of the dwellings have balconies.* No. 24 Northbrook Street at Newbury of 1724 is small but particularly ornate. The old, original house of Radley College is of 1721–7 and has as part of its door surround pilasters disappearing part of the way up in the pattern of the rustication – a Lutyens motif which also occurs at Kingston House. An interior in this English Baroque is the entrance hall and staircase of Purley Hall, dated 1719. The wall paintings covering even the underside of the staircase are *Thornhill* school. Fine slightly later interiors are at Hall Place near Hurley. But the most splendid interior of the first third of the century is the entrance 48b hall of Farley Hill, a house in its exterior still Queen Anne rather than Palladian.‡

Once Baroque drama had been discarded, the county settled down to the standard five-bay or seven-bay brick or stone houses, mostly with a centre pediment as one knows them in all counties of England. Hall Place near Hurley of the thirties has already been mentioned, Pusey House is of 1753, Calcot House near Reading (rather grander) of 1755, Ascot Place – like Buckland and Basildon with linked pavilions – probably of the 1760s, Culham Court of 1770, Faringdon House of c.1780–90, and so on to *Wyatt*'s Purley Park and *Wyatville*'s Woolley Park, Brightwalton, with a semicircle of Tuscan columns round an ample bow window. This is dated 1799.

But the county was not entirely classical and columnar. The GOTHIC REVIVAL and the Picturesque made their appearance early and left their mark. The earliest date seems to be the two pretty churchyard gateways of Newbury parish church, i.e. if they are by *Fuller White* and of 1770. Immediately after follows Donnington Grove just outside Newbury. The dates here are before 1772 and about 1785. The first designer was *John Chute* of The Vyne. At Milton House in 1776 *Stephen Wright* added

* Twitty's Almshouses at Abingdon are of 1707 and Tomkins' Almshouses of 1733.

‡ One public interior must find its place here too: the Abingdon Council Chamber of 1759, built in an addition of 1731–3 on top of the Perp St John's Hospital just across the Market Place from the Town Hall.

52a two wings, Gothic internally, and the library is the most
charming Gothicist interior in Berkshire. In 1777 *Sir Robert
9a Taylor* gave to the church of St Peter at Wallingford its delightful fancy spire, undecided as to whether it should be considered
classical or Gothic. Sandleford Priory is one of *Wyatt*'s first
essays in the Gothic: 1780–1 (with the two finest and largest
rooms in a wing attached to the back and treated entirely classi-
cally). At Buckland House about 1790 the stables were given a
Gothic façade as an eye-catcher from the house. A much more
effective eye-catcher was Strattenborough Castle Farm from
Coleshill. The former buildings here, in 1792, were not only
51a made to appear a medieval ruin but a medieval ruin repaired –
a piece of ingenuity and sophistication worth recording. Binfield
House has nice Gothic trim too, and Farley Castle, Farley Hill,
of 1809–10. In St George's Chapel, Windsor, *Henry Emlyn*
designed the charming Gothic monument to Edward IV in 1789
and the perfectly convincing *Coade*-stone screen between
crossing and chancel with its pretty fan-vault in 1790–2. He also
19 added and repaired the stalls equally convincingly. The same
can alas not be said of his contribution to the classical style. His
English Order, as demonstrated at Beaumont Lodge (now Beaumont College), Old Windsor, in 1790 is terrible, the way a pair
of columns coalesces at bottom and top into one quite inexcus-
able.

THE PICTURESQUE was given a field-day in Windsor Park.
It is the ensemble one must try to visualize – difficult now that
so much of it is inaccessible to the public. If a few items have to
be singled out, Fort Belvedere or Shrub Hill Tower, a triangular
medievalizing tower of *c.*1750, much imitated later, is one,
Cranbourne Tower of 1808 another, the wonderful ruins of
52b Lepcis Magna presented to the Regent in 1816 and re-erected
by Virginia Water a third. Virginia Water of *c.*1750 is the largest
of the made lakes of Berkshire, but most of the country houses
had their lakes, small or large, and the Thames was also called
in for picturesque siting. The Temple on the island between
Fawley Court in Bucks and Remenham, designed by *Wyatt* and
built in 1771, is not easily forgotten, and the third Duke of
Marlborough's fishing lodge and banqueting house on Monkey
Island of *c.*1744 must originally also have been a delight. It
derives its name from the monkey paintings by *Clermont* inside.
Again at Windsor, Frogmore House, given a classical remodelling by *Wyatt* in 1792, has a room with pretty decoration of
53 flowers and garlands by *Mary Moser*. At Park Place, General

Conway's estate, the cyclopean bridge at the foot of the grotto valley is placed so that coming from the grotto one sees the water of the Thames through it, although the river is not all that near. But the climax of the picturesque apparatus of Park Place is of course 'little master Stonehenge', as Horace Walpole called it, the stone circle given by the inhabitants of Jersey to General Conway in 1787 and re-erected accurately. Buckland House has a fair number of picturesque objects in its grounds as well, including an Ice House with a portico to the lake. The portico has a kind of intermittent vermiculated grotto rustication, a treatment which also occurs in the quadrant walls of Pusey House and the porch of the rectory of Kingston Bagpuize, which is dated 1723. To these large-scale ornaments two on a small scale must be added: Halfway House, that enlarged piece of Staffordshire ware, halfway between Newbury 51b and Hungerford, and Hop Castle near Winterbourne, with an octagonal centre and ogee cap, walls of whole flints and bones, and at least partly a grotto treatment of the interior.

The Medieval Revival started Rococo, turned Romantic, and finished Archaeological. The story is familiar, but that Windsor Castle, the major architectural monument of Berkshire, is more 35 than anything a monument to the transition from Romantic to Archaeological is less familiar and, as far as the layman is concerned, hardly realized at all. Yet it is true that the Windsor we see today and which remains in the memories of Continental visitors as one of the most spectacular castle ensembles anywhere is essentially the work of *Sir Jeffry Wyatville* in the eighteen-twenties. Had he not heightened the Round Tower by 33 ft, had he not heightened many of the other towers, had he not created the s front with its central gateway and recast the E front, Windsor from a distance or Windsor from within the Lower and Upper Wards would not be half as impressive as it is. The naïvety with which the early C19 believed in the possibility of making a better medieval castle out of an existing and faulty one may amaze us now. Yet this attitude – which is of course the same that has given us better picturesque landscape than nature could provide – set off Windsor on the greatest period of its social life, which is the Victorian period. The State Apartments were ready for it, their remodelling begun by *Wyatt* about 1800, but principally done by *Wyatville*. Some rooms are classical,* the Grand Reception Room is a remarkably early case of 56

* But the specially fine doors in the Crimson Drawing Room were brought 55 from Carlton House, the Regent's London house, and date from *c.*1810.

neo-Rococo, and most of the rooms are Gothic and tend to be somewhat gloomy. The scale is remarkable. St George's Hall is 185 ft long, the Waterloo Chamber (re-decorated in 1861) about 90 by 45 ft.

But before we can take our stand in the year 1837 and look forward over the second and the last third of the C19, we must see what happened in sculpture and the decorative arts at the time of Wyatville. It is true, nothing has yet been said about sculpture and decoration of the second half of the C18 either, but there is little to be said. In CHURCH FURNISHING only a little mopping up is needed – i.e. one large head of typical mid-Georgian Stained Glass by *John Rowell*, 1744, at Arborfield, and the lovely engraved clear armorial glass of 1792 by *Eginton* at Great Coxwell,* and in MONUMENTS scarcely more. One *Wilton* at Padworth (†1776), and several minor works by several other sculptors whose names the reader can try in the index, *Nollekens* e.g., *Bacon* e.g. *Canova* did an enormously heavy tablet at Speen (†1806), *Flaxman* a lot of tablets of no special value and one extremely fine one at Cookham (1810), *Westmacott* a noble one at Ruscombe (†1799), one to *Wyatt*'s design at Shrivenham (†1793), and several others, but the sculptural or perhaps rather scenic sensation of C19 sculpture in Berkshire is without any doubt that snow-white *tableau vivant*, the apotheosis of Princess Charlotte in Windsor Chapel. This is by *Matthew Cotes Wyatt* and was executed between 1817 and 1824. The basic conception is entirely Baroque, the dead body invisible under a heavy cloth except for the fingers of one hand, the mourning maidens with their heads all covered by their mantles, the rising young body in the middle, the front of the tomb-house, the large marble-carved curtain. But the whiteness and the chaste, motionless faces of the ascending princess and the two angels counterbalance that violence and result in a unison of Baroque and Classical which is typical of Romantic sculpture (and also of the Romantic cartoon).

The typical CHURCHES of the same years are Gothic, but also in their composition and their internal space still wedded to the classical Georgian ideals. Berkshire examples of this type, known as the type of the Commissioners' Churches, are the Windsor parish church of 1820–2, Hungerford of 1816, Sunninghill

---

* Berkshire has an uncommonly complete series of heraldic glass from Ockwells (*see* above) via Radley (C16) and Lucas Hospital Wokingham (*c.*1665–70) to Abingdon Town Hall (*c.*1830) and Windsor Chapel (by *Willement*).

of 1826–7,* and, after 1837, Holy Trinity Windsor of 1842–4 and Bear Wood of 1846. But Gothic was not the only medieval style admitted for inspiration. Norman had much to recommend it, just because the square, static element of the classical, which they did not want to give up yet, is more easily attained in a *Rundbogen* style than in a pointed style. So there was a brief national fashion for the neo-Norman in the forties. In Berkshire it is heralded remarkably early at Kennington in 1828. Even *Pugin* at St James Reading, in 1837–40, succumbed to the Norman, tempted no doubt by the adjoining abbey ruin.‡ The other examples are Hermitage 1835, Shaw 1840–2 (by *Hansom*), and Burghfield 1843. The Nonconformists during these same years demonstrated their anti-medievalism by keeping away from Gothic altogether and sticking to classical. Windsor has two specially good examples: the Congregationals of 1832 and the Baptists of 1839.

But the most valuable church of the pre-Victorian C19 in Berkshire is no doubt Theale, by the little-known *E. W. Garbett*, and of 1820–32. This, at a moment when Gothic almost without exception meant minimum Perp or indifferent lancets, is in a scholarly and a very ambitious way E.E. It is inspired directly from Salisbury Cathedral and makes a proud show, where it stands outside the village.

Yet how different are its tight verticals from the 'reality', i.e. the substantial, full-blooded VICTORIAN CHURCH BUILDINGS designed by those who came after Pugin. *Scott* is the oldest of these, and his Bradfield parish church of 1847–8 is a first-class example to demonstrate that change. It is Second-Pointed now, as they called it, i.e. with tracery from Geometrical to Early Decorated; it performs feats of variety and picturesqueness internally and externally, but a thicker, heavier picturesqueness now than that of the Rococo Gothic had been.§ Of the slightly younger men of the Victorian Gothic *Butterfield* did much, but nothing special, except the spiky and idiosyncratic St Nicholas' 58b

* This and the Windsor parish church have cast-iron piers.
‡ There is one more *Pugin* church in the county: Tubney, 1844–7, uninteresting architecturally, but interesting in that a Roman Catholic architect in the 1840s could be commissioned to design a Church of England church and could accept. Tubney is close to Oxford. And another Pugin P S. Messrs Betjeman and Piper report that the Presbytery at East Hendred possesses furniture and crockery from Pugin's house at Ramsgate.
§ This is not Scott's first appearance in Berkshire. He started as a designer of workhouses, and that at Old Windsor by the firm *Scott & Moffatt* is of 1835 and yet Tudor, not classical as workhouses used to be.

School at Newbury of 1859 and perhaps the odd neo-Norman nave of Ascot Priory of 1877, *Teulon* did just one duly perverse church – Leckhampstead (1858–60) – but *Street*, who lived for some early years (1850–2) at Wantage, can be studied excellently in the county, and so can *Woodyer*. Boyne Hill, Maidenhead, of 1854–7 is Street at his best, a powerful group of church, gate, parsonage, school, and schoolmaster's house, Great Fawley of 1866 is as serious and almost forbidding, and the Convent of the Wantage Sisterhood of 1855 etc. is at least eminently characteristic of his domestic style. Most attractive of his secular buildings however are the village schools such as Inkpen of 1850, and Eastbury of 1851, where period precedent is waived in favour of commodity. *Woodyer*, who liked ornate interiors, could show this in three major buildings: St Paul Wokingham of 1862–4, ornate externally as well, Christ Church Reading of 1861–2 and 1874 with the curious and wholly successful large tracery area above the chancel arch, and the surprisingly large chapel of the House of Mercy at Windsor of 1881.

Berkshire is a bonanza of High Anglo-Catholic communities. At Wantage the Sisterhood had Street's small chapel replaced by a large rib-vaulted one in 1887. The designer was *Pearson*, who also designed the large, also rib-vaulted parish church of Ascot in 1896–7. Also at Wantage *William White* did the Retreat House of St Michael in 1855. Ascot Priory was begun by *Buckeridge* in 1861 and continued by *Scott*. Other orders built too, but need not be recorded here. On the other hand Douai Abbey at Woolhampton, Roman Catholic, ought perhaps to be remembered, though its architectural record is poor, and also the public schools, like Wellington with a chapel by *Scott*, less memorable by far than the college buildings themselves to which we shall revert presently, Bradfield with a competent and externally well composed chapel by *John Oldrid Scott*, Sir G.G.'s son, and the Catholic Beaumont, Old Windsor, with a chapel most unexpectedly in a Raphaelesque style. The room is tunnel-vaulted and the decoration by *Bentley* is *alla* Loggie or Pompei. Italian also is the exterior of the spectacular Royal Mausoleum in Windsor Park, built in 1862–71 by *A. J. Humbert*, but designed as regards the Raphaelesque interior by *Professor Grüner* of Dresden, in whom Prince Albert had had much confidence. It is one of the most complete and convincing High Victorian interiors in the Italian style. The exterior is rather Romanesque instead, whereas *Humbert*'s Mausoleum for the Duchess of Kent of 1861 is a domed rotunda, of a rather French Dixhuitième flavour. Some fifteen years later the chapel of the Royal Military Academy at Sandhurst was built in a Byzantine-cum-Italian-Romanesque style (consecrated in 1879). It has since been more than doubled in size.

Much of the original CHURCH FURNISHINGS has been kept in the Victorian churches. The round stone Pulpits, the low iron Screens, the carved Fonts are too little noticed and too little appreciated.* The Reredoses are often sculptured, weakly almost without exception. The weakness of Victorian SCULPTURE is altogether a fact hardly to be denied. The monument to the Duchess of Gloucester of 1859 in St George's Chapel, designed by *Scott* and carved by *Theed*, is Victorian sculpture at its best. So is Prince Albert's Monument in the Albert Memorial Chapel by *Baron Trinqueti*, who was responsible for the design of the whole interior of the chapel in 1863–73, by far the most eminent Victorian ecclesiastical interior of Berkshire, with its Latest Classical stories on the walls, engraved in marble, and its small white marble reliefs. The total effect is eclipsed however by the gorgeous monument to the Duke of Clarence by *Alfred Gilbert*, 33 and that, though of 1892, is post-Victorian by any terms of definition one could apply to the Victorian style. It is Arts and Crafts turned Art Nouveau in the hands of a decorator of genius. The lava-like curves of structure and draperies and so much else is Art Nouveau without doubt, and earlier than nearly all Continental Art Nouveau.

The Arts and Crafts component is originally derived from *William Morris*'s patterns. Morris's influence is much greater than such a survey as this can point out. Morris's own work in Berkshire is confined to STAINED GLASS, but there – if we include that designed by *Burne-Jones* before Morris's did their own as a firm – it ranges from 1861 to the years of decline after his death. The glass in the original chapel of Bradfield College by Burne-Jones of 1862 is among the most astonishing of the century, forceful, bold in composition and colouring, and not a bit historicist. Of the same year but tender and intimate the *Morris* glass at Cranbourne. Other Morris glass at Dedworth (1863–87) and Tilehurst (1869) and then, of the seventies, and of mature excellence, at Eaton Hastings and Easthampstead (Brack-nell).‡ *Kempe*, the other familiar name in Later Victorian glass, is

* The Font in St Paul Wokingham by *Woodyer* is specially noteworthy. Its freely growing plants all along the drum of the bowl are proto-Art Nouveau in a way not infrequently found in the 1860s.

‡ One major domestic job of *Burne-Jones*'s ought also to be referred to, 61 the series of paintings of Briar Rose at Buscot Park, done in 1890.

ubiquitous in Berkshire. Nowhere can he compare with Morris, either in colouring or in composition or in the use of leading. *Gibbs* among the pre-Morris purveyors of stained glass is the one most intelligently aware of the role of leading. The county is rich in Victorian stained glass, and those who want to train themselves to recognize the handwritings of *Hardman, Wailes, Clayton & Bell,* and others can do so. Here only a few special windows need be annotated: *J. P. Seddon,* the architect and friend of the Pre-Raphaelites, designed one *c.*1877 at Sunningwell, and it is thoroughly successful. *Heywood Sumner*'s E window at Longworth is on the way from the Arts and Crafts to the English variety of Expressionism, and *Brangwyn* did a series of windows at Bucklebury in 1912 and about 1920 in his customary robust and colourful style. No other church furnishings deserve a word, except perhaps the Painting of Christ at Emmaus by *Westlake* at St John Stratfield Mortimer and the Pulpit at St Mary Wallingford by *Onslow Ford.* This is of 1888 and has bronze reliefs of saints in a marble setting.

The contrast between the character and the quality of the churches and of Victorian SECULAR ARCHITECTURE is baffling alike to the layman and the expert. By and large the churches are scholarly, and where they depart from Gothic authority, they are in their heresies thoroughly considered. Their architects knew exactly what they were doing. Licence, even major licence, is not arbitrary: it is taken advisedly. Not so in most secular architecture, especially of the pre-Morris–Webb–Shaw decades. Berkshire illustrates this to perfection. Up to the thirties classical reasonableness still prevailed, and the safeguards of the pattern-book were firm. Typical are such buildings as St George's School at Windsor of 1803, the Abingdon Gaol of 1805–11, a veritable Bastille, the Sandhurst Military Academy of 1807–12 with its monumental Greek Doric portico, and the grandiose Royal Berkshire Hospital at Reading of 1837–9 – all four incidentally public buildings, a sign of the growing importance and range of public architecture in the C19. The concomitant of such large buildings of the first third of the century is the large terraces in towns such as those opposite the Reading hospital in London Road, or those of King's Road Windsor, e.g. Adelaide Terrace, dated 1831. One need only compare this with Queen's Terrace a little further S, which is about twenty years later, to have the full impact of the change from pre-Victorian to Victorian, red brick with blue-brick diapers, shaped gables, recessions and juttings-forward, and a broken skyline.

The first sign of the change, i.e. the first sign of personal power and inventiveness getting the better of the pattern-book, is the astonishing sequence of rooms made about 1825–30 inside Kingston Lisle House. Who can have thought out this coffered-vaulted entrance passage, this groin-vaulted hall, this flying 57 staircase, their scale and their highly individual detail? We do not know. *Basevi* has been suggested, and *Cockerell* too.

But while here the elements are still derived from the Roman and the Grecian, they turned to Italianate-Villa, Tudor, Jacobean, and Frenchy soon, and to mixtures which explain the term Free Renaissance used at the time. At Windsor e.g. the Royal Waiting Room of the Southern Region station is Gothic (and internally very pretty: 1850–1), the Workshops in Great Park by *Teulon* are utilitarian but if anything Gothic too (1858–61), and the Dairy in the Home Park (by *John Thomas*, the sculptor: 1858) is 60 internally Cinquecento with a lot of shiny fayence. But all this is minor work. No major work was needed at Windsor.

On the other hand the securely rich middle class called for houses of a size and especially a number of rooms that easily outdid Georgian sizes in the county. Berkshire, after the railway had come in 1840, was near enough to London to be desirable as a county for wealthy people's country mansions. Aldermaston Court comes first, 1848–51 for D. H. D. Burr, by *P. C. Hard-wick*, totally asymmetrical, with a tower and a generally Tudor appearance. It cost £20,000. Easthampstead Park (Bracknell) is Jacobean, as big, and dates from 1860. At Englefield enlargement and remodelling took place after a fire in 1886. But the climax, and in its brazen way one of the major Victorian monuments of England, is *Robert Kerr*'s Bear Wood, begun in 1865 59b for John Walter, owner of *The Times*. This is again part-Tudor, part-Frenchy, has again an asymmetrically placed tower, and is in volume probably an equivalent of Blenheim. Nor did the pressure for houses on that scale subside. Marlston House was built for the Palmers of Reading by *Edward Burgess* as late as 1895–9, and *Waterhouse* built country houses on that scale or nearly that scale left and right. His own at Yattendon – he was Lord of the Manor of Yattendon – has been replaced, but Buckhold House of 1884–5 survives, and a whole corpus of others, e.g. round Reading University. He also designed the Reading Town Hall in 1872–5.

But by far the best of these major High Victorian buildings of Berkshire, and the one most disciplined in its layout and most consistent in its stylistic apparatus, is Wellington College 59a by *John Shaw*, begun in 1856. The style chosen is a mystery. It is derived from two sources both equally unfavoured at the time: that of William and Mary's Hampton Court and that of Louis XIII. So here is brick with ample stone dressings, here are segment-headed and oval windows, here are garlands and mansard roofs, and here above all is a firm axiality conducted triumphantly through two courtyards and ultimately punctuated by two identical towers. Did it impress Nesfield, when he turned Queen Anne, and later *Norman Shaw*? It is far from certain. Norman Shaw went over from his delightfully easy Tudor to the so-called Queen Anne only after 1865. In Berkshire he is represented by two of his Tudor houses, both exemplary of the elegance with which he could treat the Home Counties precedent: Greenham Lodge near Newbury of 1875 and Holme Grange, Wokingham, of 1883 are both imaginatively composed and, especially inside, boldly detailed.

Norman Shaw's influence on English domestic architecture was immense. It even reached as far as the Continent and America. It started off Lutyens as well as Stokes as well as Newton as well as *Baillie Scott*. By the latter there is one quite characteristic house dating from 1899 at Wantage, by *Stokes* Shooter's Hill House, Pangbourne, of 1898 and an exceedingly good new range at Ascot Priory of 1901, by *Newton* Luckley, 63 Wokingham, of 1907, but by *Lutyens* two of his best early houses: Deanery Gardens, Sonning, of 1901 and Folly Farm, Sulham- 62 stead, of 1906 and 1912. Folly Farm, however, shows him at the moment of abandoning the Arts and Crafts Tudor at which he was so supremely good and deserting to the William and Mary in which Shaw also had preceded him. Folly Farm is indeed the moment of transition; for here the William and Mary house of 1906 (added to a genuine timber-framed farmhouse) precedes the brilliant Arts and Crafts range by six years. This range, with its enormous roof, its low loggia of short piers, and its pool was Lutyens's last in that style. It was also among the last on that scale; for the First World War brought an end to the commissioning of rich men's country mansions. Berkshire has one of the most uninhibited Edwardian ones, even if designed a few years before Queen Victoria's death: *Sir John Belcher*'s Pangbourne Tower.

And there we can end – or nearly end. For the TWENTIETH CENTURY has not done much yet to the county other than covering large areas with indifferent houses and bungalows and all main roads with cars. New buildings of value which would justify inclusion on the standards so far applied all belong to the last five years: a forceful, somewhat overpowering skyscraper block of flats at Bracknell New Town by *Arup Associates* as 64 the only contribution Bracknell has so far made, a factory at Wokingham by *Yorke, Rosenberg & Mardall*, the Road Research Laboratory at Crowthorne by the Ministry of Public Building and Works (*J. Moss*), and the Army School of Electronic Engineering at Arborfield by *J. A. Ford* of the same Ministry. Add to this the fact that a private art lover has in his garden at Bucklebury two of *Henry Moore*'s reclining figures, and the survey is done.

Those who want to deepen their knowledge of the art and architecture of the county beyond what this Introduction and the following Gazetteer can do are referred to the following books. First and foremost the *Victoria County History* vols 3 and 4 of 1923 and 1924; then the accounts of country houses in *Country Life* and sundry papers in the *Berkshire Archaeological Journal*. The MHLG has completed its survey of the county, and this contains brief descriptions of far more houses than are mentioned in my gazetteer. The *Little Guide* (by F. G. Brabant, largely as written for the first edition in 1911) has just that much of historical enrichment as is missing in my pages, and Messrs Betjeman and Piper's *Berkshire*, 1949, has sensitive descriptions and a galaxy of first-rate photographs selected so as to keep away from the obvious. Having tried to do the same as far as possible, I regret to find that in the end I often chose the same subjects for the photographers as they had done.

APPENDIX: GEOLOGY

BY TERENCE MILLER

Berkshire, like its neighbours Wiltshire and Buckingham-shire, straddles the great chalk ridge of South and East England that runs down from the Wash to Weymouth Bay. The dominant geological feature of the county is thus the chalk, whether visibly present as surface rock, or lying buried beneath newer rocks, or, as in North Berkshire, w of Oxford, only comparatively recently – in the geological sense – stripped away to expose older strata below.

The structure of the chalk as a bed of rock is a sheet, 700 ft thick, dipping gently s, with its exposed upper or N edge forming the ridge which runs from White Horse Hill, by West Ilsley

Downs, down to the Thames N of Goring. This sheet passes s under the valley of the Kennet, and then turns up in a sharp wrinkle to reappear at the surface and form a second scarp face under Inkpen Beacon. In East Berkshire the quadrilateral Sonning–Henley–Farnham–Maidenhead also has chalk bedrock, and Windsor Castle stands on an outlying hump of it.

Only the N part of the chalk area – Lambourn Downs, for example – can be called 'typical chalk country', with bare, rolling grassland and clumps of beech or mixed timber. Elsewhere the pure white limestone is obscured by a jumbled deposit known as 'clay-with-flints'. This is the insoluble residue left after the weathering away of an originally thicker chalk cover. With a veneer of this kind, although the resulting soils are stony, they are capable of carrying good crops and much more extensive woodland than the bare chalk downs.

N of the chalk main scarp, with the ancient Ridgeway running along its crest, and the Icknield Way at its foot, lie the Vale of White Horse, the Berkshire Ridge, and, beyond, the valley of the upper Thames. These three strips are controlled by rock formations older than the chalk.

Immediately at the foot of the downs there is a flat shelf breaking the slope down to the River Ock. On this shelf, which is the outcrop area of a hardish sandstone (Malmstone) in the Upper Greensand formation, are Kingston Lisle, Wantage, Harwell, Didcot, and North Moreton. Parts of it carry notable cherry (and other fruit) orchards. Below this shelf the main part of the Vale of White Horse has been carved out of two adjacent clay formations, the Gault Clay (Cretaceous), and the Kimmeridge Clay (Jurassic). Neither of these is often exposed, as the surface of the bedrock is much covered by sands and gravels deposited by the meanders of river systems, both recent and ancient. The soils are cold and stiff, the fields often prominently marked by 'ridge-and-furrow', the hedges high, with strong oak trees. Much the same kind of clay land, but based on a still older formation, the Oxford Clay, underlies the upper Thames. Here, the flat river-sand and gravel terraces are wider and better defined than in the Vale. Between the two clay belts runs the North Berkshire Ridge, from Coleshill and Shrivenham, by Faringdon and Kingston Bagpuize, to Cothill and Cumnor, just outside Oxford.

This ridge marks the outcrop of relatively resistant mid-Jurassic (Corallian) limestones and sandstones, the same rocks which were formerly quarried enormously for the colleges of

Oxford. As the name suggests, certain of the limestones contain great masses of fossil corals. Parts of the ridge carry an additional capping of the much younger – but still pre-chalk – pebbly Lower Greensand. Badbury Hill and Faringdon Folly are examples of these Lower Greensand hills. Near Faringdon this sandy formation includes the famous Faringdon Sponge Bed, with a remarkable assemblage of fossil sponges, sea-urchins, and other sea creatures. Where the Coral Rag limestone forms the surface the soil is stony and good for wheat; elsewhere there is more loam, which carries orchards and hop-fields, or, in a few places, sandstone weathering down into sand-hills, as at Buckland Warren.

s of the line Hungerford–Reading–Windsor, Berkshire is made, for the most part, of rocks younger than the chalk. These younger rocks are mainly stiff yellow-brown clays and either greenish or red-brown sands, often pebbly. Isolated remnant patches of the same soft rocks also lie out on the chalk surface forward (i.e. N) of their main outcrop, as around Boxford and Hermitage, N of Newbury. There are three divisions: the oldest, the Reading Beds, mainly sandy; the middle, a thick (250 ft) sheet, of London Clay; and the youngest, also sandy, the Bagshot Beds. Of these, the Reading Beds have a relatively narrow outcrop, and the London Clay, like other clay formations, produces a rather dull and featureless landscape. In their own right, therefore, they contribute little to the Berkshire scene. Above them, however, sands and pebble-beds of the Bagshot group are responsible for many of the 'commons', gorse- or heather-covered, and with fine expanses of pine 'forest'. Considerable stretches of South Berkshire are modified – whether on a clay or sand bedrock – by spreads of sand and gravel produced originally by rivers draining off the great ice-sheet which once lay across North Berkshire. Although the main component of these Plateau Gravels and River Gravels is the familiar flint, there are, in addition, variable proportions of other, more exotic rock fragments, brought s by the ice-sheet itself, or by rivers draining from it, from the midland and northern counties. Greenham and Bucklebury Commons, and Aldermaston Park, are examples of the effect of Plateau Gravel patches; Bagshot Heath is a mixture of Bagshot sands and Plateau Gravels; Windsor Great Park, and most of the country from there w almost to Reading, is practically bare London Clay.

Berkshire has no important source of building stone of its own, but is within easy range of some of the most famous of

English freestones – Bath, Headington, and Portland. There has always been a steady flow of stone into the county, and comparatively little 'native' quarrying, with the exception of the Corallian limestones of the N, as at Cothill, near Oxford. On the other hand, as might be expected, both North and South Berkshire have an abundance of clays for brick-making – Oxford, Kimmeridge, and Gault Clays from formations older than the chalk; London Clay from the beds younger than the chalk. The chalk itself has been used, as in churches at Tilehurst, Sonning, and Waltham St Lawrence, but it is too soft for external use unless artificially protected. However, the irregular silica concretions – flints – which are scattered through the middle and upper chalk, and occur in profusion in the clay-with-flints and Plateau Gravels, have been an important building stone at least from Roman times. They were used in the Roman walls at Silchester, and appear, combined in various ways with stone, brick, or timber, in many Berkshire buildings.

The Reading, London, and Bagshot Beds, unmodified, contain no rock suitable for building. But by a natural process of patchy and irregular hardening certain sands of these formations provide isolated 'boulders' of tough sandstone – the famous Berkshire sarsens. These, left lying on the surface after the weathering away of the softer parent sand, may remain in place or be re-incorporated into river sands or gravels, or become embedded in the clay-with-flints. They may be found all over Berkshire, and have often been used as corner-stones, as stepping-stones, or gate-posts, or simply built into walls. Sarsen-built houses can be seen e.g. at Lambourn, Ashbury, and Idstone. Sarsen stones were also used in the chambered barrow 3a of Wayland's Smithy, Ashbury, and, very extensively, in Windsor Castle. Another example of a similar natural hardening process is found around Bagshot Heath, where a pebbly layer has been 'cemented' by ironstone to form a conglomeratic rock. Blocks of this are used at Wokingham church (tower) and the churches of Binfield, Warfield, and Winkfield.*

* Also Byfleet and Chobham in Surrey.

BERKSHIRE

*

ABINGDON

INTRODUCTION

Abingdon owes its existence to the abbey founded in 675. The
town grew up in front of the abbey gates with its market place
immediately outside the gatehouse – the same pattern as e.g.
Battle Abbey in Sussex. In Domesday Book no town is yet
mentioned – only 'ten traders before the gates'. The abbey
extended along the Thames. So did the town, with the church
at the far end. It makes a very fine view from the bridge, in
spite of the bloody-minded insistence of the gaol on its own
presence. The prosperity of Abingdon was first that of the
abbey, later of a flourishing woollen trade. There were bitter
struggles between abbey and town throughout the Later Middle
Ages.

CHURCHES

St Helen. The steeple rises splendidly at the s end of East St
Helens. It is a C13 steeple, which is surprising considering
the rest of the church. Doorway to the N with shafts with leaf
capitals. Smaller blank arches l. and r. Lancet windows with
continuous roll mouldings above. Pairs of lancets as bell-
openings. Perp parapet with pinnacles. Spire with one set of
lucarnes at the foot and a band above. The steeple has often
been restored. The spire was last rebuilt in 1888. To this
tower, which was always a N tower, a C13 church belonged.
This consisted of nave and N aisle. Part of the E wall still remains, but the rest was remodelled when, in the C15 and C16,
Abingdon built itself an exceedingly spacious new church
with double aisles N and s. One examines the exterior by
entering the churchyard from the tower through an Elizabethan archway. Between steeple and two-storeyed N porch
a formerly two-storeyed structure supposed to have been
the priest's dwelling. The porch has to the front three small
niches. Then (renewed) Dec windows, i.e. in the N wall of the

C13 N aisle. The w view is all Perp, four large windows, but no regularity. Also a w porch. The s side is Perp and ends on the E in a vestry or treasury, so that to the E there are five gables of different pitch and details. Those of the chancel E window are evidently Victorian. This E side borders immediately on a street. The interior has four arcades all essentially the same, with concave-sided octagonal piers, concave-sided capitals, and moulded depressed arches. The nave has a clerestory. The outer s aisle was built in 1539, according to a preserved will. The chancel details are even more blatantly High Victorian–E.E. internally than externally. They are by *Woodyer*, 1873, and cost £7,000 (PF). By him no doubt also the N doorway from the tower porch.

FURNISHINGS. FONT. By *H. P. Peyman* of Abingdon. Shown in the 1851 Exhibition. Copy in white marble of the font of Sutton Courtenay. – FONT COVER. Dated 1634. – REREDOS. By *Bodley*, 1897. – ALTAR in the inner N aisle. By *Bodley*, c.1897. – PULPIT. Dated 1636. Very good; not over-done. Angle columns, simple arched panels, but with a pedimented feature in each panel with an indicated false perspective (cf. Buckland and Shrivenham). – ORGAN CASE. 1725 by *Abraham Jordan*, with good carving. – MAYOR'S SEAT. 1706, with openwork foliage front, carved lion and unicorn instead of poppy-heads, and a small iron SWORD REST. – PAINTING. The roof of the inner N aisle is panelled, and the panels were painted about 1390. The *ensemble* is unique in England and artistically very valuable. It consists of canted sides painted with figures and a flat top part painted with delightfully traceried interlocked lozenges. The figures are set in narrow cusped panels and each pair under an ogee arch with panelled spandrels. At the foot, disregarding the panels, runs a vine trail. This motif reveals the whole as having been a Tree of Jesse. Prophets and Kings alternate, but at the E end of the N side is Christ crucified framed by the Annunciation. Jesse himself and the other earliest figures were at the w end of the s side and are not preserved. An inscription runs all along the cornice of the canted parts and tells us that the chapel was built by William Reve, and the roof repaired by William Cholsey, and that Boniface IX offered an indulgence to those helping in the repair. Reve belongs to the second half of the C13, but Boniface IX ruled from 1389 to 1404, and the indulgence dates from 1391. The style of the figures is typical of this date and may be compared with panels from screens

in East Anglia or the Despenser Retable in Norwich Cathedral.
– STAINED GLASS. In the outer N aisle W window large figures
in strident colours, early C19 (TK: c.1819?). – By *Kempe* N
1889, inner N aisle W c.1914, outer S aisle 1893. – CHANDE-
LIERS. Of brass, three large, one smaller. Two of the large
ones are inscribed 1710 and 1713, the third seems C16. –
PLATE. Cup of 1567, altered; Almsdish given in 1829. –
MONUMENTS. Brass to Geoffrey Barbour † 1417, a merchant,
demi-figure (inner S aisle W), 13 in. long. – Brass to William
Herward † 1501 (inner S aisle E), 29 in. long. – Edmund
Bostock † 1605. Nice small tablet (inner S aisle E). – Mrs
Hawkins, by *J. Hickey*, 1782. A major work by a minor
sculptor. It was a difficult job to compose a monument so as
to display six portraits. Seated woman holding books. She sits
in front of a Rococo strigillated object which may mean a
sarcophagus. Her arm rests on a medallion with the portrait
of her fiancé, the Rev. Mr Hart. L. and r. busts, above the
strigillated object two busts and an urn. The busts represent
Mrs Hawkins's father and mother, sister and cousin. – Dr
John Crossley † 1790 by *Nollekens*. Conventional, with a big
putto by an urn. – Very many more tablets.

CHRIST CHURCH, Northcourt Road. Converted by *W. Emil
Godfrey* in 1961 from the BARN of Northcourt Farm, a tithe
barn of Abingdon Abbey. The transept now has a glazed end
wall, and there is an identical window opposite. The barn itself is of stone and attributed to the C13. The roof has tie-
beams and queen-posts, probably C15 or C16.

ST MARY AND ST EDMUND (R.C.), Oxford and Radley Roads.
1857 by *G. Goldie* (GS). Tall, of nave with bellcote and chancel
and S aisle and N chapel. Geometrical tracery. The former
SCHOOL to the N. (In the churchyard MONUMENT to the 7th
Earl of Abingdon † 1928 by *Eric Gill*.)

ST MICHAEL, Park Road. 1864–7 by *Sir G. G. Scott*. Nave and
aisles, transepts, chancel, high bellcote. Geometrical tracery.
A quiet, dignified design. Round and octagonal piers, quatrefoil clerestory.

ST NICHOLAS, Market Place. An odd W front. Late Norman
doorway with three orders of shafts. Arch with roll mouldings,
one with a fillet. Though much restored, there seems to be
indication of more Norman work here, including blank
arcading, and it is not in line with the present church. This
church has to the N two lancets and traces of a third, to the S
(where the parapet is of 1881) two Dec windows. Otherwise

Perp, including the w tower, built into the older nave, and
the odd oriel or shallow chapel to the N. This is said to be of
the restoration of 1881, but the window is certainly at least
partly old. – FONT. C15. Broad, panelled stem, bowl with
quatrefoils. – PULPIT. Jacobean. The book rest is supported
by two eagles. – SCULPTURE. Small stone relief of the Crucifixion and two saints. – PLATE. Set of 1786. – MONUMENT.
John Blacknall † 1625. Two kneeling figures. Altar front with
flat strap decoration. The monument was not erected till 1684
and moved in 1881.

NONCONFORMIST CHAPELS. A most instructive set of four,
all of between 1840 and 1875. First BAPTIST, Ock Street,
1841, still purely classical, with an attached portico of Tuscan
columns carrying a pediment. Then CONGREGATIONAL,
The Square, 1862 by *J. S. Dodd* (BC), classical going Italian,
with giant pilasters and a pediment, just a little less disciplined than twenty years before. Then METHODIST, Ock
Street, 1845 by *Wilson* of Bath, Gothic in the early, modest
lancet way, and finally TRINITY METHODIST, Park Road,
by *Woodman*, 1875, full-blown churchy, with a large N
steeple and fussy Geometrical tracery, evidently to outdo
Scott's St Michael's in the same street of the 'west-end' of
Abingdon.

ABINGDON ABBEY

Abingdon Abbey, as has already been said, was founded in
675. The Abingdon Chronicle tells us that the church was
only 120 ft long, but had a w as well as an E apse, a custom
extant in North Africa (Orléansville) in Early Christian times
and in Germany from the C9 onwards (Fulda, plan for St
Gall). Further efforts ought to be made to excavate. After all,
the church was on ground not now covered by buildings. The
Danes wrought destruction. Under Aethelwold in 955 the
abbey was re-founded. Under Abbot Fabritius (1100–17) it
reached a climax of prosperity. In 1100 there were twenty-
eight monks, in 1117 seventy-eight. In the C15 and early C16
the average was about thirty. Nothing of the abbey church is
visible *in situ* at all, and little of the monastic buildings. The
w boundary of the area extended from the river N, along Stert
Street as far as the railway station. The street called The
Vineyard was indeed the abbey vineyard. The most impressive monument now is the ABBEY GATEWAY. It is of the late
C15 and has three archways, the southern one C19. The arch-

ways have depressed pointed arches with traceried spandrels. Above the middle arch a niche with an original statue of the Virgin. Two-light windows, battlements. Three bays of tierceron vaulting across the interior. The E face of the gatehouse is similar to the other. The gatehouse is attached to the church of St Nicholas, which must have been in the same relation to the abbey as was St Lawrence by the gatehouse to Reading Abbey. And as at Reading the *hospitium* of St John Baptist is close to this place, so it was at Abingdon, where the Hospital of St John is now the Municipal Buildings (*see* below). E of the abbey gateway are the Abbey Gardens. It is here, a little to the E, that the church stood. Instead there are now in the gardens a number of salvaged architectural fragments: two window-heads, one late C13, the other Dec, an artificial ruin with three-bay arcades running N–S, piers and arches identical with those of St Helen, and large E and W window frames. Too little seems known about these fragments.

The only consistent range of abbey buildings is a subsidiary one along the river, SE of the gateway and SW of the church. They consist from E to W of the Long Gallery, the Chequer, and then a lower range. The LONG GALLERY dates from about 1500. It is partly of stone, partly timber-framed. It was originally divided into divers rooms, and access to them was by a timber gallery or cloister walk, comparable to that of the Long Alley Almshouses and to the gallery of the Horseshoe Cloister and the older Canons' Cloister at Windsor. The windows are straight-headed and were never glazed. The rooms were separated from the gallery by partition walls. They had a roof with tie-beams on arched braces. To the W of this range is the CHEQUER, a square C13 block of stone *See* with buttresses and a doorway which has a two-centred arch $_{359}^{p.}$ and continuous mouldings. This leads into an undercroft with one octagonal pier. No capital, single-chamfered ribs in four bays. The room above has another doorway with continuous mouldings and two Dec two-light windows. Tall chimney with a rare and interesting top, the most interesting of its date $_{34b}$ in England. The vents are three stepped little lancets in a gable. The room inside has to the S also two windows which are blocked. Excellent C13 fireplace with stiff-leaf and other leaf capitals and a projecting hood. The room was divided in two in the C14 and a triangular lobby made with three doorways. One opened towards the river. W of the Chequer is a lower stone range and then a timber-framed gable on a stone base. Roof with two tiers of wind-braces. This range was probably the GRANARY.*

PUBLIC BUILDINGS

45b TOWN HALL, Market Square. Built in 1678–82. The 'under-taker' of the work was *Christopher Kempster* of Burford, one of Wren's City masons. It is not known whether he also designed it, or who else did. Of the free-standing town halls of England with open ground floors this is the grandest – grander decidedly than Windsor. It is also remarkably high and monumental for its two storeys. Celia Fiennes called it the finest town hall in England. Brown stone, four by two bays. Giant pilasters on very high plinths used consistently. Open arches below, the windows above of three lights arched with a transom and the mullions forming a concentric arch above the transom – Wren's pattern at Trinity Library Cambridge. Hipped roof, top balustrade, and cupola, as was used for country houses of c.1635–75. At the back a staircase tower ending in bulbous pinnacles. The stair rail is of the dumb-bell type. The ground floor was of course used as a market, the upper room as a court room. It is now absolutely plain. Balcony on four wooden Corinthian columns. – STAINED GLASS. Heraldic, from St Nicholas. Made by *J. H. Russell*, c.1830. – REGALIA. Small Mace bought in 1584; two Cups, 1639; Tankards of 1651, 1653–4, 1675, and 1681; Great Mace, silver-gilt, 1660 or earlier; small Mace, *temp.* Charles II; small Mace, *temp.* James II; large Tankard, 1700; Set of Casters, pair of Salts, and twelve Spoons, 1721; Plate, 1735; two Punch-Bowls and Ladles given in 1740; two large Cups and two Salvers given in 1744; four Salts, 1759–60; two Punch-Bowls and Ladles, given in 1760–1; four Salts, 1764–5; two Candlesticks, 1774; large Cup and Cover, 1795–6; Sets of Spoons of 1798–9, 1799, 1818, 1826–7; Strainer, 1810; Salt Spoons inscribed 1810; Strainer, 1814–15; Fish Slices, 1827–8; also later C19 plate.

MUNICIPAL BUILDINGS, Market Place. A group of buildings not originally belonging together. The range towards St Nicholas and the Abbey Gate has a rubble ground floor with restored Perp windows and a better preserved S doorway and belonged to the Hospital of St John. In 1731–3 *John Stevens* of

* The surviving range of abbey building faces THAMES STREET to the S. At the E end of this is MILL HOUSE, now the vicarage. This has a doorway with a two-centred arch, and on the attic floor blocked Perp windows.

Wantage raised the building one storey, and in this new part, in 1759, a fine Council Chamber was made. The N front has in the middle a big niche flanked by pairs of Doric pilasters, placed naïvely on brackets. The main doorway inside the Council Chamber has a pediment and is well detailed. Nice coving. Two end chimneypieces. To the W the Municipal Buildings have a successful outer staircase arrangement provided in 1958 and incorporating to the N a curious doorway with Elizabethan caryatids but C18 Gothick top parts. The continuation is of 1811. Behind, towards Bridge Street, is an irregular brick part, also of 1731 etc. This contains the staircase (with turned and twisted balusters) and the so-called Bear Room with a handsome Venetian window. The doorways have odd, rather heavy, still Early Georgian surrounds. There follows part of the former ROYSSE'S GRAMMAR SCHOOL, to which the entrance was the archway mentioned before. It is a timber-framed building which also formed part of the hospital originally. Inside is now a gallery with a stucco tunnel-vault. This dates from 1911.

POLICE, Bridge Street. 1857. Seven bays, two storeys, the windows widely spaced. A plain, honest job.

FREE LIBRARY, High Street. 1896 by *J. G. T. West*. Half-timbered, with gables, and too tall to be either historically credible or suitable within the scale of Abingdon.

GRAMMAR SCHOOL, Park Road. The oldest part is the W part: 1869–70 by *Edwin Dolby*: brick, high, clumsy, and Gothic. The range to the E of this is lighter in brick and style: 1879–80. The Chapel is of 1902, by *West*.

CONVENT SCHOOL OF ST HELEN AND ST KATHERINE, Ferndale Road. 1904–5 by *F. Pearson*, brick; the stone chapel by the same, 1922.

FITZHARRY'S SCHOOL, Northcourt Road. By *J. T. Castle*, the Berkshire County Architect, 1958–60. Good.

PRIMARY SCHOOL, E of the former. By *Bridgwater & Shepheard*, 1949–52. Is this the earliest school in England to use pre-stressed concrete?

GAOL. 1805–11, by *Daniel Harris* of Oxford. This bastille of Berkshire is impressive enough by itself; as a job of siting it is unpardonable. Hexagonal centre and radiating wings, as then usual. Brown stone, small windows.

CORN EXCHANGE, Market Place. 1886 by *Charles Bell*. Brick, and really with no definite style nor alas any personality.

ABINGDON BRIDGE. The medieval bridge, dating from 1416,

was mostly rebuilt in 1927. The first two ribbed, depressed-
pointed arches on the Abingdon side were allowed to remain.
They were widened with ribs of the older, rebuilt arches. The
view towards St Helen's church is lovely, or would be, if it
were not for the gaol.

The MARKET PLACE has of course its fair share of fine buildings,
but it has also two for which nothing good can be said: the
Corn Exchange (see above) and the QUEENS HOTEL, red and
yellow brick, of 1864, and quite unbelievably joyless. No
houses of individual interest otherwise. We must radiate from
the Market Place. To the S BRIDGE STREET with the CROWN
HOTEL, whose pretty courtyard repays a visit. Also to the S,
from behind the TOWN HALL, EAST ST HELENS runs to
the church. It is as a street perhaps the best in Abingdon –
also because it is not haunted by traffic as badly as the others.
The first notable house still belongs to the Market Place: four
bays, three storeys, early C18, the top windows with frills to
the lintels. No. 19 is timber-framed and has windows of the
so-called Ipswich type which are typical of c.1665–75 and
occur often at Abingdon. They are tripartite and straight-
topped, but the middle light has an arch below the top. Then
opposite TWICKENHAM HOUSE, built for Joseph Tomkins,
mid Georgian, of red brick, five bays, two storeys, with a
three-bay pediment. Doorway with Ionic columns and a pediment. In the frieze a Kentian head. Pretty, white Chinese-
Chippendale staircase. (Other rewarding interior features, e.g.
late C18 Gothic bookcases.) Stables on the l. with a pediment.
Nos 31–33 are early C19, Bath stone and perfectly smooth.
No. 26 is of the late C15, with overhang and two gables.
Inside, a stone chimneypiece with a lintel decorated with
cusped panels. The sides of the dormers have trefoil-headed
windows, and a similar window of three lights is in the E wall.
No. 28 is of c.1570, low and long, and originally had gables.
The doorway has a segmental pediment on composite pilasters
and a frieze running up to a point in the middle – i.e. Early
Georgian. To its r. are two small Elizabethan or slightly later
windows. Panelling, fireplaces, and original roof timbers
inside. No. 30 is Early Georgian too, of five bays, chequer
brick with two gables. The doorway similar to the previous
one. At the back some C15 evidence. The street then narrows
and has a gabled house (Nos 32–34) across the vista. Over-

hang on brackets. Opposite another house with an oversailing
upper floor. Its neighbour is No. 57, dated 1732. Chequer
brick, five bays, even brick quoins. The middle bay framed
by pilaster strips. Later doorway. So on to the steeple of St
Helen, which forms the *point-de-vue* for the later part of the
walk along the street. The last house is FELLOWS' CLOSE
(formerly Helenstow), two-storeyed with a large, arched entrance to the yard. Several pre-Reformation windows, one of
them wooden, another stone, of two lights.

In the CHURCHYARD of St Helen a small square brick box with
a pyramid roof, which is the Organ Blowing Chamber, and
three sets of Almshouses. No other churchyard anywhere has
anything like it. The centre of the three is CHRIST'S HOS-
PITAL or the LONG ALLEY ALMSHOUSES. They were built 36b
in 1446, though it is doubtful if much of that date is still
visible on the front. This front has a wooden pentice or
cloister walk. The porch is of 1605 and has pilasters with
volutes outside and a gable. The cloister windows with arched
lights may well be of the same date. The pretty lantern was
put on in 1707. The side to the river is rubble-faced and C15,
though it carries a date 1674. In the centre inside is a panelled
hall with pilasters and a bay window to the back. To the r.
of Christ's Hospital TWITTY'S ALMSHOUSES of 1707. Red
brick, also one-storeyed. Hipped roof with gable and lantern.
Seven dwellings. To the l. of Christ's Hospital and with their
back to the river the BRICK ALLEY ALMSHOUSES of 1718, 47a
built for Christ's Hospital by *Samuel Westbrooke*, mason.
Chequer brick and rubbed brick. Seven bays, the centre solid
and raised with a pediment, the sides giant arches or niches
in which are the doors and upper balconies, a very unusual
and rather modern conceit. To the river just two storeys, the
ground floor with segment-headed windows. Back from here
to the church by the s end of East St Helens, with Nos. 58–
60, John Tomkins's malthouse, of chequer brick, dated 1748.

Now from the Market Place w, i.e. along HIGH STREET. No. 10
has a charming C18 ground floor with the doorway between
two bow windows and a metope frieze running all along.
Opposite the LION INN, timber-framed, with two slightly
projecting gabled windows. The High Street ends at THE
SQUARE, not at all square. On its e side a nice timber-framed
group. We shall go on here presently. First OCK STREET,
the continuation of High Street. On the r. a deep Doric porch.
Then No. 5, with some Gothick window details, and No. 7,

with a nice doorcase with a decorated frieze. After that the grandest Abingdon house, built probably for one of the Tomkins family. Early Georgian, nine bays, three full storeys, panelled parapet. Straight-headed windows. Windows one, four, six, nine are narrower. Paired doorways (later?). Good interior features. To the l. STABLES, a deep open courtyard with, in the middle of the end range, archway, Venetian window, and cupola. The wings have giant blank arches and pediments to the street. Much more of nice houses (notably No. 28, with a rich mid C18 chimneypiece and a staircase with stucco panels and alternatingly columnar and twisted balusters). At the corner of CONDUIT ROAD, ELY'S CONDUIT, a plain brick niche, with a date 1719. This is followed by TOMKINS' ALMSHOUSES, 1733. Brick. Two rows with a characteristic frontispiece at the far end. More worthwhile houses further W: Nos 91–93 of c.1700, Nos 105–109 of the late C17, Nos 125–129 of c.1700 (three large gables), and No. 143 of c.1600 (overhang of the E wall).

From the Square BATH STREET goes N. The best house here is STRATTON HOUSE, built by Benjamin Tomkins and dated 1722. Seven bays with bays three and five narrower and blocked. Red and rubbed red brick. Segment-headed windows with frills to the lintels. Doorway with Roman Doric pilasters and a triglyph frieze. The middle window also flanked by pilasters. Staircase with thin twisted balusters. Then, on the other side, THE GABLES, timber-framed, mid C16, with three gables. Turn W from Bath Street to have a look at PARK ROAD and ALBERT PARK. This is the 'North Abingdon' in the North Oxford sense, villas and terrace houses in Gothic varieties. In the park the CONDUIT, a plain C16 stone cube with a pyramid roof (SE corner), and the MONUMENT to Prince Albert, a statue on a pedestal so high that it is almost like a column (total 48 ft). By *Gibbs* of Oxford, 1865.

Back again to the Market Place and now N along STERT STREET. No. 3 is timber-framed and of pre-Reformation date. The stone doorway, though, may be *ex situ*. The two projecting gabled upper windows and the two main gables are probably a C17 alteration. Nos 31–33 are also timber-framed and have two symmetrical gables. They are structurally C15. Then BROAD STREET on the l. Nos 12–16 with three gables. No. 32 with Ipswich windows. Stert Street narrows a little further N and No. 52, THE KNOWL, stands across, a charming timber-framed house with an oversailing upper floor and pargetting to the side, but an early C18 front of five bays and a doorway with Roman Doric pilasters, decorated metopes, and a segmental pediment. Staircase with twisted balusters. On into VINEYARD. On the l. BANBURY COURT, flats in a stepped arrangement. 1962 by *Dennis Page & Partners*. Opposite No. 21, five bays, doorway with pilasters and pediment. Then No. 45, late C18, three bays, and the second floor all three as big lunette windows. Opposite ST JOHN'S HOSPITAL, 1801. Two-storeyed, chequer brick, with projecting wings.

Then, to finish with, out along the Radley Road, to the r. into Barton Lane and to BARTON MANOR, where, next to the house, the inarticulate, two-storeyed ruin of the former barn of the abbots of Abingdon.

PAGAN SAXON CEMETERY. The site was discovered during road work in Saxton Road. The cemetery consisted of seventy-nine cremations in urns and one-hundred and twenty-two inhumation burials. Among the grave goods were numerous disc and saucer brooches, miniature toilet instruments of iron, and in male graves knives, javelins, and swords.

ROUND BARROW, s of Gosford. This large, tree-covered barrow is 60 ft in diameter and 4 ft high. Ploughing right up to the perimeter of the mound has obliterated all traces of the surrounding ditch, which is now visible only as a crop mark from the air.

ROUND BARROW, 1½ m. SW, on Sutton Wick Field. This great barrow, 150 ft in diameter and 5 ft high, has been much reduced by ploughing. No surrounding ditch is visible.

ALDERMASTON

5060

ST MARY. Nave and chancel long, under one roof; s transept, w tower with shingled broach spire. The length of the building is explained by the fact that the nave was Norman and that then, early in the C13, the chancel was thrown into the nave (see the break in the width inside), the transept was added, and a new chancel, itself long, was built. In the chancel lancets, the s transept arch pointed with only a slight chamfer. Norman the small N doorway into the former chancel and the re-set w doorway with an order of colonnettes with spiral and zigzag decoration. The capitals have pairs of birds. Inside the church an excellent large Norman head (s wall). Chancel roof with tie-beams and kingposts. – PULPIT. Elizabethan, with tester. Arabesques and blank arches. – PANELLING of the nave walls; C17. – Two CHANDELIERS of the C18. – PAINTING. Much is preserved in the s transept, though not very well. On the l. of the s window large early C14 St Christopher. On the r. C15 scene with luxuriant canopy. Also traces of C13 masonry patterns. – (PAINTING. Triptych, Adoration, Flemish, early C16.) – STAINED GLASS. In two chancel N windows C13 roundels of the Annunciation and the Coronation of the Virgin. – The rest of the chancel by *Kempe*, 1898. – Funeral HELM in the s transept. – PLATE. Cup and Cover, 1576; Silver-gilt Cup and Cover, *c*.1635; two silver-gilt Flagons, 1718; Paten, 1718; Set of 1809. – MONUMENT. Sir George Forster and his wife who died in 1526. Made probably *c*.1530. Alabaster and of the highest quality, especially the small figures. Recumbent effigies.

27   Against the tomb-chest standing sons and standing daughters under canopies. From the same hand probably as the Roos Monument at Windsor.

ALDERMASTON COURT. The house of 1636 was destroyed by fire in 1843. In illustrations it looks, with its hipped roof, rather 1660 than 1636, but 1636 is the date on a preserved tablet, and it fits the preserved woodwork. This consists of

41   the splendid staircase running through two storeys and some additional figures. These figures, all allegorical or mythological, are still as Mannerist as in 1610, besides being very good for their date. The staircase itself is memorable as being one of the earliest to have a pierced parapet instead of banisters. The parapet moreover is no longer strictly strapwork, but in a state of transition from strapwork to broad-leaved foliage and to gristly forms. The staircase is now inside *P. C. Hardwick*'s mansion for Daniel Higford Darvall Burr. He built it in 1848–51, and it cost over £20,000 (GS). Tudor style, completely asymmetrical on the main (entrance) side. Brick with blue diapers. Mullioned and transomed windows, with and without arched lights. Further back, i.e. part of the back elevation, a slender tower with close 'flushwork' of stone and brick and a kind of steep pavilion-roof top. Very spiky chimneystacks. Large rooms inside. The STABLES are C17, see e.g. the doorway with the steep open pediment. Of *c*.1636 also the grand LODGES, two-storeyed with semicircular gables. They were originally the two wings of a house.

The lodges look down the almost straight village street, which is closed visually at the bottom by the C18 inn. L. and r. all brick cottages, varying in date and shape, but none an intrusion. Behind the inn the village LOCK-UP, brick, with a shallow dome.

In the grounds of Aldermaston Court the buildings erected in 1949–61 by the Ministry of Works for the ATOMIC ENERGY AUTHORITY, impressive and architecturally well-designed structures by the *Ministry of Works* architects.

OLD MILL. Nice group of a five-bay brick house and the brick mill.

GRIM'S BANK. This great earthwork begins on Little Heath, 1 m. SE of Aldermaston Court. At this point the bank still stands 8 ft high and the W-facing ditch is clearly visible. The earthwork runs in a straight NE direction for over ½ m. and then changes to a more northerly direction for a further 300 yds to the W edge of Padworth Common. There is then a gap of some 450 yds before the earthwork resumes its course in a NE direction across the common. Presumably the vegetation at the time of the earthwork's construction was sufficiently dense to provide a natural barrier at this point. At the beginning of this second length of earthwork the bank is some 5 ft high, but traces of the ditch have been almost obliterated by infilling and ploughing. In its continuing NE course close to the summit of Raven Hill and through Old Park the bank is a comparatively slight feature, only 3 ft high. Beyond Old Park it alters course to a more northerly direction for 270 yds and then turns again NE for the final 70 yds of its length.

In Old Park and 150 yds SE of Grim's Bank is a second massive earthwork, GRIM'S BANK II. This earthwork has a bank some 8 ft high with a broad, W-facing ditch. It runs in a straight NE direction across flat country for nearly ¾ m.

Both these earthworks and the lesser bank and ditch systems associated with them in the Old Park area are regarded as boundary dykes erected in the C5 by the Britons, centred on Silchester, Hants, as a bulwark against the growing pressure of Saxon incursions.

ALDWORTH

5070

ST MARY. The church houses one of the richest collections of C14 effigies in the country. It is in fact partly of the early C14 itself. But the W tower is earlier, broader than deep, with pairs of single small lancets as bell-openings and a recent pyramid roof. The chancel side window probably *c.*1300 (cusped Y-tracery), and the S aisle properly Dec, i.e. with windows of three lights with two big reticulation units, a doorway with a typical moulding, and arcade arches of a typical moulding. The octagonal piers, however, both bases and capitals, look later C14. To the aisle they have two dogs as hood-mould stops who look as if they came straight from a comic of today. The aisle is remarkably wide, a little wider in fact than the nave. The date 1315 recorded for the re-dedication of the high altar probably refers to the chancel, but it could also refer

25a to at least six of the eight MONUMENTS to members of the de la Beche family. The six are arranged three against the N wall under identical canopies, three against the S wall under identical canopies, very similar to the others, but not quite the same, and two under arcade arches. The canopies were alas terribly over-restored by *St Aubyn* in 1871, or rather by (BC) *Earp*, who did the actual carving. They are cusped and subcusped with pierced spandrels and the cusps in a very original way not meeting at a point, but forked. Ogee gables with crockets and finial. The S canopies are divided by two buttress shafts, the N canopies by one broad one. Now the effigies themselves. One of those under the canopies is a Lady. She has an ample mantle falling in chiefly vertical folds. The others are Knights, all cross-legged, one totally defaced. The most interesting are the Lady, the Knight

25b to her E, and the easternmost Knight on the N side, the first two because they are not recumbent but turned slightly but decidedly to one side – which adds something intimate that is unusual in early C14 monuments – the third because he is represented in a most exceptional way, semi-reclining, almost like a Sansovino or an English Jacobean effigy. He leans on one elbow, his knees are pulled up, his feet are crossed, and by his feet sits a page. There is also stiff-leaf foliage to indicate the grass on which the page sits. Stiff-leaf was dead by 1300. How early can this monument be? One would not risk any date earlier than 1290, and even then it is all highly individual. The two monuments under the arcade seem later, mid C14 probably, because the two Knights have their legs no longer crossed. But that argument is not always reliable. The Lady lying next to one of them, however, must be early C14 again, or indeed late C13; for her drapery still falls in the convention of C13 Virgins, i.e. with a rounded fold across and then diagonals down. – PULPIT. Very fine, with decoration

of a Cornelis Floris type not at all common in England.* –
READER'S DESK. Also very Netherlandish, but much busier.
– BENCH ENDS. With large, very summarily shaped poppy-
heads and a nice variety of inhabitants. Three of them are
Perp, the other three Jacobean. – SCULPTURE. Head of
Christ(?). In the vestry. Mid C14 and supposed to have be-
longed to one of the monuments. Originally probably a
bracket. – PLATE. Cup and Cover, 1632. – In the churchyard
a yew-tree of 27 ft girth, called gigantic in the *Gentleman's
Magazine* already in 1760, 1798, and 1799.

ALFRED'S CASTLE *see* ASHDOWN PARK

AMBERROW COURT *see* SANDHURST

APPLEFORD   *5090*

ST PETER AND ST PAUL. Over-restored, but with a simple
Late Norman S doorway and a C13 chancel S doorway. The
nave was recast by *Ewan Christian*, the W tower, whose buttresses rise in many set-offs and which carries a square spire
with half-hipped lucarnes, by *W. Gillbee Scott*, 1885–6 (BC). –
COMMUNION RAIL. Early C18.

APPLETON   *4000*

ST LAWRENCE. A Late Norman church, as the four-bay N
arcade shows. Round piers, square abaci, the capitals not high
and two with leaf. The W respond has trumpet scallops.
Pointed arches with one slight chamfer. Perp W tower unbuttressed. – FONT. The base is part of a Norman font with
spiral decoration including beaded bands. – COMMUNION
RAIL. Early C18. – PLATE. Cup, 1659; Almsdish, 1683; Cover
Paten, 1728. – MONUMENTS. Brasses to John Goudrington
† 1518 and wife. 27 in. figures in shrouds. – Sir John Fettiplace, 1593. Stone. Recumbent effigy. Columns l. and r.
Elaborate strapwork on the back wall. – Mrs Southby † 1806.
By *R. Blore*. In the style of Bacon. Two female figures by an
urn.

APPLETON MANOR. An amazing survival. Part of a manor-
house of 1190 or 1200 with a doorway worthy of any major
church. Three orders of colonnettes. Big upright stiff-leaf

---

* In the vestry are two panels, re-used for a cupboard door, which
probably were the doors of the pulpit. The pulpit came from St Laurence at
Reading.

capitals. Round arches with deep mouldings. Through the
doorway one entered the hall, and two quite large round-
arched doorways to the service rooms have also survived.
They have one slight chamfer and rolls as hood-moulds. A
small head between the two. The hall outer walls are evident,
by one nook-shafted corner. The fireplace is a Tudor inser-
tion, though lengths of roll moulding have been re-used. In
front of the main doorway a Tudor porch with timber-
framed upper floor. The timbers are exposed on one side. To
the N of the Manor a weatherboarded barn and attached to it
a gateway.

POST OFFICE. Dated 1690. The porch has a gable or steep
tympanum with a symmetrical leaf-trail pattern in pargetting.
S of it a brick cottage, probably of the early C18, with windows
not segment-headed but half-ellipse-headed.

ARBORFIELD

7060

ST BARTHOLOMEW. 1863 by *J. A. Picton*. Nave, chancel, apse.
Flint. Early Dec style. – STAINED GLASS. Head of Aaron by
John Rowell of Wycombe; 1744. Large head, strong colours,
entirely pictorial. – PLATE. Two Patens inscribed 1793. –
MONUMENT. William Standen † 1639. Large tomb-chest with
black columns and on it the two recumbent effigies, their
small child lying across their feet. Alabaster, and feelingly
carved.

The OLD CHURCH and ARBORFIELD HALL have both gone.
Of the church one flint wall remains, and the shell of a brick
addition.

ARBORFIELD COURT, 1 m. S. Neo-Georgian of the early
Edwardian type. By *F. B. Wade*, 1906.

BARTLETT'S FARMHOUSE, 1 m. SSW. Red brick, five bays,
doorways with Roman Doric pilasters.

R.E.M.E. SCHOOL OF ELECTRONIC ENGINEERING, 1¼ m.
SE. By *J. A. Ford* (*Ministry of Public Building and Works*). An
excellent group, axial to one side, free to the other, Miesian
in style.

ARDINGTON

4080

HOLY TRINITY. The church is dominated externally by the
Victorian spire on the N tower and the Victorian N chapel, and
internally by the rich Victorian decoration of the chancel with
much stencilling. The tower and spire are by *Joseph Clarke*,
1856 (BC), the rest of the Victorian building and enrichment by

Somers Clarke (1887). But when one looks more closely, the church has a long and interesting architectural history. It starts about 1200 or a little later with the N doorway, which has a round arch of many mouldings and some dogtooth enrichment, and a small N lancet, and is continued at once, i.e. *c.*1210 or so, by the four-bay s arcade with round piers, big stiff-leaf capitals of three different varieties (one with two tiers), and pointed arches with one slight chamfer, and then the N tower to its E, whose arch towards the church is double-chamfered and has a hood-mould on stiff-leaf stops, and the chancel arch with three orders of columns, one with stiff-leaf capitals and an arch of three proper chamfers, and the arches to the s and N chapels, the one with two chamfers, the other with two hollow chamfers. There is more work of that date, but it is in confusion. What for instance is original of the two big squints? One, in the s chapel, has a pointed-trefoiled arch. And are the two responds of the arch from s aisle into s chapel *ex situ*? One has a stiff-leaf capital, the other a brilliant late C13 capital with naturalistic leaves and a dragon and a lion. The arch they carry is clearly Perp. The s doorway has, in one moulding, the charming motif of ballflowers connected by a trail.* In the aisle is one window with Y-tracery. So that dates the aisle wall as early C14. Perp the nave roof with foliage bosses on lively stone corbels. – FONT. Octagonal, with ballflowers on the base. – PULPIT. Jacobean, with blank arches. The tester is not genuine. – ARCHITECTURAL FRAGMENTS. In the porch a charming late C13 gablet with a king's head, foliage, and two dragons. – Also a Pelican corbel and the canopy of a former image. – PLATE. Cup and Cover of 1573; Flagon of 1633; Paten of 1636. – MONUMENTS. Clarke family, *c.*1635. Tablet with black columns, swags, and angels. – Robert Vernon † 1849. Two memorials, one his bust in a lavish Gothic surround, the other a large white kneeling female figure, amply draped. This is by *Baily*. – In the churchyard CROSS. The shaft is, and the part above with the 'gargoyles' seems to be, original.

ARDINGTON HOUSE. Built in 1721 (VCH). A swagger three-storeyed building of vitrified grey and red brick. Seven bays with a projecting three-bay centre. This carries a decorated pediment. The windows are segment-headed in the centre, normally oblong otherwise. Stone doorway with ears and a complex top. Is this original? The garden side is the same

* Cf. e.g. the St Albans Lady Chapel.

except for the doorway, but it has a later four-column wooden veranda. The sides are perhaps even more remarkable than the main elevation. They are of three bays only, and hence appear very high. This height and the details are decidedly Vanbrughian. The windows are set close together and all are round-arched, except for those of the second floor, which are circular. Pediment right across at the top. Entrance hall with paired fluted pilasters flanking one niche l., one r. The hall is open to the staircase behind, which is spacious and rises in two arms to return in one. Thin twisted balusters.

9060
ASCOT

ALL SOULS, South Ascot. 1896–7 by *Pearson.* Large, red-brick, E.E. Square crossing tower with a rather unexpected pyramid roof.* Equally unexpected the baptistery, which projects to the s at the w end like a porch and has two rounded angle buttresses with solid E.E. pinnacles. Main N porch, small s porch attached to the angle between nave and transept. Brick interior, with four-bay arcades, unemphasized, with a rib-vaulted crossing and sexpartite rib-vaults in the chancel and the lower s chapel. The baptistery is also rib-vaulted. It is octagonal with three open sides projecting into the s aisle. High three-light w window, broader five-light E window.

ALL SAINTS, ⅞ m. NW, on the main Bracknell road. Modest, red brick, by *T. H. Rushforth,* 1864. Varieties of C13 windows. Two-bay aisle arcades. – STAINED GLASS. *Kempe* E window 1907 (Jesse), but the rose window above by *Hardman* (BC). – The PAINTING of chancel and aisles by *Heaton, Butler & Bayne,* 1874 and 1883 (BC).

ST FRANCIS, ½ m. SSE. 1889 by *A. J. C. Scoles* (BC). Red brick, with an apse and no tower. Aisles, octagonal piers, lancet windows and windows with plate tracery.

ASCOT PRIORY, 1½ m. NW. The priory is of the Society of the Holy Trinity, founded by Priscilla Lydia Sellon, a friend of Pusey's. The society started at Devonport in 1848 and built St Dunstan's Abbey, Plymouth, in 1850 etc. The Ascot house was built as a convalescent hospital. The original buildings *See*
p.
359 are by *Charles Buckeridge* (BC) and were begun in 1861. He was followed by *Scott.* The chapel is by *Butterfield,* 1877 etc., the fine s wing by *Stokes,* 1901. Scott's is the w end at r. angles to Stokes's wing, with high plate tracery windows and formerly an open timber roof. Scott's also

* A spire was intended.

other rooms and passages in the centre. Stokes's building
is at once recognizable as his by the tower in the re-entrant
angle. The top part in particular, with its open lantern and
the sloping sides of the lantern, is delightful. The broad flat
buttresses on the r. side of the front of the range are a sensi-
tively introduced motif too. Mullioned and transomed main
windows. Large roof with hipped dormers. The CHAPEL is
surprising. It has a short, two-bay nave with aisles in the
Norman style, E.E. transepts, and a long, aisleless E.E.
chancel. Red and white stone. The shafts in the chancel must
imply the intention to vault in stone. – STAINED GLASS.
Good side windows by *Gibbs*. – The E windows by *Comper*. –
Separate LADY CHAPEL of 1935 by *Mitchell & Bridgewater*,
simple, but Expressionist Gothic, all steep arches and no
bases or capitals.

RACECOURSE. Ascot horse racing was started by Queen Anne
in 1711, but it was only taken up seriously, and indeed revived,
by the Duke of Cumberland, who kept his stud at Cumberland Lodge in Windsor Great Park. At the end of the C18 the
races were already attended regularly by King and Queen and
Prince of Wales. Of the earliest grandstands and royal stand
nothing remains. Even the Royal Pavilion as remodelled by
Sir Albert Richardson in 1936 has disappeared. The present
grandstand is a rebuilding of 1961–4, impressive in its length
and sweep, but of no structural originality or indeed enterprise. It is by Messrs *Wimpeys* architect's department
(*E. V. Collins*).

ASCOT HEATH HOUSE, S of the racecourse, on the Egham
road. By *Robert Kerr*, 1868. Red brick, symmetrical, not very
big. Two gables with bay windows under. A third gable in the
centre, and to the l. and r. a characteristic difference in the
fenestration. On the l. the staircase shows by the stepped
windows; the same motif Kerr was using at the same time at
Bear Wood.

ROYAL ASCOT HOTEL, immediately SW of the racecourse.
Seven-bay centre and long lower r. attachments. Brick and
stone dressings. Homely, and of no architectural merit.*

BUTTERSTEEP HOUSE, Buttersteep Rise, 1¾ m. SSW. By
Francis Lorne, for himself, illustrated in 1942. Whitewashed,
but originally yellow Dutch brick. Dutch otherwise as well.
The operative name is Dudok. Flat roofs. Typical apsidal
staircase projection, not with a specially wide or high window.

* Additions by *Clark & Holland*, 1871 (GS).

ASCOT PLACE, 2¼ m. N. Mid Georgian. Yellow brick. A seven-bay centre of two storeys and two three-bay pavilions with square cupolas. The centre block has a three-bay pediment and a deep porch of paired Tuscan columns. This may be a C20 addition. The interior has (or had) many such additions as well, and it is not easy to recognize what is C18 and what is germane to the house. Following the views and knowledge of Mr Frank Scarlett, the Tuscan columns at the back of the entrance hall and the staircase are original. The staircase has thin turned balusters and carved tread-ends. The fireplace in the room to the l. of the entrance hall seems trustworthy too. In the room to the r. of the entrance hall the two columns are all right but not *in situ*. The doorcase is Georgian but comes from another house.

5070

ASHAMPSTEAD

ST CLEMENT. Early C13 nave and chancel – see a few lancet windows. Weatherboarded bell-turret with shingled spire. Good roofs with tie-beams, collar-beams on arched braces, and two tiers of wind-braces. – PAINTING. Important wall paintings in nave as well as chancel. They date from *c*.1230–40. Stiff-leaf trails, scrolls, etc. Also in the nave the Annunciation, the Visitation, the Nativity, and the Annunciation to the Shepherds, all of extremely slender, supple figures under trefoiled arches. The scenes are easily recognizable, even if they are no longer aesthetically enjoyable. Above the tie-beam which separates nave from chancel Christ in Majesty, the Virgin and St John, and six seated figures.

PARSONAGE, E of the church. By *T. H. Wyatt & D. Brandon*, before 1851. Whitewashed, Tudor, with steep gables and dormers.

The house at the cross-roads NNE of the church has a castellated TOWER in the garden.

PYT HOUSE. The centre has a façade which seems Early Georgian. Arched windows between giant pilasters in the middle. Steep broken pediment. Somewhat later additions.

2080

ASHBURY

ST MARY. Of chalk and brown stone. Evidence of a Norman church with aisles is the S doorway (one order of shafts, decorated capitals, zigzag meeting along a ridge) and one shaft of the W respond of the S aisle arcade with its scallop capital and the springing of an arch lower than the present one. The

N aisle has the same shaft, but no capital or arch is left. E.E.
the W tower. The bell-openings have tracery with a spherical
triangle in the head, i.e. late C13. The situation in the transepts is difficult. They are also C13, but the windows are later
(S transept S c.1300, N transept N Dec). However the responds
of the arches from the aisles to the transepts give enough E.E.
evidence: S aisle S, N aisle N. In the S transept below the S
window a tomb recess with a cinquefoiled arch. The chancel
late C13 too, or c.1300. So are the intersecting tracery of the
E window and the tracery of the S windows. The four-bay
arcades in their present form are Perp. Piers of the four-shaft-
and-four-hollows section, the arches the easternmost double-
chamfered, the other double-hollow-chamfered. Good roof
with tie-beams, kingposts, and short arched braces. Perp N
porch of two storeys with a tierceron-star vault. At the W
end of the N aisle is a fireplace. – PLATE. Cover Paten, inscribed 1577; Spoon, inscribed 1637; Bread-holder, 1717/18;
Flagon 1778/9; Cup, 1781. – MONUMENTS. Brasses to
John de Walden, c.1350, bust only; to Thomas de Bushbury
† 1409 (10 in. and, originally, 20 in. figures); and to William
Skelton † 1448 (28 in. figure). All chancel floor.

MANOR HOUSE. Of the C15, which is rare in Berkshire. Chalk
and stone. Buttressed. Many windows with cusped ogee-
headed lights, and also one with depressed uncusped lights.
On the ground floor the old windows have transoms. They
light the hall. In addition the porch and the inner doorway
with quatrefoils in the spandrels. The porch was in its upper
part rebuilt in brick in 1697. Moulded beams inside the hall
with carved bosses. (On the first floor a room with a moulded
wooden cornice and a traceried frieze. Also between this
room and the room above the porch a screen with trefoil-
headed openings; VCH. Original roof with wind-braces; NBR.)
The village lies on the slope of the downs and is largely built of
chalk.

KINGSTONE FARMHOUSE, ⅜ m. NE. Dated 1730. Chalk front,
sarsen sides. Five-bay façade of two storeys, quite plain. Door
hood on brackets. Pitched roof.

WAYLAND'S SMITHY, 1 m. NE and just N of the Ridgeway.
This monument has long been known as one of the few
examples of a chambered tomb in the county, but excavation
conducted in 1962–3 revealed an earlier monument on the
site. This consisted of an earthen long barrow flanked by
quarry ditches and covering a mortuary house of stone and

timber which contained the remains of thirteen disarticulated and semi-articulated corpses. At a later date the mound was enlarged by the digging of a second ditch outside that of the long barrow to provide additional material to cover a chambered tomb which was added to the broader s end of the long barrow. A straight façade of upright sarsens flanked the entrance to the chamber, and further smaller sarsen slabs were set up as a kerb to support the material of the mound. After the recent series of excavations the monument was partially restored and it is now under the guardianship of the Ministry of Public Building and Works.

THREE BARROWS, *see* Idstone.

ALFRED'S CASTLE, ROUND BARROWS, and ROMANO-BRITISH SETTLEMENT, see Ashdown Park.

ASHDOWN PARK

40b Built for the first Earl of Craven, who also built Hamstead Marshall. For Ashdown we have no date, nor an architect. The style suggests about 1660. It is the perfect doll's house, proof of a longing for neatness and all-round order typical of the years after the Civil War and architecturally of the years following the Jacobean riot. The house itself is of five by five bays, very high, and has on the entrance side at some distance two detached office ranges. All this stood originally – *see* Kip's engraving – in a forest with long straight avenues in all four main directions. The source of the composition is Holland, and the style, wherever it appears in England about 1660, is also at least partly inspired by Holland. Chalk and brown stone dressings. Hipped roofs, the house itself with a balustrade on top and a belvedere cupola, just as had been done at Coleshill a little before, and earlier still (before 1638) at Chevening. The chimneys are so grouped in house and office ranges that they stand like pricked-up ears. The house has three storeys above a basement, the offices one. There is very little of adornment, just the stone balustrade to the garden entrance, and the balcony and pediment of the middle window on this and the entrance side. The windows have stone crosses, except on the ground floor, where they are given two transoms. Steep-gabled dormers. Entrance passage with a big open pediment to the doorway towards the main garden room. Between the scrolls of the pediment a bust. To the r. an arch leads to the staircase, which runs right up to the top. It has extremely strong dumb-bell balusters. Two rooms towards the gardens have leaf coving, one of them also a wreath in the middle of the ceiling. The chimneypieces are Georgian and have been brought in recently.

ALFRED'S CASTLE, on Swinley Down. This is a small, roughly circular, univallate earthwork enclosing some 2½ acres. The rampart was originally faced with sarsen boulders, many of which were removed for use in the construction of the house. The earthwork is broken by gaps on the NE, NW, and SE – the latter at least appears to be original. This earthwork lies within a very much more extensive ditched enclosure which is only visible as a crop mark from the air. The site is unexcavated, but surface finds from the area include sherds of Iron Age A and B, Romano-British, and Saxon pottery, indicating a long and complex history.

ROUND BARROWS, S of Swinley Copse. Two good bowl barrows, one covered by trees. Both are approximately 3 ft high; one is 54 ft in diameter and the other 70 ft.

ROMANO-BRITISH SETTLEMENT, in the extreme SW of the parish of Ashbury, just W of Botley Copse. The settlement stands on a slight rise to the N of a dry valley and consists of a roughly rectangular enclosure of 1½ acres bounded by a broad shallow ditch with an inturned entrance in the middle of the S side. The site lies at the centre of a group of CELTIC FIELDS, and is directly linked to these on its E side. The site is unexcavated, but large quantities of Roman pottery are to be found in its ploughed interior.

ASHRIDGE FARM see WOKINGHAM

ASTON TIRROLD AND ASTON UPTHORPE   5080

The parish boundary runs along the middle of the main S–N road, with Tirrold to the E, Upthorpe to the W.

ST MICHAEL, Aston Tirrold. C11 S doorway, similar to the W doorway at South Moreton. Earlier still, it seems, though clearly *ex situ*, the doorway from the N aisle into the vestry. These large stones and their arrangement indicate Anglo-Saxon workmanship. E.E. S transept with lancets, but the S window Dec, with flowing tracery. Later E.E. the chancel, see the stiff-leaf capitals of the priest's doorway and the bar tracery of a S window. The E window has intersecting tracery instead. Perp W tower. The N aisle with its arcade is of 1863. – SCREENS. In the S porch two lengths of timber arcading coming probably from screens, the E one early, say early C14, the W one Perp. – PLATE. Chalice, Paten, and probably Cover Paten of 1754.

ALL SAINTS, Aston Upthorpe. Nave and chancel in one. In the nave a small Norman window and the remains of a S doorway. What is the date of the timber N porch? The VCH suggests the C17. Chancel of 1859–60 (BC), by *P. C. Hardwick*. His presumably also the pretty bell-turret with spirelet. – BENCHES. Perp ends, backs, and fronts re-used.

PRESBYTERIAN CHAPEL, Aston Tirrold. 1728. Two arched windows flanked by two (altered) doorways. Hipped roof. Blue and red brick. The end walls have two windows and show two roofs. Nothing special left inside.

At Aston Tirrold the MANOR HOUSE close to the church has a lovely E front of the early C18. Chequer brick. Seven bays, segmental shell-hood on carved brackets.

COPSTILE, on the main road S of the inn, is also of seven bays. It is of red brick with brick quoins and has a straight hood over the doorway, again on carved brackets. Pitched roof.

THE FILBERTS, facing the playing fields, is dated 1745. Plain three-bay front of red brick. Pitched roof.

FISHING LODGE. C18 Gothick. The ground-floor windows with ogee arches, above quatrefoil windows.

IRON AGE HILLFORT, on Blewburton Hill. Excavations in 1949 and 1953 revealed a number of phases in the settlement of the hilltop. The earliest occupation, dating to the C4, consisted of a group of circular huts enclosed within a palisade which provided the only defence. The second phase consisted of the construction of the bank and ditch. The rampart was revetted on the inner and outer faces with timber and was separated from a V-shaped ditch by a berm. These defences were broken on the W by an entrance 37 ft wide. This work may be dated to c. 300 B.C. The fortifications were then allowed to fall into disrepair, and at a date which cannot be precisely determined (? C I B.C.) the ditch was recut and the material from it added to the existing rampart, which was now of dump construction. The W entrance was narrowed to 25 ft and the rampart flanking the gate revetted with dry-stone walling. This phase was the work of Iron Age B groups. The end of this period is equally difficult to date, but must have been some time in the first half of the C I A.D. That its end was a sudden and violent one is attested by the bodies of animals crushed by the collapsing ramparts and the burning of the gateway. This destruction could be attributed to the westward-expanding Belgae or to Roman attack.

AVINGTON

3060

St MARK AND St LUKE. A memorable little church, sheltered See p. 359 under a gigantic cedar tree. The church is entirely Norman, with nearly all the windows original: three stepped E windows, two W windows, one above the other, and also a S doorway with divers zigzags. Inside more thrills to come, the broad, rather sagging chancel arch with scallop capitals, beakhead, zigzag at r. angles, and pellets in the arch, and capitals of open-mouthed beasts. In the S doorway beakhead was also planned, but not carried out. The chancel is of two bays, and it was once rib-vaulted (cf. Devizes). The responds have scalloped capitals, the ribs of the first bay had beakhead (a unique motif?), the E corners had the ribs on brackets with more open-mouthed beasts. The SEDILIA are a plain Norman arch. Of the C13 the doorway at the E end of the nave, the 'low-side' window, and the N doorway. – FONT. Even this is Norman, and it is moreover exceptionally interesting. Tub-shaped, eleven narrow arches with figures squeezed in, including a bishop, a man and a devil, two devils, an atlas of the Italian type carrying – what? 14b

BAGNOR MANOR FARMHOUSE see SPEEN

BANISTERS see FINCHAMPSTEAD

BARCOTE MANOR see LONGWORTH

BARKHAM

7060

St JAMES. 1860–1 by *John B. Clacy & Son*; chancel and transepts 1887. S porch tower with high shingled spire on a wooden bell-stage. The older parts flint, the later stone. Pointed-trefoiled windows. The roof corbels like Japanese puzzles in which three-dimensional pieces have to be fitted in in ingenious ways. – FONT. Stone, late C18, in a Louis Seize mood. – PLATE. Paten given 1664; Flagon given 1729; Paten given 1775. – MONUMENT. Late C13 oak effigy of a lady (S porch).

BARKHAM MANOR. Red brick, Georgian, two ranges of differing date, and at the junction a handsome one-storeyed Tuscan portico with pediment. Niches l. and r.

LONGMOOR LAKE was made by John Walter of Bear Wood (*q.v.*).

BARLEY MOW INN *see*
LONG WITTENHAM

BARTLETT'S FARMHOUSE *see* ARBORFIELD

BARTON COURT *see* KINTBURY

6070   BASILDON

ST BARTHOLOMEW. The w tower of blue and red brick was
built in 1734. The rest of the church is over-restored (1875–6),
but basically genuine. It dates from the late C13; see the
cusped Y-tracery of the nave, the Geometrical tracery of the
chancel side windows (circle with trefoiled cinquefoil), and
the chancel E window of three pointed-trefoiled, steeply
stepped lights under one arch. – FONT. Octagonal, Perp,
simple. – MONUMENTS. Brass to John Clerk † 1497 and his
wife. The figures, which are 12 in. long, are in the nave floor.
– A C14 canopy, with cusped and subcusped arch, buttress
shafts, and pinnacles, was re-used outside the church for a
memorial to Sir Francis Sykes † 1804. – His monument
proper in the church is very different. It is by *Flaxman* and
has a standing, mourning widow, her face not visible. She
stands by an urn on a high pedestal. The medallion portrait
of Sir Francis is attached to the pedestal. – Sir Francis W.
Sykes † 1843. Gothic tablet by *R. Brown*. – Mrs Benyon
† 1822. By *Storey*. – Two Deverill boys drowned in 1886.
Monument in the churchyard with portrait group, the boys
in their swimming trunks.

ST STEPHEN, Upper Basildon. By *P. N. Perkins*, 1964–5. A
square set diagonally with the altar across one corner and the
seating on three sides around it. Seats for only 120, and very
spacious for that number. Pyramid roof on eight steel ribs
rising from the floor. Glazed lantern top and two odd oriels
on two sides. High porch leaning forward as an aggressively
steep gable. The church cost only £12,600.

Immediately to the E of St Bartholomew CHURCH FARM, C16,
but with a picturesque late C18(?) front with battlements and
a shaped gable.

BASILDON PARK. Built by *John Carr* for Sir Francis Sykes in
1776. The most splendid Georgian mansion of Berkshire.
Bath stone. The house itself is seven by six bays, but the
scale is large. There are in line with the entrance side three-
bay one-storey links (behind which is an enclosed courtyard),

then three- by four-bay two-storeyed pedimented pavilions, and then again three-bay one-storey walls. The composition thus stretches out considerably, but the dominance of the centre is guaranteed. This has a rusticated lowish ground floor, then a *piano nobile* with, on the entrance side, a recessed giant three-bay portico of unfluted Ionic columns and a pediment. The giant columns comprise the upper half-storey. Towards the garden and the Thames the front has only five bays, and three of them are, in the way Carr liked it, a broad canted bay window. The entry into the house is a fascinating adventure. One can go in through three arches in the rustication below the giant portico and through a door into a low ENTRANCE HALL with four columns,* and then through an intermediate room into a round GARDEN ROOM partly in the bay window. This room has columns along the walls. But from here only a small subsidiary staircase leads to the *piano nobile*. Or one ascends one of the two relatively narrow staircases inside the space behind the three arches and thus comes up to the portico and straight into the grand UPPER ENTRANCE HALL. Was perhaps an outer staircase planned? The entrance hall has splendid paired pilasters and a coved ceiling. On the walls, not in proper framed panels, medallions and sphinxes. To the l. of the entrance hall is the LIBRARY. The bookcase comes from Carr's Panton Hall in Lincolnshire. To the r. of the entrance hall the SMALL DRAWING ROOM. The chimneypiece seems Carr's, but the ceiling looks Early Victorian, and it is indeed known that *J. B. Papworth* worked at Basildon Park in 1839–44. Behind the entrance hall, in the ample centre of the house, is the STAIRCASE HALL. The staircase goes up in three flights with wide, open well. Iron balustrade of discreet motifs between firm uprights. Above a balcony and an arched gallery. The top windows are lunettes. On the walls again no actual panels but spreading stucco with griffins instead. At the NE corner of the house is the LONG DRAWING ROOM with a two-column screen of pink scagliola columns. The ceiling has a shallow segmental tunnel-vault with rather more geometrical forms. The walls have panels. Is this perhaps Papworth wanting to be in keeping with the Georgian house? The chimneypiece again comes from Panton Hall. The adjoining OCTAGON in the centre of the front towards the river is evidently by Papworth, but the

* In this room are two seated figures of Egyptian women by *W. W. Story*, the American sculptor; 1858.

DINING ROOM, in the SE corner, is once more original, with its chimneypiece. One BEDROOM on the upper floor has a groin-vaulted alcove, fine doorcases, and a fine plaster ceiling. – The EAST LODGES are octagonal with garlands just below the eaves. Gatepiers with vases. – The SOUTH-EAST LODGE is faced with alternating bands of flints and stucco and has pointed and quatrefoil windows.

THE GROTTO, $\frac{3}{4}$ m. WNW. White, informal house built by Lady Fane, who died in 1792. Inside one fine room with Adamish decoration. Lady Fane's grotto has completely disappeared and left no traces.

PEACOCK PAVILION, 1 m. SE. Built in 1956. The stonework came from Bowood in Wiltshire, i.e. a *Robert Adam* mansion. The pavilion was designed by its owner, Mr *G. Child Beale*. – The FOUNTAIN originally stood at Witley Park near Godalming and dates from the 1890s. The name of the sculptor is given as *O. Spalmach* (Studio *O. Andreoni*, Rome). – Much SCULPTURE, including a black Valkyria, cast by *Gladenbeck* in Berlin. – Also a statue of Shakespeare by *A. Salata*.

NOKE'S TOMB, Tomb Farm, $1\frac{1}{2}$ m. SW, is in ruins. It was the mausoleum of a Quaker buried here in 1699.

(At LOWER BASILDON, according to the NBR, CHURCH HOUSE FARM has a sumptuous chimneypiece with demi-figure caryatids and a tympanum representing St George and the Dragon instead of a lintel. The photograph looks as if these pieces, obviously not belonging together, might be Flemish of about 1700.)

ROMAN BUILDING. In Church Field two mosaic pavements were found and destroyed by workmen in the C19. No other remains were located, but the pavements indicate the existence of a well-appointed Roman building in this area.

ROMAN VILLA, at Ealing, $1\frac{1}{2}$ m. from Well House. The villa was of corridor type, 75 ft long and 45 ft wide. It included a hypocaust system and at least one mosaic floor with a guilloche pattern in red, blue, and white.

BAULKING

ST NICHOLAS. Long nave, chancel, and tiny bellcote. The chancel could be work of the Uffington masons. E.E. with lancets, a stepped group of three to the E, shafted inside. ANGLE PISCINA. E.E. also the very unusual stone chancel SCREEN, really just a doorway, but with openings l. and r. which may not be original. The nave doorway plain, of *c.*1200;

in the s wall two Dec windows. Nave roof Jacobean, with pendants from the tie-beams, but in fact dated 1708. – PULPIT. Jacobean (from Grittleton in Wiltshire). – PAINTING. Almost unrecognizable Nativity, N wall W, early C14.– PLATE. Cup of 1583; two Patens of 1715; two-handled covered Cup, inscribed 1723/4.

Baulking has an extremely large green.

BEAR PLACE *see* WARGRAVE

BEAR WOOD

7070

ST CATHERINE. 1846 by *Good* (BC; probably J. H. Good). The material good ashlar stone, the character still the thin one of the Commissioners' churches. Narrow w front, w tower with its w entrance the main entrance to the church. No aisles, high two-light Dec windows. The Dec details not all correct. High interior. – STAINED GLASS. In the chancel the original glass by *Wailes*; deeper colour than he used as a rule. – MONUMENT. John Balston Walter, John Walter's son, who was drowned while trying to rescue two others in the frozen lake. † 1870. The monument by *Matthew Noble*. Large angel in a sinuous stance. The relief below shows the frozen lake.

ESTATE HOUSING near the church, towards Sindlesham Green. Red brick with black diapers; gables. Even the pub conforms.

BEAR WOOD (Royal Merchant Navy School). Bear Wood was designed in 1864, i.e. a hundred years ago. As a piece of private architecture Blenheim or Hardwick could not be more remote. As far as scale is concerned, and the disregard for what we pygmies would call domestic comfort, Bear Wood is indeed nearer to Blenheim than to our poky villas. John Walter II, owner of *The Times*, bought the estate about 1830. His son John Walter III, reserved, handsome, conscientious, and of High-Church piety, got married in 1842, lost his wife, and married again in 1861. In January 1865 Mr Kerr and John Walter were working on the plans. *Robert Kerr*, then forty-two years old – Walter was forty-seven – had been a bit of a revolutionary when he was young, but had lately settled down, being appointed professor of architecture at King's College and publishing a book, *The English Gentleman's House*, which told readers all about the necessities and conventions of planning for wealthy gentlemen. The book came out in 1864. It was probably on the strength of the book that John Walter

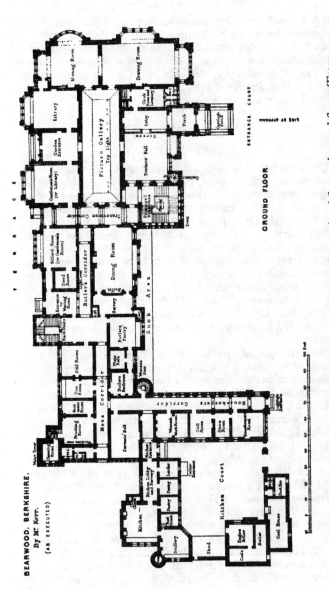

BEARWOOD, BERKSHIRE.
By Mr. Kerr.
(AS EXECUTED)

GROUND FLOOR

Bear Wood, by Robert Kerr, designed in 1864. Plans of ground and first and second floors (From Robert Kerr, *The English Gentleman's House*)

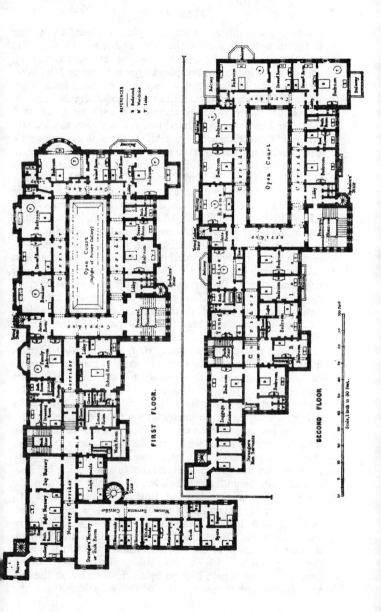

REFERENCES
B Bedstead
W Wardrobe
T Table

FIRST FLOOR.

Open Court
(Skylight of Picture Gallery)

Corridor

Bedroom

Dressing Room

Boudoir

Ante Room

Family Bedroom

Dressing Room

Work Room

Linen Room

School Room

Lady's

Principal Staircase

Bachelors' Stair

Women's Stair

Nursery Corridor

Servants Corridor

Woman Corridor

Night Nursery

Day Nursery

Strangers' Nursery or Sick Room

Bath

Nurse

Coals

Schoolmaids

Housemaids

Kitchenmaids

Cook

Scullery

SECOND FLOOR

Open Court

Corridor

Bedroom

Dressed Rooms

Balcony

Young Ladies

Governess' Stair

Valet's Stair

Bath Rooms

Principal Stairs

Bachelors' Stair

Strangers Men Servants

Loggia

Lumber

Scale, 1 Inch to 30 Feet.
10   0   10   20   30   40   50   60   70   80   90   100 Feet

selected him as his architect. The plans of Bear Wood were
in fact included by Kerr in the second edition of his book. He
must have considered them his crowning achievement to date,
and they are indeed so completely the epitome of High Victorian domestic planning that they are illustrated here. They
will also help an understanding of the following description.
The house was sufficiently complete in 1868 for a first staff
party for *The Times* to be held; but *The Architect* in 1870 still
called it 'aproaching completion'. It is of red brick with ample
stone dressings. The style is what we would now call Jacobean,
but with an admixture of French motifs. Kerr himself called
it 'of the irregular or Non-Classical type'. On the N side is
the main entrance, and at the l. end of the façade a long wing
projecting to the N. The s side has a terrace and overlooks the
lake. The centre of the entrance side is symmetrical with a
tower and a gable l. and r. Projecting in front of the tower is
a deep porte-cochère with banded pillars. But this symmetrical part is only the r. end of the façade. The l. gable is in
fact ruthlessly cut into by a second, more massive and truly
enormous tower. The details of this are quite unauthorized
by any period style. The window arrangement expresses,
again ruthlessly, the fact that in this tower the staircase rises.
The top of the tower bristles with a palisade of pinnacles.
Further l., in the corner of the façade and the projecting wing,
is a round turret with a conical roof, unmistakably French.
This also has the window arranged so as to express the staircase. The wing ends with yet another tower, this one with an
ogee cap. The w side is less interesting, though it is also
asymmetrical. Straight gables. The s side has its l. half, i.e. its
principal half, again symmetrical, with three shaped gables
between two turrets. The continuation to the r. is once more
irregular, with a tower with a pavilion roof and a sw corner
tower. The prominent chimneys have alas been replaced. The
main exit on this side has two carved angels holding babies.

The plan behind these façades is as follows. From the
porte-cochère one reaches the Entrance Hall, 43 by 27 ft,
with a screen as in great halls of old. To the l. is the Staircase,
24 by 24 by 80 ft high. From the staircase hall straight s runs
a corridor to the s front. To the l. of this is the Dining Room,
to the r. the centre of the representational part of the house:
the Picture Gallery, which can of course also be entered direct
from the entrance hall. It is 70 by 24 ft. To the r. of the hall
and gallery and facing w are the Drawing Room and the

Morning Room, to the l. of the latter and due S of the gallery the Library, the cross passage to the terrace exit mentioned above, and a second Library or Gentleman's Room. To the l. of this the cross corridor comes out, and then there is another room also called Gentleman's Room. This clearly was the Office; for it communicates with a Waiting Room for estate-business callers with its own small exit.

What went on in the E half of the house and on the upper floors is sociologically even more revealing. To the l. of the dining room followed the Butler's Pantry, with access to a corridor S of the dining room called the Butler's Corridor. Then, to the l. of the Butler's Pantry, was the Butler's Bedroom with, attached to it, the Plate Safe. Here ended the butler's territory. His corridor continued straight E as the Men's Corridor with, off it to the S, Cleaning Room, Brushing Room, Footman's Room, Gun Room, and a spacious room called Odd Room. But to the N, in the wing, ran the Housekeeper's Corridor, and behind it were the Housekeeper's Room, Store Room, Still Room, Women's Workroom. The Kitchen etc. were yet further E on the other side of a courtyard. The butler's and housekeeper's and the men's and women's quarters met in the Servants' Hall.

On the first floor in the principal, i.e. W, half of the house the area above the picture gallery formed an inner court, and was surrounded by a corridor. Along this lay the principal bedrooms, the S suite including the Boudoir. In the SE corner were the Nurseries, though the School Room was above the dining room. The ladies' maids slept to the E of this, the maids in the Housekeeper's Wing.

On the second floor the Bachelors' Rooms were above dining room and butler's quarters with direct access to the principal back stair (on the N front), the Young Ladies' Rooms – separated, one is disturbed to see, from the bachelors only by a corridor – above some of the principal S bedrooms. An internal stair, connecting this floor with the first floor only, took the young ladies to the Boudoir. At the SE corner was provision for Strangers' Men Servants.

Those who study the plans might find more enlightenment; e.g. the NE turret had the Luggage Entrance, the little French-looking turret was the Women Servants' stair.

Now one or two details concerning the interior. The Entrance Hall is in a ham Jacobean, but the normal hall exit, i.e. the exit to the gallery, was a mirror. The Picture Gallery of course is sky-lit. Drawing Room and Morning Room could be thrown into one by means of sliding doors with masterly marquetry. The woodwork was in fact made in private workshops on the estate. The brick was dug and made on the estate too. The stone is Mansfield carboniferous limestone. Gas was also produced in a private plant. The estate was 7,500 acres, including Finchampstead, Barkham, and Sindlesham. John Walter paid for the building of the schools at Finchampstead, Sandhurst, and Wokingham and for Woodyer's lavish St Paul at Wokingham. The lake to the s of the house is more than 40 acres in size. This is the lake in which, in the very year of the completion of the house, John Walter's eldest son was drowned. The house is now part of a boys' school, a fitting memorial.

HEADMASTER'S HOUSE. 1921 by *Prentice*.

CHAPEL. 1934–5 by *Sir Herbert Baker*. Red brick, with Perp windows and a flèche. The interior is an odd mixture of styles. Perp the windows and the open roof. But narrow aisle passages with arches of continuous mouldings, rather Early Christian in detail. Moreover, a rib-vaulted apse preceded by choir bays with shallow domes. A shallow dome over the lobby too.

GYMNASIUM. 1930. Opposite the chapel and forming with it and the N front of the house a *cour d'honneur*.

BEAUMONT COLLEGE *see* OLD WINDSOR

BEECH HILL

6060

ST MARY. 1867 by *Butterfield*, the N aisle 1873 (BC). Nave and chancel under one tiled roof. The walls flint with brick bands and chequers. Bell-turret, tile-hung below, weatherboarded above. The windows pointed-trefoiled and with plate tracery. Interior with exposed brick and stone dressings and patterns. The aisle arcade has square, only slightly chamfered piers and continuous arch mouldings – an early case of such simplification. High tripartite chancel SCREEN. – STAINED GLASS. Mostly by *Gibbs*, with his typical pronounced black lead lines. – N aisle NE window by *Kempe*, 1896.

See p. 359

BEECH HILL HOUSE. Messrs Betjeman and Piper give the date 1720. Brick. Seven bays and a full three storeys. Blunt top. Later porch. But inside the original staircase with carved tread-ends and a very handsome corner room with angle fire-

place, wooden surround and overmantel, panelling and door
surrounds with pilasters and friezes.

THE PRIORY. By the Loddon, with a canal or straight arm in
the garden. C16 or older parts are at the back. They are
timber-framed. The front range was added in 1648, see the
date on the porch. The façade is of brick and gabled. The
lower S range was also added. In the interior on the first floor
two splendid mid C17 chimneypieces with pilasters with
Ionic capitals, garlands, friezes with garlands, and overmantels with volutes down from halved Ionic pilasters.

BEEDON   4070

ST NICHOLAS. Flint-built. Nave and chancel, timber bell-
turret with a shingled broach spire. Nave and chancel of
c.1200–30. In the nave lancet windows and a doorway, quite
simple, but the shafts with shaft-rings and a roll moulding
keeled. The chancel arch has broad flat leaves on the responds,
and this may be the earliest feature of the church. E.E.
priest's doorway, lancet windows with continuous roll
mouldings inside as well as outside. The E end three even
lancets and a round window in the gable. The interior of the
chancel has just that extra in the shaftings and leaf capitals of
the E window and the bit of dogtooth decoration which makes
one remember the church. If the lancets in the side walls
were all still there, it would make an uncommonly complete
piece. – PLATE. Cup and Cover, 1576.

MANOR HOUSE, N of the church. Early C18, with segment-
headed windows and pilaster-strips.

ROUND BARROW, on Barrow Hill, SW of Stanmore. This large
bowl barrow still stands over 7 ft in height, although it has
been considerably reduced by ploughing. It was excavated in
the C19, when a cremation accompanied by an incense cup
and a bronze dagger were found. The group can be dated to
the C16 B.C.

BEENHAM   5060

ST MARY. 1859 by *Woodyer*, the chancel added in 1871 (BC).
Older only the brick tower, built after a fire of 1794. The
Victorian work is of flint, late C13 details. – The chancel
decoration was executed by *Miss Sharp* of Ufton Court, who
also painted the neo-Quattrocento Last Supper. – STAINED
GLASS. By *Hardman*, and typical of his style in imitation of
the early C14.

VICARAGE. Late Georgian, red brick, of three bays, the side bays on the ground floor Venetian, on the upper floor tripartite windows.

HILLFOOT, $\frac{5}{8}$ m. E. Dated 1737, and characteristic of the date in the segment-headed windows and the bold brick cornice.

BENHAM PARK see SPEEN

BERE COURT see PANGBOURNE

BESSELSLEIGH

ST LAWRENCE. In the grounds of the Manor, but by the main road. Nave and chancel in one, the roof with stone slates. The C13-looking twin bellcote is assigned to 1632 by the VCH. 1632 is the date recorded in the chancel for the beautifying and repairing of the church by William Lenthall, Speaker of Parliament. Plain, unmoulded Norman S doorway. Late C13 w and E windows (three stepped pointed-trefoiled lights under one arch), the E window with a cinquefoiled rere-arch. The other windows mostly Perp. Pleasantly unrestored interior. – Norman PILLAR PISCINA with decorated stem and top with decorated scallops. – FONT. C17, rather mid than late. Round stem with bands of rocky rustication. Small bowl with garlands. – PULPIT. C18. With tester. – COMMUNION RAIL. C18. – BOX PEWS. – TYMPANUM. With pendants. Probably of 1632. – TILES. A whole set. Are they C15? – PLATE. Cup and Cover, 1635. – (In the churchyard MONUMENT to the Rev. E. M. Walker by *Eric Gill*, 1932.)

SW of the church a lonely GATEPIER of the former house. It is typically mid C17 in style and remarkably similar to those of Sutton Courtenay Manor.

BILL HILL see ST NICHOLAS HURST

BINFIELD

ALL SAINTS. W tower of dark brown conglomerate; Perp. The prominent stair-turret with its ornate ogee top is of course Victorian. The S aisle is of conglomerate too. The N aisle is of 1848, the E end mostly of 1859, and what is pre-Reformation is Perp – except a S aisle S window which, with its cusped Y-tracery, must be of *c.*1300. The S doorway has fleurons in one moulding. Perp four-bay arcades of octagonal piers with moulded arches. The S chapel arcade looks somewhat earlier. An angel from a former house in the S chapel. – PULPIT. Dated

1628. Blank arches and arabesque. Back panel, its upper half with caryatids, and tester with strapwork cresting. – The HOURGLASS on an elaborate iron stand with the Arms of the Farriers' Company in London, leaves and grapes, a lion, a pelican, and a wolf, is probably C17 (cf. Hurst). – Victorian iron SCREENS, W, N, and S of the chancel. – STAINED GLASS. In the SE window C15 glass, whole figures. – S aisle W by *O'Connor*, 1863. Violent colours and no stylization. – MONUMENTS. Brass to Walter de Anneforde, c.1360s, bust, 9 in. – Palimpsest brass. Inscriptions of the mid C16 and on the reverse part of a figure of a bishop or abbot. – Catherine Macaulay Graham † 1791, the historian and republican. Tablet with relief profile in a circular wreath. – George Hotham † 1806. By *Westmacott Jun.* Tablet with flag and sabre.

BINFIELD LODGE, ¾ m. NW. Late C18, brick, the distinguishing feature being the end bays, which are raised and carry a pediment. Curves down from this l. and r. and between them a lunette window.

BINFIELD PARK, ⅜ m. S. Built in 1775. Brick, of nine bays and two and a half storeys, with a three-bay pediment. A smooth front. Good GATEPIERS with pediments, and below them garlands.

MANOR HOUSE, ⅞ m. SE. C18, of five bays with hipped roof. Porch on Tuscan columns. Two later three-bay wings.

BINFIELD HOUSE, ¾ m. SW. Large, two-storeyed, late C18 brick house with delightful Gothick trim, including not only ogee-headed windows and a porch on slender shafts, but a Gothic Venetian window and a window in the form of a reticulation unit.

BINFIELD PLACE, ⅞ m. SW. The remains of a Jacobean manor house. Two gabled projections (probably out of a former three), one with original bricks.

Binfield Place faces the Windsor road (B road). The village of Binfield is S of this. It has its own church.

ST MARK. By *Sir Arthur Blomfield*, 1866. The damage done by a recent fire was sympathetically repaired by *Frederick Etchells*. Red brick with black-brick trim. Nave, chancel, and transepts. Lancet windows. The interior even more patterned: red and black brick and stone. Blomfield in his early years was much influenced by Butterfield. The effect is however not strident, as in Butterfield's churches, but curiously neat.

Opposite the church MOOR CLOSE, a Missionary College. The

original building is of 1881: red brick, with a tower and
mullioned and transomed windows.

¼ m. SW of St Mark POPE'S HOUSE, Early Georgian, of red
brick. Five bays, three storeys, with segment-headed windows.
Doorway with flat pilasters but a fine open scrolly pediment
with a big shell in the open top. The side elevation has a pedimented doorway too.

BISHAM

Wooded hills form the backcloth to Bisham's two principal
buildings – the church and the abbey – which are not visually
connected, even when seen from the river which they both
border.

ALL SAINTS. The Norman W tower is immediately by the
Thames. Twin single-chamfered bell-openings. The tower
arch is round and has one respond with a multi-scalloped
capital, the other with waterleaf – which dates the tower to
c.1170–80. The rest of the church is alas inside and outside
all of the restorations, especially that of 1849 by *B. Ferrey*.
The only exception is the Hoby Chapel with its windowless
chalk wall. This is of the late C16. – REREDOS, N chapel. Four
Late Gothic painted saints, probably East Anglian; very bad.
– ROYAL ARMS. Of George III, painted, with a guilloche
frame. – STAINED GLASS. The E window of the Hoby Chapel
has interesting heraldic glass of 1609. – PLATE. Small Cup
and Paten, the latter of 1765. – MONUMENTS. Interest is
concentrated in the Hoby monuments in the S chapel. The
earliest is that of Sir Philip † 1558 and Sir Thomas † 1566. It
is of alabaster, a tomb-chest with the two bearded half-
brothers, both in relaxed, semi-recumbent attitudes. Shallow
arch behind. Long poem, worth reading in full. – Sir Thomas's
widow Elizabeth married Lord Russell who died in 1583. She
died in 1609. She kneels in widow's weeds under a canopy
with columns. Behind her children, and others outside the
columns. Also alabaster. Iron railings. – Margaret, wife of Sir
Edward, † 1605. The finest of the Hoby monuments and
indeed one of the most original monuments of the age. Again
alabaster. On the high plinth a slender obelisk crowned by a
heart. At the corners of the plinth four swans, the supporters
of the Hobys. At the foot were originally four more obelisks
(see the Buckler drawing). – The other monuments in the
church are as follows. In the N chapel Purbeck tomb with

short tomb-chest and canopy of three hanging arches on colonnettes with lozenge patterns. Pretty vault inside. Probably early C16. – Thomas Crekett † 1517. Brass, nave w wall, 16 in. figure. – George Kenneth Vansittart † 1904 aged 14. Kneeling Eton boy by *Morris Harding* under a Gothic canopy.

On the way from the church to the Abbey on the s side TOWN FARM HOUSE, timber-framed with brick infilling and a hipped roof. Then nice terraces of cottages, some timber-framed, but mostly Georgian.

BISHAM ABBEY. The house was an abbey only for three years. It was first a preceptory of the Templars, then in 1337 became an Augustinian priory, then in 1537 a Benedictine abbey. As such it was dissolved in 1540, and the estate was granted to Sir Philip Hoby in 1553. He began to build almost at once, and, after he died in 1558, his half-brother († 1566) continued. The appearance of the remaining buildings is accordingly complex and their evidence not easily understood. The s front is the most telling. Here one sees a C13 porch with a fine outer and an equally fine inner doorway and a quadripartite rib-vault. The doorways have colonnettes and extremely delicately moulded arches. On the door itself C13 ironwork. On the l. of the porch and lying a little back is the front of a range extending N at r. angles. To the s it has a good tall two-light upper window with bar tracery. The part of the front E of the porch is Hoby work, chalk below, stepped brick gables above, and windows with mullion and transom crosses and their pediments. As one enters through the porch one is in the SCREENS PASSAGE. To one's l. are five blocked arches. They went in the C13 to the kitchen and offices. The screen and the gallery above the passage may be of the C15. To the r. is the GREAT HALL of the Hobys. This was the Templars' Hall already, and evidently this Templars' house was not at all laid out like a monastery. It seems to have had the appearance of a manor house. The s wall of the hall is C13, though the chimneypiece is Hoby. The lower, stone part is very good and 39a typical of c.1560, i.e. with coupled columns and very dainty decoration. The wooden overmantel must be Later Elizabethan or Jacobean. The windows in the end walls are not original. The Hobys placed s of the original outer wall of the hall a set of rooms of theirs, the façade of which we have seen.

When the Augustinians came in, they built to the E of the hall a CLOISTER, of which only one range survives, a curious cloister indeed, low and irregular, with six arches, one and six narrow, two to five wide. The Hobys placed in front of the northern ones a canted brick bay window. The upper parts here and round the corner to the N and a projecting part to the N with large pedimented windows are all Hoby (except for the hall window already mentioned). The gables are stepped again. Slightly recessed rises a brick TOWER of an oddly irregular shape. This was being built in 1560. To the NW more C13 walling, but no features. Inside altogether, apart from the hall, not many features have been preserved.

To the S of the Abbey BARNS, one converted into a large private house, and a circular DOVECOTE.

TEMPLE MILLS, ½ m. SW, close to the river. Part of the present paper mill is the mill building of c.1790, red brick with a cupola. It has been attributed to *Samuel Wyatt*.

(WAYSIDE CRUCIFIX by *Eric Gill*, 1917. At the same time war memorial to F. S. Kelly and others.)

BLEWBURTON HILL *see* ASTON TIRROLD

BLEWBURY

Blewbury has a curious layout. The A-road called LONDON STREET runs along the S end of the village, and from it the other village houses develop along a loop filled in in the middle and having the church in its centre.

ST MICHAEL. The exterior tells this: one small Early Norman window in the nave on the N side, one larger Later Norman window in the chancel also on the N side. There is one lancet in the N transept (but the E window is Dec with flowing tracery). There is another lancet in the S transept. Dec the chancel windows (E reticulated tracery). Perp S doorway with leaf in the spandrels and the N doorway with initials in the spandrels, and Perp also the ashlar-faced W tower with a pierced quatrefoil parapet. The interior confirms and enormously enriches this first impression. First of all the Norman church, at least the Late Norman one, had a crossing with no doubt a crossing tower. The crossing piers are there, all four, solid, just with nook-shafts. These shafts have capitals with broad flat leaves or waterleaf. That allows for a date c.1170–90. The arches are single-stepped and already pointed. That is in favour of 1190 rather than 1170. Set in the crossing but on corbels a rib-vault. The corbels indicate that the vault was not at once planned. Yet here the capitals again have waterleaf. The ribs consist in section of one half-roll and two quarter-hollows. The chancel – see the large N window – belongs to the same build, and this also is rib-vaulted. The ribs are of the same section and stand consistently on corbels too. A little later this cruciform church was enlarged to the s, and it was, for no good reason, enlarged in such a way that pieces of wall were left standing between all the new aisle arcade arches. The capitals of the semicircular responds still have trumpet-scallops, but also stiff-leaf. So again, c.1190 seems the date. Also the first three arches from the E are lower than the other two, yet the higher w arches cannot mean an extension of the Norman nave; for the C11 window faces them. All arches pointed and with only slight chamfers. The N arcade is C14 and extends only opposite the E arches of the s arcade. Octagonal piers, arches with sunk convex curves. The s chancel chapel looks c.1300 in its details. – PISCINA. A piscina survives which served a rood-loft altar. It looks as if it were the re-used top part of a Norman pillar piscina. – FONT. Perp, octagonal, with quatrefoils. – STALLS. The fronts with tracery. – SCREEN. To the s schapel, an unusual design for Berkshire. Wide, ogee-headed single openings with panel tracery over. – DOORS. The door to the rood loft is Perp and very pretty. – s door with C13(?) ironwork overlaid by wooden blank pointed arches. – STAINED GLASS. E window by *Bentley*, but with one beautiful early C14 angel in the head and fragments of another. – TILES. Some medieval ones in various places. – PLATE. Chalice, 1663; Paten, undated; Cup and Paten and Paten, 1725. – MONUMENTS. Brasses to John Balam † 1496, priest, 20 in. figure; to a Knight and two wives, c.1500, 27 in.; to John Latton † 1548, 18 in.; to Sir John Daunce † 1545, his wife † 1523, and their children. The 18 in. figures lie on a low tomb-chest. – Two effigies, defaced, in the churchyard N of the w tower. – John Macdonald † 1841, aged thirteen, small brass plate with a very rustic figure of Faith looking like Britannia. Brass was a very unusual material at that time.

s of the church the WILLIAM MALTHUS CHANTRY SCHOOL, built in 1709. Red brick, five bays, with an apsidal hood. sw of the church a single ALMSHOUSE of 1738, for the oldest man in the village, and a second of 1838.

Blewbury is full of attractive timber-framed houses, but there is no reason here to single out any, except perhaps HALL BARN, sw of the church on the loop, with, at r. angles to the house, a brick wing of three bays with giant pilasters and wooden cross-windows. They have odd frilly lintels. It is probably work of c.1660.

(In SOUTH STREET is a cruck-framed cottage. NBR)

In LONDON STREET a good recent house by *Martin Sylvester*, 1963–4. The same architect is, at the time of writing, engaged on a group of sixteen smaller houses on the W outskirts.

ROUND BARROWS. These two magnificent barrows lie on Churn Down, W of the rifle range. The N barrow is 12 ft high and 108 ft in diameter; the second site, 200 ft to the SW, is 123 ft in diameter and 12 ft high. Both sites were excavated in the C19 and again in 1935. They appear to have been erected over existing pits containing Iron Age pottery and are probably of Roman date, although their purpose is obscure: neither revealed any interments.

ROUND BARROWS, on Churn Hill. The E barrow is a fine example of the bell type, 54 ft in diameter and 6 ft high, separated from its encircling ditch by a berm 20 ft wide. A small bowl barrow almost touches it on its W side.

IRON AGE HILLFORT, Blewburton Hill, *see* Aston Tirrold and Aston Upthorpe.

ROUND BARROW, Compton Down, *see* Compton.

BOARS HILL *see* WOOTTON

2080   BOURTON

ST JAMES. 1860 by *J. W. Hugall*. Nave and bellcote and chancel. Kentish plate-tracery, if you please.

BAPTIST CHAPEL. 1851 by *W. F. Ordish*. Also nave and bellcote and chancel. The details Dec.

Bourton is a mid C19 village.

PINEWOOD, formerly Bourton House, Tudor and gabled, is by *Ordish* as well, and the tender in 1845 was for £6,650 (GS).

The SCHOOL is dated 1842, and there is neo-Tudor estate housing.

BOWYER'S FARMHOUSE *see* SWALLOWFIELD

407·   BOXFORD

ST ANDREW. The W tower is of c.1692. Handsome large flint panels in brick framing. The church is mostly Victorian. N aisle of 1841, but the arcade (lozenge-shaped piers, continuous mouldings) probably by *J. O. Scott & Sons*, 1908. – FONT. Small octagonal bowl, with very simple panels, probably of

*c.*1662. – PULPIT. 1618, with its tester. – COMMUNION RAIL.
Of *c.*1700, thin, twisted balusters. – PLATE. Cup and Cover,
1786; Paten on foot, 1836. – MONUMENT. Jacob Anderton,
rector, † 1672. Tablet. The 'predella' and piers built up of
book-spines.

The church and the near-by houses form a pretty group by the
Lambourn.

On the w bank street with brick cottages, also thatched roofs,
and WESTBROOK HOUSE, five bays with a three-bay pediment into which a round-arched window reaches up. Is it
early C18?

BOYNE HILL *see* MAIDENHEAD

BRACKNELL

8060

HOLY TRINITY, Chance Road, Bracknell. 1851 and 1859 by
Coe & Goodwin. Flint, with a NE tower with shingled broach
spire. The windows E.E. to Dec. The s aisle is as wide as the
nave, and the N and s arcades are made to differ.

ST MICHAEL AND ST MARY MAGDALENE, Easthampstead.
Quite an imposing Victorian church, though coarse. By *J. W.
Hugall*, 1866–7. Only the w tower, which rises to a considerable height and has a yet higher stair-turret, is halfway up
older than Victorian. The brickwork makes a Jacobean date
probable. So the tower is finished in brick too, although the
rest of the church is ashlar-faced. E.E. details. – PULPIT.
Inscribed and dated 1631 on a large arched panel. Much
arabesque. – STALLBACKS. Late C17, fine pedimented panels.*
– SCREEN. Made up from traceried panels of the former Perp
rood screen. – STAINED GLASS. The E window and several
other windows by *Morris & Co.*, i.e. *Burne-Jones*, 1876. The
E window represents the Last Judgement. It is a noble, if
somewhat languid composition. Most figures in white robes,
the angels with wine-coloured wings, the sky dark blue. – N
aisle one window by *Kempe*, 1893. Very feeble next to the
Burne-Jones. – PLATE. Cup and Cover, 1569; Almsdish,
1659; Paten presented in 1670. – MONUMENTS. Brass to
Thomas Berwyk † 1443, demi-figure, 8 in. (nave E). – William
Trumbull † 1678, large tablet, exceptionally sober. – Elija
Fenton, poet, † 1730. Absolutely plain, but the inscription by
Pope.

ST ANDREW, Binfield Road, Priestwood. 1888. The architect

* They came from Oxford Cathedral.

is *H. G. W. Drinkwater* (BC). Small, brick, with an apse and a
tiny bell-turret.

ST JOSEPH THE WORKER (R.C.), Stanley Road. By *Clifford
Culpin & Partners*, 1961–2. The dominant feature is a steep
roof, 100 ft long. It appears as a triangle in the façade, with
the lower part open as a porch and behind it the actual block
of the church. So the roof seems to be a canopy. Low flat-
roofed aisles project l. and r. of the steep roof. A metal cross,
22 ft high, rises out of a pool.

COLLEGE OF FURTHER EDUCATION. By *J. T. Castle*, the
County Architect; completed 1963.

EASTHAMPSTEAD PARK COLLEGE, 1¼ m. W of Easthampstead
church. Built in 1860 for the Marquess of Downshire. Red
brick, large, of three storeys, in a kind of Jacobean and on a
kind of E-plan. Shaped gables, broad porch. To the r. of this
what in an original Jacobean house would represent the great
hall window (with transom), but is here the staircase window.
The fronts of the projecting wings differ, l. semi-octagonal, r.
square. To the SE also a symmetrical front: arcade of ten
arches on stumpy, square, tapering pillars.

METEOROLOGICAL OFFICE. 1959–61 by *Eric Bedford*, Chief
Architect to the *Ministry of Works*, a good group.

PERAMBULATION. Bracknell in the early C19 was called 'a
small thoroughfare hamlet', but 'adorned with many genteel
residences and delightful villas'. The thoroughfare is the
HIGH STREET. Here, near the W end, is the RED LION, of
brick with odd horizontal courses. The side elevation is
timber-framed with brick infilling. At the E end is the OLD
MANOR HOTEL, also C17, also brick, with gables, and all
much altered. Today's character of the High Street is that of
a small-town shopping street: two-storeyed buildings and no
events. But on the N side one modern terrace breaks in, with
shops and curtain walling. That is the herald of the New
Town, whose shopping centre is the BROADWAY, parallel to,
and N of, the High Street, and reached by a pedestrian
shopping lane. At the time of writing the Broadway is very in-
complete and holds out no hope of distinguished architecture.

The NEW TOWN was incorporated in 1948. It was to have no
more than 25,000 inhabitants. By the end of 1959 17,500 was
reached. Now there are 25,000, and the target has become
60,000. A plan for the town centre was made in 1963 by
G. Rhys and the chief architect to the Corporation, *E. A.
Ferriby*.

At present only the following requires notice. E of the centre, by
the roundabout at the E end of Broadway and the S end of
Warfield Road, the Meteorological Office, *see* above, and
Messrs MAC FISHERIES, 1961–2 by *E. A. Ferriby*, a curtain
wall job, and a little further S the College of Further Educa-
tion, *see* above. Yet further E, i.e. at BULLBROOK, the
CASTROL RESEARCH LABORATORIES, 1962–3 by *Lam, Biel
& Partners*, good, with an odd glazed top with tapering sides.
W of the town centre another industrial area. Little of individual
interest. Messrs FERRANTI, Western Road, is by *E. A.
Ferriby*, 1961–2. N of this blocks of flats, e.g. CAMPION
HOUSE and BRYONY HOUSE, six- and four-storeyed, and
quite good (1961–3 by *E. A. Ferriby*). Otherwise much hum-
drum housing.

New flats also at Bullbrook, e.g. BAY HOUSE, Bay Road, six-
storeyed with a group of shops (also by *E. A. Ferriby*).

The one outstanding job – outstanding in whatever New Town
it might have been placed – is POINT ROYAL, Rectory Road,64
Easthampstead, just E of the Easthampstead shopping terrace.
It is by *Arup Associates*, 1960–4, a hexagonal seventeen-
storey point-block of 102 flats for single people or couples
without children. Two sides of the hexagon are slightly
concave, and – as cannot be avoided in a hexagon – the
rooms are oddly shaped. There are six on each floor, with
staircase, lifts, etc., in the centre. The block is of reinforced
concrete, and is placed in a shallow bowl with car parking
below. The slightly up-curved rim of the bowl allows day-
lighting for the car area and also acts as a ha-ha for the block.
The structure of the block is exposed, and in fact set outside
of, and detached from, the glazing of the flats. The block
thus looks transparent at the edges, and the rooms can have
glazing right to the floor level. The finish is raw and the
ensemble very powerful. But rising as it does in lonely splen-
dour, it cudgels down the whole scale of Bracknell. As a
single climax it is placed too eccentrically, and it is also too
massive, not tower-like enough. It calls for four or five more
of identical design. They could then create their own environment.

Opposite Point Royal is the one-storeyed COMMUNITY
CENTRE of white brick; nice and clean.

Of the genteel residences mentioned in the early C19, few
remain which can be mentioned here.

OLD BRACKNELL HOUSE, Old Bracknell Lane, S of the station,

is of five bays and two storeys and has a pretty, semicircular Adamish porch.

SOUTHILL PARK, ⅝ m. SE of Easthampstead church. Large, of brick. One five-bay range C18.* The rest said to have been rebuilt in 1853. But the tower and the door look rather too Baroque for so early a date.‡

EASTHAMPSTEAD PARK, see above.

CHURCH HILL HOUSE, opposite Easthampstead church. This started life as almshouses and was rebuilt as the WORKHOUSE in 1826. The older part still exists, a two-storeyed red-brick range with a cupola.

CAESAR'S CAMP. Small univallate Iron Age hillfort of irregular plan enclosing some 20 acres. A prominent counterscarp bank is visible at some points along the defences. The two opposed entrances on the N and S are probably original, those on the E and W modern. The N part of the fort is now a public recreation ground.

BRADFIELD

6070

ST ANDREW. Except for the W tower and the N aisle by *Sir George Gilbert Scott*, 1847–8. The tower is C16 work, oblong flint panels framed in red brick. Battlements and higher stair-turret. As for Scott, he did feats of picturesque variety outside and inside this church. From the entrance to the churchyard one reads: N aisle with pointed trefoiled single-light windows, higher N chapel with geometrical tracery, vestry cross-gabled with plate tracery, and chancel with shafted lancets. The S side is again entirely different, with lancets and a S transept. Inside the consistent variety is even more striking. The N arcade is original Dec work. Low octagonal piers and double-chamfered arches. So the S arcade is of completely different form and height. Or take the N aisle windows (the W one is original) and Scott's S aisle windows, or the rib-vaulted apse. Here the AUMBRY has a shouldered lintel, the PISCINA rounded trefoil arches, the SEDILIA pointed arches. Decoration runs from zigzag to stiff-leaf. – Iron SCREENS. – STAINED GLASS. Mostly by *Wailes*, the W window signed. – PLATE. Cup and Paten, 1674; Set of 1800. – MONUMENTS. Obelisk in the churchyard to Henry Stevens, Lord of the Manor, † 1773. – Mrs Stevens † 1840. Small tablet framed to one's

* Alterations by *Soane* recorded for 1801.

‡ Goodhart-Rendel, *D.N.B.*, mentions Southill Park among the works of *Temple Moore*.

surprise in three-dimensional strapwork, something quite unexpected in Early Victorian funerary monuments.

BRADFIELD COLLEGE. Bradfield College was founded in 1850 by the Rev. Thomas Stevens, squire and rector. He used the site of Bradfield Place, and of this a number of fragments survive. They are first the lowest courses of walling and buttresses of a barn, originally 191 ft long. The best preserved buttress is at the SE corner of the school area close to the gateway. The others follow along the road to the W. Then there is some brick walling of very large bricks between the quadrangle and the church and, standing against the churchyard wall, a curious small polygonal brick building with a tiny polygonal, rib-vaulted lobby. It looks as if it might have been part of a gatehouse.

The quadrangle just mentioned is the main feature of the school. The various parts and stages along its E, N, and S sides are architecturally insignificant, but the W side is open to the country, and that is Bradfield's great asset. When the school started, it had only the N part of the E range at its disposal. This was Bradfield Place. It now looks 1840s-Tudor (except for the later tile-hanging), but the building is older. Stevens then added classrooms and dormitories in 1853 and 1862, to the S of the house, and they are the brick range with half-timbering.

In 1856 the DINING HALL was built, some way E of the house. This is a Gothic room with late C13 external details and wooden posts to divide it into a nave and aisles, and has tiles and chimneypieces with leaf decoration. But the *clou* of the room, and indeed of the school altogether, is the STAINED GLASS in the W lancets, designed by *Burne-Jones* when he was only 24 years old and made by *Powell's* shortly before 1859, before Burne-Jones had joined forces for good with William Morris. They are as a matter of fact much stronger and bolder than anything from Morris's workshops, and can only be compared with Burne-Jones's work at Waltham Abbey, Essex, of 1861. The colours are forceful, and the compositions are uncompromising too. In the l. lancet an angel, Eve, Adam delving, in the middle lancet the Tower of Babel, in the r. lancet two pages, Solomon and the Queen of Sheba, and a court scene. In the sexfoil above the Cross of St Andrew (the college is the College of St Andrew) and fishes; for Andrew was a fisherman. The E window by *Wailes* opposite is an anticlimax.

The hall belongs more to the ENTRANCE COURT than to the

buildings so far mentioned. This irregular court dates from
c.1865 (but the lengthening of Army House on the E side was
done only in 1889). The architect of these early parts of the
college is not certain. The most probable name is *Sir G. G.
Scott*, though Stevens himself was no doubt not a passive
client. Scott refers once to his strong will. Stevens had met
Scott in 1835 or 1836, and they had become great friends. A
daughter of Stevens married Scott's son John Oldrid, a
daughter of Scott Stevens's son. Another daughter of Stevens
married a Powell of the glassmakers' firm. The main buildings
ending the N and S wings of the quadrangle are Big School and
the chapel. BIG SCHOOL is of the 1860s and was completed,
with the library over, in 1872. The architect here was *John
Oldrid Scott*, but the style is the same as before. Flint and red
brick; gabled E end with lancets. Big School also is aisled. The
part between Big School and the manor house is later.

The CHAPEL is by *Oldrid Scott* as well and is architecturally
the best that the school has to offer. The W part is of 1890–1.
The building is of red brick with stone dressings in the Dec
style and has a lively short tower with recessed pyramid roof.
The narrow aisles are separated from the nave by polished
black columns. Tower, chancel, and sanctuary were added in
1901. Round the altar C17 PANELLING taken from the
Headmaster's House. The STAINED GLASS of the E window and the panels of opaque glass to its l. and r. are by
Powell's.

In the angle E of the church the WAR MEMORIAL. The panels
of slate with inscribed names added after the Second World
War are by *Will Carter*. N of the N range of the quadrangle,
between it and the church, is GRAY SCHOOLS by *W. G.
Newton*, c.1935–6, and rather anaemic.

Of other buildings of the college the best-known is the Greek
Theatre. The stage building dates from 1890 but received
its present façade in 1955.

Near the church and in the village are a number of Georgian
five-bay houses. One stands immediately NW of the churchyard, is of chequer brick, has a pedimented doorway, and,
with its timber-framed neighbour and the weir, forms a pretty
group. A second is in the village street, E of the church, by
the bridge. This is of red brick with vertical blue-brick strips.
Two more further N. One of these, HOME FARM HOUSE,
has its door-hood on brackets.

$\frac{3}{4}$ m. SW is the OLD RECTORY, by *Ould*, 1882, and in his way with timber-framing patterns of the West Country rather than of Berkshire.

$\frac{5}{8}$ m. s the WAYLAND HOSPITAL, former WORKHOUSE. This was built in 1835 and is still classical. It is on the usual work-house pattern.

$1\frac{1}{2}$ m. sw is BRADFIELD HALL, dated 1763. It is a complex building, but the centre is in order. Façade of three bays, the middle one being a canted bay window. Entrance side curi-ously informal: two bays, the Tuscan porch instead of one, and a pediment over the middle of the rather high elevation. Between the arched main windows of ground floor and first floor oval windows. Inside, a groin-vaulted entrance hall leads to the saloon. (This is two storeys in height and has a gallery on four Doric columns. MHLG) STABLES to the E with cupola.

BRADLEY FARMHOUSE see CUMNOR

BRAY   9080

The centre of Bray is still a village centre, which is a relief in this commuters' country. But, where the Café de Paris used to be, there is now a river estate of flats.

ST MICHAEL. A remarkably large church. Big and broad Perp s tower with porch and higher stair-turret. In the porch tier-ceron-vault of an unusual pattern. The inner doorway with continuous Perp mouldings. But inside the church the arcades of six bays are early C14, judging by their arches.* Low octagonal piers. The two-bay arcades to the chancel chapels early C14 too.‡ Externally the s doorway is of the same period, and so must be the (re-done) windows. Perp N and s chapels; but everything externally hopelessly over-restored. Victorian in a more positive way the chancel arch with its naturalistic decoration and the chancel roof (architect *T. H. Wyatt*, date 1859, according to BC). – FONT. According to the church-wardens' accounts of 1647, yet entirely Perp of the standard type. – STAINED GLASS. E window by *Wailes* to *Street*'s design (BC). – Chancel s by *Henry Holiday*, made by Powell, 1868. – MONUMENTS. Brass to Sir John de Foxley † 1378 and two wives. The typical ambiguity of vertical and hori-zontal representation is here especially telling. The three are seen on a bracket, and, although that implies that they are

* The E bay of the N arcade was rebuilt in 1860.
‡ Also rebuilt in 1860.

standing, he in fact has his helmet behind his head and a dog at his feet. The canopies are missing. It must have been a very fine piece when it was complete. The figures are 2 ft 6 in. long. – Brass to William Laken †1474 (s aisle), a 13 in. figure. – Brass to William Norreys † 1591. Tablet in architectural surround with an egg-and-dart frame (N aisle). – William Goddard † 1609, founder of Jesus Hospital. Large tablet with two frontal three-quarter figures. Black columns, wide open pediment. The inscription reads

> 'If what I was thou seekest to know,
> These lynes my character shall show,
> Those benefits that God me lent,
> With thankes I tooke, and freely spent:
> I scorned what plainess could not gett,
> And, next to treason, hated debt;
> Loved not those that stirr'd up strife:
> True to my friend and to my wife.
> The latter here by me I have,
> We had one bed, and have one grave.
> My honesty was such that I
> When death came, feared not to dye.'

– Brass of c.1610. Architectural surround with guilloche and a steep pediment. No name, no date. The inscription as worth while as the previous one:

> 'When Oxford gave thee two degrees in art,
> And love possest thee master of my heart,
> Thy colledge fellowshipp thow lefs't for mine
> And nought but death could seprate me from thine.
> Thirty-five yeares we livd'e in wedlocke bands
> Conioyned in our hearts as well as handes
> But death the bodies of best friendes devides
> And in the earths close wombe their relyckes hides
> Yet here they are not lost but sowen, that they
> May rise more glorious at the Judgment day.'

– William Paule † 1685. Tablet with segmental pediment on columns. A wreath round the inscription. – Mrs Hanger † 1739. By *Peter Scheemakers*. No effigy; minor.
In the churchyard the CHANTRY CHAPEL OF ST MARY. It became a school in the early C17, and it was then that the wooden cross-windows were inserted. – Outside the s wall a RELIEF of a horse. Is it Norman? – The main access to the churchyard is by a timber-framed C15 GATEHOUSE. Brick

infilling, low passageway, and above it to the outside an oriel.
Pretty lane from here to the main street. In the main street,
at the N end, and overlooking the churchyard, CHANTRY
HOUSE, C18, three-storeyed, the front later than the rest.
The front has two canted bay windows and a doorway with
Ionic columns and a pediment. Staircase with turned balusters
and carved tread-ends. Further s in the main street some C15
cottages on the l., the CROWN HOTEL, a C15 hall-house, on
the r.

At the s end of the village JESUS HOSPITAL, founded in 1627,
a large brick quadrangle with twenty-eight dwellings, with
their windows l. and r. of the doorway and their large dormer
windows exceptionally generously dimensioned. The centre of
the entrance side is higher and has to the outside a statue of the
founder and l. and r. stone cross-windows. In the centre of
the end wall the chapel with an original SCREEN. Four arches
l., four r. of the entrance. Tapering pillars, no top decoration.

BRAY WICK HOUSE, ½ m. SW. The main front is dated 1675
and has a three-bay centre and two-bay moderately projecting wings. But there are no features, except the broad
brick string course above the ground floor which projects
slightly above every window. Behind, one corner of three by
three bays is later and a little higher. (A staircase inside with
balusters looking rather earlier than 1675. In one room nice
thin Rococo stucco. Is it genuine C18 work?* NBR)

HOLYPORT HOUSE, Holyport Green, ¾ m. SW. A Queen Anne
house of five bays with hipped roof and segment-headed
windows. Earlier timber-framed rooms behind. The house
overlooks HOLYPORT GREEN with several attractive houses,
especially one picturesquely wonky-looking timber-framed
house on the W side of the Green.

Behind Holyport House is GAY'S HOUSE, also C18. Brick, of
seven irregular bays, with a porch on Tuscan columns. The
windows on the r. of the porch are arched on ground floor and
upper floor.

BRAYWOOD   8070

ALL SAINTS. 1866 by *Talbot Bury*. The church has been
demolished.

BRIGHTWALTON   4070

ALL SAINTS. 1862–3 by *Street*. Rock-faced, in the late C13

* I was not allowed to see the interior.

style, with Geometrical tracery. SW tower with big shingled broach spire. The S arcade has short quatrefoiled blackish (blue lias: BC) piers, the clerestory quatrefoil and trefoil openings. – REREDOS. By *Earp*. – STAINED GLASS. By the font glass of *c*.1863, by an unfamiliar-looking hand. Mr A. C. Sewter, the foremost expert, attributes it to *Burne-Jones*. Children presented to Christ. Strong colours, but not strident. The faces with quite some tension. – PLATE. Small, ornate Cup, German, inscribed 1610; Paten, 1729; silver-gilt Paten, 1722. – BRASS to John Newman(?) † 1517. A 14 in. figure.

SCHOOL. By *Street*, 1863. Brick and stone dressings. Half-hipped roofs. Only the main window Gothic.

RECTORY. By *Street*, 1877. Brick and tile-hanging. Dormers. Good big chimneystacks.

WOOLLEY PARK, 1¼ m. NW. A late C17 house, remodelled by *Sir Jeffry Wyatville* in 1799. Cement-faced. The main façade with a big bow with attached giant Tuscan columns. Only two bays l., two r. of it. But Victorian additions l. as well as r. At the back a Tuscan one-storeyed veranda between projecting wings. (Inside, the staircase divides into two and is lit by a dome.)

BRIGHTWELL
5090

ST AGATHA. The S doorway of *c*.1200. Capitals with leaf. Round arch with a filleted roll. Of the same time the S arcade. Three bays, round piers, octagonal abaci, single-step pointed arches. The tower arch belongs too. Two slight chamfers. But the tower itself dates from 1797. Blue headers and red brick dressings. Arched bell-openings. Parapet. The N arcade is of about 1300, and the windows are in agreement with such a date. Late Geometrical tracery. Standard elements. Early C14 chancel. Windows with Geometrical tracery, but also ogees. Similarly the PISCINA and SEDILIA still look C13 but have ogees. The hood-mould of the group has head-stops. The S aisle fenestration is Dec too. Perp clerestory. – CHANDELIER. Brass; C18. – STAINED GLASS. Fragments, including a head, N aisle. – PLATE. Cup of 1599; small Paten of 1752; large Paten of 1771/2. – BRASSES. John Scoffyld † 1507, priest, 18 in. figure (s aisle). – Robert Court † 1509 and wife, 20 in. figures (nave). – Richard Hampden † 1512 and wife, 15 in. figures (nave).

BRIGHTWELL MANOR, S of the church. Georgian; blue headers and red dressings. Three storeys, five bays, plain arched doorway.

N of the church a HOUSE with a C17 part with mullioned windows.

BRIMPTON

5060

ST PETER. 1869–72 by *John Johnson*. All flint and quite big. The tower is in fact a brick tower of 1748, faced with flint and provided with a broach spire. The style chosen for the church is Dec. Inside, piers of polished granite. Nave and aisles, transepts, and symmetrical vestry and organ chamber, the latter opened by a two-light window to the chancel. – STAINED GLASS. N transept N by *Willement*, *c.*1856 (Betjeman and Piper). – Chancel S 1859 by *Lavers & Barraud*. – PLATE. Cup and Paten, Late Elizabethan; Paten, 1800.

MANOR FARM. Next to the house the former CHAPEL OF ST LEONARD, a plain oblong flint building with a Norman N doorway (tympanum with a big cross), a N lancet, and a Dec E window of three stepped lights, nicely done.

BRIMPTON MILL. Dated 1731. Brick, of five bays, with a weatherboarded gable.

ROUND BARROW CEMETERY, in the S of the parish, close to the Hampshire border. The group consists of two bell barrows and three bowl barrows. They vary in diameter from 60 to 100 ft and in height from 4 to 8 ft.

BROADLANDS see SUNNINGHILL

BROADMOOR see CROWTHORNE

BROCKHAMPTON FARM see LAMBOURN

BUCKHOLD

6070

HOLY TRINITY. 1836 by *Sampson Kempthorne*. Nave and chancel and bellcote. Lancet windows. Cemented walls.

BUCKHOLD HOUSE (St Andrew's School). By *Alfred Waterhouse*, 1884–5. Large and quite freely grouped. Red brick and yellow terracotta. Gothic and Elizabethan forms mixed. In the entrance hall ceramic pictures by *Doulton's*, including a view of their own Gothic works at Lambeth, and also a view of Boston, Mass. – Octagonal COWSHED.

BUCKHURST PARK see SUNNINGHILL

BUCKLAND

3090

ST MARY. The church possesses an exceptionally wide early C12 nave, the dimensions of which are given by the N and S

windows fairly high up and the N and S doorways. The very
tall S doorway has two orders of shafts with one-scallop
capitals and strong roll mouldings. Hood-mould with saltire
crosses. The N doorway is lower but otherwise similar. The
nave battlements of course are later, probably Perp. The
church is cruciform with a crossing tower with E.E. lancet
bell-openings. The piers on which the tower stands are unfortunately restored beyond redemption. E.E. also the N
transept – see the remains of lancets in the W and N walls.
The chancel must be Dec, judging by the N recess with ogee
gable and ballflower decoration and the S recess minus the
leaf and fleur-de-lis friezes which must be a later cutting. The
SEDILIA and PISCINA with pointed-trefoiled heads also Dec.
But all that evidence is externally obscured by the fact that
the chancel and N and S transept windows and the nave W
window of three to five lights have mullions running dead into
the arches. The same motif with even the arches straightened
out occurs at Uffington. The VCH in both cases calls it E.E.
But can that be? On the S transept here a date 1787 is inscribed. But if the C13 is too early, 1787 is too late. It looks a
C17 repair. However, nothing is recorded, and why would such
consistent repairs have been needed? Good chancel roof with
tie-beams, kingposts, and many carved bosses. Extremely rich,
glittering S transept DECORATION with mosaics. Made in the
1890s by *Powell's* (BC). – FONT. Perp, octagonal, with
quatrefoils and tracery motifs. – PULPIT. Jacobean, similar
to that in Shrivenham church. Angle pilasters tapering. Blank
arches with fake perspectives. – BOX PEWS and PEWS,
including open balustraded fronts. – TOWER GALLERY high
up. Balustraded; Jacobean. – CHANDELIERS. In the transepts. One was given in 1733 (VCH). – SOUTH DOOR. The
ironwork is of the C12. – STAINED GLASS in the S transept,
probably part of the general decoration. It looks *Powell's*, and
the date of death recorded is 1888. – SCULPTURE. In the
piscina small Italian C17 alabaster relief of the Adoration of
the Shepherds. – Three funeral HELMETS in the N transept;
C17. – PLATE. Cup of 1565, an early post-Reformation date;
Paten of 1638; Plate of 1697; large Flagon of 1721. – MONU-
MENTS. William Holcot † 1570. Triangular niche in the
chancel N wall. He was a lay-preacher after the Reformation.
Under Mary he recanted. He made a will for his heart to be
kept in a casket in this niche. The shape may allude to the
Trinity. – Sir Edward Yate and his daughter who died in 1648.

Black and white marble altar with 'frontal' of strapwork and garlands. 'Reredos' with the same elements. The garlands are a progressive motif. Good quality. – Sir John Yate † 1658. Tablet with black columns, garlands in the 'predella'. The top already an open scrolly pediment. – Elizabeth Perfect. Coade stone, i.e. by *Coade & Seely*, 1802. Weeping putto by an urn.

ST GEORGE (R.C.). 1846–8 by *Hansom* (Mr D. Evinson) or *W. W. Wardell* (BC). Whichever it was, the church looks as if it was remodelled in the later C19. Nave and chancel, bell-cote on a mid-buttress. High N chapel with Kentish tracery. The rest of the tracery Geometrical.

BUCKLAND HOUSE. Built in 1757 etc. by the younger *Wood* of Bath for Sir Robert Throckmorton. Buckland House as built was not as large as it is now, but it was the most splendid of smaller Georgian houses in the county. *Romaine Walker* about 1910 added the wings to the house itself, not the low outer wings, and thereby doubled the accommodation. These wings as seen from the grounds project beyond the centre and look perfectly convincing. From the entrance, on the other hand, they stay in line with the centre, and the result is an unhappy crowding of link windows. Wood's design was a square and low links to outer pavilions. The square is of five bays and two and a half storeys and has an exceptionally high ground floor, exceptionally, considering that it is rusticated and that giant columns start only above it. Yet the main rooms are on the rusticated, not on the upper level. The giant columns are Corinthian and carry a pediment, and the frieze is enriched throughout by leaf garlands. The main upper windows are framed by aedicules. The pavilions cruciform but with diagonals in front of what would be the re-entrant angle. Romaine Walker, needless to say, added the unfortunate porch. It is not known whether he also altered the low ENTRANCE HALL with its coupled pilasters. He certainly re-did the STAIRCASE, though in its original place. The two fully preserved rooms in the centre block are the saloon and the adjacent room behind the stairs. The SALOON is higher than the other rooms and has a coved ceiling with medallions and swags and in the flat centre a much baro-quized stucco version of Reni's 'Aurora'. Big chimneypiece. Door-hood on brackets. The adjacent room has a Rococo plaster ceiling and a very fine late C18 chimneypiece. The centre towards the garden is oddly of six, not five bays.

Paired doors lead therefore out of the two main rooms to the open stairs and the terraces. Original also the interiors of the end pavilions. In the E pavilion the LIBRARY with a ceiling painted all in one (i.e. not in compartments) by *Cipriani* and *Rebecca* to Cipriani's design, and with decoration gone Adamish. The W pavilion on the other hand is grand in the sense of the façade. It is called the CHAPEL, but if it was that, it must have had the altar at the W end, which is unlikely. The interior is all left in stone. Corinthian angle pilasters in groups. Columns only in the W arm of the cross. The frieze again with garlands. The windows flanked by colonnettes. The chimneypiece still has a head with rays as its centre – still, as this is a William Kent motif. The room is not really vaulted. There is only a broad coving with penetrations.

In the grounds are an ICE HOUSE, N of the N end of the house and the NW corner of the Manor House, in the trees. It is largely above ground and thatched. The front is a portico of three arches, W, N, S, and has ample grotto rustication on the portico openings. By the lake is a rustic BOATHOUSE built of upright logs. Further W a pedimented EXEDRA, derelict, and a good deal further W, i.e. NW of the house, a ROTUNDA of unfluted Ionic columns with a dome. The urn inside is by Romaine Walker and commemorates the Knight of Kerry.

MANOR HOUSE. A late C16 or C17 house with mullioned and transomed windows was converted in the late C18 into Gothick STABLES to Buckland House. Of the old house the E side still has a canted bay window and a window immediately l. and a window immediately r. of it, making a total of fourteen lights. To the l. and r. of this part the Gothick architecture, i.e. windows with Y-tracery. The front towards Buckland House has polygonal angle towers and nine bays in between, the centre an archway. The façade is crenellated and the battlements rise as a shallow gable above the archway. There are of course also quatrefoil windows.

Much ESTATE HOUSING.

BUCKLEBURY

ST MARY. The churchyard is entered by cast-iron gates of 1827 (signed by the firm: *N. Hedges*). The church is of flint and possesses a very ornate Late Norman S doorway. The inner order has rosettes, faces, four-petalled flowers, etc. The next order has shafts with decorated capitals. In the arch pellets and zigzag. In the centre of the hood-mould a fearsome face crowned by an orb and a cross. C13 N arcade of three separate openings cut into the former wall. Double-chamfered arches. Perp W tower* with W doorway and W window. C18 pinnacles and spire. – FONT. Octagonal, strongly moulded, probably C14. – PULPIT. Later C17? Just panels framed by guilloche. – BOX PEWS. – COMMUNION RAIL. With twisted balusters, c.1700. – WEST GALLERY. The date 1824 might well apply to it. – STAINED GLASS. The chancel E, N, and S windows by *Brangwyn*, 1912, N aisle window by the same (date of death commemorated 1917). Strong colours, clearly and dramatically told stories, in a kind of realist Expressionism. – PLATE. Cup, 1576: Cover, 1577; Paten on foot and Flagon, 1811; Almsdish, 1824. – MONUMENTS. Sir Henry Winchcombe † 1703. Two putti and a coat of arms under a looped curtain framed by pilasters and a pedimental top. – Also three HELMS, two SWORDS, and a pair of GAUNTLETS.

RECTORY. A handsome early C18 brick façade of three bays with giant pilasters. One-bay pediment. – In the garden two large bronze figures: Reclining Figure by *Henry Moore*, 1961–2, but done in plaster c.1956. – Draped Reclining Woman, 1957–8 by the same. The setting is ideal.

BUCKRIDGES *see* SUTTON COURTENAY

BULLBROOK *see* BRACKNELL

BURGHFIELD
6060

ST MARY. 1843 by *J. B. Clacy*, a rather terrible neo-Norman effort. Brick, with a W tower. Its top stage is polygonal. A stumpy spire on top. Two unhappy porches in the angles between tower and nave. Wide nave and wide transepts. The chancel built by *Bodley & Garner* in 1892 (BC), in the Dec style, and carefully, as one would expect. The E window is above the reredos. – FONT. Cut in the C14, with blank panelling, out of a circular tub-shaped Norman font. – STAINED GLASS. The E window by *Burlison & Grylls* (BC); not at all bad. – PLATE. Cup, 1632; Paten on foot, 1714. – MONUMENTS. Early C14 effigy of a Knight, damaged, but must once have been very fine. Angels by his pillow, crossed legs. – Richard Neville, Earl of Salisbury, † 1460. Two recumbent stone effigies; defaced.

---

* On the SE buttress relief of a man with a wheel. It looks C18. It has been suggested that it might be a rebus referring to the Winchcombe family who were Lords of the Manor, and in this case might well be earlier.

OLD RECTORY, ¼ m. NW. Brick, Georgian, five bays with three-bay pediment. Door surround with pilasters, triglyph frieze, and pediment.

2090
BUSCOT

ST MARY. By the Isis, i.e. the Thames, outside the village. Perp W tower with W doorway and W window. Nave and chancel separated by a chancel arch of *c.*1200. Two orders of simple stiff-leaf; zigzag arch. In the chancel one N lancet and one low-side lancet. Unrestored N side of the church. Inside, cinquefoiled rere-arches indicate that what seem wide early C19 lancets were originally two-light windows. – PULPIT. Three panels are a re-used Flemish triptych, early C16. Two other panels English Early Renaissance, probably domestic. – LECTERN. Splendid, Spanish, C17; of wood. – STAINED GLASS. The E window by *Burne-Jones*, i.e. *Morris & Co.*, 1891: the Good Shepherd. By the same a window in the chancel on the S side; *c.*1895. – PLATE. Silver-gilt Cup and Bread Holder, 1711; Cover Paten and Flagon, 1779. – MONUMENTS. Brasses to Husband and Wife, *c.*1500, 2 ft figures. – Monument to Margaret Loveden Loveden † 1786. Two putti by a grey obelisk. At the foot relief of Charity. She is giving money to a poor man and bread to a girl. – Elizabeth Loveden Loveden † 1788. In front of an obelisk, reclining on a couch. A baldacchino above her on the r. An angel appearing from the l. and holding her hand. Both by *Robert Cooke*.

OLD RECTORY. Fine house of *c.*1700. Five by three bays, two storeys, hipped roof. Stone, and roofed with stone slates.

The VILLAGE HALL with cupola at the end of the short village street and the village WELL of four square pillars and a four-gabled roof, as well as a number of houses, were done for the Hendersons, i.e. the first Lord Faringdon, by *Sir Ernest George* in the 1890s. In the village street MANOR FARM-HOUSE, dated 1691, five bays, two storeys, hipped roof, like the Old Rectory. But wooden cross-windows and doorway on carved brackets.

BUSCOT PARK. The house may have been built about 1770. It is of nine bays and two storeys with a pedimented three-bay centre. To the N two generous symmetrical bows. In 1889 *Sir Ernest George & Peto* added a big wing and altered the house itself. The wing was pulled down and the house brought back to its original appearance by *Geddes Hyslop* just before the Second World War. The work was done for Lord Faringdon.

Hyslop also added two detached classical ranges at a distance and in axis with the house. They end on either short side in a Tuscan portico. One has a cupola, and a tunnel-vaulted passage through its centre. In this wall PAINTINGS of Labour Party and generally Socialist subject matter; and also of the family having tea. They are by *Lord Hastings* (then Lord Huntingdon), who studied under Diego Rivera, and were done in the thirties.

The entrance hall has at its back a screen of two red scagliola columns with Ionic capitals. The overdoors with recent Grecian paintings by *Elroy Haldall*. The ceilings of the rooms to the l. and r. are distinctly Adamish. In the centre room on the garden side another, more elaborate, such ceiling. Round the walls in thick gilded neo-Renaissance frames the 61 series of *Burne-Jones*'s Sleeping Beauty (Briar Rose), painted in 1890. The frames were designed by Burne-Jones too. Fine chimneypiece with detached termini-caryatid maidens. Vaulted passage along the centre of the house between the front and back rooms. In one of the two bow-fronted back rooms is yet another excellent plaster ceiling. The overmantel is in the Chippendale–Chinese fashion. The *chinoiserie* paintings, however, are recent. The staircase hall has an Adamish ceiling too. But the composition of Roman Doric columns in the window wall is Hyslop's.

BUSSOCK WOOD *see* WINTERBOURNE

BUTTERSTEEP HOUSE *see* ASCOT

CAESAR'S CAMP *see* BRACKNELL

CALCOT
2 m. w of Reading

6070

CALCOT HOUSE. 1755 for John Blagrave. A splendid seven-bay house, unfortunately provided with a later roof. Red brick, all headers. Basement and two storeys. Three-bay portico with brick pilasters carrying finely carved Ionic capitals. Pediment with a Venetian window squeezed into it. Doorway with attached Tuscan columns and a triglyph frieze. The back just as impressive. The house here forms the end of an oblong stable court with three ranges and four corner pavilions with hipped roofs. The staircase has an iron railing with scrolls, quite modest. Walls with good stucco panels. The extension to the second floor is recent. The principal room has a modest plaster ceiling. – LODGE on the Bath Road three by three bays with giant blank arches.

ALMSHOUSES. 1852. Quite pretty. Red brick and blue diapers. One-storeyed.

CARSWELL MANOR see LONGWORTH

4980
CATMORE

ST MARGARET. Two Norman doorways, the s one with a head at the top of the hood-mould. The rest of the Norman features overwhelmingly Early Victorian, an effort to make a modest Norman church showy Norman. The work is of before 1850, as in that year the church was called 'lately carefully restored' (BC). The nave roof with collar-beams on arched braces and wind-braces is of 1607. The pendants betray the date. – FONT. Tub-shaped, Norman, with a top band of defaced decoration. – PLATE. Paten on foot of 1723(?); Almsdish of 1834.

7070
CAVERSHAM

ST PETER. Norman s doorway. One order of shafts, zigzag up the jambs and in the arch, partly at r. angles to the wall. The abaci have saltire crosses. Re-set Norman window in the w wall of the N vestry. Perp N wall. The s aisle is an addition of 1878. The tower was rebuilt in 1878 (BC). Low arcades inside, with round piers. Good Perp N chapel. Panelled arches on a pier the capital of which has carved angel-busts, a Windsor motif. The chapel has a N window, now inside, a little later yet than the other N windows. The chancel was lengthened in 1924–5 by Sir N. Comper (BC). – FONT. Norman, of Purbeck marble, a round basin, but at the angles raised spurs with concave outlines. – CHANDELIER. Of brass, dated 1743. – Former WIND VANE. Dated 1663. Now on a staff. – PLATE. Silver-gilt Flagon and two Patens, inscribed 1753. The flagon is a piece of Elizabethan Revival.

The church lies above the site of CAVERSHAM COURT, now a public garden by the Thames. Of the buildings a GARDEN HOUSE remains, brick, C17, and the STABLES, also brick and C17.

The centre of Caversham is now all Reading. At the main crossing, at the angle of GOSBROOK ROAD and South Street, the BAPTIST FREE CHURCH, 1875–7 by *Waterhouse*, red brick, Gothic, and in Gosbrook Road *Waterhouse's* WEST

MEMORIAL INSTITUTE, of 1865–6, also brick and also Gothic. It was the Free Church before the present one was built. At the corner of HENLEY ROAD and PEPPARD ROAD is QUEEN ANNE'S SCHOOL, 1894 and later. It includes Amersham Hall, built as a Nonconformist boys' school by *Waterhouse*, probably *c.*1865. The chapel is by *Sir Reginald Blomfield*. At the top of Peppard Road is the entrance to CAVERSHAM PARK, a stuccoed mansion of 1850–2, in the Palladian tradition. This is, however, across the Oxfordshire border.

Finally, at the far W end of SURLEY ROW, a somewhat Italian lane, OLD GROVE HOUSE, Elizabethan, of flint set in square panels, framed by brick bands. Gables, unusual chimney-stack.

In 1964 a beginning was made on a large HOUSING ESTATE taken out of Caversham Park. It is an area of 156 acres and will in the end have 1,500 houses. The plan is entirely on the Radburn principle of strict separation of pedestrian and vehicle circulation. The designers are *Diamond, Redfern & Partners*, with *Paul Ritter* as the planner. The site runs from Peppard Road to Hurley Road.

CHADDLEWORTH
4070

ST ANDREW. The S doorway is Norman. It has zigzags up the jambs, meeting at the angle. Arch with two zigzags. Hood-mould on heads, with a nice simple trail. In the original chancel a Norman N window. In the nave an early C13 N lancet. Early C13 also the short, unbuttressed W tower. The hood-mould over the W window is re-used Norman work. To this modest church *Street* in 1851 added a chancel, deliberately unconcerned, it seems, with the scale and character of the church. His chancel is of blue and red brick, is higher, has a slate roof, and displays bigger and heavier windows. On the N side of the church two family chapels, the eastern one of 1706, the western of 1765. – The PULPIT is not Georgian, but imitation-Georgian. – RAILS to the family chapels. – Creed and Our Father. Nicely bordered WOODEN BOARDS, dated 1757. – PLATE. Cup and Cover, 1585; Cup, 1717; Paten, 1788; Salver, 1790. – MONUMENTS. Exceptionally many tablets, but no major monuments. In the chancel Thomas Nelson † 1748 with two standing putti. – In the nave on the N side two Mrs Nelsons † 1618 and 1619. Above the inscription ogee arches. – Bartholomew Tipping † 1757, big. – Chardin Musgrove † 1768, with a standing mourning female by an urn. By *King* of Bath. – On the s side two more Bartholomew Tippings † 1718 and † 1737. – In the western family chapel yet another Bartholomew Tipping † 1798. Signed Westmacott Junior, i.e. the future *Sir Richard Westmacott*. Competently and restrainedly Grecian.

CHADDLEWORTH HOUSE. Of *c.*1830. Blue and red brick. Five bays. Tuscan porch. Pedimental gable.

POUGHLEY FARMHOUSE, 1½ m. s. Now inside an Air Force establishment. This was the site of a priory of Augustinian Canons founded *c.*1160. (A part of the w range of the priory buildings is now incorporated in the E façade of the farmhouse. Blocked late C13 two-light window with pointed trefoiled lights. Small figure of a seated monk, re-set. VCH) To the ENE of the façade excavations have shown an aisleless chapel, probably with a w tower.*

ROUND BARROWS *see* Great Fawley.

³⁰⁹⁰   CHARNEY BASSETT

ST PETER. Small, next to the larger Manor House. Embattled nave. Curious Jacobean bellcote. Perp two-bay N arcade (octagonal pier, depressed double-chamfered arches). But the interesting thing of the church is the Norman work: i.e. the outer moulding of the s doorway with radially set faces, their tongues out and forking like beards, and the tympanum set up inside. This shows a standing man holding two gryphons and bitten by them. He is called in the literature Alexander, but the representation does not fit the Alexander story. – PULPIT. Perp, of wood. – STAINED GLASS. C15 fragments.

MANOR HOUSE. Centre and two projecting wings, the s wing being the late C13 solar wing of a hall-house. The centre, where the hall was, and the N wing are a C19-Tudor rebuilding. The C13 wing has a rectangular projection to the E. The ground floor has windows which are small slits, except for one two-light window under a round arch. The head is re-set. In the N wall is a doorway to the former house, and also a large fireplace with a shouldered lintel. On the upper floor was the solar, and to its E the chapel. Two-light windows in both. The chapel E window has bar tracery. In the s wall a pointed-trefoil-headed lancet. Roof with tie-beams, crownposts,

---

* Mr S. E. Rigold adds to this 'a good piece of C14 arched-braced roof with a well-preserved louvre'.

and four-way struts. In the W wall of the N wing is a re-set quatrefoil opening also of the C13.

CHERBURY CAMP. The low-lying situation of this fort would appear to render it indefensible under modern conditions. It has been shown, however, that during the life of the fort access to the low knoll on which it is constructed would have been barred by a stream on the N and W and by an extensive area of swamp on the E and SE. Access was by means of a narrow neck of higher ground on the NE. The defences consist of three concentric banks and ditches, best preserved on the NW. These fortifications are broken by gaps on the N, S, and E sides; only the last is an original entrance. This E entrance had a metalled surface in which cart ruts had been worn and gave way in the interior of the fort to a finely cobbled street. Finds from the ditches suggest that the fort was the work of Iron Age B groups, probably at the beginning of the C1 A.D.

CHAVEY DOWN
2 m. E of Bracknell

8060

HEATHFIELD SCHOOL. The school chapel is by *Street*, 1850, i.e. very early.* Nave and chancel in one, tiled roof, small bell-turret. Straight-headed three-light windows with ogee-headed lights. The interior was entirely remodelled c.1960. The school buildings, near the chapel, include a re-erected Georgian shopfront of doorway and two bow windows.

CHERBURY CAMP *see* CHARNEY BASSETT

CHIEVELEY

4070

ST MARY. Unbuttressed C13 W tower with Perp bell-stage, and a very fine C13 chancel. The E wall has three lancets, with continuous roll mouldings outside, continuous roll mouldings and shafts with stiff-leaf capitals inside. The roof has one tie-beam on arched braces with traceried spandrels.‡ The side walls have lancets. The nave is of 1873, by *J. W. Hugall*. – FONT. Octagonal, Perp, with quatrefoils. – PULPIT. Jacobean, with blank arches and arabesques. – MONUMENT. Mrs Fincher † 1688. Small. Square brass plate in a stone surround of leathery or doughy forms, more like 1650 than 1688.

* Or is this even the church by Street mentioned in the *D.N.B.* as designed for Bracknell before 1849?

‡ It probably also served the purpose of supporting the lenten veil.

CHIEVELEY HOUSE, SE of the church. Red brick, five bays, hipped roof, the doorway with a straight hood on three brackets, one of them an angel-head.

VICARAGE, N of the former. Five bays with a one-bay pediment and a hipped roof.

(PIG FARM COTTAGE. Of cruck construction. NBR)

PRIOR'S COURT, 1 m. E. Late C18. Seven bays, the first and last two raised by one storey and pedimented. In the raised part a lunette window. The centre has a porch with four (re-used?) Corinthian stone columns. (In the house some C14 STAINED GLASS, e.g. monkeys playing musical instruments – see *Newbury District Field Club*, 11, 1872.)

IRON AGE HILLFORT, in the middle of Bussock Wood. This small 10-acre fort is of univallate construction on the N and W and has two banks on the E and S, where the gentler slope would favour attack. There are a number of gaps on the E side, but without excavation it is impossible to say which are contemporary with the ramparts.

3080

CHILDREY

ST MARY. Quite a big church. The nave basically early C13 – see the two doorways, that on the S side with a hood-mould of dogtooth. But the windows are Perp and the upper windows – a heightening – Late Perp. Then the chancel, higher than the nave. This is late C13 – see the windows with pointed-trefoiled lights and a circle over. Also cusped Y-tracery and SEDILIA and PISCINA with pointed trefoiled heads. The Easter Sepulchre on the other hand must be later – late C14 at the earliest, see the Perp panelling behind the ogee gable. The foliage, however, is still near the Dec. Much oak leaf. After that the transepts – see the Dec E window and the low tomb recess in the N wall (cf. below). But the big window over this is Perp again. Broad Perp W tower with W doorway with decorated spandrels and a typical broadly moulded arch to the nave. The date of the transepts is internally confirmed by the arch into them. No chancel arch at all. – FONT. Of lead, c.1200, with small upright figures of bishops taken from the same few moulds. A very interesting piece. – SCREEN. One-light divisions; not much of it old. – BENCHES. A few old, with simple poppy-heads. – STAINED GLASS. In the N transept, much of it C15, but in small parts. – PLATE. Paten, hall-marked 1496, with the Vernicle; Cup, C17. – MONUMENTS. The low tomb recess in the N transept is Dec. It has an ogee arch, ballflower, ogee cusping, and a fine, slender cross-legged effigy, hand at his sword, shield held high up. – Purbeck marble tomb with short tomb-chest and canopy on a straight under-edge. Brasses of William Fete-place † 1516 and wife, kneeling, in shrouds against the back wall. – Many brasses: William Fynderne † 1444 and wife (chancel floor). 52 in. figures, but little of them left. High ogee canopies. Interesting inscription in distichs. – Headless priest, 12 in. figure, c.1450. – John Kyngeston † 1514 and wife, Trinity above, 30 in. figures (chancel floor). – Joan Walrond, Mrs Strongbow, † 1507(?). Small figure in a shroud, beautiful Trinity above (s transept floor).

BOWL BARROW, 50 yds NE of the Ridgeway and W of Hackpen Hill. This fine barrow is 90 ft in diameter and 4 ft high. The site was excavated in the C19, when an unaccompanied primary cremation was found.

CHILTON

ALL SAINTS. The blocked N doorway Norman, the s doorway probably too. The chancel arch is of c.1200 (unmoulded, pointed). So is the priest's doorway. The s arcade (in an odd position) must be early C13. Big round pier, round abacus, single-chamfered arches. The chancel of c.1300, see the E window of the same type as those of the s chapel of Brightwell, i.e. arches upon arches. Two N lancets with ogee-trefoiled heads. W tower 1847. – STAINED GLASS. E window designed by *J. F. Bentley* and made by *Westlake* (BC), 1873. – PLATE. Chalice and Paten, late C17.

CHILTON FOLIAT

CHILTON LODGE, W of Leverton. 1800 by *W. Pilkington*. Monumental five-bay façade of ashlar, only one and a half storeys high but generously spaced, with a giant Composite portico to which a wide staircase leads up. Pediment over the portico. The ground-floor windows l. and r. of the portico are set under blank arches. On the E side a porte-cochère, on the W side an attached wing, both said to be by *Sir Arthur Blomfield*. STABLES of brick behind.

The rest of Chilton Foliat is in Wiltshire; see *The Buildings of England: Wiltshire*, p. 151.

CHOLSEY

ST MARY. Quite a major church. Cruciform, of flint and stone and essentially Norman, with a chancel lengthened in the C13.

There must have been a similar church here already in the
C II; for the crossing tower has long-and-short quoins. They
may be Saxo-Norman overlap of course, and the crossing
piers are too much remodelled to make sure whether a Saxon
core is possible. Of the crossing arches, however, the capitals
of the W and E responds seem trustworthy up to a point, and
they are rather after than before the mid C 12. Two have
decorated scallops, one of them with two little heads inserted.
Norman moreover two S transept windows and one N transept
window, one larger nave S window, and the S doorway with
one order of shafts and zigzag in the arch. The transepts
originally had apses to the E. The arch to one remains, the
outline of the other has been excavated. So it is likely that the
Norman chancel also ended in an apse, in which case the plan
would have been that of e.g. Norman Melbourne (Derby-
shire). That the chancel is a lengthening can be seen on the N
side, where the sill frieze breaks off at a certain point. On the
S side it runs all along. The S side has five lancets and the
priest's doorway with a continuous roll moulding. The E
window is of three lights, the middle one sharper and taller
than the others and with three uncusped, unfoiled circles
above – a typical motif of c.1275. Inside the lancets are shafted,
and they stand so close together that one shaft serves two of
them. The shafts have fillets. The E window shafts are
excessively long and have shaft-rings and leaf capitals. The
SEDILIA are simply stepped seats below the lancets. Of later
contributions it is enough to list the S transept S window of the
type with arches upon arches as its tracery, i.e. a type of c.1300,
and the N transept N window, which seems of about the same
date, but is of 1877–8. The top parts of the tower are Dec; the
pretty little doorway to the tower staircase is Perp. – BENCH
END. One, with poppy-head, in the chancel. – (DRESSER.
From Trautmannsdorf Castle near Merano in the Tyrol,
c.1700. In the vestry. – SCULPTURE. A Norman piece, probably from a scallop capital, in the N wall of the intermediate
chamber of the tower.) – TILES. A few under the E crossing
arch, more in the S transept. – PAINTING. Taking the Sacrament to a Sick Person at Traù. By *A. W. Rimington*. –
STAINED GLASS. By *Kempe* chancel S 1891, N 1900. – PLATE.
Cover Paten, 1577; Chalice and Cover Paten, 1646. – MONU-
MENTS. Defaced effigy of a Lady, early C 14. – Brass to John
Mere, vicar, † 1471. A 14½ in. figure.

MANOR FARM. It is here that the materials were re-used of the

BARN which had been the largest anywhere and was de-36a molished in 1815. Its length was 303 ft, and its height 51 ft.* The roof was supported by square stone piers, about 35 ft high, with chamfered angles. The outer walls were only 8 ft high, i.e. the expanse of roof was tremendous. The date of the barn is not certain, but the early C13 or even the late C12 seems likely – cf. e.g. the chamfered angles of piers of the late C12 at Byland Abbey or the rounded angles of the piers of the late C12 Canons' Barn at Wells.

(BREACH HOUSE. By *E. P. Warren*, 1905. In the William-and-Mary style. Recessed centre with two-column veranda. Hipped roof. *C.L.*, 1909)

FAIRMILE HOSPITAL (Psychiatric), ¾ m. w of Moulsford. Built in 1867–70, designed by *C. H. Howell*. Red brick with gables and a tower. Additions by *G. T. Hind*, 1898. The George Schuster Hospital is by *Powell & Moya*, 1955–6: one-storeyed and roughly cruciform; a good, clearly articulated design.

CHURN DOWN *and* CHURN HILL *see*
BLEWBURY

CLEWER *see* WINDSOR, pp. 300, 304

COCK MARSH *see* COOKHAM

COLD ASH   5060

ST MARK. 1864–5 by *C. N. Beazley*. Nave with bellcote, chancel with polygonal apse. Brick, with bands of stone and vitrified brick. Lancets and late C13 tracery. – PULPIT. Of stone, circular, with a broad band of severely geometricized flowers, entirely in the style propagated by Henry Cole and his circle. – Low metal SCREEN. – STAINED GLASS. E by *Clayton & Bell* (BC). – Apse N and S by *Kempe* 1891.

CONVENT (Franciscan Missionaries of Mary). Red brick, with a tower. The chapel by *W. C. Mangan* of Preston, 1934–6.

(THIRTEOVER HOUSE. By *Leonard Stokes*, 1898. A large, handsome house, in Stokes's free neo-Tudor.)

COLESHILL   2090

ALL SAINTS. The church makes an odd group from outside,

* According to Professor Horn, the second largest is at Vaulerand in France (c. 233 ft), the second largest in England at Beaulieu in Hampshire (224 ft).

and is odder and more confusing inside. There is what looks
like a Late Norman respond facing not E or W but N, and
what looks like half a respond facing as improbably. They
belong to the S arcade and represent a normal round pier and
a semicircular respond cut down (when?). Capitals with flat
leaves, and also some trumpet scallops. The arch is double-
chamfered and later. To the W of this bay is another completely muddled one. To this leads the E.E. S doorway, which
has a rounded trefoiled head. The N arcade on the other
hand is perfectly normal: three bays, round piers, round
abaci, double-chamfered arches – i.e. late C13. A half-bay has
been added on the W, showing that the W tower is a later
addition. It is indeed Perp; with W doorway (hood-mould on
angel busts), W window, bell-openings with Somerset tracery,
battlements, and eight pinnacles. A vault was planned inside.
Dec the S porch, higher than nave and chancel, and Dec
the S transept – see the two ogee-headed recesses in the S wall.
The N aisle has a pierced quatrefoil parapet. But what is one
to make of the large quatrefoil E window of the chancel? Is it
C17 or C18? – The STAINED GLASS in it was brought from
Angers. It is early C16. – BOX PEWS in the S transept. –
PLATE. Two silver-gilt Cups and Patens, inscribed 1776. –
MONUMENTS. Effigy of a Lady, early C16, holding a scroll?
(S transept). – Sir Henry Pratt † 1647 and wife. White and
black marble. Two effigies, she recumbent and below, he
semi-reclining, but also dead, a little above. – Viscountess
Folkestone † 1751, by *Rysbrack*. Two putti hold an oval
medallion with two profile portraits. The whole against the
usual obelisk. – Mark Stuart Pleydell, 1802 by *Coade & Seely*.
Tall, elaborate Gothic canopy.

COLESHILL HOUSE was gutted by fire in 1952 and subsequently
entirely pulled down. What remains is only four pairs of gatepiers eminently characteristic of the mid C17. The house was
in fact built *c.*1650–62. It was designed for Sir George Pratt
by his cousin *Roger Pratt* in consultation with *Inigo Jones*.
There are also drawings for Coleshill by *John Webb*. The consultation with Jones included the architecture as well as the
plaster ceilings. The house was the best Jonesian mid C17
house in England. It had nine bays and two storeys, and a
big hipped roof, a top balustrade, and a belvedere cupola.
High, square chimneystacks with far-projecting cornices stood
prominently and symmetrically on the roof. In the roof were
pedimented dormer windows, their pediments alternatingly

42a
& b

triangular and segmental. The staircase of Coleshill, completed in 1662, was one of the most beautiful in England. Two arms rising in a spacious hall, first away from one another, then parallel up to the landing. Balusters already with leaves up the bulb at the foot. The string with thick fruit garlands. Oval niches with busts in the walls. Typically Jonesian plaster ceiling with strong beams with guilloche. In the panels wreaths. More opulent were the plaster ceilings of the saloon and the library.

The STABLES have projecting wings. Mullioned windows. The cupola looks late C18. The DOVECOTE probably dates from the time of the house and is circular.

STRATTENBOROUGH CASTLE FARM. An eye-catcher from Coleshill, 1 m. distant to the S. Dated prominently 1792. It is really a farm with barns, but the house was given a back towards Coleshill with two sham tower fronts castellated and 51a various big arrow-slits and large, unmoulded cross-windows. It is of stone, but towards the top of brick, as though it were a repair of a stone ruin, and the windows are blocked. One of the barns has a stepped gable, the other an elaborately bricked-up enormous sham window of five lights, partly ruinous. Below this window is a genuine C11 tympanum. 13 What church does it come from? It has the lamb in a circle in the middle and l. and r. wild tendrils in an unmistakable Ringerike style, i.e. an C11 Danish-Viking style.

COLEY see READING, p. 207

COMBE

3060

A very isolated hamlet S of Walbury Hill, the highest elevation of Berkshire.

ST SWITHIN. Nave and chancel. Timber bell-turret with N and S aisles, almost as in Essex. The S doorway arch may be of c.1200, the chancel of the early C13 – see the pointed chancel arch with one slight chamfer and the N lancet windows.

COMBE MANOR FARM. C18. Irregular five-bay façade with the intrusion of an older big chimneybreast. (Entrance hall with a screen with semi-elliptical openings and pilasters. NBR) On the garden wall a pretty C17 GAZEBO of brick, square, with Ionic pilasters near the angles and a pyramid roof. Raised window surrounds. The gazebo is dated 1667.

COMBE GIBBET, on the LONG BARROW on the ridge between 2 Walbury Hill and Inkpen Hill. Very high, and with a cross-

bar for two. The long barrow itself is Neolithic, nearly 200 ft
long and 75 ft wide at its broader E end, where it stands 6½ ft
high. The flanking quarry ditches are clearly visible and are
15 ft wide and 3 ft deep.

WALBURY CAMP, on Walbury Hill, at a height of 974 ft. This
is the largest hillfort in the county, enclosing an area of 82
acres. The univallate defences enclose a roughly trapezoid
area. The principal entrance, with inturned ramparts, is at
the NW corner. The fort has not been excavated, although
circular depressions in its interior suggest the former presence
of huts.

COMPTON

5080

ST MARY AND ST NICHOLAS. The W tower C13, see the S
window with plate tracery and the flat, broad staircase projection. The other details Perp. The body of the church
mostly of 1850. N aisle 1905 by *J. O. Scott* (BC). – REREDOS.
Designed by *E. P. Warren*, 1893 (BC). Gothic, with Crucifixion in the centre and much better side panels with foliage,
a chalice, and the Instruments of the Passion. – PULPIT. Of
c.1700. With garlands at the angles – an attractive piece. –
LITANY DESK. With three Netherlandish C16 panels, Crucifixion and two saints. – PLATE. Salver of 1754; Paten on foot
of 1798; Jug of the late C18; Cup probably of 1804. – BRASS
to Richard Pygott and wife, c.1500; 20 in. figures.

Much HOUSING for the Agricultural Research Station.

A cruck COTTAGE in the Wallingford Road.

PERBOROUGH CASTLE. An Iron Age hillfort on Cow Down.
The site is roughly circular in plan, the defences enclosing an
area of 15 acres. It has been considerably damaged by cultivation, which has almost completely obliterated the rampart
on the S and SW. The best preserved section is on the N,
where the bank, ditch, and counterscarp bank are clearly
visible. The only contemporary entrance appears to be that
on the N. The five large hollows in the fort's interior are
probably marl pits.

  The banks of CELTIC FIELDS are faintly visible in the interior and can be more easily seen NW of the fort, especially
in the wood to the W of Cow Down Barn.

ROUND BARROW, on Compton Down, adjacent to Grim's
Ditch, on the Blewbury–Compton boundary. The barrow is
of bowl type, 90 ft in diameter and 7 ft high, surrounded by
a clearly visible ditch 12 ft wide. A hollow in the centre

suggests that it has been opened, although no record of this work survives.

COMPTON BEAUCHAMP

ST SWITHUN. Small, by the moat of the house. Built of chalk. Nave and chancel, transepts, and thin unbuttressed W tower with pyramid roof. The tower seems C13, see the low and narrow arch to the nave. C13 also the chancel, see the N lancet and the SEDILIA, just a stone bench with low arms. The E window is Dec with reticulated tracery. – FONT. Perp, plain, with quatrefoils. – PAINTING. The gay chancel painting with vine trails and, in the window jambs, palm fronds is not rustic Regency, but by *Lydia Lawrence, c.*1900. – STAINED GLASS. In the N transept E window fine early C14 Crucifixus. In the chancel E window equally fine Annunciation and a third figure. – PLATE. Cup of 1668/9; Paten of 1737. – MONUMENTS. Several major tablets, especially Rachel Richards † 1737 and Ann Richards † 1771. The inscription of Rachel's and the putto heads in the roundel of Ann's are admirable.*

RECTORY. 1849 by *H. E. Kendall*. Chalk and limestone with steep gables.

COMPTON HOUSE. The house dates from the early C16, about 1600, the later C17, and about 1710. It is the latter date which faces one as one approaches. A tall, three-bay, two-and-a-half-storey centre with giant Doric pilasters on a ground floor with banded rustication. Top balustrade, and lower, recessed two-bay wings. All this is stone-faced. Through the centre one enters an oblong courtyard and faces a late C17 stone front of four bays and two storeys with cross-windows and a pedimented doorway. The l. and r. sides of the courtyard are lower and older and have small mullioned windows. Outside, the E, W, and S sides of the house are all brick. In the E wall is just one early C16 window of two lights with uncusped arched lights. Fine S view towards the distant gates. N of the N range, at r. angles, are separate wings of the later C17 with wooden cross-windows.

* In addition to the above, Mr Samuel Gurney mentions to me in a letter the REREDOS, ROOD, COMMUNION RAIL, etc., all by *Martin Travers*, and a piece of SCULPTURE, a head of Christ in the S transept, said to come from the C6 church of St Sergius and St Bacchus at Constantinople.

COOKHAM

HOLY TRINITY. Flint, partly mixed with stone. Low, broad w tower. Nave and aisles and chancel chapels. The nave is Norman, as one N window shows. In the early C13 the short N aisle and the N chapel were built – see their lancet windows and the wide, low arch with nailhead to the chancel.* Also a late C13 N doorway, blocked. Late in the C13 the s aisle and s arcade were built, and also, it seems, the N arcade was re-modelled. Octagonal piers, moulded capitals. The arches on the s side double-chamfered, on the N side double-hollow-chamfered. The s aisle windows with Y-tracery. C14 s chapel with two tomb recesses. The oddly placed second doorway in the s aisle should be noted. Late Perp the w tower with higher stair-turret. C18 repairs to the N chapel in brick. The roofs with tie-beams and kingposts. – STAINED GLASS. The E window of c.1840. – TILES. Plenty of medieval tiles in the chancel. – PLATE. Two Chalices and Patens of 1818. – MONUMENTS. Brasses in the N chapel to John Babham † 1458 (14 in.), floor, to William Andrew † 1503, his wife, and her second husband (16 in.), floor, to Richard Babham † 1527 and wife, kneeling (10 in.), N wall. – In the chancel on the N side monument to Robert Peake † 1517 and wife. This is a Purbeck marble monument with a canopy of three hanging arches on twisted columns (cf. Bisham). Brasses 18 in. long on the short tomb-chest. Pretty vault inside the canopy. – In the s chapel Arthur Babham † 1561. Tablet with small kneeling figures. – Sir Isaac Pocock, drowned in the Thames 1810. By *Flaxman*. White relief. His reclining body in a boat held by his niece. The oarsman in shallow relief behind. Beautifully executed, and with genuine feeling. – C. Ashwell Boteler Pocock † 1887. Bronze tablet; Arts and Crafts. – Fred Walker A.R.A., tablet with head by *H. H. Armstead*, 1877 (w wall).

The church lies close to the Thames. By the entrance to the graveyard CHURCH GATE HOUSE, timber-framed. The river is crossed by an iron BRIDGE of 1867. Shallow arch on iron columns. Low parapet with pierced quatrefoils. s of the church a good group of late C17 to early C18 houses, notably WISTARIA COTTAGE with handsome carved modillions, its neighbour EAST GATE with a door pediment on carved

* The VCH says that the Norman-looking jambs, as if of a former two-bay arcade, are 'modern'.

brackets, and the finest, TARRY STONE HOUSE. This is
chequer brick, of five bays with parapet. Doorway with segmental pediment. The window above flanked by pilasters and
with a cut-brick pattern in the lintel. Opposite the house the
TARRY STONE, a large sarsen stone. At the start of the HIGH
STREET the STANLEY SPENCER GALLERY. *Stanley Spencer*
was born and lived at Cookham. The High Street has kept its
villagey scale well, even if shops have been made in most of
the house fronts.

(FORMOSA PLACE. C18. Three storeys, five bays, the middle
ones forming a broad, shallow, canted bay. Pointed windows
with intersecting glazing-bars. NBR)

ROUND BARROWS, to the N, on Cock Marsh. A group of four
bowl barrows, the largest of which is 90 ft in diameter and
7 ft high. Three of the barrows were excavated in the C19.
Two yielded Early Bronze Age cremation burials and the
third a Saxon inhumation accompanied by a shield and an
urn.

ROBIN HOOD'S ARBOUR, *see* Maidenhead, p. 176.

COOKHAM DEAN
₈₀₈₀

ST JOHN BAPTIST. 1844 by *R. C. Carpenter*. Flint, humble.
Nave, chancel, low S aisle, and bellcote. Early C14 style. The
interior a pure white. – STAINED GLASS. In the chancel good
glass of c.1860, i.e. consciously primitive but with odd ten-
sions in the faces, almost like Toorop, i.e. perhaps influenced
by Moxon's Tennyson. The date of death recorded is 1860. –
In the N wall a *Kempe* window of 1893, still with much dark
brown and dark red.

(THE COPPICE. By *T. H. Lyon*, 1904.)

COX GREEN *see* MAIDENHEAD

CRANBOURNE
₉₀₇₀

ST PETER. 1849 by *Benjamin Ferrey*. Flint, nave with bellcote
and chancel. Dec style. The S chapel with red brick bands
c.1866. This has plate tracery. Ferrey's chancel is remarkably
ornate inside. – STAINED GLASS. A wide variety of designers
and of quality. At the top of course the W window which is by
Morris (Cana), *Ford Madox Brown* (Christ and a child), and
Webb (ornament), and of 1862. Beautifully tender scenes. Also
by *Morris*, probably himself, a one-light S chapel window of

about 1861.* In a s aisle window *Kempe* glass as early as 1878. – The two-light window with St Peter and Cornelius is of 1896 and by *Selwyn Image*, executed by *Powell*. The Rev. B. Clarke adds to this two s nave windows by *Hardman*, the s chapel E window by *Clayton & Bell*, and the chapel w window by *O'Connor* (of 1865).

FERNHILL PARK, ⅜ m. E. Partly of *c.*1740, partly of *c.*1900.

CROWTHORNE

8060

ST JOHN BAPTIST. 1873 by *Blomfield*, the chancel added in 1888–9. Red brick and black brick bands. Steep bellcote over the nave E gable. Cross-gabled aisles. Geometrical tracery. Low, apsed w baptistery. Wide interior, also red and black brick. Unmoulded brick arches. – STAINED GLASS. E and SE windows 1894 and 1889.

BROADMOOR INSTITUTION. The original plan by Major-Gen. *Joshua Jebb*. The opening was in 1863. Brick, with small arched windows. The high walls go without saying.

ROAD RESEARCH LABORATORY, 1 m. N. Big and good new buildings by the *Ministry of Public Building and Works* (*J. Moss*).

WELLINGTON COLLEGE, *see* p. 260.

CRUCHFIELD HOUSE *see* WINKFIELD

CULHAM COURT
1¼ m. E of Remenham church

7080

Built in 1770–1 for Robert Mitchell. The architect is unknown. Red brick, of five spaciously placed bays. Elegant proportions altogether. To the N and s the three centre bays project slightly and are pedimented. To the N a Venetian doorway, to the s a single doorway with pediment. Some pretty plaster-work inside, especially the ceiling of the drawing room to the N. Stone staircase with elegant, simple wrought-iron railing. (On the first floor a vaulted cross corridor.)

CUMNOR

9000

ST MICHAEL. The story starts on the s side of the nave, where there is part of a Norman corbel-frieze. At the same time or a little later the w tower was begun. It has a w doorway with one order of shafts and a round arch and an arch towards the nave with three orders of shafts, scallop capitals, and a pointed

* I owe these details to the ever helpful Mr A. C. Sewter.

arch with roll mouldings. That would take one to *c*.1200. The bell-openings are indeed lancets with continuous thin roll mouldings, two to each side. Inside the tower a splendid spiral staircase, dated 1685, instead of the usual ladder. The chancel belongs to the same time as the nave, see the one small Norman N window (with a pointed rere-arch). On the s side a later C13 window, on the E side a Dec one (reticulated tracery). Dec N aisle, especially the doorway, Dec s transept. Here again reticulated tracery, and also a window with a tri-angle top and lozenge shapes for the tracery (cf. North Hinksey and Theale). One window of *c*.1300 in the s side of the nave. Perp clerestory with a fleuron frieze. Wide nave. The N arcade Early E.E. (circular piers, octagonal abaci, arches with one chamfer and one hollow chamfer, hood-moulds with heads and leaf paterae). Dec arch to the s tran-sept. The two big tomb recesses in the s wall are cusped and subcusped, but have no ogees, whereas the PISCINA has. Two head corbels l. and r. of the E window. The chancel arch goes with the arcade arches, and the short shafts of the responds have in fact flat stiff-leaf on one capital, two rows of knob-like leaf on the other. In the chancel traces of the window of *c*.1200 which was replaced by the later C13 one. – PULPIT. A Jacobean two-decker, the clerk's part specially roomy. – STALLS. Good poppy-heads with heads, IHS, etc. – COM-MUNION RAIL. With alternating twisted and fluted balusters; Early Georgian. – Another(?) which is heavily Jacobean serves as the chancel screen. – SCULPTURE. Statue of Queen Eliza-beth I, said to have been erected by the Earl of Leicester in the garden of Dean Court Cumnor, now rather unhappy in the vestry part of the N aisle. – STAINED GLASS. Odd bits in the N aisle. – W window by *Kempe*, 1889; E window by the same, 1901. – PLATE. Silver-gilt Cup with chased ornament, 1571; Cover Paten, 1723; two Cups, 1808. – MONUMENT. Anthony Forster, *c*.1572. Forster was supposed to have murdered Amy Robsart who fell down the stairs of Cumnor Place to her death. A Purbeck marble monument of the familiar early C16 type, i.e. tomb-chest with much-cusped quatrefoils, big canopy with a quatrefoiled frieze, and quatre-foil panelling inside the canopy. The brasses against the back wall. But instead of buttresses, columns. Are they the contri-bution of 1572 to an older monument or Easter Sepulchre, or is this a case of extreme traditionalism?

THE BEAR AND RAGGED STAFF, W of the church. The front

with symmetrically projecting gabled wings looks C17, but at the back a mullioned window with arched lights, i.e. a C16 form.

BRADLEY FARMHOUSE, ⅝ m. SSE. Seven bays, two storeys, brick.

CURRIDGE
1¾ m. SE of Chieveley

SCHOOL, MASTER'S HOUSE, AND CHAPEL. One little brick group by *S. S. Teulon*, 1854–5.

CUSCOTE MANOR *see* EAST HAGBOURNE

DAVIS STREET *see* ST NICHOLAS HURST

DEDWORTH

ALL SAINTS. By *Bodley*, 1863. Plain, small brick church with a remarkably square and solid bellcote. Tracery of c.1300–30. Conventional S arcade. – STAINED GLASS. This is what makes a visit imperative for anyone walking around Windsor. The glass is by *Morris & Co.*, of 1863–87. The E window with Nativity by *Burne-Jones*, Crucifixion by *Rossetti* (made in 1861), and Resurrection by *Morris* himself. The S aisle middle window of 1873, St Anne by *F. M. Brown*, St Catherine by *Morris*. The first window from the E in the S aisle is of 1877, the N aisle middle window of 1881, and N aisle first from W and S aisle W of 1887. They are all by *Burne-Jones*. The Annunciation is specially lovely.

ST LEONARD'S HILL, 1 m. SW. The St Leonard's Hill estate has been broken up. It is now a gradually growing estate of prosperous houses in their gardens. One of the original mansions still stands: ST LEONARD'S of c. 1771 but almost entirely rebuilt in 1872 for Sir Francis Tress Barry. It looks rather 1840s, however, cemented and castellated. The other major mansion, of 1876 by *C. H. Howell*, is in ruins. It was extensive, Frenchy, with steep pavilion roofs and a square tower.

ST LEONARD'S DALE. A stuccoed Georgian house of only three bays and one and a half storeys. The side windows tripartite with a blank arch decorated fan-wise. The top centre window of lunette shape. Doorway with demi-columns.

DENCHWORTH

ST JAMES. Of dark rubble. With a NW tower, a N aisle further

E separated from the tower, and a S transept. Mostly Perp windows, one of them (chancel S) with tracery a little nicer than usual. Plain Late Norman S doorway. The interior reveals that the N aisle was originally C13 (see one respond) and the S transept Dec (see the arch with its continuous sunk-quadrant mouldings).* – PULPIT. Not Perp, but 1889. – PLATE. Chalice and Paten of 1587/8. – MONUMENTS. Brass to Oliver Hyde † 1516 and wife; 25 in. figures. – Brass to William Hyde † 1557 and wife and many children. They all kneel. – Five tablets to Geerings in the S transept, 1690 to C18.

MANOR HOUSE. Four-bay later C17 front (cross-windows), but one ground-floor window C15. Where does it come from? Early C18 shell-hood over the doorway. Near the house an oblong building known as the WOOL STORE. This is dated 1708, but still has mullioned and transomed windows. However, they are placed symmetrically l. and r. of the doorway. But, on the other hand, the doorway still has a Tudor head. The building has a hipped roof.

DENFORD

3060

HOLY TRINITY. By *J. B. Papworth*, 1830–4. Gothick. Demolished.

DENFORD HOUSE. Stone house of three bays, spaciously planned. On the entrance side the centre is recessed, and a semicircular porch is set in front of it, with paired Tuscan columns. On the S side there is a big central bow instead. Three-bay wings are added. They are dated 1839. The MHLG calls the house 1832 and by *Sir Jeffry Wyatville*. But Colvin mentions several items at Denford House as by *Papworth* and of 1827–8.

DIDCOT

5090

ALL SAINTS. In a W part of Didcot which has managed to remain villagey. The church is Dec, but much pulled about. Three-bay S arcade, Dec at least in the W respond and the second pier, though this looks as if it had been wrenched out of true into a diagonal position. One Dec S window with

* Mr Ferriday drew my attention to a 'gross attack' on *Street*, who restored the church in 1852. It came from the Rev. C. H. Tomlinson and was published in the *Building News* on 15 September 1876 and answered by Street on 20 October. Mr Tomlinson calls Street 'a certain young man from Oxford called Street'.

segmental head. The chancel is higher than the nave. Timber bell-turret with shingled spire. – STAINED GLASS. Some fragments in the w window. – MONUMENT. Excellent effigy of a mitred Abbot, probably Ralph de Dudecot † 1293/4. Purbeck marble.

ST PETER, in the New Town. 1890–8. No architect known, except for the tower, which is by *Waterhouse* (GS). The church itself with its broad lancets looks 1830 rather than 1890. – PULPIT. From Long Wittenham and originally perhaps from Exeter College, Oxford. Dated 1634 and unusual in design. No arabesques, just strapwork.

(A COTTAGE of cruck construction is near the church. Information from the Rev. J. W. Gann.)

DONNINGTON

4060

37 CASTLE. Sir Richard de Abbesbury was granted licence to crenellate in 1386. The castle he built was oblong, with four round corner towers, two square towers intermediate on two sides, a mighty gatehouse on a third sticking far out, and the fourth projected beyond the two towers with canted sides as a half-hexagon. It seems as if, apart from the gatehouse, there have been only timber buildings. The gatehouse is of three storeys and has its own round towers, an archway with a broadly moulded four-centred arch, and inside a lierne-vault in two bays, the centre of each in the shape of four kites, cusped.

CASTLE HOUSE. The house is of brick and has an C18 front, but is older. The front in fact has two gables above the Georgian fenestration. Seven bays, two storeys. High, narrow doorway with pediment.

HOSPITAL. Built in 1602, restored and re-opened in 1822. Red brick, one-storeyed, round a courtyard with a covered way on wooden posts. Central porch to the street. Big, diamond-shaped chimneys.

DONNINGTON GROVE. The house, a little Gothic gem, was built before 1772 for James Pettit Andrews, F.S.A., author of a history of England, many archaeological papers, and An Appeal to the Humane on behalf of Climbing Boys. His architect was *John Chute* of the Vyne, friend of Horace Walpole. The house is of blue brick, only three by three bays, of three storeys, and castellated. The s front has a porch projection in the middle, rising the whole height and provided with a charming porch of bamboo-thin clusters of Gothic shafts, a

Chippendale–Gothic doorway, and an oriel window above of a complex shape. The windows have mullions, arched lights, and hood-moulds. To the E the centre is a broad canted bay window. The small entrance hall has a simple Gothic plaster vault, in full contrast to the surprisingly spacious staircase hall with an arcaded gallery right round the upper floor and a central lantern. The stair balustrade is of cast iron. (On the upper floor the principal s room has Gothic plasterwork round the tops of the chandeliers.) As a N attachment about 1785 a large drawing room was added, very chastely classical. In the grounds a three-arched BRIDGE across the stream which is dammed into a lake, and a Gothick FISHING LODGE. Brick STABLES with stepped gables.

Donnington village has become part of Newbury. DONNINGTON SQUARE for instance has consistently town houses. It is not a square, but a crescent, and it must initially date from about 1840. Semi-detached houses, some under one gable, one with two gables, also one with two towers of the Italian villa style and another with two towers and Jacobean trim. Interrupting this chronological, if not visual, unity is OLNEY LODGE by *W. Hunt*, the design for it shown at the Royal Academy in 1901. Red brick and tile-hanging, Tudor, but with a low, rather Baroque angle tower and Art Nouveau lettering, quite resourceful.

DOUAI ABBEY *see* WOOLHAMPTON

DOWN PLACE
1¾ m. SE of Bray

9070

The house has an L-shaped river front, both parts Georgian. The later is of nine bays and has as its feature a wide shallow bow with Greek Doric columns, i.e. early C19; the earlier, at r. angles, has two smaller bows, a doorway between, and a pretty staircase with carved tread-ends. To the l. of the later façade a quite incongruously added Gothic one-bay bit, with a tall pointed window and a fancy Dec canopy over it.

OAKLEY COURT, immediately SE, is an eerie experience at the time of writing. It is a Victorian Gothic mansion of 1859 in full decay, with ivy half-covering the porte-cochère and greenhouses with broken panes.

At OAKLEY GREEN, I m. SE, the OLD MALTHOUSE, E of the Red Lion, is timber-framed with two gables whose bargeboards may be original (MHLG). The suggested date is C16.

4090
DRAYTON

St Peter. Perp w tower, unbuttressed. The chancel was rebuilt in 1872, but the windows are old. In the nave the
masonry is old, but the windows are all renewed. s porch of
1879 by *E. Dolby* of Abingdon, a very nice job. In the chancel
a simple doorway of about 1200 and at the e end a group of
three stepped lancet lights with continuous roll mouldings.
The s transept has lancet windows. Most windows of
the church Perp. Perp also the n arcade. The piers of the four-
shafts-and-four-hollows section. The arches four-centred. In
the nave a Piscina with dogtooth, i.e. c13 again. – Pulpit.
Jacobean, with arabesque. – (Bench Ends. Those on the s
side of the nave are mostly original.) – Sculpture. Six panels
of an alabaster altar of the familiar type and all of the familiar
iconography; c15. – Stained Glass. The e and w windows
designed by *J. F. Bentley* and made by *Westlake* in 1872. – In
the n aisle Ascension designed by *Bell* and made by *Powell*. –
Plate. Salver of 1727.
In the High Street quite a number of enjoyable houses,
ending with the Manor House. This consists of two parts,
both Georgian, the higher r. one of three bays, blue and red
brick, with a doorway with Corinthian pilasters and a segmental pediment, the l. one of red brick with pilaster strips
and stone lintels to the windows. Good iron Gate and Gatepiers.
By the Green, at the junction of the Abingdon and Sutton
Courtenay roads, the Baptist Chapel of 1834, with pointed
doorway and pointed window, and Gothic House, with
pointed windows and a lattice porch.

4000
DRY SANDFORD

St Helen. 1855 by *J. B. Clacy*. Nave and chancel and apse.
Bellcote over the e end of the nave. Lancet windows. The
interior quite dignified, with a rib-vault in the apse. – Stone
Pulpit, accessible by an outer stair, and Reader's Desk.
Church Farmhouse, s of the church. Stone, five bays, two
storeys, hipped roof.
Between this and the church a symmetrical imitation-Georgian
house, well done, but the date 1959 is a surprise. (By *E. H.
Vaux*.)
Plenty of Oxford housing.

EALING *see* BASILDON

EARLEY *see* READING

EASTBURY   *3070*

ST JAMES. 1851–3 by *Street*. Nave and N aisle under one big
roof. Bellcote at the E end of the nave. N arcade with plain
polygonal piers into which the arches die. The W window of
the aisle is round and has three spherical triangles as tracery.

To the E former SCHOOL, by *Street*. Flint with brick quoins
and bands and brick tympanum between the windows and
their pointed arches. Half-hipped roof. Much Butterfield
influence.

N of the church the brook with a little bridge, and on the other
side a little square. On it the CROSS: patterned base and long
shaft. To its W a house of blue headers and red dressings, and
NW of that a similar one dated 1791.

At the SE end of the village PIGEONHOUSE FARMHOUSE. This
has a date 1620, and to this may well belong the flint part
of the house with the mullioned windows and also the large
octagonal DOVECOTE (flint with brick quoins and pyramid
roof) with 999 nesting holes.

At the NW end of the village MANOR FARMHOUSE, brick, early
C17, with mullioned and transomed windows and a good
chimneypiece inside, with caryatids.

EAST CHALLOW   *3080*

ST NICOLAS. The W front is of 1858, with the funny stunted
tower of 1884. But behind this is a medieval church, with a
C13 N arcade of three bays (low piers, square with four demi-
columns, good moulded capitals, double-chamfered arches), a
chancel arch of the same date, and an arch to a S chapel with a
typical early C14 continuous moulding. – LECTERN. Dramatic
eagle with a snake. Is it *c.*1850, and is it Continental? –
STAINED GLASS. In N windows some C15 parts of figures.

EAST GARSTON   *3070*

ALL SAINTS. Outside the village. Basically Late Norman, see
the crossing tower (cf. Lambourn) with its E and W windows,
the S doorway with shafts with trumpet scallops or stiff-leaf
and a deeply moulded arch including a keeled roll, and the
blocked N doorway with a slight chamfer. The transepts have

Norman masonry too. The N chapel is Dec, as the continuous mouldings to the chancel show, and also the eminently curious E window of three steeply stepped lights and huge over-cusped pointed trefoils above the lower ones. The arch to the S transept is Dec also. The chancel is of 1875 (*J. W. Hugall* according to BC). The S arcade looks *c.*1900 but is in fact of 1882 (by *Ewan Christian*; BC). Not one of the crossing arches is original. – PILLAR PISCINA. Norman, *ex situ*. – PULPIT. Jacobean. A part of the back board in the vestry. – REREDOS. In the N chapel, with paintings probably by *Westlake* (*see* below). – PAINTING. On the nave E wall Tree of Jesse, by *Westlake*, said to be copied from a church at Florence. Reredos and wall painting both very creditable. – PLATE. Cup and Cover, 1576; Cup, 1675.

MANOR FARMHOUSE. Close to, and parallel with, the church. Seven bays, two storeys, brick, with a hipped roof.

EAST GINGE *see* WEST HENDRED

1080

EAST HAGBOURNE

ST ANDREW. Early C13 S arcade of three bays. Round piers, octagonal abaci, one-step pointed arches. Bases with spurs. The S chapel is of two bays and probably just a little later. Pier with coarse and heavy stiff-leaf, double-chamfered arches. C13 chancel windows, though the five-light E window and the clerestory are Perp. Chancel arch on big head corbels, one a *triciput*. Then the N arcade and N chapel arcade. The N chapel can be dated, as there are brass inscriptions to the woman 'qui fieri fecit istam capellam' and to her husband as 'fundator istius Ile', and they died in 1403 and 1414. That is eminently interesting, as the chapel is entirely Dec – see e.g. the reticulated tracery of the E window. The tower arch also is Dec, though the ashlar-faced tower appears all Perp from outside. Charming bell-canopy on top. Perp also the walls of S chapel and S aisle. Nice gargoyles, etc. Low-pitched nave and chancel roofs with tie-beams. C17 S chapel roof with pendants. – FONT. Octagonal, Perp, nothing special. – PULPIT. A little of Perp woodwork. – STAINED GLASS. Excellent, small early C14 Nativity and Virgin in a N window; much red and blue. Also fragments in the N chapel E window. – PLATE. Cup and Paten, 1664; Flagon, 1736; Cup, 1738.

Delightful group of timber-framed houses NE of the church round the village CROSS. The shaft has on one side two niches.

Much timber-framing in the main street as well, and also
No. 7, partly timber-framed, partly Georgian blue and red
brick. At the end of the main street, where it meets the B-
road, another CROSS, mostly C19, and close to it GRANGE
COTTAGE of five bays, brick, with wooden cross windows.*

CUSCOTE MANOR, ¾ m. W. Timber-framed, C17, with fretwork
bargeboards and one tripartite, typical later C17 window. The
wider middle-light is arched below the straight top of the
window, i.e. the so-called Ipswich motif.

EASTHAMPSTEAD see BRACKNELL

EAST HANNEY

4090

ST JAMES. 1856 by *Street*. Nave and chancel under one tile
roof, though with a chancel arch inside. S porch at the W end.
No visible bellcote. Goodhart-Rendel commented: 'Entirely
different from the Puginist type of nave and chancel chapel.'

EAST HENDRED

4080

ST AUGUSTINE OF CANTERBURY. Perp W tower of ashlar
with W doorway and four-light window. N aisle and N transept Dec. S aisle and S porch very Victorian, especially the
porch entrance (1860–1 by *Woodyer*). But inside, the arcades
of four bays are E.E. with piers carrying very thick, lush, and
somewhat brobdingnagian stiff-leaf capitals. C14 chancel
PISCINA with shelf and gable. The two-light opening into the
organ chamber is of course Victorian. Perp S (Eyston) chapel.
Two bays, thin piers with the four-shafts-four-hollows
moulding. The chancel roof is boarded above the altar and
has moulded rafters, purlins, and carved bosses.‡ – PULPIT.
Jacobean, with strapwork, arabesques, and a knob-like head
in the centre of each main panel. – SCREEN. To the S chapel,
tall, of one-light divisions; good. – STALLS. With tracery from
a screen dado. – CHEST. Now the N transept altar. Rich later
C16 work with heads in roundels and caryatids. Is it Flemish?
– LECTERN. What date can this be? The stem rises from a
foot with a shoe stepping on three crocodiles. – STAINED
GLASS. Bits in the S chapel. – PLATE. Large silver-gilt Cup,
1632; Paten, inscribed 1632; Flagon and Almsdish, 1783; all

* According to Mr D. R. Sherburn there is a cruck cottage at East Hagbourne.

‡ The Rev. F. G. Addenbrooke draws my attention to a *ceilure* or canopy
of honour above the former rood.

London. – BRASS to Roger Eldysley † 1439, a 25 in. figure (N transept, floor).

ST MARY (R.C.). 1865 by *C. A. Buckler*. Nave, N aisle, and chancel. Turret in the corner of the nave and a S sacristy. Spirelet. Early C14 style with Kentish tracery. – STAINED GLASS. By *Hardman*. – Also one window in the English wood-engraving–Expressionism. – Next to the church a large brick PRESBYTERY and in it light-oak furniture and crockery said to come from *Pugin*'s house at Ramsgate.

JESUS CHAPEL, at the E end of the village. Oblong, of ashlar, Perp, with a Perp E window and a W doorway with segmental arch. The Priest's House, attached to the chapel, is timber-framed and assigned to the late C15.

On the way from the Jesus Chapel to the church a number of good timber-framed houses, in particular KING'S MANOR, with brick infilling and stone slate roof. Gateway and barns. Also THE STORES, with two symmetrical gables and brick-nogging.

HENDRED HOUSE, E of the church, has a C13 chapel. The date is determined by two lancet windows. The E window is Dec. Some foreign STAINED GLASS in the windows. The house itself must be late medieval, as the chimneypiece with a quatrefoil frieze in the hall is *in situ*. The façade does not give away a date. It is regular with two short projecting gabled wings, but the consistent hood-moulds look *c.*1840. The back regularized probably early in the C19.

ROUND BARROW, in Scutchamer Knob plantation, just S of the Ridgeway. This fine barrow still stands 11 ft high and is 120 ft in diameter. It is surrounded by a ditch 5–8 ft wide and 5 ft deep. In the lowest levels of this ditch were found sherds of Iron Age pottery. No trace of a burial was found during the excavations.

ROUND BARROW, on East Hendred Down, N of the Ridgeway. The barrow is 75 ft in diameter and 2½ ft high. The site was excavated in 1934, when the bones of two horses were found overlying numerous sherds of Romano-British pottery. The barrow has no ditch, and was formed by scraping up the surrounding topsoil.

EAST ILSLEY

4080

ST MARY. Dec W tower, N aisle of 1845, the rest C13. In the chancel dogtooth hood-mould of one lancet window and pointed trefoiled windows and a pointed cinquefoiled window

with a circular one over (E). In the s aisle the w window of the
same type, the E window with plate tracery, the arcade of
three bays with round piers. Their abaci are odd and seem to
have originally been square. Also the arches have only a slight
chamfer. So while the rest is all later C13, this arcade is
probably as early as c.1200. The N arcade is of 1845. In the
chancel an AUMBRY with dogtooth. – FONT. Said to be
Norman, but very doubtful. – PULPIT. Jacobean. With the
usual blank arches and arabesques. – SETTLE. With Early
Renaissance medallions containing heads and with caryatids.
Probably assembled from odd dismembered parts. The piece
reached the church only in 1963. – COMMUNION RAIL. Of
c.1700, with alternating turned and twisted balusters. –
PLATE. Cup of 1733; Almsdish and probably Flagon 1846. –
BRASS to Katherine Hildeslea † 1606. Latinists should read
the inscription.

EAST ILSLEY HALL. Quite a swagger Early Georgian house.
Five bays, two storeys, blue and red brick. Segment-headed
windows with aprons, panelled parapet, the centre part oval.

KENNET HOUSE, opposite. Probably a little earlier, say c.1700.
Six bays, straight-headed windows. Shell-hood on carved
brackets. Staircase with twisted balusters.

EAST LOCKINGE see LOCKINGE

EAST SHEFFORD see LITTLE SHEFFORD

EATON HASTINGS

ST MICHAEL. There is no village to go with the church, which
lies close to the Thames. Brown stone. Nave with bellcote
and chancel. In the nave N wall an Early Norman window and
the remains of the doorway, with a plain tympanum. The
priest's doorway in the chancel looks c.1200. So does the
chancel arch, with an abacus with saltire crosses still Norman,
but a pointed arch with a slight chamfer. The s doorway to
the nave has a rounded-trefoiled head, i.e. is C13. So are the
chancel lancets and the SEDILIA, a recess with two shafts on
heads and with big stiff-leaf capitals. The E window (three
stepped pointed-trefoiled lights under a round arch) looks yet
a little later. The s aisle has disappeared, but its arcade is
preserved, late C13 too. Circular piers, double-chamfered
arches dying into the imposts. – PULPIT. Jacobean. –
STAINED GLASS. Small St Matthew and small Risen Christ

by *Burne-Jones*, i.e. *Morris & Co.*, 1872–4. – PLATE. Elizabethan Cup; Bread Holder of 1717–18.

EDDINGTON

3060

¾ m. NE of Hungerford

ST SAVIOUR. 1868 by *Sir Arthur Blomfield*. Nave and chancel;
bellcote. Brick. Bar tracery.

EMMBROOK *see* WOKINGHAM

ENBORNE

4060

ST MICHAEL. Nave and chancel, two cross-gabled N aisle bays,
and a small timber bell-turret. The interior reveals that the
church was originally Early Norman or Saxon and that aisles
were provided as early as the mid C12. They are of two bays
plus a W bay and were evidently (which is unusual) built N
and S at the same time. Also the W bay, which follows beyond
where the original W wall had been, must have been decided
upon at once. Evidence is the identity of style throughout.
Short round piers, square abaci, capitals with many scallops,
many flutings, or stylized leaves. Bases with spurs. Arches
with two slight chamfers. The chancel arch responds are contemporary too, though the arch is C19. E.E. chancel with
lancet windows, shafted inside, and a DOUBLE PISCINA whose
position shows that the Perp W wall runs further W than the
E.E. E wall. Terrible S side, probably of 1893 (when the N
transept was added), but re-set in it a single-chamfered
Norman doorway and the head of a small Norman window. –
FONT. Norman, tub-shaped. Narrow blank arches, and under
them mysterious vertical objects of divers kinds. – One old
plain BENCH (N aisle W). – PAINTING. In the chancel on the
N side a beautiful Annunciation. Large figures. Early C14. –
PLATE. Cup, 1663; Paten, 1679; Paten, 1801.
Nice farm buildings by the church.
ROUND BARROW CEMETERY, *see* Newbury, p. 185.

ENGLEFIELD

6070

ST MARK. The church lies in the grounds of the house, surrounded by trees, the typical High Victorian estate church.
It is by *Sir George Gilbert Scott* and was built in 1857. Scott
used a good deal of the C13 church on the spot, dating from
the time when the village was around it. E.E. the spacious S

aisle and s arcade. The E window is three stepped lancets with continuous rolls, the w wall has a small doorway (re-set?) and an over-restored foiled window above. In the s wall the main doorway with one order of shafts with moulded capitals and a whole order of what can only be described as uncarved beakheads, a surprisingly late occurrence of this motif. Inside, the E windows have Purbeck marble shafts with rings and leaf capitals. To the l. a beautiful image bracket with three bands of E.E. decoration. The s lancets, two pairs of them, are also shafted (not Purbeck) and have leaf capitals. The w pair is largely C19, and it is altogether uncertain whether the s aisle really went as far w as is supposed. The s arcade anyway stopped short of the present w bay, which is Victorian. The rest is E.E., with circular piers with stiff-leaf capitals, circular abaci, and well moulded arches. In the nave N wall a re-set length of an E.E. arch. Scott's church has a N tower with a stone broach spire and two tiers of lucarnes. It makes the church stately, not regional, and eminently Victorian. – PILLAR PISCINA (N chapel). Norman, with decorated base, shaft, and top. – SCREEN (between N chapel and chancel). Of one-light divisions. – PLATE. Cup and Cover, 1577; Paten and Paten on foot, 1821. – MONUMENTS. In the s aisle in recesses Knight with crossed legs, early C14, and Lady, wholly re-cut, C14. – Also in the s aisle Mrs Benyon † 1777. [31a] By *Thomas Carter*.* An excellent, surprisingly Berninesque scene with the lady on the ground collapsing and women attending to her. Big drapery behind. – Also two completely unenriched yet perfect tablets: † 1789 and † 1805. – In the chancel N wall Purbeck marble monument to Sir Thomas Englefield, c.1500. Large tomb-chest with enriched quatre-foils. Canopy with pendants, cresting, and vaulting inside. The brasses were on the E wall, not the tomb-chest lid. So the monument probably served as an Easter Sepulchre. – On the nave N wall Marquess of Winchester † 1675, a large tablet of black and white marble, very simple, without any curly decoration, and – strangely enough – without name or date. Instead a poem and then in beautiful italics a passage from Dryden. – Richard Benyon † 1854. Relief of the three Maries at the Sepulchre in a Gothic surround. – In the N chapel: Small alabaster tablet of 1605 to John Englefield, his wife and son. One recumbent effigy, two kneeling ones below. Several

* Mr Gunnis, with his customary kindness, allowed me to publish this attribution, which is based on a bill he has found in the Benyon papers.

obelisks. – Milburg Alpress † 1803. Small tablet with a very small kneeling woman and her sturdy little boy by an urn.

RECTORY. Near the church, also in the grounds, wholly on its own. Stone, Tudor, gabled. By *P. C. Hardwick*.

ENGLEFIELD HOUSE. 'Englefield House is a handsome Elizabethan structure, completely modernized inside and out', says the VCH. The paragraph on the house ends: 'The whole exterior now presents a not unpleasing example of the mid-Victorian Elizabethan style.' That clearly will not do. There is no mention of the date – 1886 – when a fire made rebuilding necessary, nor a mention of the architect responsible – *Richard Armstrong* of London. Nor is there a reference to the fact that when Dance painted the house in the late C18 and Constable in 1832, its front did not look materially different from what it looks like now, except that the front door is now closed and Victorian pinnacles stand against the sky. The S and W fronts look Elizabethan, but they cannot according to their style be of before 1559, and between 1559 and 1589 the owner, Sir Francis Englefield, was away from England as a Catholic, and the temporary occupants were hardly likely to rebuild. Then, in 1589, it went to the Earl of Essex, and after his execution in 1601 it remained with the Queen and then the King until 1611. Between 1611 and 1622 it was the Earl of Kelly's. From 1635 onwards it belonged to the Marquess of Winchester. When was it built, then? It does look Elizabethan rather than Jacobean, and so 1590–1600 is perhaps the most probable date. Three-storeyed stone façade with flint patternings. Central porch and two bay windows. The windows of ground floor and first floor with pediments. Round the corner on the W side another bay window, a slender four-storeyed porch tower, and another narrower bay window. The E front has the massive Victorian entrance tower with porte-cochère. This is ashlar-faced and replaces a tower apparently in brick like the W tower. To its r. C18 brickwork is exposed, and a big blocked archway. This represents the place where up to the Victorian time the main road passed the house.* In the corresponding part of the W front there is also C18 work, i.e. a ceiling and a chimneypiece.‡

* Mr W. J. Smith, the County Archivist, to whom I owe the information on the fire and the rebuilding, has few Bunyan papers for the mid century. But the new road was built in 1854, and Murray's *Handbook* in 1860 calls the mansion 'recently built' and briefly mentions the tower.

‡ *The Beauties of England and Wales* say that the house was modernized by Paulet Wright. He died in 1779.

Of the same time the ceiling of the large dining room in the E corner of the front. The principal rooms of the house are large and Victorian, notably the hall under the tower, running up through two storeys and open to a wide gallery or corridor on the ground as well as the first floor. Their decoration was not included in Armstrong's bill of 1886, which amounted to £2,556 17s. The LODGES in the road have the date 1862.

FAIRMILE HOSPITAL see CHOLSEY

FARINGDON

2090

ALL SAINTS. One of the richest churches of Berkshire. It is set across the top of the Market Place and against the trees of the grounds of Faringdon House. Nave and aisles, transepts with appendages, chancel and N chapel, and low crossing tower. The odd details of the tower are of 1645. The nave is Norman, as is at once shown by the clerestory windows, the corbel frieze of the N aisle, and the flat buttresses at the W end. The W doorway and the five-light W window of course Perp. Long early C13 chancel with lancet windows, in the E wall three, separated and slightly stepped. Also priest's doorway, still round-arched with one slight chamfer. The evidence of the transepts is complicated outside as well as in. The S transept with its W chapel is a Victorian job anyway (1853 by *Hugall*). The N transept is C13, but its W chapel is C14 (reticulated tracery of the N window), and the baptistery and vestry attachments W and E are again Victorian, though the baptistery doorway is a re-set Norman piece with a big crenellation frieze in the arch. The jambs with two odd flat lobed bands, each lobe hollowed in the middle. Very good Perp N aisle windows, just two, but each of six lights with a transom. Perp N chapel. Inside, the arcades which correspond to the clerestory windows turn out to be a little later than these would have made one expect. Round piers with elementary stiff-leaf capitals and octagonal abaci. Round arches with mouldings. The responds differ, the W responds being stiff-leaf corbels, the E responds one semicircular, the other flat. That looks *c.*1200. So the W buttresses probably belonged to the nave before it had aisles. Richly shafted crossing arches also of *c.*1200. The capitals mostly big upright stiff-leaf, but also still trumpet-scallops. Pointed arches. In the chancel SEDILIA with cinquefoiled pointed arches, buttress shafts, and pinnacles, dogtooth and coarse crocket leaves. The

PISCINA has a moulded-trefoiled arch, i.e. belongs to the
date of the chancel, whereas the sedilia must be of the later
C13. The arch from the N transept to the former N aisle with
its billet frieze belongs to the time of the arcades, the arch to
the N chapel is C15 (as is the arcade of the chapel towards
the chancel: octagonal pier, double-chamfered arches), but
the arch is set within a larger C13 arch. The details between
transepts and W aisle of course Victorian. – FONT. Octagonal,
with Perp tracery motifs of different patterns. – SOUTH DOOR.
C13. Splendid, with agitated scroll-work, several parts ending
in dragons' heads. – STAINED GLASS. In the S transept W chapel
by *Wailes* (TK). – S transept E by *Kempe*, 1888. – PLATE.
Salver, 1721; large Flagon, 1733; large Cup and Paten. –
MONUMENTS. In the chancel: Brasses on the N wall to Thomas
Faryndun † 1396 (13 in.), his wife Margaret † 1402 (13 in.),
John Parker † 1485 and wife (25 in.), Katherine Pynchepole
† 1443 (13 in.), John Sadler † 1505 (13 in.). – In the N chapel
three standing monuments, described by Lord Torrington as
'lumbering marbles'. Jane Pye † 1706. By *Edward Stanton*.
White marble and black columns, no effigy, putti on the open
curly pediment. Top urn. – Anna Pye † 1729. Grey marble;
no figures. – Henry Pye † 1749, their husband. Obelisk with
portrait of his son in oval medallion. Vase below. – N transept:
Sir Thomas Unton † 1533. Alabaster. Two effigies on a tomb-
chest. Shields in wreaths in fields of colonnettes and shell
arches, i.e. Early Renaissance. – Purbeck marble monument
with the usual flat-bottomed canopy, with a trellis vault inside.
Against the back wall kneeling brasses of Sir Alexander
Unton † 1547 and wives. – Sir Edward Unton † 1583. Large
tablet of alabaster and touch. Twin arches, no effigies, but small
allegorical figures. – Sir Henry Unton † 1596. Alabaster and
touch tablet. The life-size kneeling lady now detached from any
monument belonged to this one. – Henry Purefoy † 1686. Standing monument with two weeping, naked putti. Cherubs' heads
in flat relief above. Vase at the top. In the style of Gibbons.

FARINGDON HOUSE, N of the church, with a direct and perfect
view towards it. Begun *c.*1780 and called by Lord Torrington
in 1785 not yet finished. Five bays, two storeys, top balustrade, and hipped roof. Stone, stuccoed. The centre bay
raised to two and a half storeys and framed by a giant arch.
Broken pediment. Tuscan porch with niches l. and r. L. and
r. of this front, pedimented doorways start quadrant walls.
The garden side is different. Here a two-armed open staircase

rises to a terrace which rests on five elliptical arches. Otherwise, except for three pediments – two windows and the doorway – there is no decoration. Fine entrance hall with a two-armed staircase which rises to a landing on three arches. Broad frieze at half-height. Elegant stucco work, especially the overmantel with an urn in the dining room. – ORANGERY of three glazed bays with a pediment. The arrangement in front with four splendid urns of *c*.1700 is recent.

Next to the church good GATEPIERS, apparently of the mid C17 (cf. Coleshill), and a three-bay Early Georgian house with segment-headed windows.

PERAMBULATION. On leaving the church one should first have a look at two houses along the churchyard in CHURCH STREET, one Early Georgian, of brown stone, two bays, with a raised pedimented centre and an arched window sticking up into the pediment, the other, called CHURCH FARM HOUSE, also Early Georgian, of five bays, with segment-headed windows and an ample shell-hood over the door. Then straight into the MARKET PLACE. It is L-shaped and has along its sides no houses of special interest, except the CROWN HOTEL, which, behind its Georgian front, hides a very pretty courtyard with an early C14 range and an open Jacobean staircase. This leads to the front rooms, one of which has a decorated plaster ceiling. In the BELL HOTEL opposite also minor plasterwork. On the W side of the hotel a mullioned window. But what makes the Market Place is the TOWN HALL in the middle, late C17, on Tuscan columns, with a hipped roof. From the Market Place E, through London Street to LONDON ROAD, and at its end SUDBURY HOUSE, handsome, colour-washed, with two symmetrical bows. From the Market Place W to a road fork at which the CORN EXCHANGE, 1863, in a funny debased Gothic with a totally unmonumental, asymmetrical front. The r. fork is GLOUCESTER STREET, with several C18 houses including OAKLEA, *c*.1700, of four bays with a hipped roof. Then along a l. turn, GRAVEL WALK, lies WESTBROOK HOUSE, Early Georgian. The doorway has alternating rustication, the first-floor windows are segment-headed except for the middle one, which is straight but has a moulded surround. (The house is said to have a date 1705 inside. MHLG) Just beyond the turn into Gravel Walk, in LECHLADE ROAD, i.e. the immediate continuation of Gloucester Street, the FRIENDS' MEETING HOUSE, early C18, small, with a big hipped roof.

WORKHOUSE (former), Ferndale Street. 1846 by *Foder* of London.

LORD BERNERS' FOLLY. 1935 by the *Duke of Wellington*. Brick tower, 140 ft high, with an arcaded look-out room and an octagonal top with battlements and pinnacles. It must be the last of the follies.

7060

FARLEY HILL

ST JOHN EVANGELIST. 1890–2 by *G. Truefitt*. The tender was for £1,535 (GS). Red brick, roof reaching low down. Turret with spirelet at the SE corner of the nave. Wide nave, brick, with a wagon roof. It is a well-enclosing interior. Tripartite chancel arch.

FARLEY HALL. Built about 1730. Brick, still in the tradition of Queen Anne. A fine, spread-out composition culminating in the circular lantern with its diagonally set coupled columns. The centre of the house is of seven bays with a slight three-bay projection to the entrance, a very deep one to the garden. Straight-headed windows, panelled parapet. This centre is connected by three-bay links with lower four-bay pavilions. The doorway to the entrance has fluted composite columns and an ornamental bolection frieze. To the garden there are
48b Ionic columns instead. The entrance hall is the climax of the house. It is about square, and reaches up the whole height of the house. The cupola moreover is open. One looks up into its pilasters and windows. The ceiling round the cupola is painted with mythological scenes in the Veronese tradition by *Lanscroon*. They represent the Triumph of Cybele, Venus and Vulcan, Neptune and Amphitrite, and Jupiter and Juno. On the back wall at first-floor level five painted rural scenes put in much later. They are by *J. F. Nollekens*. On the other walls at the same level a wooden communication balcony. The doorways, two l., two r., are excellent on ground and first floors. On the ground floor they have Doric pilasters and pediments, on the first floor Ionic pilasters and no pediments. Good chimneypiece with a large central head. In the middle room towards the garden handsome doorways too. They are balanced in the opposite wall by two shell niches. Behind that blank wall lies the staircase, accessible from the entrance hall. It has column balusters and carved tread-ends. In the dining room garland decoration along the top of the walls and on the chimneypiece, again with a head. Splendid overmantel with a large urn in relief. The doorways have open scrolly

pediments with shells in the middles. Stucco ceiling with a central painting of deities.

FARLEY CASTLE. Built in 1809–10 by *W. Fellows*. A brick castle with Gothick windows, brick hood-moulds, turrets, and battlements. Quite sizeable and asymmetrical in composition. To the NE a MONUMENT. Column with a sundial and the lead figure of Father Time. Dated 1723.

HALL'S FARMHOUSE, ¾ m. E. Brick, and originally of five bays. Between each ground-floor window and that above it a sunk panel. In addition brick quoins not only to the angles but l. and r. of every window – a motif which Sir John Summerson would no doubt list as Artisan Mannerism. When was the house built? About 1675? Hipped roof. Later doorway.

FARNBOROUGH   *4080*

ALL SAINTS. Ashlar-faced Late Perp W tower. The church of flint. The nave is Norman, see the one N window and the simple N doorway. – C13 PILLAR PISCINA. – On the E wall two identical MONUMENTS, tablets of † 1668–83.

RECTORY. Grey vitrified bricks and red-brick dressings. Five bays, panelled parapet. Segment-headed windows. The house was built in 1749. The porch with set-in columns; the upper storey with a round-arched window and the top lantern are later, say *c.*1800.

FAWLEY *see* GREAT FAWLEY

FERNHAM   *2090*

ST JOHN. By *J. W. Hugall*, 1861 (GR). Nave with bellcote and chancel. Brown stone and stone-slated roof. E.E. details. – STAINED GLASS. E window († 1867) by *Wailes* (BC).

FINCHAMPSTEAD   *7060*

ST JAMES. The church has a wide view to the S over Hampshire. 1b Brick tower, built in 1720, yet still with the bricks laid in English bond. Arched bell-openings, square pinnacles. The body of the church is Norman. Two N windows are exposed inside, and the E end is an apse. Also there is a nicely decorated PILLAR PISCINA. Perp chancel arch and N windows. The small N doorway is Perp too, but dated 1590. The room into which it leads has a wide arch to the chancel, and that also could well be of 1590. – FONT. Norman, tub-shaped, with beaded diagonal bands. – PLATE. Silver-gilt Cup and Paten,

1591. – MONUMENTS. Elizabeth Blighe † 1635 and her little daughter. Small brass plate. Mrs Blighe is standing, holding the child by her hand and placing her other hand on a skull which lies on a column. – Richard Palmer † 1670. Tomb-chest with black marble lid.

EARTHWORK. The church stands on a rectangular platform enclosed by a bank in which the S and E walls of the churchyard stand. The site is unexcavated and cannot be precisely dated.

Near the church a gabled and enormous red brick house, looking like a rectory.

WEST COURT, 1¼ m. W. Late C17 brick house of seven bays with a hipped roof. Inside, the staircase with twisted balusters is preserved but re-used. Re-used also a Jacobean overmantel and Jacobean panelling with pilasters.

BANISTERS, 1¼ m. SW. 1683. Long, even brick façade with tiled roof. Two-storeyed porch. Horizontal (later) windows. Brick frieze below the eaves. The porch has brick pilasters below and an oriel above.

NEW HALL, 2 m. WSW. White, picturesque group of buildings by a ford.

1 m. E of Finchampstead is a ¾ m. long AVENUE of high red-woods.

FRILFORD
1 m. NW of Marcham

4090

Two big mid C19 stone villas, one with a pair of chalet gables, the other with a pair of Jacobean shaped gables. Why should they have been built here?

IRON AGE AND ROMAN SHRINES, see Garford.

PAGAN SAXON CEMETERY, on Frilford Heath, N of the river Ock. From the mid C19 large numbers of graves have been discovered in the area. Both urned cremations and inhuma-tions are represented. The cemetery is a poor one, however, and grave goods few. They include small saucer and cruci-form brooches and iron knives.

FRILSHAM

5070

ST FRIDESWIDE. Mean brick W tower and less mean brick S porch, both said to be 1834. Genuine Norman N doorway with one order of shafts, scallop capitals, and a lintel with seg-mental underside. The S doorway plainest Norman. Two renewed Norman N windows, one belonging to the then nave, the other to the then chancel. Nave roof with tie-beams,

collar-beams on arched braces, and wind-braces. – PULPIT.
Simple, Jacobean. – READER'S DESK. Also simple, also
Jacobean. – SOUTH DOOR. With minor early ironwork over-
laid by minor battening. – PLATE. Chalice, flat semi-globular
Bowl, and Cover Paten, only the latter inscribed 1712.

s of the church a pleasant, utilitarian MILL house.

FRILSHAM HOUSE, 1¼ m. ENE. By *S. Gambier Parry*, 1896.
Neo-William-and-Mary, brick with brick quoins and a symmetrically gabled façade. The building is L-shaped, and the
other arm of the L has a long irregular front.

FURZE HILL *see* LITTLE COXWELL

FYFIELD

4090

ST NICOLAS. Of about 1200 the N and W doorways. They have
deeply moulded round arches, and the capitals of the shafts
go from trumpet-scallop (N) to upright stiff-leaf (W). Dec
chancel, the E window of four lights with reticulated tracery.
The priest's doorway has a hood-mould on unrestored heads.
Much was done to the church after a fire in 1893. That
explains the s side and the octagonal part of the tower. But
the comical s porch with its outsize pinnacles seems to be of
1867–8, by *J. C. Buckler* (BC). Perp N arcade with octagonal
piers and an arch moulding not of a usual section. In the
chancel an ornate Perp PISCINA and an ornate Perp pedestal,
a CREDENCE TABLE, it is assumed. – MONUMENTS. Sir John
Golafre † 1442. Effigy above, corpse below. A terrifying
representation. – Lady Katherine Gordon, the White Rose
of Scotland and widow of Perkin Warbeck, † 1527. Tomb-
chest with elaborate decoration set in a high recess with
straight canopy. But how much of this is original? Nearly all
of it is of a composition material harder than stone, and probably dates from after the fire of 1893. Even the openwork
spandrels and the scale are not convincing. – George Dale
† 1625. With an incised bust. He points to a skull. – In the s
transept parts of rescued late C17 to C18 tablets.

FYFIELD MANOR. A remarkable survival. A stone house of
*c.*1320 complete with its hall, porch, and service wing. Only
the solar wing is missing. The porch doorways have mouldings
and decoration (ballflower) typical of the date. At the former
high-table end of the hall, doorways of the same mouldings
to the former chamber and the former staircase to the solar.
In the opposite wall of the hall, i.e. in what was the screens

passage, three doorways formerly to buttery, kitchen, and pantry. Above these, visible by its timber work from outside, a solar. Mighty tie-beams, queen-posts, cusped arched braces, and cusped wind-braces. Three bays. Above the porch a small wooden two-light window with one reticulation unit. Externally the evidence of the great hall is concealed by an Elizabethan front with three-light windows and three (or four) gables.

MANOR FARMHOUSE, by church and manor. Of *c*.1700. Five bays, two storeys, hipped roof. Doorway with straight hood on brackets.

WHITE HART. The chantry founded by Sir John Golafre († 1442; see above), with the priest's house attached. C15. The hall is the full height of the house and has a roof with collar-beams on arched braces and wind-braces. The priest's house has always been two-storeyed. It has its staircase at the back. The present dining room was the priest's study, the present public bar the kitchen.

4090

GARFORD

ST LUKE. Nave and chancel in one, plus a N aisle, and a timber bell-turret. There was apparently previously a C13 W tower. Some old windows are also re-used (e.g. lancets in the chancel), and the nice C13 S doorway with continuous roll mouldings. But mostly the church is by *Edwin Dolby* of Abingdon, 1880. – (SCREEN. C15 parts are incorporated. – HOURGLASS STAND. Wrought iron. VCH)

IRON AGE AND ROMAN SHRINES, in the field W of Noah's Ark Inn. The earliest structures revealed by excavation were a number of timber-built round huts, associated with Iron Age A pottery, and grain storage pits. Towards the end of the prehistoric period a small shrine or sacred enclosure was constructed. It consisted of a horseshoe-shaped ditch enclosing a double row of timber uprights beside one of which an iron ploughshare had been deliberately buried. In front of these posts was a square-cut pit containing the votive offerings of a miniature bronze sword and shield.

At the end of the CI A.D. a Romano-Celtic temple was built on the village site, overlying one of the earlier Iron Age huts. The temple consisted of the usual square cella with sides 25 ft long enclosed within a portico 55 ft square. The site appears to have been venerated well into the C5.

Also in the CI a second religious building was erected on

the site of the earlier Iron Age shrine 80 ft to the S. This was
a stone-built, circular structure 36 ft in diameter. The precise
nature of this building is uncertain, but in view of its position
overlying the earlier shrine it may be regarded as religious in
function and reflecting the continuity of worship on the site.

GOOSEY

ALL SAINTS. At the SW end of a wide green with houses on
both sides which are almost too small. Nave and chancel in
one, roofed with stone slates. C19 bell-turret. The roof inside
with tie-beams and kingposts with two-way struts. – STAINED
GLASS. Some C15 work in a S window.

GRAZELEY

HOLY TRINITY. 1850 by *Benjamin Ferrey*. Flint. Nave, chancel,
bellcote, late C13 details. – (STAINED GLASS. E window by
O'Connor.)

GREAT COXWELL

ST GILES. At the end of the village. Nave of *c*.1200. The N wall
has two small lancets. In the S wall a jolly lot of odd windows,
the earliest early C14 (with cinquefoiled rere-arch). The
chancel N side of the same date as the nave, though the
chancel arch must be mid C13, the S window with bar tracery
(a spherical triangle) later C13, and the E window (three
stepped pointed-trefoiled lights under a round arch) late C13.
Inside the E window two plain lancet niches. Do they go with
the N side ? A window like the E window also in the tower W
wall, but the top of the tower is Perp; battlements and gargoyles. – PULPIT. Jacobean. – COMMUNION RAIL. Later
C17, with flat balusters of dumb-bell outline. – NORTH DOOR
with impressive, large-scale tracery. It might well be of *c*.1300.
– STAINED GLASS. In the E window clear glass panes with
engraved shields. 1792 by *Eginton*. – PLATE. Chalice inscribed
1680; Paten probably of the same date. – BRASS to William
Morys, *c*.1500; 18 in. figures.

COURT FARMHOUSE. Late C17 stone farmhouse. Front of five
bays, the ground-floor windows with stone crosses. Pitched
roof. To the farmhouse belongs the magnificent BARN which *See p.* 359
William Morris (whose country-house was only a few miles
away at Kelmscott) called 'as noble as a cathedral'. It is of
stone and roofed with stone slates, and is 152½ ft long and
51 ft high. The date is C13. The buttresses are still shallow,
also in their set-offs. Entrances by a transept and an archway

opposite the transept. The archways are segment-headed and have two continuous chamfers. Posts divide the barn into nave and aisles. The collars and straight braces, transverse as well as longitudinal, are strong and serviceable and entirely utilitarian.

GREAT FAWLEY

3080

ST MARY. 1866 by *Street*. A serious, almost forbidding church with a beautiful view to the N over the Downs. Small, rock-faced stones. Nave and aisles, higher chancel. S tower with pyramid roof, apse. Later C13 window details, but in no way an imitation-late-C13 church. Three-bay arcades, low circular piers of dark marble. Vaulted chancel, the ribs on marble shafts, the windows also marble-shafted. Stone PULPIT and low stone SCREEN, both with the use of marble. – REREDOS with Crucifixion, by *Earp*, the mosaic work by *Salviati*. – STAINED GLASS. One excellent two-light window by *Morris*, especially fine the round Nativity in the tracery circle. Probably of *c.*1866.

SOUTH FAWLEY MANOR HOUSE. An imposing Jacobean house, built in 1614 by Sir Francis More. Front with two gables and a third a little recessed. Porch under one half of the second big gable. Two orders of pilasters, the upper exceedingly elongated. Round the l. corner one more gable, and then an embattled tower containing the staircase. Good, solid woodwork with heavy vertically symmetrical balusters. The staircase leads up through two storeys.

ROUND BARROWS, in a N–S line on the S spur of Woolley Down. All three sites were excavated some years ago, with inconclusive results. The N barrow produced an unaccompanied inhumation, but in the others no trace of interments was found. On the evidence of the pottery the excavators inferred that the barrows were constructed in the Iron Age.

GREAT SHEFFORD

3070

ST MARY. The only church in Berkshire with an original round tower. It is probably Norman.* In the chancel E wall remains of a former Norman triplet. The S doorway is Norman too, though it is pointed. Shafts with beast's-head capitals. Arch with zigzag at r. angles to the wall. So the arch was probably made pointed from being originally round. Perhaps it was done early in the C13, at the time of the nave N lancet

* The top stage of the tower is octagonal.

and the N doorway with its two slight chamfers, the tower
arch of three chamfers (the inner on small heads),* and the
lancet windows in the chancel. In the chancel also one window
of *c.*1300 (cusped intersected). – FONT. Norman, tub-shaped,
with four bands of foliage, one and two complementing each
other, three a running pattern, four individual symmetrical
figures. – REREDOS. 1912. Painted by *Byam Shaw.* – PLATE.
Paten of 1728; Cup of 1730; Flagon of 1815. – In the churchyard CROSS with, at the angles of its base, heads.
(MANOR FARMHOUSE. Probably C16. Angle buttress at the
NE corner. MHLG)

GREENHAM
4060

ST MARY. By *Woodyer,* 1875–6. Flint, lancet windows, an
arrow of a bellcote. Fine unified interior, especially the
chancel. This has at the E end five closely set lancets shafted,
a prettily painted roof, and painted and stencilled decoration
round the arch and on the walls. Stencilling also on the nave
and aisle walls. All this painting is of after 1888, the year
when a N aisle was added. The baptistery is of 1895 (BC). The
aisle and the baptistery piers are of marble. The work up to
1895 is all Woodyer's. – STAINED GLASS. The Tree of Jesse
is Netherlandish of 1618, but made to look C20 by setting the
figures in clear glass.

GREENHAM LODGE. By *Norman Shaw,* 1875. A fine view to
the N. Red brick, inspired evidently by Shaw House, but only
in making the façade symmetrical on the E-pattern. Norman
Shaw the motif of the twin enormous windows at the ends of
the short wings. Twice at each end four lights with four
transoms. The porch doorway moreover a typical Shaw piece,
white in a Baroque variety. Inside, the hall-screen, the
panelled staircase to its l., and the Great Hall to its r. deserve
attention. The hall is panelled high up, but there is still space
on the long wall for three oriels to look into it. The chimneypiece is something tremendous. The overmantel stretches
right up to the closely beamed ceiling with panels of gilt
leather. The whole of this overmantel stands on two columns.

GRIM'S BANK *see* ALDERMASTON

GRIMSBURY TOWER *see* HERMITAGE

* The transition from the square W end of the nave to the roundness of
the tower is by squinches.

GROVE

⁴⁰⁹⁰

St James. 1901 by *P. A. Robson* (GR). With an odd bellcote in an odd place. Derelict at the time of writing. – FONT. Of wood, said to have been used by Dr Pusey.

Grove Farmhouse, ⅜ m. ESE. Dated 1684. Chequer brick, three bays, wooden cross-windows, doorway with bolection moulding.

(Orchard View is a cruck cottage. NBR)

HAINES HILL *see* ST NICHOLAS HURST

HALFWAY HOUSE *see* KINTBURY

HALL PLACE
1½ m. SSE of Hurley

⁸⁰⁸⁰

Built *c*.1730–5 for William East, a wealthy London man. The architect is not known. The estate is entered from the E by a castellated LODGE with arrow slits of shapes typical of the Gothick of 1760 or so. A straight avenue takes one to the house, others go S and N, and one used to go E. At the end of the N avenue a lead STATUE of Diana on a high base. The house is of red brick and has its façade on the entrance side. Seven bays, basement and two and a half storeys, parapet. At the angles giant pilasters. One-storeyed three-bay links lead to five-bay wings projecting at r. angles. The drawing room is very splendid. Stucco ceiling and stucco wall panels, some with big intertwined dolphins, two with profile portraits in cartouches. They are no doubt the work of the Italian *stuccatori* who worked in such places as Ditchley and Sutton Scarsdale. There they are *Artari*, *Vassali*, and *Serena*. Door frames with Corinthian pilasters and pediment. Sumptuous chimneypiece. On the mantelshelf two big volutes. At the top, below a baldacchino with looped-up curtains, two putti holding a portrait medallion. In the anteroom to this room a more classical chimneypiece with two eagles on the top. In another room a chimneypiece the overmantel of which has a relief in an elaborate frame on which perch two eagles.

⁴⁹

^{48a}

HALL'S FARMHOUSE *see* FARLEY HILL

HAMPSTEAD NORRIS

⁵⁰⁷⁰

St Mary. Quite large. Short broad w tower with flatly projecting staircase. In spite of the Perp doorway, window, arch to the nave, and battlements surely an early tower. The nave sw quoin even looks Saxon. s doorway of c.1200, simple, with a billet hood-mould. The N doorway of the same time, still simpler. E.E. chancel with lancets and in the E wall three widely spaced lancets with continuous roll mouldings inside. Nave roof of 1635 with collar-beams, arched braces, and pendants. Chancel arch of 1879–80 (by *Arthur Baker*; BC). – FONT. 1768. Of semi-globular shape. The stem and foot meant to be Gothic. – SCULPTURE. Knight on horseback, the figure over 2 ft high. C13. He is charging; prancing horse. It is an excellent piece of sculpture, but what can it have belonged to? – PAINTING. Beautiful, if faded, large seated C13 figure of the Virgin against an arch. – MONUMENTS. John James † 1818. By *Westmacott*. Grecian and quite plain, but with an inscription worth recording

> Could stone articulate, could earth declare,
> What noble virtues are recorded here
> The widowed voice might now be spared to raise
> Its feeble numbers, to an husband's praise.
> Yet how instructive is it to relate,
> The painful history of that husband's fate.
> A fate – that in its mournful progress told
> A lesson, equally, for young and old,
> So young, so gifted, and alas! so blest
> By fortune, nature; By the world carest.
> Struck in the opening of his brightest day
> To fatal malady, became a prey.
> Ah loved and more than my existence prized
> Heaven mark'd thee for its sweetest sacrifice
> Two lingering years, brought on the fatal hour
> And all the misery, fate had in its power.
> When to the world, and to his weeping wife
> A long farewell, announced departing life.
> Still with the tears the joyful accents fell
> From lips where truth was ever wont to dwell
> Dying he said 'See what devotion gives!
> I know, I feel, that my redeemer lives.'

– Lowlsey Family. In the churchyard. Square monument of cast iron. Seven steps with inscription and an iron spire. Mid C19. – CROSS in the churchyard. Base only, but with Perp panelling.

MANOR HOUSE, to the E. Irregular, with one stepped gable. Doorway with pilasters and pediment. Long, aisled, weather-boarded BARN.

ROMAN VILLA, *see* Hermitage.

4060

HAMSTEAD MARSHALL

ST MARY. C18 W tower of brick. Plain Late Norman S doorway, C14 N aisle, the E and W windows round-arched, with Late Dec tracery. Perp N arcade of two bays. Wide depressed arches, the responds with broad shafts and broad hollows. Good restoration by *Sir Charles Nicholson*, 1929. – FONT COVER. Jacobean; openwork. – Two-decker PULPIT. Early C17. With tester. – BOX PEWS. – WEST GALLERY on columns of bottle-like entasis. – COMMUNION RAIL. Of *c*.1700. – PLATE. Cup and Paten given in 1622.

MANOR HOUSE. Built for the Earl of Craven by *Sir Balthasar Gerbier c*.1660, on the pattern, it is said, of Heidelberg Castle to please Elizabeth of Bohemia (and the Palatinate). Continued by *Winde*. Burnt in 1718. Kip's engraving of a solid block, eleven by eleven bays, three storeys high, with dormers, a hipped roof, and three belvedere cupolas, looks emphatically English of *c*.1660 and not a bit like Heidelberg. All that

42d & e remains is a number of pathetic GATEPIERS, some on their own, some still attached to garden walls. Three pairs are of stone, one with balls on top, the other two with urns and pineapples. Gibbonsish garlands in small panels. The other

42f pairs of brick and decidedly early C18. As for the earlier, it is interesting to note that, according to Mr Gunnis, *Thomas Strong*, one of Wren's masons, worked at the house in 1675.

MOUNDS, in the park. These three large mounds are probably castle mounds rather than barrows.

MILL. Early C19. The house has a raised centre with chamfered corners, i.e. it is an elongated octagon.

HARE HATCH *see* WARGRAVE

HARTLEY COURT *see* SHINFIELD

4080

HARWELL

ST MATTHEW. *The Times* in 1962 reported that to the W of the present tower remains of a nave had been found. The walling showed herringbone laying, so that an C11 date is likely. At the same time a pewter CHALICE was found which dates from *c*.1200. It has a cambered lid with a raised cross whose arms are chalices and whose foot is stepped. It may have come from the tomb of the man to whom the plain N and S doorways are due, and the three-bay arcades with round piers, early, i.e. upright, stiff-leaf capitals, octagonal abaci, and single-chamfered arches and the transepts with lancet windows (N smaller than S) and arches corresponding to the arcade responds – elements all of c.1200. The W tower may have been begun at the same time, but the bell-openings have plate tracery of elementary motifs, and that is mid-century. There is an excellent Dec chancel, less so outside, as the five-light E window is over-restored, than inside. Here the chancel arch has two lively horizontal figures instead of capitals, and by the side of the priest's doorway sits a yet jollier little man with a bottle. Dec SEDILIA and PISCINA too.* – SCREEN. The shafts with shaft-rings probably early C14 like the chancel, but the top parts Perp. – COMMUNION RAIL. Of c.1700; twisted balusters. – CHANDELIER. Brass. Dated 1766. The centrepiece moulded, not a ball. – PLATE. Pewter Chalice, see above; two Chalices and Patens given in 1724.

GEERING ALMSHOUSES, on the main S–N road (the A-road). 1715. One-storeyed, brick, with a recessed centre with an arcade of three widely spaced arches and small segment-headed windows in the wings. The tops of the wings still have shaped gables. The centre of the recessed part is raised, with the parapet curving up to it.

The best house of Harwell is MIDDLE FARM. It has its C14 hall with embattled central truss, kingpost, and fourway struts, and a little pargetting of 1589, when a floor was put into the hall. The front and back doorways with the former screens passage also survive, and two of the doorways from this to the kitchen and offices. The service wing may represent a hall of the late C13. Also tie-beams, crownposts, and fourway struts. One barn has crucks. Several other good timber-framed farmhouses.‡

ATOMIC ENERGY RESEARCH ESTABLISHMENT, 1½ m. SW. It started in 1946 and now covers 441 acres, plus 93 of housing, playing fields, etc., plus 100 of research laboratories of other bodies. Two reactors, Dido and Pluto, and the improbable-looking Tandem Generator are the most prominent objects. Among the other buildings none is outstanding.

* Messrs J. M. Fletcher and P. S. Spokes draw attention to the original ROOFS, scissor-braced in the S transept, with crownposts and two collars in the nave, with octagonal crownposts in the chancel. Their dating is c.1220–40 for transept and nave, c.1305 for the chancel.

‡ Mr J. M. Fletcher of Harwell has listed the following CRUCK COTTAGES at Harwell and obtained provisional radiocarbon datings for them: in CHURCH LANE LE CARILLON, c.1425, and DELL COTTAGE, c.1445, in SENNINGS LANE SCHOOL HOUSE, c.1600.

HATFORD

St George. Norman n window, s doorway, chancel arch, and
priest's doorway. The doorway has scallop capitals, one with
a small head, and zigzag in the arch. The window has an
inner roll moulding. The chancel arch has scallop capitals
too, and a one-step arch. All this points to *c*.1130–50. The
priest's doorway is late c12 (one slight continuous chamfer).
Late c13 several other windows (chancel s, nave s, and
especially chancel e: three stepped pointed-trefoiled lights
under one arch). Also late c13 a tomb recess in the chancel n
wall. The church is ruinous, and the w end has been converted
into a MAUSOLEUM for the Rev. Samuel Paynter † 1893. Red
granite sarcophagus, four grey granite columns carrying a w
gallery. – PANELLING. Jacobean. On the e wall. – MONU-
MENT. Defaced effigy of the late c13(?). His hands hold his
heart.

Holy Trinity. 1873–4 by *W. Wigginton* at the expense of the
rector. Small, with a sw porch tower. Walls of grey crazy
paving. Nave and short chancel. Details late c13. – PLATE.
Cup and Cover, 1581; Paten, inscribed 1640.

s of Holy Trinity a terrace of six cottages. Brown stone. Big slate
roof with two tiers of irregularly arranged dormers. Said to
be by *Street* (D. Cole).

HEATHLAND
2 m. sse of Wokingham

St Sebastian. 1864 by *Butterfield*. Nave and chancel in one.
Red brick and blue brick diapering. Small bell-turret with
Jacobean balusters. Timber s porch. n aisle on two plain
wooden posts. – STAINED GLASS. w window by *Gibbs*.

The NINE MILE RIDE runs e–w from s of Easthampstead to
s of Arborfield Garrison. It is a ride originally cut through
Windsor Forest, and it does not seem to represent a prehistoric or Roman road. Still in 1928 the *Little Guide* called
it 'remarkably lonely, as it hardly possesses a single house'.
Now it is for long stretches lined with bungalows. Who
allowed them in? The result is ribbon development at its
most fatal and fatuous. The tourists' pleasure is spoiled by
the bungalows, and the bungalow dwellers' by the tourists' cars.

HERMITAGE

Holy Trinity. 1835, in the Norman style, i.e. long, round-headed windows and a Norman w porch. The chancel by *Maurice Hulbert* (BC) is enterprising for 1887, with brick dressings exposed inside. – FONT. Neo-Norman.

GRIMSBURY TOWER, ½ m. SE. Inside an earthwork stands an octagonal brick tower with battlements and a pyramid roof behind. The ground-floor windows are pointed, the upper ones have an odd shape of ogee curves leading to a moulded top.

ROMAN VILLA, in a field on Well House Farm, below the high ground of Cold Ash. The site was discovered during ploughing operations in the C19. No plans were made of the structures found, but they included a substantial building, 108 ft long, containing at least one mosaic pavement. The villa appears to have been destroyed by fire at the end of the C3.

HILLFOOT see BEENHAM

HINTON HOUSE see ST NICHOLAS HURST

HINTON WALDRIST   3090

ST MARGARET. Essentially later C13, though much re-done. The s transept s window (three stepped pointed-trefoiled lights under one arch) is typical of the late C13. In the rere-arch two little fluted corbels. The w tower is Dec. – PLATE. Cup of 1725; large Paten of 1809. – MONUMENT. John Loder † 1701. Good cartouche.

HINTON MANOR. Early C18 front of five bays and two storeys. Door-canopy on elegant brackets. The E side of the house has early C17 details, including two cross-windows. The house stands in a moat, and this and a MOTTE to the SW are supposed to belong to a motte-and-bailey castle.

EARTHWORK, in an oak copse on Windmill Hill. The site is rectangular in plan and is enclosed by a single bank and ditch with traces of a counterscarp bank in places. The area enclosed measures 270 ft by 60 ft. The site is unexcavated, but on the analogy of similar structures in the area may date to the C1.

HOLME GREEN see WOKINGHAM

HOLYPORT HOUSE see BRAY

HOP CASTLE see WINTERBOURNE

HUNGERFORD   3060

ST LAWRENCE. 1816 by *Pinch* of Bath. Large and uninspired.

Bath stone exterior with aisles and an apsed chancel. Many
9b clumsy pinnacles, especially big on the W tower. The windows
have intersecting tracery. The piers with their carved capitals
and the arches are of 1880–1. – FONT. Octagonal, Perp, with
quatrefoils. – STAINED GLASS. In the S aisle W window glass
of c.1816, typical, with its deep yellows.* – The E window by
Lavers & Westlake, 1887 (BC), and not an ornament. – MONU-
MENT. Defaced and footless Knight of c.1350 (N aisle E).

The VICARAGE is a C17 cottage with wooden mullioned and
transomed windows and later additions.

Visiting Hungerford from the Bath Road, one starts at the
corner of the BEAR HOTEL, low, white, with a Tuscan porch,
and RIVERSIDE, brick of c.1800, a cube of three storeys and
three bays with parapet and tripartite windows. Only the
WESLEYAN CHAPEL opposite the two on the N of the Bath
Road is somewhat painful: 1868–9 by *Willson & Wilcox* of
Bath. Pale blue and red brick, with a (ritually) SW turret and
heavy E.E. tracery. Then S across the Kennet, Nos 12–13
BRIDGE STREET, five bays and a pair of identical doorways,
with broken pediments. Across the canal and into the HIGH
STREET. The house on the l. is a delight, with an iron bridge
as access to the first floor and other decorative iron work. Bow
window to the canal. Opposite a timber-framed cottage. The
High Street is wide and nearly straight. The scale and
character are undisturbed, though shops of course have
invaded many of the ground floors. Specially pleasant No. 11
of four bays with alternating blocks of rustication for the
window surrounds, No. 16 of six bays with a hipped roof, and
the house opposite with a nice doorcase. Then the railway
bridge and to the r. to the Green, at the end of which stands
the church. Back, and then alas the TOWN HALL. This is of
1870, not detached, only three bays wide plus a tower bay, fussy
and with an undefinable cap on top of the tower. The ground
floor of the three bays is a loggia. Red brick and yellow terracotta.‡ To the l. down PARK STREET, to the HOSPITAL,
former WORKHOUSE, of 1840, still in a utilitarian sub-
classical style, with pedimental gable (no longer a real pediment), brick, fifteen bays long. Back to the High Street and
on the r. No. 27 with four gables, three large, one small

* The Rev. K. Tagg tells me that the glass until recently had the signature
of *W. Collins*, Wilkie Collins's father.

‡ Mr Angus Marshall, the Town Clerk, tells me that the architect was
Ernest Prestwick of Leigh in Lancashire.

(C17?), No. 28 of five bays, blue and red brick, No. 107 opposite, also blue and red, but three widely spaced bays. The windows have blank segmental arches with free motifs. The CONGREGATIONAL CHURCH is of 1840, stuccoed, with giant pilasters and no pediment. No. 33 is the most ambitious house: five bays, blue headers and red dressings, and four (not original) gables. No. 34 has two minimum Venetian windows on the ground floor – and that is the end.

THE YEWS, New Town. Early C18, blue brick and red dressings. Segment-headed windows.

STANDEN MANOR, 1¾ m. SSW. Early C18. Blue headers and red dressings. Six-bay front with the end pairs of bays somewhat projecting. Parapet, hipped roof, segment-headed windows, widely spaced. On the side a big bow has later been inserted.

NORTH STANDEN FARM. The C13 chapel has been demolished.

HURLEY

HURLEY PRIORY was founded before 1087 as a Benedictine house. What remains of it is the nave of the church, now the parish church (see below), and the refectory range to its N. The latter is part of an inhabited house now and has to its S, i.e. towards the cloister, two Norman-looking doorways not regarded as medieval by the VCH, and small pointed-trefoil-headed windows over, and to the N the remains of three large early C14 windows. Excavations have shown that the church initially had a long aisleless chancel and an apse, was lengthened in the C13 and given a straight E end and a straight-ended N aisle, and lengthened again in the C14, when it got new chapels. Beneath the crossing interesting evidence of the Saxon predecessor of the church was found. It seems to represent a crossing and two turrets or towers to its immediate E. The E range of the cloister was found in a C13 state, with the chapter house oblong, its doorway enriched by colonnettes. The dormitory above it stretched as usual a good deal further N than the N wall of the refectory. E and SE of the chancel remains of Ladye Place, a Tudor mansion, were found, including a crypt of two naves and four bays below a wing projecting W from near the S end. This has been regarded as the infirmary undercroft. To the W of the church are a round DOVECOTE and a BARN, both assigned to the C14.

ST MARY is no more than the oddly long and narrow nave of the priory church. The proportions are decidedly Anglo-Saxon.

The windows of the church are Norman (except for one large Dec s window), and so are the doorways, except that that to the w is partly and that to the E entirely of *Hakewill*'s restoration of 1852. Hakewill also did the neo-Norman stone SCREEN separating the altar space from an E vestry. – FONT. C15, with coarse blank panelling. – BENCH. Just one old one with poppy-heads. – PAINTINGS. Moses and Aaron from the reredos; C18 (by the w door). – PLATE. Cup of 1655 with Cover of 1635; Paten on foot of 1693; and Flagon of 1695. – MONUMENTS. John Lovelace of Ladye Place † 1558 and his wife † 1579. A typical Early Elizabethan monument, i.e. with columns and no figures. Superstructure with arms and two eagles as finials. – Richard Lovelace † 1602 and his son Sir Richard. Upper parts of the figures only. From a lost monument (vestry). – Viscountess Ashbrook † 1810. By *Flaxman*. Tablet with two kneeling putti. – Lt-Commander Hipolyto J. Da Costa † 1823. By *Theophilus Clifford* of Marlow. White and black marble tablet; large.

HOUSE, 250 yds s. By *Hartry, Grover & Halter*, 1963–4. Small and architecturally convincing.

HURST *see* ST NICHOLAS HURST

2080

IDSTONE
¾ m. sw of Ashbury

A hamlet of chalk, Sarsen, and brick. Specially rewarding the Rectory Farmhouse and the Parsonage Farmhouse. At the entry to the hamlet from the B-road a later C17 three-bay house, formerly the TRIP THE DAISEY INN, with a recent relief showing a hound doing just this. Symmetrically placed mullioned windows.

THE THREE BARROWS, s of Old Ditch, on Idstone Down. These three bowl barrows all measure approximately 50 ft in diameter and 5 ft in height. The central and western examples have depressions in their centres, although there is no surviving record of their excavation.

INHOLMES *see* WOODLANDS ST MARY

3060

INKPEN

ST MICHAEL. Nave and chancel in one; tile-hung bell-turret. Plain C13 s doorway, the hood-mould on two defaced heads. Traces of a large s window. Interesting restoration and remodelling by *Clayton Crabbe Rolfe* of Oxford, 1896, i.e. the s

porch, the charming Arts-and-Crafts Gothic s window with
its partially flying rere-arch, and the N arcade with the lozenge-
shaped piers and continuous mouldings. The nave must have
been much widened, as the timber posts of the bell-turret
now stand free. – PLATE. Set of 1758. – Silver-gilt Chalice
and Paten, given in 1903; designed by *Bodley*. – MONUMENTS.
Effigy of a Knight, the legs lost. Defaced, but it looks late C13.
– Tablets of *c*.1738 and *c*.1763.

OLD RECTORY. Built about 1695. Seven bays, but in a typical
c.1700-way the windows next the centre are much slimmer
than the others. Hipped roof with dormers with triangular
and segmental pediments. Sashed windows, but at the back
still some of the original wooden mullion and transom crosses.
Entrance hall with two arches on a Roman Doric column and
the staircase behind.

WEST COURT HOUSE, ¼ m. NE. Red brick. The N part with
the porch early C18, the s part later C18.

SCHOOL, 1 m. NE. By *Street*, discussed in *The Ecclesiologist*58a
in 1850 and indeed most remarkable for that date. Brick,
tile-hung gables and tile-hung blank pointed arches above
windows. It is all so informal and domestic and un-
High-Victorian that it seems an immediate preparation for
Shaw.

KIRBY HOUSE, 1¼ m. ESE. Fine entrance side of 1733. Five
bays, two storeys, segment-headed windows. Parapet and
pedimental gable with an arched window. Brick. Blue headers
and red dressings. Raised brick quoins. The doorway must be
recent, but there is a splendid doorcase round the corner
which was perhaps originally here. Columns and carved
brackets for the hood. The house of 1733 here borders on a
higher addition of 1761. This also has a five-bay façade, but
all is more widely spaced. The staircase is of 1733 and has
turned balusters and carved tread-ends.

LONG BARROW, Gallows Hill, *see* Combe.

KENNINGTON

ST SWITHUN. Cruciform, of yellow brick, free neo-Georgian.
By *Lawrence Dale* and the Vicar, the Rev. *S. S. Davies*, 1956–8.
Central altar inside.

The old church stands to the l. of the new. It is in the Norman
style, of 1828, by *Daniel Robertson*, an early date for neo-
Norman. It is a plain rectangle without separate chancel, but
with a Norman bellcote. Plain long windows. The w doorway

is startlingly well imitated, even to a capital with a little
Sagittarius.* Two orders of columns. Roll mouldings.
(MANOR HOUSE. Dated 1629 on a beam. Stone ground floor
with C16 two- to four-light windows with round-arched lights.
Timber-framed upper floor, also of 1629, with Late Georgian
windows. In two back rooms fine plaster ceilings, vine,
pomegranate, strapwork, and arabesque.)

KILN GREEN see WARGRAVE

₄₀₉₀

KINGSTON BAGPUIZE

ST JOHN BAPTIST. 1799–1800 by *John Fidel* of Faringdon, but
apsed and internally altered by *E. Dolby* in 1882. W doorway
with inset Tuscan columns and above atrocious little Dolby-
Norman windows. Pediment. Pretty cupola with wooden
columns. The side windows and E window set in large blank
arches. – PLATE. Paten, 1724/5; Cup, Paten, and Flagon
1727/8. – MONUMENTS. Edmund Fettiplace † 1710. Inscription below canopy with two putto-heads and two urns. – John
Blandy and wife, 1762. Obelisk with two oval portrait
medallions.

KINGSTON HOUSE. The date must be about 1720. Tall brick
house. Seven-bay centre with raised pedimented three-bay
centre. Lower wings. Quoins. Vases on top. The ground-floor
windows all arched, the upper ones segment-headed. Doorway with rusticated surround in which the flanking pilasters
partly disappear (cf. Radley House). It is a Lutyens effect,
two hundred years ahead of its time. Triglyph frieze. The
window above with curves widening down towards the sill.
The entrance side (former back) is identical, but has a simpler
doorway. The side elevation is of four bays with a four-bay
pediment. The original entrance hall has two discreetly decorated stone chimneypieces. Behind it the staircase (now
entrance) hall. The wooden staircase rises in two arms (as it
used to do at Coleshill) and reaches an upper balcony or
gallery in the middle of which is a spacious shell niche. Pretty
turned balusters with fluted bulbs near the foot (also as at
Coleshill). In one room a beautiful Rococo chimneypiece. –
In the garden a SUMMERHOUSE of chequer brickwork with a
lower storey, which has a shallow brick dome. The back faces
a terrace, and to that side the upper floor is ground floor. It

* I hear from the Rev. S. S. Davies that this is a rebus of the name of the
builder: Bowyer.

has a few steps leading to a doorway and l. and r. not apses but halved apses – a very curious motif. – Very good iron GATES.

STONE HOUSE, in the Faringdon road. Of *c*.1700. L-shaped, the main part of five bays with stone mullion-and-transom-cross windows.

RECTORY, ½ m. S. Built in 1723. Five bays, two storeys. The middle bay stressed by alternating rusticated giant pilasters. Porch with rocky grotto rustication similar to that of *c*.1750 at Pusey House. Mr Colvin has recently found that the house was designed by *Dr Clarke* of Oxford.

BRIDGE, 2 m. N. Six semicircular approach arches and then six pointed medieval arches, the middle one widest, and with ribs and traces of ribs.

KINGSTON LISLE
3080

ST JOHN BAPTIST. Small, with a timber bell-turret with spire-let. Norman chancel, see one N window. Nave of *c*.1200, see the N doorway and buttressing. The chancel E window is Dec (reticulated tracery) and has inside niches l. and r. C17 nave roof with tie-beams and pendants. – PULPIT. Later C17 with tester. – BENCHES. The ends straight-topped with tracery and arms, Instruments of the Passion, etc. – SCREEN. Jacobean; simple. – PANELLING. Chancel E wall, Jacobean. – NORTH DOOR. With splendid iron hinge-work of *c*.1200. – PAINTING. Large figures of St Peter and St Paul in the jambs of the E window. In the head of the Norman window roundel with head of Christ. On the N wall Herod's Feast and Be-heading of St John. All these are C14. – STAINED GLASS. Chancel S. A little with a head. – PLATE. Chalice and Cover, 1576; Paten, 1640.

KINGSTON LISLE HOUSE. The architectural history of the house, the interior of which is most ingenious and dramatic, is oddly obscure. The only fact known is that the house appears on a trade-card of *c*.1830. This is the card of a builder of Lechlade, *Richard Pace*. Mr Colvin reports that wings etc. were added in 1812. That is all. The centre of the house has seven bays with arched windows and attic windows over. Three-bay pediment, former doorway with Gibbs surround and stone bands and keystones. That is mid Georgian, and so is the modestly Rococo plasterwork of the former entrance hall. The garden side instead looks early C19, with three bays of widely spaced tripartite windows and a broad doorway with Greek Doric columns. Of the wings one has a big bow and contains the billiard room, the other has the present entrance at its end. This leads to a monumental passage with coffered tunnel-vault. At the far end of this are two windows, very high up, because the conservatory used to be here. One of the windows is in front, the other on the l. Facing the latter is the entrance to the centre of the house, and here a very large, functionally quite unnecessary procession of rooms has been created to continue at r. angles what the entrance hall had begun. The first part has a vault with fans in the corners, the second has sculpture placed boldly on the cornice, the third has an oblong groin-vault, and the last a half-vault with fans. In the latter two parts of the composition the staircase rises. Two flights of it are flying, and the balustrade is of wrought iron with S-scrolls. The staircase arrangement is such that it can connect the most unexpected levels. It is not known who designed this fascinating procession of spaces and could convince the client of such a waste of space. Messrs Betjeman and Piper suggest *Basevi* or *Cockerell*. The most likely date is c.1825–30.

ROUND BARROW, N of Kingston Lisle and E of Fawler. Large round barrow, 75 ft in diameter and 7 ft high. The mound is now covered by trees.

KINTBURY

ST MARY. Not a small church. Nave, transepts, chancel, W tower. The restoration of 1859 has made the church virtually Victorian. Norman S doorway with zigzag arch, what little is original of it. C13 W tower, broad, with clasping buttresses. One-light bell-openings. Tower arch to the nave with nook-shafts carrying stiff-leaf capitals. Later C13 N transept, though the arch looks early C13 (one slight chamfer). However, the N window has intersecting tracery. The S transept is of brick, was built in 1713, but is thoroughly victorianized. – PLATE. Flagon of 1683; Almsdish of 1688. – MONUMENTS. Jonathan Raymond † 1711. Not easily seen. Two busts and an urn on a pedestal between. – This motif was then taken up by *Peter Scheemakers* and *Thomas Scheemakers* who made the monuments to Sir Jemmet Raymond † 1754 and Jemmet Raymond † 1767 respectively. The former also has two busts and a raised urn between, the latter has on the pedestal the bust of the husband, and the busts below are of two wives. – Brass to John Gunter † 1624 and wife. She has her hat on.

WALLINGTONS, $1\frac{1}{8}$ m. SW. Early C17, but far too drastically restored in 1892. Front with two gabled wings. Four gables on the side elevation. Mullioned and transomed windows.

BARTON COURT, $\frac{5}{8}$ m. NNW. 1772. Chequer brick, of two and a half storeys. Five-bay front, the centre window Venetian.

LODGES of Kintbury House, 1 m. N, on the Bath Road. Gothic, one-storeyed, white and pretty, but not half as pretty as

HALFWAY HOUSE, the favourite of all travellers on the Bath 51b Road. It is a late C18 toll-house on the turnpike and looks exactly like a Staffordshire piece. A square with four corner towers, castellated, with round-arched and pointed-arched windows.

KIRBY HOUSE see INKPEN

KNOWL HILL   8070

ST PETER. 1840, with a flint chancel by *W. Scott Champion* of 1870. The old part is by *J. C. & G. Buckler*, of brick, with lancet windows and a hexagonal bell-turret with spirelet standing on a shallow projection. – STAINED GLASS. Three saints by *Hardman* from St Michael Oxford, as restored by *Street* in 1854.* – MONUMENT. Jane E. Smith † 1852. By *William Theed*, 1854. Small white standing figure.

LAMBOURN   3070

ST MICHAEL. A large and interesting church with a prominent crossing tower. Late Norman from the W end to the crossing, i.e.: W wall with doorway, two orders of shafts, one with shaft-rings, arch with two zigzags meeting to form three-dimensional lozenges, hood-mould on beasts' heads. Remains of the window above with a continuous roll moulding. Circular window in the gable. Then the aisle W windows and the lower parts of the crossing tower. The plain N and S doorways look a little later. C13 N transept, see the E lancet. The N window is Perp. Dec S transept, see the S window. Perp chancel E window, Perp tower top with three-light bell-openings, polygonal angle buttresses, and pinnacles, and Perp the only ornate part of the church, the outer S chapel with battlements and pinnacles. The inner S chapel E window looks *c.*1800. Now the interior. All four crossing arches are in a good Late Norman state. Keeled shafts, Late Norman capitals, pointed arches with three slight chamfers. The four-bay arcades can

* Information received from the Rev. Basil Clarke.

hardly be earlier, yet still have square abaci for their piers, i.e. this early feature was kept long. Round piers, bases with spurs, capitals with scallops, also Norman foliage. Round arches with two slight chamfers. The arches from the aisles to the transepts pointed with one slight chamfer. The N arch disturbed by a Perp inner flying buttress for the crossing tower (when the top was put on). Typically Dec arches (sunk quadrant mouldings, continuous) from the W to the N chapel and from the chancel to the S chapel. Perp arches from the chancel to the N chapel (four shafts and four wide hollows, four-centred arches), from the outer to the inner S chapel (shafts and deep wave), and from the S chapel to the W. This arch has a hunt in small figures in the hollow of the arch and heads and flowers in the hollow of the jambs.

FURNISHINGS. FONT. Later C17, with swags (N chapel). – PILLAR PISCINA. Norman, with leaf capital, later used as a stoup (N aisle). – SCULPTURE. Small Mannerist profile relief of Charles I with two angels l. and r. Alabaster, from Lambourn Place ('King and Martyr'). – STAINED GLASS. In the N chapel C16 figure and bits. – Outer S chapel, c.1855, by *Willement.* – S and N aisles by *Kempe,* 1890 and 1894. – PLATE. Silver-gilt Chalice-Cup, 1587; Paten, inscribed 1631; Flagon, secular, inscribed 1701; Almsdish, early C18; Bread Holder, 1746–7. – MONUMENTS. John of Estbury † 1372, and his son. Brasses, demi-figures, 14½ in., S chapel. – Sir Thomas Grandison and wife. Brasses, demi-figures, 14 in. long; also S chapel. – John Estbury † 1508. Good brass figure, 33 in. long, on a tomb-chest with shields in round panels. – Sir Thomas Essex † 1558 and wife. Alabaster. Effigies on a tomb-chest with shields and very elementary balusters. At his feet a dolphin (N chapel). – Thomas Garrard † 1583 and wife. Tablet with kneelers (chancel N). – Thomas Garrard † 1619 and wife. Brasses, she wearing a hat (chancel S). – Charles Garrard † 1710. Tablet with two putto heads at the foot (S transept). – CURIOSUM. The village STOCKS in the N chapel.

Round the church much to see. The former VICARAGE to the SW, a Jacobean composition, brick, with two big side and a smaller middle gable, but the fenestration all Later Georgian, round-headed windows with Y-glazing bars, and in the centre two Venetian windows. To the N the wall with many sarsen stones. In it a small C17 doorway from Lambourn Place, with strapwork at the top. Then the very picturesque ALMS-

HOUSES of 1852, by *T. Talbot Bury*, castellated façade with
a higher turret. This display leads not to a bishop's palace,
but to the sweet cloister of the almshouses, small, low, and of
timber. Behind the almshouses down a lane to the WESLEYAN
CHAPEL of 1835, brick, three bays, round-arched windows.

To the E of the church the MARKET PLACE. In it the VILLAGE
CROSS, steps and tall shaft genuine. At the principal corner the
RED LION. Façade of light grey sarsen stones in brick frames.
Round the corner in NEWBURY STREET different: blue and
red brick and giant brick pilasters. In the street two specially
good houses: IVY HOUSE of three bays, blue headers and
red dressings, broad doorway with Tuscan columns, triglyph
frieze and pediment, and No. 21, six bays, with narrower
windows l. and r. of the pretty Adamish doorcase. Columns
and pediment with fan-motif in.

In the HIGH STREET, running S from the Market Hall, also
two attractive houses: No. 3 with pargetting in simple
patterns and a doorway with a fan-motif in the pediment, and
COLLEGE HOUSE, Early Georgian, of light grey sarsen stone
with brick dressings, seven bays, segment-headed windows,
l. and r. of the door narrower windows, three-bay pediment.
Also in the High Street, like any other house, *Street*'s SCHOOL,
Gothic, blue and red brick, of 1850, nothing particular.*

BROCKHAMPTON FARM, ¾ m. SE. The l. part flint with mullioned and transomed windows, the r. part five bays, not
regular, with segment-headed ground-floor windows. Blue
headers and red dressings. The windows are sashed, but
originally had wooden crosses, see the side and the back.

THE SEVEN BARROWS, on the downs to the N. This fine cemetery of twenty-four round barrows includes examples of bell,
bowl, and disc barrows and two twin barrows – two mounds
surrounded by a common ditch. Excavations conducted on a
number of these sites in the C19 recovered several crouched
inhumation burials accompanied by beakers and urn cremations.

LONG BARROW, just N of Seven Barrows Farm, at the S end of
a wood, on the boundary of Lambourn, Sparsholt, and Kingston Lisle parishes. The mound is orientated E–W and is 220 ft
long. It expands to a width of 70 ft at its E end, where it still
stands 4½ ft high. There are flanking quarry ditches, 15 ft
wide, round the S end of the barrow. At the E end numerous

---

* The NBR notes one cruck cottage on the authority of Addy, and *C.L.*
has illustrated one (29 October 1927). It may be the same.

sarsens project from the mound and suggest the presence of a chamber at this point.

MEMBURY CAMP. Only the NW corner of this fort is in Berkshire, the remainder lying across the county boundary in Wiltshire. The fort is of univallate construction, enclosing an area of 32 acres. The defences are broken by an entrance on the NW. The site has been damaged by cultivation and is now much overgrown.

LECKHAMPSTEAD

4070

ST JAMES. By *S. S. Teulon*, 1858–60. A 'hard' church and a wilful one in some features. The church has a crossing tower, but it is no more than a timber bell-turret. Also it has transepts, but they are no more than glorified dormers in so far as their end walls are flush with the nave wall and the aisle roofs go on below them. The church is of flint, with red-brick dressings including broad bands. The chancel is surprisingly short for 1860. The inside is all brick, red, yellow, black, and with diapers. The chancel arch stands beyond the crossing, and the crossing is no more than two pairs of cusped braces. – FONT. Norman, of cup shape, with leaf friezes at top and bottom. – PULPIT. Jacobean, with two tiers of the familiar blank arches. – COMMUNION RAIL. The balusters partly turned, partly twisted. Early C18. – STAINED GLASS. E window by *Lavers & Barraud* (BC). – PLATE. Elizabethan Cup; Paten on foot, 1723.

LETCOMBE BASSETT

3080

ST MICHAEL. Norman chancel, see one N and one S window. The N doorway, though it is probably re-set, would prove a Norman nave. One order of shafts, capitals with the four Signs of the Evangelists in the four big scallops of the two capitals. Tympanum with a pattern of incised squares, perhaps not original. The chancel arch narrow and the abaci of the responds decorated with crisp, close leaf trails. Chancel E and S windows later C13 with elementary bar tracery. Nave and S aisle, including S arcade, 1861 by *Butterfield*. Thin W tower, also later C13?

See
p.
359

HILLFORT, on Segsbury Down, just N of the Ridgeway. This Iron Age fort is of univallate construction with a slight counterscarp bank which can be traced for some 200 yds on the NW. The area enclosed is about 26 acres. The rampart was probably faced with sarsen, and sarsen blocks are still

visible projecting out of the turf. Probably only one of the gaps
in the defences is original. It is marked by the out-turning
of the rampart. Sherds of Iron Age A and B pottery have
been found on the surface in the interior of the site, and a
Saxon burial was discovered in the s stretch of rampart in the
C19.

BOWL BARROW, at the junction of Letcombe Bassett and
Lambourn parishes, just E of Stancombe Farm. The barrow
is 45 ft in diameter and 4 ft high and is surrounded by a ditch
12 ft wide. The site is now covered by trees. Excavations in
the C19 produced no evidence of a burial beneath the mound.
To the NE is a second ditched bowl barrow, 41 ft in diameter
and 4 ft high. The depression in the centre of the mound
marks the position of the C19 excavation.

LETCOMBE REGIS
3080

ST ANDREW. Nave and chancel and W tower. The tower,
except for the top, is C13 work. Lancets and two-light bell-
openings with a polygonal shaft and a leaf capital. Tower arch
with one slight chamfer. The s windows Victorian, on the N
side Perp windows and smaller ones over them, as though
the s side had had a Perp aisle with clerestory. – FONT. Tub-
shaped, Norman, with a scalloped top band. – STAINED
GLASS. Some original fragments, including one small Christ
in Majesty. – PLATE. Elizabethan Cup and Paten; Flagon of
1720.

ROMAN VILLA, see Wantage.

LEVERTON
3070

A sweet model village of c.1800, or at least a sequence of five
pairs of thatched cottages in a row.

CHILTON LODGE, see Chilton Foliat.

LINDEN HILL see WARGRAVE

LITTLE COXWELL
2090

ST MARY. Nave with bellcote on the E gable, and chancel. The
bellcote is really the most interesting thing here. It is a genuine
later C13 double bellcote with plate tracery. Norman nave,
see the plain s doorway. Norman chancel, see the plain
priest's doorway. The responds of the chancel arch are
Norman too. One nave s window of c.1300. The others Perp,
as is the transomed four-light window in the chancel. The

chancel E window is Victorian, but the niches to its l. and r. inside are in order. – WEST GALLERY. With remains of the former rood screen. – CHANDELIER. Brass. Moulded centre. Dated 1729. – PLATE. Cup and Cover, 1584.

CHURCH HOUSE, E of the church. Brick, Early Georgian. A remarkable house of five bays. The end bays low, with an arched window and a rising parapet. The next bays with canted bay windows and the centre with a Tuscan porch. The parapet rises above the middle pedimentally, and there are three oval windows in it above the three middle bays. All this is very typical of c.1720.

IRON AGE HILLFORT. This badly damaged site lies on Furze Hill, with commanding views over the Vale of White Horse. The site was described in the C19 as being rectangular, but now only a length of double ditch on the w side is well preserved.

LITTLE SHEFFORD
3070

HOLY INNOCENTS has recently been demolished.

OLD CHURCH. This also looks disused. It is small, of nave and chancel with a small timber bell-turret. One Norman N window. Otherwise Perp windows. – STAINED GLASS. In the E window two figures of the early C16. – PLATE. Set of c.1630–40. – MONUMENTS. Sir Thomas Fettiplace † c.1442. Alabaster. Two recumbent effigies on a tomb-chest with angels holding shields. Wide-spread wings. – John Fettiplace † 1524. Purbeck tomb recess with tomb-chest and canopy. The canopy is straight and stands on quadrants. Vaulted inside. Brasses against the back wall, kneeling.

LITTLEWICK GREEN
8070
3 m. ssw of Maidenhead

ST JOHN EVANGELIST. 1893 by *E. J. Shrewsbury*. Nave and chancel and bellcote; also transepts. – REREDOS. A most surprising and interesting early Quattrocento PAINTING of the Adoration of the Magi, North Italian, with many contacts with Germany. Could it be from Verona? The panel would seem a *cassone* in a photograph, but is 10 ft long. Also many attractive and unusual iconographic features.

VILLAGE WELL. C17. The posts with the roller and its handles are all complete. Tiled roof.

LITTLE WITTENHAM
5090
The village lies under the Wittenham Clumps, indeed two clumps on the hill, and the church is close to the river Thames.

ST PETER. The w tower is Dec below, Perp above, and has a
higher stair-turret. The body of the church is of 1863, by
C. Buckeridge. Nave and chancel, E.E. style. – Typical round
stone PULPIT. – STAINED GLASS. E window by *Clayton &
Bell* (BC). – PLATE. Chalice and Paten Cover, 1577–8; Flagon,
1696–7; silver-gilt Cover Paten, 1714–15. – MONUMENTS.
Brass to David Kidwelly † 1454, a 14½ in. figure. – Brass to
Cicely Kidwelly † 1472, good. The figure is 35 in. long. Both
chancel floor. – In the chancel a tomb recess. The tomb-chest
has quatrefoils. Depressed arch and buttress-shafts. On the
tomb-chest brass to Geoffrey Kidwelly † 1483, a 2 ft 6 in.
figure. – Sir William Dunche † 1611. Only parts remain,
especially the two effigies of alabaster, she recumbent, he on
his side with his head supported by his arm. Also two obelisks.
– William Dunche and his wife. Jacobean brass plate. The
date of death is left open.

SINODUN CAMP, on Castle Hill, commanding a fine view of
the Thames valley. The hill has been defended by the construction of a roughly heart-shaped enclosure consisting of a
deep ditch and high outer bank. There is a single entrance on
the w. Little is known of this fort, which is unexcavated,
although Iron Age and Roman pottery have been found in
the ploughed interior and a ROMANO-BRITISH SETTLEMENT
lies 200 yds w of the entrance to the camp. Pottery from this
site suggests occupation from the C1 to the C5.

LITTLEWORTH
3090

THE ASCENSION. Built in 1839. Architect: *H. J. Underwood.*
Nave and bellcote, w porch. The chancel rebuilt in 1876. In-
side PAINTED INSCRIPTIONS in a nice mid C19 Book of
Hours style.

RADCOT BRIDGE, 2¼ m. N of Faringdon. Three ribbed arches,
the first and third pointed and quite possibly C14. The
middle arch later. This is the best medieval bridge in Berkshire.

LOCKINGE
4080

ALL SAINTS. Norman N doorway, with a big crenellation frieze
in the arch. In the s chapel a re-done and re-set Norman
window. The chancel of the early C14. The E window has Y-
tracery, and l. and r. of the coarse chancel arch are ogee-
headed niches. Plain SEDILIA without ogees. Some original
paint left. The arch to the s chapel looks earlier than the
6*

rest of the chancel. The w tower dates from 1564, the s
aisle from 1886. – PULPIT. Jacobean, with blank arches and
arabesque. A ledge on corbels for putting books or notes on.
– WEST SCREEN. Made up of Jacobean panelling. – NORTH
DOOR. Good, heavy ironwork; C14? – SCULPTURE. Relief of
the Annunciation; Italian, C17. – CHANDELIERS. Three, of
brass, from Corfu, C17 or C18. – STAINED GLASS. E window
designed by *Lady Jane Lindsay* (BC). – PLATE. Cup, 1576;
Paten, 1677. – MONUMENTS. Mrs Grace † 1633. With
kneeling effigy. – Many tablets.

The mansion was pulled down after the Second World War. The
ORANGERY remains, close to the church, among barns. Blue
and red brick, Early Georgian, with seven segment-headed
glazed openings.

The village of East Lockinge is a village of estate housing of
the 1860s.

WEST LOCKINGE FARM, ½ m. NW. Georgian. Blue and red
brick, five bays, hipped roof, and later enlargements.

LONGCOT

ST MARY. W tower of 1722, a rare date for Berkshire. Arched
windows. Nave and chancel are C13 work. Evidence is the
fine N doorway with stiff-leaf captals and a moulded trefoiled arch, one chancel N lancet, and perhaps also the chancel
arch. The N windows of the church a nice mixed lot, including
one two-light Dec and one four-light Perp. – PULPIT. Jacobean. Many motifs, also knob-like heads as pendants of
paired blank arches.

LONG WITTENHAM

ST MARY. Basically a Norman church. One chancel N window
survives, and the chancel arch. Wide single-step arch on decorated capitals, one with two monsters. E.E. the chancel, as
shown by one lancet, the s arcade of four bays with round piers,
stiff-leaf capitals, and double-chamfered arches. It makes no
allowance for the s chapel or transept, which is indeed a little
later – say of *c.*1275 as against *c.*1250. Good s window of
three pointed-trefoiled lights with two trefoils and a big sexfoiled circle. Dec s and N aisle walls, the N wall with one
window with cusped intersecting tracery and a doorway with
a characteristic moulding. The N arcade has standard components. The capitals are likely to be C14. Perp clerestory
and perhaps s porch. The porch is of timber and may go

back to the C14. – FONT. Of lead, circular, Late Norman. A broad band of rosettes and wheels, just two moulds repeated all the time. Below, a narrower band of small figures of a bishop under an arch. – The font was later encased and the Jacobean FONT CASE now serves as a table. – Jacobean also the FONT COVER. – PULPIT. Simple, Jacobean too. – What is more surprising is that the STALLS with their poppy-heads are Jacobean. – Jacobean SCREEN to the S transept. This and the stalls come from Exeter College Chapel, Oxford. – TILES. Some C15 tiles round the font, some S aisle E. – PLATE. Cup and Cover of 1576. – MONUMENTS. In the S transept an amazing monument. It is a PISCINA of pointed-trefoiled 17b form, but the top of the arch cannot be seen, because it is hidden by two small angels with wings standing up. And the piscina itself has in front of the basin a miniature effigy of a Knight. It must be of about the same time as the S window. – At the E end of the S aisle a plain Dec tomb recess.

CRUCKFIELD COTTAGE (No. 18), S of the village cross, is of cruck construction. It is L-shaped, with three pairs of crucks in the longer arm of the L.

CHURCH FARM contains one blade of a cruck truss and its BARN two complete bays. Mr J. M. Fletcher bases the dating of the cruck truss of the farm to c. 1440 and of the barn to c.1550 on a provisional radiocarbon investigation.

BARLEY MOW INN, $\frac{7}{8}$ m. N. Three bays of cruck construction. Crucks are here visible externally.

ROMANO-BRITISH SETTLEMENT. In the fields immediately adjacent to Northfield Farm are numerous crop marks indicating the presence of ditched enclosures and a variety of circular and rectangular buildings of an extensive settlement. Some of these features were excavated in the C19 and produced Romano-British material.

LONGWORTH

ST MARY. Nave with clerestory, embattled S aisle. Several late C13 windows. The rest, including chancel and W tower, all Perp. However, inside a much earlier story. The original nave was enlarged to the N, by one and then another C13 aisle arch. The arches stand on corbels and have two slight chamfers. Then, in the late C13, a complete four-bay S aisle was built (round piers, round abaci, double-chamfered arches), and the N aisle was lengthened by two bays. Finally both aisles were cut off when the W tower was built. Perp N chapel of one bay. – REREDOS. Arts and Crafts, the paintings by *Kate Bunce*, the much more attractive beaten metal frames by her sister (BC). – SCREEN. Jacobean, with extremely elongated columns and strapwork top. – STAINED GLASS. The large Crucifixus in a cyclamen-coloured robe with vines rising l. and r. is by *Heywood Sumner* and as early as 1900 – again very much Arts and Crafts. – PLATE. Tall Cup, no marks; small Paten on foot, inscribed 1629; tall Flagon (by *W. Fawdrey*); Chalice, 1721; silver-gilt Almsplate. – MONUMENTS. Brass to John Hinde, rector † 1422, demi-figure, 12 in. – Brass to Richard Yate † 1498 and wife, in their shrouds, 27 in. figures. – William Bowles † 1801. By *Westmacott*. Seated young man and two standing women, one comforting the other. – In the churchyard s wall a simple Perp doorway.

OLD RECTORY. Three parts, one gabled, c16, with a mullioned window with arched lights, the second Early Georgian, four bays, brown stone and raised brick window frames, the third late c18. The doorway of this part, however, seems to belong to the second part.

BARCOTE MANOR, ½ m. NE. Brick mansion in the Tudor style, built in 1875. A very irregular composition with many gables. The staircase window makes one think of *Kerr*.

CARSWELL MANOR, 1 m. ENE. The w range contains genuine early c17 work (e.g. mullioned and mullioned and transomed windows), the rest is partly of 1840 but mostly of 1898. Parts of the staircase are early c17, and so is the handsome DOVE-COTE with its four gables.

LOWER BASILDON *see* BASILDON

LUCAS HOSPITAL *see* WOKINGHAM

LUCKLEY *see* WOKINGHAM

LYFORD

ST MARY. Rubble-built. Nave and chancel and timber bell-turret set on strong braced and scissor-braced posts visible inside. In the chancel N and s lancets and one low-side window with pointed-trefoiled head. Lancets also in the nave on the s side. With them goes the N doorway (one continuous chamfer). The upper windows are Perp and indicate a heightening. – PULPIT. Jacobean, with the usual blank arches. In them large stylized tulips. – SCREEN. By the turret-posts. Perp, with single-light divisions; modest. – BENCHES. A few, the ends undecorated.

LYFORD MANOR. Dates 1617 and 1621. Of dark rubble. Gabled, irregular.

HOUSE, NE of the church. Chequer brick, five bays, dated 1717. (LYFORD GRANGE. Edmund Campion was arrested here.)

LYFORD MANOR FARM. Timber-framed. The core a later C16 range of two rooms divided by a wall with two back-to-back fireplaces (cf. Priory, Marcham). S and NW additions of the early C17, staircase addition later C17. (See Spokes and Jope: *B.A.J.*, 1959)

ALMSHOUSES. Brick, three sides of a courtyard. The oldest parts look no older than Georgian.

MACKNEY *see* SOTWELL

MAIDENHEAD

8080

The centre of Maidenhead lies less than a mile W of the bridge across the Thames which connects Berkshire with Buckinghamshire. The Bath Road traffic used it and then, until the Maidenhead by-pass was built, ended in a hopeless jam in the High Street. So the axis of Maidenhead runs E–W. It is not a town of architectural events and what minor events there are lie between the centre and the bridge.

ST ANDREW AND ST MARY MAGDALENE. The church of 1822–5 by *Busby* (of Brighton) has recently been pulled down* and a new church was built in 1964–5. It is by *Lord Mottistone & Paul Paget*, and according to the design‡ in a rather thin and spiky modern style, basically Gothic in outline. – PLATE. Two Flagons, 1629; Chalice and Paten, 1657; Paten, 1725.

ALL SAINTS, All Saints Avenue, Boyne Hill. 1854–7 by *G. E. Street*. The two W bays by *A. E. Street*, 1907–11. Before that time the steeple stood clear and the group was even more remarkable than it is now. It is a group of varied outline and frontages consisting of steeple, church, and gate to a courtyard with parsonage, parsonage stables, schoolmaster's house, and school house. The whole is of brick, the church with stone stripes, the other buildings with vitrified blue brick stripes etc. The style is c.1300 or, as *The Ecclesiologist* wrote in 1854, 'an ornate Geometrical Middle Pointed'. The interior of the

* The old building had been condemned as unsafe by the Diocesan Surveyor.

‡ Seen at the time of writing.

church red and blue brick. The coupled trefoil clerestory windows do not stand above the arches below, but they are symmetrically placed all the same. The E window is set high up. Stone PULPIT and low stone SCREEN. *The Ecclesiologist* summed up: 'We have seldom been more pleased with a design than with the one before us'.

ST JOSEPH (R.C.), Cookham Road. 1884 by *Leonard Stokes*. Brick, flint, and stone. Gothic. Aisleless with transept. Over the S transept a tower with a spike.

ST LUKE, St Luke's Road. 1866–70 by *G. R. Clarke*. Large, rock-faced. Plate tracery. The prominent spire 1894 by *J. O. Scott*. – STAINED GLASS. E window by *O'Connor*, 1871.

ST MARK, St Mark's Road. 1873 by *Charles Cooper*.

ST PAUL, High Town Road. 1887–9 by *E. J. Shrewsbury*. Red brick.

ST PETER, St Peter's Road, off Furze Platt. 1897 by *E. J. Shrewsbury*. Red brick, with a short, embattled SE tower, added only in 1961.

METHODIST CHAPEL, Castle Hill and King Street. 1859. Yellow brick, and rather like a Commissioners' church.

TOWN HALL, St Ives Road. 1960–2, pale red brick and stone. Remarkably large, and in a weak, retardataire neo-Georgian, i.e. what would have been conservative already in 1936. By *North & Partners* with *Sir Hubert Worthington*. – REGALIA. Small silver-gilt Mace, London, 1604; large silver-gilt Mace, London, 1776; Cup, Dublin, c.1775; Cruet, London 1801; silver-gilt Cup, c.1810.

POLICE STATION, Broadway. 1906 by *J. Morris*, the County Surveyor. Very red, i.e. brick and terracotta with typical battered buttresses. Asymmetrical tower (cf. Wokingham). Quite fun.

FREE LIBRARY, opposite the town hall. Small, pretty, in a free Baroque with a cupola. By *Arthur E. McKewan* and *G. H. V. Cole*, 1904.

CLOCK TOWER, King Street. 1897 by *E. J. Shrewsbury*. Brick and stone, fancy Tudor, with a wooden lantern. No architectural merit.

ST MARK'S HOSPITAL, the former WORKHOUSE, 1 m. W. 1836 by *Cooper & Son*.

The only sensible PERAMBULATION is from the corner of King Street and High Street first for a few minutes W to see the villas of c.1840 and then on the way out towards Reading (i.e. in CASTLE HILL and the BATH ROAD) and then E along the

HIGH STREET, where the small-town shopping has suddenly been given a jerk by a group on a large-town scale. Two rows of two-storeyed shopping terraces leading to an eight-storey office block on very high stilts (by *Ian Fraser & Associates*).*

The best houses of Maidenhead are further E in BRIDGE ROAD. First SMYTHS ALMHOUSES of 1659, a row in dark brick, one storey and gabled dormers. Nice coat of arms. To the r. additional ALMSHOUSES, 1895, redder brick and a number of pavilions. Further E a few pretty Georgian brick houses, the best OLDFIELD LODGE, lying back behind a wall with gatepiers decorated by nice paterae. Lodge with pointed windows. Yellow brick house with handsome Venetian doorway and windows. These houses are on the S side. On the N side lying back some 50 yards behind other houses RAY LODGE. Tall and stately, red brick. To the S one-storeyed portico of four wooden Roman-Doric columns with pediment. To the N tall thin Tuscan columns as a colonnade coming forward above the outer stairs to the main entrance. Two-bay pavilions l. and r. Back to the S side, and hideous between these Georgian houses the former SHOWBOAT roadhouse, white and modernistic, of 1932–3 and already a complete period piece. By *E. Norman Bailey* and *D. C. Wadhwa*. Just before the bridge a road leads S to the REITLINGER MUSEUM, formerly OLDFIELD, a typical rich Maidenhead house of *c*.1895. Black and white, extensive and irregular. Further S on the FISHERY ESTATE of the 1880s more such houses. Back and to the BRIDGE, a beautiful piece of 1772–7 designed by *Sir Robert Taylor*. Seven main water-arches with rocky rustication on the voussoirs. Fine balustrade. The bridge cost £19,000. To its S the RAILWAY VIADUCT by *Brunel*, 1837–8. Brick, with two long semi-elliptical arches said to have been the largest brick span ever (128 ft each). It is the bridge which appears in Turner's *Rain, Steam and Speed*.‡

* Since writing this a second high block, eleven storeys, glass and brick ¡nfilling, has gone up in the High Street a little further E, on the site of the old town hall. This is by *Hildebrand & Glicker*.

‡ As the inverted triangle of streets of which the High Street is the base remain intolerably congested by local traffic even after the completion of M4 a plan for central redevelopment was commissioned from Lord Esher of *Brett & Pollen* in 1961. This plan proposes a loop road cutting N from the station across back land W of King Street, and then E along the S edge of Kidwells Park to join the old A4 a little W of Smyth's Almshouses. This will enable the High Street (where pavements are only 4 ft wide) to be cleared of traffic and paved from wall to wall. Pending this improvement, an extension of the shopping centre S on to the back land inside the triangle has already begun,

NORDEN FARM, Altwood Road, s of the Bath Road. The survival of a farm. Behind a screen of black weatherboarded
barns a plain Late Georgian brick house of three bays with a
Tuscan porch. New housing around.

ROBIN HOOD'S ARBOUR, in Maidenhead Thicket, just s of
the road to Stubbings House. The site is a sub-rectangular,
ditched enclosure covering ¾ acre. The area is defended by a
single bank and ditch with a counterscarp on the w and s. A
section cut through the N line of the defences proved the
ditch to be 16 ft wide and 2 ft 9 in. deep. The gap in the w
defences is original, and from it a track led to a sunken paved
stockyard in the interior. The scanty finds included sherds of
Belgic pottery dating from the early C1.

ROMAN VILLA, at Cox Green, between Northumbria Road and
the Maidenhead by-pass. The site was discovered from the
air, and nothing is now visible on the ground, for much of
the area is covered by a housing estate. The villa was excavated in 1959 and shown to have a fairly complex building
history. The earliest structure, built in the early C2, consisted
of a simple rectangular building, 63 ft long and 26 ft wide,
divided into a small living room and a large hall which probably
served both as kitchen and cattle shed. In the mid C2 a
corridor was added to the NE, the original building provided
with further partition walls, and a bath suite built on its
SE end, the whole forming a villa of winged corridor type.
The main feature of the third building phase, which cannot
be precisely dated, was the provision of a greatly elaborated
bath wing. In the final phase, in the late C4, this bath building
was once again simplified. The villa lay within a ditched
enclosure which was probably dug at the same time as the
third building phase of the villa and had silted up during
phase four.

MARCHAM
4090

ALL SAINTS. 1837 by *William Fisher* of Oxford. He used the
C13 w tower (unbuttressed, one-light bell-openings), the N
chapel E wall with its three widely spaced, stepped lancets,
the arch from the N chapel to the chancel with stiff-leaf

with two-storey shops and the two blocks of offices referred to on p. 175. S of
the latter a new central square is to be formed, with a Central Library and
more shops, all served by a large three-decker car park projected into the
centre from the loop road over the top of King Street.

responds, and the Perp S doorway with a continuous frieze of large, individual leaves in one jamb and arch moulding. The vault inside the tower with hollow-chamfered ribs on four face corbels is a Perp addition to the tower too. Otherwise symmetrical arrangement of tall, transomed, straight-headed Perp windows of 1830 proportions. Equally characteristic of 1830 is the interior, one large, wide space. What distinguishes it is the E end, where the chancel and N chapel now appear like twin chancels, their W arches treated identically. – BENCH ENDS. Plain, straight-headed, with linenfold panelling. – PLATE. Elizabethan Cup. – BRASSES to Edmund Fettiplace † 1540 and wife. Kneeling 15 in. figures.

The HOUSE S of the churchyard has some mullioned windows.

MARCHAM PARK (Denman College). Of the early C19. A seven-bay, two-storeyed stone house. The side is of six bays with symmetrically arranged tripartite windows. Stone staircase with wrought-iron balustrade of simple S-shapes.

PRIORY, ½ m. SE. An oblong range with mullioned and mullioned and transomed windows with arched – lights C16 no doubt, and according to external appearance first half, though Messrs Spokes and Jope prefer c.1570. The doorway moulding, however, is of a Dec type. Inside, the wall through which lead the two doorways to the former offices. The hall is divided into two rooms by a fireplace opening into both. Next to this in the far room is a spiral staircase.

MARLSTON

5070

CHURCH. Mostly by *Butterfield*, 1855. Nave and chancel, bell-turret with shingled spire. Lancets and Dec windows. Of the medieval church the N doorway of c.1200. One order of shafts with scallop capitals. Arch with a slight chamfer and a roll moulding. The S doorway, heavily pointed-trefoiled, is Butterfield's. – PILLAR PISCINA. Norman, with decorated scallops. – STAINED GLASS. E window by *Kempe*, 1901.

MARLSTON HOUSE (Brockhurst School). By *Edward Burgess*, 1895–9, for the Palmers of Reading. Large, of brick with stone dressings. Rib-vaulted octagonal porch, big Elizabethan hall window to its l. The garden side with four gables and three canted bay windows in a very odd, very deliberate, syncopated rhythm. In the hall very high overmantel, with elongated pilasters and caryatids yet higher up.

MEMBURY CAMP *see* LAMBOURN

5060

MIDGHAM

St Matthew. From the Bath road it seems to lie on the hill
   entirely on its own. 1869 by *John Johnson*. Flint; nave, chancel,
   N chapel, and a SW spire. The interior sumptuous with
   polished granite piers, one exceeding fat to help support the
   tower. Roof on brackets with faces, chancel arch with angels.
   And so on. A two-light window opens into the organ chamber.
   The carving was done by *Farmer & Brindley* (BC). – STAINED
   GLASS. E window *Ward & Hughes* (BC); nothing to commend
   it. – PLATE. Paten hallmarked 1531, with the Vernicle.

4090

MILTON

St Blaise. Unbuttressed W tower with an unmoulded round
   arch to the nave, called C18 by the VCH. Nave, N aisle, and
   chancel almost entirely by *Woodyer*, 1849–51. The chancel
   higher than the nave and more ornate. Strange coal-hole
   composition. – STAINED GLASS. Fragments of old glass in
   several windows. – E window by *O'Connor*, 1851. – PLATE.
   Plate, London, 1679; Cup, London, 1765.

Milton House. The C17 centre is most interesting. What is
   its date? 1660? 1670? Can it be much later? It is called
   newly built in 1696. Five bays, a high three storeys, brick of
   not specially careful quality. Giant pilasters above ground-
   floor pilaster strips. The giant pilasters have Ionic capitals
   and waistbands; which turn out to be raised panels with
   fleurs-de-lis. Odd flat raised upper quoins. The garden side
   identical with the entrance side. Short wings of 1776 by
   Stephen Wright, with oblong projections in the middle on the
   entrance side, canted on the garden side. Nice one-storey
   offices. Inside, one room has a plaster ceiling of the time of
   the house. Panels with wreaths, round and oval, in a very
   satisfying pattern, of Inigo Jones derivation. Oak and laurel.
   Original and equally characteristic one chimneypiece with two
   rustic maidens with cornucopias in the overmantel and thick,
   compact garlands l. and r. of the fireplace. It may be by
   William Bird (cf. Pusey). The chimneypiece in the room with
   the plaster ceiling is late C18 with a splendid Kentian overmantel of *c.*1740. Also original the staircase through all floors
   with sturdy turned balusters. In the l. wing the library and
52a the chapel, both Gothick, and the library quite delicious –
   absolutely complete with fireplace, bookcases, and window
   decoration, including odd pendants. The chapel is plainer.

Thin-ribbed ceiling with pendants. In the windows STAINED GLASS, the side windows Netherlandish C16, the altar windows English late C14 bits and pieces from Steventon village. The glass was put in in 1772. – VESTMENTS. Bishop Challoner's vestments of 1760 are preserved in the house.

MONKEY ISLAND
⅞ m. SE of Bray

9070

Access by way of a suspension footbridge. On the island a hotel and a house. They were the third Duke of Marlborough's fishing lodge and pavilion and were built *c.*1744. He owned the estate of Whiteknights outside Reading. The fishing lodge has rusticated walls (of wood?). In the centre is a raised octagon with lunette windows and a room in front of it with a canted bay window. In this room paintings of monkeys fishing, shooting, etc., by the monkey specialist *Clermont*. The house, known as the Temple, has a r. part of three bays with rusticated ground floor with giant columns above with a large Venetian window. The ground floor was originally open where there are now arches. (Inside lively stucco decoration of Neptune, sea deities, etc.) Added on the l. a plain lower five-bay house.

MORTIMER COMMON *see* STRATFIELD
MORTIMER

MOULSFORD

5080

ST JOHN BAPTIST. By *Sir G. G. Scott,* 1846.* Small, by the Thames. With a bell-turret with shingled broach spire. The N arcade, low, with arches dying into the octagonal piers, looks late C19, but no work at that time is recorded. – PLATE. Chalice of 1774.

OLD VICARAGE. At the time of writing in the course of conversion into an Old People's Home. The architect is *H. A. J. Darlow.*

FAIRMILE HOSPITAL, *see* Cholsey.

NEWBURY

4060

Leland calls Newbury one of the three most important cloth towns in Berkshire, the others being Reading and Abingdon. The climax of the trade is marked by the life and the riches of John Smallwood, alias John of Winchcombe, alias Jack of Newbury.

* According to the VCH. His fee was £64.

He lived around the year 1520, and a fanciful C17 chronicle of his life tells us of his two hundred looms and the two hundred men, the two hundred pretty boys, the two hundred maidens and hundred women who worked for him. Nor was he the only wealthy clothier. We hear of others including the Dolmans, and under Queen Elizabeth Thomas Dolman was the – apparently much envied – leader of the trade (*see* Shaw House, p. 213). In the C17 and C18 the national importance of Newbury may have decreased, but local prosperity does not seem to have suffered much. Newbury in any case had the additional advantages of a situation on the Bath Road. The plan of the town clearly expresses this dual situation. The town itself has as its spine the s–n streets s and n of the river Kennet, but at the very n end the Bath Road crosses from e to w.

6 ST NICHOLAS. The church is the great monument of the wealth of Newbury in the Late Middle Ages. It is a Perp church throughout, large, ashlar-faced, and the work of one generation. It was built c.1500–32, the nave at the expense of John Smallwood. The church is embattled throughout. The w tower has massive polygonal buttresses and big pinnacles with their own battlements and pinnacles. On it a date 1532. The windows are of four to six lights and of three lights in the clerestory. The arcades have five bays, and the piers are of a variety of the standard section of four shafts and four hollows in which the shafts towards nave and aisle are trebled. Only one pier, the second from the e on the n side, is different. It has a wave moulding instead of the plain hollow and a capital band all round instead of capitals only for the shafts. The chancel arch and the pretty chancel roof are of 1858 (*Woodyer*). The nave roof is Perp and has the initials of John Smallwood. – PULPIT. Unusual and quite splendid. Above the familiar blank arches square panels with thick leaf frames. The pulpit was presented in 1607. – GATES to the chancel. Low, of iron, 1704. – STAINED GLASS. All by *Hardman*, designed by *Powell* and *Maycock* (BC). Not good. – MONUMENTS. Brasses to John Smallwood † 1519 and wife, 27 in. figures. – Griffith Curteys † 1587. With kneeling figures under arches (chancel s, outside). – Many tablets in the church. – CURIOSUM. Charity Boy, painted on board and cut out. He comes from a school founded before 1713.

From the street the churchyard is entered by two very pretty Gothick archways. It is likely that they are connected with a payment to *Fuller White* in 1770.

St George, Wash Common, Andover Road. The old church humble red brick, the new Italian in taste, white, pantile-roofed. Tunnel-vault with penetrations. By *F. C. Eden*, 1933 etc. The w end is not yet built.

St John, Newtown Road. 1955–7. By *S. E. Dykes-Bower*. Red brick, large, in a kind of neo-Romanesque, neither period nor modern.

St Joseph and the Sacred Heart (R.C.), London Road. The old, small, featureless red brick church of 1864 stands by the side of the new, large, inappropriately Early Christian or Byzantine or Italian Romanesque, equally red church with its separate high campanile. Only the top of the campanile goes a kind of free Renaissance. The church has a semicircular porch with green marble columns and inside the area round the altar space developed in the Byzantine way of the inscribed cross, i.e. a groin-vaulted crossing, high, short chancel and transept bays, and lower corner features with balconies. Central altar; canopy on marble columns. The church is of 1923–8 by *W. C. Mangan*.

St Mary, Speenhamland, London Road. In 1876–9 *Street* added the present chancel to a church of 1830. In 1911 etc. *A. E. Street*, the son, replaced the church by a new and larger one. No tower. Ashlar facing. Geometrical tracery. Imitation Perp piers inside. The best thing about the church is the chancel decoration. This was done by *Burlison & Grylls* in memory of someone who died in 1884 (BC).

Methodist Church, Northbrook Street. 1837–8. Stone-built, in the lancet style.

Town Hall, Market Place. 1876–81 by *James H. Money* (BC). He imitates Waterhouse. Blue and red brick, a tower on the l., a much higher one on the r., differing in a characteristically Victorian way. The peculiar hardness of it all is very similar to Waterhouse's.* The building cost was estimated at a mere £4,345 (GS).

Museum, Wharf Road. The most interesting house in Newbury. Built in 1626–7. Commonly called the Cloth Hall, but it was built (with money left by John Kendrick of Reading) as a municipal cloth-weaving workshop to give employment to the poor. Three wings were intended, but only one was built. Timber-framed, the ground floor with six columns carrying segmental arches, each with a pendant. One would

* PLATE. Two silver-gilt Maces, one C17, the other 'somewhat later' (VCH).

assume that they were originally open, but the doorway to the W is original with its straight hood on brackets. Massive overhang. Top gables. The building is continued to the E by the so-called CORN STORE, a long timber-framed building with an outer upper gallery. Originally the Kennet wharf was close to it. This extremely interesting structure has been ruined by the town, which put a snack-bar and other shops and offices in, all in connexion with the messy bus-station-cum-car-park in front of it. What is the date of the Corn Store? Mr R. Neville Hadcock suggests c.1660–80.

GRAMMAR SCHOOL, Enmore Road. 1885 by *Power & Hughes*. Red brick, nearly symmetrical. Tudor.

58b ST NICHOLAS SCHOOL, Enmore Road. 1859 by *Butterfield*, and as original and aggressive a job as any of his. The school stands at a corner and has a tower there. This tower is set back from the two ranges between which it stands and has moreover canted sides. On top of that the upper windows towards Enmore Road are dormers under four shark-teeth-sharp gables.

CORN EXCHANGE, Market Place. 1861–2 by *J. S. Dodd* (BC). Stone, restrainedly Italianate. Three bays, with pairs of giant pilasters, only the angle ones differing from the others. Pediment all across. Arched windows.

FALKLAND MONUMENT, Andover Road. 1878. Granite obelisk on a high base, with minor Gothic details below.

PERAMBULATION. We start in the Market Place, which is of Victorian interest chiefly and of minor interest at that. Apart from the Town Hall and the Corn Exchange the principal building is the WESTMINSTER BANK. Broad and stone-faced along the N side. It is of 1864, by *J. Chancellor*, and was to cost £3,653 (GS). The style is that at the time called Italian Gothic. To the E of this, in WHARF ROAD, No. 5 is the first of many Early Georgian houses to come: red brick, five bays, three storeys, segment-headed windows, parapet with one blank lunette in the middle. Later doorcase.

First S, along CHEAP STREET, with little to see. Nos 33–4 keep the bargeboards to the gables, dated 1679. The ST MARY'S ALMSHOUSES of 1864 are poor-man's Gothic. No. 8 has a straight hood on carved brackets above its side entrance.

From the S end of Cheap Street W by Station Road and then a little S or by St John's Road and then a little N to an interesting corner. On the E side of NEWTOWN ROAD, facing a green, RAYMONDS BUILDINGS, or Lower Raymonds Buildings, dated 1796, a long range of plain, classical almshouses. Twenty-five bays, two storeys, pedimental gable in the centre. Across the street, just s of the new Christian Science church, UPPER RAYMONDS BUILDINGS, 1826 and Gothic. Straight-headed two-light windows, and in the raised middle a giant arch. To the immediate E of this range of almshouses, in ARGYLE ROAD, is a remarkable group of buildings. At the N end of the short street on the E side is a high Early Victorian house attached to which, with its E end on Newtown Road, is the LITTEN CHAPEL, a small Perp chapel with two small genuine Perp windows and an original roof. The E end is cut off by the road. The chapel is said to have been connected with the Hospital of St Bartholomew and later served as the Grammar School. It has a handsome roof with collar-beams, queen-posts, and wind-braces. In Argyle Road itself ST BARTHOLOMEW'S HOSPITAL, a U-shaped brick building of two storeys with a hipped roof. It dates from 1618, but the windows have mullion and transom crosses, and this looks later C17 and could go with the date 1698 on the cupola. Opposite BARTHOLOMEW MANOR HOUSE (with a front of 1927–8, but the building behind medieval, Tudor, and Queen Anne, including e.g. an Early Tudor chimneypiece opposite the porch. The building may have been farm buildings originally, was made into a house in the C16, and became Raymond's Almshouses in 1676). The similar-looking house next to it is all restoration.

N of Argyle Road runs BARTHOLOMEW STREET towards the N, the Kennet, the town hall, and, in its N continuation, ultimately to the Bath Road. In Bartholomew Street the EIGHT BELLS, C16, one-storeyed, with three gables. Gothick window details. No. 28, much renewed, is of six bays, Early Georgian, with a pretty doorway (a staircase with twisted balusters and a room with nice late C18 stucco and chimneypiece; NBR). By the bridge, a good finish, a house with a broad, shallow canted bay window and the main windows with semi-elliptical heads. Opposite opens WEST MILLS, running along the side of the parish church. Here ST NICHOLAS HOUSE, Early Georgian, five bays, with semi-elliptical window heads, aprons below the windows, a parapet with arched panels, and a doorway with a pediment on carved brackets. Staircase with one twisted, one fluted, one plain baluster to each step. To its W a house with a porch on Tuscan columns and a frieze with decorated metopes. The HUNT ALMSHOUSES of 1729, rebuilt in 1817, are quite plain, but have a blank oval on the front. Then on the other side the good group of the MILL and after that No. 22, early C18, low, brick, with a big moulded brick frieze above the ground floor, and Nos 23–29, C17 cottages, called The Old Weavers' House.

Back and across the BRIDGE (one arch, balustrade) and into Northbrook Street, but first into NORTHCROFT LANE for the humbly Gothic three-bay CHILDS ALMSHOUSES of 1821. In NORTHBROOK STREET the best C18 houses of Newbury. It must have been a swagger street before shops invaded it and traffic killed it stone-dead. Nos 91–92, on the W side, is the most ambitious house, brick, seven bays, three storeys, giant pilasters, parapet – i.e. Early Georgian. Then on the other side No. 8, dated 1669, also brick, and very typical of its date in the articulation by pilasters for each floor. Two top gables. Staircase balusters a transition from the Jacobean to the dumb-bell shape. Nos 13–14 (Woolworth) is again Early Georgian, but quite plain. Nos 23–24 is timber-framed with brick nogging, as is visible along the N side. It is called Jack of Newbury's house, and it may indeed have been his. Inside an original roof with tie-beams, queen-posts, and windbraces. No. 26 is of four bays, later C18, with pilasters framing the two middle bays. No. 61, on the other side, has a particularly pretty Adamish doorcase. Then, opposite, the former LITERARY INSTITUTION, dated 1834, stone, with Soanian incised ornament above, but details on the ground floor which tend to get a little looser. No. 24 is dated 1724. It is quite small but uncommonly ornate. Three bays, Composite pilasters on the upper floor and a Venetian window. Cypher and date. The parapet rises in the centre to a segmental shape. Northbrook Street continues as BROADWAY, and here no more needs attention than the Georgian shop front of No. 19. At the top of Broadway is the CLOCK TOWER, with a colonnaded base like a market cross. It dates from 1929.

The clock tower marks the place where Newbury meets the Bath Road. Along this wealthy houses also spread already early in the C18. First E, that is in LONDON ROAD. No. 40 has a flat Gothic three-bay front with battlements. The doorway has an ogee arch and thin tripartite shafts, the windows are straight-headed. Then, at r. angles to the road, a threebay house with blue brick headers and red brick dressings and an arched middle window, and, forming an L with this,

DOWER HOUSE, early C18, very massive, of seven bays and three storeys, with the angle pairs of bays raised to a fourth floor and given pediments. These parts are red brick, the centre three bays blue and red with segment-headed windows. Plain doorway. The house was an inn originally. It is abandoned at the time of writing but ought to be preserved. Nothing after that.

Back to the clock tower and now E. In OXFORD STREET on the N side, hidden behind houses, the former THEATRE of 1802. On the S side No. 27, once more Early Georgian, five bays, segment-headed windows, but round-arched ground-floor windows and mid-window, and, a little further on, THE HIGH HOUSE, Late Georgian, of three storeys. Opposite is No. 2 BATH ROAD, a very fine house of five bays, blue and red, with strong angle pilasters, a three-bay pediment, and again segment-headed windows. The house has a date 1720 on the roof. The porch with Roman Doric columns and a pediment is later. SPEEN COURT, mid C18, blue headers and red dressings and with angle pilasters, was quite grand too, but has been spoiled by additions. GOLDWELL also mid C18, and also altered. It has its brick quoins, however, and the banded brick rustication of the ground floor. CASTLE HOUSES, Early Georgian, is not attractive to look at now. SPEEN HILL HOUSE is early C19, of three bays, with a porch, rendered. A fine cedar tree in the garden. After that the road passes on into Speen (see p. 224).

One outer item. In TYDEHAMS, off the Andover Road, two Early Modern houses, THE HAVEN, by *Thomas Tait*, 1929, a very early date for England, and SHEPHERDS, by *Pakington & Enthoven*, of 1934. It is typical that The Haven is still symmetrical, Shepherds is not. The source of the first is blatantly Peter Behrens's house of 1926 at Northampton, of the second Le Corbusier as broadcast in England by Connell, Ward & Lucas.

ROUND BARROW CEMETERY, on Wash Common. Three mounds here have the appearance of being Bronze Age bowl barrows, though since the mid C18 they have been thought to cover the remains of those killed in the battle of Newbury in 1643. The largest mound, in the side of the copse, is 120 ft in diameter and 9 ft high. The two smaller ones are surmounted by memorial stones to the victims of the battle.

NEW HALL see FINCHAMPSTEAD

NINE MILE RIDE see HEATHLAND

NOKE'S TOMB *see* BASILDON

NORTH HINKSEY

The part by the church is still villagey, in spite of all the Oxford development around.

ST LAWRENCE. A Norman church, Norman the s doorway with one order of columns, scallop capitals and many zigzags in the arch, Norman the blocked N doorway and two N windows, Norman a re-set chancel s window. The chancel arch also seems Norman, but it is in fact by *John Macduff Derick* (BC). The W tower, short and unbuttressed, looks Norman too, but is in fact E.E., as shown by the W lancet. In the nave s wall a Dec window with a triangular head and lozenge tracery (cf. Cumnor and Theale). – FONT. Octagonal, of the pattern-book type, i.e. with eight different tracery designs, including reticulation. They are all Dec except for one, which is on the way to Perp. – PLATE. Cup and Cover, 1582; Paten, inscribed 1681. – MONUMENT. William Fynmere † 1677. Tablet with oval centre, garlands, etc., and two putti at the top. Probably by *William Bird* (cf. Pusey). – In the churchyard CROSS with the shaft still complete.

In the village Cottage No. 9 is symmetrical with one mullioned window l. and r. of the doorway, probably late C17.

One field SW of the Southern By-pass opposite the SW exit of the village street is the CONDUIT, dated 1634 on a buttress, but built in 1616–17 to supply water to the conduit house at Carfax (now in Nuneham Park). The conduit was given by Otho Nicholson, and the water passes below the river. Square, *c.*18 ft long, ashlar-faced with a pitched roof.

WESTMINSTER COLLEGE. By *Seely & Paget*, 1957–9. A large composition in grey brick and buff stone, in a mildly blocky neo-Georgian. The centre is the chapel with a white weatherboarded gable and bell-turret looking as if it had come straight from Connecticut. Below the chapel the library. If one considers the date of the design, it is surprising that the architects should have been happy in the tradition of C19 historicism, but it is more surprising that the client, an educational body, should not have insisted on something of this century. The large STATUE looking towards Oxford is by *John Matthews*.

NORTH MORETON

ALL SAINTS. A voussoir stone (?) with beakhead decoration on a window ledge and the round s arcade piers are all that remains of the Norman church. The present church is mostly mid C13 to earliest C14. There are first the s arcade arches, double-chamfered, the chancel arch which corresponds, and the s chapel arcade of two bays, where the arches are hollow-chamfered. The w respond of this arcade is a three-quarter column and has a rich stiff-leaf capital. The s respond of the arch into the chapel also has stiff-leaf, and it looks as if some re-using had here taken place. This s chapel was then re-modelled and perhaps lengthened and widened. This may be connected with the foundation of a chantry in the church in 1299. To this date clearly belongs the large E window of a rare but not unique type: five lights, with, as its tracery, arches upon arches, diminishing to four, three, two, and filled by trefoils or quatrefoils (cf. e.g. the Wells Lady Chapel). The w window of the chapel, which is higher than the nave, has the same type of window reduced to three lights. Pretty frieze at the top outside with beasties. Angle PISCINA with ogee arches which otherwise are missing. Ballflower as well, which also occurs on two image corbels l. and r. of the E window. The chancel windows are late C13 too, see the Y-tracery and the details of the E window of three stepped pointed-trefoiled lights; Dec windows in the s aisle and the nave wall. Perp w tower of enormous stones. Pierced quatrefoil parapet. The arch to the nave with concave-sided responds. – STAINED GLASS. In the s chapel E window about the best glass in 18a Berkshire. It is contemporary with the window and the chapel to which it belongs. The dominant colours are yellow, green, and brown. There are fifteen scenes altogether, and elaborate canopies. The scenes are from the lives of Christ (centre light), the Virgin (s light), and St Nicholas, St Peter, and St Paul. – Fragments also in the nave N and s aisle s.

Several worthwhile timber-framed houses, the most attractive COBBS COTTAGE with two gables and an oriel under one of them.

OAKLEY GREEN see DOWN PLACE

OCKWELLS MANOR HOUSE
¾ m. WSW of Bray
8070

Ockwells Manor, built by Sir John Norreys some time between 1446 and 1466, is the most refined and the most sophisti-cated timber-framed mansion in England. It is true that its

perfection is partly due to the C20 restoration by *Fairfax Wade*,
but the façade, i.e. the E side, is in fact largely original. The
near-symmetry, but not-quite-symmetry, is certainly as it was
devised in the C15. The façade has two main gables over the
wide end bays, the l. one a little larger than the r., two minor
gables, of about the same size, but the l. one, belonging to the
porch, coming a little further forward than the other, which
represents the hall bay window, and the even hall windows,
one band (five plus five) of them, between the minor gables.
So the plan of the house seems the standard manor-house
plan and perfectly clear in the façade, clearer in fact than it
will turn out to be when one studies the interior. The hall
windows with plain arched lights are intact, the more playfully detailed windows belonging to the gabled bays are mostly
of the restoration, but the lacy bargeboards are again in fairly
genuine condition. To return to the anomaly of the plan
already referred to, the standard arrangement would be that
chamber and solar are to the r. of the hall, pantry, buttery,
and kitchen to the l. The former is the case at Ockwells, but
the kitchen and the buttery and pantry are in a separate W
range separated from the front range by a small courtyard.
The house originally had a chapel which came forward from
the SE angle of the façade. All that remains of it is a brick
wall with some plain windows and two doorways. The W and
S sides of the house are also brick, not half-timber. The NE
range is C19 or C20.

From the porch the HALL is entered through a doorway
the spandrels of which are carved with a griffin and an antelope. In the hall the screen is plain. The hall has an open
timber roof with collar-beams, arched braces, and one tier of
wind-braces. The roof rests on moulded posts, and the braces
are moulded too. Big stone chimneypiece. In the windows a
famous set of armorial STAINED GLASS, eighteen shields in
all. Behind the hall is the courtyard. The exit from the screens
passage leads into a dog-leg CLOISTER which runs along the
S and W sides of the courtyard and has uncusped arched
lights. The function of the cloister is to connect the screens
passage with pantry, buttery, and kitchen. Of this arrangement the most telling witness is now a serving hatch as big as
those at Hampton Court and with iron hinges. No satisfactory
explanation has yet been given for the shifting of the offices
from their customary position, nor is it known where the two
doorways in the S wall of the hall led.

In the room with the hatch is a chimneypiece with the date 1673, but judging by its style clearly of c.1550. The WEST PARLOUR has an Elizabethan chimneypiece with caryatids and a Spanish gold and red leather wall covering. A simpler Elizabethan chimneypiece with pilasters to the overmantel in the chamber beyond the high-table end of the hall. Jacobean STAIRCASE and yet another, simpler, Elizabethan chimneypiece in the solar.

To the E of the former chapel is a GATEWAY with a room above whose wooden window has tracery, and beyond the gateway is a BARN, of the same time as the house and also timber-framed. Near by a circular brick DOVECOTE with buttresses.

OLD WINDSOR

9070

Excavations at Kingsbury carried out in the last ten years have revealed the site and many details of the Anglo-Saxon and Norman town.

ST PETER. A C13 flint church by the river Thames. w tower with lancets, doorway, and tower arch with slight chamfers. The same slight chamfers for the s doorway and the chancel doorway. One genuine lancet in the chancel too. Handsome C14 nave windows, straight-headed. *Scott* restored the church in 1863–4, and his are the fine big shingled broach spire and the substantial timber porch. – FONT. Octagonal, Perp, recent. – PAINTINGS. Some original C13 ornamental painting in the chancel, more in the same style, but of the Scott time. – STAINED GLASS. Medieval bits in several windows. – s aisle one by *Kempe*. – PLATE. Set of 1701; Chalice and Paten 1750. – MONUMENTS. Mrs Sheridan † 1817, *Coade* stone; in the churchyard, s of the church. – Charles A. Murray † 1895. Recess with tomb-chest and recumbent effigy. Two members of the family upright against the back wall.

BEAUMONT COLLEGE. The Society of Jesus bought the estate in 1854 for its novices. The school was established in 1861. It started with Beaumont Lodge as its building, a house designed by *Henry Emlyn* of Windsor and built in 1790. It is of nine bays with a recessed giant portico and would be a Georgian mansion like many others, if it had not been for Emlyn's ill-advised invention of, and plea for, an 'English order' incorporating the Star of the Garter. That alone, if for example confined to the capitals, might have been innocuous, but Emlyn's idea was to couple columns, let them grow out of one painful squashed common lower part, and hide the place of the splitting by the Garter Star. Alas right at the top the columns remember again that they are Siamese twins and share one pair of volutes in the capital. Good staircase round an apsed space with an iron handrail. The range to the r. of the mansion is of 1865 and may be by *Hansom*. The range was extended to the E in 1870, also probably by Hansom. The CHAPEL was designed by Hansom in 1870. But the mural decoration in a highly surprising Raphael style, i.e. with 'grottesche' of the Pompeian and the Vatican loggie kind, is by *Bentley*, 1873–6. In the same years he did the high altar, reredos, tabernacle, and throne. The HIGH ALTAR is a ciborium with two angels, the REREDOS is in the Venetian Renaissance style with five painted saints, but also little pediments and garlands.* The room is tunnel-vaulted and articulated by pilasters. Penetrations in the vault. In 1884 *Bentley* enlarged the chapel by a low N aisle. Piers and segmental arches dying into them and the segmental aisle vault glazed in the centre of each bay.

ST JOHN'S (Beaumont College Preparatory School). By *Bentley*, 1888. Brick and yellow stone. French Renaissance. A symmetrical front with, l. and r. of the entrance, two short polygonal turrets and, on top, a white lantern turret. Gabled angle pavilions. On the l. the chapel projects, with Perp windows and a small turret on the side away from the façade. On the r. at an obtuse angle the kitchens and infirmary. The back is rather more Georgian in style.

OLD WINDSOR HOSPITAL, the former WORKHOUSE. 1835 by *Scott & Moffatt*. Not classical; already Tudor. Red brick with diapers. Gables and dormers. A symmetrical composition with a raised three-bay centre, two canted bay windows, and a cupola.

(THE PRIORY contains a small octagonal room in which a date 1762 has recently been found. This belongs to the conversions carried out for Dicky Bateman, as Horace Walpole calls him, by *J. H. Muntz*.)

6060   PADWORTH

Church and house close together.

ST JOHN BAPTIST. Nave and apsed chancel, timber bell-turret. Roughcast. Entirely Norman. N and s doorways with decorated colonnettes and arches and also capitals with leaves

---

* The wing to the l. of the house of 1790 is by *Adrian G. Scott*, 1937.

and with volutes. The chancel arch quite grand in its proportions, tall, and again with busy leaf capitals. – COMMUNION
RAIL. C17. – (PAINTING. On the E wall of the nave traces of
a large St Nicholas with the miracle of the three boys below.
Also, on the r. of the saint a recumbent figure.) – STAINED
GLASS. In the apse by *Kempe*, 1891. – PLATE. Cup and Cover,
1664; Cup, 1742. – MONUMENTS. Mrs Loftus Brightwell
† 1711, standing monument with a big base and two putti l.
and r. of a coat of arms on the top. – Christopher Griffith
† 1776. Signed by *J. Wilton*. Large female figure bending over
an urn with a portrait medallion.

PADWORTH HOUSE. Built *c*.1769 by *J. Hobcraft*. Cemented
brick. To the S seven-bay centre with lower three-bay wings,
to the N nine and five bays respectively. The centre of the
centre is pedimented on both sides. Doorway with Tuscan
columns on the S, Ionic columns on the N side. Triangular and
segmental pediments respectively. Plasterwork by *Joseph
Rose*, especially the principal saloon and the entrance hall.
In this the staircase runs up in three flights, the second right
above the doorway. Very elegant stucco panels. The top
landing carried on Roman Doric columns and itself with
Adamish columns. The space below the landing is groin-
vaulted; so is the landing itself. Good fireplace in the saloon.
A Gothick fireplace comes from the fishing lodge.

FISHING LODGE, ½ m. N. A charming Gothick façade with an
ogee-headed doorway between two niches and an embattled
gable.

HOUSE, Padworth Common. By *Raymond Lockyer*, 1961. Well
planned; modest appearance. The house cost just over £4,000.

GRIM'S BANK, *see* Aldermaston.

PANGBOURNE

607

ST JAMES. Brick tower with brick quoins. That fits the year
when it was built: 1718. The battlements have stone angles.
The church is of 1866, by *J. Woodman*. It is a spacious
building with Late Geometrical to Dec tracery, and the
strictly naturalistic capitals and the two-bay arcade to the
organ chamber the Victorians liked so much. – PULPIT.
Jacobean, with large blank arches and much arabesque work.
– PLATE. Cup, 1677; Flagon, 1692; Paten, 1698; Cup, 1737. –
MONUMENTS. Sir John Davis † 1625. Large, of grey stone,
three recumbent effigies, coupled Tuscan columns l. and r.
and a pediment. – Three daughters of Sir John Suckling

† 1658–61. Remarkably reticent and classical. Black and white marble tablet with an open segmental pediment.

By the w end of the church stands CHURCH COTTAGE by *Stokes*, *c.*1900. A little to the E of the church is THE SQUARE. Here, and along the bit of Whitchurch Road to the railway arch, a group of houses and shops also by *Stokes*, *c.*1900, a nice quiet, yet varied composition. Grey headers and red brick the r. building, roughcast the l.

Again by *Stokes* at the start of SHOOTER'S HILL, i.e. the Oxford road, a big house of 1898, the symmetrical façade with a bold upper overhang carried on two bay windows. Gables above and small Venetian windows in them; this also a happy composition. Further along Shooter's Hill a sequence of more run-of-the-mill Late Victorian houses, locally known as the Seven Deadly Sins.

PANGBOURNE TOWER (Nautical College), 1¼ m. SW. By *Sir John Belcher*, 1897–8. A very ambitious mansion, in a very free William and Mary style. Red brick, but the top of the high, massive porch tower on the entrance side of stone. The garden side is symmetrical, with a slightly recessed centre and outside the wings two lower porch bays with ogee caps. Above the centre of this façade appears a piece of balustrading and a belvedere cupola. Behind the whole of the recessed centre is one long room and behind that, i.e. along the entrance side, runs a gallery with a middle bay window. The doors to the gallery in its ends are of onyx.

E of the college DAVOLI, a new house by *K. G. A. Feakes*, very good in the new architectural idiom of the 1960s: two mono-pitches rising and defeated in their rise by two steep square chimneys of differing height.

PORT JACKSON, Lower Bowden, 1¼ m. WSW. By *Arnold Mitchell*, 1901. Brick and tile-hanging, asymmetrical and gabled.

BERE COURT, 1½ m. SW. Early Georgian, brick, of seven bays. Doorway with Tuscan columns and a triglyph frieze. The window above it round-arched. Entrance hall with charming stucco decoration. Three arches at the far end. Staircase starting in one arm and returning in two. Rather heavy cast-iron balustrade.

7080

PARK PLACE
1⅜ m. SSE of Remenham church

The present house is by *Thomas Cundy*, 1870, in a rather dreary French Renaissance with a tower over one corner of the façade. Pavilion roofs. This house takes the place of that of

(a) *Scenery:* Maidenhead, river Thames

(b) *Scenery:* Finchampstead Ridges

I

Scenery: Combe Gibbet

(a) *Prehistory:* Ashbury, Wayland's Smithy (long barrow and chambered tomb)

(b) *Prehistory:* Uffington, White Horse, first century B.C. (?)

(b) *Church Exteriors*: Windsor Castle, porch into the cloister, c. 1350

(a) *Church Exteriors*: Warfield church, east window, Decorated

4

Church Exteriors: Windsor Castle, St George's Chapel, begun 1475

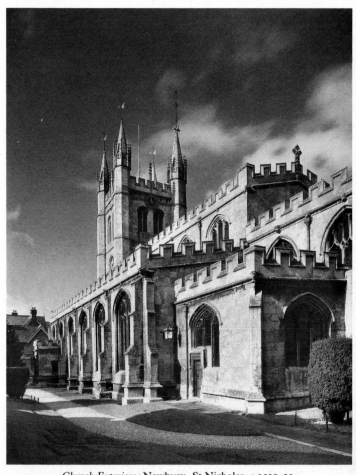

Church Exteriors: Newbury, St Nicholas, *c.*1500–32

Church Exteriors: Sunningwell, west porch, c.1560–70

(a) *Church Exteriors*: Ruscombe,
south aisle, 1638–9

(b) *Church Exteriors*: Uffington,
transept east windows, 1677–9(?)

8

(b) *Church Towers*: Hungerford,
by John Pinch, 1816

(a) *Church Towers*: Wallingford, St Peter,
spire by Sir Robert Taylor, 1777

9

Church Interiors: Windsor Castle, St George's Chapel, begun 1475

(a) *Church Interiors:* Abingdon, St Helen, fifteenth and sixteenth centuries

(b) *Church Interiors:* Shrivenham, 1638

Church Interiors: Windsor Castle, chapel (demolished), by Hugh May, 1684–6

Anglo-Saxon Doorway: Coleshill, Strattenborough Castle Farm, tympanum, eleventh century

(a) *Norman Doorway:* Charney Bassett, south doorway, tympanum,
eleventh century

(b) *Church Furnishings:* Avington, font, twelfth century

14

Church Furnishings: Hampstead Norris, relief of a knight on horseback,
late thirteenth century

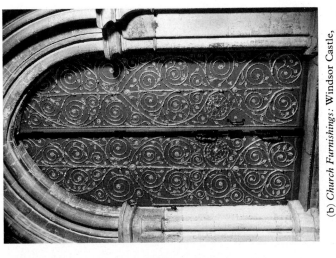

(b) *Church Furnishings*: Windsor Castle, St George's Chapel, door of Henry III's Chapel, by Gilebertus, mid thirteenth century

(a) *Church Furnishings*: Uffington, south door, thirteenth century

16

(b) *Church Furnishings*: Long Wittenham, piscina-monument, late thirteenth century

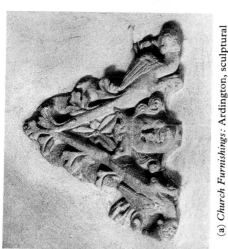

(a) *Church Furnishings*: Ardington, sculptural fragment, late thirteenth century

(b) *Church Furnishings*: Warfield,
screen and rood loft, fifteenth century

(a) *Church Furnishings*: North Moreton,
stained glass, c.1300

18

Church Furnishings: Windsor Castle, St George's Chapel, choir stalls, mainly by William Berkeley, 1478–85

(a) *Church Furnishings:* Abingdon, St Helen,
painted ceiling in north aisle, *c.*1390

(b) *Church Furnishings:* Littlewick Green, Adoration of the Magi,
North Italian, early fifteenth century

(a) and (b) *Church Furnishings:* Windsor Castle, St George's Chapel,
west window, stained glass, early sixteenth century

(a) *Church Furnishings:* Stanford-in-the-Vale, wooden font and cover, early seventeenth century

(b) *Church Furnishings:* Binfield, hourglass stand, seventeenth century

Church Furnishings: Stratfield Mortimer, St John, Christ at Emmaus,
by N. H. J. Westlake

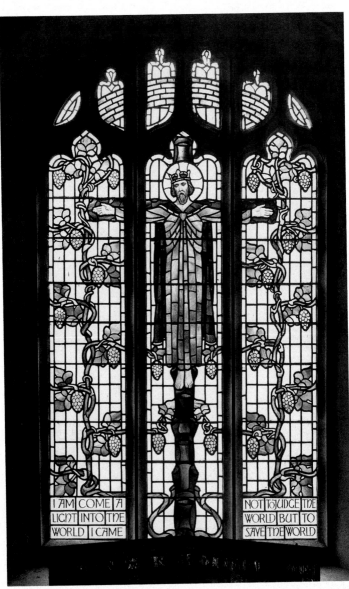

Church Furnishings: Longworth, stained glass by Heywood Sumner, 1900

The text within the stained glass reads:

I AM COME A LIGHT INTO THE WORLD I CAME

NOT TO JUDGE THE WORLD BUT TO SAVE THE WORLD

(a) *Church Monuments:* Aldworth, members of the de la Beche family, early fourteenth century

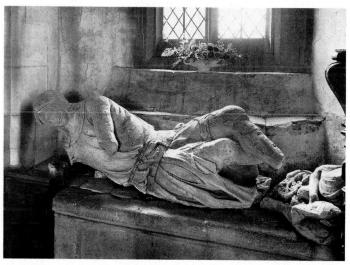

(b) *Church Monuments:* Aldworth, one of the de la Beche family, *c.*1290

25

(a) *Church Monuments:* Sparsholt,
oak effigy of a lady,
early fourteenth century

(b) *Church Monuments:* Fyfield,
Sir John Golafre †1442

Church Monuments: Aldermaston,
Sir George Forster and wife (detail), *c.*1530

(a) *Church Monuments:*
Shottesbrooke, William
Throkmorton †1535

(b) *Church Monuments:* Windsor Castle,
St George's Chapel, the Earl of Lincoln †1585
(*Copyright Country Life*)

Church Monuments: Bisham, Lady Margaret Hoby †1605

(a) *Church Monuments*: Bisham, Lady Elizabeth Hoby †1609

(b) *Church Monuments*: Reading, St Laurence, John Blagrave †1611

(a) *Church Monuments*: Englefield,
Mary Benyon †1777, by Thomas Carter

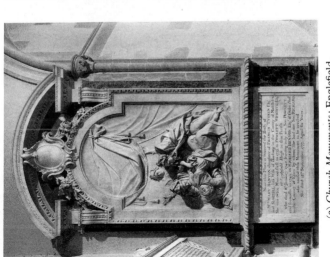

(b) *Church Monuments*: Speen,
Margrave of Anspach †1806, by Antonio Canova

31

Church Monuments: Windsor Castle, St George's Chapel,
Princess Charlotte †1817, by M. C. Wyatt

Church Monuments: Windsor Castle, Albert Memorial Chapel,
Duke of Clarence †1892, by Alfred Gilbert, detail

(a) *Abbeys:* Reading, twelfth century

(b) *Abbeys:* Abingdon, The Chequer, chimneystack,
late thirteenth century

34

(a) *Secular Buildings:* Windsor Castle, as in the sixteenth century. Engraving

(b) *Secular Buildings:* Windsor Castle, air view

(a) *Secular Buildings:* Cholsey, Manor Farm, barn, *c.*1200. Engraving

(b) *Secular Buildings:* Abingdon, Christ's Hospital,
1446 and seventeenth century

Secular Buildings: Donnington Castle, licensed 1386

Ockwells Manor House, 1446/66 (*Copyright Country Life*)

(b) Windsor Castle, Queen Elizabeth's Gallery, chimneypiece, 1583

(a) Bisham Abbey, great hall, chimneypiece *c.*1560, overmantel *c.*1600
(*Copyright Country Life*)

39

(a) Shaw House, completed 1581

(b) Ashdown Park, c.1660

Aldermaston Court, staircase, 1636 (*Copyright Country Life*)

Gatepiers (a, b, c, *Copyright Country Life*) (a) and (b) Coleshill House, by Roger Pratt, *c.*1650–62 (c) Sutton Courtenay, Manor House, mid seventeenth century (d) and (e) Hamstead Marshall, by Thomas Strong (?), 1675(?) (f) Hamstead Marshall, early eighteenth century

42

Swallowfield Park, doorway, by William Talman, 1689/91

Wokingham, Lucas Hospital, 1665 *(Copyright Country Life)*

(a) Windsor, town hall, by Sir Thomas Fitch, c.1687, completed by Wren, 1689–90

(b) Abingdon, town hall, built by Christopher Kempster, 1678–82

45

Windsor Castle, Queen's Presence Chamber, *temp.* Charles II,
carving by Grinling Gibbons

(a) Abingdon, Brick Alley Almshouses, built by Samuel Westbrooke, 1718

(b) West Hanney House, 1727 (*Copyright Country Life*)

(a) Hall Place, c.1730–5, chimneypiece
(*Copyright Country Life*)

(b) Farley Hill, Farley Hall, c.1730, entrance hall
(*Copyright Country Life*)

Hall Place, c.1730–5, drawing room, Italian stucco work (*Copyright Country Life*)

49

(a) Speen, Benham Park, by Capability Brown, 1772–5, portico

(b) Basildon Park, by John Carr, 1776, gates

(a) Coleshill, Strattenborough Castle Farm, 1792

(b) Kintbury, Halfway House, late eighteenth century

(a) Milton House, library, 1776 (*Copyright Country Life*)

(b) Windsor Castle, Great Park, Virginia Water, ruins from Lepcis Magna, erected 1826

Windsor Castle, Home Park, Frogmore House, 1792,
room decorated by Mary Moser

(a) Sandhurst, Royal Military Academy, by John Sanders, 1807–12

(b) Reading, Royal Berkshire Hospital, by Henry Briant, 1837–9

Windsor Castle, Crimson Drawing Room, door from Carlton House, *c.*1810

Windsor Castle, Grand Reception Room, by Sir Jeffry Wyatville, *c.*1820–30

Kingston Lisle House, staircase, *c.*1825–30

(a) Inkpen, school, by G. E. Street, 1850

(b) Newbury, St Nicholas School, by William Butterfield, 1859

(a) Wellington College, by John Shaw, 1856–9

(b) Bear Wood, by Robert Kerr, designed in 1864

Windsor Castle, Home Park, Dairy, by John Thomas, 1858

Buscot Park, *c.*1770, parlour, paintings by Sir Edward Burne-Jones, 1890

Sulhamstead, Folly Farm, by Sir Edwin Lutyens, addition of 1912 (*Copyright Country Life*)

Wokingham, Luckley, by Sir Ernest Newton, 1907

Bracknell, Point Royal, by Arup Associates, 1960–4

the Conway family, and the interest of Park Place is its grounds as beautified by General Conway, who bought the estate in 1752. In his time the grounds were 900 acres in size. To his period belong the handsome obelisk piers close to the entrance to the house, and the OBELISK W of the house, but not the seeming obelisk E of the house which turns out to be the little top SPIRE of St Bride's in the City, erected by Mr Fuller Maitland in 1837. Conway work also the CYCLOPIC BRIDGE at the foot of HAPPY VALLEY (now part of the grounds of a house of that name). This was built in 1781–6. The stones said to come from Reading Abbey are in fact much too cyclopean for that. Every stone, Horace Walpole writes, was placed by the general's own direction. The stones came from fourteen different counties, and the bridge cost £2,000. On the river side they are conglomerate and form voussoir stones. At the top of Happy Valley the GROTTO, six tunnel-vaulted entries into a cross-tunnel-vaulted long, low room with niches. Here also, it is said, stones from Reading Abbey were used. From here the Thames looks through the bridge as if it were immediately beyond. In fact there is plenty of space and e.g. a pretty early C19 COTTAGE with bargeboarded gables which was built as a boathouse. Yet a little further s an estate called TEMPLE COMBE and in this the DRUIDIC TEMPLE, called by Horace Walpole 'little master Stonehenge', a STONE CIRCLE found in Jersey in 1785 and brought over as a gift to General Conway in 1787. The stones were all re-erected accurately, and Walpole is right, as usual, when he calls the monument 'very high-priestly'. The circle stood originally on Mont de la Ville, St Helier, Jersey. In its original form the tomb was covered by a mound of earth revetted with drystone walling, but only the megalithic structure was erected in the park. In its present form it consists of a stone-built passage 15 ft long and 5 ft wide roofed with four capstones leading to a circular area enclosed by a ring of thirty upright slabs against which are built five cells roofed with capstones but open to the centre. The diameter of this circle is now 27 ft, although a contemporary plan made before its removal from Jersey shows it to have been originally 21 ft in diameter. Some slight additions appear to have been made to the monument as a number of the stones are of a sandstone unknown in Jersey but outcropping in Berkshire.*

* The house was rebuilt in 1963–4 to designs of *Hadley & Partners*. Large, and all living quarters on one storey. A curvaceous design.

PEASEMORE

ST BARNABAS. The w tower is of red brick and carries an
inscription: 1737 Will Coward Gent. built ye tower. The
top of blue brick, however, and the recessed spire are of 1842,
the date when the rest of the church was built, also of blue
brick. In 1866 *Street* added the chancel (GS), and on that
occasion probably also altered the windows and provided the
N porch. – REREDOS. By *Earp* (BC). – FRONTAL. Five
Netherlandish panels, C17 clearly by their ornament, but still
entirely Mannerist in the figures. They are rustic but very
forceful and deserve a careful look.

PERBOROUGH CASTLE *see* COMPTON

PORT JACKSON *see* PANGBOURNE

POUGHLEY FARMHOUSE *see* CHADDLEWORTH

PRIESTWOOD *see* BRACKNELL

PRIOR'S COURT *see* CHIEVELEY

PURLEY

ST MARY. Re-set inside the church is the Norman chancel
arch. Single-scallop capitals, strong roll moulding, abacus
with saltire crosses in chip carving – i.e. first half of the C12.
Of the early C13 a re-set lancet and doorway in the vestry. In
the chancel a partly original lancet on the N side. The w
tower is of brick and dated 1626. But mostly the church is of
1870, by *Street*, and it is not a church that could contribute
to his fame. – FONT. Norman, on short, stubby columns,
decorated in different ways. – PLATE. Almsdish of 1683;
Chalice and Paten of 1733. – MONUMENTS. Anne Hyde
† 1632, tablet with small, stiff reclining figure on her side and
a baby in the same position. Two obelisks. – Pretty tablet of
coloured marbles, date of death 1772. – Good Grecian group
of a family turning towards an urn on a high pedestal. On it
the portrait of the deceased. A genius with an extinguished
torch stands by the pedestal. This commemorates Anthony
Storer, who died in 1818. No signature of a sculptor of this
well-done monument.

The church is reached along a regrettable bungaloscape.

PURLEY PARK, ¼ m. sw. By *James Wyatt*, c.1800. Five-bay
façade of Portland stone. Porte-cochère of pairs of Tuscan
columns. The centre bay with the porte-cochère is framed

by giant pilasters. Towards the Thames semicircular bow with detached wooden columns. On this side the house has only three bays. Entrance hall with two fluted Ionic columns. Staircase with a spare iron balustrade of an unusual design of interlocking ovals. Two delicate stucco ceilings.

PURLEY HALL, 1½ m. WSW. The front with two symmetrical canted bay windows and mullioned and transomed windows is of the early C17. The entrance side has a porch of 1869, the E front Early-Victorian-looking trim. Inside a fine if small entrance hall with grisaille wall-paintings in the *Thornhill* style: standing figures, trophies, etc. The staircase has slender twisted balusters and carved tread-ends. Its underside is part of the painting scheme. All this seems to be of c.1700, but on a rainwater head is a date 1719. Late Georgian SUMMER HOUSE by the lake; stone and flint rustication. 'Venetian' opening under a pediment. Inside a niche. Probably of the same time the LODGES. Whole flints and brick bands, circular windows, battlements.

PUSEY

3090

ALL SAINTS. Built about 1745–50 for J. A. Pusey, who died in 1753. Oblong, with N and S transeptal chapels and a W porch. The top of the tower looks a remodelling of c.1840 – see the Italian villa type of roof, and the Grecian acroteria. It is in fact not on the Buckler drawing. The windows are arched, but the three principal windows Venetian. The chapels are separated from the nave by beautiful Venetian screens. Also a W doorway into the S chapel, internally pedimented. – SCULPTURE. Small German Entombment relief, c.1500. The background openwork traceried windows. – MONUMENTS. Incised slab to Henry Doggett and wife † 1480. – M. Dunch † 1679 by *William Bird*. Tablet with two awkward weeping putti. – The comparison with the neighbouring tablet of 1707 is telling. – Jane Pusey † 1742 and J. A. Pusey † 1753. By *P. Scheemakers*. Large monument with reredos background. In front of it young woman seated on the ground. Above bust of the husband in a medallion.

PUSEY HOUSE. Built in 1753. Stone, of five bays and two and a half storeys with two-storey wings and quadrant walls to entrance as well as garden. They have niches with busts and end in pedimented features. The niches have grotto-like vermiculated rustication. The doorway on the entrance side has Tuscan columns and a triglyph frieze. Entrance hall with a screen of columns to the l. Staircase with simple lyre-type wrought-iron railing. In the garden a Chinese BRIDGE across the lake and a square TEMPLE with a low dome. Quatrefoil frieze at the top of the square. In the temple a STATUE of Mrs Brotherton, née Pusey, dated 1759, and busts on tapering pillars in the four corners.

QUEEN ANNE'S MEAD *see* SWALLOWFIELD

RADCOT BRIDGE *see* LITTLEWORTH

RADLEY

St JAMES. Mostly Perp, and curious in that the s arcade has sturdy and high wooden posts instead of piers and longitudinal arched braces instead of arches. Unbuttressed small w tower. Embattled s aisle. The diagonal chancel buttresses have pinnacles, and along the chancel N and s sides runs a fleuron frieze. – FONT. Norman, drum-shaped, with blank arches on colonnettes. – STALLS. C17, with C17 MISERICORDS, mostly with cherubs' heads. The surprising date may be connected with the damage suffered by Radley in the Civil War. – PULPIT. The Late Perp canopy is a rarity. It is said to have belonged originally to the Speaker's chair in the House of Commons. The broad back panel has partly Flamboyant and partly linenfold patterns. – STAINED GLASS. Much very interesting heraldic glass of the C16, supplemented very skilfully by *Willement*. In the E window also larger parts of an early C16 composition, French or Flemish. – In the w window a large portrait which also looks early C16. – PLATE. Paten, 1571; Cup, 1605; Almsdish, c.1700; Flagon, 1705; Brass Almsdish, probably Flemish C16, with the Virgin and Child and the Signs of the Evangelists. – MONUMENTS. Sir William Stonhouse † 1631 and his son † 1632. Large standing monument by *Nicholas Stone*. Recumbent alabaster effigies of husband and wife, he behind and a little above her. The son kneels large on the r. Other children in relief below. Shallow back arch and open top pediment. – Sir George Bowyer † 1800. By *Nollekens*. Tablet with circular inscription in a laurel medallion. Gun, flag, etc., below. – Davis family, c.1822. Dainty triptych with an urn. By *J. Lock* of Abingdon.

RADLEY COLLEGE. The nucleus is RADLEY HALL, built in 1721–7 by *William Townesend* of Oxford as mason and perhaps architect. Nine-bay house of red brick with stone dressings and especially quoins of even length at the angles and the angles of the centres. None of the centres have pediments. Three and a half storeys. Arched ground-floor windows. The entrance doorway has a rusticated surround in which the flanking pilasters partly disappear (cf. Kingston House). Volutes down the window above. To the garden good, simpler doorway with carved brackets. Radley College was started in 1847. Of that year is the very odd CAMPANILE (architect *Howard*), of brick, square in plan, but set diagonally and with far-projecting buttresses.* E of Radley Hall and connected with it by a covered walk is a forecourt with the CHAPEL l. (s) and the DINING HALL r. (N). This group is by *Sir T. G. Jackson*, the covered walk of 1891, the chapel of 1895, the dining hall of 1910. The boys' house opposite is of 1886. Older buildings to the N, i.e. round the campanile: SCHOOL, W of it, of 1848, UPPER DORMITORY W of this, of 1849, the OCTAGON attached to it on its W side of 1857, GALLERY DORMITORY, SW of the campanile, of 1859, and the GYMNASIUM, E of the campanile, also of 1859. Many later additions, those of between the two wars mostly by *H. I. Merriman & A. B. Knapp Fisher*. The NEW LABORATORY, E of the main older group, is by *W. G. Newton*, 1937, of concrete, with a radiating plan and horizontal windows, inspired by the same architect's laboratory at Marlborough. Eight CLASSROOMS were added in 1960–1. They are by *Gollins, Melvin, Ward & Partners*, a straight-forward curtain-walling job, uncommonly well detailed.

WICK HALL, 1 m. SW. Built *c.*1700. Five bays, the ones l. and r. of the doorway narrower. Two storeys, hipped roof. Wooden cross-windows. Fine shell-hood over the door. Staircase with twisted balusters. (Jacobean screen in the drawing room, and another in the library. NBR)

READING

7070

INTRODUCTION

Two basic facts must be considered to understand the history of Reading: its position characterized already by William of Malmesbury as a potential *diversorium ad populosiores urbes Angliae* for all travellers, and its Cluniac abbey founded by Henry I in 1121 and the king's favourite monastic establishment. A castle also existed but was destroyed already in 1151.

---

* They were added in 1855 to create ball-courts.

Later the cloth trade supported Reading, as it supported so many English towns. Leland states that the town 'standith by clothing', and Archbishop Laud's father was a Reading clothier. Defoe still called Reading 'very large, wealthy, handsomely built'. Of his time the evidence must now be sought out.

READING ABBEY

The abbey was founded as a Cluniac house by Henry I. It was colonized from Lewes and was for 100 monks. In 1305 there were 65, in 1445 only 35. The time of Henry I was probably the climax. Much survives, but all except the inner gatehouse in so fragmentary a state that is of little architectural even if of much picturesque value. The extent was considerable. It starts where the Perambulation on p. 204 is going to start, by the Market Place. The church of St Laurence (p. 199) was the parish church *ante portas* of the abbey, with the outer gate formerly attached to its s flank. N of the church, now entered from Valpy Street or a passage N of St Laurence's churchyard, is part of the HOSPITIUM of St John Baptist, a range of flint with a polygonal stair-turret of brick on the N side. The range dates from 1486, when it was converted into a school. A good deal further E than St Laurence, at the E end of Forbury, is the INNER GATEHOUSE (Abbey Gate). This is of the late c13, but was drastically restored by *Scott* in 1869. Flint and stone, with angle turrets. The outer N arch is pointed, the inner round. The s arch is round too. Remains of a rib-vault with fillets on the ribs. Large lancet windows. What survives of the church and the ranges round the cloister is E of the abbey gate, s of the Catholic church, and immediately W of the gaol. It is as follows. Nothing of the nave and aisles of the CHURCH except the SE respond of the nave, where it is attached to the N arch of the s transept, walling of the s transept quite high up, remains of the two E chapels of that transept, and, just s of the Catholic church, of the two E chapels of the N transept, nothing of the chancel with its ambulatory which would now be inside the gaol, then s of the s transept the tunnel-vaulted SLYPE and a room above, s of this the CHAPTER HOUSE, oblong and apsed, and, visible quite high up, the W wall of the DORMITORY s of the chapter house, the high s wall of the REFECTORY W of the dormitory wall, i.e. s of where the cloister lay, and the REREDORTER, at r. angles to the s end of the dormitory, i.e. across a drain split off the Kennet. Finally, back in the streets

34a

of the town, s of Abbey Square, something of the ABBEY MILL incorporated into the present Abbey Mills. C12 arches, one with zigzag, one with a single chamfer, and two smaller ones. The south gate to the abbey precinct lay at the w end of Abbey Square.

But by far the most interesting survival of the abbey is the CAPITALS and other fragments now mostly in the Reading Museum, but some also in the Victoria and Albert Museum. They are partly ornamented with beaded bands, rather wildly entwined, partly figured. One particularly strange capital has two bearded angels, another the earliest surviving representation of the Coronation of the Virgin. The size of the capitals makes it clear that they were originally in the cloister. Their style derived from that of the Canterbury crypt. Their date may be c.1130. Henry I was buried in the chancel of the church in 1136. The piers and the voussoirs of the arches were carved too. One fragment in the Victoria and Albert Museum shows beakhead, and probably represents the earliest occurrence of this motif in England. It can be regarded as the child of West French and Viking parents. Fragments from the abbey were used after the dilapidation and demolition all over the Reading region.

CHURCHES

ST LAURENCE. The church looks down the Market Place. Originally the outer abbey gate was immediately attached to its s flank. Early C12 the SE quoins of the nave, a small s window in the nave, and fragments of a doorway re-set in the N aisle. In 1196 the Hospitium of St John Baptist was founded (see above), and probably in connexion with this the church was enlarged, see the E wall of the chancel with three lancets, shafted inside, and the nave s doorway, still with waterleaf capitals. Round arch with a filleted roll. A little later the w respond of the N arcade with its arch springer (i.e. a N aisle was built) and the N chapel arcade of three bays with round piers and early stiff-leaf capitals still keeping close to the bell and close to the upper edge. Perp w tower with polygonal buttresses and a tall arch to the nave and a lower one to the N aisle which embraces the tower. The outer aisle wall has straight-headed windows. Of the same time the E respond of the N arcade. But the arcade itself was rebuilt in 1522. Perp also the nave roof with tie-beams and kingposts. – FONT. Octagonal, Perp, of 1522, nothing special. – PULPIT. A fine piece of the C18, with inlay work. – BENCH ENDS. With tracery panels and poppy-heads (chancel). – ORGAN CASE. By *Byfield*, 1741. Supported on big neo-Elizabethan posts. – PLATE. Flagon and Almsdish, 1631; two Cups and Patens, 1637; Flagon, 1638; Patens, 1701 and 1708; Almsdishes, 1735 and 1752; Wine Strainer, 1730/1; Head on a staff, 1790/1. – MONUMENTS. Brass to John Kent and wife, early C15. Demi-figures, 12 in. long (N chapel). – Brass to a man, early C16, 23 in. figure (ditto). – Brass to Walter Barton † 1538, 2 ft figure. Palimpsest (ditto). – Thomas Lydall † 1608. Low diptych with kneeling figures and three columns (N aisle). – John Blagrave † 1611, author of *The Mathematical Jewell*. Demi-figure, frontal, with sphere and quadrant. In the surround five small figures, l., r., and above. They represent the five regular geometrical solids. – Mrs Hamley † 1636. Kneeling figure (s wall). – Ann Haydon † 1747. Still with the figure kneeling. – Dr Valpy, 1838. Life-size standing figure high up under a giant arch. By *E. C. Hakewill*, executed by *Samuel Nixon* (BC). – Along the w half of the s wall Blagrave in 1619 built an arcade known as Blagrave's Piazza. It was six arches long and was pulled down in 1868.

ST AGNES, Northumberland Avenue. 1938 by *E. Ravenscroft*. Red brick, with an Italian low-pitch roof to the crossing tower.

ALL SAINTS, Downshire Square. 1865–74 by *St Aubyn*. E.E., with a bellcote over the E end of the nave. Ornate w doorway. Ornate mosaic w wall inside by the font. Very ornate chancel of 1889–90 with an apse. Fine tall proportions internally. – PULPIT. Of wrought iron.

ST BARTHOLOMEW, London Road. The church is by *Waterhouse*, 1879, the chancel by *Bodley*, 1881. Blue and red brick, lancet windows, bellcote. Low round polished granite piers. The finest thing is the chancel E wall with its Dec window high up.

CHRIST CHURCH, Christchurch Road. By *Woodyer*, 1861–2, enlarged 1874. An exceptionally rewarding High Victorian church and very typical of Woodyer. Big, with a NW porch steeple. E.E. style. The clerestory with bold blank tracery. The crockets of the gable over the porch entrance have remained uncarved and look like the New Brutalism. Inside, the arcade piers very personal, with closely set Purbeck shafts and big capitals with ever so many gablets and naturalistic flowers. Eastlake in 1872 called them 'difficult to accept as agreeable in an artistic sense'. The clerestory has openwork-cusped rere-arches. But the most astonishing and successful feature is the openwork tympanum in the chancel arch, an arched band of trefoils carrying reticulation. – The PULPIT is no doubt by Woodyer too. – Richly sculptured REREDOS by *Birnie Philip* (BC). – STAINED GLASS in the chancel and clerestory by *Hardman*, 1868 (BC).

ST GILES, Southampton Street. 1873 by *J. P. St Aubyn*, except for the C13 aisle walls and the Perp tower. The tower now carries a spire. Flint. Very rich E.E. chancel. – SCULPTURE. Fragments in the tower, including a large Norman capital. They probably come from the abbey. – STAINED GLASS. In the S chapel by *Powell's*, designed by *Wooldridge*, 1872. – PLATE. Silver-gilt Chalices and Covers of 1599 and 1618; Paten, 1632; three Flagons of 1636, 1637, and 1639. – MONU-MENTS. Brass to John Bowyer † 1521 and wife; 19 in. figures. – Uncommonly many C18 tablets, including some of un-common design (e.g. Thomas Paterson † 1746).

GREYFRIARS. The Franciscans arrived at Reading in 1233 and went to their present site in 1285. Money for the *opus fratrum minorum* was bequeathed in 1311. That fits the details of the church. It was in fact almost entirely reconstructed in 1863 (by *Woodman*), but on sufficient evidence. Nave and aisles, transepts, but no chancel. Everything E of the chancel arch remained destroyed. The N transept was built wholly afresh. Of the piers, which are square with semicircular projections, most are original. Moulded arches. In the transept windows intersecting tracery. The large W window with reticulated tracery. The big E bellcote is of course of 1863. – (TILES. In a showcase. With sporting themes.)

ST JAMES (R.C.), Forbury Road. 1837–40 by *Pugin*, in the Norman style which he would never have chosen even a few years later. His reason must have been proximity to the abbey ruins. The S aisle and the ambulatory round the apse are recent (*W. C. Mangan*, 1925). The N aisle was completed only in 1962 (*H. Bingham Towner*). – FONT. A C12 stone found on the abbey site. Block with interlacing.

ST JOHN EVANGELIST, Watlington Street. 1872–3 by *W. A. Dixon*. Big, with a SW spire. E.E. Coarse and rock-faced. The window dressings in buff and red stone.

ENGLISH MARTYRS (R.C.), Tilehurst Road. 1926 by *W. C. Mangan*. Brick. Demonstratively Italian. With a NW campanile and an octagonal crossing tower.

ST MARY (Episcopalian), Castle Street. 1798, but mostly 1840–2. The original architect was *R. Billing*. A fine Grecian façade with six giant Corinthian columns and a pediment. The cupola has been lost. The portico etc. is by *H. & N. Briant* (BC).

ST MARY, St Mary's Butts. In the N wall a Norman doorway, re-set. S arcade of *c.*1200. Four bays, round piers, capitals in the transition from waterleaf to stiff-leaf, octagonal abaci, round arches with one big chamfer. At the E end of the N aisle an arch of *c.*1300 which must once have connected a N transept with an E chapel. The chancel is of 1864, the N aisle is of 1872. The W tower is as late as 1550–3: chequer flint and stone, with polygonal buttresses. – FONT. Octagonal, with quatrefoils, but not Perp. It was given in 1616. – SCREEN. Under the tower arch. With a band of 1631. – PAINTING. Christ and the Syro-Phoenician Woman. Attributed to *Lodovico Carracci*. Given by (the later) Dean Milman. Large (S aisle). – PLATE. Silver-gilt Cup and Cover, 1592; two silver-gilt Patens, 1626; Flagon, 1628; large Flagon, 1652; Chalice and Cover inscribed 1661; silver-gilt Spoon, 1668; large Bowl, 1767; Almsdish inscribed 1776. – MONUMENTS. William Kendrick † 1635. Two kneeling figures facing one another. Top pediment, segmental and broken, already with a thick garland between, i.e. on the way from Jacobean to classical. – John Monk † 1809, by *Flaxman*. The expiring man in a chair fortified by a standing figure of Faith.

ST PETER, Church Road, Earley. 1844 by *J. Turner*, the aisles and chancel 1882–3. Grey vitrified brick. NW tower.

ST STEPHEN, Rupert Street. 1864–6 by *William White*. Enlarged (S aisle and chapel) 1886. Brick, with bellcote and plate tracery. E.E. Brick exposed inside. The capitals naturalistic or stylized.

CEMETERY. 1842–3 by *William Brown*. Classical entrance gate and chapels with a Tuscan portico and pediment.

PUBLIC BUILDINGS

SHIRE HALL, Forbury. 1904–11 by *Hall & Warwick*. Stone. Free Palladian and quite lively. Not big.

MUNICIPAL BUILDINGS, Blagrave Street. 1872–5 by *Waterhouse*. Addition by *Thomas Lainson*, 1879–82. Blue and red brick. Large, Gothic, and asymmetrical, with a tower at the S end. Inside an Italianate concert hall, in fact the plain brick town hall of 1786 minus one bay.

TELEPHONE EXCHANGE, Minster Street. By *Stokes*, illustrated
in 1908. Five bays, symmetrical, not really in any period style.

UNIVERSITY, Whiteknights Estate. The Whiteknights Estate
belonged to the Englefields from 1606 to 1798 and then to the
Marquess of Blandford, later fifth Duke of Marlborough.
He had famous ornamental grounds with rare plants, described by Mrs Holland in 1819. His library was even more
famous. He overspent on it all, and in 1819 a twenty-three-
day sale of the library was held. The estate went to Sir Isaac
Lyon Goldsmid, bullion broker, in 1849. He was the first
Jewish baronet (1841). In 1867 the estate was divided into
six leaseholds.

Reading University started as a University Extension
College in 1892. It moved to London Road in 1904, the site
having been made available by the Palmer family (of Huntley
& Palmer). The same family gave an endowment of £150,000
in 1911. The college became the University of Reading in
1926 and acquired the new site in 1947. Of the six large
villas, or indeed country houses, on the estate four were by
Waterhouse: Erleigh Park 1859, Whiteknights 1868, Foxhill
(for himself) 1868, and The Wilderness 1873. The first of
these three is demolished and only the lodge remains. The
second and third exist, but the fourth also has gone, though
its stables survive. Foxhill is N of the lake, Whiteknights W
of Foxhill. Whiteknights Park, W of the narrow S part of the
lake, can only be attributed to Waterhouse. Mr Stuart Smith
has found no office evidence on the house. The new buildings
are disappointing, when compared with buildings of the same
years of other universities, old and new. There is really not
one that needs a detailed appreciation. Faculty of Letters by
Easton & Robertson, Cusdin, Preston & Smith, completed
1957, Physics by the same, completed 1960, Sedimentology
by the same, 1962, Library by the same, 1963, Whiteknights
Hall by *Stanley Meirick,* University Grants Committee's
Architect, 1964.*

TECHNICAL COLLEGE, King's Road. By *Lanchester & Lodge*,
1950–5. Terrible, in the tamest squared-up neo-Georgian of
between the wars. – In front of the entrance every year a
different piece of sculpture is displayed.

---

* For the old buildings Mr Stuart Smith gave me all the information,
for the new, Mr J. F. Johnson. In a letter from Mr Johnson I was told that
in the meantime Windsor Hall and the Department of Chemistry have been
completed. They are also by *Easton & Robertson, Cusdin, Preston & Smith.*

READING SCHOOL, Erleigh Road. 1865–71 by *Waterhouse*. Red brick, long symmetrical front, Tudor. The centre is the hall and this – as we are *c.*1870 – has an asymmetrically placed turret. The chapel, also by Waterhouse, was added in 1873. Many later additions.

LEIGHTON PARK SCHOOL, Shinfield Road. The core is Pepper Manor, but much has been added. *Waterhouse* extended the main building on the SE in 1890 and built Grove House at the N end of the site in 1892–4. This has since also been extended. Townson House with the Libraries, etc., N of the main building, and Peckover Hall, to the NW of the former and E of Grove House, are by *Fred Rowntree*, 1910. Much more since, and especially after the Second World War.

ROYAL BERKSHIRE HOSPITAL, London Road. 1837–9. By *Henry Briant*. A splendid building. Bath stone. Monumental block with a giant portico of six attached Ionic columns and a pediment. The wings were added in 1861, and a further l. wing at r. angles with an end pavilion with Doric pilasters, perfectly in harmony with the original work, followed in 1881–2. This and also the Greek Doric colonnade with an upper floor are by *Morris & Stallwood*, a remarkable feat of keeping in keeping, at a time when this was very rarely done. The r. pavilion is of 1882 too, but the connecting link was only provided in 1912. Good, if not large, staircase under a lantern. The CHAPEL is in the state of 1882.

BATTLE HOSPITAL, Oxford Road. The former WORKHOUSE. 1866–7. Red brick, gabled, i.e. Elizabethan.

GAOL, Forbury Road. 1842–4. Red brick, castellated and symmetrical. By *Scott & Moffatt*.

STATION. 1840. A nice Italianate job of yellow brick with pedimented windows and a cupola.

PERAMBULATION

The town developed on the river Kennet, away from the water-meadows of the Thames. We start in the MARKET PLACE. It is a triangular space of no visual distinction. In the middle the SIMEON MONUMENT of 1804, a triangular pillar, designed by *Soane* and characteristic of him in all its details. On the W side the former CORN EXCHANGE, 1854 by *J. B. Clacy & F. Hawkes*, free, debased Renaissance, quite small, and then a timber-framed house with two oriel windows. On the S side No. 52 with giant pilasters, early C19. On the E side Messrs SUTTON'S, High Victorian Gothic, three generously spaced bays only, with a French pavilion roof. By *W. & J. T. Brown*, 1870–3. At the NW corner No. 25, also with giant pilasters, and also early C19. The house curves round and leads out of the Market Place. From this place to the N to Blagrave Street and the railway.

To the E to FORBURY GARDENS and the MEMORIAL to those fallen in the Afghan wars, an enormous lion by *George Simonds*, 1886. S of the gardens the new building of the PRUDENTIAL ASSURANCE, by *Fitzroy Robinson & Partners*, 1963–4, with an inner courtyard which will one day become a trunk road.

To the W from the N end of the Market Place along FRIAR STREET, with some early C18 houses with segment-headed windows on the N side. Then turn N into STATION ROAD to gaze at Nos 7–25, fantastic Latest Victorian, with a diversity of steep gables and very varied detail altogether. Yellow and red brick, by *Joseph Morris & Son*, 1901–3. At the station corner the GREAT WESTERN HOTEL, opened in 1844, a quiet, small palazzo.

At the W end of Friar Street turn l. and go down West Street to ST MARY'S BUTTS. N of the church the VICARAGE, five bays, 1727, with segment-headed windows,* and the house on its r., also Early Georgian, with a door canopy on sumptuously carved brackets. E of the church the DISPENSARY of 1840, a nice five-bay palazzo with short lower wings. The quoins are diamond-cut. Bath stone. Old houses also on the S side.

Now out to the W, first briefly along OXFORD ROAD, then along Castle Street. In Oxford Road minor early C19 expansion, e.g. MANNSON HOUSE with a Tuscan porch. Much more in CASTLE STREET. First still timber-framing and Early Georgian houses, especially No. 19, of five bays, with segment-headed windows and a doorcase with pilasters and a segmental pediment. The former CONGREGATIONAL CHAPEL with its Soanian ornament and its pedimental gable is of 1837, by *J. J. Cooper*. More Georgian houses, also of Bath stone. Then the VACHEL ALMSHOUSES, two rows of cottages at r. angles to the street. 1864–5 by *W. H. Woodman*. After that No. 63, HOLYBROOK HOUSE, mid C18, of five bays, with a very ambitious heavy doorcase. Columns mightily blocked. Laurel frieze. Carved spandrels. Keystone head. (Staircase with turned balusters, decorated Hall, Rococo ceiling in the Music Room, large garden down to the Holy Brook. MHLG) More Bath stone terraces. Then the street becomes CASTLE

* Pretty fireplaces and staircase (NBR).

HILL, and among further terraces, low Italianate villa gables begin to appear. The continuation of Castle Hill is BATH ROAD. At its beginning some brick houses of 1800, e.g. BRUNSWICK HOUSE (former Blue Coat School), five bays, three storeys, Tuscan porch.

Back to St Mary's Butts and S, down BRIDGE STREET. The only noteworthy house is SEVEN BRIDGES HOUSE, the original Simonds house by the brewery. Five bays, Roman Doric porch. By *Soane*, 1790. Off to the E, in CHURCH STREET, some minor Georgian houses. However, one of them, No. 8, has giant angle pilasters, though it is only two bays wide. It must be of c.1720. The continuation of Bridge Street is SOUTHAMPTON STREET, with more Late Georgian terraces. Note the doorways with set-in Doric columns. Parallel with Southampton Street, reached from the end of Church Street, is LONDON STREET, a wide Georgian street with many original houses left. Nos 73–79 are the best. No. 73 has odd door-hood brackets sideways as well as forward. The fine Grecian stone front with attached giant Ionic columns between angle pillars and a pediment was originally the SCIENTIFIC INSTITUTION, 1843 by *W. Brown*. At the N end of London Street to the E Queens Road with QUEEN'S CRESCENT, a long Bath stone crescent of 1832 etc., by *J. J. Cooper*. Then the HIGH BRIDGE of 1788, one arch with vermiculated rustication on the voussoirs, and so, by Duke Street, back to the Market Place.

Now E. First KING STREET with the GEORGE HOTEL, with its picturesque courtyard, and with BARCLAYS BANK opposite boasting a rich doorway in its palazzo front. The house is by *Henry and Nathaniel Briant*, 1838–9. Then follows KINGS ROAD. On the S side KENNET HOUSE, by *Cecil Elsom & Partners*, recent and decent. Then good groups of stone houses of c.1830, classical, also with pairs of tall bows as if they were copied from Brighton, and also with low Italianate gables. From the far end of Kings Road one returns along LONDON ROAD, seeing the development backward. The early C19 went out as far as No. 113, but there are plenty of High Victorian villas even further W, especially on the S side. On the N side good houses of c.1830–40 round ELDON SQUARE. Yet further W a white terrace with giant pilasters of only six bays, and then the best of all, Nos 45–65. This is, according to Mr Sherburn, of 1825–35, by *Richard Billing*. The doorways again have set-in Doric columns. Terraces also opposite, one of twelve bays with pediments over the end bays. A little before, off to the N in WATLINGTON STREET, is WATLINGTON HOUSE. The garden side is dated 1688 (rainwater-heads). Five bays, two storeys, hipped roof. The upper middle window is at a lower level than the others (staircase) and has a brick pediment. (Staircase with strong twisted balusters. Entrance hall with fluted pillars and two arches. NBR) The entrance side is C18. Back to the Market Place by Queens Road or Kings Road, and that finishes the perambulation of Inner Reading.

OUTER READING

CALCOT, *see* p. 109.

CAVERSHAM, *see* p. 110.

TILEHURST, *see* p. 242.

No proper perambulation can be suggested. The following individual items may be picked out.

S of London Road along REDLANDS ROAD, where No. 76 is said to have been designed by *May Morris*, William Morris's daughter. Also in Redlands Road ST ANDREW'S HALL (University Hostel), formerly EAST THORPE, by *Waterhouse* for Alfred Palmer, 1880. Additions, but the main rooms unaltered.* Again in Redlands Road SOUTH HILL, an attractive group of three pairs of houses, early C19, the side pairs a little canted forward. These side pairs have very clumsily detailed Greek Doric entrances. Then, just N of Christchurch Road, in HIGHGROVE STREET an old CONDUIT house of brick, 9 by 6½ ft in size.

SW and W, off WENSLEY ROAD at Coley is COLEY PARK FARM with a brick BARN (of six bays, dated 1619. Queen-post trusses. MHLG). To its W, just S of the Bath Road, a group of high-rise flats, by *C. H. A. Willett*, 1957–8. Of COLEY FARM itself only the massive gatepiers are left, at the N end of COLEY AVENUE, i.e. also in the Bath Road. N of the flats is Prospect Park and in it, placed on a hill, PROSPECT HOUSE, early C19. Stuccoed. Centre of five bays with a colonnade of unfluted Ionic columns and wings lying back a little. They have bow fronts and shallow domes. Nice staircase with simple iron balustrade.

Reading has much new housing other than what has been

* Mr Stuart Smith kindly told me of this.

mentioned. The town is growing rapidly, thanks to a position just far enough from, and just near enough to, London.

REMENHAM

7080

St Nicholas. Virtually of the time of the Victorian restoration (*Roland Plumbe*, 1870). But one large Dec two-light window on the N side is original, and the W tower with its polygonal buttresses (cf. Henley) is of 1838. Also, the apse represents a Norman apse of the past. – STAINED GLASS. In the apse by *Kempe*; 1909 (BC). – TILES. Ancient tiles by the pulpit. – IRON SCREEN. Presented by Sir John Noble of Park Place (*see* p. 192). The screen is a gate shown in 1873 'at the Siena exhibition'. (Does this not mean Vienna?) Elaborate, with vine trails. – Two BRASSES under the tower, † 1591 and † 1622.

TEMPLE, on Temple Island. 1771 by *James Wyatt*. An ornament belonging originally to Fawley Court across the river. It is extremely pretty and commands a full view of the mile to Henley. White, with a shallow bow front and an open cupola with columns. A perfectly harmless cottage behind.

REMENHAM COURT, ¼ m. s. White, with two symmetrical bows and a veranda on columns. Is is of *c*.1840?

CULHAM COURT, *see* p. 124.

ROBIN HOOD'S ARBOUR *see* MAIDENHEAD

ROOKS NEST *see* WOODLANDS ST MARY

RUSCOMBE

7070

St James. The chancel of flint is Norman. The small windows are pointed outside, but the rere-arches are round. Two windows in the E wall. The rest of the church, nave and tower, is of brick and was built in 1638–9. The two parts are not of the same build, see the difference in the brickwork and the way the W wall of the nave cuts through the buttresses of the tower. Interesting details of the three-light brick windows (cf. Winkfield, 1629) and bell-openings. The heavy wagon roof of the chancel is dated C14 by the VCH. – Between nave and chancel, inside, the C17 TYMPANUM with the Commandments. – Also of *c*.1639 the PULPIT with tester. – Two very simple C17 PEWS. – PAINTING. In the chancel, in the window jambs, traces of figures, assigned to the C13, but either very faint or restored into the likeness of Fra Angelico. – PLATE. Cup, 1630; Flagon, Paten, and two Almsdishes, 1821. –

MONUMENTS. Several C18 tablets, e.g. a purely architectural one, rather 1733 than 1774. – Richard Neville Neville † 1793 by *Flaxman*, simple, with two heraldic medallions with ox-heads. – Sir James Eyre † 1799, by *Sir Richard Westmacott*. A noble piece with a large asymmetrically placed standing female figure by an urn and a branch of weeping willow.

NORTHBURY FARM, formerly Ruscombe Manor. Timber-framed with brick infilling. Early C17. Front with three gables. It is only a part of the manor house.

ST LEONARD'S HILL *see* DEDWORTH

ST NICHOLAS HURST

7070

ST NICHOLAS. Flint with a brick tower. Mostly Victorian. The tower of 1612, Gothic, with C19 cupola. Norman N arcade, evidently tampered with and now inexplicable in more than one way. Norman W respond with multi-scallop capital and square abacus. Thin Norman circular pier with similar details, but the lower part of the pier fatter than the upper and ending in a collar as of a chipped-off capital. E respond as the others but with a capital too small, made for a tripartite respond and with what looks like chipped-off stiff-leaf. Unmoulded arches. Early C13 N doorway with two slight chamfers. The lancets of the N aisle would go with it. S arcade of 1875. In the C14 a W bay was added to the N arcade. Pretty head details. Also C14 heads on the vertical strips which must formerly have supported roof beams. – REREDOS. By *J. D. Sedding*, 1872. Alabaster, florid, with two biblical scenes: Expulsion and Nativity. – SCREENS. Perp, but much re-done. The top cresting openwork Jacobean and very enjoyable. – PULPIT. Simple, Elizabethan, with the usual blank arches. – HOURGLASS on a delightful wrought iron stand dated 1636. – PLATE. Silver-gilt Cup, Paten, and Flagon, 1611–12. – MONUMENTS. Purbeck marble wall tomb of the early C16 with canopy on a flat arch. Tomb-chest with quatrefoils. Later brasses († 1578) against the back wall (N chapel). – To its W brass plaque to Alse Harrison † c.1600, with the lady in a four-poster. She died in childbed. – Lady Savile † 1631. Long, tripartite, with three groups of kneeling figures. Each group under lifted curtains. Angels hold them l. and r. Alabaster and touch (N chapel). – Henry Barker † 1651. Recumbent effigy, very well done. A praying child on the l., a frightening skeleton on the r. Top with open curly pediment. Alabaster (N wall of chancel). – Sir Richard Harrison † 1683 by *William Stanton* (signed). Large tablet with kneeling figures facing one another. She with a lively, if a little awkward turn. Behind them a standing man, like an apparition. The group in a recess with a trefoil arch. Segmental top pediment. White and grey marble (chancel s).

s of the church BARKER'S ALMSHOUSES, founded in 1682. Brick, flat, one-storeyed, with dormers. Entirely pre-classical.

E of the church the CASTLE INN, a pretty group, seen from the churchyard.

HURST HOUSE, ¼ m. NW. Mostly of 1847, but with some materials of a preceding house said to be of 1530. Only the four heavy, straight-topped wooden doorways inside can be of that date. The scanty remains of mullioned windows and the brick chimneys must be Elizabethan. So is the fine panelling with pilasters in one room.

HURST LODGE, ⅝ m. NE. C18 five-bay front with three-bay pediment and a heavy recent door surround. Older bits behind. One side has cross-windows and dormers, i.e. probably dates from the later C17. The back is gabled.

HINTON HOUSE, 1⅛ m. NE. Built before 1589. Brick with blue brick diapering. Entrance side with two gables and a polygonal bay window with porch between. Mullioned and transomed windows. Chimneystacks octagonal or lozenge. The house was originally much larger. (Inside, a room with pilaster panelling and an elaborate overmantel and another with panelling and overmantel above the former. VCH)

STANLAKE PARK, 1⅝ m. NNE. Brick. Late C16. Three-gable front, the centre a little recessed. Mullioned and transomed windows. A canted C18 part later set into the similar back of the house.

HAINES HILL, 1½ m. NE. A large house formerly of H-plan with several courtyards. The oldest parts are late C16 or early C17. Of that time is the long gallery, but the ends of this were re-done in 1716. The front of the house is of 1760, and the servants' wing of c.1825. The front has nine bays with a three-bay pediment and a porch on Tuscan columns. The back has gabled wings, but in the recessed centre is a large bow no doubt also of 1760. One side of this back part has three shaped gables (NBR). The interior decoration dates partly from c.1716, partly from c.1760 (VCH).*

* I have not seen this house myself, as Mr A. Godsal refused my request to see it.

HIGH CHIMNEYS, Davis Street, 1 m. SW. Brick, dated 1661 by scratching in on several bricks. Yet still the same type as Stanlake Park. Gabled, with recessed centre. Front and back almost identical, i.e. H-shaped. The windows, as against those of Stanlake Park, have wooden mullion and transom crosses. The doorways with canopies on scrolly, coarsely carved brackets.

BILL HILL, 1½ m. SE. Early Georgian. Blue bricks with red-brick dressings. Segment-headed windows, those of the first floor with stone keystones. Doorway with open pediment and the characteristic lines along the frieze leading up to a central point. Angle pilasters in three orders (giant pilasters would have been more typical). One-storey three-bay wings projecting at r. angles and connected by low links. Fine early C 19 staircase with sparse, delicate iron balustrade. Gatepiers of brick with square urns and original wrought-iron gates. On the B road running S an oval STONE with a palmette at the top and an inscription commemorating the making of the road by subscription. The date is 1770. (The stone was moved here from Marchfield, Binfield. MHLG)

(HATCHGATE FARM. Barn of cruck construction. NBR)

SANDFORD see WOODLEY

SANDHURST 8060

ST MICHAEL. 1853 by *Street*, and enlarged in the sixties by *Woodman*. Coursed brown rubble. SW tower with wide open porch entrance and in it an imitation Norman doorway based on something real which had survived. Uninspired interior. – FONT. Furiously Norman, 'executed by one of the daughters of the late Rector'. – Much PAINTING on the walls. – MONUMENTS. Lady Farrer † 1892. Convincedly Athenian. She is seated in a chair, the family standing opposite. – A Jacobean brass († 1608).

ROYAL MILITARY ACADEMY, 2 m. ESE and really belonging to the Camberley area, i.e. the largest military area in England. The original building 1807–12 by *John Sanders*, after the [54a] academy, established in 1789 at High Wycombe, had moved to Sandhurst from Marlow. This original building is like a mansion, white, with a splendid portico and facing landscaped grounds and a lake – an appropriate place for young gentlemen to spend some formative years in. The portico is severely Greek Doric – a relatively early use of the order – and of six columns with a pediment. On either side twelve bays plus seven-bay wings plus three-bay pavilions, the outer blocks connected with one another and the centre by pillars. Large plain entrance hall and behind it, in axis, the former chapel, large as a ballroom, with segmental vault and an intruding Victorian Perp chancel window. The present CHAPEL is an independent brick building on an amazing scale and in an amazing style. It ought probably to be called Byzantine. As it now is, it consists of a nave of three bays, a chancel, and transepts, but at the start it was orientated differently, and the transepts were the whole building. Their front is Italian Romanesque rather than Byzantine, and it was consecrated in 1879. It was designed by *Captain Henry Cole*.* It had a short nave of two bays with weakly octagonal arcade piers, a crossing, a chancel like the nave, and an apse. Then, in 1922, Capt. *A. C. Martin* F.R.I.B.A. conceived the extension, and this was completed in 1937. Now one enters from the w through a feeble atrium and finds oneself in a church of three Byzantine inscribed-cross units, i.e. units of a square with a sail-vault plus a tunnel-vaulted nave continuation to the w and E plus four corner pieces. The new E end is an apse again, but the old chapel remained with its apse as transepts. The old apse with its MOSAICS and its marble revetments is the most sumptuous part of the building. Otherwise the interior is mostly white. One side apse at the E end has a good MOSAIC by *Boris Anrep*. – STAINED GLASS in the original apse E parts (four windows) by *Powell's*, in the w part (two windows) by *Laurence Lee*. – In the original apse two recent STANDS for books of remembrance by *Sir Hugh Casson*. – The very imaginative and lively ORGAN CASE is by *Sir Hugh Casson* too. It dates from 1950.

AMBERROW COURT, ½ m. N. 1885 by *W. Ravenscroft*. Light purple brick, C17 style, with gables, and an animated composition, with the porch set at an angle and a principal four-light window – a free version of the Ipswich type popularized by Norman Shaw. The arch here is segmental.

SANDLEFORD PRIORY

4060

The priory was founded for Augustinian Canons c.1200 and seems always to have remained small. Of the priory buildings one roof survives, but this is part of a large room of the house

---

* I owe the name to Mr Nicholas Taylor.

as rebuilt by *James Wyatt* in 1780–1. Wyatt appears Gothic
here, not classical, as in the Pantheon in London, and Sandleford is supposed to be his earliest Gothic country house.*
Symmetrical façade, cemented, seven bays, the outer pairs
with embattled gables, the centre bay raised squarely and
also embattled. Yet the ground-floor windows are round-
arched. To the side a broad bow. At the back a wing extends
with the two largest rooms, the first an oval preceded and
followed by a small lobby with a screen of two columns to the
oval, the second a large oblong with a final broad tripartite
window with a segmental top. All this is classical and Adamish,
though the exterior of the segment-headed end window has
an ogee arch. It is above this large room that the C14 timber
roof is preserved, a roof with closely set arched braces of Dec
moulding, running up to a moulded longitudinal beam from
which raking struts go up to the rafters. The entrance hall of
the house is small, and it is followed by a larger room at the
back which has thin shafts to the ceiling, a token of a former
hall. What would then have been the screens passage is fan-
vaulted in stucco.

SCHOOL GREEN see SHINFIELD

SEGSBURY DOWN see LETCOMBE BASSETT

SEVEN BARROWS see LAMBOURN

SHAW   4060

ST MARY. 1840–2 by *J. Hansom*, in the Norman style, i.e. long
round-headed side windows of the lancet type, and a shocking
w front with a very powerful w window, equally unauthorized
long bell-openings, and a spire. The chancel is by *Butterfield*,
of 1878. It is of flint and has late C13 windows. The interior
of 1840 is characterized by the thin barn roof, that of 1878 by
painted decoration. – MONUMENT. Sir Thomas Dolman
† 1711. Enjoyable writing-master's writing.

SHAW HOUSE. The largest Elizabethan mansion in Berkshire,
built for Thomas Dolman, clothier, and completed in 1581.
Red brick, E-front, gabled. The projecting wings have four- 40a
light single-transomed windows, but to the inner sides only
large chimneybreasts. The recessed centre has three gables

---

* But Sheffield Park, Sussex, was in all probability begun well before
1779.

and a middle porch with two unfluted Ionic pilasters and a pediment. Greek inscription saying: 'Let no jealous enter'. The window above projects a little too and has a stone surround with the Latin inscription: 'The toothless envies the eater's teeth, and the mole despises the eye of the goat' – a highly unpleasant motto – and a pediment. The fenestration of the centre ought to be appreciated. It still stresses externally the place where the great hall lies. To the r. of the porch are three two-transomed windows, to the l. one and two one-transomed ones. The mullions incidentally are of an unusual and elegant H-section. The side has two symmetrical canted bay windows and a middle doorway with pediment on pilasters. The back has projecting wings too. Along the centre runs an C18 arcade, with a middle porch with a semi-elliptical head. There are no Elizabethan interiors. The internal features of the house are of the late C17 and the first half of the C18. The former date is that of the staircase with twisted balusters. The excellent stone fireplaces are of the latter, and the Rococo ceiling of the staircase is the latest part worth mentioning.

See
p.
359

SHELLINGFORD

3090

ST FAITH. A very satisfying church. It has a Norman chancel arch with good decorated capitals and a single-step arch. Late Norman the s doorway with two orders of shafts, zigzag in the arch meeting at the angle. The hood-mould stands on beasts' heads but already has dogtooth decoration. Traces of a Norman N doorway too. The priest's doorway also of two orders, but the shafts have shaft-rings. Zigzag in the arch. Partially unbuttressed E.E. w tower with lancets, that to the s exceedingly long. The recessed spire was added in 1625 and rebuilt in 1852. The arch to the nave is broad and has a slight chamfer. Dec chancel, reticulated tracery in the E window. But to the N a three-light Perp window. This was originally probably the N window of a chapel; for inside the soffit of the arch and the jambs are decorated with quatrefoils. May be a tomb stood here. The nave s side has a three-light Dec and two four-light Perp windows, the latter with tran-soms. – FONT COVER. Jacobean. – PULPIT. Broad arched panels; not over-decorated. – BOX PEWS. By *Frederick Etchells*, c.1948. The Georgian Group has won, and things have come full circle. It is not so long ago that restorers almost automatically cast out box pews. – STAINED GLASS. In the E window two crowned female heads and more. Also old bits in the chancel and nave s windows. – PLATE. Silver-gilt Cup and Cover, 1597; Paten on foot, 1641. – MONUMENTS. In the chancel indent of the large brass to John of Bluebury, priest, who died in 1372. – Mrs Mary Packer † 1719. Large architectural composition. White and grey marble. At the lowest stage alternatingly blocked pilasters. Above a sarcophagus, a bust and two putti. – Sir Edward Hannes, physician of Queen Anne. Large tablet of reredos type with bust and putti. – Second Viscount Ashbrook † 1780. By *W. Tyler*. Brown, white, and grey marble. Obelisk behind a sarcophagus above which two putti by an urn in a diagonally rising composition. – Third Viscount, 1802 by *Flaxman*. Much smaller and plainer. Urn on a pedestal.

A long, low, even range sw of the church has several late medieval straight-headed windows. Two lights, arched tops. Probably early C16.

SHELLINGFORD HOUSE, nw of the church. A symmetrical two-gabled front of five bays. Mullioned windows with hood-moulds. On the upper floor they run 2, 2, 4, 2, 2 lights. It all points to the mid C17. (The staircase with dumb-bell balusters and columns as newel posts and at the same time supports for the flights above confirms that date. NBR)

(The house formerly called THE GATEHOUSE, according to the Rev. D. G. Peck, has a good stucco ceiling of the early C17.)

SHINFIELD   *7060*

ST MARY. The church has a Norman doorway with one order of colonnettes, thin scallop capitals, and a hood-mould on heads. The chancel is Dec, see the elementary flowing tracery of the two-light windows. The s chapel window has mullions and a transom, and the chapel is indeed dated 1596. The brick tower is yet later. It is dated 1664. It is broad, has polygonal clasping buttresses, several lively brick friezes, and a chamfered, round-arched doorway. Wide nave, wide aisle, Victorian arcade. The s chapel has a nice canted boarded ceiling with bosses. – FONT. High Victorian, with naturalistic leaves. The church was in fact restored in 1857. – PLATE. Almsdish of 1761. – MONUMENTS. Hugh Steward. Purbeck marble tablet with a coat of arms, an inscription on a scroll, and a sword below. On the hilt the date 1576. – Edward Martin † 1604 and wife. Tablet with small kneeling figures. – Henry Beke, wife and daughter. Dated 1627. Quite a swagger alabaster tablet. To the l. and r. of the three kneeling figures

angels holding drapery open. The clothes also are amply
draped.

SCHOOL GREEN, ½ m. SE. The SCHOOL founded in 1707 is
still there, and it is effectively flanked by an extension of 1860
with a bellcote and another of 1889. The old building is of
four bays plus the middle doorway and two storeys. Wooden
cross-windows.

HARTLEY COURT, 1½ m. NW. The front Late Georgian, white,
of five bays, with the first, third, and fifth tripartite. Hipped
roof.

SHIPPON

1 m. NW of Abingdon

ST MARY MAGDALENE. 1855 by *Sir G. G. Scott*. Nave and
chancel. Bell-spirelet on the nave E gable. Geometrical tracery.
MANOR HOUSE, E of the church. Early C18. Five bays, two
storeys, hipped roof. Doorway with pediment.

SHOTTESBROOKE

ST JOHN BAPTIST. In 1337 Sir William Trussell established
a college here, and the large and impressive church must be
the immediate consequence of this. It is Dec throughout, a
cruciform design with windows of flowing tracery, mostly
just of two lights, but the E window of five with quite an
exuberant pattern, and the N transept N window of three,
decidedly wilful. The church is of flint, the chancel of
knapped flint. The crossing tower carries a recessed spire
with lucarnes right at the foot. Inside, the N and S crossing
arches are triple-chamfered on the barest responds, just with
a slight chamfer. But the E and W arches must be a later re-
working. They are Perp in the responds, though Dec in the
arch mouldings. In the chancel simple, ogee-headed SEDILIA
and PISCINA. Opposite an ogee-trefoiled doorway. In the
N transept below the N window are two tomb recesses, no
doubt one William's. They have four pendant ogee arches
each and a straight top and are separated by a steep-gabled
niche with a bracket for an image and a pretty tipped-up
vault inside. – FONT. C14 too. Ogee-headed panels, no separate
foot or stem. – STAINED GLASS. Original bits in many
windows. – E window by *Hardman* (BC). – PLATE. Paten,
1709; Paten, 1712; Chalice, 1714; Flagon, 1762. – MONU-
MENTS. Late C14 brass to a lady, 3 ft 6 in. – Brass to Richard
Gyll † 1511, 25 in. Both N transept floor. – Also late C14 the

excellent brass to a Priest and a Layman, 4 ft figures under canopies. – William Throkmorton, priest, † 1535. Moustached 28a stone figure carved into a stone block so that he appears to lie in his coffin. A band of stone is left standing across his waist, and on this are brass inscriptions. – Sarah Cherry † 1714. Small, bad bust under a baldacchino. – Also Cherry tablets of † 1699 and † 1703.

The COLLEGE has virtually disappeared. Thomas Hearne still saw 'the two spacious halls with their chimneys and the parlours and other remains' (*Gent. Mag.* 1840). The village which must have existed has also gone. So the church now looks the typical Victorian estate church, lying as close as it does to the house and in its grounds.

SHOTTESBROOKE PARK. Castellated brick mansion recently relieved of forty-one rooms including the fine staircase and drawing room. These were late C18, as the whole indeed appears to be. In fact the brickwork is partly Tudor. Polygonal angle-buttresses. The side where the rooms were demolished has been very handsomely tidied up by *Viscount Esher (Lionel Brett)*. – By the side STABLES with a pretty cupola. Two long radiating avenues in front of the house.

SMEWINS, ¾ m. SE. Timber-framed house with two gables. Brick infilling. C16?

SHRIVENHAM   2080

ST ANDREW. This is an extremely interesting church, because it represents a personal solution to the building of a large church, when few were built. There was on the spot a church which was cruciform, and of this the central tower on its four arches (many continuous broad mouldings) remains and demonstrates a date about 1400. The roof line of the old continuation is also still visible, but that is all. All the rest was removed in 1638, when Lord Craven decided to build afresh. He built a large oblong outside the four arches, of nave and aisles and chancel and chapels, and added a W porch. This has entrances from N and S with four-centred heads and hood-moulds on big stops. The porch has a pediment too, the only classical feature. In the E wall of the church, set symmetrically at the ends of the chapel, are also two such entrances. Otherwise all is long, straight-headed Perp windows, with cusped arched lights and no tracery, of three, four (two plus two), and five lights. That is all. Inside, the arcade has double-chamfered 11b round arches on Tuscan columns with an excessive entasis,

reminiscent of a certain bottle-shape. – FONT. Of Purbeck
marble, C12, octagonal, with two shallow blank arches on
each side – a familiar type. – PULPIT. Very good, and unusual. The usual blank arches made the pretext for false perspectives (cf. Buckland). Angle columns and balusters. Large
tester. – BENCHES. Simple, straight-headed, and pleasant. –
PANELLING. Nearly all the way round, plus a more decorated
surround for the tower-stair doorway. – PLATE. Cup of
1577/8; Cup of the early C17; Flagon, 1624; two Patens,
1636; two Plates with allegorical figures, foreign. – MONU-
MENTS. Defaced effigy in the S aisle. Is it C13? – On the
chancel E wall two nearly identical tablets: † 1713 and † 1734.
– On the chancel W wall pretty tablet with garlands: † 1721. –
Rothesia Ann Barrington † 1745. By *Thomas Paty* of Bristol.
Coloured marbles. Obelisk and simple urn. It looks later. –
Second Viscount Barrington † 1793. Designed by *James
Wyatt* and carved by *Richard Westmacott*. A circular base
and an urn on top. Now supported by a Victorian angel bust.
– Admiral Barrington † 1800. With a big flag. By *Flaxman*. –
Russell Barrington † 1840. By *T. Denman*. A roundel with a
sweet ivy wreath.

In the main street ELM TREE HOUSE, a fine specimen of about
1700. Five bays, two storeys, hipped roof, later Tuscan porch.
Wooden cross-windows. Staircase with twisted balusters.
Next door the variedly grouped SCHOOL, Gothic of 1863.

STATION. 1840. Very small. Flint with Tudor windows and
roofs far projecting like a canopy on the entrance as well as
the platform side.

ROYAL MILITARY COLLEGE OF SCIENCE. The college was
founded as the 'Advanced Class' at Woolwich in 1864, became
the Artillery College in 1885, the Military College of Science
in 1927, and moved to Shrivenham only in 1947. The main
group of blocks is over 1200 ft long, of red brick, neo-
Georgian, and entirely symmetrical. In addition garden-
suburb-like housing. The officers' mess is BECKETT HALL,
built in 1831–4 in a Tudor style for the sixth Viscount
Barrington. The architect was *W. Atkinson*. The main rooms
have plaster ceilings. In the centre the hall with a covered
ceiling, the centre panels glazed. Close to the house by the
lake is a SUMMER HOUSE, square, with a big (renewed)
pyramid roof and stone cross-windows. Each side has two,
close to a middle doorway. This does seem original work of
c.1635.

SHURLOCK ROW

8070

1½ m. sw of Waltham St Lawrence

ALL SAINTS. 1870 by *J. Sharp*. Brick, with transepts, a low
apse, and lancet windows.

GREAT MARTINS. Brick, with two C17 gables and a considerable enlargement of c.1830 on the l.

SILWOOD PARK *see* SUNNINGHILL

SINDLESHAM

7050

SINDLESHAM HOUSE (Salvatorian Fathers). Plain Georgian
seven-bay front, stuccoed, with a three-bay pediment, a
Tuscan doorway, and two one-storeyed bows.

   Behind the house the new CHAPEL, 1963–4 by *R. J. Beswick*
of Swindon (and of the firm which won third prize in the
competition for Coventry Cathedral). Square, with one of the
fashionable folded roofs.

SINDLESHAM MILL, ⅝ m. NW. Pretty group. Three-storeyed
brick mill, long, with the ground-floor and first-floor windows
tied together by giant arches.

The GREEN is triangular, and along it runs Bear Wood estate
housing.

BEAR WOOD, *see* p. 79.

FOREST GRAMMAR SCHOOL, Winnersh, 1 m. N. Recent and
good.

SINODUN CAMP *see* LITTLE WITTENHAM

SMEWINS *see* SHOTTESBROOKE

SONNING

7070

ST ANDREW. Visually the church is Victorian (by *Woodyer*,
1853 and 1876 etc.). Really original parts are only the shaft of
the Norman PILLAR PISCINA inside, with spiral bands, the
bases of the N arcade piers, E.E., the lower part of the Perp
tower, and the arch N of the chancel. The VCH builds up a
whole architectural history, with C13 N aisle walling, early C14
S aisle walling, late C14 E parts of the N chapel, chancel E parts,
and aisle arcade piers on both sides. Pretty chancel decoration
by *Bodley*, 1903–6. – Very ornate REREDOS with figures in
tiers, Dec in style, as is the E window. By *Woodyer*, 1875 (BC)
and very characteristic of him. – SCREENS to N and S chapels.
Perp single-light divisions, much restored. – STAINED GLASS.

E window by *Hardman*, 1869 (BC). – One N window by *Kempe*,
1893. – CHANDELIER of brass, two tiers, dated 1675. – PLATE.
Two silver-gilt Almsdishes of 1661 and an undated silver-
gilt Spoon. – The church has a splendid set of MONUMENTS,
starting with the brass on the chancel floor of Laurence Fyton
† 1434, a 38 in. figure. – Several more brasses on the chancel
floor, all Barkers, † 1546, † 1549, † 158 ?. – Also a child † 1627.
– In the S aisle fragment of an Elizabethan monument: six
small kneeling figures. – Lady Litcott † 1630 (S chapel),
kneeling below curtains. Columns l. and r. Red and black
marble. – Lady Anne Clarke † 1653 (N chapel). Demure bust
in an oval recess with garlands. Segmental pediment at the
top. – Charles and Elizabeth Rich † 1665 and 1656 (S chapel).
Large, with twisted columns; no figures. – Sir Thomas and
Thomas Rich † 1667 and 1663 (tower). A very remarkable
monument, called by the *Ecclesiologist* in 1853 'the vilest
paganism imaginable' (BC). Two large white identical urns on
a black marble slab which is carried by four sad white putti. –
Sir Anthony Barker † 1630 and his son † 1675 and grandson
† 1694 (S chapel). Above the inscription two putti under a
baldacchino. – William Barker by *Sir R. Westmacott*, c.1796
(Gunnis). A standing female figure drops a flower on an altar.
Not an inspired piece. – Canon Hugh Pearson, 1883 by
Frederick Thrupp. White recumbent effigy under an elaborate
Gothic canopy linking chancel and N chapel.

The S wall of the churchyard is of Tudor (and later) bricks
and reminds us of the fact that at Sonning was a PALACE of
the Bishops of Salisbury. This was excavated in 1916, and
evidence was found of the late C15 gatehouse, a large forecourt, the great hall, earlier C15, with porch and square bay
window, the C13 solar range to its N stretching E, a small
irregular court E of the hall and S of the solar, more chambers to
the E of the court, and the kitchen some distance S of the hall.
N of the church is the Thames BRIDGE, probably later C18, of
eleven brick arches increasing in size to the centre. From
here THAMES STREET winds along and has on its N side
FALCON HOUSE, Georgian, of brick, irregular, on its S side
Lutyens's DEANERY GARDENS, built for Edward Hudson,
the owner of *Country Life*, in 1901. The theme which started
Lutyens off was the ancient wall to the street, which he did
not want to break. So one enters by very small arched doorways. The principal one of these leads into a low groin-
vaulted passage which takes one to the front door of the house

proper. On the r. is an inner courtyard formed by the front of the centre of the house and a wing projecting to the old wall. In the courtyard a small pool with what Mr A. S. G. Butler calls 'a chaste piece of sculpture'. The vaulted passage belongs to a second wing, symmetrical with the other. The main front of the house is to the s, and its principal feature is a glorious bay window (of Norman Shaw inspiration). It projects by three lights and has a six-light front. This bay lies in axis with the hall fireplace and the pool in the courtyard. But that axiality is broken by the entrance passage, which, as we have seen, is asymmetrically placed in one wing. However, the passage also is followed through to the s front, where it is represented by a deeply moulded arched exit. To the r. of this stands as a very dramatic accent a chimney with three bold and high stacks set diagonally. The composition is as splendid as that of similar elements at Tigbourne Court in Surrey of 1899. The hall inside, behind the big bay window, has wind-braces showing up in the walls.

At the top of Thames Street is PEARSON STREET. Here the ROBERT PALMER COTTAGES, brick, of 1850, a set of alms-houses. Then cottages and one five-bay house of c.1700, with a doorway decorated by pilasters and a triglyph frieze. Then the corner of the HIGH STREET with divers pretty timber-framed cottages and Georgian houses, e.g. the WHITE HOUSE with Soanian incised ornament. At the bottom the timber-framed BULL HOTEL by the entrance to the churchyard. At the top, i.e. in Pearson Street, across the view up the High Street, THE GROVE, early C18, with three gables. The door-way has a canopy with pendants as fine as those of Queen Anne's Gate, London.

At the s end of Pearson Street a C17 brick house on the r., and *en face* the Victorian GATES and LODGE of Holme Park. This is now the Reading Blue Coat School and has kept two figures of Charity Children, a bluecoat and a greencoat boy.

SOTWELL

ST JAMES. 1884 by *S. R. Stephenson*. Like a Surrey church. Nave and chancel, timber bell-turret and shingled broach spire. In the N wall inside a stone which looks like a Norman capital.* – PLATE. Cup of 1780; Paten of 1836.

* The Rev. R. Gibbs writes that in addition the following remain from the preceding church: C14 roof timbers, two C14 windows in the N wall, parts of two C12 ones in the N and S walls, and part of a C13 doorway in the N wall.

SMALL'S HOUSE, Mackney, ½ m. sw. An extremely interesting
Elizabethan or Jacobean stone house. The street front is of
two symmetrical gables and three widely spaced bays, with
a four-centred head to the doorway and three- and two-light
mullioned windows. The back is slightly different, in so far
as here was the entrance to the hall, i.e. there are four bays,
with the doorway not in the middle and with a four-light
window to its l. The sides have far-receding centres so that
deep narrow courtyards are formed and only a small core
remains in the middle of the house. Here the staircase is
placed. It originally had no direct access from the street doorway. Strange also is the placing of the hall fireplace in the
wall where one would expect in a large house the screens
passage, a Yorkshire custom unexpected here.

SOUTH FAWLEY MANOR HOUSE see
GREAT FAWLEY

5000
SOUTH HINKSEY

The part by the church is still villagey, in spite of all the Oxford
housing around.

ST LAWRENCE. Nave and chancel and unbuttressed w tower.
The present chancel is simple and pleasant Georgian work.
The rest basically C13, see the chancel arch responds and
some windows. – SCULPTURE. Miniature ivory pediment with
St John and other figures. Is it continental of *c.*1850?* –
PLATE. Chalice and Paten, *c.*1636.

SOUTHILL PARK see BRACKNELL

5080
SOUTH MORETON

ST JOHN BAPTIST. In the w wall a narrow C11 doorway. The s
aisle has a s lancet and a s cusped lancet and other indications of
the same style, i.e. one must assume that the aisle was added
already in the early C13. Otherwise most windows Perp. Dec
the nave w window (reticulation), Perp the s aisle buttresses
with shields in panels. The church has a bellcote of 1849.
Inside, the arcade is of two parts separated by a C19 arch said
to replace a small round-arched doorway. The two w bays are
of *c.*1200 (round pier, octagonal abacus, single-step arches),

---

* Canon A. G. Whye tells me that an identical pediment is at St Aldate's
Rectory at Oxford.

the E bays of the C13 (round piers, double-chamfered arches).
– PLATE. Paten, 1584; Chalice, 1786.
THE HALL, NE of the church, on the main road. Seven bays,
blue and red brick. Windows with stone keystones. Panelled
parapet.

SPARSHOLT

3080

HOLY CROSS. The N doorway is of the late C12, with its waterleaf as well as stiff-leaf capitals, its round arch, the odd, still
Norman motif of the arch moulding, and the hood-mould still
on beasts' heads. The S doorway seems a little later, though
the arch is also still round. Stiff-leaf capitals. C13 W tower
with later shingled broach spire. Typical late C13 bell-
openings. Good early C14 chancel of chalk. Long Dec
windows, parapet with cusped wavy fields. Dec also the S
transept.* The S window is of four lights and has reticulated
tracery. Nave S windows Dec and Perp. In the church the
Dec contribution is confirmed. For instance the chancel arch
and S transept arch both have continuous chamfers. Moreover the chancel has its full equipment of EASTER SEPULCHRE,
S tomb recess, SEDILIA, and PISCINA, all with ogee arches,
with cusping and head cusps, and in the S wall of the S transept are two tomb recesses of the same kind. With one goes a
tomb-chest with small 'weepers'. Chancel roof on stone
corbels with the four Signs of the Evangelists. – REREDOS.
This is the lower part of a former E window. – SCREEN
to the S transept. Shafts with shaft-rings instead of mullions,
and cinquefoiled, not pointed, arches – i.e. C13, an exceptionally early date for a wooden screen. – BENCHES. In the
chancel. The ends straight-topped and with tracery and
emblems. – NORTH DOOR. With original iron scrollwork of
the late C12. – STAINED GLASS. One head in a nave N
window. – PLATE. Chalice and Paten of 1613(?). – MONU-
MENTS. In the chancel tomb recess Knight, crossed legs,
hood of mail, praying hands, two angels by his pillow.
Clearly early C14, i.e. of the time of the chancel. – In the S
transept, not *in situ*, three over-lifesize oak effigies, also early
C14. Knight, the legs not crossed, and two Wives, one wearing 26a
a wimple. – Brass to William Herleston, priest, early C15.
The figure is in the top of a cross and 25 in. long. – Lady,
12½ in., and upper half of Man, originally 21 in., both
*c.*1510–20, and all three on the chancel floor. – Sir George Hyde

* A N transept has disappeared.

† 1623. Tablet with strapwork (s transept). – John Pleydell † 1591 and his wife † 1623. Of chalk. Wide tablet, oval, with much carving around, strapwork, heads, etc. Strapwork top.

MANOR HOUSE, s of the church. Blue and red brick. Early Georgian (VCH: c.1722). Five bays, segment-headed windows. Three-bay pediment.

BOWL BARROWS, on the sw spur of Sparsholt Down. Two well-preserved bowl barrows, 90 ft and 27 ft in diameter and 6 ft and 2 ft high respectively.

SPEEN

4060

ST MARY. 1860 and 1878. Flint and stone. w tower with pyramid roof. Medieval the N arcade piers, round, of Purbeck marble. Double-chamfered arches. Also the Dec E window with flowing tracery of a popular pattern. – PULPIT. Jacobean. The sounding-board only. The rest is now at Aldbourne in Wiltshire. – STAINED GLASS. Medieval bits in the N chapel. – Uncommonly many MONUMENTS of interest. John Baptiste Castillion, a Piedmontese, † 1597. Recumbent effigy with praying hands. Shields on the tomb-chest. Alabaster. – Lady Elizabeth Castillion † 1603. Stone effigy with farthingale and widow's hood. – Jonathan Hicks and his wife who died in 1713. The monument with extremely lively decoration of garlands, putti, skull, hourglass, trumpets, etc., is no doubt by *Jonathan Hicks* himself, who calls himself a 'freemason and carver'. – William Craven and his mother who died in 1717. Big base and rich coat of arms and drapery above. – Thomas Wyld and his son. By *Bacon*, 1791. Kneeling female figure with a small urn for the son. Profile medallion for the father at the foot of the large tablet. – Margrave of Anspach † 1806. By *Canova*. His wife was a Baroness Craven. Enormously heavy tablet with a kneeling, amply draped female figure by an amphora. – William Brinton † 1823. By *Chantrey*. Altar with a profile medallion.

31b

MONUMENT at the corner of the A-road and the street to the church. A truncated column and a metal ball. This is said to have nothing to do with the Battle of Newbury and to have been a lamp post.

The houses along the main road are the immediate continuation of those of Newbury. They start with the three-bay, three-bay pediment, yellow brick SPEEN LODGE. Then, after some desolation, SPEEN MANOR with a nice doorcase, the HARE AND HOUNDS, dated 1756, with a five-bay NE front with pedimental gables, LEIGHTON LODGE, blue brick with two canted bay windows, and so to SPEEN HOUSE, stuccoed, with a central bow window up the whole three storeys.

ELMORE HOUSE, SW of the church. Brick. Early C18, five bays, two storeys, hipped roof, with lower three-bay wings.

BENHAM PARK, 1 m. W. 1772–5 by *Lancelot (Capability) Brown*, who also laid out the gardens. Brown had gone into partnership with *Holland* in 1772. Built for the sixth Earl of Craven. Three storeys, stone, nine bays, with a portico of four un- 50a fluted Ionic columns and no pediment. The central room has two grand chimneypieces with carved wooden overmantels and a delicate plaster ceiling. Several nice details in other rooms. The GATEPIERS and LODGES at the NE corner, i.e. on the A-road, are excellent too. The piers each have two pilasters with banded vermiculated rustication, a niche between, and a pediment. – At the NW corner the GATEPIERS have trophies on top and are said to come from Hamstead Marshall.

BAGNOR MANOR FARMHOUSE, 1⅛ m. NNW. C17; altered. Jacobean staircase (MHLG and NBR).

SPEENHAMLAND *see* NEWBURY, p. 181

SPENCERS WOOD   706b

ST MICHAEL. 1908 by *S. Slingsby Stallwood*. Red brick, also inside. Bellcote. Dec windows.

SCHOOL. 1890. Pretty. Grey vitrified brick and red brick patterns. Gables with bargeboards.

CONGREGATIONAL CHAPEL. 1902–3 by *W. Ravenscroft*. Red brick, with a tower, and cosy to look at.

STANDEN MANOR *see* HUNGERFORD

STANFORD DINGLEY   5070

ST DENYS. Flint, with a weatherboarded bell-turret. Brick chancel of *c.*1768 (Kelly). Inside, the church is both more interesting and more eloquent. To the original church a N arcade of two bays, one small and round-arched, the other wider, higher, and pointed, was added in the late C12. The piers are nook-shafted. Shortly after, in the early C13, the same was done on the S side. The capitals now had stiff-leaf. Soon also a W bay was added on the N side, allowing for a wider nave. The W lancet of the aisle is original. The chancel arch also is of the same type. The s doorway may be of the time of the s arcade. One order of shafts with stiff-leaf capitals. The arch very odd, trefoiled, but a rosette cuts into the top foil. – SOUTH DOOR. With the old hinges. – PAINTING. Remains of C13 wall painting. Masonry and scroll patterns. Also a King in the jamb of a N window. – BRICKS. Very interesting encaustic bricks, not tiles, now built into the N respond of the chancel arch. – PLATE. Paten, 1697; Chalice, 1718. – MONUMENTS. Brass to Margaret Dyneley † 1444, a 19½ in. figure. – In the churchyard elegant urn on a pedestal to Richard Carter † 1773.

GARDEN HOUSE, ¼ m. s. Five-bay Georgian house with a pedimented doorway.

RECTORY, sw of the former. Chequer brick, early C18, also of five bays. Three dormers in the roof with alternating pediments. Doorway with Ionic pilasters intermittently blocked. Big keystones and broken pediment.

STANFORD-IN-THE-VALE

3090

ST DENYS. Quite a large church, with quite a high w tower. The earliest evidence is the s doorway, still with trumpet-scallop capitals, i.e. late C12, and the N doorway with crocket capitals, probably of the same date. Then the w tower. The arch to the nave triple-chamfered, the bell-openings twins. These features indicate the late C13. The tower ended with a corbel-frieze, but was heightened later. Dec chancel with the E and one s window provided with tracery which includes the spiked trefoils usually called Kentish tracery. Perp N porch higher than the aisle. Crenellated s porch also Perp. Low nave with Perp crenellated clerestory. C14 aisles with straight-headed windows. The N aisle is continued as a vestry, unnoticeable outside. C14 also the arcades, with octagonal piers and double-chamfered arches which die into the piers. Traces of the C14 clerestory below the present one (above the spandrels, not the apexes of the arches). In the chancel an extremely interesting PISCINA with shelf and PYX CANOPY over. This also is probably Dec.* – FONT. Jacobean, the whole font encased in wood panels and provided with a wooden cover as well. – PULPIT. Jacobean, roomy, with close arabesque decoration. – STALLS. A few, plain. – STAINED GLASS. In the heads of chancel E and s windows original, i.e. early C14, figures. –

22a

* The pyx canopy is locally supposed to have been a RELIQUARY originally.

PLATE. Cup and Cover, London, 1585; Paten on foot, London, 1711; large Flagon, London, 1752.* – MONUMENT. Brass to Roger Campedene † 1398, rector. Oversized demi-figure, 28 in. long.

The village spreads out and has e.g. two greens. s of the church MANOR FARMHOUSE, early C18, four bays, brown stone and red brick dressings, two storeys, hipped roof. (Some nice interiors. The BARN is dated 1618 and has a tie-beam roof. NBR) N of the church RECTORY HOUSE, stone, C18, of three bays with a hipped roof. Further N, i.e. at Upper Green, STANFORD HOUSE, red brick, very high, three widely spaced bays of small windows. One-bay projection with pediment. Doorway with Tuscan columns and pediment. To the s, i.e. along the street towards the Wantage road, PENSTONE'S FARMHOUSE, a fragment, part C17, part early C18, i.e. with mullioned and with segment-headed windows. Then COXE'S HALL, dated 1733, and quite a dramatic Early Georgian front. Brick, roughcast. Five bays, segment-headed windows. One-bay projection carried up higher and provided with a pediment. The doorway and main window in the projection are round-arched. (Staircase with thin twisted and turned balusters. NBR)

MILL FARM, ½ m. s. Georgian, five bays, rubble, with raised brick window surrounds.

STANLAKE PARK see ST NICHOLAS HURST

STEVENTON
4090

ST MICHAEL. The earliest piece is one s arcade pier which is round and has a stiff-leaf capital. It seems to tell of a smaller church. The present dimensions belong to the early C14. s porch tower – see the bell-openings; s aisle – see the windows; N side – ditto; chancel – ditto. The Perp E window is over-restored. The w doorway, though round-arched, is Perp. Inside a curious muddle. The tower arches really have no capitals – just abaci slabs. One of them has ballflower (which suits the date), one fleurons. The s arcade between the tower and the E.E. pier is shapeless. The wide arch E of the E.E. pier has two hollow chamfers. – FONT. Octagonal, Perp, nothing

* The Flagon has an inscription: 'As an humble testimony of their Unfeigned thanks to Almighty God, For the Recovery of their three Children, Thomas, Sohpia and Charlotte from the Small-pox by Inoculation Anno 1752'. The interesting thing is, as the Rev. H. S. Fry points out to me, that this of course is many years before Jenner.

special. – PULPIT. Jacobean, the tester now a table. –
BENCHES. With plain panels. Also a front with blank tracery.
– ALMSBOX. 1633. On a hefty baluster. – STAINED GLASS. E
and chancel N windows by *Warrington* (BC). – PLATE. Silver-
gilt Cup and Cover, London, 1571. – BRASS to Richard Do
† 1476; 14 in. figures (chancel floor).

There was originally an alien Benedictine cell at Steventon.
It lay S of the W end of the CAUSEWAY, the memorable
feature of the village, a paved raised tree-lined way from
church to green along which are all the houses of interest,
starting with THE PRIORY, a timber-framed house with two
differently projecting gables and behind it a hall which is
supposed to have been the guest hall of the priory. It seems
early C16 and has one central hammerbeam truss with tracery
spandrels and a fireplace inserted later. Two tiers of wind-
braces. Contemporary service wing. The solar wing is late C14,
with a kingpost roof. It is in good condition too. A N extension
from the solar wing has been assigned to the late C15. Along
the Causeway then, all on the S side, a number of worth-while
houses, all timber-framed. Nos 103–107, part late C14 (W wing
with kingpost roof) and part C17, with two equally projecting
gable wings; Nos 77–81, also part medieval and part C17 with
a stout chimneybreast to the street and a picturesque polygonal
bay on its immediate l.; No. 67, early C17, though dated 1657,
very pretty, with a little pargetting and under the l. gable an
oriel, under the r. a canted bay. Fretwork bargeboards. Then
come No. 57 with four steep gables and Nos 39–43 with
crucks and cross-bracing in the gable, very well and completely
preserved.* Further along, beyond the green, in MILTON
LANE, an L-shaped house with wooden cross-windows, one
of chequer brick with segment-headed windows, and a big
thatched one with two gables on slightly projecting wings.
The spacious GREEN has along its E and NW sides mostly
council housing.

SCHOOL. By *Street*, 1864 and 1871. Addition of 1900.

(By the station COTTAGES in the Tudor style, of c.1840. They
were built for the Great Western, and board meetings were
held in them, as they were about halfway between London and
Bristol. J. Betjeman and J. Piper)

STOCKCROSS

4060

ST JOHN. 1839. Blue brick, with W tower, transepts, and lancet

* I am grateful to Mr S. E. Rigold for help on the dating of these houses.

windows. The chancel was lengthened in 1864 (BC). The church was almost entirely re-fitted by *Sir Ninian Comper* (BC). – STAINED GLASS. Comper's anaemic E window replaces that which is now blind and hard to see. – In two side windows assembled bits of former glass.

Some early C20 ESTATE HOUSING.

STRATFIELD MORTIMER   *6060*

ST MARY. 1869 by *R. Armstrong*, the W end with two surprising flying buttresses. Vestry 1896 by *E. Swinfen Harris*. Quite a stately church, and certainly a busy exterior. Rock-faced, with a SE steeple. Broach spire with two tiers of lucarnes. Geometrical tracery. Five-bay arcades with round piers and naturalistic capitals. Small foiled clerestory windows. Much blank arcading in the chancel. – REREDOS. The paintings 1868 by *O'Connor*, better known for stained glass. – STAINED GLASS. Behind the organ a mixed lot, including small English C15 pieces. – Also a mixed lot of Victorian glass, most interesting the W window with large figures by *Clutterbuck*. – PLATE. Complete Set of 1869. – MONUMENTS. In the chancel a 6 ft 6 in. coffin-lid with an inscription referring to Aegelwardus, who is mentioned in the Anglo-Saxon Chronicle and died in 1017. An eminently important piece. – Brasses to Richard Trevet † 1441 and wife, 27 in. figures.

ST JOHN, Mortimer Common. 1882 by *William Rhind*, but this refers only to the present aisle. Nave and chancel and W tower by *Swinfen Harris*, 1896. Red brick. The W tower has four top gables. Lancet windows, nice boarded roof. – REREDOS. A painting by *Nathaniel H. J. Westlake*: Christ at Emmaus, in the Nazarene tradition. Christ strictly frontal. Behind him a cloth held by angels. Westlake was a pupil of Dyce and Herbert and later specialized in stained glass. – STAINED GLASS by *Kempe*, chancel and S aisle SE.

Just W of St Mary the SCHOOL of 1869, rock-faced, with a high tower crowned by a saddleback roof.

MORTIMER HILL, halfway between Stratfield and Mortimer Common. Georgian. Front with doorway between two canted bay windows. The doorway has pilasters, a triglyph frieze, and discs in the metopes.

MORTIMER HOUSE, ⅜ m. N. 1774. Blue brick headers and red brick dressings. Five bays, two storeys. The centre projects a little. Contemporary additions to the l. Terrible later porch.

Fine staircase with a wrought-iron railing with s-scrolls. On the walls decorative friezes. Glazed circular lantern.

ROUND BARROW CEMETERY, on Mortimer Common. This group of four Early Bronze Age barrows includes a very fine bell barrow with a mound 80 ft in diameter and 6 ft high surrounded by a ditch 9 ft broad and 1 ft deep.

WOKEFIELD PARK, ⅞ m. NNE. Large, but of at least two periods. The centre of seven bays with two-bay projecting wings is probably Early Georgian. The staircase with twisted and fluted balusters looks that date. It rises behind a screen of fluted Ionic columns. This centre and the articulated five-bay wings are all cemented. Are the additions and the remodelling of the centre *c.*1820 or later?

STRATTENBOROUGH CASTLE FARM
see COLESHILL

5080   STREATLEY

ST MARY. Short Perp w tower. The rest of 1865 by *Charles Buckeridge.* – REREDOS. 1893. Designed by *Pearson* (BC). – PAINTING. The Mourning of Christ. After *van Dyck*, the picture in the Berlin gallery. – PLATE. Paten, 1715; Cup, 1716. – BRASS to Elizabeth Prout † 1440, a 20 in. figure (chancel N wall).

In the HIGH STREET STREATLEY HOUSE, late C18, of five bays and three storeys, red brick, smooth, with a big doorcase of unfluted Ionic columns and pediment. Also some other Georgian houses higher up ending in ELM LODGE across the top, and some Georgian cottages below. But charming as they are, surely the most attractive architectural feature of Streatley is *W. Ravenscroft*'s conversion of old malthouses into a village hall, a tower and two private houses l. and r. This group of brick with tile-hanging and gables, built rather late for its style in 1898, lies between church and High Street and is varied and cosy.

8080   STUBBINGS
                         2½ m. W of Maidenhead

ST JAMES THE LESS. 1850–4 by *R. C. Carpenter*. Flint; nave, chancel, and N aisle; bellcote. Windows mostly of single lights with ogee tops. In the chancel encaustic PAINTING.

6070   SULHAM

ST NICHOLAS. 1838, with an E end of 1875. The church is

flint and stone, with a w tower, lancet windows, and the apse
of 1875. Between nave and chancel a triple screen, i.e. three
arches nearly the full height. – FONT. The bowl is of marble,
semi-globular and of 1733. – PLATE. Paten, 1680; Paten on
foot, 1691; Cup, 1729; Almsdish, 1732; Flagon, 1751; small
Flagon, early C19. – MONUMENT. Small tablet to Jane Wilder
† 1845. It comprises an incised panel showing her in prayer
at a prayer desk, not strictly in profile. A very charming
period piece. – John Wilder † 1892, rector for fifty-six years.
The memorial is an enriched CROSS in the churchyard,
Gothic of course, and of 1892.

SCHOOL. 1892. The windows a nice mixture of Gothic and
Baroque. The architect may have been the incumbent, the
Rev. *J. Wilder*, Provost of Eton College.

(At the w end of the village the STOCKS. VCH)

SULHAMSTEAD

6060

ST MICHAEL. 1914 by *E. J. Munt*; flint, Gothic, and really of
no architectural interest at all. Moreover, redundant now.

RECTORY. Brick, Georgian, of five bays, with pedimented doorway.

FOLLY FARM. *Lutyens* made this house in two campaigns out
of a timber-framed cottage existing on the site. The two campaigns took place in 1906 and 1912 and were undertaken for
two different owners. Oddly enough, i.e. in contradiction to
Lutyens's development, the first was classical, the second
Tudor–Arts-and-Crafts. Lutyens had done Monkton House,
Singleton, in Sussex in a classical style already in 1902, the
courtyard of Papillon House in Leicestershire in 1903, and
Nashdom at Taplow much more monumentally in 1905. Here,
at Folly Farm, he built a complete William-and-Mary house
from the s end of the cottage to the E, a front with a two-
storeyed hall in the centre and two symmetrical projecting
wings. The next owner wanted much more space, and Lutyens
provided it by returning to his early Arts and Crafts style,
handled in few other cases as brilliantly as in this belated one.
The addition is to the w of the house of 1906, which was left
entirely intact. The new wing runs w and then turns s–N, w
of the cottage. This s–N part in the end became the largest of
the house. Visually the climax is the pool with the roof 62
extending low down over the cloister. From the s the house
is thus frankly of two periods which the layman may well
read as Tudor, with mullioned and transomed windows and

a weatherboarded gable, and William and Mary, of grey and red brick. In the garden Lutyens, as so often, collaborated with *Gertrude Jekyll*, his earliest patron and promoter.

SULHAMSTEAD HOUSE. Early C19, white, of two storeys. Nine bays with a three-bay giant Ionic portico.

TYLE MILL. 1937–8 by Lutyens's disciple *A. S. G. Butler*.

BRAZENHEAD COTTAGES, ⅛ m. N of Folly Farm. Once one house. Timber-framing and brick infilling, C17, a nice composition with gabled projections l. and r.

SULHAMSTEAD ABBOTS

6060

ST MARY. Flint, a small village church with a timber bell-turret. The church may be of *c.*1200 altogether, though only the chancel windows and the N arcade remain as features. The windows are small, pointed outside, round inside, the arcade has an original W respond and two original arches with only a slight chamfer. The third arch is C14. – FONT. Norman, tub-shaped, with blank arcading. – MONUMENT. Brass to Ralph Eyer, 1524 (when he was still alive). It has the following inscription:

Extremum vitae finem, meditare, Viator
Tam cito cum videas omnia nata, mori,
In coelum converte oculos, amplectere laudem
Damnosasque Evae despice blanditias.

One wonders what the congregation thought of the accursed blandishments of Eve.

SUNNINGDALE

9060

HOLY TRINITY. The chancel 1860 by *Street*, the rest 1887–8 by *J. Oldrid Scott*. The coarser character of the work of 1860 is externally at once noticeable. Oldrid Scott is competent, but not attractive here. It is a big church with a steeple over the crossing and E.E. details. The GATES to the churchyard, of cast iron, are obviously older. They must belong to the previous church, which was built in 1839. – STAINED GLASS. One S window by *Kempe*, 1892. – MONUMENT. Prince Victor of Hohenlohe-Langenburg † 1891. Alabaster. By his daughter, *Countess Feodora Gleichen*. Recumbent effigy in relief. Italian Renaissance style.

COWORTH PARK FARM. Timber-framed and gabled. The MHLG calls it C15 and earlier.

SUNNINGDALE PARK, ½ m. N. Classical, of nine bays with attached portico, but a lush fancy-Gothic hall with gallery on columns round the upper floor. Large staircase. All this was done by *W. E. Lord* for Sir Hugo Cunliffe-Owen in 1930.

CHARTERS, ⅞ m. WSW. By *Adie, Button & Partners*. 1938. A typical case of the C20 style adopted willy-nilly, just in order to be up-to-date. The result is motifs only in an ensemble not conceived in the C20 spirit. White and cubic it is, and horizontal windows, even breaking round corners, it has, but the great hall in the centre has a front to the S with the giant pillars of the Fascist brand and the French windows to its l. and r. are of Georgian proportions. The interior was originally almost entirely period, and the model farm had pitched roofs with blue glazed tiles.

SUNNINGHILL

9060

ST MICHAEL. 1808 and 1826–7. Yellow brick. W tower with a re-used Norman zigzag arch to the doorway. Wide S aisle, its W front flat-topped and crenellated, its windows with Y-tracery. The same in the N aisle. However, some of the windows were made Geometrical in 1888, when the chancel and S chapel were built in yellow brick with red-brick trim by *W. H. Crossland*, the architect of the Royal Holloway College. They are imitation-Perp and have complicated pinnacles. Interior of 1828 with thin cast-iron columns. Wide aisles, their stucco roofs original. The nave roof evidently of 1888. The chancel roof extremely busy, with cusping. – PLATE. Chalice of 1711; Patens of 1703, 1715, and 1834. – MONUMENTS. In the S aisle one by *King* of Bath († 1783). – In the churchyard columns to Sir H. R. and Lady Popham. She died in 1866. Relief with nautical instruments and names of battles: Copenhagen, Cape of Good Hope, North of Spain, Buenos Ayres.

CORDES HALL, in the middle of the village, ½ m. S. 1902 by *Joseph Morris & Son*. Brick and roughcast, with remarkably inventive brick windows crowned by curved hood-moulds and cross gables. Top lantern.

SILWOOD PARK, ½ m. E. Red brick and huge. Free Tudor with a freer tower. According to *The Builder* designed by *Waterhouse* in 1876. Executed with alterations by *S. Tugwell* of Bournemouth. It was meant to cost £22,800 (GS), but in fact cost £27,500.

TITTENHURST PARK, ¾ m. E. 1737, with additions. The

8*

exterior looks *c*.1830. White, two-storeyed, with a pretty Ionic porch. In the garden two weeping blue Atlas cedars, an extreme rarity.

BROADLANDS, 1 m. w of Sunningdale Station. By *Minoprio & Spencely*. Published in *Country Life* in 1934, and there shrewdly analysed as belonging to the 'middle' as against the 'left' of the modern style in its English form. The left is characterized as Corbusier–Mendelsohn–Connell–Chermayeff –McGrath, the middle as Stratford Theatre and Oliver Hill's Morecambe Hotel. *Country Life* praises Broadlands as 'not led away by the functionalist bogy'. It is brick, with a flat roof and a top frill of projecting brick ornament. Motifs of Spanish-Mission and Tudor can be noticed. The house replaces one by *Norman Shaw*, fortunately not one of his best.

(BUCKHURST PARK, 1 m. NE. Alterations and additions by *Edward Power* in 1873 etc. cost £6,000 (GS). In a mixture of styles. One part with neo-Tudor windows, another neo-Georgian with a veranda of columns. NBR)

4000
SUNNINGWELL

ST LEONARD. Mostly Perp, except for the jewel of a w porch. Ashlar-faced N transept tower and ashlar-faced s transept. Several straight-headed windows. The chancel is structurally earlier, see one blocked C13 s window. The w porch is
7   supposed to have been given by Bishop Jewel of Salisbury, who died in 1571 and was rector of Sunningwell about 1551. It is seven-sided, with the entrance from the N, where it looks a regular octagon. At the angles are unacademic unfluted Ionic columns. The windows are small, Gothic, and cusped. Originally the porch carried a steep-pitched roof. – PULPIT. Very simple, Jacobean. – BENCH ENDS. With enormous, summary poppy-heads. Rather post- than pre-Reformation. – STAINED GLASS. The E window is most interesting. The design and the colouring are obviously inspired by the Pre-Raphaelites and Morris, but it is equally obviously not theirs. Adoration of the Shepherds and the Magi. The Virgin holds up the Child to them. Smaller figures below. Dark blue background of the main scene. Excellent leading pattern. The answer to the mystery of the attribution is that the window was designed by *J. P. Seddon*, who was a friend of Morris and the Pre-Raphaelites and restored the church in 1877. The glass, according to TK, was made by *S. Belham*. – PLATE. Cup of 1660.

BEAULIEU FARMHOUSE, SE of the church. What can the date of the porch doorway be? The four-centred doorhead looks late C16 or early C17. But can the open segmental pediment be earlier than *c*.1660? The forms are all very thin.

SUTTON COURTENAY

5090

ALL SAINTS. Late Norman W tower, broad, with clasping buttresses. The doorway is imitation, but the window above is genuine, with zigzag. Simpler windows N and S. Bell-openings, twin, pointed, under a round arch, zigzag jambs. Then a corbel-frieze, and above a Perp top storey. The arch towards the nave is wide and single-stepped. Also Late Norman the responds of the chancel arch, with decorated scallop and intertwined-band capitals. The present arch is later, but could not the S arcade E arch, evidently tampered with, have been the chancel arch? It is now pointed but need not have been originally. Big zigzag and crenellation motifs. The rest of the S arcade and the whole N arcade of the notably wide nave C14 with standard elements. C13 chancel with lancet windows. A lancet, but cusped, also the N aisle W window. Is it late C13? Late C13 anyway the N aisle E window and also the identical S aisle E window (spherical triangle in the top). The other N aisle and the S aisle windows wide and Perp. The clerestory is puzzling. While the S side is Perp, the N side has two decidedly Dec windows and three others which could be early C14 too. Charming Perp S porch of brick, two-storeyed. – FONT. Norman, tub-shaped, with narrow arcading and odd tripartite leaf motifs at foot and top of each arch. – FONT COVER. Jacobean. – PULPIT. Jacobean, with back post instead of back panel, and tester. None of the usual arabesques. – STALLS. Three in the chancel; plain. – SCREENS. The rood screen with one-light divisions and the dado openwork with the same simple tracery patterns. Was it always open? – Also simple N and S parclose screens. – BOX PEWS. One is dated 1633. It is quite plain. – SOUTH DOOR. Perp, with tracery. – CHANDELIER. Of brass. Dated 1821; still a Baroque pattern. – PAINTING. A number of C17 inscriptions, one with the naïve representation of six widows and their benefactor, another, rather grander, with three Doric pilasters. – STAINED GLASS. Fragments, huggermugger, in many windows. – PLATE. Cup and Cover, 1584; Paten inscribed 1624; small Cup, 1812; large Flagon, 1822. – MONUMENTS. Three Perp tomb-chests with quatrefoil fronts: chancel N, used as an altar in the S aisle, and in the churchyard S of the chancel. – In the chancel N wall large tomb recess of the late C13. In it effigy of a priest, ruthlessly re-cut. It was probably early C14.

Sutton Courtenay is a large village and a rewarding one, both for the picturesque and the architectural traveller. Immediately W of the church is NORMAN HALL, a most remarkable example of a manor house of c.1190–1200. It is a plain stone rectangle, but has an excellent S doorway with one order of shafts, roll mouldings, and nailhead and dogtooth details. There is also, not quite in line, a N doorway with a continuous roll moulding and a small N doorway further E which is Perp and has charming little carvings up the jambs and the arch. Inside, on a beam, is the date 1626. This could apply to a renewal of the top part of the doorway. The hall was illuminated by lancet windows, of which some remain complete and some in traces. Roof with tie-beams, collar-beams on arched braces, and two tiers of wind-braces.

MANOR HOUSE, SW of the church, S of Norman Hall. The house as it is now, pink-washed, gabled, and bargeboarded, has great charm, in spite of its quite considerable size. It is U-shaped, open to the back garden and the river with two far-projecting wings framing a not too wide courtyard. This pretty picture hides the archaeological evidence (or conjecture), which is of the S wing being the C13 hall range (like Norman Hall) of the Courtenays and the E range being a C15 extension. In the S range the tie-beam roof with crown-posts and massive curved braces is hidden. Only the N range tells its story. It is the story of an enlargement of about 1670, and that date is made certain by the consistent use of Ipswich windows (for the term see Abingdon, p. 58). They belong to the first floor; for the ground floor is an open loggia with unfluted Ionic columns. On the first floor the windows are separated by pilasters. Garlands on their bases. On the outer side of the range the motif is repeated, but not original. Inside, a small Jacobean staircase with decorated string. In front of the E front a pair of GATEPIERS of the mid C17, almost identical with the one at Besselsleigh and similar to the piers at Coleshill. To the N a BARN with exposed timber on a stone base.

42c

THE ABBEY, S of the church. On the other side of the road, also in its own grounds. This never was an abbey, but it was a grange of Abingdon Abbey. It is a courtyard house with the W, N, and S sides of the C14. The W front is pretty and probably early C19 or Early Victorian from outside, with its castellated centre and its two gables. But in the l. gable is a genuine large window of the early or mid C14 with flowing tracery (the opposite number on the r. is not original), and round the corner to the N medieval windows continue. But inside, behind the battlements, is the original great hall, with its open roof with one mighty cruck truss carrying a kingpost and four-way struts. Specially massive purlins. The doorways to the front and the back have characteristic Dec mouldings too. The place where the solar staircase ran from the former high-table end can also be located by an upper doorway with a plain continuous chamfer. The room beneath the solar has moulded beams. – In the hall a screen made up of copious Jacobean panels.

Sutton Courtenay has plenty of enjoyable houses. Only the following can here be referred to. Going N from the church, first the ALMSHOUSES of 1820, one-storeyed, with the centre a little stressed. Then opposite COURTENAY LODGE, C18, chequer brick, of five bays with a hipped roof. Doorway with a hood carved inside with a basket held by two putti and foliage l., r., and top. Then gabled houses, one with two Ipswich windows, and opposite THE WHARF, an C18 core but mostly by *W. Cave*, *c.*1912. Neo-William-and-Mary with hipped roof and slightly projecting wings. One more good house round the corner, in Appleford Road, MILL HOUSE. This has to the W a whitewashed front with giant pilasters, probably early C19, to the street a porch.

S from the church in the MILTON ROAD a charming gabled house of 1631 with two oriels, their posts carved, and further S a fine group: No. 53 with two heavy ground-floor bay windows and a heavy doorway, Early Georgian alterations of an earlier house, No. 76 with a sweet symmetrical Gothick front and opposite a good bigger timber-framed house. In the DRAYTON ROAD GOSLINGS, timber-framed, with two low four-light windows probably original, and GILBOURN'S FARM, closer to Drayton than to Sutton Courtenay, also timber-framed, but with a doorway with segmental pediment on pilasters.

(BUCKRIDGES, ½ m. SSE of the church. 1631. Gabled, irregular, with steeply gabled oriels and chimneystacks set diagonally. NBR)

SUTTON WICK FIELD *see* ABINGDON, p. 61

7060

SWALLOWFIELD

ALL SAINTS. Flint. Nave and chancel in one; tiled roof. Bell-
turret with brick-nogging. The nave is Norman, see the N
and S doorways. The N doorway has two orders of colonnettes
with scallop capitals and a round, moulded arch with zigzag.
The chancel is Dec, see the elementary flowing tracery of the
side windows. The E wall is Victorian. Two Perp nave
windows. Late medieval also the sturdy timber supports of
the bell-turret. They include scissor-bracing. – STAINED
GLASS. A three-light nave window by *Hardman*. – In the N
transept *Holiday*, 1884, not good. – PLATE. Flagon, 1639;
Paten, 1651; Paten on foot, 1719. – MONUMENTS. Brass to
Margery Letterford, mid C15 – a 15 in. figure. – Brass to
Christopher Littcott † 1554, 28 in. figures (both chancel
floor). – John Backhouse † 1649 and members of the
Backhouse family (1669). Two large tablets with black
columns, but not identical. – Funeral HELMS. – Sir Henry
Russell † 1852. Tablet with ogee top. Profile in roundel.
White marble.

SWALLOWFIELD PARK is not sufficiently known in its architectural history. What is known, is that the second Earl of
Clarendon rebuilt it in 1689–91, that he employed *Talman*,
and that in 1820 *William Atkinson* remodelled the house for
Sir Henry Russell. What is Talman's? Certainly the monu-
43　mental doorway re-erected in the garden. This ornateness is
Talman's quite specially, and compares for instance with
Drayton in Northants. Pilasters with garlands, corbels or
brackets instead of capitals, broken segmental pediment with
swags or drapes in it. The doorway once belonged to the
house. The house is H-shaped with the wings projecting
little to the entrance, much to the garden. Panelled parapet.
This is essentially Talman's house, but internally the only
feature characteristic of him is the surprising oval vestibule
in the middle of the garden side with its stucco ceiling. The
remains of one staircase (carved tread-ends, column posts)
could also be his. The porte-cochère on the entrance side is
of course Russell's. Two pairs of Tuscan columns. The
entrance side is the S side. The E side is nine bays long and
has a three-bay centre with giant pilasters. That also is something of which 1690 was well capable (see e.g. Talman at
Chatsworth in 1687–96). To the W a complex and interesting
development of the outbuildings. They are of exposed brick,

the house is cemented. There is first an arcaded courtyard open to the w. It has nine by seven bays. Against the s side of the arcading stands a small house and the short side of the long flat stable block. Between the two the courtyard is entered by an archway with coupled giant brick pilasters. The stables have three archways, the middle one flanked by single pilasters, the outer ones each endowed with only one pilaster, as on the other side short wings project. The windows are segment-headed and have just one wooden mullion. The parapets are panelled. All this looks late C17.

Of the gardens of Swallowfield John Evelyn wrote that they were 'as elegant as 'tis possible to make a flat by art and industrie and no mean expense'.

BRIDGE in the grounds. Five plain arches.

LODGES. High Victorian. Brick with diapers.

BOWYER'S FARMHOUSE, ½ m. w. Dated 1749. Blue and red brick, five bays, wooden cross-windows. It certainly looks earlier.

QUEEN ANNE'S MEAD, 1¼ m. NW. A pretty three-bay front of chequer bricks and a front garden visible through an C18 wrought-iron gate.

SWINFORD BRIDGE   4000

Three approach arches either side and three larger mid-arches, the latter with rusticated voussoirs and balustrade. The bridge was built in 1777.

SWINLEY DOWN see ASHDOWN PARK

TEMPLE MILLS see BISHAM

THATCHAM   5060

ST MARY. Flint, quite big, with many gables, largely of the restoration of 1857 (by *Thomas Hellyer*). Original the Norman s doorway with zigzag, at least in a few parts. Original also the N arcade, clearly early C13. It is puzzling. The first bay is low, the others higher. The piers and arches have only a slight chamfer. There is a sign of a former w wall E of the first bay. Perp N aisle with its windows. – STAINED GLASS. s aisle w by *Powell's*, 1865, i.e. before they developed their characteristic Walter-Cranish style. – MONUMENTS. Tomb-chest with quatrefoils (s chapel) to Sir William Danvers † 1504. – Nicholas Fuller † 1620. Alabaster tablet with kneeling figures, the children below the parents.

CHAPEL, at the E end of the main street (A4). Founded in 1304, but the straight-sided arch to the S doorway Late Perp (cf. Theale, i.e. Oxford), the S and N windows probably C17, and the W porch Victorian. Two original, pretty niches l. and r. of it.

In the main street near the chapel on the N side a three-storeyed, three-bay house of brick and then a thatched timber-framed cottage.

Close to the church the VICARAGE, Early Georgian, of five bays, blue brick with red dressings. THATCHAM FARM, W of the Vicarage, is a handsome brick group with its outbuildings.

THATCHAM HOUSE. Victorian Gothic, brick and stone dressings, with an eccentrically placed turret.

MESOLITHIC SETTLEMENT, on a low terrace, just W of the Mow Brook and N of the railway embankment. The evidence from this site suggests temporary and intermittent occupation by groups of Maglemosean hunter-fishers. No traces of dwellings have been found, and the settlement is marked by hearths and a scatter of flint tools and flint-knapping debris. The flint equipment includes burins or gravers for antler and bone working, and a large series of small blades or microliths which served as arrowpoints or barbs in composite hunting weapons. Pollen samples and radiocarbon dates indicate settlement by Mesolithic groups from c.6000 to c.4000 B.C.

6070
THEALE

HOLY TRINITY. 1820–32 by *E. W. Garbett*, the tower by *John Buckler*. This is a church as remarkable for scale as for style. Regarding scale, it was all paid for by Mrs Sophia Sheppard, sister of Dr Routh, President of Magdalen College Oxford and Rector of Theale. Regarding style, the pattern is patently Salisbury Cathedral, and that was not a pattern likely to be chosen in 1820. 1820 looked to the Perp, 1840 to the late C13 and early C14. The early and mid C13 had no popularity. Lancet windows were used freely, but not to make up E.E. ensembles. Garbett's church is very tall, and seems more so by its pairs of very slender lancets in each bay and by the Salisbury buttresses. The tower is also E.E. It is open in a passage on the ground floor and is connected with the church by what seems to be a transept but houses a library. The façade of the church is also modelled on Salisbury, but the W porch gives the real date away. It is much too high and narrow

in its proportions. Besides, such a w porch is not correct E.E.
cathedral style. The porch is stone-vaulted. So is the handsome w gallery inside. The principal vaults however are of
plaster. It is a great pity that *Oldrid Scott* added the apse. –
STAINED GLASS. In the apse by *Kempe*, 1892. – MONUMENT.
The 'chantry chapel' is that of Bishop Waynflete, removed
from Magdalen College Oxford in 1830 by Dr Routh. Two
doorways in the same style and probably also from Magdalen.
Characteristic straight-sided diagonals in the tracery and
straight-sided arches to the doorways (cf. Cumnor, North
Hinksey). Inside, the cenotaph of Mrs Sheppard.

RECTORY, E of the church. Stone, classical, 1830, five bays with
a three-bay pediment. Also built by Mrs Sheppard.

In the main street, near the E end, on the s side, some nice five-
bay Georgian houses.

TIDMARSH   6070

ST LAURENCE. The church possesses a splendid Norman s
doorway. The orders are all continuous and all ornamented:
zigzag, chain, also trails and scrolls. The hood-mould has as
its apex a fearsome head (of Christ ?) in a rounded trefoil, the
top foil more than semicircular. c13 w lancets, c13 chancel
lancets, and c13 polygonal apse, a great rarity in English
parish churches. Madeley in Herefordshire is a parallel, but
it is later. This one, from the apse arch and the supports of
the (recent) plaster rib-vault (triple shafts with fillets, stiff-
leaf capitals), is mid c13 at the latest. As impressive as the
apse are the heavy timber supports of the bell-turret and its
shingled pyramid roof. They have upper scissor bracing, and
the posts as well as the tie-beam and arched braces are robustly
decorated with motifs immediately derived from the Norman
doorway. This is by a Victorian rector's wife. At first one would
call it c17. – FONT. If c12, then entirely re-cut. – PULPIT. If
c15, then only in very minor parts. – COMMUNION RAIL.
c18. – PAINTING. In the jambs of one N and one s lancet
faded c13 single standing figures. – PLATE. Cup of 1749;
Paten on foot. – MONUMENTS. Brass to Margaret Woode
† 1499, 19½ in. long. – Brass to Henry Leynham † 1517, 3 ft
long. – Robert Hopkins † 1834. By *Whitelaw*. Big tablet with
a small urn.

OLD RECTORY. 1856. Brick. Symmetrical three-bay front with
steep gables. Gothic casement windows, but brick-filled
tympana. Was *Street* the architect ?

6070

TILEHURST

St Michael. s aisle of the early c14 (windows with Y- and intersecting tracery). Brick tower of 1737 with clasping buttresses, the rest 1856 by *Street*, including the rather wild spire with angle pinnacles, flying buttresses, and very large lucarnes. Flint church, not specially attractive outside or inside. – STAINED GLASS. Chancel E and S by *Wailes*, 1856, designed by *Street* (TK). – In the S aisle E window of 1869 by *Morris*, a Virgin and large angels on a patterned, deep blue ground. – PLATE. Silver-gilt Chalice and Cover, 1573; silver-gilt Flagon and Almsdish, 1737. – MONUMENTS. Brass to Gavin More † 1479 (13 in. figures). – Sir Peter Vanlore of Utrecht, a merchant, † 1627. Two recumbent effigies, praying. Children below and also, frontal, l. and r. Back arch with good strapwork and trophies. Alabaster.

St George, St George's Road. 1885–6 by *Sidney Gambier Parry*. Chancel 1893. Brick, with lancets and the bellcote over the nave E end. Polygonal apse. – (PULPIT. Jacobean; from Sonning.)

Church of Jesus Christ of Latter Day Saints, Readway. Modernistic, with thin tower carrying a spike.

At the S end of Church End Lane survives a timber-framed farmhouse. It ought to be kept. Down Kentwood Hill on the E side Kentwood Farmhouse, later c17, brick, with a hipped roof and wooden cross-windows.

TITTENHURST PARK *see* SUNNINGHILL

8070

TOUCHEN END
1¾ m. SE of White Waltham

Holy Trinity. 1862 by *J. Turner*. Brick. Nave with bellcote and chancel. In the Dec style. The aisle windows all low, segment-headed, and of three lights, with reticulation units. Wooden posts between nave and S aisle, on the pattern of Winkfield. – STAINED GLASS. 1959, in an attractive, un-exacting Expressionism. Designed by *Colin Shewring*.

4090

TUBNEY

St Lawrence. 1844–7 by *Pugin*. It is in no way distinguished and might be by anybody. But the fact remains note-worthy that about 1845 so close to Oxford a Catholic architect could be chosen for an Anglican church.* Nave with bellcote and chancel. The bellcote on a mid-buttress. Minimum ogee-headed one- and two-light windows. Thin trussed rafter roof, in the chancel with an embattled wall-plate. The stencilled PAINTING of the chancel roof could well be Pugin's. – FONT. Given to the church by Queen Adelaide. Octagonal. Carved bowl supports and four carved panels.

TUBNEY HOUSE. The entrance side is plain Late Georgian but with two embattled pedimental gables over the ends. The side has all the windows with hood-moulds, probably Latish Georgian. But towards the garden is one C17 mullioned and transomed window and a canted bay window with steep Gothic openings. Also more battlements. Inside an ample staircase, apparently early C18.

TWYFORD

7070

ST MARY. 1846 by *Ferrey*, enlarged considerably in 1908–10 by S. S. Stallwood (BC). Flint, E.E., with a NW tower. Quite large. By Ferrey the S aisle and arcade. To the W of the church a ruinous tower said to belong to a former chapel of St Swithun.

In the HIGH STREET several nice houses, e.g. by the bridge the POLEHAMPTON SCHOOL house, plain, brick, of five bays. The school was founded in 1721.

In LONDON ROAD is APSLEY HOUSE, Early Georgian, rustic but very charming. Blue-brick headers and red-brick dressings. Five bays, segment-headed windows. The sill-zone with some elephant leg decoration. Pedimented doorway. A little further out the HARRISON ALMSHOUSES of 1640, a one-storeyed row with a porch. Projecting wings at the back.

UFFINGTON

3080

ST MARY. A church of *c.*1250 with a crossing tower. Its top storey turns octagonal, and a further storey was added after 1740. The windows of the church are mostly lancet pairs, and also triplets. Below these groups blank circles or roundels, for consecration crosses. Access to the church is by one grand and two unusual porches. The S porch is on a cathedral scale. Outer and inner doorways have mature stiff-leaf capitals. On

---

* The Rev. F. E. Rusby tells me that Pugin wanted a tower, but the cost of £645 was too much. In the end, the church cost £649, and Pugin received a fee of £30.

the buttresses niches with continuous mouldings. In the buttress gablets small figures. In the top gable also a figure composition. Large, unfinished panelled pinnacles l. and r. Rib-vault inside, the rib profile not one of the current ones. A second doorway with shallow porch leads from the E into the S transept. It is tunnel-vaulted. Is it explicable by the fact that the manor belonged to Abingdon Abbey? Was a house perhaps attached or close by in a monastery fashion? The third doorway is the priest's doorway, and that also has the uncommon feature of a gable. To its l. incidentally a three-light Dec window with reticulated tracery. Yet another curious fact is the very large sexfoiled circular window above the N doorway into the nave. Why was this made? The three lancet windows in the W wall of the nave have very odd tops, and these seem to belong to a restoration of 1677–9.* It is tempting to attribute to this date also the weirdest of all features of Uffington, the E chapels of the transept, two N, one S. They are of three lights with steep triangles, not arches, and the mullions simply running into them (cf. Buckland). It looks like Lethaby or E. S. Prior and certainly not like the C13. Would 1678 be an answer? Internally all is mid C13 again. Much shafting in the chancel. Original SEDILIA and PISCINA. Groups of triple wall shafts indicate the intention to vault. Springers indeed survive. The capitals of the shafts are polygonal, as though they were Perp. But they are not; for they recur in the impeccable transept E arcades. Each of the three chapels has a big PISCINA. The transept windows are shafted too. Finally the crossing arches, and they present something odd once more, the abaci with concave hollows as if they were Perp. It is all round a highly idiosyncratic style we find at Uffington, but surely not idiosyncratic enough for the transept E windows. – READING DESK. The ends are two bench ends. – SOUTH DOOR. C13, with very elaborate hinges. – PLATE. Cup of 1583. – MONUMENTS. Edward Archer † 1603. Stone, of reredos type. Two columns, straight top with strapwork. – John Saunders † 1638. Semi-reclining effigy, stiffly on his side. Coffered arch. Strapwork on the back wall.

(FRIENDS MEETING HOUSE, ¼ m. SE, i.e. E of Garrards Farm. 1711.)

S of the church UFFINGTON SCHOOL, a small oblong building

* The Rev. Basil Clarke quoted to me the churchwardens' accounts for 1677–9: 'Payd to *John Deane* for ye end wall of ye Church, pulling it downe & setting it up £25. 00. 00.'

of 1617* with mullioned windows. The building is of chalk, as is nearly the whole of Uffington.

VICARAGE. Asymmetrical, with gables and Gothic details. According to Messrs Betjeman and Piper by *Kendall*, 1849.

THE WHITE HORSE, ¼ m. NE. This great chalk-cut representa-3b tion of a horse is some 360 ft long and 130 ft high. It is the only undoubted prehistoric hill figure in England. The stylized treatment of the horse finds parallels in the horses on Belgic ceremonial buckets and on their coinage. The Uffington horse was probably cut in the C1 and may have served as a tribal emblem. It has never ceased to impress and puzzle people. Celia Fiennes praised its 'perfect proportions', Francis Wise in 1738 the 'skill in Opticks' of its makers and its durability, and Robert Dodsley in 1744 reported that it was supposed to have been made by Hengist. The horse had to be scoured every so often, and this, in the C17 at the latest, developed into a ceremony with all kinds of revels. In our less merry century the grooming of the horse is done by the Ministry of Public Building and Works.

BARROW. Just above the White Horse is an elongated pillow mound, 70 ft long and 40 ft wide, flanked by quarry ditches. The site was excavated in the C19, the central depression marking the position of this work. Forty-six Romano-British inhumation burials were recovered, and also an urned crema- tion, the latter perhaps a Bronze Age interment beneath a pre-existing round barrow.

UFFINGTON CASTLE, on White Horse Hill. The fort is of univallate construction with a single entrance on the NW. Little is known of the site, which has not been scientifically excavated, although some work on the ramparts in the C19 showed them to be faced with sarsens. The form of the ramparts suggests that the fort is the work of Iron Age A groups, although a silver coin of the Dobunni was found in the interior.

ROMANO-BRITISH SETTLEMENT, in the saddle joining Uffington and Woolstone Downs. The site consists of a small rectangular enclosure defined by a shallow ditch, 4 ft wide, with an inner and an outer bank visible at the SE corner. The site is unexcavated, but sherds of Roman pottery have been found in its ploughed interior.

MOUND, *see* Woolstone.

* Also dates 1634 and 1637.

UFTON GREEN *see* UFTON NERVET

6060

UFTON NERVET

St Peter. 1861–2 by *R. Armstrong*. Early C14 style with shingled spire. – STAINED GLASS. E window 1862 by *Clutterbuck* (BC), still pictorial in the early C19 way. The nave windows by *Lavers & Barraud*, grisaille, i.e. brown outlines and some little yellow. – PLATE. Cup, Elizabethan. – MONUMENTS. Richard Perkyns † 1560. Early Elizabethan at its best. Unfortunately only the canopy is left: two fluted columns and a delicately decorated frieze. – Francis Perkyns † 1635. Two recumbent stone effigies on a tomb-chest with kneeling children, all badly preserved. – A very ancient yew-tree s of the church.

St John Baptist, Ufton Green, ⅞ m. NW. All that remains is one flint wall with a marvellous huge hat of ivy.

Ufton Court. Built *c.*1570–80. Large, timber-framed, with many gables. An E façade, with porch gable, each projecting wing with four side gables and one front gable and the connecting pieces between porch and wings with four gables each. That sounds perfectly symmetrical; in·fact, it isn't, as of these latter gables those on the r. are in one plane, those on the l. not at all. The façade has two overhangs with moulded bressumers. The first-floor windows are slightly projected on brackets and have shallow pediments. The porch is deep and has ornamental front posts and also side balusters. It still leads into a screens passage and to an exit. The garden side was brick-faced in the early C18, but the doorway and the big chimneybreast tell of the still medieval arrangement of the Elizabethan hall. In the hall a thin-ribbed plaster ceiling with heavy pendants. Queen Anne panelling. In a room to the N also thin-ribbed plasterwork. It is divided by beams with carved decoration still entirely Early Renaissance, i.e. rather 1540– than 1580–looking. In the NE room modest mid C18 stucco and a mid C18 chimneypiece. (s of the screens passage the Elizabethan staircase, and s of this a small service room connected with the large kitchen by a hatch which is pre-Reformation in date and proves that at least this part of the house must structurally go back that far. The kitchen was originally open to the surviving trussed rafter roof. The SE wing must originally have held the chapel on the upper floor, and there are three ingenious priest holes. Francis Perkyns, who died in 1616, was indeed a recusant. VCH)

UPPER BASILDON see BASILDON

UPTON

5080

ST MARY. Flint-faced, nave and chancel and a timer bell-turret. In the chancel two Norman windows, not identical. In the nave one Norman window. Norman chancel arch with saltire-cross frieze in the abaci.

WADLEY HOUSE
1¼ m. E of Faringdon

3090

Two parts, a plain seven-bay façade of 1768 with a doorway and Tuscan columns and a pediment, and behind it an L-shaped C16 part with mullioned windows with uncusped arched lights, especially one in the gable facing E. A farm building has three large Gothick quatrefoils.

To the N a three-bay red brick house with a one-bay pediment.

WALBURY CAMP see COMBE

WALLINGFORD

6080

The first charter was given to Wallingford in 1155 by Henry II, who had here concluded the treaty with Stephen which ended the civil war and secured him the succession. But Wallingford had a guild merchant before then, and the castle also was in existence and had indeed been in prominence, as the Empress Maud had taken refuge in it in 1142. It is not known when the town was laid out, but its plan shows clearly that it is a made town. It is roughly square, with rounded corners, and its streets are roughly parallel or crossing at r. angles. The main crossing is that of Castle Street running N–S and continued in St Mary's Street with the High Street running due W from the Thames bridge. The castle fills the NE quarter, the NW quarter is still mostly open (Bull Croft), the Market Place lies in the line of St Mary's Street S of the main crossing. Ramparts are preserved along the E and S sides and half the N side. Wallingford had ten or eleven parish churches in the C12, but only four in the C15. Now there are three. There was also a small Benedictine priory.

ST MARY, immediately S of the Market Place. A flint church of 1854 (by *David Brandon*) except for the W tower. The tower has polygonal angle buttresses.* – PULPIT. By *Onslow Ford*,

* It received pinnacles in 1660, and these (or copies) may be re-installed.

1888. Marble, with bronze reliefs of saints. Marble decoration also in the chancel, but of 1901. – STAINED GLASS. N aisle w by *Willement*, 1856. – PLATE. Paten, 1833. – MONUMENTS. Walter Bigg † 1659. Large tablet. The flat carving and the garlands and swags all typical of *c.*1660. Top segmental pediment with a skull. – (Thomas Renda † 1722. Signed by *E. Stanton & Horsnaile the Elder*. Gunnis) – In the chancel telling comparison between the tablets † 1746 and † 1826.

St LEONARD. A Norman church, ill-treated by *Hakewill* in 1849, who added the totally uninspired w tower and the s arcade. But the church is genuinely Norman, see the herring-bone masonry on the N side, the N doorway, and, after all, in spite of recarving, the splendid arches E of the nave and W of the apse. They are tall and wide and have decoration of small motifs such as saltire crosses, stars, etc. The capitals and abaci of the w arch are basket-weave, those of the E arch have two heads. – PAINTING in the apse. By *G. D. Leslie*, 1889 (BC). – PLATE. Two Chalices, Paten, and Flagon, 1812.

St PETER. Nave and tower 1760–9. The delightful spire was designed in 1777 by *Sir Robert Taylor*. It is not known if he also designed the rest. Flint tower, square, with an open Gothic octagonal bell-stage and the spire growing in a historically quite unauthorized curve out of it. The spire is openwork too, in four stages. It is rather cheeky for Sir Robert, but entirely convincing. The nave is of stone, with arched windows and a segmental vault. The apse was added in 1904 and is unfortunate. – STAINED GLASS. The E window is by *Morris & Co.*, of *c.*1918, and shows what the firm had come to twenty years after Morris's death. – PLATE. Silver-gilt Chalice and Paten 1769 and Almsdish 1777. – MONUMENT. Sir William Blackstone, the jurist, is buried here. Slab in the floor and Gothic monument of *c.*1841 outside on the s wall.

FRIENDS' MEETING HOUSE, Castle Street. 1724; a simple brick cottage.

CASTLE. The castle fills the NE quarter of the town. It has two ditches to N, W, and S, and one to the E, where the Thames was a further defence. On the N side the town ditch formed a third enforcement. The motte is at the s end of the inner bailey. On it mixed remains of masonry. More on the E side, with one early C14 window. More also to the SW. The masonry here belongs to the collegiate church of St Nicholas. It is of the early C16 and has one straight-headed three-light window. The whole is picturesque, but historically not very rewarding. The area is now the grounds of CASTLE HOUSE, a large gabled Tudor house of 1837.

TOWN HALL. 1670. To the Market Place the open ground floor has four sturdy columns, the upper floor just a Venetian window, and the roof appears pyramidal. To the sides five bays and a hipped roof. – REGALIA. Mayor's Badge, *temp.* Charles I; a silver-gilt Mace by *Thomas Maundy*, 1650; silver-gilt Cup and Cover by *Charles Shelley*, 1668; Shield, probably London, 1750–1.

CORN EXCHANGE, Market Place. Just one item in the terrace of the E side of the square. 1856, in a restrained Italianate. Stone, three bays, the windows arched pairs.

PERAMBULATION. This will have to fan out from the MARKET PLACE. On the E side LLOYDS BANK, of 1915 (by *F. W. Shann*), but looking entirely c.1830, of five bays. The middle window is arched and has a reeded surround. Pedimental gable. On the W side Nos 14 and 15, blue and red brick, with plain Venetian windows. Down S by ST MARY'S STREET. Not much to be seen, except the flat W terrace of ST LEONARD'S SQUARE, blue and red brick, c.1800, and Nos 28–29 of a similar character but with a minimum Venetian window on the second floor. The street then becomes READING ROAD and leaves the old town. Immediately on the E down a service road to the river and here ST LUCIANS, the most interesting house in Wallingford. It is of brick and pargetted and has a symmetrical W front with three gables and two castellated bay windows and looks Elizabethan. On the N a handsome range of outbuildings.

Continuing a little on the Reading Road on the E side AUGIER'S ALMSHOUSES. They are of 1681 and have three gables. The Gothic glazing bars are obviously early C19, but are the ogee head to the foundation tablet and the big Tudor roses on the other gables and the W porch really 1681?

Now N from the Market Place, again along ST MARY'S STREET. Here the WHITE HART, c.1500, with two gables and Gothic details at their foot. No. 1 is the corner to the High Street. Early Georgian, of five bays and three storeys, blue and red brick, with segment-headed windows and a parapet. This is the next point for fanning out from. To the N in CASTLE STREET a C16 timber-framed house with gables and overhang. To the W HIGH STREET in its less eventful part. At once on the N side Nos 62–63, blue and red brick, segment-headed windows, then No. 35, the Municipal Offices, low, widely spaced, red

brick with angle pilasters and a parapet, early C19. Near the
end, where the street stops being a town street, on the s side,
FRANK H. JENKINS'S GARAGE, etc., a good modern job by
Hancock Associates, 1961–2, black steel and glass, no fashionable gimmicks. After that a house with a Greek Doric porch
on the same side and one on the N side preceded by FLINT
COTTAGE, C17, with three even gables and mullioned and
transomed windows.

Finally to the E from the junction of St Mary's Street and
HIGH STREET. On the N side at once the former LAMB
HOTEL, Early Georgian, blue and red brick, of two and a half
storeys, quite plain, with a middle archway. Then the WEST-
MINSTER BANK, five bays, three storeys, plus one-bay
additions l. and r. The five-bay part has angle pilasters. Later
Georgian. After that the GEORGE INN, C16 or C17, with
two gables and an oversailing upper floor. In the yard an C18
brick part with a re-set wooden C16 doorway and a Venetian
window above. Off s for a moment into WOOD STREET for
No. 12, blue headers and red brick, segment-headed windows,
three storeys. On in the High Street, No. 74 with handsome
C18 stabling with a cupola behind, and on the s side Nos 17–19,
C16, picturesque, with an overhang. (Cellar beneath, vaulted
in quadripartite bays, partly C14. MHLG) No. 75 again blue
headers and red brick, three storeys, five bays. No. 76 lies
back, is of stone, and has a Greek Doric porch, i.e. *c.*1820.
Then the *clou* of Wallingford, CALLEVA HOUSE, Early
Georgian. Five bays, three storeys, blue and red brick.
Segment-headed windows. Upper giant brick pilasters on
ground-floor pilaster strips. Parapet. Doorway with pilasters,
triglyphs, and segmental pediment. (Staircase with slim
twisted and fluted balusters and carved tread-ends.) Opposite
the castellated GATES of Castle House (*see* above).

Here we are close to WALLINGFORD BRIDGE, a bridge of
altogether seventeen arches, though only five of them span the
river. Three of the arches are medieval and ribbed, perhaps
C13, but the three middle ones with the handsome balustrade
date from 1809. The arches to the l. and r. of these three are
of 1751.

To finish with, a walk down THAMES STREET, opposite the
Castle Lodges, is recommended, though the houses look their
best rather from the Oxfordshire side of the river. First a
stately three-bay one, with a stone E front and lunette windows
on the second floor. Then CASTLE PRIORY, with a five-bay

river front and good interior work. Then on the w side of the
road a group of five houses and studio flats by *Morton &
Lupton.*

WALLINGTONS *see* KINTBURY

WALTHAM ST LAWRENCE   8070

ST LAWRENCE. Approached under a majestic yew tree. W
tower of flint and stone blocks, the doorway Perp, but the w
window of *c.*1300 (finely detailed in cusped intersecting
tracery). The very top early brick. The body of the church
flint, with all details Victorian. The s transept front of 1847
with a rather bleak Victorian window. Internally, however, the
church demonstrates a Norman origin. Two-bay arcades N and
s with unmoulded arches separated by pieces of wall. Of the
responds two have a very elementary row of flat leaves. These
arcades of the short Norman church were continued E by two
standard Dec bays. No chancel arch. – FONT. Perp. Octagonal.
No separate foot or stem. Panelled sides. – PULPIT. 1619.
Only the back panel with caryatids in its upper part is original.
– SCREEN. The tracery heads are original and show that this
was a Dec, not a Perp screen. – RAILING to the baptistery.
Jacobean, and presumably not *in situ.* – CANDLE BRACKETS.
C17, and very pretty with their decorative S-curve decoration.
– PAINTING. On a N pier an early C14 figure and ornamental
scrolls. – STAINED GLASS. E window by *Wailes,* probably of
1847, when the chancel was re-decorated. – W window by
Kempe, 1877. – One N aisle window signed by *M. Schneider* of
Regensburg, 1866. Why go to him? The glass is not even
technically adequate. – PLATE. Chalice and Cover of 1661;
Paten of 1783; Chalice of 1795. – MONUMENTS. Sir Henry
Neville † 1593 and two wives and one daughter. Alabaster.
Four kneeling figures. Flat top. – Katherine Thomas † 1658.
A memorable monument. Urn of a curiously organic shape,
somewhat like an inverted pear, on a short marble column,
placed in a niche – no ornament whatever. – Dorothy Lewis
† 1687. A pretty, scrolly cartouche. – Capt. Henry Neville
† 1809. By *Sir R. Westmacott.* With a military still life.
From the church s the BELL INN, an impressive piece of C14
timber-framing. Attached to it a C15 timber-framed cottage
with exposed brick infilling. Then IVY BANK FARMHOUSE,
L-shaped and also timber-framed. Opposite a good recent
brick house painted white. 1960–1 by *Paul Cornwall-Jones.*

After that COLTMANS, gabled Elizabethan or Jacobean brick, and KELLINGHAMS, again timber frame and brick infilling. At the s end of the main street by the war memorial PARADISE, brick, C18, with an irregular but attractive front and a side with tripartite windows. By the same green PARADISE FARM-HOUSE, C15 gable and C18 otherwise, and BORLASES, much altered but with a C15 core. The hall has its timber roof with wind-braces.*

₄₀₈₀

WANTAGE

ST PETER AND ST PAUL. The church can only narrowly be reached from the Market Place, and that is just as well. It is a large cruciform building with a crossing tower and dates essentially from the later C13. Externally this is visible as follows. The bell-openings of the tower are of two pointed-trefoiled lights with a circle over. Of the same date, it seems, the upper chancel windows, unless they are entirely of *Street*'s restoration of 1857. Street lived at Wantage from 1850 to 1852, when he moved to Oxford. He settled down in London in 1855. The chancel of the church was lengthened at the Perp time and the small s doorway then put in. The s chapel and transept E chapel are of course Perp too and can boast sub-stantial gargoyles. This part and the corresponding N chapel alone are ashlar-faced. In the w wall of the s transept, to return to the C13, is a lancet. Otherwise more external Perp: nave windows and two-storeyed s porch. The w wall belongs to a lengthening of 1877 (by *Butterfield*); hence its prominent middle buttress. Inside the church, the arcades (except for the w bay) again C13. Round piers, round abaci, double-chamfered arches dying into the piers. The sw respond belongs to the same build, the NW respond is Perp. Roof supports of stone Perp too. Arch from the s aisle into the transept C13, but interfered with, from the N aisle Perp. But the s respond of the N transept E aisle (of two bays) has stiff-leaf and really seems the earliest feature of the church. The s transept E arcade is of the type of the nave arcades. The crossing arches are heavy and triple-chamfered, i.e. late C13 also. The arches from the chancel to the chapel are clearly Perp, but differ. Both sides have the familiar four-shafts-and-four-hollows section, but the N capitals are concave-sided. – PULPIT. Of 1857, i.e. probably designed by *Street*. – SCREENS. To the chancel chapels, of

* (FOUR ELMS. Above the door relief of four elms by *Eric Gill*, c.1926. Robert Gibbings then lived in the house.)

one-light divisions, Perp. – STALLS. The ends with tracery and big poppy-heads, the seats with MISERICORDS. On the misericords a pelican, a double eagle, shields, and mostly leaves. – CHANDELIER. A splendid piece with two tiers of arms; dated 1711. – STAINED GLASS. N transept E by *Willement*, 1848. – PLATE. Cup, London, 1571; large Cup, London, 1624; two Patens, London, 1722; large Almsdish, not English, inscribed 1725; two large Flagons, London, 1744. – MONUMENTS. Sir William Fitzwarin † 1361. Two alabaster effigies. Formerly with a canopy above the tomb. – Brass to Sir Ives Fitzwarin † 1414, a good 5 ft figure. – Brass to a Priest, c.1330 (2 ft). – Brass to a Man, early C16 (17½ in.). These are in the N transept. – Brass to Walter Talbot and two wives † 1522 (18 in.). This is in the S aisle. – William Wilmot † 1684. Wide tablet with columns and an open segmental pediment. Two frontal demi-figures, both at ease with one hand on the breast. A baby, pathetically upright, between them. The monument, which is signed by *William Bird* of Oxford, is supported on three angel busts. – John Stamp † 1728 and his wife 1741. The latter date must be valid, according to the Rococo detail. The two vases may even be an addition of c.1784. By *John Townsend Jun.*

METHODIST CHAPEL, Newbury Street. 1848 by *R. W. Ordish*. Modest Dec; stone.

CEMETERY. The CHAPEL is by *Butterfield*, 1850 (BC), a plain oblong building, of stone, with a circular E window. At the time of writing it seems doomed.

ST MARY'S CONVENT, Faringdon Road. Of the Anglican order of the Wantage Sisterhood, founded by Elizabeth Lockhart, inspired by W. J. Butler, later Dean of Lincoln. Stone buildings, the original ones by *Street*, 1855–6. They lie behind and to the l. of the present gatehouse, and the wing to the r. with which they form a courtyard was added in 1860. Street's designs are of course Gothic and of course unornamental. It is interesting, however, to see that his dormer windows are not at all Gothic and rather C17. Behind this is the original chapel, also by Street, and built in 1858–61. It is a plain oblong room with lancets on the N side and a large (altered) E window. The chancel side walls have arcading below and a circular window above. In 1866 and 1871–2 the refectory was built. It was altered in 1900. In 1878 the Noviciate was erected N of Street's buildings. This is by *Butterfield*, a long range with tall stone windows with segmental arches. In 1887 a new larger chapel was begun. It is by *Pearson*, with Geometrical tracery, high and rib-vaulted in stone. It originally went only as far as the screen and was lengthened in 1900. The curious, somewhat fussy re-arrangement of the E end, with stone piers acting as a canopy over the altar and three little vaults l., centre, and r., is by *Comper*, 1923.

RETREAT HOUSE, Priory Road, SW of the church. Also called ST MICHAEL'S. 1855, and initially by *William White*, probably changed in the process of building (BC). A very picturesque, though of course heavily picturesque, house of brown stone with thin brick motifs and pointed brick tympana above the windows. Porch set diagonally in an angle. The apsidal end of the upper chapel is an addition by *A. B. Allin*, 1888 (BC). Two larger, flat-fronted buildings were added yet later.

URBAN DISTRICT COUNCIL OFFICES, Portway. Inside the remains of the MARKET CROSS of 1580, with small defaced figures under arches.

ST MARY'S SCHOOL, Newbury Street. The main buildings lie right along the street, from l. to r.: new building of 1962 by *Lewis & Reedman*, brick, with the fashionable over-heavy concrete beams etc. and low bands of windows and an equally typical N view. Then *Butterfield*, 1874–5, but obviously heightened. This was done in 1900. Butterfield has small trefoil-headed windows. Then a five-bay Early Georgian house of blue and red brick with segment-headed windows and a pedimented one-bay centre projection. Doorway with brick pilasters and pediment. After that the CHAPEL, by *Ponting*, 1898–9. Red brick, fancy Gothic, with the motifs of several phases; asymmetrical turret with spire. The apse has a wooden tierceron-vault.

CHURCH SCHOOL, Church Street. 1850 by *Woodyer* (BC). Coursed stone with a hipped tower top.

KING ALFRED GRAMMAR SCHOOL. Stone, with two projecting wings. Gothic, and not symmetrical. By *J. B. Clacy*, 1849–50 with later additions. (The hall is attributed to *Butterfield*.) The Norman doorway of the former Latin School building in the churchyard was re-used. Little however is original. Arch with beakhead and lozenge decoration.

See p. 359

ST KATHERINE'S SCHOOL, Ormond Road. By *A. M. Mowbray*, 1897 (BC). Brick.

PERAMBULATION. We start in the MARKET PLACE. Its S side is excellent, and with its blue and red C18 brick houses a summing up of the regional Georgian style. The Market Place is nicely irregular in shape, particularly successfully to the w. The SE corner is No. 1, Early Georgian, three-storeyed, with segment-headed windows with aprons. Panelled parapet. No. 6 blue and red, this time the blue bricks all headers. Nos 7–8 also has blue headers and again a panelled parapet. No. 10 is a little lower, No. 11 stands forward a little and has a hipped roof. Segment-headed windows, aprons. Then, considerably back, the BEAR HOTEL of six bays with a pedimental gable in which, in a semicircle, the name in early C19 Egyptian letters. After that the Market Place narrows. Nos 29–30 stands across. To the Market Place it has a Victorian roof with Victorian dormers, but to the side a nice doorcase with scrolly open pediment on scrolly brackets and a (repainted) date 1708. No. 33 starts the N side. It has five bays to the S and once more segment-headed windows. At the back they still have the original mullion and transom crosses. Nothing after that, except that the E side makes quite a nice, uneventful *finale*. Off now to the E from the NE corner: WALLINGFORD STREET, with the best house in its garden derelict, and another, ROCKWELL HOUSE, of five bays, with wavy decoration of the bricks of the window lintels. Then S from the SE corner, down NEWBURY STREET. The best houses are both early C18, one now part of St Mary's School, the other opposite, also belonging to the school, which is of five bays and three storeys, yellow brick (an unusual choice) with red dressings, segment-headed windows, parapet. Then STILE'S ALMSHOUSES of 1680, brick, one-storeyed, with a hipped roof. Five very widely spaced bays.

From the Market Place w to the church and to its N the VICARAGE, 1850 by *Street*. Stone, asymmetrical, varied window shapes (and various periods of Gothic imitated). Gables.

From the NW corner of the Market Place straight N is GROVE STREET. At the corner of Mill Street yet another Early Georgian three-storeyed five-bay house of blue and red brick with segment-headed windows. Hipped roof. Another, humbler one of the same type further on, and then DALKEITH HOUSE, detached, of the early C18, but with two shallow late C18 bows. Now down MILL STREET with more blue and red, especially No. 20 of eight bays with brick aprons to the windows. Opposite, Nos 25–37 Victorian Gothic ALMSHOUSES, 1867 by *J. P. Spencer* (GS). One more blue and red five-bay house with segment-headed windows, and so to the convent. In DENCHWORTH ROAD, N of the convent, is WHITE

LODGE, one of the rare houses by *M. H. Baillie Scott*, Voyseyish in style and dating from 1899. Characteristic unmoulded mullioned window, and very characteristic gable pulled low on one side.

THE HAM, Ickleton Road, opposite the end of Ham Road which is the s continuation of Denchworth Road. Early Georgian, of three plus one bays. Venetian doorway and window. Hipped roof. At the back a wide canted bay window.

ROMAN VILLA. The site was discovered in a field on Chainhill Farm and excavated in the C19. The villa was of corridor type, 80 ft long and 36 ft broad, divided into five rooms of varying dimensions. A hypocaust system was found in the s room. Coins from the villa suggest an occupation from the early C2 to the beginning of the C4.

WARFIELD

8070

ST MICHAEL. One of the most rewarding churches around. Built of dark brown conglomerate. The N aisle E.E., as the N lancet and traces of more lancets establish. The rest mostly Dec, namely the N chapel and the chancel. The chapel windows have cusped Y- and cusped intersecting tracery. Y-tracery in the chancel too, but also one of the most ambitious designs of flowing tracery in Berkshire. Perp w tower of conglomerate and much stone. Short recessed spire. Perp N arcade of five bays (octagonal piers, double-hollow-chamfered arches), Perp arch to the s transept. The chancel arch on the other hand and the arches to the N chapel are Dec. They have consistent continuous mouldings of typical breadth and details. The chancel is most lavishly appointed, and, although much is over-restored (by *Street*, 1872–5), the effect is still of the most generous. SEDILIA and PISCINA with ogee arches, crocketed gables, and much foliage. The pattern continues into a screen behind the altar, creating a narrow vestry or relic chamber between altar and E wall (cf. e.g. Blakeney and Great Yarmouth in Norfolk). This screen is entirely of 1872–5, but is supposed to be based on original evidence. On the N side the EASTER SEPULCHRE has alas been mostly hacked off. In the N chapel were originally three tomb recesses with canopies, much as at Aldworth or Winchelsea. Excellent N aisle and nave roofs with tie-beams, collar-beams on arched braces, and wind-braces; heavy C14 timbers. – SCREEN to the N chapel. Four-light divisions, which is rare in Berkshire, and substantial parts of the rood-loft, which is rarer still. – BENCHES. Some ends have tracery which was probably originally part of the rood-loft. – STAINED GLASS. In the head of the E window some early C14 censing angels. The rest of this window by *Burlison & Grylls*, 1889 (BC). In the S transept S window some fragmentary C15 figures. – In the N aisle W window one C15 figure. – MONUMENTS. Thomas Williamson † 1611. Alabaster tablet with kneeling figures. – Small kneeling figures also in two fragmentary tablets in the N chapel. – John Walsh † 1797. Lifesize female figure with an extinguished torch standing by an urn in front of an obelisk. Unsigned. – Sir John B. Walsh † 1825. By *Bacon Jun.* and *Samuel Manning*. Large tablet. Half-naked male figure on a Greek couch with Faith(?) standing by.

To the SE the VICARAGE, 1862 by *Poulton & Woodman*. Red brick, gabled and varied.

To the S the PARISH ROOM, C17, timber-framed, and, at r. angles to it, ST MICHAEL'S COTTAGE, C16 or C17, also timber-framed.

WARGRAVE   7070

ST MARY. Burnt down in 1914 and rebuilt by *W. Fellowes Prynne*. What remained of the old building was only the brick W tower of *c.*1635 etc. Polygonal buttresses and (re-set) Norman N doorway with one order of colonnettes with zigzag which look as if they were *ex situ,* and with scalloped capitals and a hood-mould with shallow lobes. In the fire a former Norman N arcade was revealed: plain, slightly chamfered piers and plain arches. – FONT. Octagonal, Perp, with cusped quatrefoils. – STAINED GLASS. One S window, mildly Expressionist, by *John Hayward,* 1962. – PLATE. Cup and Cover Paten, probably first half of the C17; Flagon, 1709; Paten presented in 1763; Paten, 1837. – (In the SE corner of the churchyard the HANNEN MAUSOLEUM, designed by *Lutyens.*)

In the village timber-framed cottages and Georgian brick houses, the best of the latter WARGRAVE HOUSE at the corner of High Street and School Lane and the former VICARAGE in High Street. More striking the Norman-Shavian contributions, especially WOODCLYFFE HALL, High Street, with a typical Shaw oriel under the gable, and the WOODCLYFFE HOSTEL in Church Street. The former is of 1901–2, the latter of 1905. Both are by *Cole A. Adams.* Did he also do the LITTLE HOUSE and the adjoining THAMES COTTAGE, both in the HIGH STREET? Also in the High Street, behind the White

Hart, the CONGREGATIONAL CHURCH of 1835, stucco, Gothic, with an embraced w tower. Further N the High Street becomes HURLEY ROAD, and here on the E side CHAPEL HOUSE of c.1800, white, with ogee-headed and quatrefoil windows, and FORD HOUSE, originally a tea-house of an adjoining mansion. Late C18, with a Gothic colonnade or veranda, on the E side, returning on the N and S.

⅜ m. NE of the centre of Wargrave, in an elevated position overlooking the river, is WARGRAVE MANOR, early C19, white, with a broad bow in the centre, a long colonnade or veranda, and recessed two-bay wings. From here further NE, at Crazies Hill, CRAZIES, a house incorporating two two-storeyed pedimented porticoes of Tuscan columns, the cupola, and the entrance hall with Tuscan columns from the former Henley Town Hall, built in 1790.

½ m. E, at Holly Cross, FOX STEEP, a house by *Oliver Hill* of c.1923, all waney elm and roofs at odd levels, a Hansel and Gretel fantasy.

From Wargrave to the E, 1½ m. away, HARE HATCH, with the OLD HOUSE, E of the Horse and Groom, red brick, with a pediment to the N, and a little S of it THE HILL with a red three-bay front to which one-bay wings and a canted bay, used on the ground floor as a porch, have been added a little later. Further E, two houses on the N side of the main road. First HARE HATCH HOUSE, five bays, brick, the doorway and middle window in one giant blank arch, and on the side elevation two symmetrical canted bay windows. Then THE GRANGE, handsome, also red brick, of two and a half storeys. These four houses all appear to be late C18.

Yet further E, at KILN GREEN, on the S side of the road, CASTLEMANS, earlier Georgian and rather bleak. Tall, five bays, parapet. Then N of the road, from W to E, ¾ m. away the convent, ½ m. away Bear Place, ¼ m. away Linden Hill. The CONVENT OF THE GOOD SHEPHERD was Endelles Manor or Yieldhall and is by *John Belcher*, 1894, brick and half-timber. Gabled. Nice group of the porch and a brick tower. Very lively to the other side as well, with bay windows of different shapes and in different planes. BEAR PLACE is Georgian, red brick, with two symmetrical bow windows. The MHLG reports the existence of a contract of 1784 to build the house for £843. LINDEN HILL is stuccoed and less regular, but also has a front with two symmetrical bows. The tower is C19.

WASH COMMON see NEWBURY, pp. 181, 185

WASING

5060

ST NICHOLAS. Long nave and lower chancel, the timber bell-turret midway along the nave. These curious features find their explanation in the fact that the medieval church ended where the bell-turret is and the W part is an C18 enlargement. Another is the S transept. The dates of the enlargements are not quite clear. Dates 1761 (W porch), 1826 (W window), and 1839 (S transept) occur, yet these parts all look 1761 with their arched windows. The lancets in the chancel mark that part as C13, the nave windows are Perp. Coved C18 ceiling. But the very pretty plaster treatment round the windows inside seems impossible for the C18. It looks *c.*1875, the date of a restoration. The chancel arch certainly belongs to that time, but is not at all pretty. – PULPIT. Jacobean. – STAINED GLASS. The Moses probably early C19 or perhaps *c.*1835. – Many pieces of brought-in C16–17 glass, including some of 1649. – PLATE. Cup of 1671.

WASING PLACE was burnt out in the Seond World War. It was by *Hobcraft*, of 1770–3. A new house has since been built from the old materials, five bays with a five-bay pediment and a semicircular porch. The STABLES are charming, a symmetrical front with blank pointed arches and battlements.

WATCHFIELD

2090

ST THOMAS. 1858 by *Street*. Steep roof, down low over the narrow N aisle. Steeply gabled bellcote on a mid-buttress: the details late C13. Nothing of interest inside. – PLATE. Cup probably of 1636; Paten inscribed 1711.

WAYLAND HOSPITAL see BRADFIELD

WAYLAND'S SMITHY see ASHBURY

WELFORD

4070

ST GREGORY. 1852–5 by *T. Talbot Bury*, the round tower and the spire with eight dormers exact replicas of the medieval predecessor, Norman and E.E. Ornate vaulted porch. Elephantine tower arch, uncarved. Recesses in the aisles as if for tombs. Long vaulted chancel of three bays, lancets, wall arcading, black marble shafts. A piquant stone PULPIT comes out of the

wall at the corner of N aisle and chancel arch. – FONT. Norman,
tub-shaped, with intersecting arches. – PLATE. Set of 1737. –
MONUMENTS. Brass to John Westlake, rector, † 1489, 17 in.
figure. – Brass to John Younge c.1530, 16 in. figure. Both at the
back of the sedilia. – Mrs Anne Parry † 1585. Kneeling figure;
alabaster (s aisle w). – Francis Mundy † 1678. Oval, with
coarse carving around. – Elizabeth Mundy † 1689. Bust in a
round-arched recess, a little like Wilhelm Busch's Widow
Bolte. – Thomas Shirley † 1780. Big standing monument
without figures. Draped urn on a high base.

WELFORD PARK. The seven-bay W front of three storeys, brick,
with giant pilasters stretched to the utmost of their capacity, is
an early C18 refacing, or at least partly so; for some of it is
brick in Flemish, some in English bond, and round the corner
the house continues in English bond and is, with its hipped
roof and its extremely curious brick details, something like
1660–70. The windows have raised frames and are vertically
connected by a raised vertical band standing on the centre of
each lower window. At the back this house has two projecting
wings, but a big bow has later been set between them. The
staircase with turned balusters, bulbous below.

8060

WELLINGTON COLLEGE

59a Wellington College was founded in 1853 as a national memorial
to the Duke, who had died in 1852. It was to be a school for
orphans of officers, and all the money was voluntarily subscrib-
ed. Fees should range from £10 to £20 *per annum*. The foundation stone was laid in 1856, the school was opened in 1859. The
first headmaster, Edward White Benson, ended as Archbishop
of Canterbury. The architect, *John Shaw*, is by and large
unknown, though Wellington College alone ought to have
secured a lasting reputation for him. He was over fifty when he
was recommended for the job by *William Burn*, the architect,
and commissioned. Burn knew Shaw's Royal Naval School at
Deptford, now Goldsmiths' College, begun in 1843, which is in
itself as remarkable a job as Wellington College: an extremely
restrained, decidedly Italian design, with a giant middle portal
as its only decoration. Commercial buildings by him are fussy
and undistinguished. Wellington College is distinguished, it is
not at all restrained, and some people may well call it fussy too.
However that may be, for the history of Victorian architecture
it is highly important; for it is in a style made up of Christopher Wren's Hampton Court and Louis XIII, and that

mixture, purged of all fussiness, was going to be re-introduced by Nesfield at Kinmel Park some ten or twelve years later and to start the so-called Queen Anne fashion. Wren, according to *The Builder* (1, 1843, 218), had interested Shaw already in his early days.* It is remarkable that *The Builder* recognized Wren in Shaw; for *The Times* in 1859 called Wellington College 'a handsome edifice in the decorated Italian manner or mixed style'. *The Times* also liked its 'ruddy, cheerful glow'. Cheerful one may well call it, remembering the grim Gothic starkness of contemporary public schools. But the remarkable thing is that Wellington College, in spite of *The Times*, is just not Italianate in the sense of the 1850s nor the purer Cinquecento of Barry in 1850 (Cliveden).

Wellington College is built of red brick and Box stone. The estimates, excluding the chapel, were for sums ranging from £36,000 to £46,000.

In plan Wellington College has something of the axial flourish of Greenwich. For schools such axiality was by no means common, though the Woodard schools, in their unaccommodating Gothic way, also possessed it. But the tradition of the Victorian public school is one of less formal composition, collegiate in the Oxford and Cambridge way. The plan of Wellington College is of two square courtyards, one behind the other, with wings coming out at the N and S angles. The W and E ranges are higher than the N and S ranges and the cross range between the courtyards. In this cross wing is (or was) Large School, in the S range the Dining Hall with richly garlanded dormers and a lantern, in the N range in the middle the main entrance. It has giant columns and a pediment, and above it is a high clock-turret or lantern. The higher W and E wings have mansard roofs and in their middle, i.e. where the cross range meets them, each a high tower. The duality is reminiscent once more of Greenwich. In the upper storeys here are the dormitories. The two courtyards are arcaded.

We must now try to define the motifs which Shaw chose and connect them with the general picture of the style of the college. The mansard roofs of course are French, and the window surrounds on the main floor of the E and W ranges with their busy rhythm of brick trim are Louis XIII too. Also such things as the tower tops may have been intended to suggest France. On the other hand the hipped roofs of the other ranges, the segment-headed windows, the main portal (cf.

* 'The style of Wren of which Shaw has proved himself a master before.'

Trinity Library, Cambridge), and the dormers are William and Mary, and the arches of the cloisters are just Victorian and nothing else.

On the N front bronze STATUES of military heroes by *Theed*. The sculpture of the s front and the cloisters also by *Theed*.* The persons were selected by Prince Albert, who all the way along took a very close interest in the building.

Shaw had intended to have his chapel project from the s range s at the E angle and to match it by the infirmary projecting from the w angle. But this was not done. Whether Benson flinched from Shaw's style for a chapel or whether he flinched from a s orientation, in 1860 he went to *George Gilbert Scott*, a safe man and Gothic, and asked him to design the chapel. Shaw, very handsomely, agreed. Prince Albert, who had first thought of a reduced copy of Eton Chapel and then of a basilica (i.e. probably something Early Christian with round arches, as it was liked in Germany), in the end also agreed. The chapel was built in 1861–3 and faces E. It breaks the grand Baroque axiality of Shaw, and is of red brick, in the Geometrical style, with a main apse, a N chapel apse, and a very slender spire. However, the chapel apse and the aisles were added later, in 1886 and 1899 (by *Arthur Blomfield*). Arcading and rising amphitheatrical seating. Capitals with naturalistic foliage. The chapel is connected by a short Gothic arcaded passage to a big Gothic porch facing s, and this in its turn is connected to the main building by a longer colonnaded passage. – STAINED GLASS. W window by *Lusson*.‡ – In the apse by *Hugh Easton*, 1954, quite unbelievably behind the times, and moreover terribly genteel and thin-blooded. – (WAR MEMORIAL to the First World War. By *Lutyens*.)

The chapel is now part of a later E group of school buildings. N of the E end of the chapel dormitories of 1886 by *Arthur Blomfield*. At r. angles to these, i.e. opposite the N side of the chapel, Dining Hall, Common Room, etc., by *G. J. Blomfield*, 1906–7. Behind the range of 1886 further additions of 1927 and 1940.

WEST CHALLOW

ST LAURENCE. Nave and chancel in one, roofed with stone slates. Genuine early C14 double bellcote. Nice porch with

---

* Except for Count Alten by *F. W. Engelhard*, 1861.
‡ So Mr Nicholas Taylor tells me.

bargeboards of the C15. Simple N doorway of *c.*1200, with one order of shafts. – FONT. Tub-shaped. The decoration of the rim can hardly be Norman. – PULPIT. With some simple Jacobean panelling. – SCREEN. In good condition; one-light divisions. – STAINED GLASS. Old bits in the E window. – PLATE. Paten of *c.*1500 with the monogram of Christ; Chalice, 1605/6.

MANOR FARM. A dramatic early C18 front. Blue and red brick. Five bays, segment-headed windows. Stone keystones. Parapet. The centre bay is carried up one half-storey higher and crowned by its own parapet.

WEST COURT *see* FINCHAMPSTEAD

WEST HANNEY

4090

ST JAMES. Nave and lower chancel. Sturdy N transeptal tower. In the nave two Norman N windows. Also the Norman eaves line. N doorway Norman too, with various lobed decoration of the arch. Tower, end of the C12, with lancets, a doorway to the W, and, next to it, a lancet cut through a buttress. The arch to the church is triple-chamfered. The responds still have one trumpet-scalloped and one fluted capital. The E window, however, is Dec (reticulated tracery). Fine E.E. chancel arch. Rich stiff-leaf capitals on short shafts supported by heads. In the S transept late C13 windows with pointed-trefoiled heads. The S aisle follows after the S transept. Straight-headed Dec windows. Doorway with Dec moulding on – strangely enough – gablets. Blank-traceried parapet. Five-bay arcade. Square piers with demi-columns. Arches with the unmistakable sunk-quadrant mouldings. – FONT. Norman, tub-shaped, with neat vertical bands of rosettes. – PULPIT. Jacobean in style, but the (separate) back panel dated 1649. – SCREEN. Perp, one-light divisions. – COMMUNION RAIL. C17. – STAINED GLASS. Old bits in the S aisle. – BRASSES to a Priest, 4 ft figure, late C14; to John Cheynie † 1557, still with black-letter inscription; to John Ashcombe † 1592 and two wives, and to other post-Reformation people.

WEST HANNEY HOUSE (Old Rectory). Dated 1727 (MHLG).47b Blue and red brick. Six bays, two storeys, with a raised two-bay centre. The parapet curves up to it, and it has its own parapet. Segment-headed windows with stone keystones. The parapet is panelled. The four-bay side elevation has a raised two-bay centre too. Fine staircase with three turned balusters to the step.

WEST HENDRED

4080

HOLY TRINITY. By the brook, in a dip. Dec w tower, Dec N aisle doorway, Dec chancel with nice, steeply gabled buttresses. The arcades of three bays with octagonal piers and double-chamfered arches also possibly C14, though more probably later. – PULPIT. Jacobean. Spacious and panelled right to the ground, i.e. without foot or stem. – FONT COVER. Dated 1630. – Similar details in the re-used panels of the READER'S DESK and the PANELLING of the E wall. – BENCHES (N aisle). Straight-topped, with tracery. – COMMUNION RAIL. Later C17, with dumb-bell balusters. – TILES. Exceptionally many medieval slip-ware tiles in chancel and nave. – STAINED GLASS. Many small bits. – PLATE. Paten, 1662 or 1664; Flagon, 1674; Cup of C17 shape, 1787.

N of the bridge METHODIST CHAPEL, brick, 1830, with pyramid roof. SE of the bridge brick HOUSE of the early C18 with segment-headed windows still with wooden mullion and transom crosses.

(GINGE MANOR, East Ginge, 1¼ m. S. Partly C17, partly early C18. The S front of the latter date; five bays, doorway with straight hood on carved brackets. Also of that date the staircase with twisted and fluted balusters. MHLG and NBR)

WEST ILSLEY

4080

ALL SAINTS. Nave and chancel pre-Victorian, the chancel apparently C18. Victorian bellcote and N aisle and other alterations. The E window has a date 1878. The Victorian work is late C13 in style. C14 nave roof with tie-beams and collars, also wind-braces. – PULPIT. Jacobean; a fine, quiet piece. – BENCH ENDS. Two poppy-heads.

WEST WOODHAY

3060

ST LAURENCE. 1883 by *Sir Arthur Blomfield*. Nave and chancel in one, SE tower with pyramid roof. Plate tracery on lancets. – SCULPTURE. Three exceedingly pretty Rococo putti of wood. Bought in Scotland. – STAINED GLASS. The chancel windows by *Morris & Co.*, 1883 and 1890. – In the nave S side typical *Powell* glass.

WEST WOODHAY HOUSE. The house is a bit of a mystery.

There are three tablets recording the date 1635, and the stone doorway, now set in a porch, goes well with that date. But the appearance of the house otherwise, especially from a distance, would suggest 1675 rather than 1635. Two somewhat project-ing wings recessed centre, hipped roof with dormers, no decoration, except raised brick quoins. The windows are sashed but probably originally had wooden mullion and tran-som crosses. Also, the brick bond is still English, and the windows have thin raised moulded brick surrounds. Can it after all be 1635? It would be yet earlier than the demolished Aldermaston Court (1636), Chevening in Kent (pre-1638), and Inigo Jones's house for Lord Maltravers (1639).* – Good GATES and GATEPIERS with vases.

WHITE WALTHAM   8070

ST MARY. Flint, and dominated by the gross W tower of 1868 with its higher stair-turret turning circular at the top. Yet the building is old. Inside is a re-used unmoulded Norman arch (S of the tower), and the S doorway has two Norman capitals. Fine early C13 chancel with lancets N and S, and in the E wall three widely spaced stepped lancets with a round window in the gable. Inside, the E lancets have continuous rolls, and between them are odd high and very narrow niches also with rolls. The DOUBLE PISCINA has trefoiled arches on a de-tached column. Late C13 the N aisle W window (a quatrefoil done in plate tracery). Dec S transept S and one E window. The N transept is of 1889. The interior is even more High Victorian than the exterior. – STAINED GLASS. S transept S by *Mayer* of Munich, and so German! Big figures. – PLATE. Paten of 1694; Chalice of 1702; Flagon of 1709. – MONUMENTS. On the chancel floor two brasses to ladies: Margaret Hille † 1465 (14 in.) and Joan Decons † 1506 (18 in.). – In the tower standing monument to Constantine Phipps † 1723, by *W. Palmer*. No effigy, no figures; excellent workmanship. – Sir Benjamin Tebbs † 1796. Woman by an urn in front of an obelisk.

By the church a big aisled BARN. Another BARN with adjoining timber-framed cottages with brick infilling. Also W of the church the STOCKS and WHIPPING POST.

WICK HALL *see* RADLEY

* The whole substantial addition of 1880–1 has been pulled down. (Some original features inside.)

3070

WICKHAM

ST SWITHIN. Projecting Anglo-Saxon sw tower. Flint with ample mortar. Long and short quoins. Windows with outer splay. Bell-openings twin with mid-wall shafts. Victorian top, Victorian nave and chancel, Dec, by *Benjamin Ferrey*, 1845–9. Ferrey made the interior very sumptuous, again Dec, especially the tower screen with much tracery and the canopies l. and r., all a background to his FONT. Also foliage capitals, a Dec REREDOS, Norfolk angels supporting the nave roof, and elephants (yes) supporting the aisle roof. They are of papier-maché and were shown at the Paris Exhibition of 1862. – PLATE. Set of 1804.

OLD RECTORY. An older house converted and much enlarged by *Ferrey* and provided with a spectacular Gothic bay window. The ARCHITECTURAL FRAGMENTS from Welford church which adorned the garden have all been destroyed.

WINDMILL HILL *see* HINTON WALDRIST

9070

WINDSOR

WINDSOR CASTLE

INTRODUCTION

35a & b Windsor Castle is the premier castle of England. It is also England's largest castle. It covers about 13 acres. It has been a castle since William the Conqueror, but the first stone buildings were put up by Henry II between 1165 and 1179. Its position is excellent from the point of view of commanding the Thames Valley and of defence. The cliff on which the castle stands is impressively steep to the valley. The climax of the defence arrangements is the round keep. It stands on an artificial motte or mound and is accompanied by three baileys, one to the w, a smaller one in the middle, and the third to the E. The W bailey is called the Lower Ward, the middle one the Middle Ward, the E bailey the Upper Ward. This was no doubt already so at the time of William, and Henry II's walls followed the pattern. Since then the castle has grown steadily with, as a special impetus, the foundation of the Order of the Garter by Edward III in 1348 and with a large rebuilding programme by Charles II. But the architectural climax was the Romantic era from about 1800 to about 1830, and the social climax was, one is tempted to say, the age of Queen Victoria. The early C19 has given us the fairy picture of the castle from a distance, e.g. the M4 motorway. The castle contained a collegiate church with its college, and this college survives and occupies a third of the total area. The separate existence of the college and the castle must always be remembered.

By way of a preliminary exploration the castle ought to be circumambulated. Practically to most users of this book this will not be possible, as part of the circumference is not accessible to the public. What the tour will help to establish as firmly as ought to be done here from the start is that essentially all the features of the walls are C19–Romantic. Once this has been said, it can be pointed out that the three mighty rounded towers towards the town, i.e. Thames Street, and the walling between them are Henry III's, that Henry II's walling is most prominent in the Winchester Tower, NW of the round keep with stone blocks and narrow flint bands, in some walling to its W and its E, and especially the walling of the E side, and that the keep itself is in its lower parts Henry II too. Further towers of Henry III are on the S side, recognizable by their broad, big rounded projection (Henry III's Tower, Edward III's Tower – a perverse name). Charles II's work – he did much more than is preserved, as we shall see – is best visible in the square Victoria Tower at the SE corner and the NW part of the State Apartments, i.e. NE of the Round Tower. That range then recedes and has Henry II walling, but after that projects again and is pure George IV. The finer points of the outer walls cannot here be described.

We enter now by Henry VIII's Gateway, and shall look at the castle from there to the far E range.

HENRY VIII'S GATEWAY has to the outside broad polygonal towers. The archway has a four-centred head and continuous mouldings. Above it is the king's coat of arms and at the top are workable machicolations. The vault is simple: quadripartite with ridge-ribs. To the inside there is a large eight-light window, straight-headed and transomed, the lights still cusped. The turrets here are much thinner.

On leaving the gatehouse one has the first full view of the LOWER WARD, with the chapel facing full on, the one major building of fine buff ashlar limestone, Henry III's walling on the l. except for the tower in the SW corner all hidden by *Salvin's* building of 1862, the Horseshoe Cloister w of the chapel, and the quarters of the Military Knights, or at first the Poor Knights, the *milites pauperi* or *milites veterani*, a part of the Garter foundation. Their quarters continue the line of the gatehouse towards the Round Tower. Their first length is ashlar-faced and is an addition of Queen Mary Tudor to the further (ragstone) range of Edward III. The two ranges were over-restored by *Blore* in 1840–50. In the distance on the r. are the Round Tower and the Upper Ward.

It can be assumed that the chapel will be looked at first.

ST GEORGE'S CHAPEL

5The chapel was built to replace Henry III's chapel further E (on which more later) and its enlargement by Edward III, needed when the Order of the Garter was created in 1348. The new chapel was begun in 1475 and built from E to w. Progress was slow. By 1484 the chancel without its vault and the chancel aisles with their vaults were ready, the transepts and the nave minus the w bay begun. By 1503 the s transept was ready to receive the burial of Sir Reginald Bray. His munificence made it possible to complete the nave.* The w bay and w front were an afterthought, but all seems to have been ready by 1511. The contract for the chancel vault dates from 1506. The spasmodic building activity is due to the political vicissitudes of the decades in question. Eton and King's Chapels were willed and begun by Henry VI in 1449 and 1446, i.e. they were Lancaster jobs. Edward IV started St George's Chapel, and work had indeed all but stopped at Eton and King's about 1461. It was only resumed, *c.*1470 and 1477 respectively, when Edward felt safe and settled enough. In 1475, as we have seen, he started St George's Chapel. Henry VII had little interest in his Yorkist predecessor's initiative and probably changed his mind only

* The gradual completion is visible internally, by a change of stone descending from the N transept to floor level, which is reached one bay E of the w front. That the chancel aisles must have been in full operation in the 1480s is evident from the dates of the transfer of the bodies of John Schorne and Henry VI and the date of Edward IV's monument.

when he had decided to adapt the chapel of Henry III and Edward III as his tomb-house. That was in 1494. The master masons were *Henry Janyns*, documented from 1478 to 1484, but perhaps the original designer, and *William Vertue*, documented for the chancel vault. The chapel is 237 ft long as against Eton's *c.*190 and King's *c.*290. There has been so much restoration, chiefly in the last hundred years, that details can only rarely be accepted as the original carvers' work.* St George's Chapel differs from these two and the earliest major royal chapel, that of St Stephen in the palace of Westminster, in that it has a prominent transept. This transept – that is the most striking and a quite unexpected feature – is placed half-way down, not further E, as was the scarcely abandoned custom. The nave has seven bays, the chancel has seven bays. The transept has polygonal ends, which is again unexpected. A tower over the crossing was intended but never built. It would have been oblong, like that of Bath Abbey, begun in 1499. The balance between W and E with the transept in the middle is one of the signs of the impending Renaissance, or rather the readiness of England to receive the Italian Renaissance and its insistence on symmetry. The only feature which detracts from a full appreciation of symmetry is the difference between the polygonal chapels at the W and the E ends. The latter is an actual addition to the seven bays, the former corresponds to the first of the seven bays and caused this bay to be made wider than the others. The result, as we see it today with its three projecting polygonal bays, is curiously similar to Palladian or Baroque compositions. What obscures this prophetic harmony a little is the fact that the W chapel is one-storeyed and has an ogee roof, whereas the E chapel has two upper floors and a flat top.

The details are all very sumptuous, but the basic arrangements are uniform and repetitive. All the aisle windows are of four lights, with two embattled transoms and four-centred heads. All the clerestory windows are of four lights too, but in a two plus two arrangement, and have one embattled transom and

* Mr Maurice Bond, to whom I am extremely grateful for most generously given help, listed the major restorations for me as follows: *post* 1682, *Wren* removing the original King's Beasts and repairing roof and vault; 1782–92 *Emlyn* repairing stonework and adding screen, stalls, and staircase to the Royal Pew; 1841–5 *Blore*, including the reconstruction of the W window; 1863 *Scott* reconstruction of the E end of the chancel; 1866–72 *Scott* new W approach; 1878–86 *Pearson*, including new buttresses, parapets, gargoyles; 1920–30 *Brakspear*, complete restoration, new King's Beasts.

two-centred arches. The buttresses have niches, and there are flying buttresses above. Above the aisle windows is a frieze of beasts and then elaborate openwork battlements. Above the clerestory windows is a frieze as well, and then an openwork parapet. The upper buttresses end in plain pinnacles, or rather shafts, on which stand the royal beasts. The same system applies partially to the W chapel and completely to the transepts. In the re-entrant W angle of the transept is a porch provided in 1926, in the re-entrant E angle Bishop King's Chapel, a curious little excrescence of 1492–6.

The W front is grand enough, but was made yet grander by the wide staircase added in 1866–72. The façade is dominated by its fifteen-light window with four transoms and a four-centred head. The doorway is relatively small. Blank panelling l. and r., and a pretty frieze above. The three STATUES above the window are of *Coade* stone and were placed in 1799. Big angle-turrets with ogee caps. The N side of the chapel is fundamentally the same as the S side, but simpler in many details. The E side cannot be seen, owing to buildings to which we have to turn later. The E window is of fifteen lights too, but quite different in its design. Whereas the W window is even throughout, the E window is divided into four–seven–four with much larger panels and only two transoms plus a third at the level of the springing of the side arches. The chief tracery motif of these side arches incidentally is a square.*

10   The INTERIOR of St George's Chapel is wide rather than high. The effect is due partly to the consistent use of four-centred arches. In the case of the vault this is carried so far as to give the impression of a coved ceiling, flat all along the centre. The other dominant element of the chapel is the insistence on line rather than mass. In detail this ought to be observed. The arcades are high, much and thinly moulded, and, to the nave at least, entirely continuous in their mouldings, i.e. without any capitals. Above these follow blank panelling with pretty heads, a frieze, and then the clerestory windows whose two-centred arches can hardly be noticed, as the vault seems to cut into them. This vault is the marvel of the chapel, a complex design divided clearly into coving and ceiling. The ceiling part is emphasized by two straight longitudinal ribs running parallel to the ridge rib. The area of these three is

---

* Inside, the E window is surrounded by a moulding with angels making music.

arranged as stars with quatrefoiled circles as infillings and many bosses. The coving part has its ribbing of the palm frond, i.e. tierceron, type with liernes only in one small part. There are thirteen such ribs from each springer, three plus three into the penetrations for the clerestory windows, the next to the outer longitudinal ribs, the next the real diagonals establishing a basic normal quadripartite vault, the sixth just up the liernes, the seventh the transverse arch.

The aisles are treated quite differently. Here there are fan-vaults, and fan-vaults, at the time when the chapel was designed, were indeed still very exceptional for major vaults. The aisle walls are panelled and a frieze with battlements runs above them. The panelling is linked to the windows by vertical roll-mouldings, three to each bay, l., centre, and r.

The sw (Beaufort) and nw (Urswick) chapels have vaults starting with six little fans and leading up to a central star – a very handsome variation on the theme of the – it will be remembered: earlier – principal vaults.

The crossing has the one major fan-vault in the chapel. The crossing arches are broad and panelled, as is the inner surround of the w window as well. In the transepts the nave system continues, and it is delightful how the vaulting star fits in with the polygonal ending dictated by the polygonal end-walls of the transepts. The only difference in the elevation is that the e wall has in the inner bay a frieze of angel busts emphasizing the fact that here altars must have stood. In the s transept two niches with canopies of the reredos are indeed still *in situ*.

The chancel system is again the same, except that the aisle fan-vaults have octagonal instead of circular centres and the nave vault has a pendant as the centre of each star. There is only one anomaly in the chancel. The last two n bays are low, because above them the upper chantry of Edward IV was put in which later became the Royal Pew. It is accessible by a small newel staircase in the wall. It has an oriel to the w and a much wider one to the chancel. To the e of this yet another oriel was provided by Henry VIII some time probably in the 1520s. This is of wood, and extremely interest-ing in that it combines Gothic arches and panelling with Renaissance balusters. The fan-vaults of this low part of the aisle beneath the watching chamber have the central circles like the nave and not the octagons of the chancel, and Mr Harvey wonders whether this whole two-storeyed arrangement might not be an afterthought. The conversion to being the

Royal Pew belongs to George III and was done in 1785 by *Henry Emlyn,* a carpenter attached to Windsor Castle who developed into a gentleman and an architect.

The ambulatory behind the altar is a spot of great piquancy for the architectural historian. Henry III's chapel of *c.*1240 stood E of the present one, as will be seen later. This was its W entrance. The E wall of the ambulatory has three arches unmistakably E.E. The capitals have gone, but the bases and the moulded arches are eloquent enough. And, while this takes us for the first time to the beginnings of the Gothic in the castle, the other details of the ambulatory take us to the end. The cypher of George III will be noticed above the N doorway, and the panelled segmental vault also is his. The doorway leads into the VESTRY, and from here one can reach the STAIRCASE to the Royal Pew, early C19, with a nice cast-iron railing. It leads to a Gothick ante-room and then to the pew itself with the oriel. The niche in the N chancel aisle N wall by the start of the ambulatory is not explained.

In the S chancel aisle the corresponding niche has something to do with the SE chapel, which was originally the chapel of John Schorne, rector of North Marston in Buckinghamshire, who conjured the devil into a boot, died about 1290, and was transferred to St George's Chapel when Bishop Beauchamp of Salisbury became Dean in 1478. In the niche in question is a small squint to the E with a contemporary wooden grille. The chapel has a vault like those of the SW chapels, which were, as we have seen, in fact built later. Above the chapel is a room with a quatrefoil peep-hole down into the S chancel aisle. This is presumably connected with the years of the cult of Henry VI and control over pilgrims.

FURNISHINGS. St George's Chapel is as rich in furnishings as a cathedral, and in such cases the tradition of *The Buildings of England* is to discuss them topographically rather than chronologically or by types of objects. We start from the E end.

CHANCEL. REREDOS. Of alabaster, with carved scenes. 1863 by *John Birnie Philip.* – STAINED GLASS. The E window by *Clayton & Bell*; dull. – The two big CANDLESTICKS in the Italian Renaissance style are copies of two of the four made for Henry VIII and now in St Bavon at Ghent. They are of the 1530s. – MONUMENTS.* The exquisitely fine iron grille be-

---

* The monuments are treated fully and authoritatively in Shelagh M. Bond: *The Monuments of St George's Chapel,* one of the admirable *Historical Monographs relating to St George's Chapel.*

longed to the monument of Edward IV, † 1483, and is by *John Tresilian*. It is all a filigree of tracery. – Opposite, white marble recumbent effigies of Edward VII and Alexandra, 1919 by *Sir Bertram Mackennal*. To the N aisle, against the tomb-chest two small allegorical figures in the Alfred Gilbert tradition.

STALLS. The stalls were provided in 1478–85, the principal 19 carver being one *William Berkeley*. They consist of three tiers, the topmost for the Knights of the Garter and the dean and canons, the middle one for the Military Knights, the minor canons, and the choirmen, the lowest for the choir boys. Behind the top row are high, elaborate canopies with helmets and crests on them. In addition to the rows along the N and S walls, there are four return stalls each side to the W, against the screen. Between them and the N and S stalls is a short piece without seating. The N and S sides originally had twenty-one stalls each, but two each side were added in 1786–90 by *Henry Emlyn*, who made some other minor changes and did a great deal of repairing and extra carving – amazingly skilfully. In front of the stalls are desks, the lowest tier of them being of the C19. The desks are divided into blocks, and each block-end has a poppy-head with a scene to the W and a scene to the E and small figures of prophets. The desk fronts have blank tracery and scenes in tympana and spandrels carved in relief. Moreover, all the stalls have misericords, the elbows of the seats have carving, and an inscription – largely Psalm XX – runs along the front of the upper desks. It is impossible, within the scope of *The Buildings of England*, to list all the sculpture. Fortunately there is Montague R James's guide: *The Woodwork of the Choir*, 2nd ed., 1955. The following is no more than a summary. It is arranged in the order of Montague James's guide. First the link-pieces between return stalls and N and S stalls. They each have three figures and in addition vertical strips with small figures. The large ones are N: St George, St Katherine, the Virgin; S: St John Evangelist, St Edward, St Edmund(?). Of the small figures a number are by *Emlyn*, and it is not always easy to recognize them as such. – Then the other woodwork, N before S. The N return stalls have poppy-heads of the life of Edward III and of St George and the Dragon, all by *Emlyn*, and also demi-figures of Prophets in pulpits, some original, some by *Emlyn*. In the spandrels of the desk fronts are e.g. Doubting Thomas, the Ascension, Pentecost, and (in three scenes) the Last Judgement.

Among the misericords are a gatehouse and a mermaid. –
N stalls from W to E. On the poppy-heads are along the upper
row scenes from Christ's Passion ending with the Crucifixion
and along the lower row the continuation to Emmaus (not all
in the correct chronological order). The small Prophets here
are all by *Emlyn*. Among the scenes on the desk fronts are
many animals and grotesques, e.g. a lizard, two snails, a sala-
mander, and a scene with the fox, a monkey as a doctor, and a
cat and a rabbit pouring something into the fox's mouth, then
(E block) an army camp, a cow and a boar, a cat and a squirrel,
a bull playing a lute, the Fifth Trumpet (from *Revelation*), a
ship, a fox and an ape, St John Baptist and the Lamb etc., and,
at the E end, *Emlyn*'s entertaining George III and Queen
Charlotte at a Thanksgiving in St Paul's on the occasion of the
king's recovery in 1789, first driving to St Paul's in a coach,
then the ceremony inside the cathedral. The misericords of the
N stalls have e.g. Samson and the Lion, an eaglet, griffins, an
Amphisbaena, a dog chasing rabbits, an owl mobbed, and
(lower rank) men in armour, a Wild Man, a friar, an antelope,
an elephant and castle.

Now the s return stalls. On the poppy-heads again Edward
III and St George, all by *Emlyn*, the small Prophets again
largely original (including David and Moses) and a few by
Emlyn. On the desk fronts the Annunciation (Sovereign's
Desk), Visitation, Magi, Circumcision, Crucifixion, Resurrection, Women at the Sepulchre, and Harrowing of Hell. The
misericord of the Sovereign's Desk is iconographically unique:
the Meeting at Picquigny between Edward IV and Louis XI.
Then a gatehouse. The s stalls (W to E) have partly the rarely
told story of St George, partly scenes from the life of the
Virgin and the Last Judgement. They are all original and the
most worthwhile pieces, though the figures are stocky and
the telling is naïve. One thought of contemporary stalls in
Germany such as those at Ulm fixes the level of aesthetic value
at Windsor firmly. Among the prophets here are probably
(upper row) Isaiah and Jeremiah. The desk fronts have e.g. the
Coronation of the Virgin, the Journey to Emmaus, and the
stories in the two side spandrels (these three by *Emlyn*),
the Nativity and the Visitation, then (E block) stories of the
martyrdom of a mother and child (Cyriacus and Julitta?) and
at the E end the Attempt on King George III's Life in 1786
(two tympana and four spandrels). Of the s side misericords
the following may be singled out: a jester with bagpipes, two

dogs, two wyverns, two wrestlers, two lizards, two dragons, four dogs, Wild Man, cockatrice, unicorn, apes and grapes, rose bushes, and (lower row) three monks and a fox, monkeys, 'Who sups with the devil . . . ', three groups from the Dance of Death, the pelican, pedlar and apes, two men gambling and quarrelling, two boys at a game.

THE GARTER STALL PLATES.* The seven hundred plates form a 'heraldic storehouse of the highest artistic excellence', unequalled in Europe, wrote St John Hope. In accordance with a statute of the Order of the Garter the plates have been placed on the backs of the knights' stalls, originally at death, but, from at least 1489 onwards, within a year of installation. They are of copper or brass, with gilded or silvered surfaces on which the arms of the knights have been richly enamelled or painted. The earliest is that of Ralph, Lord Bassett (s side, Stall 13), erected c.1390 in a stall in the original chapel, and transferred with some ninety other plates to the new choir about 1483. The finest plates are probably those dating from the C 15; and, notably, a group of twenty-seven erected c.1421 which are cut out to the shape of the heraldic design; of these, the plates of Hugh Stafford, Lord Bourchier (N 19), Sir Sanchet Dabrichecourt and William Lord Latimer (both s 25) are superb examples. The plates of the first half of the C 17, although large in size and somewhat florid in design, are finely engraved; those of Charles I as Prince of Wales (s 3), Count Palatine of the Rhine (s 5), and King Gustavus Adolphus II of Sweden (s 3) are typical. During the C 17 enamel was replaced by paint, and except to heraldic specialists, the later painted plates are of very much less appeal. A revival of enamelling in 1908 symbolized a return in some degree to earlier standards, as has the occasional use in recent years of the cut-out shape. The plates of Earl Baldwin (s 27) and of Sir Winston Churchill (N 23) are, for instance, a marked improvement on those of such of their predecessors as Benjamin Disraeli, Earl of Beaconsfield (N 25), and the third Marquess of Salisbury (s 18).‡

LECTERN. Early C16; of brass, with two desks. A mighty piece, probably Netherlandish.

* This account was kindly contributed by Mr Maurice Bond, and I am extremely grateful to him for it.

‡ The eighty-seven surviving plates of before 1485 were splendidly reproduced by Hope in his *Stall Plates of the Knights of the Garter* (1901); and a complete list is provided by E. H. Fellowes in *Knights of the Garter* (St George's Chapel Monograph, 1939, with supplement, 1963).

16b   EAST AMBULATORY. DOOR to Henry III's former chapel,
C13, with extremely elegant ironwork, much more spaciously
done than usual. The ironwork is signed: *Gilebertus*. – Stone
SCREEN like that of a chantry chapel to hide the access to a
staircase. Probably by *Brakspear*. – SPIRAL STAIR by *Brakspear*, very successful. – MONUMENTS. Theodore Randue
† 1723. Excellent; of the reredos type; no effigy, no figures,
hardly any ornament. – Col. Brudenell † 1768, pretty tablet. –
Robert C. Parke † 1815. By *Humphrey Hopper*. Small group
of the dying officer, his horse, and a helping soldier.

NORTH CHANCEL AISLE. FONT. Fragment of a Purbeck
marble font of the time of Henry III. It was round and had
heads at the angles. One remains, and some flat stiff-leaf.
– DOOR. With outstanding ironwork, a rose and a square
piece round the keyhole. – STAINED GLASS. By *Willement*;
mostly heraldic. – MONUMENTS. Edward IV. Standing wall-
monument, made in 1789 by *Emlyn*. Gothick, with large brass
lettering. – Earl Harcourt † 1830. White statue by *Sievier*,
1832. Relief scenes l. and r. on the high base. – Chantry Chapel
of Lord Hastings † 1483, the chantry established in 1503.
Stone screen ; inside PAINTINGS of the story of St Stephen;
provincial. On the w and e walls niches with canopies and angel
friezes. Lierne-vault with star shapes. – Sir John Elley † 1839.
Big white block with bust by *R. Trentanova* of Rome, 1815.
– Dean Gerald Wellesley † 1882. By *J. E. Boehm*, 1883–4.
White marble; recumbent effigy.

SOUTH CHANCEL AISLE. LINCOLN CHANTRY. This was
originally Master John Schorne's Chapel (*see* above). The iron
GRILLE is C15 work. – MONUMENTS. Edward Earl of Lincoln
28b   † 1585. Alabaster. High tomb-chest. Two recumbent effigies,
he on a half-rolled-up straw mat. Children kneeling against
the tomb-chest. Also helm and gauntlets of alabaster. Achievement against the w wall.* – King Edward VII *see* Chancel.
– Henry VI. Black slab to commemorate the place where the
king was laid to rest after his coffin had been transferred from
Chertsey Abbey in 1484. His HELMET above. – The HELMET
of Charles Brandon a little further w. – ALMSBOX. Of iron,
with letters H in black letter. H stands no doubt for Henry,
and this remarkable box was in all probability made to receive
offerings at Henry VI's tomb. – OXENBRIDGE CHANTRY.
Canon Oxenbridge died in 1522. The chantry is much like the

* Above this chapel two upper rooms with HEADS and HELMS of some of
the Garter canopies.

earlier Hastings Chantry, and it ought to be noted that there is not a sign of the Italian Renaissance yet, except in the PAINTINGS, dated 1522, which are in the Antwerp style of c.1520. – PAINTINGS. Four large panels of standing Kings. Part of Bishop King's Chantry, c.1495. – MONUMENT to the Duchess of Gloucester, 1859, signed not only by *W. Theed* but also by *Sir G. G. Scott* as designer. Tomb-chest of several marbles, polished, inlaid brass cross. Above four snow-white reliefs in the quatrefoil shapes of Ghiberti's Baptistery doors.

BISHOP KING'S CHAPEL. Bishop King of Bath and Wells, † 1503, was a Canon of Windsor. However, that is not enough of an explanation of why he alone should have been allowed a chapel so visibly sticking out of a perfectly uniform chapel. The King Chapel was built in 1492–6. The tomb is in the open arch between chapel and aisle. Interesting wall decoration of mottos and patterning, very harshly done, without any arch, curve, cusp, or foil. – STAINED GLASS. Heraldic panels; C15. – On the floor three BRASSES. Canopy of William Magge, first warden of the College, 1380. – The other two brasses of the 1630s.

CROSSING. ORGAN GALLERY. A handsome 'veranda-screen'. Designed by *Henry Emlyn* and made of *Coade* stone in 1790–2. Horace Walpole called it 'airy and harmonious'.

NORTH TRANSEPT (Rutland Chapel). Large Perp stone SCREEN. – MONUMENTS. Lord Roos † 1513 and wife. Grand alabaster monument with recumbent effigies, about as good as any made of that material at that time in England. Against the tomb-chest mourning knights one side, mourning ladies the other, and angels holding shields. All in the shallow ogee-headed recesses which are found so frequently in the alabaster monuments of the early C16. – Brass to Canon Honywoode † 1523. A plaque with the kneeling dean presented by St Katherine to the Virgin. – Copper-gilt plaque to the Duchess of Exeter and her husband. He died in 1483, she in 1476. Two kneeling figures and the Trinity over. – Charles Okes † 1860. Tablet with a most remarkably geometricized ship.

SOUTH TRANSEPT (Bray Chapel). Large Perp stone SCREEN. It has the Bray rebus, a hemp-bray, in the frieze. The same in the N transept screen, since, as has been said, Sir Reginald Bray was responsible for more than his chapel. – MONUMENTS. Frame of Robbia coloured fayence. It must date from the early 1520s, but its context is not recorded. The nearest to it are of course *Giovanni da Majano*'s roundels at

Hampton Court, and they date from 1521. Giovanni is indeed
the most likely author of this frame. – Sir William Fitzwilliams
† 1551. The typical Purbeck marble tomb of the early C16 with
pendant (ogee-headed) arches. Ornamented angle colonnettes.
A pretty device is the way in which the tomb-chest is detached
from the canopy. – Sir Richard Wortley † 1603. Alabaster
tablet set in the Robbia frame. – Bishop Giles Tomson † 1612.
Also alabaster. Frontal demi-figure with a formidably Assyrian
beard. He was indeed 'moribus gravis'. In a shell niche.
– Bishop Brideoake † 1678. Semi-reclining effigy, white,
between black columns. Large, wide-open segmental pediment. A large vase of curiously organic shape in it. Signed by
William Byrd of Oxford. – Prince Christian Victor of Schles-
wig Holstein. By *Emil Fuchs*, 1902. Père Lachaise rather than
England. Large, white angel with a sword. – In the centre the
Prince Imperial, son of Napoleon III, † 1879. By *Boehm*.
Recumbent effigy, white on a white sarcophagus. Long French
inscription.

21a
& b   NAVE. STAINED GLASS. W window, with sixty-five figures.
the majority of them largely original early C16 work, a rare and
impressive survival.

NORTH AISLE. FONT. Of wood, mid C17. Foot with four
sirens, stem a short column, cover with thin garlands along the
edges. A curiously inexpensive, undemonstrative piece for St
George's Chapel. One would like to know its story. – MONU-
MENTS. King Leopold of Belgium. By *Boehm*, 1878. White
statue. Lively face. – King George V and Queen Mary. 1937
by *Sir William Reid Dick*. The effigies of marble, very un-
lively and yet not monumental. The design of the monument
by *Lutyens*.

32   NORTH WEST (Urswick) CHAPEL. Iron GRILLE of c.1510–
20. – Princess Charlotte † 1817. By *Matthew Cotes Wyatt*. If
proof were needed that the Romantic decades could combine
the sensational with the chaste – here it is. A snow-white
scene acted by life-size figures. Below, the princess dead
on a ledge covered entirely by a heavy sheet from under which
only the fingers of one hand hang down. To the l. and r. four
mourning women, all completely hidden by their mantles.
Above, the princess ascending to heaven, one breast bare, and
two angels l. and r., one holding the still-born baby, the other
crossing his arms. All this takes place in front of a stone tomb,
the entrance to which is scarcely visible because of a large white
curtain. The monument is perhaps the most complete state-

ment of one ideal of funerary sculpture of the early C19. The effects are very strong, but the whiteness and the emotionless faces that are seen make it safe in the church. The folds also are disturbed only in a few places. – PAINTINGS. Two very good panels of bishops of c.1500. Influenced by Goes? – STAINED GLASS. Behind the monument. Large figures, strong colours; probably early C19.

SOUTH AISLE. FONT. Designed by *J. L. Pearson* and made in 1888.

SOUTH WEST (Beaufort) CHAPEL. Iron GRILLE of c.1510–20. By *Jan van den Einde* of Malines. – SCULPTURE. Small Spanish C13 Virgin. – MONUMENT. Earl of Worcester † 1526. Alabaster. Two recumbent effigies. An angel stands stiffly at their heads. His feet rest against a goat, but about them also two little bedesmen. – STAINED GLASS. Largely by *Willement*, probably c.1845–50.

VESTRY. PAINTING. Large, dramatic Last Supper by *Benjamin West*. – Large numbers of TILES, some possibly of Chertsey, others of Penn make, 1355, from the Aerary.

PLATE.* Secular Dish with rose in the centre, gilt, 1548; pair of Flagons, 1576 and 1583; pair of Chalices and Covers, 1612 and 1616; Chalice, 1612; pair of large Flagons with St George, 1660; three large gilt Basons with Christ blessing a child, Christ washing St Peter's feet, and the Last Supper, all 1661. Also of 1661 two large gilt Patens; another Paten; two Flagons; pair of large Chalices, gilt, 1667; also a pair of Candlesticks of c.1660 and a pair of larger Candlesticks of c.1694 (by *A. Nelme*).

LOWER WARD

HORSESHOE CLOISTER, W of the chapel. It is not a cloister in the usual sense of the word, as it is open towards the chapel. The horseshoe shape is in fact unique. It was built in 1478–81 as houses for the Priest Vicars, who sang the services as predecessors of the present Minor Canons. It is timber-framed with brick-nogging and prominent ogee-shaped diagonal braces. Each vicar had a separate house. There are altogether twenty-one of them. The houses have a newel stair by the entrance and the chimney in the outer back wall. In front of the houses runs the cloister walk. It has depressed-ogee-headed openings. Nearly everything that meets the eye is

* One volume of the *Historical Monographs* already referred to is E. A. Jones: *The Plate of St George's Chapel* (1939).

Scott's of 1871. Behind the Horseshoe Cloister to the NW is Henry III's CURFEW TOWER, finished off by *Salvin* in 1863 in a Carcassonne way. Inside a splendidly strong rib-vault: one quadripartite bay and a six-ribbed apse, as it were, with seven deep pointed-tunnel-vaulted niches in the thick walls. From here a SALLYPORT exit to the town in the thickness of the wall. Many steps; pointed tunnel-vault.

Behind the Horseshoe Cloister to the N the CHAPTER LIBRARY, once the HALL OF THE VICARS, provided in 1415–16, a large room with an open timber roof. The tie-beams are original. The chimneypiece has Denton's rebus, i.e. probably came from Denton's Commons, a range built in 1520 and demolished in 1859.

In the gap between the Horseshoe and the chapel appears MERBECK, as they now call it. It was probably a canon's house, and is like a manor-house. Hall-house type, though of the projecting solar and office wings much is Victorian. Timber-framing and brick-nogging. The hall has a four-light window with transom and uncusped lights and a fine roof with collar-beams, arched braces, and wind-braces. Chimneypiece with a big hood and a curious, rather bleak frieze. The l. extension of the house has a bold overhang.

To the r. of Merbeck an irregular early C18 brick house and then a memorable stone patch with one N window of the Great Hall of the C12, reconstructed by Henry III. Segment-headed arch and stepped inner arch. During the reconstruction of the house behind this wall in 1965, beneath the internal C17 and C18 plaster walls, extensive medieval work was discovered. The house in fact comprises the block of domestic royal chambers, dating from the C12 and C13, which stood between the Great Hall and the castle wall. On the first floor immediately above the cliff is the main chamber, perhaps as reconstructed *c*.1225; stone walls, fireplace, fragmentary wall paintings, including an upper layer of C15 plainsong music. On the second floor, set in a later wall, a tall cylindrical chimney, C12 or early C13, one of very few surviving, with later C13 scissor-beam roof trusses alongside. These discoveries are important in that little survives elsewhere in the castle of pre-Edward III date, and very little in the country at large of the fabric of Henry III's royal lodgings. To the E an interesting canon's house of 1660. Brick with giant pilasters. Even the Ionic capitals are of brick. It is very characteristic of the mid C17. These houses were canons' residences.

Another one, Georgian, stands across facing W. This has a hipped roof and forms the W end of the Canons' Cloister, on which *see* below.

Back to the chapel and looking S the range of the Military Knights already referred to. At its E end is **Henry III's TOWER**, remarkable because its two high upper windows with their round arches and transom-like balustrade represent the one survival of *Hugh May*'s work for Charles II, a compromise externally between classical and medieval. He started work in 1675; for this is the date of the warrant to pull down what was to be replaced.*

The area E of St George's Chapel is particularly interesting. Here once more the epochs mix. There is a Perp doorway immediately E of St George's Chapel, and this ought to be taken. It leads into a passage with a panelled segmental vault. The blank arches in the W wall correspond to the three arches of entry to **HENRY III's CHAPEL** which were noticed in the E ambulatory of St George's Chapel. They probably led into a galilee, and the chapel itself followed E of it. It has in the past been suggested that the wall in question was the actual W wall of the chapel and the wall opposite did not originally exist. This is disproved by the wall **PAINTING** of a head the style of which is clearly Henry III. The quality is outstanding. Further evidence for the chapel itself is the **CLOISTER** to its N, a cloister which is now of the time of Edward III. The chronology must be carefully watched. Of Henry III's time the sumptuous doorway from the cloister to the passage into the galilee just mentioned. Stiff-leaf capitals, richly moulded arch. Also of his time the equally rich blank arcading to the E of this dooway, i.e. along the S wall of the cloister-walk. The cloister arches themselves with rather heavy Perp tracery belong to the work of Edward III in connexion with the Order of the Garter. At the corners piers with canopied niches. Edward III's work started in 1350, but already in 1344 he had erected the mysterious **ROUND TABLE** of wood, 200 ft in diameter. If only we knew where to look for it and what it was like. The mason was William of Ramsey (of the St Paul's chapter house), the carpenter William of Hurley. Altogether Edward III spent on Windsor the fabulous sum of £50,000. Henry III a hundred years before had spent *c.* £15,000.

The most interesting surviving job of Edward III's years is the **PORCH** from the W into the cloister. It is singularly unre- 4b

* *See* also State Apartments, p. 288.

stored and a prime example of the transition from Dec to
Perp. Wall panelling still with ogee-headed and ogee-footed
quatrefoils. Charming outer door-surrounds, blank cusped
and subcusped and again with occasional ogees. Two bays of
ingenious lierne-vaulting with the basic diagonal and ridge-
ribs interrupted by lozenges as if they opened and closed
scissor-wise. This porch has a s doorway which now leads into
the vestry and would originally have led on to the galilee of
Henry III's Chapel. The s side of this doorway, now inside
the vestry, was originally cusped, and the arch has a frieze of
small quatrefoils. The remaining features of Edward III's in
the cloister are doorways with hood-moulds on pretty bracket-
like stops.

In the cloister s walk a wall PAINTING of a royal head. It
must be of c.1270 and is of the very highest quality. – MONU-
MENT. In the cloister w walk Ann Aldworth † 1695. Cartouche with bust at the top and three putto-heads.

Above the w cloister walk is the original LIBRARY, now
divided into the Chapter Room and the Chapter Clerk's
Office. The Office has a C15 ceiling with bosses, the original
Treasury or AERARY (1353–5), the Muniment Room, lying
above Edward III's porch, a typical mid C14 rib-vault with
diagonal and ridge-ribs only and hollow-chamfered ribs.
Plain big bosses – all solid and no frills. – Good medieval
TILES here.

From the N cloister walk a passage leads to the CLOISTER of
1353 with the houses for the canons and the vicars of the
College (see below). It is a long narrow cloister with a timber
arcading towards the centre. The arches have disappeared.
Scott, in crossing the cloister by a middle passage, reconstructed them. The residences along the N side are built against
Henry II's wall and into Henry II's Winchester Tower. From
the terrace here the HUNDRED STEPS lead down into the town
by way of a C19 barbican at bottom level.

The cloister E walk borders on what was Edward III's
GARTER CHAPTER HOUSE of 1350–2. This is now the ground
floor of the DEANERY. Its upper wall, flint and brick, appears
above the cloister. The upper wall dates from the time of
Dean Wren, Sir Christopher's father. One C14 side window is
still in good order. It is Perp, of four lights with one transom
and a quatrefoil frieze at the foot. Between the chapter house
and the Chapel of Henry III is a VESTRY with a tierceron-
star-vault. Walls with blank cusped and subcusped arches.

Henry III's Chapel was replaced by the present ALBERT MEMORIAL CHAPEL. But when was this done? St John Hope dated it all *temp*. Henry VII, though he had to admit that no records survive. Mr Harvey recently has made out a good case for *temp*. Edward III. His intention was to provide a chapel for his two new foundations of 1348: the college of secular canons, consisting of Dean, 12 Canons, 13 Priest Vicars, 4 Clerks, 6 Choristers, and 26 Poor Knights,* and the Order of the Garter, consisting of the Sovereign and 25 Knights Companion. The remodelling (or rebuilding) of the chapel took place in 1350–4.‡ Another argument in favour of Edward's time is the polygonal apse, which fits the c14 better than the c15 – see e.g. Lichfield or the Greyfriars at New Winchelsea. The four-centred arches of the windows are in contrast to the arches of St George's Chapel, and their tracery is more akin to that of Edward's chapter house than to any of St George's. Henry VII may still have gone over it when he decided to make it a grand chantry chapel for Henry VI following on E of St George's Chapel. It is aisleless and has four-light windows with two transoms, and pretty pierced battlements. The doorway by which we entered this whole area is probably Henry VII. Four centred-arch, thin continuous mouldings. A second doorway leads into the chapel proper. Above the former a transparent repetition of the four-light windows of the chapel with the sky looking through. The chapel has a lierne-vault, with two long, straight ribs, parallel to the ridge-rib, but also simpler than in St George's. The chapel was unfinished when Henry VII died. Cardinal Wolsey, Canon of Windsor, with his knack for doing things grandly and showily, took the chapel over and finished it in 1514. He wanted it for his own monument, which he ordered in the new Renaissance style from *Benedetto da Rovezzano* in 1524 and which is now in the crypt of St Paul's. After his death Henry VIII held on to the chapel, as he held on to Hampton Court, and had the tomb converted for his own use, but he was ultimately buried in St George's Chapel, and so this chapel fell into disuse and decay. The sarcophagus was left lying about, and the candlesticks (*see* above) were sold. Charles II for a time thought of replacing it by a chapel to his

* Actually, however there were never more than three Poor Knights before the mid c16.

‡ The original REREDOS of Nottingham alabaster was so big that eight horses had to pull it.

martyred father, and *Wren* designed a domed rotunda in 1678. In 1810 George III had a vault made beneath it as the tomb house for his family. He intended to make the chapel the Garter Chapter House.

The first look into the chapel is one of amazement. This is not Henry VII, it is a Victorian shrine, and Queen Victoria did indeed convert it into an Albert Memorial. The original impression can no longer be obtained. The room is now dominated by *Gilbert*'s masterpiece, and it is impossible to overlook it. If one succeeds, then it will be seen that the chapel as remodelled in 1863–73 and redecorated by *Baron H. de Trinqueti* of Conflans was restrained as well as rich. Round the walls below the windows runs a band of large stories told in etched marble (i.e. really line drawings like the cartoons for paintings) and separated from one another by white marble reliefs. Below is a dado of coloured marbles. The etched marble executed by *Jules Destréez* is classical in style in a sense which is familiar from mid C19 France and Germany but not England. To the l. and r. of the entrance standing angels; in the tympanum Entombment. The vault is decorated by *Salviati* mosaic. – REREDOS. Marble, with Christ rising, and two angels; good. By *Sir G. G. Scott*; the sculpture by *Trinqueti*. – STAINED GLASS. By *Clayton & Bell*. – MONUMENTS. Duke of Clarence † 1892. By *Alfred Gilbert*. The Duke was the son of the Prince of Wales. Gilbert was summoned to Sandringham and commissioned. The Prince, future Edward VII, apparently approved of this exceedingly daring, radically novel monument. It was all but complete in 1898. Then, however, Gilbert's procrastination got worse, his troubles mounted, he was declared bankrupt in 1901, moved to Bruges, and did not return to London till 1926. It was only after that date that he made the five missing statuettes (St Hubert, St Nicholas, St Catherine of Siena, St Etheldreda, St Catherine of Egypt). The monument has the recumbent bronze effigy on a high marble sarcophagus. A large upright bronze angel holds a crown above the Duke's head. The fabulous thing is the grille around the monument. The ornament as well as the small figures are totally post-period-imitation – the nearest England ever got to Continental Art Nouveau. The iconographical daring is as great as the aesthetic originality. Iconographically a Tree of Jesse is meant. – To the E Cenotaph to Prince Albert. By *Trinqueti*. White recumbent effigy, two angels kneeling by his head. Figures on the tomb-chest as well. They are largish

33

angels at the corners, and allegories of Justice, Truth, Love, and Charity. – To the W Duke of Albany † 1884. Also white, but generally simpler. By *Sir J. E. Boehm*.

Past the apse of the chapel one sees on the l. again the DEANERY, with a courtyard open to the S and having on its W side the C14 chapter house (*see* above) and on the E side work of c.1500. The courtyard represents part of the line of the DITCH between Lower Ward and Middle Ward.

MIDDLE WARD

One enters between early C19 ranges and has at once the Round Tower in front.

ROUND TOWER. It stands on an artificial mound and was originally surrounded by its own ditch, of which something remains on the S side. The tower is of the type known as a shell keep, that is a high, circular or nearly circular wall (102 by 95 ft) with only lightly constructed buildings inside. This wall is in its lower parts of the time of Henry II, but the top 33 ft are by *Wyatville*, put on to counteract the effects of the heightening of the S and E ranges of the Upper Ward and of many towers. The main interest of the interior lies in the timber-framed building erected by Edward III in 1354–61 inside the shell. The principal floor has C19 two-light windows with two-centred arches and a transom. There are small straight-headed windows of two lights below, and these look original. To some of the upper windows corresponds the hall inside, with an open timber roof. On the level below are some sturdy timber posts. The staircase with vertically symmetrical dumb-bell type balusters and the details of the ring corridor at the upper landing seem to belong to the remodelling by *Hugh May* for Charles II.

The Round Tower can be reached in two ways. If, on approaching from the Lower Ward, one forks r., one finds oneself in a dramatic *Wyatville* passage between walls and then in front of a *Wyatville* range across from which a closed corridor ascends the mound.

If instead one forks l., one passes the small MAGAZINE TOWER of 1857 and a gateway to the NORTH TERRACE. This, which allows an inspection of the N side of the castle, dates from the 1570s and is one of the few contributions to the castle of Queen Elizabeth I. The Norman Gateway is the entry to the Upper Ward.

UPPER WARD

The NORMAN GATEWAY is not Norman. It dates from 1359,
except for the l. one of the big round towers, which is by
Wyatville. The centre part is of brown stone and has machicolations. The entry arch has the characteristic sunk-quadrant
mouldings and a groove for the portcullis. Two-bay vault inside with diagonal and ridge-ribs.

On emerging from the gateway, the irregular buildings to
the s finish in the corridor and staircase up the mound to the
Round Tower. Parts of the group are mid c14, one part is late
c15, the rest being Wyatville's.

The range on the N side is more telling. It is the one now
used by the ROYAL LIBRARY. It consists of two parts. The
higher, r. part is the earlier. This dates from 1497. It is of three
widely spaced bays and three storeys. The side bays each have
one oriel window high up. The centre is a much larger oriel
window of complex plan: oblong with canted corners, and in
the middle a further canted projection. This liking for projections of unusual plan is expressed also on the outer side of the
range, where the w end is an oriel of a triangular plan with a
point in the middle and convex lobes l. and r. A fashion for
such oriels ensued and is principally represented by Henry
VII's Chapel in Westminster Abbey. The range w of this is
dated 1583. It is lower, and has to the s three canted oriel
windows, to the N a nearly symmetrical front also with oriels,
the middle one attached to a big square projection.

As one moves on E, one has in front the w end of the N
range of the Upper Ward, the range with the State Apartments.
Turning s, out of the irregular and comparatively small court
in which one has been standing, one reaches the Quadrangle.
This is a very large oblong courtyard, about 375 by 230 ft.
Although the buildings around are of divers dates, the early
c19 has impressed its stamp upon them indelibly. There is
little to distinguish between what *James Wyatt* did for George
III from 1796 and what his nephew *Sir Jeffry Wyatville* did
from 1820 to 1830 for George IV, except that Wyatt used
Portland stone for his windows, Wyatville for all his dressings
a brown stone. Wyatt was made Surveyor General after
Chambers's death in 1796 and finished work at Windsor when
George III moved in in 1804. The king was insane from 1810
to his death in 1820. Wyatville began in 1820. It is said that
Wyatville's work alone cost over one million pounds.

What characterizes all the work of the first third of the c19 is a curious and unmistakable unison of contrived variety with yet maintained uniformity. A lively skyline of battlements and towers, an interruption every so often of the walls by entrance features of several shapes and – especially on the E front – by bay windows and oriel windows is not enough. The long straight walls towards the quadrangle between the various features remain, and their even fenestration provides an un-medieval, really Georgian, rhythm, as does the stone walling, made to appear more even than it is.

In detail the ranges round the quadrangle consist of the following. The NORTH RANGE is much wider than the other two. It had ever since Henry II represented the principal living quarters of the castle. The width allowed for inner courts, of which one is now filled in by *Salvin*'s Grand Stair-case, a second and larger one by the Waterloo Chamber. A third still exists S of the Kitchen. The walls of the Waterloo Chamber, the walling S of it towards the quadrangle, and much walling N of it is in fact still Norman, but there are no features left to show it. The medieval Great Hall was along the S front of this range.

The SW part of the N range, looking S, W of the Porte Cochère, and looking W is of the time of Edward IV, even if the windows are *Wyatt*'s. The NW range of rooms facing the North Terrace, and there four storeys high, is what remains of Charles II's remodelling of 1678 etc. Evidence of these latter dates will be found inside. The Porte Cochère is of course *Wyatville*'s (date 1827), as are the Visitors' (or Equerries') Entrance in the NE corner and the Sovereign's Entrance in the SE corner. Wyatville also added, for convenience's sake, the long corridor along the inner sides of the E and S ranges. He heightened these two ranges to provide more acceptable servants' quarters, but kept the heightening recessed behind the line of the corridors so as to preserve the dominance of the N range. Most of the main windows of the N range are of a standard two-light type, but above the Porte Cochère are four-light windows to S, W, and E, and towards the N terrace, above the entrance into the range, is a large five-light window. On this side the polygonal Brunswick Tower at the NE corner is entirely *Wyatville*'s. It is connected with the bay with the five-light window by another corridor of Wyatville's. The SE corner tower, called Queen's Tower, is a *Hugh May* addition or alteration, as a string course shows. In front of the whole E front is the SUNK GARDEN, made by *Wyatville*, with along its

N side the former ORANGERY, also *Wyatville*'s, and remorse-
lessly Perp in its glazed openings. In the sunk garden a
splendid stone VASE with the Judgement of Paris by *E. Pearce*,
c.1680–90. The principal accent of the S front of the S range is
George IV's Gateway (foundation stone 1824), a state exit
towards the Long Walk, which looks of spectacular length
from here. The gateway is *Wyatville*'s, though its E tower is in
fact of Edward III's time. The W end of the range, a strong
round tower, called Edward III's Tower, however, is entirely
C13 work. Broadly speaking, what the S and E ranges represent
is Norman outer walls against which originally there were no
buildings or wooden buildings and then a thin range of building of the time of Edward III. It is in front of this that
Wyatville made his additions.*

The quadrangle is permanently surveyed by the equestrian
MONUMENT of Charles II at its W end. This is of 1679,
bronze, and stands on a high stone base. On the base reliefs by
Grinling Gibbons, garlands, coats of arms, etc. The statue was
carved in wood by a German and then cast by *Josias Ibach*, also
a German. In the inscription he adds to his name 'Stada
Bramensis 1679 FVDIT'. This probably means Stade, not too
far away from Bremen.‡

THE STATE APARTMENTS

The State Apartments are entered from the North Terrace by a
Wyatville doorway leading to a long Wyatville cross-VESTI-
BULE, divided by slim imitation Perp piers into a nave and
aisles, and vaulted. The vestibule ends to the S in the grand
porte cochère. Turning E from here (not open to the public)
one is in a long two-naved C14 undercroft with octagonal piers
and single-chamfered ribs. The continuation of this is a room
with single-chamfered wall shafts and single-chamfered ribs,
also probably C14. To its N is a vaulted corridor with hollow-
chamfered ribs. A little way to the N of this is the monumental
KITCHEN, dated 1828 and about 70 by 30 ft in size. Its walls
are *temp.* Charles II and it runs through two storeys. The open
timber roof and lantern lighting of course are *Wyatville*'s. The

---

* Are the two tall windows in the Clarence Tower facing W two more
surviving of *May*'s work? Their proportions are like those in Henry III's
Tower in the Lower Ward (*see* p. 281).

‡ At Stade, as the Municipal Archivist, Dr Wirtgen, kindly informs me,
there was indeed an organ maker Nicolaus Ibecchius of Marburg, *floruit*
c.1640–50.

public turns W from the S end of the vestibule, along another two-naved C14 undercroft, identical with the former, and then N into *Salvin*'s GRAND STAIRCASE, made in 1866. It fills the former open Brick Court and is in the Early Dec style, has a large lantern, and is somewhat arid. The vault of the GRAND VESTIBULE adjoining it to the E on the upper floor is by *Wyatt* and much more lively. Fans and a lantern. This was the staircase hall before Salvin's. Against its N wall under a wooden canopy is a seated figure of Queen Victoria by *Boehm*; 1871. The walls of the room are actually C14 work, i.e. Edward III had at least three if not four ranges round Brick Court.

It is advisable to turn from the staircase first N; for here is the first of the three surviving rooms of the rebuilding in 1677–8 by Charles II. It is the KINGS' DINING ROOM (former State Ante-Room). The ceiling is by *Verrio* and represents a Banquet of the Gods. Like all Verrio's work it lacks sparkle, let alone brio. The wood-carving is by *Gibbons* and *Henry Phillips* and, needless to say, done superbly. Phillips since 1661 had been the King's Master Carver in wood, whereas Gibbons became Master Sculptor to the King in 1684. The room is square with a W and an E alcove. These have skylights, probably of Salvin's time; for before he built the staircase, there was of course enough light from Brick Court. The room has a later C18 chimneypiece of white marble with coupled Tuscan columns.

To the E and facing N follows the KING'S DRAWING ROOM (former Rubens Room). Here and in the following rooms all that remains of Charles II's time is the top cornice. The ceiling is *Wyatville*'s. Now W, along the N side. One more room here has a later C18 chimneypiece. The *Wyatville* ceilings are very instructively post-Georgian, even if some are of George IV's reign (as George IV's Brighton Pavilion is post-Georgian). But those of the King's Dressing Room, the King's Closet, and the Queen's Drawing Room (former Picture Gallery) are in fact William IV's, with dates 1833 and 1834. The ceilings are still in geometrical panels on the Georgian system, but garlands tend to be thicker and looser, branches lusher, leaves more naturalistic.

In an irregularly octagonal CABINET, E of the Queen's Drawing Room and joining it to the King's Dining Room, are *Gibbons* coats of arms and oval panels with heads in relief. They are re-set. From the Queen's Drawing Room W one could enter the ROYAL LIBRARY (not open to the public). The

first and largest room has the date 1834 in the plasterwork. w
of this is QUEEN ELIZABETH'S GALLERY of 1583 with a rich
broad banded plaster ceiling, said to be a copy of the original
one. If that is so, it would be a very early case of broad bands
39b instead of thin ribs. Original, however, the splendid chimneypiece of stone, wth tapering pillars with strapwork l. and r. of
the opening and columns, pilasters, and niches in the overmantel.

The QUEEN'S BALLROOM (former Van Dyck Room) is s of
the Queen's Drawing Room and faces w. Though the room
was remodelled by *Wyatt*, the ceiling is of the *Wyatville*
period. The chandeliers are English and were ordered in 1804.
Back now to the s side to see the other surviving rooms of the
Charles II period: the QUEEN'S AUDIENCE CHAMBER and
the QUEEN'S PRESENCE CHAMBER. The ceiling by *Verrio* of
the first represents Queen Catherine of Braganza in a chariot
drawn by swans to the Temple of Virtue, that of the second,
much darker one, represents the queen under a canopy spread
by Time and surrounded by Virtues. The carvings are again
46 by *Gibbons* and *Phillips*. Both rooms have good late C18
chimneypieces. That in the Presence Chamber was brought
from Buckingham Palace by William IV and is by *Bacon*,
dated 1789. It has extremely elegant long corbels l. and r. of the
opening, and on the mantelshelf a clock with two semi-
reclining figures.

E of the Presence Chamber and s of the Grand Vestibule is
the GUARD ROOM, including the deep square projection above
the porte cochère, and E of the Guard Room ST GEORGE'S
HALL. The s wall of this – minus of course the features and
especially the windows – is *temp.* Edward III, the N wall
partly that and partly Norman. The Norman part was outer
wall towards the courtyard, where now the Waterloo Chamber
is. St George's Hall is 185 ft long. Before Wyatville it was two
12 rooms. The w half was *Hugh May*'s glorious CHAPEL of
1684–6, the most Baroque interior of England, it has been
said. It was swept away by Wyatville in 1829. The low-
pitched timber roof is in fact of plaster. At the E end is a
canopy for the throne, a gallery, and wood panelling. No-one
would call it very festive. One realizes this particularly force-
56 fully as one proceeds into the GRAND RECEPTION ROOM, N
of St George's Hall; for here *Wyatville* for once went Rococo,
and though the detailing is all somewhat riotous, the effect is
certainly gay. w of this room is the GARTER THRONE ROOM,

facing N and with Norman N and S walls. The details, and particularly the ceiling, are Wyatville's, but the plentiful carved panels and foliage hangings are *Gibbons*'s and come from Hugh May's chapel. W of the Throne Room and past the Ante-Throne Room one would again be in the King's Drawing Room.

Finally, between the Throne Room and St George's Hall, lit only from above, as it was built by *Wyatville* in the place of an open court, the WATERLOO CHAMBER. Its date is 1830, but it was re-decorated by *Blore* in 1861. It was built to hang *Sir Thomas Lawrence*'s portraits of some of those who helped to defeat Napoleon. The room is vast, but it tends to be gloomy and would be more so if it were not for the splendid chandeliers. The lantern lighting is interesting, with its curiously nautical raking profile. Again *Gibbons* panels and foliage hangings are re-used.

THE EAST AND SOUTH RANGES

These are not open to the public.

In the E range the most interesting room is the DOMESTIC CHAPEL, E of St George's Hall and N of the Visitors' (or Equerries') Entrance. It is by *Blore* and was made in 1842. The sanctuary was enlarged and the octagonal lantern made in 1852. The result is a curious indeterminate shape, with the sanctuary to the N. Gothic wood panelling. – SCULPTURE. A very fine terracotta group of the 1870s by *Dalou*: an angel and children, the latter being Queen Victoria's grand-children. – Along the E front of the E range runs a number of State Rooms, the most impressive being the GREEN DRAWING ROOM (carpet by *Grüner*) and the CRIMSON DRAWING ROOM with its excellently crisp decoration, especially of the doors, which came from the Regent's Carlton House. Both ss these drawing rooms are *Wyatville*'s. The Gothic furniture in the STATE DINING ROOM may be part of that designed by *Pugin* in 1827 for *Morel* the decorators, when Pugin was only fifteen years old. Other furniture in this series of rooms was also originally at Carlton House. W of the rooms runs Wyatville's corridor, to end at the SE corner of the quadrangle by the SOVEREIGN'S ENTRANCE and the odd-shaped staircase behind it. This leads to the most private flat of the royal family, which is in the SE corner of the castle. Some rooms here and in the adjoining guest suites and guest rooms of the S range on to Edward III's Tower have been refurnished very recently by *Sir Hugh Casson*. Also in the s range is the QUEEN'S AUDIENCE CHAMBER. This dates from 1860–1.*

THE MEWS

The Royal Mews or stables are visually part of the town rather than the castle. They extend along and E of St Alban's Street and were built in a gothicizing but on the whole sensibly utilitarian way by *Blore* in 1839–42. The RIDING SCHOOL has two-light windows with Y-tracery. The largest entrance is by a gateway at the s end opposite the post office. To the same group belongs BURFORD HOUSE, originally built by the Duke of St Albans for Nell Gwynn, but so thoroughly blored that not a single feature of the house as illustrated by Kip can be recognized.

THE PARK

Windsor Forest in the Middle Ages was a vast expanse of woods and heath extending from Reading to Chertsey and from Guildford into Buckinghamshire. Such wood and heath land could be called a park; for a park in the Middle Ages was simply enclosed or reserved hunting country. Park became what we mean by it only in the course of the c17 and even more the c18. At Windsor the distinction of the park into Home Park and Great Park is an arbitrary one. The difference is really only that the Home Park is closed to the public,‡ whereas large parts of the Great Park are accessible, even if few of the buildings.

Home Park

From the castle the predominant feature is, and even more was before the tree disaster, the LONG WALK. This is three miles long and was made in 1685 and planted with elm trees. Unfortunately they had to be felled in 1945. The trees now are planes and chestnuts, and a final decision on what thinning out will be best is to be made later. Its *point-de-vue* is the equestrian statue of George III which belongs to Great Park.

In the Home Park the buildings are as follows.

* The PLATE of Windsor Castle – as against St George's Chapel – cannot here even be summarized. Readers must be referred to E. Alfred Jones: *The Gold and Silver of Windsor Castle*, 1911, a sumptuous folio with 103 plates and a complete, amply annotated list.

‡ Except for the meadows N of the Datchet road.

FROGMORE HOUSE. Out of an early C18 house which had seven
bays and two or already two and a half storeys *Wyatt* in 1792
made the present house for Queen Charlotte. The lower wings
are also initially Wyatt's, and so is the veranda or arcade
towards the garden. This has seven bays, now glazed, and
Tuscan columns. The wings were enlarged early in the C19 by
big bow-fronted pavilions and the porte cochère on the entrance side, of two pairs of columns, was possibly also made
then. Inside, there is a handsome staircase starting in one arm
and returning in two. It has a wrought-iron balustrade. Also
there is a pretty room decorated by *Mary Moser* with flower 53
garlands on walls and ceiling. On the first floor a gallery runs
from front to back. This is decorated in a rather crude
Pompeian manner, perhaps by *Princess Elizabeth*, one of
George III's daughters. Close to the house are the STABLES,
with two towers with cupolas, framing the archway.

The beautiful grounds of Frogmore House were probably
devised by *Sir Uvedale Price*, the great amateur–expert of the
Picturesque. His father was Vice Chamberlain to the Queen.
There is a lake, and there is a GOTHIC TEMPLE by *Wyatt*,
really a small pavilion with attachments designed in a ruinous
state. The windows are Perp. The interior is Early Victorian,
with niches and a panelled ceiling. Also in the grounds the
TEA HOUSE, High Victorian probably, two cottages set at r.
angles with central Tudor brick chimneys and surrounded by
wooden verandas.

NW of Frogmore House is FROGMORE COTTAGE, plain, two-
storeyed, early C19, and behind this an INDIAN KIOSK taken
by Earl Canning in 1858 from the Kaiserbajh at Lucknow.

W of Frogmore House are the two mausolea which have changed
the character of that part of the park so decisively.

MAUSOLEUM OF THE DUCHESS OF KENT. 1861 by *A. Jenkins
Humbert*, the architect of Sandringham. Begun during the lifetime of the Duchess. Domed rotunda with rusticated substructure and above detached columns of pink granite with
bronze bases and capitals. Copper-covered dome. The detail is
French rather than English. The interior is by *Grüner* (see
below). Walls with heraldic painting on scarlet ground and
blue glass above with stars. The STATUE of the Duchess is by
the younger *William Theed*.

ROYAL MAUSOLEUM, i.e. mausoleum of Prince Albert and
Queen Victoria. 1862–71 by *A. J. Humbert* and Professor
Grüner of Dresden, Prince Albert's favourite specialist in

decoration. Grüner also did the initial sketch for the whole
building. The building cost £200,000. It is externally in the
Romanesque style, i.e. with *Rundbogen*, and in plan a Greek
cross with low convex ambulatories in the re-entrant angles,
which results inside in an octagon with four arms.* The whole
is crowned by a dome. The centrality is mitigated by an E
portico of three arches. In front of this two life-size bronze
STATUES of Angels, one with a sword, the other with a
trumpet. They are by *Georg Howaldt* of Brunswick. The outer
GATES and the inner DOOR, the former bronze, the latter brass,
were designed by *Grüner* and are of outstanding workmanship
(*Potter & Sons*).

The style of the interior is a rich Italian High Renaissance,
deliberately Raphaelesque, and for this style, less at home in
England than in Germany, the mausoleum is a key monument.
In Germany the style was handled most skilfully by
Semper in Dresden, and the interior of the mausoleum was
indeed designed by *Grüner*, who lived in Dresden, had
published a book on Italian fresco decoration in 1844,
and had started a Raphael corpus with Prince Albert in 1853.‡
Tunnel-vaulted arms, giant pilasters for the main piers, niches
with large statues between them, painted Evangelists in the
spandrels above. The STATUES are by *Heinrich Bäumer*
(David), *Hermann Hultzsch* (Isaiah), *Gustav Kuntz* (Daniel),
Friedrich Rentsch (Solomon), all of Dresden. Rentsch's is the
most classical. The others turned out more Baroque. The
Evangelists were painted by *Nicola Consoni*. In the dome below
the tripartite windows oval medallions painted by *Pfänder*
from Consoni's designs. The gilded ribs rest on papier-maché
angels by *Hultzsch*. The STAINED GLASS in the mausoleum is
by *Ion Pace*, and a replacement of c.1909. The large PAINT-
INGS in the four chapels or cross arms are again by *Consoni*,
after Raphael compositions. On the vaults of the chapels more
painting: by *Julius Frank* and *Pfänder*, again Raphaelesque.
The pretty relief medallions in the spandrels of the arches are
the work of *Pietro Galli*, who also did the excellent RELIEF of
the Deposition on the altar frontal. In the centre is the
MONUMENT to the Queen and the Prince Consort, 1864–8,
two white marble effigies by *Baron Marochetti*, high up on a

* Mr Winslow Ames tells me of the Coburg Mausoleum at Coburg, an
octagon with wings built in 1846 and seen by Queen Victoria in 1860.

‡ Passavanti's *Raphael* had come out in 1839, confirming and spreading
the cult of Raphael in Germany.

big tomb-chest, with four large kneeling bronze angels at the
corners of the tomb-chest. In the l. and r. transepts MONU-
MENTS to Princess Alice Grand Duchess of Hesse and her
child by *Boehm*, 1878–9, and to the Duke of Kent, Queen
Victoria's father, also by *Boehm*, 1874. White marble effigies.
The group of Princess Alice and the child, both asleep, is on
the pattern of Chantrey's popular Sleeping Children. – Also a
white STATUE of the Emperor Frederick III † 1888, by
Boehm, and a white group of Victoria and Albert in Anglo-
Saxon costume by the younger *Theed*, 1867. She looks
admiringly up to him.

CROSS to Lady Augusta Stanley † 1876 of blue granite in the
style of the Anglian crosses. The cross is directly in front of the
Duchess of Kent's mausoleum.

To the SSW of Frogmore House is SHAW FARM, Italianate in the
Osborne way and utilitarian. The two LODGES s of it are by
Wyatville. Of much greater interest and appeal is Prince
Albert's DAIRY of 1858. Nobody will be enthusiastic about its
exterior, but the colourful fayence (*Minton's*) interior has so
much charm, with its panels of putti and its medallions of
children of the royal couple. The interior design and probably
some of the execution is by *John Thomas*, Albert's favourite
sculptor. By him personally very probably the fountains with
herons carrying a shell on which is a human figure carrying a
smaller shell. The dairy belongs to Prince Albert's HOME
FARM, which has an eminently typical but unattractive tower.
The buildings, according to the *Ill. L. News*, were designed by
Mr G. A. Dean, 'the well known agricultural architect and
land agent'. Opposite the Home Farm is the AVIARY, with
bargeboarded gables.

ADELAIDE LODGE, ⅓ m. NE, is the only surviving part of the
original ROYAL LODGE, built for the Regent by *Nash*. It is
picturesquely bargeboarded and was re-erected here in 1831.
For Royal Lodge otherwise, *see* below.

PARK STREET GATES and other HOME PARK LODGES. Tudor,
by *Wyatville*, yellow brick and stone.

Great Park

Windsor Great Park is still 4,800 acres in size, as against Richmond Park, the largest London Park, which has only just over
2,000. Hyde Park even at the time of Henry VIII had less
than 700.

The Long Walk ends at the EQUESTRIAN STATUE of George III

known as the Copper Horse. This is by *Westmacott*. The statue was made in 1824–30 and with its granite base stands over 25 ft high. Westmacott received £18,712 for the statue. The figure in studied disarray. An equally straight walk, nearly as long and, to the N, with a steady view of the Round Tower, leads from QUEEN ANNE'S GATE (the lodge is of stone and has bargeboards)* at the s end of King's Road to Ascot. This is called QUEEN ANNE'S RIDE and goes through between THE VILLAGE and Prince Albert's WORKSHOPS. The workshops are sound utilitarian brick structures, by *Teulon*, 1858–61. The village is by *S. Tatchell*, of the 1930s, in the garden-suburb style. From here the public road, the King's Road, can be reached in three ways, two ending in LODGES which were built in 1952 and 1960 (*R. Tatchell*). By the Ranger's Gate is RANGER'S LODGE, a simple white Regency house. The third way out is further s, by SANDPIT GATE, Gothic, stuccoed, embattled, with a turret, and all rather square, and then past FOREST LODGE, a larger Georgian brick house of nine bays, the side thirds two-storeyed, the centre a half-storey higher. On the ground floor in the centre and the centres of the wings Venetian windows. The higher middle part of the house has giant pilasters. FOREST GATE is the place where the public road is finally reached. This is of the same type as Sandpit Gate. Beyond the public road to the NW two more buildings belonging to the Great Park, the FLEMISH FARM, an insignificant building of Prince Albert's years, and CRANBOURNE TOWER, all that is left of Charles II's Cranbourne Lodge, a high, polygonal Late Georgian brick tower with a yet higher stair-turret and pointed windows. On the ground floor a handsome room with a polygonal liernevault of plaster and the date 1808.

But the centre of Great Park is the other side of the Copper Horse, not w, like Queen Anne's Ride, but E. It is here that the precinct of ROYAL LODGE lies. This is entered by two neo-Georgian LODGES by *Tatchell*, grand and chaste. They form a group with three cottages each side of the entrance. The Royal Lodge itself is a large, pink-washed, rather institutional building with a three-storeyed centre and two-storeyed wings and some minimum Early-Victorian-looking Tudor detail trying

---

* N of the gate, i.e. strictly outside the park, are Estate COTTAGES of 1853, red and blue brick with gables, and most probably by *Teulon* (*see* in the text a little further on). Yet further N a group of between-the-wars COTTAGES, nicely composed, with a squat tower.

to be in harmony with the one surviving feature of the 1820s, *Wyatville*'s Dining Room (now drawing room), originally added to Nash's cottage orné (*see* above: Adelaide Lodge). This has five windows with ogee tops and Perp tracery. The garden was remodelled by *G. A. Jellicoe* in 1932–5. In the garden a COTTAGE, about half real size, built and furnished entirely for Queen Elizabeth I I as a child. Door, one little bay l., one r., thatched roof.

Also in the gounds of Royal Lodge the CHAPEL by *Teulon*, 1863–6. It has a nave and a chancel, a lower s transept, and a s aisle whose windows have odd cross-gables. High open kingpost roof inside, round piers with typically High Victorian leaf capitals, complicated timbering of the aisle roof. – STAINED GLASS. In the E window 1863. – W and one N window by *Kempe*, 1902 and 1905. – EMBROIDERY. Florentine Frontal assigned to the C15. Presented by Queen Mary, George V's queen.

s of Royal Lodge is CUMBERLAND LODGE (University of London), built at the time of Charles I I and inhabited in the mid C18 by the Duke of Cumberland of Culloden fame and Ranger of Windsor Park. Of the original building very little, if anything, remains. The house was damaged by fire in 1811, restored by *Wyatville*, much enlarged in 1870 by *Salvin*, and again remodelled in the C20. On the far side are Gothick details. Long STABLES with cupola. In axis with the turreted Gothick side of the house, some ¾ m. away, is the OBELISK commemorating Culloden. Close to this axis, a little off to the E, ALMSHOUSES of *c.*1950.

A little w of Cumberland Lodge the ROYAL SCHOOL, a one-storeyed village school, symmetrical, of brick, with pretty, fancy glazing bars. It was established in 1845.

Further away, s of Cumberland Lodge and rather pathetically on its own, the stiff EQUESTRIAN STATUE of Prince Albert, given by the women of England. It is by *Boehm*, 1887–90.

This leaves two important parts of Great Park which lie by the A30 and s of it: Virginia Water and Fort Belvedere.★

VIRGINIA WATER is a large, eminently picturesque, many-fingered lake made for the Duke of Cumberland about 1750 and enlarged later in the C18. It is about 120 acres in size. It was planned by *Thomas Sandby*, who also arranged for the CASCADE close to the Wheatsheaf Hotel. A little further w are

★ They are actually in Surrey.

52b the RUINS, i.e. columns from Lepcis Magna presented to the Prince Regent in 1816, intended for the portico of the British Museum, but finally re-erected at Virginia Water in 1826. The red brick bridge of the Ascot road cuts most unhappily through the remains. The pine trees on the other hand do them good.

Near the NE tip of Virginia Water a TOTEM POLE from British Columbia was re-erected in 1958 to mark the centenary of that province. It is 100 ft high.

FORT BELVEDERE started life as a triangular tower called Shrub Hill Tower some time before 1757. The angles had polygonal turrets. It was built for the Duke of Cumberland. The architect was *Isaac Ware*. The triangular shape which was later imitated by other such towers was chosen here, it is said, to give views of Windsor Castle, St Paul's, and the Hogsback, which at that time was still the s boundary of Windsor Park. In 1827–9 *Wyatville* extended this tower into a castellated, picturesquely irregular residence. The prominent main tower is a heightening of Wyatville's too. In the two original turrets which are not taken up by the staircase are still plaster ceilings of c.1750. The hexagonal centre room has recently received a new domed ceiling.

(CLOCK CASE, E of the road to Egham. A square tower of brick on an eminence. It is said to have been built by the Duke of Cumberland for an observatory, and there is a letter of 1812 of which Mr R. Mackworth Young kindly sent me a copy, stating that it is part 'of the Old Gate Way of Whitehall which stood at the entrance of the narrow part of Parliament Street', i.e. the King Street Gate, *temp.* Henry VIII.)

THE TOWN

CHURCHES

ST JOHN BAPTIST, High Street. 1820–2 by *Charles Hollis*, under the supervision of *Wyatville*. The chancel was rebuilt and enlarged by a polygonal apse in 1869–73 in the Dec style by *Teulon*. The church is of brown stone and in its proportions and details typical of 1820. W tower with oversized pinnacles. Two vestibules l. and r., as if aisles were embracing the tower. They are straight-topped and embattled. Windows of many shapes and types, rather arbitrary, even if one forgets those altered by Teulon. The interior has preserved its three galleries and its slender iron piers. Iron also the roof, with its traceried spandrels. – CHANCEL DECORATION. *Salviati* mosaic. – SCREEN. High wooden screen, designed by *Sir Arthur Blomfield*, 1898. – RAILINGS to the S chapel. By *Grinling Gibbons* himself, made for the chapel at Windsor Castle. Balusters and three openwork panels. Two of them have pelicans, the third foliage. The balusters are vertically symmetrical and have leaves round the bulbs. They probably were part of the communion rail. Gibbons was paid for work in the King's Chapel in 1680–2. – PAINTING. Last Supper by *Francis de Cleyn*, a German from the Baltic who came to England in 1623 and died in 1658 (W gallery). – STAINED GLASS. Early C20. No artists seem to be recorded. – PLATE. Silver-gilt Chalice, 1573; Chalice, 1629; two silver-gilt Flagons, 1635; silver-gilt Paten, 1637; silver-gilt Alms-dish, 1732; two Chalices, 1777. – MONUMENTS. Edward Jobson † 1605. Small tablet with kneeling figures (S aisle). – Richard Braham † 1618. By *Edward Marshall*. Angels and allegorical figures in the Mannerist style (N vestibule). – Rebecca Southcot † 1642. Demi-figure, not quite frontal, in a scrolly surround (N vestibule). – Mrs Nazareth Pagett † 1666. By *Marshall*. Black columns, black inscription. At the top two busts, at the foot engraved skull with wings (main vestibule). – Hartgill Baron † 1673. Garlands of books l. and r. 'Predella' with a heart and two owls. He was secretary to Prince Rupert. – John Hounslef † 1722. Coarse cartouche still in the C17 tradition (N vestibule). – Dr Hale † 1728. Reredos tablet. No figures (S vestibule). – Sir Thomas Reeve † 1735. By *Peter Scheemakers*. Standing monument. Two busts before an obelisk. Two putti l. and r. (N vestibule). – Topham Foot † 1712. Reredos and a weak bust. By *P. Scheemakers*, i.e. between *c*.1730 and *c*.1780. – Thomas Scourfield † 1765. With a totally asymmetrical Rococo cartouche at the foot (W wall). – Elizabeth Grope. By *T. Sharp*, 1832. Mourning woman over a sarcophagus (S aisle).

ST AGNES, Spital, Winkfield Road. 1874. Brick, lancets, a curious plan, with a short nave and a prominent S transept with E aisle. – FONT. Norman, drum-shaped. Intersecting arches and stylized long leaves hanging down under them.

ALL SAINTS, Dedworth Road, *see* Dedworth, p. 126.

ALL SAINTS, Frances Road. 1862–4 by *Sir Arthur Blomfield*, and a typically early work of his: inspired by Butterfield but just that much smoother. Red brick and blue-brick bands. No tower. Pointed-trefoiled lancets and plate tracery. Big plate-tracery W window. Big Geometrical E window. Spacious interior without tension. Round piers with fancy shaft-rings. Red, yellow, and blue brick walls. Large clerestory.

ST ANDREW, Barry Avenue, the parish church of Clewer. The village, as described on p. 304, has been nearly submerged by Windsor, but the church and the graveyard have preserved their village character. Flint, with a very short W tower with shingled broach spire. The ground floor has Norman windows, and inside there is indeed prominent Norman work: the arch from the S aisle E, unmoulded, and perhaps the original chancel arch and the S arcade of round piers with square abaci and flat leaf capitals including waterleaf. That dates this work. The tower arch has similar capitals, but the pointed arch may not be in its original state. The N arcade is by *Woodyer* (*see* p. 305); 1858. Most of the exterior is also his, though the church is in fact medieval almost entirely. – FONT. Norman, tub-shaped. Arches with elementary leaves in the spandrels. Flat zigzag frieze at the top. – REREDOS. Sculpture of Christ in Majesty and Saints. Designed also by *Woodyer*. – Tall wooden SCREEN. Victorian. – BENCH ENDS. Two with poppy-heads, very bare (nave W). – STAINED GLASS. By *Kempe*, S aisle, 1902. – PLATE. Silver-gilt Flagon, 1626. – MONUMENTS. In the churchyard Quarter-Master Edward Adams, 1819. With a military still life, including an evidently live horse. – Earl Harcourt † 1830. By *Sievier*. Excellent Grecian tablet. Snakes l. and r. The foliage elements are just getting richer and more florid. – Canon T. T. Carter † 1901. Miniature bronze relief with recumbent effigy and the piers of the canopy quite detached in front of it. By *W. Bainbridge Reynolds*.

ST EDWARD (R. C.), Alma Road. 1867–8 by *C. A. Buckler*. The estimate was for £4,000 (GS). Of ragstone. Large, but without a tower. Late Geometrical tracery. High clerestoried interior.

ST STEPHEN, Vansittart Road. 1874 by *Woodyer*. Very plain. Yellow brick, no tower. Low aisle windows. They and the clerestory windows have the motif of detached shafts or piers inside in front of the windows. – REREDOS. Large and impressive, with Christ upright below a crocketed gable and between coupled shafts with rings.

HOLY TRINITY. 1842–4 by *Blore*. In the middle of a square, in the isolation the C19 liked. A big, clumsy yellow-brick job. W tower with spire, embraced. Wide interior with galleries set between the quatrefoil arcade piers. They carry four-centred arches. Small clerestory. Transepts.

CONGREGATIONAL CHURCH, William Street. 1832 by *Jesse Hollis* (BC). A fine, proud chapel, still undisturbed classical. Yellow brick, three bays with a three-bay pediment. Tuscan porch. Arched upper windows.

BAPTIST CHAPEL, Victoria Street. 1839. Equally proud and equally classical, but quite different. Stuccoed. Giant Ionic pilasters, tall arched windows, frieze with symmetrical palm fronds. Pediment.

PUBLIC BUILDINGS

TOWN HALL (or Guildhall), High Street. Designed *c.*1687 by 45a *Sir Thomas Fitch.* The execution after his death in 1689 supervised by *Wren.* Completed in 1690. Cost £2,000. Brick and stone dressings. Three by six bays. The ground floor open as usual. Tuscan columns carrying a straight entablature on the long W side, semi-elliptical arches on the N and S show sides. On these sides the upper floor has pilasters, four of them, but the angle ones not at the angles, where quoins seem to have arrived first. Wren would not have done that. In the centre of the N side in a niche Queen Anne and the date 1707, in the centre of the S side Prince George of Denmark and the date 1713. This statue was given by Christopher, Sir Christopher's son. Inside the open ground floor also Tuscan columns. They don't touch the ceiling, an anomaly explained by legend as the sign of Wren's secret insistence on knowing more about the security of structure than the council who insisted on the columns. The upper floor all altered.* The E part of the town hall was added *c.*1830 on the site of the Shambles.

GENERAL POST OFFICE, *see* p. 303.

EAST BERKSHIRE COLLEGE OF FURTHER EDUCATION, Claremont Road. By *Bridgwater, Shepheard & Epstein*, 1954–*c.*66. A satisfactory design, modern, and placed well in its surroundings.

ST GEORGE'S SCHOOL, Datchet Road. 1803.‡ Yellow brick, long front, with two three-bay pedimented pavilions and an eleven-bay centre with a colonnade and a top lantern. The angle pavilions have arched windows set in blank arches.

EDWARD VII HOSPITAL, St Leonard's Road. 1909 by *A. W. West.* Two-storeyed centre with a mansard-tile roof. Three-bay pediment and cupola. The curious arched window above the pediment is a sign-manual of the Edwardian decade.

* REGALIA. Small Cup, 1627; silver-gilt Mace and Cup, 1660; Mayor's Chain and Badge given in 1820 and enlarged in 1830.
‡ This is the choir school of St George's Chapel.

Combermere Barracks. The Guard Room, Museum, H Q
Offices, Naafi Shop, and Junior Ranks and Sergeants' Messes
are by the War Office Architects' Department (*Sir Donald
Gibson*, architect in charge *D. Wager*), 1960–4.

Southern Region Station. By *Sir William Tite*, 1850. Red
brick, Tudor, with blue brick diapers and patterns, including
1851, V R, P A. At the far end of the platform access to the
Royal Waiting Room, a bijou of a few rooms with a turret and
spirelet. Windows Tudor with arched lights. The main room
has a bay window, canted and ending in a point, i.e. imitated
from Henry VII's Chapel at Westminster Abbey, and inside a
ribbed ceiling with a pendant.

PERAMBULATION

The town of Windsor certainly started and grew on the doorstep
of the castle. The area of town hall and parish church is
minute, about a quarter of the area of the castle. As one leaves
Henry VIII's Gateway one is in Castle Hill. The big
Georgian stone house opposite with the later Gothic porch is
no preparation for that small area, nor is the Early Victorian
shop of Nos 10–11. But then Church Street and Market
Street branch off it, and they give the true picture of size and
scale. In Church Street a delightful mixture of things, ending
in the Early Victorian front of the Ship Hotel across, in
Church Lane. Nos 4, 5, 6 are late C17. No. 6 has a square
timber-framed bay resting on big carved brackets. No. 7 is
timber-framed. The house at the corner of Church Lane
has a roughcast early C18 front and round the corner a timber
overhang. This has one thin buttress-shaft with bracket, a
sign of pre-Renaissance origin. Opposite the Masonic Hall,
formerly Free School, built in 1725–6. It is of brick, in the
Late-Wren–Hawksmoor style, see especially the short side
elevation to St Alban's Street. There is here a pediment right
across and above it two chimneys connected by an arch. To
Church Lane the house has seven bays and segment-headed
windows. Doorway with pediment on brackets and narrow
arched windows l. and r. Above an arched window instead of
the doorway and niches instead of the windows. At the corner
of Church Lane and Market Street the former Guildhall
of Holy Trinity, built in 1518, and now the Three
Tuns.
From Church Lane to the town hall and past it to the N. Next to
it huddles a tiny one-bay house, datable apparently to *c.*1718.

Now down to the river by THAMES STREET. The walk starts
with the WHITE HART HOTEL of 1890, lifted straight out of
Kensington.* Four storeys and an angle turret. Then some early
C18 houses, especially Nos 18–20, made inconspicuous by their
shop-front. By the bend on the castle side Messrs COURAGE'S
offices, yellow brick, seven bays, two and a half storeys, three-
bay pediment, doorway with Tuscan columns and pediment,
all reasonable and serviceable. To its r. the MONUMENT to
Prince Christian Victor of Schleswig-Holstein † 1900. Standing bronze figure by *W. Goscombe John*, 1903, in an aedicule.
Lower down on the same side, at the corner of Datchet Road,
the MONUMENT to George V, 'first sovereign of the House of
Windsor', low, broad, restrained, and a little too demonstratively monumental. Centre the crown on a blocky base.
L. and r. wide, shallow basins. 1936 by *Lutyens*.

Opposite the SOUTH WESTERN HOTEL, C17, with three gables
and an oversailing upper floor. Finally, shortly before the
bridge, on the other side, the OLD HOUSE HOTEL, late C17,
recessed, with two differing wings. The centre is of seven bays
and only one and a half storeys, with a pedimented three-bay
projection and a pedimented porch on Tuscan columns. *Wren*
is supposed to have lived here (when?).

Back to the town hall and now in the opposite direction along the
HIGH STREET. Again the occasional Early Georgian brick
house, then the CASTLE HOTEL with a handsome early C19
cast-iron blacony. No. 13 is curious, with the large upper
studio-like windows and the cast-iron balconies of about 1840.
Then a very fine late C18 front with four stucco reliefs of putti
representing the four seasons. No. 4 again has good early C19
railings. Opposite a bigger and prouder Victorian group: the
WESTMINSTER BANK, of stone, Latish Classical, by *Cronk
Blomfield*, 1910, then a house of 1886 in the Kensington Queen
Anne, and the gabled Tudor POST OFFICE of 1885–7 (by the
Office of Works).

The continuation of High Street is PARK STREET, a very complete Georgian street, thanks partly to Georgian imitation.
But Nos 12–16 deserve notice, three-storeyed, stuccoed, with
angle pavilions with giant attached columns and centre with
arched windows and a continuation to the r. in a rounded
corner to Sheet Street. Also noteworthy Nos 23–24, late C18,
opposite, with a pair of doorways with alternatingly blocked

* The architect apparently was *R. Robson* (*Builder*, 23 November 1889).
I owe this information to Mr Spain.

pilasters, arched windows on the top floor, and a parapet. The best group, especially in terms of doorways, is right at the end on the r.

SHEET STREET is dominantly Victorian and culminates in the ROYAL ALBERT INSTITUTE, 1879–81 by *Bacon & Ingress Bell*. Tudor Gothic; red brick and stone. In VICTORIA STREET, round the corner just a little: THE LIMES, three-bay stucco with giant Ionic angle pilasters, early C19, the WINDSOR ALMSHOUSES of 1862, yellow and red brick, Gothic, with steep gables and dormers, and No. 67, High Victorian Gothic but dated 1888. Victoria Street continues w as Clarence Road, from which branches CLARENCE CRESCENT, a neat piece of planned development by *William Bedborough*, c.1845. Two-storeyed houses with angle pilasters, elegant iron balconettes, and pillared porches, a large communal garden across the road completing the layout.

After this detour we must return once more into Sheet Street, where HADLEIGH HOUSE now re-establishes the Georgian lead. The house lies back from the street. It belongs to the later C18 and has five bays and two and a half storeys, a doorway with Adamish Ionic columns and a pediment, and good wrought-iron garden gates. Opposite the WINDSOR MOTOR COMPANY, good and recent (by *Challen & Floyd*), timber and glass. Again opposite, a yellow-brick Early Victorian terrace, called YORK PLACE (Nos 51 etc),* and so into KINGS ROAD, where more such terraces. Nos 39–63 are called BRUNSWICK TERRACE and so must be earlier, c.1795–1800.‡ Also they are red brick exposed. Three storeys and basement. First-floor verandas. Nice houses opposite too; white: especially the ROYAL ADELAIDE HOTEL, fag-end of classical, with tripartite windows bending round corners. ADELAIDE TERRACE, dated 1831,§ is stuccoed, eighteen bays long, with a four-bay pediment on two plus two pilasters, quite an acceptable compromise. Yet further out EDINBURGH GARDENS, new housing by *Edward Whiteley*, and QUEEN'S TERRACE, fiercely Jacobean, red and blue brick and shaped gables. By *Teulon*, exhibited at the Royal Academy in 1849.

That leaves only one outer stretch – in what used to be the village of Clewer. From St Andrew, the Clewer parish church,

* The Rev. Basil Clarke has found out that this is by *Robert Tebbott*, who died in 1850.

‡ George III married Caroline of Brunswick in 1795.

§ Adelaide had become queen in 1830.

s there is first at the N end the OLD MILL HOUSE in Mill
Lane. Red brick, Late Georgian, the windows in giant blank
arches. Then, amid the recent crop of suburban houses, type
1930s and type 1950s, THE LIMES, timber-framed, with a
brick front of six bays but the timbering with brick infilling
visible towards the church. After that the YOUTH HOSTEL,
1707, four bays, brick, with a very good wrought-iron garden
gate.

Further s, in HATCH LANE, to conclude with, the HOUSE OF
MERCY, by *Woodyer*.* Begun by him in 1853 and continued to
his death. He never charged a fee. The material, needless to
say, is brick, the style that joyless Gothic which for schools,
hospitals, and convents was almost a matter of course. The
original chapel of 1857 is small and has as its only enrichment
an E window with Geometrical tracery. The present chapel
dates from 1881 and is astonishingly grand and lavish. Nave
and aisles of five bays with very high round piers. Ornate chancel with apse. Lively and original patterning of red and black
brick and stone in the chancel. The high vault looks proud but
is of canvas. – High SCREEN. – Large carved stone REREDOS
and REREDOS of the s aisle. – STAINED GLASS by *Hardman*.
– MONUMENTS to the foundress Harriet Monsell † 1883, a
large brass on the chancel floor, and to Canon T. T. Carter,
rector of Clewer and the first warden, † 1901, a recumbent
alabaster effigy under a canopy. Designed by *Bodley*. Canon
Carter's brick house opposite, like a very large rectory, is to be
demolished. – An extension by *Woodyer*, built in 1873, runs N
from the NE angle of the original quadrangle, an extension of
1874, also by *Woodyer*, continues the original street front to the
s. Large extensions of 1926 by *Cecil Hare* lie s and SE of the
latter.

WINKFIELD   9070

ST MARY. An interesting and confusing church. The brick SW
tower is of 1629. The windows also all of brick. Their motifs
are worth remembering (cf. Ruscombe). This tower was built
inside a church of *c*.1300 of which a few windows survive.
The walls of the church are of a dark brown conglomerate,
except that the brickwork of the tower extends a little further
N along the w wall. Whatever happened inside these conglomerate walls is obliterated by the fact that about 1592 the area
was divided in two by a row of octagonal wooden columns

* Now called Convent of St John Baptist.

carrying longitudinal arched braces instead of arches. Whether the C14 church had already been two-naved cannot be said. The twin arrangement did not interest nor worry *G. E. Street* when in 1858 he rebuilt the chancel so that it looks tripartite into the bipartite nave. The lavish chancel decoration is by *Woodyer*. The TILES and Botticelli quotations are signed E. I. and dated 1890.* – FONT. Octagonal, richly carved, and entirely High Victorian. It is by *Bentley* and dates from 1863. – PULPIT. Handsome and simple; given in 1707. – High Victorian iron SCREEN with high candlesticks. – STAINED GLASS. In the s chapel s by *Kempe*, 1883. – s chapel E, the foiled window by *Moberley* (*Powell's*), 1860. – MONUMENTS. Thomas Montague † 1630. Brass plate, showing him three-quarter figure distributing alms (by the pulpit). – Many tablets, e.g. Thomas Wise, master mason to King Charles the Second, † 1685. – An entertaining comparison is Sir Thomas Theophilus Metcalfe † 1822 and Lord Metcalfe † 1846, the first Gothic, the second Grecian, but both by *Bedford*.

At WINKFIELD STREET, ½ m. NW, two good houses. NEWINGTON HOUSE is late C18, three-bay front, widely spaced, parapet with two urns. Four oval paterae between ground floor and first floor. A little further NE KNIGHT'S HALL, timber-framed with brick infilling, with original C16 (or C15?) timber roof.

About 1¼ m. E of these WINKFIELD PLACE, facing Windsor Forest. Five bays, two and a half storeys, porch with pediment on Tuscan columns.

1 m. NW from here, i.e. about 1½ m. N of the church, NEW LODGE by *Talbot Bury*, 1858 (BC). Symmetrical Gothic façade with three gables but with an asymmetrically placed enormous tower. Gothic interior features.

1¾ m. NW of the church CRUCHFIELD HOUSE, C18, with an early Victorian classical façade of seven bays and three storeys. The first-floor windows all with pediments. Rusticated angle pilasters.

Then s of the church first ASCOT PLACE, 1 m. SE. For this *see* Ascot, p. 70. At the sw corner of the estate KEEPER'S COTTAGE, timber-framed with brick infilling; C15.

WINNERSH *see* SINDLESHAM

---

* The Rev. Basil Clarke tells me that the tiles were designed by *Woodyer* and painted by *Mrs Daubeny*, wife of the Vicar.

WINTERBOURNE

4070

ST JAMES. Tower of blue and red brick, dated 1759. Plain arched openings. Battlements. The N chapel is C18 too. It was built in 1712. The chancel now looks all the work of a Mr *Hudson,* who restored it in 1895. The rest of the church is by *Hugall,* 1854, but a few old parts were re-used: notably a lancet window in the chancel S wall and the chancel E window, which is early C14 (cusped intersecting tracery but with ogee-headed lights).

WINTERBOURNE HOUSE. Later Georgian, of red brick. Recessed centre with a porch of two pairs of Tuscan columns. The projecting wings carry pediments. Behind, some older timber-framing.

BUSSOCK WOOD (now Phillip's Hill House), 1¼ m. ENE. By *Mervyn Macartney,* 1907. Red brick, William and Mary style, large.

HOP CASTLE, 1¼ m. NNW. A Georgian hunting lodge, and the most delectable of follies. Built of rough, whole flints with plenty of bones. The centre of the house is an octagon. This is covered by a roof of ogee outline. To its l. and r. lower wings with urns at the corners. In them are just two small rooms. Behind the octagon the entrance hall. Its walls and those of the staircase into the basement are covered with pebbles and shells – grotto-fashion. The octagon has small niches in its sides.

WOKEFIELD PARK *see* STRATFIELD MORTIMER

WOKINGHAM

8060

ALL SAINTS. A Victorian church externally, if it were not for the fact that the W tower and the clerestory are of dark brown conglomerate. But all the details are of *Woodyer*'s restoration of 1864–6. Even a Norman S doorway is provided, it is said, on the strength of a few surviving stones. But inside the arcades of five bays are medieval. The pier bases are Norman, the round piers themselves may be C13 in their lower parts, but they were lengthened when the clerestory was built. Their present details of capitals and moulded arches point to *c.*1400. – FONT. Octagonal, Perp, the underside of the bowl with intertwined tree branches. – STAINED GLASS. E window by *Hardman.* – PLATE. Set of 1729. – MONUMENTS. Elizabethan brass plate with kneeling couple in an architectural surround with a guilloche frieze in the pediment. – Edward Colton † 1682. By *Woodruff*. Two black columns, open scrolly pediment, no figures. – Humphrey Cantrel. Late C17. With pretty putto heads and putti.

ST PAUL, Reading Road. 1862–4 by *Woodyer*, a prosperous High Victorian, 'West-end' church. The building was given by John Walter of Bear Wood. Rock-faced stone. NE porch steeple with spire, bristling with pinnacles on the buttresses. The tracery of the tower is C13 plate tracery. The rest is a free, not very attractive Dec. The aisles were added in 1874. The arcades have quatrefoil piers with thin shafts in the diagonals and naturalistic leaf capitals, fern, geranium, etc. The clerestory has an original arrangement of rere-arches on detached shafts. In the chancel N is different from S. On the S side e.g. a very odd, very low clerestory. – FONT. A very original piece, eight-lobed, and with a decoration of freely growing waterlilies with intricately intertwined stalks. It is one of the not so infrequent cases of the High Victorian anticipating the Art Nouveau. – STAINED GLASS. Mostly by *Hardman*.

ST SEBASTIAN, *see* Heathland.

TOWN HALL. Gothic, by *Poulton & Woodman*, 1860. Red brick with blue brick and stone dressings. Flèche. The front to the N is fairly consistent, with its row of gables. The E side is irregular. To the S, i.e. the Market Place, a curious composition of a single-storey semicircle flanked by two windowless blocks.

PERAMBULATION. The town hall is roughly triangular, as it stands on an island in the MARKET PLACE which is also roughly triangular. No houses of great interest, the best on the E side Nos 21 and its neighbour, the former red, of five bays, with a pretty doorway with set-in Doric columns, the latter white with tripartite windows. S of these, in DENMARK STREET, on the same side, just one timber-framed house with oversailing upper floors, oriels, and gables; C17 probably. To the N, i.e. the church, one can go by two streets, PEACH STREET, with one group of C17 cottages with overhangs, or ROSE STREET, which is more rewarding. It is long and fairly wide and starts with a high C18 brick house of three bays facing up northward and ending with a white one of three bays facing downward. In between only minor things, but one group of timber-framed C16 and C17 cottages ought to be preserved. The whole area is decaying and will evidently be redeveloped. At the N end Rose Street narrows, and the approach to the church is visually very successful. At the very end on the w side a corner house, timber-framed, with the timbers visible to Wiltshire Road, tile-hung to Rose Street.

The best houses are w of the Market Place in Broad Street and Shute End. BROAD STREET is as wide as a market place. On the N side the YOUTH EMPLOYMENT OFFICE, red brick, Late Georgian, with five bays plus two projecting ones. On the s side BARCLAYS BANK, the most ambitious house of Wokingham, late C18. Five bays plus low one-bay wings. The centre bay has the doorway with Tuscan columns, a lunette window above, and a top pediment. Again on the N side OXFORD HOUSE, early C18, four bays, with a good shell-hood, and COLBOURN HOUSE, five bays, Later Georgian. At the corner of RECTORY ROAD the POLICE STATION with its Tudor details and the characteristic and quite original tower. Strongly battered buttresses, Baroque doorcase, spire with concave outline. It is of 1904, by *Joseph Morris*, County Surveyor from 1872 to 1905, and very similar to the police station of Maidenhead. The end of Broad Street is TUDOR HOUSE, C16, pretty and much restored. Timber-framed. Two symmetrical gables. On along SHUTE END. The N side is called THE TERRACE, because it lies higher up than the s side. The bank of grass is visually very effective. The bigger houses, however, are on the s side. No. 6 and No. 8 are two good pieces, 6 lower, with panelled parapet, 8 of three storeys with a doorway with pediment on pilasters. Of the several nice Georgian houses on the terrace side Nos 29–31 deserves a mention. It is a pair, with the two doors under one segmental arch.

Much ought to be picked up at Wokingham outside the area of the old centre. Going in a circle clockwise from N to N the start is ASHRIDGE FARM, ⅔ m. N of the church. Gabled, C17, timber-framed. Fine central chimney of four stacks with star-shaped tops.

In BRACKNELL ROAD, i.e. E of the centre, ST CRISPIN'S SCHOOL, the first built by the Ministry of Education's own team of researchers into rational school building (*David Medd, Mary Crowley*) under the direction of *S. A. W. Johnson Marshall.* The school was built in 1950–3. The work was inspired by that of the Hertfordshire Architect's Department. The school is of light steel construction, the components to modular sizes. A free group rising from one to four storeys. In the four-storey block are class rooms above the entrance hall and library. To the r. the dining hall, and then in the higher cross-wings gym and hall. To the l. a looser grouping of low crafts-rooms and labs. By the side of the main entrance PAINTINGS by *Fred Millett* on the composition slabs, including a modular girl.

At HOLME GREEN, 1½ m. SE, LOCK'S HOUSE, Early Georgian, of five bays, blue headers and red dressings, segment-headed windows, hipped roof with pedimented dormers, doorway with pediment on fluted Doric pilasters, and HOLME GRANGE, an extremely good design of *Norman Shaw*'s of 1883. It is of the Home Counties brick-and-tile-hanging type, but the picture of the entrance front with its gables and dormers of different sizes and directions and the off-centre porch must be seen to be appreciated. To the garden the centre is a big chimney-breast, and this is followed by a transomed bay window set at a corner so that the narrow side is parallel with the chimney.

1 m. SSW is the LUCAS HOSPITAL, the best building of Wokingham without any doubt. It was built in 1665 and is very progressive for that date. Brick. Long front with two projecting wings. Two storeys, the windows wood-mullioned. In the centre a steep three-bay pediment with a coat of arms in a cartouche and cornucopias. Small cupola. The wings end with large arched windows. The r. one contains the chapel, the l. the hall. In the CHAPEL wooden chancel arch of reredos type with a large open segmental pediment. – COMMUNION RAIL. Of dumb-bell type. – STAINED GLASS. In the E window grand coat of arms, yellow, white, some blue.

W of the Hospital LUCKLEY, by *Sir Ernest Newton*, 1907. Inspired by the Elizabethan E-type of façade, but in the long, low, stretched-out façade, the proportion of bare wall to window, the porch with its segmental hood on Ionic columns, and the circular window to its r. entirely free, and unmistakably early C20.

In MOLLY MILLARS LANE, ¾ m. SW, new factories, the best A. JOHNSON & CO. by *Yorke, Rosenberg & Mardall*, a fine, clean Miesian job. Steel frame and blue brick without windows for the production area, steel frame and white brick, stretchers only, for the office area. The fenestration here is arbitrary, a compliment to 1960 v. the Mies tradition. Good also the inquiry pavilion at the entrance to REDYNE LTD, by *J. G. Fryman*. Circular core with four arms coming out diagonally. The rest is a glass box, set under it.

⅞ m. W the HOSPITAL, the former WORKHOUSE, built in 1850, red brick, minimum Tudor.

MILL CLOSE, Emmbrook. Flats of three storeys in rows. 1960 etc. by *G. V. Hives & Sons*.

GLEBELANDS, in Glebelands Road, off Rectory Road (*see* Police, above), is, like Luckley, by *Sir Ernest Newton*. It is of 1897, also Tudor, also E-shaped, but only just on its way out from historicism, e.g. by the simplified door-hood. The centre towards the garden is a typically Newtonian polygonal bay window with a chequer pattern.

The TITHE BARN HOTEL of 1904, near by, is a telling contrast: the conventional *v.* the unusual and progressive affluent house of the turn of the century. Half-timbered.

WOODLANDS ST MARY

3070

ST MARY. 1851 by *T. Talbot Bury*, with SW turret carrying a spire.

INHOLMES, $\frac{7}{8}$ m. S. 1905–7 by *Leonard Stokes*. Sizeable, and in a correct neo-Georgian.

ROOKS NEST, $\frac{3}{4}$ m. NW. Early C17. E-shaped façade. Flint, but the central porch of brick. Round to the r. big brick chimney. The details all over-restored.

WOODLEY AND SANDFORD

7070

ST JOHN EVANGELIST. 1873 by *Woodyer*. Flint; E.E. With new Reading housing everywhere around. Nave, chancel, and N aisle. S porch in the westernmost bay of the nave with a towering two-tier bellcote turned S. This is the one remarkable feature outside. The remarkable feature inside is the tall, tripartite, somewhat bleak stone SCREEN.

CONGREGATIONAL CHURCH, $\frac{1}{2}$ m. S. Minute, Gothic, with low spire; stuccoed. 1834.

SCHOOL, Howth Drive. By *R. Sheppard, Robson & Partners*. A good, clear design.

SANDFORD MILL, $1\frac{1}{2}$ m. ESE. A very pretty group of white weatherboarded mill and separate miller's house in the trees.

GEORGE INN, by the Loddon Bridge, on the Reading–Wokingham road. Handsome, three-bay, Late Georgian brick house with tripartite windows.

WOOLHAMPTON

5060

ST PETER. 1861 by *John Johnson*. Bellcote with spire on a flint stump. E.E. details, very gross inside, especially the chancel and the two-bay arcade to the low transepts. Fancy timber

porch. – FONT. Evidently part of the rebuilding. – STAINED
GLASS. w window by *Willement*, 1861. – PLATE. Set of 1813.
RECTORY, ¼ m. NW. Tower-like Early Georgian house of three
bays, basement, principal floor, half-storey, three-bay pedi-
ment, attic, and hipped roof. Blue brick with red dressings.
The blue brick all headers.

The present village is not by the church but along the Bath road.
On the s side a nice mixture of houses, including a timber-
framed one with overhang and a five-bay Georgian one. Also a
Gothic DRINKING FOUNTAIN of 1897.

Up the hill to the church past KENNET ORLEIGH on the E, THE
COURT on the w, both by *Mervyn Macartney* c.1910–15, the
former symmetrical neo-Tudor with touches of the neo-
William-and-Mary, the latter neo-William-and-Mary. Then
WOOLHAMPTON HOUSE. (The s wing mid Georgian, the w
part older, with a Georgian front and a later top storey, to the
E Georgian and Victorian. In 1848 *Vulliamy* worked at
Woolhampton House.)

DOUAI ABBEY. English Benedictines went to Paris after the
Suppression and moved on to Douai after the French Revo-
lution. From here they went back to England in 1903 and
took over the Catholic Diocesan College founded in 1838.
The CHAPEL of that school still exists. It dates from 1848
and is by *G. J. Wigley*, a humble building of nave and chancel,
but with a rich REREDOS by *Gabriel Pippet*. – The altar itself
is by *Sebastian Pugin Powell*, 1912–13. – SCULPTURE. Virgin
and Child, demi-figure, stone. In an Italian Baroque style. –
STAINED GLASS. The still pictorial Crucifixion in the E
window no doubt of c.1849. Most of the glass in the chapel
looks French.

  E of the chapel a block of 1884–6 (top floor 1910), continued
to the s in 1888 and on a large scale (with the gatehouse and the
entrance tower) in 1893–5. This latter enlargement is by
F. A. Walters. The long extensions of the original buildings
towards the new church are by *Pugin Powell* and date from
1914 and 1922. Of 1935–6 the E extensions *by J. D. Kendall*.

  The ABBEY CHURCH is by *J. Arnold Crush* and was begun
in 1928. Most of the nave has not yet been built. Tall start of
the nave, with clerestory, lower apsed chancel. All brick, but
very white stone inside. The interior more conventional than
the exterior, but neither of great architectural interest. Dec
style.

  Recently (1963) *Frederick Gibberd* has been commissioned

to design a lower nave and a complete abbey l. and r. of the church. The foundation stone was laid in 1964.

WOOLLEY PARK *see* BRIGHTWALTON

WOOLSTONE   2080

ALL SAINTS. Nave, chancel, s transept, bellcote. Late Norman N doorway, waterleaf capitals, hood-mould on beasts' heads. Small lancets N and s. One N window early C14 with nicely cusped Y-tracery. The s transept s window is late C13, of two lights with pointed-trefoiled heads and a trefoiled circle. In the chancel N wall two Dec windows. Inside, the chancel arch (two slight chamfers) looks early C13, the s transept arch goes with the s window. – FONT. Of lead. Circular, with strange, rather bleak and disorderly patterns; C14 probably. – CHANDELIER. Brass, with one tier of arms. – PLATE. Cover Paten, 1581.

SE of the church a Georgian HOUSE of six bays with hipped roof.

DISC BARROW, on Woolstone Down. The barrow has a central mound 25 ft in diameter and 1½ ft high, standing on a platform 50 ft in diameter. It is surrounded by a ditch and external bank. 200 yds N is a bowl barrow 21 ft in diameter and 3 ft high. A second bowl barrow, 2 ft high, lies 180 yds to the NW.

MOUND, just below Uffington Camp, on the Woolstone–Uffington border. This very large circular mound is probably the motte of a MOTTE AND BAILEY CASTLE.

WOOTTON   4000

ST PETER. Nave and chancel and recent timber bell-turret. Mostly Perp, but the E window Dec. – TILES. A number displayed on one wall of the porch. They are probably of the C14. – CHANDELIER. Brass, apparently C18. – STAINED GLASS. E window by *Kempe*, with his wheatsheaf, c.1900. – PLATE. Paten with the Vernicle, c.1500. – Chalice, Flagon, Almsdish of 1786.

BOARS HILL, the villa suburb of Oxford, belongs to Wootton. The villas are embedded in green, much as in Surrey.

RIPON HALL. Gothic. Built in the 1890s for the then President of Trinity College, Oxford. Enlarged for Lord Berkeley in 1902–4 (tower, hall). The recent shingle-hung addition by *M. & D. Dove*, 1963–4.

WYTHAM

ALL SAINTS. The entrance to the churchyard is by a small
doorway from Cumnor Place. It is Perp with a two-centred
arch, but has an inscription in Roman letters. The church was
rebuilt in 1811–12 by Lord Abingdon, using materials from
Cumnor Place. Nave and chancel, unbuttressed w tower.
On the N side one late C14 window. On the s side Dec windows. Chancel E Dec as well. These four windows again come
from Cumnor. They are all four of two lights with usual
flowing patterns. One has a wheel of four mouchettes. The
nave roof on good corbels including a bagpiper. – COM-
MUNION RAIL. C18. – STAINED GLASS. Old bits (C15) nave
N. – Chancel s foreign roundels, etc. Chancel E Adoration of the
Shepherds, C18. – PLATE. Cup, 1594; Paten on foot, 1693;
Flagon, 1709; Paten on foot, 1722. – BRASS. Robert de Wytham † 1406 and wife. Fragmentary; originally c. 30 in. long.

WYTHAM ABBEY. Originally built in the early C16 with two
courtyards. One of them is now covered over and contains
the main staircase. Though the house looks generally the
result of the remodelling of 1809–10 by *Thomas Cundy* (BC),
there is plenty left of the early C16, especially on the w side.
The embattled oriel window is certainly in order. It establishes
the motif of straight-headed windows with arched lights. Such
windows also occur on the E side, the climax of which is the
gateway tower. Straight-sided pointed arch with continuous
mouldings and two separate oriels over. A polygonal turret
behind. The s side is not original. Rumour has it that Cundy's
front was taken down and rebuilt c.1870. The porch is of
c.1925., The whole, whatever the dates, is picturesquely
irregular.

YATTENDON

ST PETER AND ST PAUL. Of the building of c.1450 of which a
former inscription reported the nave roof remains, with tie-
beams, collar-beams on arched braces, and two tiers of wind-
braces. The rest appears entirely Victorian. The short shingled
broach spire e.g. is of 1896. – PULPIT. Jacobean, with the
usual blank arches and plenty of arabesque. – Two BENCH
ENDS with linenfold panelling. – STAINED GLASS. In the
chancel N by *Powell*, 1874, designed by *Burrow*. – PLATE.
Paten of 1713; Chalice of 1722. – MONUMENT. John Harris
† 1743. Tablet with an oval still life of death and eternity.

w of the church two good Georgian houses, THE GRANGE and
the MANOR HOUSE, the former of 1785, the latter with an
outer stair to the pilaster-framed door. A little further w the
former READING ROOM, given and designed in 1878 by
Alfred Waterhouse, Lord of the Manor. By him also the WELL
HOUSE, now bus-shelter, 1876. Waterhouse himself lived at
Yattendon Court, where his new mansion was begun in 1878.
This, however, was demolished in 1926 and replaced. Also by
Waterhouse the SCHOOL of 1891.

Of Georgian houses two more deserve a glance, both E of the
church: the RECTORY, of five bays, with a curious doorway,
where a kind of apron, as they are used in early C18 houses
below the window-sills, appears as a tympanum. E of this
THE MALTHOUSE, a roughcast three-bay cottage with
Gothic glazing bars.

GLOSSARY

ABACUS: flat slab on the top of a capital (q.v.).

ABUTMENT: solid masonry placed to resist the lateral pressure of a vault.

ACANTHUS: plant with thick fleshy and scalloped leaves used as part of the decoration of a Corinthian capital (q.v.) and in some types of leaf carving.

ACHIEVEMENT OF ARMS: in heraldry, a complete display of armorial bearings.

ACROTERION: foliage-carved block on the end or top of a classical pediment.

ADDORSED: two human figures, animals, or birds, etc., placed symmetrically so that they turn their backs to each other.

AEDICULE, AEDICULA: framing of a window or door by columns and a pediment (q.v.).

AFFRONTED: two human figures, animals, or birds, etc., placed symmetrically so that they face each other.

AGGER: Latin term for the built-up foundations of Roman roads; also sometimes applied to the banks of hill-forts or other earthworks.

AMBULATORY: semicircular or polygonal aisle enclosing an apse (q.v.).

ANNULET: see Shaft-ring.

ANSE DE PANIER: see Arch, Basket.

ANTEPENDIUM: covering of the front of an altar, usually by textiles or metalwork.

ANTIS, IN: see Portico.

APSE: vaulted semicircular or polygonal end of a chancel or a chapel.

ARABESQUE: light and fanciful surface decoration using combinations of flowing lines, tendrils, etc., interspersed with vases, animals, etc.

ARCADE: range of arches supported on piers or columns, free-standing: or, BLIND ARCADE, the same attached to a wall.

ARCH: round-headed, i.e. semicircular; pointed, i.e. consisting of two curves, each drawn from one centre, and meeting in a point at the top; segmental, i.e. in the form of a segment;

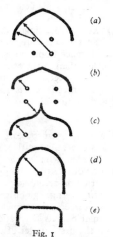

Fig. 1

pointed; four-centred (a Late Medieval form), see Fig. 1(a); Tudor (also a Late Medieval form), *see* Fig. 1(*b*); Ogee (introduced *c.*1300 and specially popular in the C14), *see* Fig. 1(*c*); Stilted, *see* Fig. 1(*d*); Basket, with lintel connected to the jambs by concave quadrant curves, *see* Fig. 1(*e*) for one example; Diaphragm, a transverse arch with solid spandrels carrying not a vault but a principal beam of a timber roof.

ARCHITRAVE: lowest of the three main parts of the entablature (q.v.) of an order (q.v.) (*see* Fig. 12).

ARCHIVOLT: under-surface of an arch (also called Soffit).

ARRIS: sharp edge at the meeting of two surfaces.

ASHLAR: masonry of large blocks wrought to even faces and square edges.

ATLANTES: male counterparts of caryatids (q.v.).

ATRIUM: inner court of a Roman house, also open court in front of a church.

ATTACHED: *see* Engaged.

ATTIC: topmost storey of a house, if distance from floor to ceiling is less than in the others.

AUMBRY: recess or cupboard to hold sacred vessels for Mass and Communion.

BAILEY: open space or court of a stone-built castle; *see* also Motte-and-Bailey.

BALDACCHINO: canopy supported on columns.

BALLFLOWER: globular flower of three petals enclosing a small ball. A decoration used in the first quarter of the C14.

BALUSTER: small pillar or column of fanciful outline.

BALUSTRADE: series of balusters supporting a handrail or coping (q.v.).

BARBICAN: outwork defending the entrance to a castle.

BARGEBOARDS: projecting decorated boards placed against the incline of the gable of a building and hiding the horizontal roof timbers.

BARROW: *see* Bell, Bowl, Disc, Long, *and* Pond Barrow.

BASILICA: in medieval architecture an aisled church with a clerestory.

BASKET ARCH: *see* Arch (Fig. 1*e*).

BASTION: projection at the angle of a fortification.

BATTER: inclined face of a wall.

BATTLEMENT: parapet with a series of indentations or embrasures with raised portions or merlons between (also called Crenellation).

BAYS: internal compartments of a building; each divided from the other not by solid walls but by divisions only marked in the side walls (columns, pilasters, etc.) or the ceiling (beams, etc.). Also external divisions of a building by fenestration.

BAY-WINDOW: angular or curved projection of a house front with ample fenestration. If curved, also called bow-window: if on an upper floor only, also called oriel or oriel window.

BEAKER FOLK: Late New Stone Age warrior invaders from the Continent who buried their dead in round barrows and introduced the first metal tools and weapons to Britain.

BEAKHEAD: Norman ornamental motif consisting of a row of bird or beast heads with beaks biting usually into a roll moulding.

BELFRY: turret on a roof to hang bells in.

BELGAE: Aristocratic warrior bands who settled in Britain in two main waves in the C I B.C. In Britain their culture is termed Iron Age C.

BELL BARROW: Early Bronze Age round barrow in which the mound is separated from its encircling ditch by a flat platform or berm (q.v.).

BELLCOTE: framework on a roof to hang bells from.

BERM: level area separating ditch from bank on a hill-fort or barrow.

BILLET FRIEZE: Norman ornamental motif made up of short raised rectangles placed at regular intervals.

BIVALLATE: Of a hill-fort: defended by two concentric banks and ditches.

BLOCK CAPITAL: Romanesque capital cut from a cube by hav-

Fig. 2

ing the lower angles rounded off to the circular shaft below (also called Cushion Capital) (Fig. 2).

BOND, ENGLISH or FLEMISH: see Brickwork.

BOSS: knob or projection usually placed to cover the intersection of ribs in a vault.

BOWL BARROW: round barrow surrounded by a quarry ditch. Introduced in Late Neolithic

times, the form continued until the Saxon period.

BOW-WINDOW: see Bay-Window.

BOX: A small country house, e.g. a shooting box. A convenient term to describe a compact minor dwelling, e.g. a rectory.

BOX PEW: pew with a high wooden enclosure.

BRACES: see Roof.

BRACKET: small supporting piece of stone, etc., to carry a projecting horizontal.

BRESSUMER: beam in a timber-framed building to support the, usually projecting, superstructure.

BRICKWORK: *Header:* brick laid so that the end only appears on the face of the wall. *Stretcher:* brick laid so that the side only appears on the face of the wall. *English Bond:* method of laying bricks so that alternate courses or layers on the face of the wall are composed of headers or stretchers only (Fig. 3a). *Flemish Bond:* method of laying

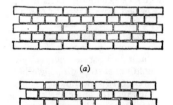

(a)

(b)

Fig. 3

bricks so that alternate headers and stretchers appear in each course on the face of the wall (Fig. 3b).

BROACH: see Spire.

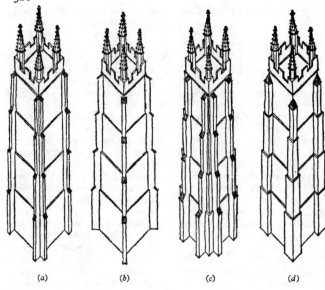

(a)   (b)   (c)   (d)

Fig. 4

BROKEN PEDIMENT: *see* Pediment.

BRONZE AGE: In Britain, the period from *c.*1800 to 600 B.C.

BUCRANIUM: ox skull.

BUTTRESS: mass of brickwork or masonry projecting from or built against a wall to give additional strength. *Angle Buttresses:* two meeting at an angle of 90° at the angle of a building (Fig. 4*a*). *Clasping Buttress:* one which encases the angle (Fig. 4*d*). *Diagonal Buttress:* one placed against the right angle formed by two walls, and more or less equiangular with both (Fig. 4*b*). *Flying Buttress:* arch or half arch transmitting the thrust of a vault or roof from the upper part of a wall to an outer support or buttress. *Setback Buttress:* angle buttress set slightly back from the angle (Fig. 4*c*).

CABLE MOULDING: Norman moulding imitating a twisted cord.

CAIRN: a mound of stones usually covering a burial.

CAMBER: slight rise or upward curve of an otherwise horizontal structure.

CAMPANILE: isolated bell tower.

CANOPY: projection or hood over an altar, pulpit, niche, statue, etc.

CAP: in a windmill the crowning feature.

CAPITAL: head or top part of a column.

CARTOUCHE: tablet with an ornate frame, usually enclosing an inscription.

CARYATID: whole female figure supporting an entablature or other similar member. *Termini Caryatids:* female busts or demi-figures or three-quarter figures supporting an entablature or other similar member and placed at the top of termini pilasters (q.v.). Cf. Atlantes.

CASTELLATED: decorated with battlements.

CELURE: panelled and adorned part of a wagon-roof above the rood or the altar.

CENSER: vessel for the burning of incense.

CENTERING: wooden framework used in arch and vault construction and removed when the mortar has set.

CHALICE: cup used in the Communion service or at Mass. *See also* Recusant Chalice.

CHAMBERED TOMB: burial mound of the New Stone Age having a stone-built chamber and entrance passage covered by an earthen barrow or stone cairn. The form was introduced to Britain from the Mediterranean.

CHAMFER: surface made by cutting across the square angle of a stone block, piece of wood, etc., usually at an angle of 45° to the other two surfaces.

CHANCEL: that part of the E end of a church in which the altar is placed, usually applied to the whole continuation of the nave E of the crossing.

CHANCEL ARCH: arch at the W end of the chancel.

CHANTRY CHAPEL: chapel attached to, or inside, a church, endowed for the saying of Masses for the soul of the founder or some other individual.

CHEVET: French term for the E end of a church (chancel, ambulatory, and radiating chapels).

CHEVRON: Norman moulding forming a zigzag.

CHOIR: that part of the church where divine service is sung.

CIBORIUM: a baldacchino.

CINQUEFOIL: *see* Foil.

CIST: stone-lined or slab-built grave. First appears in Late Neolithic times. It continued to be used in the Early Christian period.

CLAPPER BRIDGE: bridge made of large slabs of stone, some built up to make rough piers and other longer ones laid on top to make the roadway.

CLASSIC: here used to mean the moment of highest achievement of a style.

CLASSICAL: here used as the term for Greek and Roman architecture and any subsequent styles inspired by it.

CLERESTORY: upper storey of the nave walls of a church, pierced by windows.

COADE STONE: artificial (cast) stone made in the late C18 and the early C19 by Coade and Sealy in London.

COB: walling material made of mixed clay and straw.

COFFERING: decorating a ceiling with sunk square or polygonal ornamental panels.

COLLAR-BEAM: *see* Roof.

COLONNADE: range of columns.

COLONNETTE: small column.

COLUMNA ROSTRATA: column decorated with carved prows of ships to celebrate a naval victory.

COMPOSITE: *see* Order.

CONSOLE: bracket (q.v.) with a compound curved outline.

COPING: capping or covering to a wall.

CORBEL: block of stone projecting from a wall, supporting some feature on its horizontal top surface.

CORBEL TABLE: series of corbels, occurring just below the roof eaves externally or internally, often seen in Norman buildings.

CORINTHIAN: *see* Order.

CORNICE: in classical architecture the top section of the entablature (q.v.). Also for a projecting decorative feature along the top of a wall, arch, etc.

CORRIDOR VILLA: *see* Villa.

COUNTERSCARP BANK: small bank on the down-hill or outer side of a hill-fort ditch.

COURTYARD VILLA: *see* Villa.

COVE, COVING: concave undersurface in the nature of a hollow moulding but on a larger scale.

COVER PATEN: cover to a Communion cup, suitable for use as a paten or plate for the consecrated bread.

CRADLE ROOF: *see* Wagon roof.

CRENELLATION: *see* Battlement.

CREST, CRESTING: ornamental finish along the top of a screen, etc.

CRINKLE-CRANKLE WALL: undulating wall.

CROCKET, CROCKETING: decorative features placed on the sloping sides of spires, pinnacles, gables, etc., in Gothic architecture, carved in various leaf shapes and placed at regular intervals.

CROCKET CAPITAL: *see* Fig. 5. An Early Gothic form.

CROMLECH: word of Celtic origin still occasionally used of single free-standing stones ascribed to the Neolithic or Bronze Age periods.

Fig. 5

CROSSING: space at the intersection of nave, chancel, and transepts.

CROSS-WINDOWS: windows with one mullion and one transom.

CRUCK: big curved beam supporting both walls and roof of a cottage.

CRYPT: underground room usually below the E end of a church.

CUPOLA: small polygonal or circular domed turret crowning a roof.

CURTAIN WALL: connecting wall between the towers of a castle.

CUSHION CAPITAL: *see* Block Capital.

CUSP: projecting point between the foils in a foiled Gothic arch.

DADO: decorative covering of the lower part of a wall.

DAGGER: tracery motif of the Dec style. It is a lancet shape rounded or pointed at the head, pointed at the foot, and cusped inside (*see* Fig. 6).

Fig. 6

DAIS: raised platform at one end of a room.

DEC ('DECORATED'): historical division of English Gothic architecture covering the period from *c*.1290 to *c*.1350.

DEMI-COLUMNS: columns half sunk into a wall.

DIAPER WORK: surface decoration composed of square or lozenge shapes.

DIAPHRAGM ARCH: *see* Arch.

DISC BARROW: Bronze Age round barrow with inconspicuous central mound surrounded by bank and ditch.

DOGTOOTH: typical E.E. ornament consisting of a series of four-cornered stars placed diagonally and raised pyramidally (Fig. 7).

Fig. 7

DOMICAL VAULT: *see* Vault.

DONJON: *see* Keep.

DORIC: *see* Order.

DORMER (WINDOW): window placed vertically in the sloping plane of a roof.

DRIPSTONE: *see* Hood-mould.

DRUM: circular or polygonal vertical wall of a dome or cupola.

E.E. ('EARLY ENGLISH'): historical division of English Gothic architecture roughly covering the C13.

EASTER SEPULCHRE: recess with tomb-chest, usually in the wall of a chancel, the tomb-chest to receive an effigy of Christ for Easter celebrations.

EAVES: underpart of a sloping roof overhanging a wall.

EAVES CORNICE: cornice below the eaves of a roof.

ECHINUS: Convex or projecting moulding supporting the abacus of a Greek Doric capital, sometimes bearing an egg and dart pattern.

EMBATTLED: *see* Battlement.

EMBRASURE: small opening in the wall or parapet of a fortified building, usually splayed on the inside.

ENCAUSTIC TILES: earthenware glazed and decorated tiles used for paving.

ENGAGED COLUMNS: columns attached to, or partly sunk into, a wall.

ENGLISH BOND: *see* Brickwork.

ENTABLATURE: in classical architecture the whole of the horizontal members above a column (that is architrave, frieze, and cornice) (*see* Fig. 12).

ENTASIS: very slight convex deviation from a straight line; used on Greek columns and sometimes on spires to prevent an optical illusion of concavity.

ENTRESOL: *see* Mezzanine.

EPITAPH: hanging wall monument.

ESCUTCHEON: shield for armorial bearings.

EXEDRA: the apsidal end of a room. *See* Apse.

FAN-VAULT: *see* Vault.

FERETORY: place behind the

high altar where the chief shrine of a church is kept.

FESTOON: carved garland of flowers and fruit suspended at both ends.

FILLET: narrow flat band running down a shaft or along a roll moulding.

FINIAL: top of a canopy, gable, pinnacle.

FLAGON: vessel for the wine used in the Communion service.

FLAMBOYANT: properly the latest phase of French Gothic architecture where the window tracery takes on wavy undulating lines.

FLÈCHE: slender wooden spire on the centre of a roof (also called Spirelet).

FLEMISH BOND: see Brickwork.

FLEURON: decorative carved flower or leaf.

FLUSHWORK: decorative use of flint in conjunction with dressed stone so as to form patterns: tracery, initials, etc.

FLUTING: vertical channelling in the shaft of a column.

FLYING BUTTRESS: see Buttress.

FOIL: lobe formed by the cusping (q.v.) of a circle or an arch. Trefoil, quatrefoil, cinquefoil, multifoil, express the number of leaf shapes to be seen.

FOLIATED: carved with leaf shapes.

FOSSE: ditch.

FOUR-CENTRED ARCH: see Arch.

FRATER: refectory or dining hall of a monastery.

FRESCO: wall painting on wet plaster.

FRIEZE: middle division of a classical entablature (q.v.) (see Fig. 12).

FRONTAL: covering for the front of an altar.

GABLE: *Dutch gable:* A gable with curved sides crowned by a pediment, characteristic of *c.*1630–50 (Fig. 8*a*). *Shaped gable:* A gable with multi-curved sides characteristic of *c.*1600–50 (Fig. 8*b*).

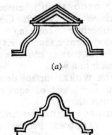

(a)

(b)

Fig. 8

GADROONED: enriched with a series of convex ridges, the opposite of fluting.

GALILEE: chapel or vestibule usually at the W end of a church enclosing the porch. Also called Narthex (q.v.).

GALLERY: in church architecture upper storey above an aisle, opened in arches to the nave. Also called Tribune and often erroneously Triforium (q.v.).

GALLERY GRAVE: chambered tomb (q.v.) in which there is little or no differentiation between the entrance passage and the actual burial chamber(s).

GARDEROBE: lavatory or privy in a medieval building.

GARGOYLE: water spout projecting from the parapet of a wall or tower; carved into a human or animal shape.

GAZEBO: lookout tower or raised

summer house in a picturesque garden.

'GEOMETRICAL': *see* Tracery.

'GIBBS SURROUND': of a doorway or window. An C18 motif consisting of a surround with alternating larger and smaller blocks of stone, quoin-wise, or intermittent large blocks, sometimes with a narrow raised band connecting them up the verticals and along the face of the arch (Fig. 9).

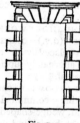

Fig. 9

GROIN: sharp edge at the meeting of two cells of a cross-vault.

GROIN-VAULT: *see* Vault.

GROTESQUE: fanciful ornamental decoration: *see* also Arabesque.

Hagioscope: *see* Squint.

HALF-TIMBERING: *see* Timber-Framing.

HALL CHURCH: church in which nave and aisles are of equal height or approximately so.

HAMMERBEAM: *see* Roof.

HANAP: large metal cup, generally made for domestic use, standing on an elaborate base and stem; with a very ornate cover frequently crowned with a little steeple.

HEADERS: *see* Brickwork.

HERRINGBONE WORK: brick, stone, or tile construction where the component blocks are laid diagonally instead of flat. Alternate courses lie in opposing directions to make a zigzag pattern up the face of the wall.

HEXASTYLE: having six detached columns.

HILL-FORT: Iron Age earthwork enclosed by a ditch and bank system; in the later part of the period the defences multiplied in size and complexity. They vary from about an acre to over 30 acres in area, and are usually built with careful regard to natural elevations or promontories.

HIPPED ROOF: *see* Roof.

HOOD-MOULD: projecting moulding above an arch or a lintel to throw off water (also called Dripstone or Label).

Iconography: the science of the subject matter of works of the visual arts.

IMPOST: bracket in a wall, usually formed of mouldings, on which the ends of an arch rest.

INDENT: shape chiselled out in a stone slab to receive a brass.

INGLENOOK: bench or seat built in beside a fireplace, sometimes covered by the chimneybreast, occasionally lit by small windows on each side of the fire.

INTERCOLUMNIATION: the space between columns.

IONIC: *see* Order (Fig. 12).

IRON AGE: in Britain the period from *c.* 600 B.C. to the coming of the Romans. The term is also used for those un-Romanized native communities which survived until the Saxon incursions.

JAMB: straight side of an archway, doorway, or window.

KEEL MOULDING: moulding whose outline is in section like that of the keel of a ship.
KEEP: massive tower of a Norman castle.
KEYSTONE: middle stone in an arch or a rib-vault.
KING-POST: see Roof (Fig. 14).
KNEELER: horizontal decorative projection at the base of a gable.
KNOP: a knob-like thickening in the stem of a chalice.

LABEL: see Hood-mould.
LABEL STOP: ornamental boss at the end of a hood-mould (q.v.).
LACED WINDOWS: windows pulled visually together by strips, usually in brick of a different colour, which continue vertically the lines of the vertical parts of the window surrounds. The motif is typical of c. 1720.
LANCET WINDOW: slender pointed-arched window.
LANTERN: in architecture, a small circular or polygonal turret with windows all round crowning a roof (see Cupola) or a dome.
LANTERN CROSS: churchyard cross with lantern-shaped top usually with sculptured representations on the sides of the top.

LEAN-TO ROOF: roof with one slope only, built against a higher wall.
LESENE or PILASTER STRIP: pilaster without base or capital.
LIERNE: see Vault (Fig. 21).
LINENFOLD: Tudor panelling ornamented with a conventional representation of a piece of linen laid in vertical folds. The piece is repeated in each panel.
LINTEL: horizontal beam or stone bridging an opening.
LOGGIA: recessed colonnade (q.v.).
LONG AND SHORT WORK: Saxon quoins (q.v.) consisting of stones placed with the long sides alternately upright and horizontal.
LONG BARROW: unchambered Neolithic communal burial mound, wedge-shaped in plan, with the burial and occasional other structures massed at the broader end, from which the mound itself tapers in height; quarry ditches flank the mound.
LOUVRE: opening, often with lantern (q.v.) over, in the roof of a room to let the smoke from a central hearth escape.
LOWER PALAEOLITHIC: see Palaeolithic.
LOZENGE: diamond shape.
LUCARNE: small opening to let light in.
LUNETTE: tympanum (q.v.) or semicircular opening.
LYCH GATE: wooden gate structure with a roof and open sides placed at the entrance to a churchyard to provide space for the reception of a coffin. The word lych is Saxon and means a corpse.

LYNCHET: long terraced strip of soil accumulating on the downward side of prehistoric and medieval fields due to soil creep from continuous ploughing along the contours.

MACHICOLATION: projecting gallery on brackets constructed on the outside of castle towers or walls. The gallery has holes in the floor to drop missiles through.

MAJOLICA: ornamented glazed earthenware.

MANSARD: see Roof.

MATHEMATICAL TILES: Small facing tiles the size of brick headers, applied to timber-framed walls to make them appear brick-built.

MEGALITHIC TOMB: stone-built burial chamber of the New Stone Age covered by an earth or stone mound. The form was introduced to Britain from the Mediterranean area.

MERLON: see Battlement.

MESOLITHIC: 'Middle Stone' Age; the post-glacial period of hunting and fishing communities dating in Britain from c. 8000 B.C. to the arrival of Neolithic communities, with which they must have considerably overlapped.

METOPE: in classical architecture of the Doric order (q.v.) the space in the frieze between the triglyphs (Fig. 12).

MEZZANINE: low storey placed between two higher ones.

MISERERE: see Misericord.

MISERICORD: bracket placed on the underside of a hinged choir stall seat which, when turned up, provided the occupant of the seat with a support during long periods of standing (also called Miserere).

MODILLION: small bracket of which large numbers (modillion frieze) are often placed below a cornice (q.v.) in classical architecture.

MOTTE: steep mound forming the main feature of CII and CI2 castles.

MOTTE-AND-BAILEY: post-Roman and Norman defence system consisting of an earthen mound (the motte) topped with a wooden tower eccentrically placed within a bailey (q.v.), with enclosure ditch and palisade, and with the rare addition of an internal bank.

MOUCHETTE: tracery motif in curvilinear tracery, a curved dagger (q.v.), specially popular in the early CI4 (Fig. 10).

Fig. 10

MULLIONS: vertical posts or uprights dividing a window into 'lights'.

MULTIVALLATE: Of a hill-fort: defended by three or more concentric banks and ditches.

MUNTIN: post as a rule moulded and part of a screen.

NAIL-HEAD: E.E. ornamental motif, consisting of small pyramids regularly repeated (Fig. 11).

Fig. 11

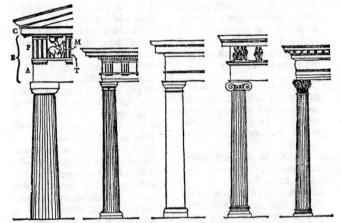

Fig. 12. Orders of Columns (Greek Doric, Roman Doric, Tuscan Doric, Ionic, Corinthian) E, Entablature; C, Cornice; F, Frieze; A, Architrave; M, Metope; T, Triglyph.

NARTHEX: enclosed vestibule or covered porch at the main entrance to a church (*see* Galilee).

NEOLITHIC: 'New Stone' Age, dating in Britain from the appearance from the Continent of the first settled farming communities *c.* 3500 B.C. until the introduction of the Bronze Age.

NEWEL: central post in a circular or winding staircase; also the principal post when a flight of stairs meets a landing.

NOOK-SHAFT: shaft set in the angle of a pier or respond or wall, or the angle of the jamb of a window or doorway.

NUTMEG MOULDING: consisting of a chain of tiny triangles placed obliquely.

OBELISK: lofty pillar of square section tapering at the top and ending pyramidally.

OGEE: *see* Arch (Fig. 1c).

ORATORY: small private chapel in a house.

ORDER: (1) *of a doorway or window:* series of concentric steps receding towards the opening; (2) *in classical architecture:* column with base, shaft, capital, and entablature (q.v.) according to one of the following styles: Greek Doric, Roman Doric, Tuscan Doric, Ionic, Corinthian, Composite. The established details are very elaborate, and some specialist architectural work should be consulted for further guidance (*see* Fig. 12).

ORIEL: *see* Bay-Window.

OVERHANG: projection of the upper storey of a house.

OVERSAILING COURSES: series of stone or brick courses, each one projecting beyond the one below it.

OVOLO: convex moulding.

PALAEOLITHIC: 'Old Stone' Age; the first period of human culture, commencing in the

Ice Age and immediately prior to the Mesolithic; the Lower Palaeolithic is the older phase, the Upper Palaeolithic the later.

PALIMPSEST: (1) *of a brass:* where a metal plate has been re-used by turning over and engraving on the back; (2) *of a wall painting:* where one overlaps and partly obscures an earlier one.

PALLADIAN: architecture following the ideas and principles of Andrea Palladio, 1518–80.

PANTILE: tile of curved S-shaped section.

PARAPET: low wall placed to protect any spot where there is a sudden drop, for example on a bridge, quay, hillside, housetop, etc.

PARGETTING: plaster work with patterns and ornaments either in relief or engraved on it.

PARVIS: term wrongly applied to a room over a church porch. These rooms were often used as a schoolroom or as a store room.

PATEN: plate to hold the bread at Communion or Mass.

PATERA: small flat circular or oval ornament in classical architecture.

PEDIMENT: low-pitched gable used in classical, Renaissance, and neo-classical architecture above a portico and above doors, windows, etc. It may be straight-sided or curved segmentally. *Broken Pediment:* one where the centre portion of the base is left open. *Open Pediment:* one where the centre portion of the sloping sides is left out.

PENDANT: boss (q.v.) elongated so that it seems to hang down.

PENDENTIF: concave triangular spandrel used to lead from the angle of two walls to the base of a circular dome. It is constructed as part of the hemisphere over a diameter the size of the diagonal of the basic square (Fig. 13).

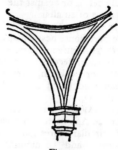

Fig. 13

PERP (PERPENDICULAR): historical division of English Gothic architecture covering the period from c.1335–50 to c.1530.

PIANO NOBILE: principal storey of a house with the reception rooms; usually the first floor.

PIAZZA: open space surrounded by buildings; in C17 and C18 England sometimes used to mean a long colonnade or loggia.

PIER: strong, solid support, frequently square in section or of composite section (compound pier).

PIETRA DURA: ornamental or scenic inlay by means of thin slabs of stone.

PILASTER: shallow pier attached to a wall. *Termini Pilasters:* pilasters with sides tapering downwards.

PILLAR PISCINA: free-standing piscina on a pillar.

PINNACLE: ornamental form crowning a spire, tower, buttress, etc., usually of steep pyramidal, conical, or some similar shape.

PISCINA: basin for washing the Communion or Mass vessels, provided with a drain. Generally set in or against the wall to the s of an altar.

PLAISANCE: summer-house, pleasure house near a mansion.

PLATE TRACERY: *see* Tracery.

PLINTH: projecting base of a wall or column, generally chamfered (q.v.) or moulded at the top.

POND BARROW: rare type of Bronze Age barrow consisting of a circular depression, usually paved, and containing a number of cremation burials.

POPPYHEAD: ornament of leaf and flower type used to decorate the tops of bench- or stall-ends.

PORTCULLIS: gate constructed to rise and fall in vertical grooves; used in gateways of castles.

PORTE COCHÈRE: porch large enough to admit wheeled vehicles.

PORTICO: centre-piece of a house or a church with classical detached or attached columns and a pediment. A portico is called *prostyle* or *in antis* according to whether it projects from or recedes into a building. In a portico *in antis* the columns range with the side walls.

POSTERN: small gateway at the back of a building.

PREDELLA: in an altarpiece the horizontal strip below the main representation, often used for a number of subsidiary representations in a row.

PRESBYTERY: the part of the church lying E of the choir. It is the part where the altar is placed.

PRINCIPAL: *see* Roof (Fig. 14).

PRIORY: monastic house whose head is a prior or prioress, not an abbot or abbess.

PROSTYLE: with free-standing columns in a row.

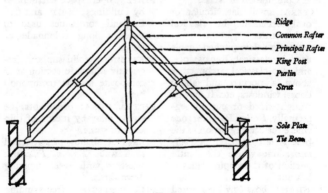

Fig. 14

PULPITUM: stone screen in a major church provided to shut off the choir from the nave and also as a backing for the return choir stalls.

PULVINATED FRIEZE: frieze with a bold convex moulding.

PURLIN: see Roof (Figs. 14, 15).

PUTHOLE or PUTLOCK HOLE: putlocks are the short horizontal timbers on which during construction the boards of scaffolding rest. Putholes or putlock holes are the holes in the wall for putlocks, which often are not filled in after construction is complete.

PUTTO: small naked boy.

QUADRANGLE: inner courtyard in a large building.

QUARRY: in stained-glass work, a small diamond- or square-shaped piece of glass set diagonally.

QUATREFOIL: see Foil.

QUEEN-POSTS: see Roof (Fig. 15).

QUOINS: dressed stones at the angles of a building. Sometimes all the stones are of the same size; more often they are alternately large and small.

RADIATING CHAPELS: chapels projecting radially from an ambulatory or an apse.

RAFTER: see Roof.

RAMPART: stone wall or wall of earth surrounding a castle, fortress, or fortified city.

RAMPART-WALK: path along the inner face of a rampart.

REBATE: continuous rectangular notch cut on an edge.

REBUS: pun, a play on words. The literal translation and illustration of a name for artistic and heraldic purposes (Belton = bell, tun).

RECUSANT CHALICE: chalice made after the Reformation and before Catholic Emancipation for Roman Catholic use.

REEDING: decoration with parallel convex mouldings touching one another.

REFECTORY: dining hall; see Frater.

RENDERING: plastering of an outer wall.

REPOUSSÉ: decoration of metal work by relief designs, formed by beating the metal from the back.

REREDOS: structure behind and above an altar.

RESPOND: half-pier bonded into a wall and carrying one end of an arch.

RETABLE: altarpiece, a picture or piece of carving, standing behind and attached to an altar.

RETICULATION: see Tracery (Fig. 20e).

REVEAL: that part of a jamb (q.v.) which lies between the glass or door and the outer surface of the wall.

RIB-VAULT: see Vault.

ROCOCO: latest phase of the Baroque style, current in most Continental countries between c.1720 and c.1760.

ROLL MOULDING: moulding of semicircular or more than semicircular section.

ROMANESQUE: that style in architecture which was current in the C11 and C12 and preceded the Gothic style (in England often called Norman). (Some scholars extend the use of the term Romanesque back to the C10 or C9.)

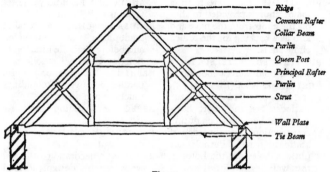

Ridge
Common Rafter
Collar Beam
Purlin
Queen Post
Principal Rafter
Purlin
Strut
Wall Plate
Tie Beam

Fig. 15

ROMANO-BRITISH: A somewhat vague term applied to the period and cultural features of Britain affected by the Roman occupation of the C 1–5 A.D.

ROOD: cross or crucifix.

ROOD LOFT: singing gallery on the top of the rood screen, often supported by a coving.

ROOD SCREEN: see Screen.

ROOD STAIRS: stairs to give access to the rood loft.

ROOF: *Single-framed:* if consisting entirely of transverse members (such as rafters with or without braces, collars, tie-beams, king-posts or queen-posts, etc.) not tied together longitudinally. *Double-framed:* if longitudinal members (such as a ridge beam and purlins) are employed. As a rule in such cases the rafters are divided into stronger principals and weaker subsidiary rafters. *Hipped:* roof with sloped instead of vertical ends. *Mansard:* roof with a double slope, the

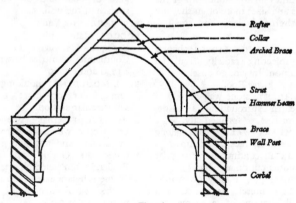

Rafter
Collar
Arched Brace
Strut
Hammer Beam
Brace
Wall Post
Corbel

Fig. 16

lower slope being larger and steeper than the upper. *Saddleback:* tower roof shaped like an ordinary gabled timber roof. The following members have special names: *Rafter:* roof-timber sloping up from the wall plate to the ridge. *Principal:* principal rafter, usually corresponding to the main bay divisions of the nave or chancel below. *Wall Plate:* timber laid longitudinally on the top of a wall. *Purlin:* longitudinal member laid parallel with wall plate and ridge beam some way up the slope of the roof. *Tie-beam:* beam connecting the two slopes of a roof across at its foot, usually at the height of the wall plate, to prevent the roof from spreading. *Collar-beam:* tie-beam applied higher up the slope of the roof. *Strut:* upright timber connecting the tie-beam with the rafter above it. *King-post:* upright timber connecting a tie-beam and collar-beam with the ridge beam. *Queen-posts:* two struts placed symmetrically on a tie-beam or collar-beam. *Braces:* inclined timbers inserted to strengthen others. Usually braces connect a collar-beam with the rafters below or a tie-beam with the wall below. Braces can be straight or curved (also called arched). *Hammer-beam:* beam projecting at right angles, usually from the top of a wall, to carry arched braces or struts and arched braces. (*See* Figs. 14, 15, 16.)

ROSE WINDOW (or WHEEL WINDOW): circular window with patterned tracery arranged to radiate from the centre.

ROTUNDA: building circular in plan.

RUBBLE: building stones, not square or hewn, nor laid in regular courses.

RUSTICATION: *rock-faced* if the surfaces of large blocks of ashlar stone are left rough like rock; *smooth* if the ashlar blocks are smooth and separated by V-joints; *banded* if the separation by V-joints applies only to the horizontals.

SADDLEBACK: see Roof.

SALTIRE CROSS: equal-limbed cross placed diagonally.

SANCTUARY: (1) area around the main altar of a church (*see* Presbytery); (2) sacred site consisting of wood or stone uprights enclosed by a circular bank and ditch. Beginning in the Neolithic, they were elaborated in the succeeding Bronze Age. The best known examples are Stonehenge and Avebury.

SARCOPHAGUS: elaborately carved coffin.

SCAGLIOLA: material composed of cement and colouring matter to imitate marble.

SCALLOPED CAPITAL: development of the block capital (q.v.) in which the single semi-circular surface is elaborated into a series of truncated cones (Fig. 17).

Fig. 17

SCARP: artificial cutting away of the ground to form a steep slope.

SCREEN: *Parclose screen:* screen separating a chapel from the rest of a church. *Rood screen:* screen below the rood (q.v.), usually at the W end of a chancel.

SCREENS PASSAGE: passage between the entrances to kitchen, buttery, etc., and the screen behind which lies the hall of a medieval house.

SEDILIA: seats for the priests (usually three) on the S side of the chancel of a church.

SEGMENTAL ARCH: *see* Arch.

SET-OFF: *see* Weathering.

SEXPARTITE: *see* Vault.

SGRAFFITO: pattern incised into plaster so as to expose a dark surface underneath.

SHAFT-RING: motif of the C12 and C13 consisting of a ring round a circular pier or a shaft attached to a pier.

SHEILA-NA-GIG: fertility figure, usually with legs wide open.

SILL: lower horizontal part of the frame of a window.

SLATEHANGING: the covering of walls by overlapping rows of slates, on a timber substructure.

SOFFIT: underside of an arch, lintel, etc.

SOLAR: upper living-room of a medieval house.

SOPRAPORTE: painting above the door of a room, usual in the C17 and C18.

SOUNDING BOARD: horizontal board or canopy over a pulpit. Also called Tester.

SPANDREL: triangular surface between one side of an arch, the horizontal drawn from its apex, and the vertical drawn from its springer; also the surface between two arches.

SPERE-TRUSS: roof truss on two free-standing posts to mask the division between screens passage and hall. The screen itself, where a spere-truss exists, was originally movable.

SPIRE: tall pyramidal or conical pointed erection often built on top of a tower, turret, etc. *Broach Spire:* a broach is a sloping half-pyramid of masonry or wood introduced at the base of each of the four oblique faces of a tapering octagonal spire with the object of effecting the transition from the square to the octagon. The *splayed foot spire* is a variation of the broach form found principally in the south-eastern counties. In this form the four cardinal faces are splayed out near their base, to cover the corners, while the oblique (or intermediate) faces taper away to a point. *Needle Spire:* thin spire rising from the centre of a tower roof, well inside the parapet.

SPIRELET: *see* Flèche.

SPLAY: chamfer, usually of the jamb of a window.

SPRINGING: level at which an arch rises from its supports.

SQUINCH: arch or system of concentric arches thrown across the angle between two walls to support a superstructure, for example a dome (Fig. 18).

SQUINT: a hole cut in a wall or through a pier to allow a view of the main altar of a church from places whence it could not otherwise be seen (also called Hagioscope).

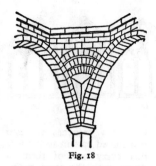

Fig. 18

STALL: carved seat, one of a row, made of wood or stone.

STAUNCHION: upright iron or steel member.

STEEPLE: the tower of a church together with a spire, cupola, etc.

STIFF-LEAF: E.E. type of foliage of many-lobed shapes (Fig. 19).

Fig. 19

STILTED: see Arch.

STOREY-POSTS: the principal posts of a timber-framed wall.

STOUP: vessel for the reception of holy water, usually placed near a door.

STRAINER ARCH: arch inserted across a room to prevent the walls from leaning.

STRAPWORK: C16 decoration consisting of interlaced bands, and forms similar to fretwork or cut and bent leather.

STRETCHER: see Brickwork.

STRING COURSE: projecting horizontal band or moulding set in the surface of a wall.

STRUT: see Roof.

STUCCO: plaster work.

STUDS: the subsidiary vertical timber members of a timber-framed wall.

SWAG: festoon formed by a carved piece of cloth suspended from both ends.

TABERNACLE: richly ornamented niche or free-standing canopy. Usually contains the Holy Sacrament.

TARSIA: inlay in various woods.

TAZZA: shallow bowl on a foot.

TERMINAL FIGURES (TERMS, TERMINI): upper part of a human figure growing out of a pier, pilaster, etc., which tapers towards the base. See also Caryatid, Pilaster.

TERRACOTTA: burnt clay, unglazed.

TESSELLATED PAVEMENT: mosaic flooring, particularly Roman, consisting of small 'tesserae' or cubes of glass, stone, or brick.

TESSERAE: see Tessellated Pavement.

TESTER: see Sounding Board.

TETRASTYLE: having four detached columns.

THREE-DECKER PULPIT: pulpit with Clerk's Stall below and Reading Desk below the Clerk's Stall.

TIE-BEAM: see Roof (Figs. 14, 15).

TIERCERON: see Vault (Fig. 21).

TILEHANGING: see Slatehanging.

TIMBER-FRAMING: method of construction where walls are built of timber framework with the spaces filled in by plaster

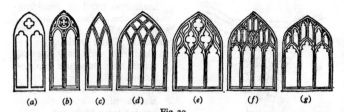

or brickwork. Sometimes the timber is covered over with plaster or boarding laid horizontally.

TOMB-CHEST: chest-shaped stone coffin, the most usual medieval form of funeral monument.

TOUCH: soft black marble quarried near Tournai.

TOURELLE: turret corbelled out from the wall.

TRACERY: intersecting ribwork in the upper part of a window, or used decoratively in blank arches, on vaults, etc. *Plate tracery: see* Fig. 20(a). Early form of tracery where decoratively shaped openings are cut through the solid stone infilling in a window head. *Bar tracery:* a form introduced into England *c.*1250. Intersecting ribwork made up of slender shafts, continuing the lines of the mullions of windows up to a decorative mesh in the head of the window. *Geometrical tracery: see* Fig. 20(b). Tracery characteristic of *c.* 1250–1310 consisting chiefly of circles or foiled circles. *Y-tracery: see* Fig. 20(c). Tracery consisting of a mullion which branches into two forming a Y shape; typical of *c.* 1300. *Intersecting tracery: see* Fig. 20(d). Tracery in which each mullion of

a window branches out into two curved bars in such a way that every one of them is drawn with the same radius from a different centre. The result is that every light of the window is a lancet and every two, three, four, etc., lights together form a pointed arch. This treatment also is typical of *c.* 1300. *Reticulated tracery: see* Fig. 20(e). Tracery typical of the early C14 consisting entirely of circles drawn at top and bottom into ogee shapes so that a net-like appearance results. *Panel tracery: see* Fig. 20(f) and (g). Perp tracery, which is formed of upright straight-sided panels above lights of a window.

TRANSEPT: transverse portion of a cross-shaped church.

TRANSOM: horizontal bar across the openings of a window.

TRANSVERSE ARCH: *see* Vault.

TRIBUNE: *see* Gallery.

TRICIPUT, SIGNUM TRICIPUT: sign of the Trinity expressed by three faces belonging to one head.

TRIFORIUM: arcaded wall passage or blank arcading facing the nave at the height of the aisle roof and below the clerestory (q.v.) windows. (*See* Gallery.)

TRIGLYPHS: blocks with vertical

grooves separating the metopes (q.v.) in the Doric frieze (Fig. 12).

TROPHY: sculptured group of arms or armour, used as a memorial of victory.

TRUMEAU: stone mullion (q.v.) supporting the tympanum (q.v.) of a wide doorway.

TUMULUS: *see* Barrow.

TURRET: very small tower, round or polygonal in plan.

TUSCAN: *see* Order.

TYMPANUM: space between the lintel of a doorway and the arch above it.

UNDERCROFT: vaulted room, sometimes underground, below a church or chapel.

UNIVALLATE: of a hill-fort: defended by a single bank and ditch.

UPPER PALAEOLITHIC: *see* Palaeolithic.

VAULT: *Barrel-vault: see* Tunnel-vault. *Cross-vault: see* Groin-vault. *Domical vault:* square or polygonal dome rising direct on a square or polygonal bay, the curved surfaces separated by groins (q.v.). *Fan-vault:* late medieval vault where all ribs springing from one springer are of the same length, the same distance from the next, and the same curvature. *Groin-vault* or *Cross-vault:* vault of two tunnel-vaults of identical shape intersecting each other at r. angles. Chiefly Norman and Renaissance. *Lierne:* tertiary rib, that is, rib which does not spring either from one of the main springers or from the central

boss. Introduced in the C14, continues to the C16. *Quadripartite vault:* one wherein one bay of vaulting is divided into four parts. *Rib-vault:* vault with diagonal ribs projecting along the groins. *Ridge-rib:* rib along the longitudinal or transverse ridge of a vault. Introduced in the early C13. *Sexpartite vault:* one wherein one bay of quadripartite vaulting is divided into two parts transversely so that each bay of vaulting has six parts. *Tierceron:* secondary rib, that is, rib which issues from one of the main springers or the central boss and leads to a place on a ridge-rib. Introduced in the early C13. *Transverse arch:* arch separating one bay of a vault from the next. *Tunnel-vault* or *Barrel-vault:* vault of semicircular or pointed section. Chiefly Norman and Renaissance. (*See* Fig. 21.)

VAULTING SHAFT: vertical member leading to the springer of a vault.

VENETIAN WINDOW: window with three openings, the central one arched and wider than the outside ones. Current in England chiefly in the C17–18.

VERANDA: open gallery or balcony with a roof on light, usually metal, supports.

VESICA: oval with pointed head and foot.

VESTIBULE: anteroom or entrance hall.

VILLA: (1) according to Gwilt (1842) 'a country house for the residence of opulent persons'; (2) Romano-British country houses cum farms, to which the description given in (1)

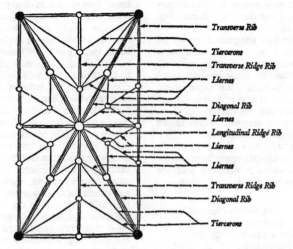

Transverse Rib

Tiercerons

Transverse Ridge Rib

Liernes

Diagonal Rib

Liernes

Longitudinal Ridge Rib

Liernes

Liernes

Transverse Ridge Rib

Diagonal Rib

Tiercerons

Fig. 21

more or less applies. They developed with the growth of urbanization. The basic type is the simple corridor pattern with rooms opening off a single passage; the next stage is the addition of wings. The courtyard villa fills a square plan with subsidiary buildings and an enclosure wall with a gate facing the main corridor block.

VITRIFIED: made similar to glass.

VITRUVIAN OPENING: A door or window which diminishes towards the top, as advocated by Vitruvius, bk. IV, chapter VI.

VOLUTE: spiral scroll, one of the component parts of an Ionic column (*see* Order).

VOUSSOIR: wedge-shaped stone used in arch construction.

WAGON ROOF: roof in which by closely set rafters with

arched braces the appearance of the inside of a canvas tilt over a wagon is achieved. Wagon roofs can be panelled or plastered (ceiled) or left uncovered.

WAINSCOT: timber lining to walls.

WALL PLATE: *see* Roof.

WATERLEAF: leaf shape used in later C12 capitals. The waterleaf is a broad, unribbed, tapering leaf curving up towards the angle of the abacus and turned in at the top (Fig. 22).

Fig. 22

WEALDEN HOUSE: timber-framed house with the hall in the centre and wings projecting only slightly and only on the jutting upper floor. The roof, however, runs through without a break between wings and hall, and the eaves of the hall part are therefore exceptionally deep. They are supported by diagonal, usually curved, braces starting from the short inner sides of the overhanging wings and rising parallel with the front wall of the hall towards the centre of the eaves.

WEATHERBOARDING: overlapping horizontal boards, covering a timber-framed wall.

WEATHERING: sloped horizontal surface on sills, buttresses, etc., to throw off water.

WEEPERS: small figures placed in niches along the sides of some medieval tombs (also called Mourners).

WHEEL WINDOW: *see* Rose Window.

INDEX OF PLATES

INDEX OF ARTISTS

INDEX OF PLACES

ADDENDA
(AUGUST 1965)

pp. 55 and 147 [Abingdon, The Chequer, and Great Coxwell barn.] In their excellent paper in *Medieval Archaeology*, vol. 8, 1964, Messrs J. M. Fletcher and P. S. Spokes discuss crown-post roofs, i.e. roofs in which the kingpost is replaced by, as it were, a kingpost truncated at the level of the collar-beam. Some of their findings could already be incorporated in the text, but in addition attention must be drawn to the Abingdon Chequer (p. 55), whose roofing is of *c*. 1340, and to the explanation of the grandeur of the Great Coxwell barn (p. 147) by the fact of Great Coxwell Manor belonging to the Cistercian Abbey of Beaulieu in Hampshire.

The following additions were very generously communicated to me by Mr Paul Thompson, who is working on a Butterfield biography.

p. 68 [Ascot Priory.] Mr Thompson gives the date of the chapel as 1885.

p. 75 [Avington.] The church was restored by *Butterfield* in 1847, and he also designed at the same time the former RECTORY opposite the church.

p. 84 [Beech Hill.] The PARSONAGE is by *Butterfield* too.

p. 166 [Letcombe Bassett.] SCHOOL. By *Butterfield*. *c*. 1860.

p. 214 [Shaw.] SHAW–CUM–DONNINGTON SCHOOL. 1875 by *Butterfield*; master's house 1883.

p. 254 [Wantage, King Alfred Grammar School.] The back buildings are by *Butterfield*, 1872.

Unless otherwise stated, the author is Nikolaus Pevsner. The date given is the date of the latest revised edition.

* Revised edition to be published by 1990.

‡ Revision starting.

§ The revised texts of *London 2: Except the Cities of London and Westminster* and *Middlesex* are incorporated as appropriate in the new volumes *London 2*, *London 3*, and *London 4*, all by Bridget Cherry.

Another Glass of
Champagne

Jenny Kane

To the people behind the characters of Amy, Jack, Rob, Phil, Paul, Kit, and Peggy.
You know who you are.
Thank you.

To all my friends at Jurassic Costa in Devon, for serving me an insane amount of coffee while I wrote this novel.

And to Greg Rees, who has supported me throughout the writing of the entire *Another Cup of ...* series. Without Greg, Amy, Jack, and Kit would never have made the leap from my imagination to five separate stories.

Jenny x

Prologue

Sticking her head out of the bedroom window, Amy took a huge lungful of fresh air. Even though her morning sickness had passed with merciful speed, the aroma of the paint she and Paul were decorating their spare room with was making her decidedly queasy.

'I thought this was supposed to be odourless paint?'

'It is.' Paul smiled at his wife as he put down the yellow paint-covered roller. 'Why don't you take a break? There's not much left to do now.'

Amy leaned against the windowsill. 'I'm fine – and anyway, it's my own fault. I should never have got on my hands and knees to paint the skirting board. Thank you for not saying "I told you so," by the way.'

Sinking onto the chair Paul had placed in the middle of the decorating chaos, Amy rubbed a palm over her bump in wonder. It seemed to be getting bigger by the hour, never mind by the day. 'Have Phil and Rob managed to make any contact with Jack yet?'

'Not a word.' Paul scraped the remains of the paint from the roller tray onto his brush and dabbed at a patchy place on the wall. 'Rob hasn't had any replies to his texts and emails. He reckons Jack is probably somewhere really remote with no Wi-Fi.'

'Hmmm. Well, I hope he resurfaces soon, or I'll have had this baby before he even knows I'm expecting one.'

Paul stretched his arms above his head to loosen the muscles cramped from painting. 'He'll turn up sooner or later. Jack always does.'

JUNE

In which we catch up with the regulars of Pickwicks Coffee Shop.

There are many changes afoot...

Chapter One

Saturday 4th June 2016

The beep of the low battery warning on Kit's laptop snapped her out of the daze she had been lost in for the last half an hour.

Grateful that the sound had gone unnoticed by Peggy, who was zipping around the tables of Pickwicks Coffee Shop serving customers, Kit shut down her computer. She didn't bother pressing the 'save' button first, because she hadn't typed a single word worth saving.

Kit checked her watch. There were about twenty minutes until Amy was due to arrive for a chat and a cuppa. It would be good to see her friend; Kit just hoped Amy wouldn't want to talk about her pregnancy too much. She wasn't sure why, but she couldn't face baby talk today. It certainly wasn't because Amy went on and on about her impending motherhood. In fact, now she thought about it, Amy talked about it surprisingly infrequently, especially considering she was coming to parenthood so late in life.

Digging her diary from her copious shoulder bag, Kit flicked through its pages. The deadline for the completion of the novel she was supposed to be working on was drawing ever closer. It was already impossibly close when she factored in that she was four weeks behind her schedule.

Despite the warmth of the day, she shivered as she wrapped her hands around her mug of coffee. She was *never* behind schedule. Peggy, Pickwicks' owner and her good friend, often joked that she was as punctual as a full stop. But recently, her mind seemed to drift off into a world of its own without the slightest provocation, and she didn't seem to have the power to stop it.

It wasn't that her ever-fertile imagination had stopped working, or even that her mind was constantly throwing ideas for future books at her – it had always had done that. This was a new, far more disconcerting feeling of a disconnection from the words that always lived in her head.

If she was honest, this lack of control over her writing frightened the life out of her. Although it hadn't been that many years since Kit had won her first proper publishing deal – she had since been lucky enough to have a short string of novels published – she sometimes felt life had been very much easier when she'd been a struggling writer of erotica. All she'd had to do back then was produce a couple of short stories a month for an American website. The ideas had never stopped, and if ever she got stuck over a particular story request, Peggy was always ready with a saucy suggestion.

Those days were well and truly gone, and suddenly Kit missed their simplicity.

Only once before had she felt this off-kilter. That had been when Amy first arrived in Richmond, innocently tipping Kit's relationship with Jack – their mutual friend *and* mutual ex-boyfriend – into total confusion. Not least because Jack, now happily gay, had never told Kit when they'd been together that he'd once loved another girl. It hadn't mattered that their own doomed relationship had been years before – Kit had found her always low self-confidence rocked to the extent where she began to doubt everything and everyone in her life.

Still, Kit told herself as she sat a little straighter in her wooden chair, *that's all history now*. The situation between herself, Amy, and Jack had felt insurmountable at the time, and yet it had worked out for the best in the end. *And so will this. It's only writer's block, for goodness' sake, it happens to every writer at some point! You're going to be fine.*

'My goodness, woman, you look like the proverbial beached whale!'

Amy grinned at the teasing smile on her former boss's face. 'Thanks, Peggy. I know I can rely on you to be ready with a huge compliment!'

2

'Huge is the word, and you are more than welcome!' Taking advantage of a lull in custom, Peggy followed Amy to where Kit was working, and pulled out a chair for her friend before sitting down herself. 'So how long have you got to go now?'

'Only two months, which is nothing like as long as I need to get ready, or even get my head around what's happening to me! I have far too much to do before the baby comes, although we've almost finished decorating the nursery at last. I haven't even managed to find anyone to cover my job at Home Hunters yet.'

Amy thanked Megan, Pickwicks' chief waitress, as she delivered a tray of drinks and half a huge carrot cake for the three friends, before asking Kit, 'I don't suppose that lovely husband of yours fancies coming back to the business while I'm on maternity leave?'

Kit shook her head. 'Not a hope. It did cross my mind after Phil gave up running Home Hunters that he might have withdrawal symptoms and want to go back, but he took to running the bookshop like a duck to water. I can't see him ever going back. And he wouldn't have the time, to be honest. Did I tell you that they're so busy now, he and Rob have employed a guy to help them with their new educational courses at Kew?'

Amy beamed. 'No, you didn't. That's fantastic! I bet Jack would be thrilled for them if he was here.' Suddenly pensive, she picked up her cup, 'I don't suppose either of you have heard from Jack?'

Peggy shook her head as Kit said, 'Not a word. I thought he'd keep in touch with you though, Amy, even if he went quiet on the rest of us.'

'Paul says he'll turn up eventually, but I'd rather like to be able to tell Jack about this bundle,' Amy patted her stomach, 'before he or she stops being just a bump in my jumper. I might ask him if he wants to be godfather.'

Kit nodded. 'Jack is godfather to the twins, and although he's a dreadful role model on the morals front, both Thomas and Helena have always found him great fun, and say that having a gay godfather is, and I quote, "Well cool".'

Peggy had never understood the loyalty Jack's two ex-

3

girlfriends felt for him considering how appallingly he'd treated them both. She certainly wouldn't want anyone who'd stood her up on her wedding day – albeit only in the role of usher – to be a godparent to *her* child, but she simply asked, 'How long has he been AWOL for?'

Amy frowned. 'It must be more or less four years since I last saw him, and about twelve months since I last spoke to him. It's not so much being AWOL as missing in action. How about you, Kit?'

Peggy and Amy exchanged glances as they saw Kit staring blankly into her soup bowl-sized cup of black coffee.

'Kit? You with us?'

'What? Oh, sorry, guys. I didn't get much sleep last night, I phased out for a minute. What was the question?'

Peggy had noticed how distracted Kit had been lately, although instinct told her that she shouldn't ask her friend about it yet. 'When did you last hear from Jack, honey?'

'I'm not sure, must be at least a year. That is very Jack though, isn't it. I bet he'd get a kick out of the fact that we're all back here wondering where he is and if he's OK.'

Amy, who'd had similar thoughts herself, grimaced. 'I wouldn't be surprised – although I'd like to think that at his age he's finally grown out of playing those games.'

Kit and Peggy laughed in unison. 'No chance!'

'I assume he's either still travelling around the world – or working in someone's garden, using that horticultural qualification he got after Paul and I got married.'

'Sounds possible, and of course,' Kit let her inner storyteller go in a way she wished she could on paper, 'if Jack has spent all the inheritance his grandfather left him, he could have got a job in the grounds of some posh house, had a torrid affair with the heir to the manor, and be in the middle of a society scandal.'

Amy smiled as Peggy divided the carrot cake into mountainous slices. 'That sounds entirely possible, and I sort of hope it's true! The boyfriend bit, I mean, rather than the scandal bit.'

Pulling her plate closer, Kit shrugged. 'I'm not sure he'd risk another relationship, not after Toby hurt him like that. I suspect

4

he's reverted to full-on sleeping around mode.' Realising she had sounded rather curt, she added, 'I'd like to be wrong though. If he settled down a bit, he might come home.'

Megan, laden with a tray of used cups and saucers, walked into Pickwicks' kitchen just in time to see Scott pull open the dishwasher, ready to put in a pile of baking tins. 'Room for a few more bits and pieces?'

Peggy's husband winked at her. 'For you, anything!'

'Thanks, Scott.' Megan began to stack the china between the trays.

Leaning his tall frame back against the sink, Scott stretched out his right leg which, ever since he'd been involved in a road accident several years earlier, had a tendency to stiffen up as soon as he stood still. 'How busy is it out there?'

Megan frowned; Scott suddenly looked unusually serious. 'Empty customer-wise. It's just Amy, Kit, and Peggy chatting at the moment. Everything alright?'

'Wait there a second.'

As Scott disappeared, a sense of foreboding crept over Megan. Did Peggy and Scott have bad news? Were they going to cut her hours? Guilt played around in the back of her mind. Had they worked out that she was considering hunting for a new job? They couldn't have, she hadn't told anyone. But if she and Nick were ever going to move in together, let alone save up for a home of their own, then she was going to have to start earning more than she did as a waitress…

Feeling more irrationally disloyal with every tick of the wall clock, Megan was relieved when Scott and Peggy came into the kitchen.

'Kit's keeping an eye on the shop for us.' Peggy smiled at her waitress. 'No need to look so worried, honey, we aren't about to sack you or anything. We've come to a decision, and we wanted you to be in the know, as it could affect you directly.'

'Affect me?' Megan looked from Scott to Peggy. 'How?'

Scott dug his wife in the ribs. 'Don't freak the girl out by being so mysterious, woman. Explain properly.'

'Sorry, Megan, but we don't want anyone else knowing, not yet anyway. This is just between the three of us, OK? Top secret.'

'Um, yes. Right.'

'The thing is ... we're doing well at Pickwicks, and have been for the last few years, and a lot of that is thanks to you and your hard work. We've been mulling over the idea of opening another branch for a while now, and we've decided to go for it. So, assuming we can find suitable premises, we'd like you to manage the new place. What do you think?'

Chapter Two

Staring out of the train window, Jack exhaled a long, slow breath. Was this how Amy had felt when she had first come to Richmond after her years of self-imposed exile in Scotland? Sort of excited, but absolutely terrified at the same time?

Jack wondered if, once he'd worked up the courage to go and see her, Amy would notice the parallels between their situations. A smile crossed his face. However she reacted, she would forgive him for not being in touch over the past few years. Amy always forgave him. For everything.

In his mind, he'd left Richmond for a good reason. Although he knew Amy accepted he'd needed to leave, he was less sure she understood why – which was why he'd decided to break off even phone and email contact with her. It was also why he hadn't told any of his friends where he was; just to see if that helped.

It wasn't that Jack *wasn't* happy for Amy and Paul to be living the fairytale, but the fact that they were together, while he was still alone, was sometimes hard to take – especially when he knew Amy's love could have been his if only he'd been prepared to risk it all those years ago. This nagging thought – one he accepted was utterly ridiculous, as he knew that he'd never have been able to ignore his sexuality, even for Amy – made him a rather less kind human being than he would have liked. He knew that until he could get past feeling he was missing out on something that all his friends took for granted, they were better off without him and the chip on his shoulder.

Amy would understand, he was sure. Kit, on the other hand, might not be as understanding…

7

Jack's smile disappeared. Years ago, back when they were dating, Kit would have forgiven him anything – but since Amy had come back into his life, and both women had become good friends in their own right, Kit had become much stronger. Jack had learnt that Kit had always hated how he could make her doubt her strength and resilience. These days she was so much more equipped to deal with him and his bullshit – and he knew it.

Perhaps he shouldn't be coming back. After all, he knew he was as emotionally messed-up as ever – but he had to go somewhere, and anyway, whether he wanted to admit it or not, he'd been getting homesick.

Plus he'd had to get away from Kent…

Opening his eyes, Jack sighed as the train's sudden slowing announced that they were arriving at St Pancras. Here he was again. Back in London, fleeing from yet another cock-up in his love life, and with nowhere to call home. He wished he hadn't so rashly sold his place in Mortlake – he'd got far less than it was worth, too, in his haste to make a clean break.

There were several Tube connections to Richmond Jack could have chosen to see his old friends straight away, but as he stood in the bustling station, he found himself unable to move a step further.

It wasn't like him to be assailed by doubt, but this time it was different. Whatever he did, he always managed to upset people. He never meant to; usually he never even saw his offences coming. On this occasion however, he knew that if he was going to go ahead with his latest plan and really make it work, he was going to cause trouble for some of his friends.

And yet, the more he thought about it, the more he was sure it was the right thing to do.

Heading into the first coffee shop he came to in the station's sizable shopping corridor, Jack ordered a gigantic latte and much-needed Danish, and forced himself to think sensibly.

He had known that his days as assistant chef at Kennedy's Bistro were numbered, but over the last few days the tension between him and Gareth, the head chef and owner-manager, had moved far beyond the usual levels of simmering dislike and bad language found in any professional kitchen, and had become unpleasantly personal.

They should never have spent the night together. Angrily, Jack cut his Danish into four pieces, taking his annoyance at his own stupidity out on the soft, sticky pastry.

He hadn't seen it coming, though. One evening, three weeks ago, after a particularly tough shift in the kitchen when everything that could have gone wrong had gone wrong, the angry banter between and Jack and his boss had taken a step into physical contact, with Gareth slapping him around the face.

They'd been the only two people left in the kitchen, and Jack's retaliation, grabbing Gareth by the collar of his shirt to tell him in no uncertain terms exactly what he thought of him, had led to them tripping. Before he'd known what was happening, Gareth had been knocked backwards, Jack had fallen on top of him, and they were exchanging hard, angry kisses.

Still shocked by his actions, and astounded that Gareth hadn't sacked him on the spot but had joined in with the heady episode – which had ended up with them spending a very ill-advised night together – Jack sighed into his glass mug.

The next morning, Gareth had suggested they make their partnership more of a permanent thing. Horrified, Jack had rejected Gareth's offer of a relationship with no tact whatsoever, and his boss had reverted to his normal state of barely controlled hatred, further fuelled by his hurt pride. Jack had recognised there and then he'd have to leave, and the sooner the better.

Knowing that Gareth would never give him a good reference, Jack had realised he'd have to buy his own place if he wanted to stay working as a chef. As soon as the idea of buying a restaurant had come into his head, he'd known it was precisely the right thing for him to do. He'd loved owning and running the Reading Nature bookshop in Kew. Well, he had until Toby had come along, made Jack fall in love with him, and then screwed him over … Shaking his head to dispel the image of his ex, who'd run off with another, far richer, man

9

after they'd been together for nearly three years, Jack swallowed hard. At least he knew his old shop was in good hands: his friend Rob, and Kit's husband Phil, who now owned Reading Nature between them, were making a real go of it.

Jack missed his old friends far more than he'd imagined he would. Over the past few days, he'd regretted cutting himself off from them so completely, even though it had felt like the only thing to do at the time. So, after two days of researching restaurants for sale in London, Jack had made another impulsive decision – but he was determined that this one would last. This was something he would stick with for the rest of his life.

When he'd arrived at work yesterday to tell Gareth that he was giving in his month's notice, Jack had walked in to the kitchen to overhear the chef bad-mouthing him to one of the waiting staff about something he hadn't actually done. With one look at Gareth, Jack quit there and then. He turned on his heel, returned to his rented bungalow, and phoned the estate agent responsible for the restaurant he was interested in.

Taking a gulp of his latte, Jack watched the throng of afternoon travellers. He couldn't help but speculate about where they were all going, and if any of them had managed to mess up their lives as often as he had.

This time though, *this time*, he *was* going to get it right.

Knocking back the rest of his coffee and pastry, Jack got up and started talking to himself under his breath. 'First things first. I will head to the estate agent's office, then I'll grab the Tube to Hounslow and book into my hotel, and then tomorrow I'll go to Richmond and face reality. Tomorrow I will decide which friend to say sorry to first.'

Hope and relief vied for top billing in Megan's head as she cut a path through her fellow Underground travellers to meet her boyfriend, Nick.

Megan and Nick had been an item ever since they'd met at a charity auction held at Pickwicks. Scott and Peggy had been raising money for the Royal Free Hospital, as the hospital's Spinal Ward had done so much for Scott after his accident that

10

he and Peggy had wanted to thank them. Megan had been in charge of liaising with the ward administrator – Nick.

For a while now, Megan had secretly been hoping he'd ask her to live with him. Now he had, though, the fact London was a ridiculously expensive place to live had stolen some of their joy. The need for Megan to earn a higher wage was becoming increasingly urgent if they were ever going to afford the rent on a decent-sized place for two, rather than continuing to live in different communal houses.

Although the thought of moving in with Nick was wonderful, Megan had been plagued by thoughts of disloyalty to Peggy and Scott – how could she leave Pickwicks? She loved the work, the customers, and the friends she worked with. Now, perhaps, she could have the best of both worlds: working for Peggy and Scott, but with more responsibility *and* higher wages. She hadn't accepted their offer yet, saying she'd need to talk to Nick first, but she couldn't imagine saying no. She felt as if a weight was being lifted from her shoulders.

'Hey, you!' Nick kissed Megan on the top of her head as she flew into his arms the second he walked out of the hospital reception. 'You look happy.'

'I am! You will never guess what Peggy and Scott are planning.'

Brimming with excitement, Megan told Nick all about their offer to make her manager of 'Pickwicks 2'.

'I honestly can't believe that they want me to run the new café! I've always fancied having a go at working on something for myself.'

'Really? You never said. You're a great artist, why don't you try and make a go of that on your own?'

'Thanks, babe, but it isn't easy to start up a business in London finance-wise. That's why I didn't mention it before – I'd far rather we used our money to move in together. Anyway, this new café idea could be the perfect solution all round. Maybe Peggy would even let me put a few of my pictures on the café walls to sell?'

Keeping his girlfriend close as they weaved their way through the crowds thronging the city streets, Nick gave her one of his huge grins. 'That's brilliant! It'll certainly help us save up for a deposit. Would the wages be higher than you're currently on?'

'That was the impression I got, although I didn't like to ask. I mean, I haven't said I'll do it yet. I wanted to tell you first.'

'How long until this goes ahead? I don't want to rain on your parade or anything, but it could be a while before this all happens. Do they have any premises in mind?'

Megan felt herself deflate a little. 'Um, not yet. But surely they wouldn't have told me if they weren't definitely going to do it?'

'Sorry, I didn't mean to put a downer on things. I just want us to move in together sooner rather than later.'

Reaching up on her tiptoes, Megan kissed her boyfriend on the lips. 'I know; it's OK. I do too. How about I explain our situation to Peggy properly? I haven't told anyone we're house-hunting, I didn't want to jinx it. I'll tell Peggy and Scott I'll take the job if they have somewhere in mind to open in the next three months, but if they can't find an appropriate place for new premises soon, I will have to look for work elsewhere.'

Even as she said it, Megan felt bad. 'You don't think that sounds too pushy and ungrateful, do you?'

Chapter Three

Desperate to make up for the time she'd wasted at Pickwicks, Kit went straight to her study when she got home, determined to write at least five hundred words before Phil came back from work.

Getting comfortable in her leather desk chair and booting her computer into life, she watched the document, with the words *Chapter Five* written on the next new page, open. Kit placed her fingers on the keyboard.

And nothing happened.

She'd heard many authors talk about writer's block, but had been rather dismissive of it, believing it was merely a mood that could be walked off, or a blip that could be solved by taking a quick break. Now she knew different. And although the syndrome certainly manifested itself in different ways for different people, Kit now appreciated precisely how frustrating and debilitating it could be. She could visualise the words in her brain – she could almost touch them – but for some reason they resolutely refused to come out of her fingers, through the keyboard, and onto the screen.

Her fourth novel was due to her publisher in only three months' time, and although it was completely plotted out in her head, and she knew exactly what was going to happen, she just couldn't write it down.

'Damn!' Kit swore at the screen, which was still empty but for the chapter heading, and flicked back to chapter four to re-read the end in the hope it would kick start her brain. She had gone over that paragraph so many times in the past week that she could recite it blindfold.

'What the hell is wrong with me?'

Leaning back in her seat, Kit closed her eyes and spoke sternly to herself. 'Come on, what *is* the matter?' Employing some of the breathing exercises she'd picked up at the one and only yoga class Peggy had managed to drag her to, she tried to slow her pulse. It seemed to be permanently racing these days, as though she was always anxious – which of course she was – but she wasn't really sure why. *Something* had to be behind her word block.

Continuing to talk to the room in general, she tried to rationalise her thoughts. 'OK, is it Phil spending so much time at the shop that's getting you down?'

Although Phil had worked long hours at Home Hunters, since he'd taken over the Reading Nature bookshop with Rob it had ruled his life during the weeks and most weekends since. But he was so happy and passionate about what he was doing. Kit knew that she didn't begrudge Phil a minute of his time at work.

'No, he's happy, so I'm happy.' She mentally crossed marital disharmony off her list. 'So, is it Jack's absence?'

Although Kit had missed her best friend like mad when he'd first disappeared to go and travel the world, she knew she hadn't missed all his drama. Anyway, she'd have had less time to disappear off for random coffee stops with him these days – and when there was time, she had more friends than ever to have coffee with. Now she considered it she realised, with some surprise, that it had been a while before she'd even noticed Jack's calls and emails had stopped.

'Not Jack, then. Not this time!' She rolled her eyes at her past irrational behaviour concerning her long-ago ex. 'So what is it? Come on, Kit. Concentrate!'

She addressed a notion that she knew had passed through her head on more than one occasion. 'Am I worried that this novel won't sell as many copies as the last one?'

Even as she asked herself the question, she started to laugh. 'Of course I'm worried about that! I always am. I was worried about the last one, and the one before, and *definitely* the first one. That sort of worry is normal and healthy. It's a trademark

14

of being a writer!'

Crossing another issue off her list, Kit murmured to herself, 'So, is it the children?'

She felt her pulse accelerate slightly, and a flickering of unease crept up her spine. She opened her eyes with a sigh. She'd been fine about the twins leaving home – hadn't she? Kit had enjoyed going through the UCAS forms with Helena and Thomas, had shared in their excitements and their panics as they'd battled their way through their A levels.

They'd worked hard, and she was optimistic they'd get the grades they needed to go to their chosen universities. It had been great fun exploring Bath with Helena and Exeter with Thomas while on their respective open days. Kit was bursting with pride for both of them, and had no trouble accepting that they were more than ready to get on with making their own way in the world now they were eighteen.

The tears welled up at the corner of Kit's eyes. She hadn't noticed them coming, but now they were washing down her cheeks in a sudden torrent of salty water. 'Is it as simple as that? Am I sad about the twins leaving?'

She wiped away her tears with the back of her hand, and yelled at her laptop, 'Well of course I am, it's normal! But that doesn't mean I'm not happy for them. Why the hell would that stop me writing?'

Lowering her voice, Kit angrily grabbed a handful of tissues from the box on her desk, and tried to rationalise her thoughts further. 'This situation will allow me to write more. I'll have so much extra time when I'm not cooking for them, or washing and ironing their clothes and…'

Dissolving into a new bucket of tears, and without being able to help it, Kit pulled her feet onto the chair seat, cradling herself against the grief she had no idea she'd been carrying, for the loss of something that hadn't actually gone yet.

Phil found his wife sat on the sofa watching repeats of *Friends* on the television, a mountain of screwed-up tissues littering the carpet, and a half-drunk bottle of white wine by her side.

'Kit?' You OK, love?'

15

'Oh, hello. Sorry, I didn't hear you come in. Good day at the shop?'

'Busy. The tourists are starting to arrive in droves now, which can only be good.' Phil's gaze fell on the large empty packet of chocolate buttons. 'You obviously haven't had such a satisfying day.'

Sitting next to his wife, he eased her up against his shoulder and wrapped an arm around her. 'Come on, Kit, what's up? I can't remember the last time I saw you in front of the television before seven o'clock at night, and certainly not with wine rather than coffee.'

'It's the twins.'

'What about them? Where is Helena, anyway?'

'She's at one of her friends' houses, I'm not sure. And God knows where Thomas has reached on his travels. And that's just it, you see.'

'That's just what?' Not for the first time, Kit's inability to explain herself out loud, when she could express herself so clearly in writing, baffled her husband.

'I'm never going to know where they are ever again!' As Kit disappeared into the comfort of Phil's shoulder, fresh tears soaked through the cotton of his shirt.

'So what's brought this on then? You've known the twins were going to leave home ever since they decided on their A level choices.'

'I know – and I *don't* know – if that makes sense. The thing is, until a couple of hours ago I didn't have a clue what was bothering me, I just knew that something wasn't right. Honestly, I've been so excited for the kids. I *am* excited for them.'

'But?'

'But … it's going to be so strange without them here, Phil. You'll miss them too, won't you?'

'Of course I will!. But what's brought this on today? You were fine this morning. Anyway, you'll have much more time to do things like that Scottish literary festival you did just before Christmas. Isn't that what you've always wanted?'

'I thought it was.' Kit took a sustaining gulp of wine, which joined the liquid already sloshing around inside her; the packet of chocolate buttons was an inadequate buffer. 'But … I haven't been able to write. Not for ages now.'

'What?' Phil frowned, 'How d'you mean? You're always tucked away with that computer! What have you been doing, then?'

'Staring blankly into space, mostly.' Kit hauled herself off the sofa and fetched a glass for Phil before passing him the bottle of wine. 'I am *so* behind with my latest book, yet I kept convincing myself it was only a temporary glitch – but the days kept adding up, and now I'm weeks, if not months, behind. Today,' she blew her nose again, 'I finally got fed up with being so feeble, so I made myself face up to things. I made a list of possible worries, trying to discover what was blocking me. It hadn't occurred to me it was premature empty nest syndrome.'

Phil couldn't help but smile. 'Typical Kit! Always in a hurry for everything.'

'Oi!' Kit poked him playfully. 'That's what Jack says about Amy!' Already feeling a bit better for simply sharing her problem, she added 'I've been looking forward to having some time for just the two of us. That's what makes this so odd.'

'Me too. And of course it'll be strange here for a while, but with Thomas already off backpacking around Europe and Helena more or less living at her friends', they've hardly been here since their exams finished anyway.'

'I know.' Kit's stomach made a weird gurgle. 'Oh, I'd better have something to eat before I fall over! I've not drunk that much wine on an empty stomach for a very long time.'

Phil wrapped his wife in his arms. 'Come on, Mrs Lambert, I'm taking you out for a curry. Go and wash your face and brush your hair, and you'll feel much better in no time.'

Staring at her bleary-eyed reflection in the mirror, Kit splashed her face with cold water. Phil was right: getting out and having some food along with a change of scene would do her the world of good.

She felt tired with the relief of having uncovered what was bothering her.

As long as that is *the problem.*

Kit squeezed her eyes closed against the new voice of doubt in the back of her head. 'Of course that's it.' She spoke directly to her reflection as she dried her face, shutting out the insistent voice asking, *Or is there something else going on here?*

Taking some deep breaths, Kit suddenly found herself thinking about Amy, who'd discovered she was pregnant at forty-three, just when she and Paul had given up on having a family. Kit was delighted for her friend, and very much looked forward to lots of cuddles with a new baby. But as she stared hard at herself in the mirror, Kit had to acknowledge that, just as Amy would be starting her family life, her own would be ending…

'I think this one has to be our first choice, don't you?'

Scott passed Peggy one of the two sets of café details he had printed out. 'It's far enough away to not take trade from Pickwicks, but not so far away that we'll be travelling miles between the two.'

Peggy rested her feet on the coffee table in front of the sofa they sat on and flicked her way through the pages she'd read many times before on the computer screen. 'The rent is about right as well. Shall we?'

Scott put his much longer legs up next to his wife's. 'I think we should.'

A mixture of excitement and nerves shot through Peggy. 'We can make this work – can't we?'

'We can. We'll have to work damn hard though.'

'That'll hardly be a change for us then, will it!' Peggy picked up her mug of hot chocolate and cuddled into Scott's side. 'Megan certainly seemed pleased. I know she said she'd have to talk to Nick, but she'll say yes, won't she?'

'I'm sure she will. Megan is a fabulous waitress, but she deserves more of a challenge. It'll be hard to replace her at Pickwicks, mind.'

'We said that about Amy though, didn't we, and we found Megan. I've already got my eyes on a couple of the younger regulars for future waiting staff. In the short term, while we're setting the new place up, I wondered about asking Kit's daughter if she'd like a part-time job.'

Scott beamed his bright white smile. 'That's a fabulous idea! I bet Helena could use the money if she's saving up for university.'

Leaning forward, Scott scooped up a couple of the tablets he'd had to take every evening to keep his lower muscles moving. Knocking the medicine back with a glass of water, he caught Peggy looking at him. 'What?'

'Every now and then I can't believe we've made it his far, not after I nearly lost you.'

Scott pulled his wife up off the sofa, 'I'm here. We made it. Together, and we'll do this together as well. We'll get the new café set up, make an extra income, and then we can kick Plan C into life.'

Peggy hugged Scott tightly. 'Plan C?'

'Yes, Plan A was opening Pickwicks, Plan B is Pickwicks 2, or whatever we call it, and Plan C is buying a bungalow we can retire to.'

'Now that is a plan I like!'

'A five-year plan, OK? Pickwicks 2 this year, and retirement in five years, in time for your sixtieth birthday, and before my legs decide they *really* don't want to do stairs anymore.'

A cloud passed over Peggy's face, but Scott kissed it away. 'It's OK, love, we *will* do this. Life won't floor us ever again.'

Chapter Four

Sunday 5th June

Waking in his hotel room bed, Jack's first thought was that out of all of his friends, it was Amy he should visit first. The appointment to see his potential restaurant wasn't until the following morning, so he had the whole day to carry an olive branch to Amy and then Kit – not to mention Rob, Phil, and Paul if he had time.

'But what do I say to her,' he asked the ceiling, 'after I've bought Amy a black coffee, how do I explain that I left her in the lurch again because I found seeing her happy difficult? That makes me an awful friend.'

Punching the over-plump pillow with his fist, Jack threw back the duvet and sat up. 'You *are* an awful friend. You've proved that over and over again. It would serve you right if Amy called your bluff and told you to sod off.'

It was only eight o'clock in the morning. There was no point in going straight to Amy's house, she and Paul wouldn't be up yet and, anyway, he had the sudden need for a proper dose of fresh air. It was time to get his mind straight.

'Right, Jack, are you listening? You are going to grab a coffee, get dressed, and go to Kew. If walking around the Gardens doesn't clear your head, then nothing will.'

Jack's next thought was that, even though he was in London again, he hadn't spent the best part of the previous evening in a nightclub, and consequently hadn't woken up in a stranger's bed that morning. This was progress. 'Perhaps I'm growing up at last. Maybe if I told Amy that I haven't come back and immediately screwed a man a fraction of my age she'd be proud of me.'

Even as he said the words he realised what an idiot he was. 'Enough! Enough of being a fortysomething teenager.'

Having gobbled down his breakfast at a speed that was guaranteed to give him indigestion, Jack made a beeline for Hounslow East Tube station, and headed towards Kew Gardens. Full of determination that this return to London was the move that would see the start of a new life, a better life, Jack looked affectionately along the road at the pub-like sign which hung outside his old bookshop, Reading Nature.

When he'd first purchased the shop with his grandfather's money, it had never occurred to Jack that he'd want to sell it one day. He'd instantly loved it, with its single bay window, and its Victorian feel. As he walked past now, he could see what a positive effect Phil and Rob were having on the place without him. For a split second Jack felt a twinge of regret, but he knew in his heart that, although it had taken him a long time to find what he wanted to do, he'd been born to be a chef. His head was so full of plans and ideas for his restaurant that he couldn't imagine working with books now. He was happy for Reading Nature to be in such good hands.

As he strolled past the bookshop Jack's head, always full of snippets of songs, was suddenly alive with Dionne Warwick's classic, 'Walk on By'. Immediately he was cross with himself.

He must *not* do that anymore. He knew his comparison of every situation to a pop lyric made him seem flippant even when he was trying to be sincere. Jack winced as he thought back to how he'd used songs to tell both Kit and Amy he couldn't be with them before he'd had the courage to admit to his sexuality; even to himself. *Although*, cutting himself a little slack, he thought, *if I hadn't sent Amy that mixtape then she would never have moved to London in the first place. Still, I really, really must not do that anymore!*

The morning after he had slept with Gareth, a whole compilation worth of songs had lined themselves up in his brain, all of which summed up the situation he found himself up in or the way he felt about it. And before common sense had the chance to kick in, Jack was blurting out lines from George Michael's 'Fastlove'.

The look Gareth had given him was an equal mix of hurt and anger, and in that moment Jack had finally seen what Kit and Amy had been telling him for years. He couldn't keep expressing himself without thinking, not saying what he truly meant, or someone was going to punch him, either through rage or out of sheer frustration.

There and then, Jack had promised himself he wouldn't do the 'song thing', as Kit called it, ever again – but he'd only been back in London a day and he was doing it again. *This has to stop.* It was high time he started using his own words to explain his emotions; he just had the feeling it was going to be a lot harder than it sounded.

Turning through the gates of Kew Gardens, Jack headed toward the Terrace Coffee Shop. He stopped and stared at the café for a while before going inside to place his order. This was where he'd first met Amy again, after she'd returned from living in Scotland.

She'd lived up there for over a decade, having exiled herself largely as a result of the way he'd treated her, and she'd only come back south after he'd sent her a letter explaining why he'd walked out on their relationship – together with, in typical Jack fashion, a tape full of music that summed up his feelings about her. Even now, after so much time had passed, Jack couldn't believe how well Amy had welcomed him back into her life. She'd always been wonderful, especially considering how thoughtlessly he'd treated her.

Sitting outside in the early morning sunshine with an insanely strong double espresso, Jack's mind swirled with both regret and practicality. He knew if he was going to build a better life, a new one where he never hurt anyone, or was hurt by anyone, ever again, then he'd have to come to peace with his own guilt over the way he'd treated Amy and Kit. They might have forgiven him, but he hadn't forgiven himself.

'So,' he muttered under his breath as the sun's rays beat down on his outstretched legs, 'the new me is going to open a restaurant, be a better friend, take no one for granted, remain single as I am a danger to young men everywhere and,' he took a deep sigh, 'probably piss Peggy and Scott off massively in the process, making me no better than the man I was before. Damn! But I can't see what else to do.'

Putting his empty cup down on the table, Jack looked up in time to see an attractive man talking to a group of eager small children on a patch of grass not too far from the café. Smartly dressed, with a good-quality camera hanging around his neck, the man was crouched on the grass so he was at eye level with the children. He was smiling broadly, and whatever it was he was saying to his young charges, they were obviously finding it hilarious.

It was unusual to see a man of that age – Jack surmised he was late twenties – in trousers and not jeans, outside of work. Jack found himself looking at the scene more closely, and grinning along with the children. He'd have laid money on the man having received a public school education. The way he held himself, the neat cut of his dark brown hair, and the tone of his voice gave his background away. *Guess I could be wrong, but I bet I'm not.* Contradicting his decision to keep away from all forms of emotional entanglement, Jack found himself thinking that he'd quite like that, but he wasn't sure if 'that' meant a man who could make him laugh – or a child of his own.

Rupert felt a rush of contentment as he began his solo Sunday lunchtime walk around Kew Gardens. He still couldn't get over how lucky he'd been to get the job at Reading Nature. It had been pure chance. He had entered the shop one day to buy a book on wildlife photography, and walked straight into a conversation between the owners about needing new staff.

This morning's lesson, teaching a group of local children about the magic of Kew in the summertime, had been great fun and as satisfying as usual. When Phil and Rob had first explained what sort of assistant they were looking for, Rupert wasn't sure he'd have the confidence to share his knowledge of nature and photography with the general public. However, teaching small groups about the joy of natural history had quickly become the favourite part of his job.

Even though it took up every Sunday morning, the enthusiasm of the local children who formed Reading Nature's

Kids Club, and their love of tracking squirrels, learning about trees, and spotting birds was boundless. The sense of reward he felt each time he made a child giggle as he pointed out the difference between different sorts of tits was priceless.

Rupert hadn't told his family about his new job as the liaison officer between Reading Nature and Kew Gardens. He knew his mother would be pleased for him, but his father, a wealthy City trader, hadn't forgiven his only son for not following in his footsteps, or at least not finding a profession he could show off about to his associates at the antiquated Gentlemen's Club he attended.

Since studying Law at university, a degree that he had undertaken at his father's insistence, Rupert had gone from one minor job to another until he'd finally stood up to his father and said that a career in the legal profession was not for him. The meeting in his father's study had been short and unpleasant, and Rupert couldn't see how the rift it had caused between them could ever be healed.

His father – always a father and never a dad – refused to understand how Rupert could be content to have no real ambitions in life. It was true that he hadn't cared for anything in particular, not until he'd taken a photography course on a whim and fallen in love with the art form.

'Photography,' his father had declared, in a voice that was laced with prejudice and would brook no argument, 'is the province of pointless arty types, eternal students, and time-wasters.'

Rupert had always been private about all aspects of his life, and shared very little with anyone, but now he was a virtual recluse outside of working hours. He was almost sure his mother suspected that his lack of ex-girlfriends indicated he was gay, although he'd never told her about his one brief boyfriend, which was an experience he was trying hard to forget. If she did know, his mother would never say anything, for although she loved his father, she was very much in his shadow. Rupert was convinced she'd never be able to handle his reaction to having a homosexual son. She was almost as bad as Rupert himself when it came to not being able to stand up to his father and his antiquated attitudes. No, much better to remain celibate and not put his mother in a position of having to take sides between her husband and her only child.

Rupert also suspected that Rob and Phil assumed he was gay. He was grateful that they respected his privacy, and hadn't asked him anything about his sexual preferences.

A slight movement to his right caught Rupert's attention as he paced softly through the quietest parts of the gardens. A robin was perched on the edge of a branch, almost within touching distance. Moving slowly, in almost total silence, Rupert lifted his camera and hoped that the bird wouldn't move as he prepared to take a shot. The national photography competition he intended to enter would be closing soon, and he still hadn't got the dream shot he wanted. Maybe this would be it?

Chapter Five

Monday 6th June

Jack knew he'd taken the coward's way out the day before. Despite all his good intentions when he'd woken up on Sunday morning, he hadn't gone to see Amy or Kit.

He had told himself it was because he wanted to view the outside of his potential restaurant and go through the financial proposal he had to present to his accountant. The cold light of Monday morning saw Jack being more honest with himself. He hadn't gone to see Amy because, as it was the weekend, Paul would probably have been there. For his first meeting with Amy in years, even though he and Paul were pretty good friends in their own right, he wanted to see her alone. And he hadn't gone to visit Kit because he'd promised himself he'd go and explain himself to Amy first.

As Jack walked toward the Home Hunters office, hoping Amy would be able to spare an hour or so for a coffee stop like they used to in the old days, he practiced what he was going to say in his head.

Right: you do not *tell her you left because you found it difficult to see her so happy with Paul when you were so unhappy yourself. Otherwise you tell her the truth – well,* almost *the truth.*

Tell her that you've missed her, that you needed to take time away from the place where Toby broke your heart, and that one place you visited just led to another, and somehow rather than months passing, years went by.

With a bubble of happy excitement growing inside him at the prospect of seeing Amy again, Jack squashed down the anxiety that his presence would not be warmly received this time, and pushed open the door to the Home Hunters office.

Jack leaned against the stone wall outside the office and tried to breathe normally.

Amy hadn't been there. Her PA, a very attractive young woman who'd introduced herself as Lauren, had said Amy was having an antenatal check at the doctors today.

An antenatal check!

Amy was pregnant!

Of all the scenarios he'd pictured; of all the reactions he'd imagined he'd have to face on his return, Amy being pregnant hadn't crossed his mind. She was in her forties, for goodness' sake!

Once upon a time Jack had wondered if he and Amy would have kids together. It had only been a fleeting thought, perhaps, but if he was going to be anyone's father, Amy would have been their mother.

Jack's head started to crowd with visions of the man in the park surrounded by happy children, Kit's twins playing with him when they were younger, how his niece and nephew loved spending time with Uncle Jack...

He was pulled out of his self-pity by a sound from across the other side of the street. A young mother, pushing a pram, was dragging a screaming toddler along after her. She looked exhausted, and about ready to lie on the ground and start screaming herself.

OK, life, thanks for the reality check!

As soon as he walked through the door and found himself standing in the foyer of the empty Italian restaurant, Jack knew it was the right place for him. Politely asking the estate agent if he could wander around on his own for a while, Jack moved slowly through the main dining area, taking in the faded tablecloths, the dated artwork, and the tatty chair covers.

Immediately he replaced his regrets over not having children with images of new furnishings, modern paintings, and potential colour schemes. The whole place needed a refit, to lift it from the budget restaurant it had been to the luxurious place he intended to campaign for a Michelin star from.

Pushing open the swing-back kitchen door, Jack found a smile spreading over his face. Compact, but not cramped, the kitchen was everything he'd hoped for. Two sets of twin sinks lined one wall, an industrial-sized dishwasher and freezer stood next to each other opposite them, and a large square free-standing preparation area waited in the middle of the space, with a utensil rack hanging above it. A vegetable cupboard, storage larder for fresh and packaged ingredients, and spaces to hang saucepans and their culinary preparation companions, all sat waiting to be filled.

It would need a lot of work. A hell of a lot of work. It would also cost Jack all the remaining money from his inheritance. For the first time in his life, he was going to have to really work for a living. But then, for the first time in his life, Jack wanted to do just that.

Heading up the narrow stairway that was separated from the back of the kitchen by a tiny hallway, Jack investigated the flat which would become his home if he took the place on.

Spacious, it covered the entire area of the bistro below. Jack converted the space in his head. With its two bedrooms, living room, dining area, kitchen, bathroom and small study, it was more than big enough for a single man.

There was one problem, however.

Jack walked back downstairs and stood in the doorway of the restaurant. He looked along the road, to a spot a couple of hundred metres away where a sign, placed by a narrow alley, directed passers-by to the coffee-and-cakes delights of Pickwicks. Jack knew that in order to make ends meet, let alone pay for all the new equipment and staff he'd need, he would have to open for afternoon coffee and cakes, too, as well as for evening meals…

Peggy and Scott would kill him.

That was if Amy and Kit didn't do it first.

Returning to the reception of what once had been the unimaginatively named Richmond Trattoria, Jack could already see the place alive with diners. He *had* to do this. It felt so right. Surely Peggy would understand? Anyway, she and Scott specialised in quick meals and coffee-break cakes. He would be cooking exclusive dinners based on carefully thought-out menus designed to stretch his guest's palates. He had no need to worry at all. There'd be no overlap in trade.

After all, Pickwicks already had a loyal clientele, mostly pensioners, and they were hardly his target demographic anyway...

Jack turned to the patiently waiting estate agent.

'I'll take it.'

If he'd had a jacket on, Jack would have turned up the collar. He felt like he was parachuting over enemy lines. As he edged along the shop-lined alley that led to Pickwicks, he wasn't sure why he wanted to see the place. If he was spotted peering through the window by Peggy or Kit there was no way he could avoid going inside, and he wasn't ready for that yet. Especially now he'd done something that he knew could potentially damage trade for Peggy and Scott, no matter what he told himself.

With his promise to himself that he would see Amy first echoing in his ears, Jack hovered at the edge of the shop next to Pickwicks and stared through the window, keeping his body shielded by the blinds that protected the late morning coffee swillers from the early summer sunshine.

Kit was at her usual table.

Peggy was hanging cups on hooks behind the counter.

Scott was out of sight – probably making some of his delicious scones in the kitchen.

Megan was chatting to a table full of pensioners.

Jack didn't know Megan as well as her colleagues, but he knew she was intelligent, good at her job, and obviously popular with the customers. It seemed a shame that she was making ends meet as a waitress when he was sure she was capable of so much more.

I'm going to need someone front of house at my new place...

Jack left the thought hanging in his head to come back to later, just as Peggy suddenly looked up from what she was doing. Flinging himself out of view, hoping that he hadn't been

30

spotted, Jack hurried back down the alleyway and out onto Richmond's main street.

He couldn't help laughing at his own mad behaviour, yet he was still relieved that he hadn't been spotted. The girls would have wanted to grill him about what he'd been up to, and they'd want to talk about Amy's condition, and he wasn't sure how to arrange his facial features for that discussion yet.

He had to go and find Amy. He couldn't put it off any longer, but he found that his palms were sweating slightly at the prospect. Knowing he was being ridiculous, Jack wiped his hands down his jeans and walked towards his friend's home on Princes Road. If Amy's clinic appointment had been that morning, she should be home by now. He wanted to see her before her workmates at Home Hunters tipped her off that he'd been looking for her.

Chapter Six

Monday 6th June

Peggy gave her head a shake. She couldn't possibly have seen Jack outside the window. She hadn't had a lot of sleep – her mind had been too full of all the plots and plans she and Scott had made over the weekend. Her eyes must have been playing tricks on her.

Glancing across at Kit's corner table, Peggy noticed that the writer's hands didn't seem to be making contact with the keys. Now she thought about it, she couldn't remember the last time she'd actually seen Kit's fingers anywhere near the keyboard. Picking up the coffee jug, she went to make sure her friend was OK.

'Kit, you looked miles away!'

Forcing out a smile as Peggy poured a fresh quota of black coffee into her huge cup, Kit shrugged. 'I was just trying to work out which words to put down first. Brain's a bit sluggish today, I'm probably tired.'

'Me too, I'm even hallucinating Jacks!'

'You're doing what?'

'I could have sworn I saw Jack through the window a minute ago.' Peggy sat down. 'Mind you, I've had next to no sleep, and the sun was in my eyes, so it was probably some random Jack-shaped bloke.'

Kit gave her friend a more genuine smile. 'And the fact he's probably backpacking around a jungle or something sort of makes it even more unlikely to have been him.'

She suddenly had an urge to confide her concerns, but the opening of the café door heralded the day's first lunchtime diners, sweeping Peggy back into service.

Slipping off her shoes, Megan sank down on the bench in the tiny garden at the back of Pickwicks' kitchen. Relieved to be on her break after a very busy hour of serving sandwiches and soup, Megan flipped open the sketchbook she'd recently taken to carrying around with her at all times, like when she'd been an art student.

She'd had a few vague ideas about taking commissions for portraits to earn some extra cash to contribute to her and Nick's house rental fund, and Megan had been practising doing mini drawings and speed sketches whenever she could to improve her confidence.

Encouraged by Nick and her friends, Megan had got into the habit of sitting outside during her lunch break with a large pad and some sketching pencils. Today, holding a photograph that Scott had covertly passed to her, she set to work. She was about to begin a portrait of Peggy and Scott as a surprise for Peggy's birthday on the twentieth of August.

Certain she wouldn't be disturbed by Peggy, who was holding the fort in the café on her own, Megan began to sketch the outline of her artwork. It seemed impossible now that she'd forgotten how satisfying it was to create a picture from scratch.

By the time Peggy had fulfilled the hunger-fuelled requirements of the last lunchtime diner, Kit had dismissed the idea of sharing her empty nest feeling with her friend. After all, she knew that Peggy and Scott would have loved children, and it seemed churlish to complain about something her friends would have loved the opportunity to face but never had the chance.

Since talking to Phil, Kit had felt a lot better, and although the words were still forming a logjam in her head, at least she knew she wasn't going mad now.

'I've gone right off tuna mayonnaise.'

Kit got up and took the heaped up tray of empty sandwich plates from Peggy. 'Has that been the favourite filling of the day then?'

'Unbelievable, isn't it. It's always popular, but for some reason best known to the shopping public of Richmond, it has been the must-have order today. Scott's had to re-mix the filling

34

three times.'

'Tell you what, you sit there and rest your feet while guarding my computer, and I'll take this out to the kitchen.'

When she got back, Kit found Peggy looking thoughtful. 'Why have you closed your work down, honey? I usually steal a read of your latest work in progress when I think you're not looking.'

'I haven't got much done today.' Kit mumbled. 'It's been a mulling-things-over sort of day.' Changing the subject, she said, 'Scott says there are some sandwiches ready for your lunch when Megan comes back through.'

'Good, I'm starving.'

'Are you and Megan managing alright with only two of you on the serving team? It's already busy, but by July it's going to be packed between eleven and two.'

'Actually, Scott and I were talking about that over the weekend. Would your Helena fancy giving us a hand and earning some money before she heads off to university? Where's she going again?'

Flinching slightly, and hoping Peggy hadn't noticed, Kit said, 'She's aiming for Bath to do Chemistry, and Thomas is hoping to be off to Exeter. Assuming they get their grades, that is.'

'Of course they will. What's Thomas going to study?'

'History.'

'Sounds good. So, do you think Helena will want the job? It would save me a lot of bother with adverts and stuff.'

Kit nodded. She knew exactly how much time it took to go through interviews and training staff for Pickwicks, so someone who was already familiar with the layout would be a real advantage to Peggy. 'I'll ask her. Helena's bank balance could certainly do with a top-up. Goodness knows it's time she stood on her own two feet financially.'

Megan came back into the café and Peggy got up to go and have her lunch before another influx of customers forced her to forego her only real break of the day. As an afterthought, she turned back to Kit. 'If you'd rather your daughter wasn't here during the day, just say. I mean, this is your office after all!'

'I don't mind at all. I'll ask her this evening, assuming she comes home She seems to live at her mates' houses these days.'

'Making the most of seeing her friends before she heads west, I suppose.' Peggy waved as she disappeared into the kitchen, to what Kit hoped wasn't a tuna sandwich, before she could see the tell-tale glint of tears fighting to form at the corner of her friend's eyes.

Cross with herself for being so emotional, Kit looked at her screen. Peggy had opened a new document and typed the words *You can talk to me, you know. Love Peggy xx* across the top of the page.

Kit should have known that she couldn't hide anything from Peggy. The manageress knew her habits better than anyone, having been host to them for the past decade or so. Kit didn't even want to guess how many cups of coffee, scones, and slices of toast she'd consumed at that table in that time. Just the thought of the amount of butter she'd spread over her early-morning snacks was enough to make her feel as though her hips were expanding right there on the seat.

Making her mind up to talk to Peggy soon, she picked up her mobile and sent Helena a text, telling her about the possible employment opportunity at Pickwicks.

Kit wasn't sure if she actually did want Helena around all day while she was writing. *But then*, she thought, *I'm not exactly writing now, am I.*

Chapter Seven

Monday 6th June

It seemed a lifetime since Amy had first come back into Jack's world and they'd sat, side by side, on her sofa at eight Princes Road, eating pizza and watching the same movies they'd enjoyed in their student days, back when they'd been a couple. Before he'd broken her heart. Before she'd run away to Scotland.

A chill ran down Jack's back as he walked towards Amy's home as he realised his friends might have thought *he'd* run away this time.

He stopped dead, narrowly avoiding being walked into by the people on the pavement behind him. Did they think he'd run away, not once but, worse, twice? No one had said anything, but it suddenly seemed so obvious to Jack that his absence while Amy got married definitely looked like running away – and his leaving again a year or so later, while he hadn't planned it that way, looked like him fleeing the scene again.

Why hadn't seen it like that until now?

Jack had considered his periods of time away from Richmond as self-preservation. He'd simply been removing himself from the scene of hurt, so that his emotions didn't have the chance to get the better of him. But as he headed towards the house of one of his closest friends, the idea that his friends might have seen his leaving of the area as weakness or failure began to gnaw at his brain.

As he got closer to Amy's house his pulse began to beat faster. He knew it was important to get his reaction to her forthcoming motherhood right – but what was right? He hadn't been nervous about seeing her; in fact, he'd been looking forward to it. He *had* been apprehensive though, in case she saw his last year as silence as a personal affront, and he was prepared to receive a telling off. He smiled to himself for a moment. Being told off by Amy was a bit like being savaged by a snail.

Unless, of course, she'd changed…

Reminding himself that Amy didn't have a mean bone in her body, Jack took a deep breath. She would listen to him before she passed judgement.

Drawing nearer to the end of terrace where she lived, he became aware of a woman walking towards him, her arms laden with heavy shopping.

Amy?

Standing still, he struggled to comprehend what he was seeing. In his head he'd pictured Amy looking like she always used to; perhaps with a slight swelling to her stomach denoting her impending motherhood. It hadn't crossed his mind that not only was Amy pregnant, but she might have the baby any second now.

Jack tried not to stare, but he couldn't help it. He'd never seen Amy look so attractive.

Amy squinted into the sunshine. It wasn't the first time she'd thought she'd seen Jack when he wasn't there. In those long days of getting over him as a boyfriend, she'd seen him everywhere she looked. Somehow his features had been reflected in every male face, his words in every song she heard; his voice echoed in every place she'd visited.

She was seeing things now because she'd been thinking about Jack a lot lately, worrying about how he was. Hoping to talk to him about her fears about becoming a mother so late in the day. Fears she hadn't even confessed to Paul. *It's your addled pregnant woman's brain playing tricks on you, girl.*

Or was it?

She stopped dead.

Hang on a minute.

Jack?

Amy's smile mirrored the feeling that started in her heart

and filled her from top to toe. Dropping her shopping, she called out to him, opening her arms wide in welcome, 'If you want this to be like the movies, you'll have to be the one to run to me. I can't: whales don't run!'

Grateful for the ice-breaker, her grin contagious, Jack dashed forward and wrapped Amy in a gentle cuddle, scared to squeeze her too tightly. 'It is *so* good to see you!'

'You too.' Amy held him briefly, before abruptly drawing back and giving him a sharp clout around the ear. 'Where the bloody hell have you been?'

Dumping Amy's shopping bags on the kitchen table, Jack apologised for the third time in as many minutes for not having been in touch.

'I get it, Jack. You've said you're sorry for the lack of contact. You haven't told me why yet, though. I know you'll have your reasons, and as far as you're concerned they'll be good reasons, even if no one else would think so. But what are they?' Amy automatically put the kettle on as she signalled for Jack to sit at the table.

'You'll understand though, won't you?'

Amy nodded her head ruefully. 'Probably. But then I've always been an idiot where you're concerned, Jack Brown.'

'Ouch.'

Resting her back against the kitchen sink, she regarded him carefully. 'I was worried about you. So was Kit. What did she say when you saw her?'

'I haven't seen her yet. I only just got back.'

Amy tried not to feel pleased that he'd come to see her first, and failed. 'Coffee, I assume? Do you still have it the same way?'

'Yes please, and yes.' Jack looked around him. The kitchen had changed since he'd last been there. It was no longer painted starkly white, but a warm cream colour. It was then that he picked up the faint aroma of fresh paint. 'You've been decorating?'

'Yes.'

'Why? This place was lovely as it was.'

39

'Oh, I can't think!' Amy couldn't prevent the sarcasm escaping from her lips. 'Could it be because Paul and I want our child to live in a house that is clean and fresh, with a perfect room of its own, adapted especially for his or her needs?'

Passing Jack his coffee and putting her own mug down in front of her, Amy slid into a seat as gracefully as her current size would allow. Seeing the shocked expression on her friend's face, Amy spoke more gently. 'Honestly, Jack! We haven't all been stuck in a timewarp waiting for when you came back. Life carries on, even when you aren't here to help it along. Whether you like it or not, things change.'

Silent for a second, Jack pointed at Amy's cup. 'Like you not drinking coffee. What the hell is that stuff?'

'Fruit tea. Cranberry and orange, to be precise.'

Jack couldn't help but laugh. 'I never thought I'd see the day.'

'You only got a coffee for old times' sake. I can't even stand the smell right now, and I can't drink it at all. Makes me feel awful. It's quite common to go off coffee in pregnancy, apparently.'

'That must be a nightmare for you! I've never known you have anything other than coffee or the occasional hot chocolate. Certainly never tea.' Jack pulled his mug as far away from her as he could, and put his hand over the top, as if to protect her from its delicious aroma.

Appreciating the gesture, Amy said, 'You aren't kidding. I mostly have cold drinks, but sometimes I crave a warm one. Hot chocolate is out because it gives me and the bump indigestion.'

Jack, who Amy noticed had been avoiding looking at her swollen belly, swallowed carefully, 'So when is it due then?'

'My *baby* is due on the twenty-sixth of August.'

Jack almost choked on his coffee. 'Blimey, that's ages yet. I mean, you're so big I thought it must be sooner, and … Ouch!' He drew his leg up and hugged it. 'You kicked me!'

'Yes, I bloody well did! I am not *that* big. I'm actually quite small for someone seven-ish months gone, so less of the cheek. Now, enough small talk. Where the hell have you been, and why the radio silence?'

'Cooking? But what about the horticulture course you did? Amy observed Jack shrewdly over her glass as he explained where he'd been for the past year. 'Didn't you want to be a gardener?'

'I did love gardening. It was great to be able to spend so much time outside, and I enjoyed the course, but I'm a bit old for that game now.'

'Too old for gardening? You're kidding. Gardeners always seem to be elderly.'

'Not these days – and not professional gardeners. There's a big difference between those who do it for a living and those who potter around in their own back gardens.'

'I guess so … but cooking? I know you were always a good cook, even when we were students, but I never had you down as a Jamie Oliver type.'

'I'd rather be Paul Hollywood.'

'I'm sure you would, but this is real life!' She stuck her tongue out at him.

'Pregnancy has made you feisty, Mrs Donahue.' Jack stretched his legs out beneath the table, 'What is it about Paul Hollywood that everyone finds so sexy anyway?'

Amy had to resist the urge to rush around and take Jack's temperature. 'Excuse me? He is good-looking, capable, unflappable, *and* he can cook. What a silly question.'

'I can cook.'

'I have no doubt you're a good chef, but how about the good-looking, capable, and unflappable bit?'

Jack looked hurt, and Amy took pity on him. 'I was only joking! Now come on, there is something you're not telling me. Spit it out before you have to dash back to Kent to prepare dinner at Kennedy's, or whatever you said it was called?'

'Yes, Kennedy's. Except I'm not dashing back. I quit. I'm here to stay this time.'

'That's fantastic! I'm so glad. I've really missed you, and now you're here you can be …' Amy stopped talking as she caught the tell-tale look on his face. 'Hang on, you quit? You

41

were just telling me how much you love your new vocation. What have you done?'

'Well, the thing is…'

Amy sighed. 'Oh no, Jack, not again.' She shook her head sadly, 'Go on then, tell me everything. Who was he this time?'

Getting up from her seat to relieve the cramp that being sat in one place for so long had given her, Amy listened to Jack's explanation. Pacing the kitchen, she tried to get her head around what he was saying.

'Let me get this straight. You're here to start a restaurant of your own after you accidentally slept with your old boss – Gareth, did you say he was?'

'Yes.'

'Gareth, much to your astonishment and horror, declared a hidden passion for you and, unable to handle the rejection, subsequently made your life hell, so you quit.'

'Correct.'

'And now you've decided that you never want to risk hurting anyone or, be hurt by anyone else, ever again, and have taken yourself off the dating radar completely.'

'Correct.'

'And this plan means you'll work for yourself, only employ women or straight men, and basically hide in your kitchen chopping parsley.'

'Correct again … but a little flippant.'

Amy looked her friend squarely in the face. 'Flippant is pretty much all I can manage, Jack. All my worry genes are being employed elsewhere right now.'

Chapter Eight

Monday 6th June

Jack scrambled off his seat and crossed the kitchen at speed. 'I'm so sorry, Amy.' He gave her another careful hug. 'I've been doing it again, haven't I?'

'Doing what?'

'Talking about me. Hogging the conversation with my problems. I haven't even asked how you are.' He shook his head, 'I was so determined not to do that. But you're so easy to talk to and I...'

Amy laughed and raised her eyebrows.

'And now I'm doing it again!' Jack bit his bottom lip coyly and batted his eyelashes in a deliberately silly way to get her forgiveness. 'So tell me, Mrs Donahue, how are *you*? I know you always wanted children, but ummm ... forgive me, there is no delicate way to ask this...'

'Aren't I a bit old to have a baby?'

'Well ... *you* said it.' Jack took Amy's hand and led her into the living room, indicating that she should lie on the sofa. 'But yes, that is what I was going to ask, albeit more subtly. Come on, feet up.'

'I'm not an invalid, Jack.'

'And yet you will put your feet up!'

Amy allowed herself to be fussed over for a while, 'To tell you the truth, Jack, I'm scared stiff.'

'Really? I assumed you'd be delighted.'

'I am. We both are.' Amy sighed. 'Look at that book.' She pointed to an open book on the coffee table that sat on the floor between where she lay and Jack sat in an armchair. 'Is that or is that not the single most terrifying book you have ever seen in

43

your life.'

Jack flicked through the pages of a week-by-week pregnancy guide. His face went a bit pale, and Amy couldn't help but laugh. 'Now, do you see why being flippant is pretty much my only way of coping with the knowledge that a human being is under construction inside me, while simultaneously making me feel like I've swallowed the spin cycle of a washing machine?'

'Is that how it feels then?'

'Sometimes.'

'Hard to imagine that is all happening inside you right now. Jack pointed to a picture of a seven-month-old foetus. 'What did the nurse or doctor or whoever say at your check-up this morning?'

'How did…?'

'Don't worry, I'm not stalking you. I popped into Home Hunters to see you. A very pretty girl called Lauren told me that's where you were. She seemed nice.'

'She is. Lauren was the first member of staff I took on myself. She's my PA, and darn good at her job.' Amy paused. 'So, you already knew I was pregnant then?'

'Yes, but I imagined you only *just* pregnant, I wasn't prepared for the full-on in bloom bit. You look incredible, by the way. I've never seen you looking so beautiful.'

Blushing, Amy wiped a stray blonde hair from her forehead. 'Thanks, although you wouldn't have been saying that through the morning sickness phase. I looked green and gaunt, and was a hormonal nightmare and regular bitch. I have no idea how Paul put up with me.'

'Because he loves you, of course.' Jack felt a sudden stab of jealousy towards Paul, though he instantly dismissed it. 'So, tell me, what *did* the nurse have to say this morning?'

'I'm fine. All is on course for August. My weight and blood pressure are good. It's my constant worrying they can't fix.'

Amy gave a half-smile as she recalled the expression on the health visitor's face when she'd confessed she felt totally fine apart from her non-stop anxiety. 'She told me that however tired and anxious I was now, it was nothing compared to how tired and concerned I'll be when the baby arrives, so I should consider it practice!'

'That's awful. Fancy saying that to you!'

'Would you rather she'd lied to me?'

'Well, no. I suppose I assumed they'd have to be reassuring. Her honesty seems a little brutal.'

Suddenly he had the urge to ask Amy if she'd ever imagined what their kids would have been like – if they'd stayed together. But he didn't. He was fairly sure he didn't need to. Instinct told him that Amy was wondering that very thing right now.

From the back of his mind came an image of the man at Kew Gardens, together with all the happy children listening to him. 'Just imagine what it'll be like in a year or two. You'll be able to take your child to Kew, drive to the coast to build sandcastles, teach them things, go to cafés, and do the stuff that you enjoy doing, but with someone who will love you always, no matter what.'

Although she tried, Amy couldn't quite hide the concern she suddenly felt for her friend. 'Are you OK, Jack?'

'Sure,' he mumbled. 'I would have liked kids one day, that's all.' He sat up and put a bright smile on his face. 'But I've made my bed and all that stuff. Tell me, do you know what colour Donahue it is going to be?'

'Colour?' Amy laughed. 'Oh, no, we don't know if it'll be a pink or a blue Donahue. Neither of us wants to know until the day.'

Smiling his approval, Jack asked, 'Why are you so worried anyway? You'll be a brilliant parent. You were born to be a mum.'

'Thanks, Jack.' Amy motioned for him to join her on the sofa. 'Sometimes it's a lot to take in though. Paul and I got together at a time when we had both given up on finding someone to have children with. We talked about IVF and adoption, but neither option felt right, although I couldn't logically tell you why. So when I fell pregnant naturally it was quite a shock.'

'I bet! A nice shock though.'

As he sat next to her, Amy tucked her head into Jack's

shoulder, a position that felt as comfortable now as it had years ago. 'It's not the birth that concerns me, although I can't say I'm looking forward to it, it's the coping afterwards. No sleep, nappies, feeding. And then there's work.' Amy was talking faster and faster as all her fears poured out. 'What if I can't find anyone to do my job while I'm on maternity leave? And what if I change my mind about wanting to go back to Home Hunters once the baby is here? Although we need the money, so…'

'Calm down, Amy, come on.' Jack smoothed her blonde bob. It was a much shorter style on her than he was used to, and he found he missed how long her hair had been before he went away. 'It's all going to be OK. What does Paul say about all this?'

'Well, I haven't liked to bother him…'

Jack sat up straighter. 'You're kidding! Why not?'

'He's so excited about being a dad. I don't want to ruin that for him.'

'He isn't daft, Amy. Paul must know you have concerns. I'm sure he has plenty of his own. I wouldn't be at all surprised if he was having similar panics.'

'You think so?'

'Positive. I would be if the woman I love was about to give birth and I was going to be responsible for two people instead of one for the rest of my life.'

Amy lifted her head and looked at him. 'My God! You make it sound terrifying!'

'Sorry, Amy, but it is terrifying. For Paul and for you. But it is also miraculous and incredible.' He touched the end of her nose affectionately. 'I was just trying to make you see that you need to talk to your husband, because I bet you're both harbouring very similar concerns.'

Leaning forward, Amy kissed Jack's cheek. 'Thanks, hun. You're right.' Swinging her feet to the floor, she slowly got up. 'I'm glad you're back. You *are* back to stay? For real?'

'I am. For real.' Jack tapped the sofa seat next to him. 'Sit back down, woman, you're supposed to be resting.'

'That's very sweet of you, but one of the problems of pregnancy needs addressing.'

He frowned. 'You OK?'

'I'm fine,' Amy grinned, 'but I'll be even better when I've had a pee.'

Jack felt proud of himself. Rather than unintentionally making things worse, as he often seemed to, his chat with Amy had left him feeling as if he'd actually helped her and Paul.

As he headed to the Tube, he thought about what Amy had said as, having made her promise not to tell anyone else he was back until he'd had a chance to see them in person, he'd left her tucking into a banana and sugar sandwich.

'Jack, you are going to see Kit now, aren't you? You remember what happened last time you didn't tell her everything?'

He knew she was right, but he wasn't quite ready for another heart-to-heart yet. Still in a mild state of shock at finding Amy so heavily pregnant, and cross with himself for feeling that way, he headed towards Reading Nature rather than travelling back to his hotel.

As he walked along, Jack was disturbed by how much he minded missing out on the earlier stages of Amy's pregnancy. He could have helped her out with shopping when she felt too sick to look at food, could have rubbed her back and made her feel better, and…

'Idiot, of course you couldn't. That's Paul's job now. Snap out of it, Jack, for goodness' sake. You're pathetic.'

Deciding that he'd only go into the shop if he could see that Phil wasn't there, he made a contingency plan to go on to Kew for another head-clearing walk before heading to the bank later that afternoon. It wasn't that he didn't like Phil … but as he was Kit's husband, their relationship had never been perfect, to say the least.

Although Rob would probably give him a hard time about disappearing, Jack hoped he was there. Right from when they'd first met at university, Rob, his closest male friend, had always had the knack of making him see sense – providing he was in the mood to listen.

He was in luck: as Jack tentatively glanced through the bay

window, he saw that Rob was alone, and quickly headed in.

'Rob?'

'Oh my God! The bad penny!' Rob came out from behind the counter and embraced Jack. 'Phil said you'd walk through the door one day as if you've never been away, and he was right.'

'Annoyingly, Phil is nearly always right. How you doing? Debbie and the kids OK?'

'Great, thanks, but to what do we owe the pleasure? You passing through, or are you back for good?' Before Jack even opened his mouth in reply, Rob added, 'And I beg you, do *not* make a reference to the Take That song, there's a good chap!'

Jack gave the Scout salute. 'I don't do the lyrics thing anymore. Scout's honour!'

Rob laughed. 'I happen to know you were never in the Scouts, so I dread to think where you learnt to do that!' Walking through to the shop's compact kitchen area, he put the kettle on. 'Come on then, spill the beans – why has the prodigal returned?'

As Rob listened to Jack telling him that he'd stayed away far longer than he'd intended to, and explaining that he'd got into cookery and was looking for a restaurant nearby, he couldn't help but suspect that there was something more to his friend's obvious unease than being wary of his reception after so long away. Stopping himself from asking if there was yet another failed relationship behind Jack's abrupt return, he asked instead, 'You seen the girls yet?'

'I've just come from Amy. I'll see Kit this evening. Don't tell her I'm back, I'd hate her to hear second-hand.'

'No problem. Amy's looking great, isn't she? Pregnancy suits her.'

'She does indeed. It must be very exciting for her and Paul. I was lucky to catch her at home; she'd been for a check-up at the clinic.'

'All good, I hope?'

'Nothing but the usual anxieties about being a parent.'

Rob's eyes narrowed, suspecting his friend was less thrilled about Amy's forthcoming parenthood than he was declaring –

but at least he was saying all the right things for once.

'Right then.' Jack put down his empty mug, 'I have to shoot off. I've got an appointment at the bank. Pub for a pint soon?'

'For sure.' Rob followed his friend to the front door. 'Don't leave it too long before you see Kit, will you?'

'That's what Amy said.'

'I'm sure she did.'

'I've already said – I'm going to see her this evening, after the bank thing.'

'Well, make sure you actually do.'

Trying not to feel annoyed – after all, Rob was justified if his past form was anything to go by – Jack simply nodded.

As he pushed the shop door open, the young man he had seen at Kew walked through, giving him a brief smile of thanks for holding it open.

Hesitating, Jack hovered outside the shop, his breath snagged in his throat. Should he go back in and introduce himself? Was fate giving him a nudge?

Striding off down the road, he gave himself yet another talking to. *I am not going to be that sort of man any more. I am better off alone.* And anyway, the last thing he needed was for Rob to witness him attempting to chat someone up – especially if he was knocked back.

Three steps later, his phone burst into life.

'Hi, Jack, it's Amy. Fancy coming over for a meal with me, Paul, Kit, and Phil soon? I've got something to ask you.'

Chapter Nine

Tuesday 7th June

'Are you sure, Scott? What if Helena picks up on it when she comes over later?'

Scott stacked freshly decorated cupcakes onto an old-fashioned cake stand as he tried to reassure his wife. 'I'm sure Megan won't say anything. After all, she hasn't even told us if she wants the job yet, has she?'

Peggy had been keen to share with Kit the news about the second branch. She didn't like keeping secrets from her friend, and she hoped that if she shared something private, Kit might open up a bit about what was troubling her, too.

'I know it isn't in your nature not to discuss things with your friends, but I'm scared of jinxing it. I want our plans to work. After all, if this new café doesn't prove to be the investment we hope it will, we could end up not getting the retirement we hope for,' Scott said.

Peggy embraced her husband. He was always so positive and lively, it was easy to forget sometimes that he worried about the future as much as she did.

'OK, love, we'll say nothing to Kit for now.'

'Not really an option today, anyway.' Scott inclined his head towards Kit's corner. The seat she occupied every morning was vacant, the coffee Peggy had placed on her regular table twenty minutes earlier, ready for her daily at nine o'clock arrival, was fast growing cold.

Peggy frowned. 'What time is it?'

'Half past nine.' Scott smiled at his wife. 'Don't look so concerned. It's Helena's first training session at ten, Kit probably stayed home late so she can walk in with her.'

51

'Yes, that's probably it.' Peggy tried to sound convinced, but she wasn't. Kit was always at her desk by five past nine at the absolute latest. She checked her mobile to make sure there weren't any texts from Kit saying she'd been delayed, but there was nothing.

Taking away the cold coffee, Peggy was distracted by the arrival of Megan and a handful of customers who all drifted through the front door at the same time. Adopting her perfect hostess smile, she set off to work.

Peggy had never seen Helena look nervous before. The eighteen-year-old had exuded an occasionally unsettling overconfidence ever since she was a little girl, and Peggy had to hide the amused smirk that was threatening to shine in her eyes. It was reassuring to know that the teenager wasn't as cocksure as she always made herself out to be.

'Thanks for coming, Helena. Did your mum tell you what the job involves?'

Helena pushed her shoulders back to show she wasn't apprehensive in any way. 'Being a waitress for a few hours a day?'

'And are you genuinely interested? I won't lie to you, it's very hard work. I can only afford to pay you minimum wage, and you'll have to work some weekends. I thought you'd like to earn some money before university, but if you aren't up for it, then I can advertise in the local paper.'

Helena, who hadn't wanted to come along at all and was perfectly happy living off handouts from her parents, had been horrified when her mum had suggested that she might like to earn her own money. She had been even more surprised when her mum had added that, although she and her dad would happily help both her and Thomas with their uni fees and rent, they weren't able to be their sole supporters any more. It was time, her mum had told her rather more curtly than she normally would, that she stood on her own two feet.

Her usual indignation hadn't worked on her mum this time, and Helena could see that it wouldn't work on Peggy either. 'Thanks, Peggy. I'd like to give it a try, if you'll have me.'

Peggy grinned. 'No problem! So, first things first. Go through to the kitchen, give your hands a thorough wash, get Scott to give you an apron, and then ask Megan to introduce you to the fine art of stacking a tray with dirty dishes and filling the dishwasher. Then once the lunch rush has passed, I'll show you how to work the coffee machine. Yes?'

Trying not to look shocked, Helena, who'd assumed she was only coming along to hear Peggy offer her the job and tell her how many hours she'd have to do, and then go home for a few more hours' sleep, found herself heading through to the kitchen as requested.

'Oh, Helena?'

The teenager turned back to Peggy.

'Is your mum alright, honey? She isn't at her desk.'

'She was in bed when I left. Said she's got a cold or something.'

Peggy wasn't convinced. If Kit's arm fell off or she had double pneumonia, she would still turn up to write her books. Something wasn't adding up.

After dishing out a few more pots of tea and slices of fruit cake, Peggy left Megan in charge and snuck out to call Phil. His phone was off, which meant he must be working with a group at Kew. She took the plunge and called Kit, but the mobile rang and rang with no answer.

Turning over in bed, Kit pulled Phil's pillow closer, cuddling it in the absence of her husband's warm body. There seemed little point in getting up today. Helena would be working in Pickwicks, and she didn't want to make her daughter any more self-conscious than she'd be anyway, by sitting at her usual corner table.

Telling herself that a day spent curled up under the duvet with her headphones turned up full blast, reading books that other people had written and ignoring the world, would do her good, Kit switched her phone to silent and left her emails unchecked. Feeling in dire need of a brain recharge, she convinced herself that if she had a day off – a day away from being her normal self – then tomorrow she'd be able to write

53

again.

With only a mild pang of guilt, Peggy had left teaching Helena how to use the coffee machine to Megan and, once the post-lunch lull began, had made her way to Kit's house. She'd tried phoning her friend on and off all day, but had got no response.

Knowing she was probably being irrational – Helena didn't seem at all concerned about her mother, and Phil would never turn his phone off if he was concerned about his wife – Peggy still couldn't dismiss the nagging feeling that all was not well with Kit.

As she turned into the secluded driveway that led up to Phil and Kit's comfortable semi-detached home, Peggy stopped dead.

Jack! She hadn't been imagining things after all. She *had* seen him peering through the café window. Now it all made sense. Who else had the ability to throw Kit off-kilter like this? Jack had to be at the bottom of this. *How dare he turn up after so long and upset her friend again!*

'What the bloody hell are you doing here, Jack?'

Startled, Jack spun around on Kit's doorstep. 'Peggy!'

Unable to stop herself, Peggy marched forward. Images of history repeating itself took control of her tongue. 'How dare you come back and upset Kit again! Don't you ever learn anything from your mistakes? You almost destroyed her marriage a few years ago, don't you dare take her down that road again!'

Jack shook his head viciously, his face pale as he took in Peggy's ire. 'What are you talking about? I haven't even seen Kit yet. And I wouldn't upset her for anything.'

'Come off it, Jack! I saw you stalking her through the window of Pickwicks the other day!'

Jack ran an agitated hand through his short spiked hair and forced himself not to raise his voice. 'Oh … I thought you might have seen me. I wasn't stalking anyone. I just wanted to … I don't know, really. I've missed you all, OK? I wanted to make sure everyone was alright, but I didn't have time to chat at that moment.'

'You expect me to believe that?'

'Yes I bloody well do, actually!' Then, taking hold of his temper, Jack added with deliberate calm, 'Why are *you* here, Peggy? Is there something wrong with Kit? I must admit I hadn't expected her to be back from writing at Pickwicks yet. I was just passing, and thought I'd call by on the off-chance.'

Hands still on her hips, Peggy moderated her tone a fraction. 'Forget why I'm here. Why are you here, Jack? Here in Richmond, I mean.'

Not wanting to provoke Peggy further by telling her about his restaurant plans – a confession that suddenly seemed more daunting than ever – he said, 'I missed my friends. I'm going to be working back in the area, and I wanted to tell Kit I was here in person, rather than her hearing it from someone else. I figured I owed her that much after being out of touch for so long.'

Jack could tell Peggy wasn't entirely convinced, so he pushed on, 'I've only been here a couple of minutes, but I can't get a reply from the front door. The lights are on so I'm pretty sure someone's in.'

Peggy, knowing she'd probably overreacted to Jack's presence, tore a piece of paper from the notebook she kept in her handbag, wrote a quick message asking her friend to get in touch, and posted it through Kit's letterbox.

'I have to get back to the café. Are you staying here to see if she turns up?'

'I can't, I have to get over to my hotel. I need to try and extend my stay for a few days while I sort out some more permanent accommodation.' Jack crossed his fingers inside his trouser pockets in defence of the half-lie he'd just told Peggy. 'I'll come back and check on Kit later. I'd like to see Phil and the kids as well.'

'Well, I can tell you that Thomas is in Europe, backpacking with his mates, and Helena's learning the ropes at my place.'

'Really? Helena's working?'

Peggy laughed; it seemed she wasn't the only one who was taken aback by such an out-of-character development. 'She needs money for university.'

Jack sighed. 'I'm getting old. Amy is starting a family and Kit is getting ready to lose hers. Where does the time go?'

Peggy stopped walking and looked at Jack with renewed respect. 'You might just have answered a few questions for me in that one sentence.'

'Excuse me?'

'Are you heading back Richmond way?'

'Yes, my hotel's just the other side, in Hounslow. Why do you ask?'

'Because I've been worried about Kit, and I suspect you've just told me what the problem might be. I'll fill you in on the way.'

Kit, oblivious to the people who had just left her doorstep, rolled over in her sleep. She had drifted off in her cosy nest, but her dreams were full of stray words chasing her down narrow tunnels in the dark.

Chapter Ten

Tuesday 7th June

Three hours later, Jack walked back up the driveway to Kit's home. Taking a deep breath, not sure what sort of reception he'd get, and fully briefed by Peggy that Kit hadn't been behaving like her usual self, Jack knocked on the door.

'Jack! Hello, disappearing godfather person!'

Taking a step back, Jack looked at Helena properly. 'Blimey –'

Helena held up her hands as if to stop the next part of Jack's sentence. 'Yes, I have grown, and I'm sure you can't believe it. I am eighteen and not five anymore. Shock! Horror! Stop the presses!'

Jack grinned. 'I get the feeling you aren't keen on those sorts of comments.'

'Got it in one. You here to see Mum?' Helena flicked her newly streaked purple and black hair away from her eyes, and stepped back to allow Jack entrance, 'She's in the kitchen with Dad.'

Not sure whether he'd be welcome or not, Jack allowed Helena to lead him into the kitchen.

'Hello, stranger.' Kit got up off her wooden chair and wrapped him in a hug.

'You knew I was coming?' Jack found he was disappointed to be robbed of the element of surprise.

Phil gestured Jack to the nearest seat. 'Oh, you know Rob; he can't keep a secret to save his life.'

'It wasn't Peggy who told you'd I'd come then?'

Kit frowned. 'No, why?'

'You didn't get her note?'

'Note?' Kit looked at Phil. 'Did you see a note?'

Helena suddenly appeared sheepish. 'Oh, umm, maybe it's this?' She pulled a folded piece of paper, with *Kit* written across the front, from her pocket. 'Sorry, Mum, I saw it on the mat when I got in. I was going to give it to you, but I was so knackered after a day at Pickwicks that I forgot.'

Phil rolled his eyes. 'A day? Helena, you did four hours. If you think that's a day's work you're in for a shock when you do a full shift tomorrow.'

'Alright! I said I'm sorry.' Helena slammed the note down on the table and stalked off.

Kit gave a half-smile. 'That's better. I was worried she'd had a total personality transplant for a minute. I know Peggy is good at bringing out the best in people, but she's not that good that fast!'

'It could be that she's smarting from having Peggy tell her that, attractive though her new floppy haircut may be, it's unhygienic for serving food and will have to pinned back.' Phil shook his head affectionately.

Laughing, Kit said, 'Good for Peggy.' As she unfolded the note, her face blanched slightly and she muttered under her breath, 'Damn. I'd better make a call. Excuse me.'

Jack nodded. 'Good idea. She was really worried. It must have been weird for her to see someone else sitting in your seat.'

Kit frowned. 'You knew Peggy had been here?'

'I popped by here as well this afternoon. Peggy turned up shortly after I did. We met on the doorstep.'

Annoyed with herself, Kit tapped her friend's number into the kitchen phone. 'Typical, no one ever knocks on this door, and then I miss two welcome guests on the same day.'

Just as she was about to hang up, the phone was answered.

'Peggy! I'm so sorry. I decided to have a no technology day. I've heard people say how good they can be for recharging the creative batteries, so I relaxed, put in my headphones, and got lost in a book. I even had a nap! I didn't mean to worry you.'

Jack and Phil exchanged glances as Kit disappeared into the hallway to continue the call in private.

'Is Kit OK? Peggy was in quite a state when I saw her earlier.' Not sure he should share Peggy's theories or not, Jack left his query there, but Phil didn't seem to mind.

'Bitten off a bit more than she can chew on the deadline front. You know Kit; she's having a little panic. She'll be fine. I'm glad she had a day off. Did her good. She'd take much more time off if it was up to me.'

'Kit has always worked too hard. Addicted to what she does, I suppose.'

Phil laughed. 'You aren't wrong! Coffee and words: an addictive combination, that's for sure. Anyway, how are you, mate? Rob said you're a chef now. Is that right?'

'It's right. I loved running the bookshop, and enjoyed the gardening, but this – it's hard to explain. I feel so right doing it. I've never looked forward to going to work more.'

'I can understand that. I loved running Home Hunters, but Reading Nature has become a passion. And it's paying off. Did Rob tell you we've hired a new guy to help us? And that we've got a contract with Kew to promote both the gardens and our shop?'

'No, he didn't! That's brilliant.'

As Kit came back in, Phil added, 'Actually, Jack, our new guy, Rupert, is coming over for a takeaway and a chat about work in a bit. Fancy staying as well? You can meet him, and we can have a proper catch-up. We're always up for fresh ideas to help us expand your former empire.'

Despite her claims to the contrary, Jack wasn't convinced that Kit was OK. The moment Phil left to fetch them a Chinese takeaway, he wasted no time. Reaching forward, he linked his fingers with his friend's.

'Look, Kit, I came over to do the whole, "I'm sorry I've been out of touch for so long, and I've missed you" speech – which I am and I have, but I think we can take all that as read. You have to tell me what's going on. Don't give me any crap about needing a day off either. You've never needed a day off in your life.'

Kit opened her mouth to reply, but Jack got in first. 'And

don't give me any rubbish about it being "nothing" either. I'm going to nag until you tell me, so you might as well spit it out.'

Drawing her hands away from Jack, Kit wrapped them around her mug of coffee. 'OK, I'm busted. You always did see through me.'

'Not this time. It was Peggy. She said you didn't go to the café this morning. Weirder still, she said she couldn't remember the last time she'd actually seen you type words onto the screen. So, what's going on?'

'Writer's block,' Kit replied so softly that Jack didn't hear.

'Pardon?'

Shouting in frustration, Kit yelled, 'Writer's block, OK? I've got bloody writer's block!' She sagged back into her seat, half shocked at herself for yelling, half relieved to have finally admitted it out loud.

'All writers get that sometimes, don't they?' Jack couldn't quite see why this was a crisis. 'Surely you just go for a walk, have a change of scene, and shrug it off?'

Kit closed her eyes and rubbed her temples. How could she explain this to someone who didn't write? She hadn't understood the concept herself until now.

'Trust me, Jack: I've tried to walk it off lots of times.' She sighed. 'It's like the worst brain freeze you can imagine. I hardly like to use the word paralysed, but that's how my mind feels. I can sense all the words queuing up in my head, but they will *not* come out of my fingers.'

Jack could hear the distress in her voice. If she couldn't write, then she wasn't Kit. 'You don't feel like you, do you? Not without having control over your words.'

Kit was stunned. 'That's it exactly. I hadn't even worked that bit out for myself, wow …' She got up and threw her arms around her ex. 'Thank you!'

'What for? I only stated the obvious.' Hugging her back, he said, 'So I guess the plan now is to find out why you feel blocked?'

'I'm pretty sure I know what the problem is, but I've been stuck for so long now that I can't seem to break the habit of being blocked.'

'Tell me. Tell me all about it, talking it out might be the answer.' Jack's heart went out to her. If he couldn't cook anymore, he'd hate it. He might have found his passion fairly late in life, but now he had, he couldn't imagine what it would be like if he was unable to do it anymore.

'I'm sure this is all wrapped up with the twins moving on and ...' Kit got no further as the unmistakeable clatter of Phil returning broke through their chat.

Suspecting that Peggy had got her theory about Kit's unhappiness spot on, Jack said, 'Tell you what, why don't I take you for an old-fashioned coffee stop tomorrow, and we can talk at our leisure?'

'I would love that, thanks, Jack. I'm so glad you're home. You are back properly now, aren't you?'

'I am. I promise.'

Kit clapped, 'Good, because I want your opinion about Rupert.'

Instantly suspicious, Jack asked, 'Why?'

There was no time for Kit to answer, however, for Phil walked in laden with bags of takeaway, together with the man Jack had seen with the group of children in Kew Gardens and followed by a freshly washed and provocatively dressed Helena.

Chapter Eleven

Peggy had told herself that, whatever happened, she must not fall in love with the café they were about to view in case things went wrong, but within seconds of entering the vacant building she had broken that promise.

The premises she, Scott, and the rental agent now stood in were smaller than the agents' particulars had led them to believe, but undeniably perfectly proportioned. With the same Dickensian feel to its exterior as Pickwicks, the café had a wide, airy bay window with sills deep enough to fill with jugs of fresh flowers. It was also nicely laid out and decorated well enough to need very little doing to it before being re-opened.

The kitchen had already been declared adequate by Scott, who was currently wondering if he could cook enough in the Richmond kitchen to stock both cafés, or if they would have to hire an additional cook as they'd originally planned.

With no other independent coffee shops nearby, Peggy and Scott were sure they could provide Mortlake with a new and delicious alternative to the usual café chains, just as they did at Pickwicks. Encouraged by the fact the café had only closed down because the previous tenant had retired, and not because the business had failed, a nod of approval from Scott and an excited smile from Peggy soon told the agent that a decision had been reached.

'You wish to rent the property?'

'We do.' Scott took his wife's hand, 'However, we'd like you to ask the landlord if he is open to a reduction in the monthly rent. The café is lovely, but it isn't as big as stated on paper, and it won't accommodate as many customers as we'd imagined.'

Making a note on his tablet, the agent said, 'I can certainly enquire about that for you, Mr and Mrs McIntyre. As space equals income in a place like this, which of course translates into your ability to pay the rent, I can't see there being a problem with it.'

Out in the bright sunlight of Mortlake's main street ten minutes later, Peggy felt optimistic. 'We really are going to have a second branch, aren't we?'

Kissing the top of her long black hair affectionately, Scott said, 'There's only one question now.'

'Only one? I can think of thousands!'

'OK, so can I. But the main question is obvious: what shall we call it?'

'I have no idea! "Pickwicks 2" isn't exactly catchy, is it?'

Peggy held her husband's arm tighter. 'Oh, hell, this is so grown up!'

'You aren't kidding.' Scott was about to add that it would also be worth the risk and all the extra hard work they'd have to put in, when his mobile rang.

'Blimey, that was quick. Are you sure…'

Peggy made impatient *what's happened?* gestures at Scott, who gave her a thumbs-up as he carried on listening, before saying, 'Would Monday afternoon be convenient? About four o'clock … Fine … We'll see you then. Thank you for acting so promptly, Mr Baxter.'

Standing as he saw Kit weaving through the tables, Jack pointed to the two large Americanos and heavily sugared Danish pastries he'd purchased in anticipation of her arrival. He was pleased to see she didn't look as tired or drawn as she had the evening before.

'I wasn't sure this place would still be here.' He gestured around the department store café, which had been their regular haunt for years before he had gone on his travels. 'Thankfully it seems to have ridden out the recession, although I'm not sure how.'

'I can't remember the last time they changed the awful art on the walls!'

'Does anyone ever buy this stuff?'

Kit smiled affectionately at her friend's expression as he studied the tacky paintings that were hanging optimistically for sale on the cream walls, contrasting sharply with the garish carpet and dark wooden furniture. Then, returning to the matter in hand, she studied his face carefully, 'Are my instincts correct, then?'

Jack, who hadn't slept much at all, his head full of the night before, nodded as he took a sustaining draught of coffee. 'Oh yes. Spot on.'

'Damn!' Kit, who'd been convinced she was right but had genuinely hoped her instincts were wrong this time, groaned. She didn't want her own romantic history to repeat itself – especially not for her only daughter.

The previous evening, Jack had been surprised when Helena had joined him, her parents, and Rupert for dinner. But his surprise hadn't lasted long. It was soon painfully obvious that his goddaughter had a serious crush on her father's new colleague.

The fact that Helena had, while Phil had gone to fetch the takeaway, taken a shower, washed her striking new hairdo so that it looked attractively soft, and dressed in a miniskirt – which could possibly have doubled as a belt – and a suggestively low-cut top, before returning to the table that had been set for four and adding a fifth set of cutlery, had spoken volumes. Her parents, who'd assumed Helena would help herself to a portion of food and then promptly disappear into the living room to consume it in front of the television as usual, had worn expressions of amazement that had almost embarrassing.

Rupert hadn't known where to look, but not for the reasons that Helena evidently hoped for. Jack had instantly understood precisely which question Kit had been about to ask him. He also saw that Helena's gaydar was as appalling as her mother's had been.

Throughout the evening, Helena had more or less ignored everyone else at the table, keeping her smiles and blatantly suggestive fork-fiddling for Rupert's eyes only. It had been painful to watch. Jack had wondered if she was aware of how obvious she was being. Knowing Helena, he suspected she did.

Phil and Rupert had talked about the bookshop, the new natural history lessons, and the nature trail sessions Reading Nature ran in conjunction with Kew Gardens. Jack was fascinated to learn about the association Rob and Phil had built up with the world-famous gardens. Helena, he noted, had listened especially carefully to the list of future dates when Rupert would be teaching, alone, away from the watchful eye of her father.

To compound the problem, Jack, who had been wondering about the man in the gardens more than he would have liked to admit, had a suspicion that Rupert was not yet entirely comfortable with his sexuality. He was certainly giving out mixed signals. Jack couldn't help feeling sorry for Helena, but he felt even sorrier for Rupert. It would be no easy task fending off Helena Lambert if she was on a mission to get her man. And if Rupert was at the stage where he'd much rather be straight, just to make it easier to deal with his family and life in general, then he might very well give in to Helena's persuasions. Something, Jack knew, from far too much experience, he'd live to regret.

Kit took a bite of her Danish, sending icing sugar clouds into the air between them. 'So, what should I do?'

'What can you do?'

Shrugging, she drank her coffee. 'I don't want her to have to go through what ...' She coloured, deciding against finishing her sentence.

'It's OK, I understand. You don't want Helena to go through with Rupert what you went through with me. To be frank, neither do I. It would ultimately be awful for both of them, and no offence, Kit, but I can't see Helena being as forgiving or understanding as you were.'

'Neither can I.'

Jack experienced a small hit of guilt at the thought of what else he was going to have to ask Kit to forgive him once she knew he was opening his restaurant so near to Pickwicks, but for now he stuck to the subject of Rupert.

66

'What sort of background does he come from? He comes across as a bit public school.'

'You got it in one. Wealthy parents. Daunting father by all accounts. Apart from that he hasn't said much about his life. Keeps himself to himself. Phil and Rob haven't been able to find out about his home life; apart from the fact he's single.'

Keeping the flutter of hope he felt inside his chest at the news that Rupert was unattached to himself, Jack said, 'I got the impression he was a private person. All he talked about last night – alongside his polite non-answers to Helena's barrage of personal questions – was work. I must say, I take my hat off to the man for dodging all her skilful enquiries. Has your daughter considered a career in MI5?'

Kit snorted a laugh. 'She wants to be a teacher.'

'She'll be bloody good at it. Bet she'll terrify the kids into working hard.' Jack caught the look on Kit's face. 'Sorry, that came out wrong. I didn't mean to be rude about Helena.'

'I sometimes wish I was more like her. I have no idea where her assertive side comes from. Not Phil or me, that's for sure! And Thomas is as laid-back as they come.'

'Mix-up at the hospital maybe?' Jack winked, 'Except, of course, that purple hair apart, she is so like you it's startling. She's a very beautiful young woman.'

'Flattery will get you a refill. More coffee?'

'Please.'

Watching Kit queue up for the drinks, Jack's mind returned to Rupert. He knew he could be reading things wrong, but the more he thought about it, the more convinced he was that Rupert was stuck in the not-wanting-to-disappoint-his-parents trap. If he came from a wealthy, traditional family, then he probably didn't want to let them down by not giving them grandchildren. Remembering his own struggles with such feelings, Jack had the urge to help. *But how can I help?* I always mess things up when I try to make things better, especially as I find Rupert attractive. Damn. I wish I'd never seen him teaching those kids. I might not have fancied him at all then.

Jack knew he was in denial. In the quiet of the night before he had daydreamed about going on long walks with Rupert, hand in hand, talking about nature, taking photos, planning restaurant menus together ... It had disturbed him how romanticised his thoughts had been. Somehow, the happy pictures Jack's imagination created while he was awake were far more disturbing than his usual night time visions of lustful bedroom encounters.

Sighing to himself, a whole nightmare of potential emotional turmoil spreading out ahead of him in his mind, Jack thanked Kit as she put a brimming coffee cup in front of him.

'So, what should I do about Helena?'

'Does she know you suspect Rupert's gay?'

'Yes. She told me I was being ridiculous, and gave me the whole, "you don't want me to be happy" routine. You remember the one; I'm sure every teenager uses that against their parents at some point.'

Jack, who could remember almost that exact sentence flying from his own youthful mouth on several occasions, nodded bleakly. 'Then all I can suggest is you let it run its course.'

'But what if...'

Jack raised his hand, 'Kit, Helena isn't you, and Rupert isn't me. Helena is far more self-aware than you ever were, and I get the impression that Rupert has far more common sense, and is a much nicer man, than I have ever been. I don't think he'll lead her on. I suspect he finds the whole thing a bit embarrassing.'

'And if the gay thing wasn't enough of a problem, he is way too old for her.'

'How old is he then?'

'Thirty. Twelve years older than Helena. I know that isn't really a massive gap at our age, but it is at hers – if that makes any sense.'

Keeping quiet the thought that the age gap between Rupert and himself was a similar one, Jack said, 'It makes sense. We all change a lot between eighteen and thirty.'

Kit ran a hand through her short red hair. 'I don't want her to get hurt.'

'I don't think there's any way you can prevent that. I wish there was.' He sighed before changing the subject, 'But there is something we can tackle, isn't there.'

She frowned. 'There is?'

'Your writer's block. You were about to tell me last night, before the arrival of the takeaway, about how the kids leaving home is affecting your work.'

Shifting uncomfortably in her seat, Kit cradled her coffee. 'It is silly, isn't it? I knew they were leaving, I've known for ages, but now it all seems so real. What am I going to do with my time? What am I for if I'm not there for the twins?'

'And Amy is having a baby.' Jack left the sentence hanging in the air for a second before saying, 'I take it the fact that one of your closest friends is starting a family when you feel as if you are about to lose yours hasn't helped.'

Kit gaped at him. 'How the hell did you work that out?' She coloured, feeling ashamed, 'I am an awful human being.'

'No you aren't. And if you are, then so am I!'

'You are? Why?'

'Let's just say that it was a bit of a shock when I found out that Amy was pregnant. Not that I resent her and Paul their happiness one bit, but, well …' Jack flicked his gaze at Kit's to make sure she wasn't looking at him with disgust before he carried on, 'I've made many mistakes over the years, but on the whole I don't regret my life – but if I'm honest I would have loved children. Seeing the woman I thought I might have children with one day expecting someone else's…'

He shook his head abruptly. 'I can't even finish that sentence. I never deserved her, and some things aren't meant to be. I mean, can you imagine me as a father! Poor child would be scarred for life.'

Kit moved around the table, and sat next to him, putting her hand on his knee. 'Oh, Jack, we're a right pair, aren't we.'

'We sure are.' Jack knocked back the remains of his coffee. 'And now I have to head into the wilds of the city. I have a potential restaurant to view. You want walking to Pickwicks? I may pop in and say hello to everyone on the way.'

'Thanks, but I'm off home. I need to phone my publisher. I have some explaining to do.'

Peering through the doorway of Pickwicks, Jack was surprised to find it was relatively quiet, with no sign of either Peggy or Scott. Helena, her hair pinned neatly back, was serving a group in the far corner of the café, and Megan was wiping tables near the door.

'Hi, Megan, how you doing?'

'Hello, Jack, I heard you were back. Long time no see. I'm good. You?'

'Great, thanks.' Jack, still in two minds if he was doing the right thing or not, said, 'Actually, Megan, could I have a word in private sometime soon?' He passed her a card with his phone number on it. 'Can you give me a quick ring? I might have a job for you. Keep it under your hat for now, I don't want to upset Peggy or cause you any trouble.'

Chapter Twelve

Saturday 11th June

Sitting in the opulent café of the Victoria and Albert Museum, Megan was trying to distract her troubled conscience by sketching some of the abstract patterns from the nineteenth-century architecture around her.

She half-wished that she'd already agreed to the new job Peggy had offered her before Jack had made his offer. She felt torn between what she felt she ought to do, and what her dwindling bank balance told her she should do.

How could she possibly choose? Peggy and Scott still hadn't told their friends that they were investing in another branch, let alone that they wanted her to run it for them. Scott hadn't wanted to jinx things by announcing anything before the contract had been agreed.

If she did agree to the job at 'Pickwicks 2', then she would be the manager, responsible for everything that went on at the new café. Jack, on the other hand, had offered Megan the post of head of staff and floor manager of a classy restaurant, with greater responsibility, a far larger wage, and fresh challenges. It wasn't that she no longer enjoyed her waitressing job, but a nagging feeling that she could be doing more with her life had planted itself in her head, and she hadn't been able to shift it.

Trying to weigh up her options, Megan ran everything through her mind one more time as she drew soothing strokes of charcoal across her paper. She critically examined the picture she was creating. It was good, but she knew she'd been capable of better when she was an art student. If only she could make her art pay … but until she and Nick had a place of their own there was nowhere with enough space for her to create the large-scale pieces she used to work on. Besides, she thought with a sigh, the chances of them being able to rent anywhere big enough to swing a cat, let alone squeeze an easel into, were slim – and renting studio space in London cost enough to make your hair curl...

When she'd been out with Nick yesterday evening, he'd advised her that she had nothing to lose by listening to what Jack had to say. She could always say no to whatever he was proposing.

She had never been very good at saying no...

Laying down the charcoal pencil she was using to shade the section of window she was reproducing on paper, Megan sighed again. Jack was due to join her at any minute, and she still had absolutely no idea what her answer was going to be. Although Jack had made his employment proposal sound glittering and un-refusable, she had a feeling she hadn't got the full story from him yet, and until she had all the facts she wasn't going to agree to anything at all.

Jack could see Megan sitting on a bench at the edge of the café. He watched her for a while. Unlike Kit or Amy always did, she did not have a steaming cup of coffee before her, but some sort of notebook, which she was staring at intently, before looking up at the high-windowed ceiling.

'I'm impressed.' He had walked quietly through the packed tables of tea drinkers. He spoke softly, not wanting to make Megan jump and therefore ruin the exquisite detail she was adding to the drawing. 'I had no idea you could draw.'

'Oh hello, Jack. Sorry, I didn't hear you arrive.'

'That is beautiful. Where did you learn to do that?'

'I went to art college, and it's always been a hobby. Do you really like it?'

'Yes.' Jack sat and marvelled at the softness of the strokes before him. Somehow, Megan had captured the very essence of the tiny portion of window mullion she'd been sketching. It was almost tangible, as if he touched the picture he'd feel the real stonework. 'You could make a living from pictures like this, you know. Ever considered making art your career?'

72

'There's nothing I'd like more, but artists in London are ten a penny. It isn't that simple. You have to know the right people to be in with a shot, and I don't.'

He inclined his head silently, as if he was about to say something else, but then turned to the matter in hand instead. 'Have you thought about my offer? It was entirely genuine, and as of last night, the premises I've been after are mine, all but for the exchange of the final piece of paperwork.'

Megan kept her eyes on her charcoal smudged fingers. 'The thing is, Jack, I would like to, but…'

'You don't want to let Peggy down.'

'Exactly. She and Scott have been very good to me.'

'Which is why I asked you confidentially. I didn't want to put you on the spot in front of your colleagues. They were wonderful when Amy gave up her waitressing job for pastures new, weren't they. I'm sure Peggy would understand that you'd welcome the opportunity for promotion. I can't imagine she thought you'd stay a waitress for ever.'

Megan looked uncomfortable; not wanting to break her word to Peggy, but not sure how else she could explain her quandary.

'Jack, I am going to have to break a confidence here. I am asking you to respect that.'

'Go ahead.'

'Peggy and Scott have taken on a new branch. A second Pickwicks coffee house.'

'They have?' Jack frowned. 'Peggy never said.'

'Did you tell Peggy you had a restaurant opening soon?'

'Good point. Go on.'

'Well, the thing is, they've asked me to be the manager for the second branch. I haven't told them if I'll do it or not yet, but…'

Jack finished off the sentence left hanging in the air, 'But she asked first, and you are a very kind and loyal person.'

'That's pretty much it, yes.'

'I need a coffee. Can I get you anything?'

Waiting in the queue, Jack was unable to decide if it would make his opening of a restaurant on Pickwicks' doorstep more or less acceptable to Peggy and Scott if they had another café elsewhere. He hadn't yet told Megan where his new venture was based. Once he'd done that, she'd probably stay with Peggy anyway, and yet Jack couldn't dismiss the feeling that she was more than tempted by his offer.

As he returned to their table, he knew one thing for sure: artistic talent like Megan's should not be wasted. And he knew someone who would love her style. Someone he knew had the sort of money to pay for her art … well, maybe he'd cross that bridge when he came to it.

Sitting back down, Jack smiled. 'Tell me about your art.'

Grateful to be able to put off the final moment of decision-making, Megan began to tell him all about her projects at college; about how she'd dreamt of having an exhibition in a gallery one day, and about her trip to help her friend Izzie sort a crisis.

'I'm not sure I know Izzie?'

'Sorry, Jack, I forgot you were away. Izzie, or Isadora if her mother is listening, set up her own art and coffee place in an abandoned medieval church in the Cotswolds. It's *so* picturesque.'

Detecting a note of wistfulness in her voice, he asked, 'What was the crisis?'

Megan smiled at the recollection, 'A tree went through the church roof just before a famous choir were supposed to give their annual Christmas concert there. I ran the centre while Izzie got the place fixed up.'

'Did it all get sorted in time?'

'It was a near-run thing, and very eventful!' She poured herself a cup of tea. 'Why do you ask, Jack? I hadn't got you down as being into art.'

'You'd be astonished by what I like!' He wiggled his eyebrows at her, playfully flirty.

Megan laughed. 'No I wouldn't! Amy and Kit are my friends too, remember!'

The mention of his friends took Jack back to the point of his enquiries. 'Do you produce bigger pieces, or do you like to work on miniatures like those?' He gestured towards her sketchbook.

'Actually, the bigger the better.' Megan found herself getting more enthusiastic and animated as she told Jack about the huge canvases she'd produced for her end of year project at college. They'd virtually been installations; abstract works of mad bright colours with small areas of intricately worked architectural features. 'They were totally insane, looking back, but I loved them. I haven't worked in large scale for a very long time.'

'But you'd like to? If you had the space, I mean?'

'I would, but as I said, that isn't an option. Nick and I can't even afford to rent a place together, let alone a place with studio space for me to indulge in splashing paint on canvases which I'd probably never sell anyway.'

Jack's eyes returned to her sketchbook. 'Would you mind if I had a look through that? You can say no, I understand that it might be private.'

Not quite sure where their conversation was leading, Megan pushed the sketchbook across the wooden surface, and sat uneasily while Jack took his time to study each and every page. Most of the pictures were of tiny details of buildings, tree bark, close-ups of leaves and flowers, and even the corner of the coffee machine at Pickwicks.

Suddenly Jack stopped and looked up. 'This is Peggy!'

'Yes. I did a few preliminary sketches. I'm drawing a portrait of her and Scott as a surprise for her birthday in August. You won't tell her, will you?'

'Of course not.' Jack tore his gaze from the pictures. 'I can't believe Peggy is going to be fifty-five. She hasn't changed since I first knew her.'

'It's staying busy that does it.' Megan thought about her boss flitting around the café with twice the energy of her staff, even though they were nowhere near her age. *Peggy*. Her expression darkened. 'Jack, I'll be honest, I would like to take you up on your job offer, but how can I? Peggy's been so good to me.'

Closing the sketchbook, Jack looked at Megan. 'I know she has, but although Peggy would miss you, she's not the sort of person who'd hold you back if you wanted to expand your horizons.'

'Can I think about it a bit longer?'

'Shall we say I need an answer by next Monday evening? That way, I can advertise if you say no.' Jack shifted a little in his seat. 'And of course, you ought to visit the restaurant, to see if you would actually like to work there.'

'Thanks, Jack, that's really kind of you. When is good for a look round?'

'I'll text you the address and we can sort a visiting time between your shifts at Pickwicks.'

Megan glanced at her watch. 'Talking of which, I ought to head Richmond way now.'

As she got up, packing her possessions into a shoulder bag, Jack said, 'Suddenly I find I have two propositions for you instead of one.'

'You do?'

'Yes, the first – which is not dependent on the second – is if you would consider providing me with six square canvases showing architectural close-ups for the walls of my new bistro. They would look stunning in there. The second, as you already know, is to come and work for me as front of house manageress. I'd also be able to offer you working hours which would provide you with time to paint – as well as some studio space…'

Chapter Thirteen

Sunday 12th June

Helena stroked her short purple skirt into place and taking a step back, examined the tan of her long bare legs in the bathroom mirror, right down to her black beach shoes.

Taking a brush from her shoulder bag, she ran it through her hair, smiling at the purple and black effect that, despite having to pin it back at work, she loved. Then, making sure her small chest was shown off to its best under her figure-hugging black T-shirt, Helena looked herself straight in the heavily kohled eyes and said, 'Go get him, girl!'

Rupert sat on the warm grass near the café with his young charges. Opening his palms in front of him, he displayed the earthworm he'd temporarily removed from the wormery he'd brought along to Kew.

Laughing along with the children, as they instantly divided into those who recoiled with cries of 'Yuck,' and those who crawled nearer with murmurs of 'Cool!', Rupert had just begun explaining how useful worms were to gardeners and farmers, and how much fun it was to keep a wormery, when he had the feeling he was being watched – and not just by his young audience.

His heart sank as he saw the vision in black and purple leading against a tree behind where his group were sat. Thinking fast, knowing that escape was not an option, Rupert fixed his fading smile in place, and passed the worm carefully around for those who wanted to touch it. 'Be very, very gentle. Remember worms are living creatures, they work hard for us, and so we should respect them.'

A young boy put his hand up, 'Rupert, is it true that worms will turn into two worms if you cut them in half?'

'An excellent question, Jason. No, that's a myth, I'm afraid. Sometimes the nerves in their bodies will keep them wriggling for a little while after they've been cut in half, but no, they will not survive.'

Wondering how many of his charges had experimented in that area, Rupert asked Jason to pass the wormery nearer. 'Worms don't like the heat, and as it is a very warm day, we should return this little chap to the cool earth now.'

Rupert was about to place the creature back in its home, when he suddenly had an idea. He knew there was no way he was going to get out of there without Helena insisting they spent some time together. Perhaps he should put her on the spot.

'Unless of course our grown-up observer would like to hold the worm?'

His expression challenging, daring her to say no in front of the children, Rupert offered the worm up towards Helena. 'May I introduce you all to my boss's daughter?' He waved a hand towards the tree against which Helena lounged. 'Say hello to Helena, everyone.'

Helena cursed inwardly as all the children chorused, 'Hello, Helena.' It had been her intention to keep this trip to see Rupert to herself. Now Rupert had introduced her to his class, probably believing he was being kind, she'd have to tell her parents she'd been to Kew.

Smiling back at them, Helena politely declined holding the worm, a species she had never been able to bring herself to touch. Watching Rupert with the children was an education in itself. He was so good with them. She smiled to herself. He was fantastic boyfriend material.

As Rupert dismissed his class into the waiting arms of their parents, he ignored the hovering spectre of Helena for a moment, and sat down at the nearest table. Pulling a ledger from his rucksack, he made a few notes about the session, including the number of attendees, and the new ideas for future classes that had come to him as he'd led the children on their mini wildlife odyssey. Then he checked his mobile, and was only partly surprised to see a missed call from his mother, as well as a text, asking her son to come and visit soon. Sighing, Rupert left the message unanswered and put his phone away.

When he couldn't put it off any longer, he looked up. Helena was nowhere to be seen, and for a fleeting second Rupert was swamped with relief. The last thing he wanted was to make small talk with a young woman who, for reasons he couldn't begin to fathom, obviously found him attractive. All he wanted to do was head off in search of more opportunities to take shots for the photography competition he wanted to enter.

His relief was short-lived. A few seconds later Helena pushed open the double swing doors of the café, holding a tray containing two cans of cola and two glasses filled with ice.

Knowing he couldn't blank her after she'd kindly bought him a drink, and not losing sight of the fact that she was Phil's daughter (he didn't want her reporting back to her father that he'd been mean), Rupert stifled a groan and prepared to delay his photographic session for an hour or so.

'Those kids really love what you do, don't they?'

Rupert's face reddened as Helena sat down and made a play of crossing and uncrossing her undeniably attractive legs as she got comfortable on the chair opposite him. 'Do you think so?'

'Sure. None of my teachers ever made me laugh or captured my attention like you did with that lot. That's quite a gift.'

'Thank you.' Rupert undid the ring pull of his drink. 'And thanks for the drink. What I do is a bit different to normal teaching, though. I mean, you *have* to go to school, and the things you're required to learn are set in stone. The children who come along to Kew all want to be here, and they all enjoy being outside and learning about nature.'

'Makes sense.' Helena looked about her properly for the first time. With the sun shining it was easy to see why her parents and Rupert loved this place so much. She, though, was a city girl through and through, and had never been one for the great outdoors. Maybe she just needed someone to show it to her properly … 'You love it here as well, don't you?'

'I do.' Rupert felt relieved; talking about his work was safe ground. 'I couldn't believe it when your dad gave me the job. It

79

really is dream-come-true stuff. I've adored Kew Gardens since I was a boy. I bet you've spent a lot of time here a lot as well.'

'Mum used to bring us when we were small; Thomas and me, I mean. She liked us to run around and exhaust ourselves as much as possible before talking us home to bed.'

'Sounds sensible to me.' Rupert grinned; he could well imagine Helena and her twin brother being a total handful. 'I might even have seen you guys playing here. Between terms at university I spent a lot of time at Kew trying to work out what I wanted to do when I grew up.' Pushing his point home about the age gap between them, Rupert added, 'When I was eighteen or nineteen you were probably six or seven, so it's possible I witnessed the odd game of catch between you and Thomas.'

Not liking how the conversation had escaped from her, an image of her childhood self not being the one she wanted in Rupert's head, Helena said, 'So what do you usually do once your lesson is over?'

'Oh, I stay.' Rupert tapped his backpack. 'I go for a long walk, take photographs, and generally enjoy being on my own for a while out of the madness of London.'

Not missing the mention of him wanting time alone, Helena felt a little awkward. Running a finger down the side of her cold glass, she licked the accumulated moisture off her fingertip. 'You don't like London?'

'It's OK. Bit too crowded for me. I like open spaces.' Rupert glanced around him, hoping that the parents who'd lingered with their children to buy refreshments didn't assume Helena was his girlfriend. He wished she'd cover herself up a bit as well; he thought she was asking for trouble walking around dressed like a gothic Barbie doll.

A glimmer of an idea to escape from his current uncomfortable situation slid into his mind. Fully aware that the real answer to the question was that she was there to see him, Rupert asked, 'How come you're not in full shopping mode on Oxford Street this morning then, Helena? You meeting your mates here later for a drink or something?'

'Umm, yeah. That's right.' Helena took refuge in her drink.

Rupert clearly wasn't interested in her yet. She was sure her mum was wrong about him being gay, though. Her mum was just paranoid after going out with Jack last century. The way Rupert had been eyeing her legs earlier, and the way his gaze kept dropping to her cleavage, was enough to tell her *that*.

Determined to give him the opportunity to get to know her well enough to fall for her properly, she rallied. 'I'm early, though. Mum is obviously worrying about something again, so I thought I'd let my folks sort out whatever's wrong without me hanging around.'

'That was kind.' Mentally awarding her a point for tactics, Rupert stretched his legs out. Perhaps he could bore her into giving up on him? 'Would you like to walk with me while you wait, or are you staying here? I was planning to head over to the greenhouses on the other side of the gardens today.'

Hope leaping in her heart, Helena treated him to her best smile. He'd just asked her to walk with him. That sort of made this a date. 'I'd love to. Thanks, Rupe.'

'Helena, there is something you should know before we set off.'

Her breath caught in her throat. Was he about to tell her he wasn't interested, or ask her out, or kiss her, or…

'I *hate* being called Rupe. OK?'

She exhaled slowly, partly relieved, partly disappointed. 'Oh. OK.'

Chapter Fourteen

Monday 13th June

Rupert kept his eyes fixed on the computer screen at the end of the shop counter, trying to decide what to do about Helena.

He had finally shaken her off after an hour of walking around the far recesses of Kew Gardens and listening to a barrage of questions about his family, his life, why he was working for her dad when he could be a rich lawyer, and some none-too-subtle enquiries about his last girlfriend, which he somehow managed to dodge by the strangely well-timed sighting of a (totally mythical) Triple-Tailed Warbler in a hedge to his left.

By the end of their conversation (a conversation which had basically been a monologue by Helena, with only the occasional punctuation of a one- or two-word answer by himself), Rupert had felt thoroughly grilled. Replaying everything that had been said in his head, he reassured himself that he hadn't said too much, hadn't led her on, and hadn't confirmed if he was gay or straight, nor had he given her any reason to expect anything from him. Still, he couldn't shift the uneasy feeling that she wasn't going to give up easily.

Unable to understand what she saw in him, Rupert groaned inwardly. Should he have told Helena that he was gay?

He closed his eyes and stretched his arms out to try and relieve some of the tension building in his limbs. He wasn't ready to say it out loud yet. Not even when he was the only one there to listen, although deep down he knew there was no doubt. When he'd sat at the table with Jack and their mutual friends the other night, for example, he had been filled with enough excited curiosity about the very attractive openly gay man opposite him to confirm his preferences.

Opening a sales spreadsheet, Rupert failed to focus on the numbers before him, musing instead on the more immediate personal crisis. Should he tell Phil that Helena had been at Kew? Surely it would all blow over if he left it alone? She was merely a teenager with a crush … although at eighteen, wasn't she past the silly crush stage? He didn't want to get Helena into trouble with her parents, but at the same time he didn't like the idea of keeping secrets from his boss. Especially as, after years of not knowing what he wanted to do with his life, he felt he was finally on the right career path.

Trying to distract himself from his thoughts, Rupert found himself tuning into the speculative conversation that was going on between Phil and Rob as they redid the shop's window display behind him.

'He hasn't told you why he's really back then?' Phil frowned as he tried to balance a cuddly blue tit on the edge of a book display.

'Just that he was ready to come back, and that he missed his friends.'

'Do you buy that?'

'Yes, but I doubt that's all there is to it.' Rob picked up a set of children's picture books and passed them to his business partner. 'The fact Jack returned without making a big theatrical fuss, or letting us know he was on his way first, makes me think he's running away from something.'

'You mean *someone*?'

'Very probably.' Rob stepped back to examine the display. 'Every time I think Jack has grown up, he goes and proves me wrong. I wish he could find someone to scratch whatever itch it is he has.'

Phil grunted. 'Do you think that'll ever happen?'

'No. Although I'd love to be proved wrong.' Rob placed a pot of fake flowers in the corner of the window. 'The chef thing was unexpected, mind.'

'Kit said he used to be a good cook.'

'Jack was always the one who did the big meals at uni. His roasts were a bit legendary, to be honest, but I had no idea he'd head in that direction job-wise.'

'I'm not sure he did either.' Phil laid one final book on the display. 'The way he was talking over our takeaway the other night convinced me he's happy, though. Seems Jack has finally found a passion that isn't going to break anyone else's heart.'

Rob nodded. 'Well that's something at least. Let's face it, Jack might be a great bloke, but there can't be many members of the gay community left for him to sleep with in London.'

Accepting a signal from Phil saying he was about to make tea, Rupert got up from his stall and went into the kitchen to collect his mug, returning just in time to hear his employers listing all Jack's past dating disasters. He moaned inwardly. A small part of him had thought that getting to know Jack might be fun – might be what he needed to help him stop battling his internal demons – but on the other hand he didn't like the idea of one-night stands, and never had. Whereas Jack seemed to thrive on them...

Even though he'd decided that, for the sake of his mother, he'd stay single, that didn't mean he didn't want to work out who he was. He'd thought Jack could help, but by the sound of it the man was obviously someone to stay away from.

Which was a shame, because ever since they'd met at Phil's place, Rupert's mind had drifted to thoughts of Jack far more frequently than was sensible.

Megan's conscience was keeping her awake at night. How could she possibly let Peggy and Scott down? They were so excited about securing the new premises for the next Pickwicks café, and had even discussed her going to view it so she could get a feel for her new place of employment – all without letting her get a word in edgeways.

She and Nick had talked about little else over the weekend. And although she was excited at the prospect of having her first artist's contract, she was in a dither.

Patient as ever, Nick's soft Irish tones had repeated the same phrases of encouragement. 'Whichever job you choose, your wages will rise. The important thing is for you to be happy.'

Kind though this was, Megan couldn't help wishing that,

every now and then, Nick would decide for her.

That afternoon, as the lunchtime rush disappeared into the less hectic trade of late afternoon teas, and Peggy began flicking through a brochure of café equipment, she knew she couldn't put it off any longer. With her palms sweating slightly, she went into the kitchen.

'Do you have a minute, Scott?'

Megan's boss glanced up at her, thinking she seemed very pale. 'You OK, sweetheart?'

'I'll get back to you on that in a minute.'

'Ahhh.' Scott put down the cloth he'd been cleaning his worktop with, washed his hands, and followed his chief waitress into the main café.

'Peggy, can I have a quick word please?' Megan, with Scott following behind her, checked that Helena could cope in the café on her own, and took a deep breath.

'You OK, Megan?' Peggy exchanged glances with her husband. 'You look a bit shaky.'

'I have something to tell you. Something I should have told you already, really. But I promised I wouldn't say anything. And then – well, I haven't known what to do.'

Megan was speaking far faster than she intended to, and the professional edge she'd been determined to keep to her voice had already been nudged out by a hint of panic. 'And of course, I'd already promised you two that I wouldn't say anything about the new café, and then this happened, and I don't know what to do because I could do with the extra money, but I don't want to let you down because you're my friends, and you've been so good to me, but now what with the art and everything…'

Scott laid his large, slightly floury hand gently on Megan's shoulder. 'Hey, slow down! Now, take a second.' Shooting a warning look at his wife, who was obviously ready to jump in with a comment before Megan had told the whole story, Scott said, 'We are indeed your friends, which means you can tell us whatever it is without worrying. Come on, what's the matter?'

With an appreciative smile at Scott, Megan dived in. 'You know Jack is back? Did you know he was opening a bistro?'

Wary, Peggy exchanged another look with her husband. 'I knew he'd been working as a chef. I didn't know about that. Go on.'

'Well, he's offered me the job as front of house manager. It was only a day or so after your job offer, but I couldn't tell him that because no one knows about Pickwicks number two, and I wasn't supposed to tell anyone about Jack's venture, as he didn't want to say anything about it for the same reasons as you haven't told anyone.'

'In case the rental deal falls through?' Scott passed Megan a glass of water.

'Yes. Although I think he is planning to buy rather than rent.'

'He would.' Peggy looked grim. 'And I imagine you're very tempted by Jack's job offer. He'll be able to pay you higher wages than we can, I have no doubt.'

Megan swallowed, and nodded quietly. The anger she could see on Peggy's face was justified, but made her feel awful. 'I have a loyalty to Pickwicks, and I don't want to let you down, but I need to earn enough so Nick and I can find a home of our own.'

Scott smiled at her. 'I know; and we do understand. You've been worth your weight in gold these last few years, but if the time has come for you to move on, then so be it. When do you have to tell Jack by?'

'Next Monday. He's invited me to visit the restaurant on Wednesday.'

'You haven't seen it yet?'

'I don't even know where it is, to be honest.'

'So you might take one look at the place and decide you don't want to work there anyway?'

'Yes.' Megan sighed. 'I am completely torn. I hate this. I really hate it.'

Peggy wrapped her waitress in her arms, cuddling her close. 'It's OK, Megan. I admit I'm furious, but not with you. Perhaps if we'd already made it public that Pickwicks was getting a second branch, Jack wouldn't have thought it was OK to poach our staff. Still, he should know better.'

'Scott?' Megan peered up at her other employer. 'What do you think?'

'I'm also annoyed at Jack, but not surprised. He's always been a decent businessman, and he knows a good worker when he sees one. For him this won't be poaching, but simply trying to get the best person for the job.'

Megan gulped. 'Do you want to withdraw your offer? I'd understand after I've been so disloyal.'

'What are you talking about? You haven't done anything wrong! You were put in an impossible position by both us and Jack. The choice is yours and yours alone.' Scott gave her his dazzling smile. 'You must do what's right for you and you alone. If you go with Jack there'll be no hard feelings. Obviously we would love you to front the new café, but we won't be able to match Jack's wages. We will be able to offer you more sociable hours than he can, though, and if you find out how much holiday he's offering you, then I'm sure we can better it.'

Megan looked from Peggy to Scott and sniffed back tears of gratitude. 'You are so kind. Thank you both.'

'Not at all. Whatever you decide we won't think any less of you. And in the meantime, you could give Helena a hand?' Peggy nodded towards a large group of pensioners who had just come through Pickwicks' front door. 'The poor girl is drowning in customers over there!'

Chapter Fifteen

Wednesday 15th June

Jack read the text with mixed feelings.

*Don't forget: dinner tonight – my place – with Kit and Phil.
7pm. DON'T BE LATE. Amy xx*

His intentions to visit Amy once more before the mini dinner
party had dissolved, due to the necessary preparations for the
opening of the restaurant, planning his forthcoming menus, and
checking on Kit. With a sense of guilt caused not only by his
neglect of Amy, but by the fact that he'd have to tell them
everything about his new bistro soon – including its location –
Jack sent a quick, positive reply as Megan honed into view.

He had agreed to meet Megan at the end of the lane that
divided Pickwicks from Richmond's main street. He knew she
thought he was being kind in escorting her from her place of
work to the site of the new bistro. He wasn't sure how she'd
react when she realised he wasn't being chivalrous as much as
walking her across the road. He wouldn't have been surprised
if, when she saw how close to Pickwicks it was, she turned right
round and walked away.

'Hi, Megan, thanks for coming.' Jack noticed she appeared a
little uneasy. 'You OK?'

'I had to tell Peggy and Scott you'd offered me a job. I'm
sorry, Jack. I had to.'

Jack grimaced. 'I understand. Do they know I know about
their expansion plans as well?'

'Not yet.' Megan's voice reflected how miserable she felt, 'I
feel like a double agent, and I can't say I like the sensation very

much.'

'I'm sure. Well,' Jack started to walk down the road, 'anyway, let me show you the bistro, then if you like the place you can make a more informed decision.'

'OK. Is it far away?'

'Not far, no.' Jack stopped walking and turned to face her. 'When we get there, whatever your initial instincts, will you promise me you'll give the place a proper look over? Even if you say no, I'd like your opinion as an experienced waitress and a potential diner.'

Suspicious, Megan agreed as Jack began to move again, only to stop five steps further along the road.

'Here?' Her brow furrowed as she looked up at the building before them.

'Here.'

'My God, Jack! It's on the bloody doorstep. Are you insane? Peggy will throttle you.'

Megan stood in the doorway of the abandoned Italian restaurant. She was stunned. She'd assumed they'd be travelling at least one Tube stop away. They were only a few hundred metres from the café where she'd just hung up her apron.

'Seriously? You aren't joking?'

'I'm not joking, and don't worry. I can handle Peggy.'

'You might be able to, but I can't! How would I ever be able to look her in the face again if I was stealing customers from her?'

Jack unlocked the front door and pushed it open, 'I thought that might be your reaction but, and I mean no offense to the Pickwicks clientele by this, I *am* hoping to attract a rather different set of customers.'

'Even so, I'm not sure I can…'

'Why not come in and have a look anyway, and give me your opinion? I'd like to talk to you about your art as well.'

Megan hated that she instantly loved the place. In her mind's eye she could already see the restaurant buzzing with life. She could smell the food and, more pertinently, she could picture her art on the wall. Jack had been right; her style of work would suit the part-painted, part-exposed brickwork walls very well.

Taking a step back, Jack said nothing, letting her explore by herself at her own pace. After a while, Megan came and sat down with him. 'It's perfect, Jack. I'd like to have been able to say I hate the place. That would have made my life a lot easier. But I don't. If you get the menu right, then this place has the potential to do well.'

'Thanks, that means a lot to me. However, I have a feeling there is a "but" hovering on the tip of your tongue.'

'But ... I can't take the job.' Megan studied her clasped hands as they rested on the table. 'If this place wasn't so close to Pickwicks I'd have said yes. The job appeals. In fact, I would have loved it, but I can't. I wouldn't be able to live with myself if I was responsible for taking trade from Peggy.'

'I won't really do that, you know. I'll be open afternoons and evenings, not mornings.'

'But you'll do lunches or afternoon teas, won't you? I mean, you'd have to for the place to pay.'

'I knew you'd see that I'll have to do afternoon teas at least. That's one of the reasons I wanted you to work for me. You know the trade.' He held up his hand to stop Megan having to defend her decision. 'However, I had a suspicion that once you knew I was so close by, you'd say no, and I respect you for that. Now then, let's move on to more positive things. Your art. Walk this way.'

Puzzled, Megan got up and followed Jack up the stairs to a small room at the back of the flat above the restaurant.

'Would this room do you as a studio?'

Megan's jaw dropped open. 'But...'

'But nothing. I want you to do me six pieces of art. I know neither you nor Nick have the room for you to be able to work on them at home, and you don't have the money to rent working space, so as I do have the space it makes sense for you to use it.'

She was still struggling to decide how she was supposed to respond as Jack carried on talking, 'There's a large window, and the light in here is fairly good, but you'll probably need to get a daylight bulb for the evening. The walls are already white, so that's good. I was intending to pull up the carpet later on, so it won't matter if that gets paint-spattered, and there's plenty of room for an easel or a floor-standing canvas to be worked on in here. Would that do you? What do you think?'

'Jack, I can't. I appreciate the offer, but I can't afford to rent a room this size.'

'You misunderstand me; you won't be paying rent. You'll be painting me six amazing pictures for the walls downstairs, for which I will pay you half what they are worth in exchange for letting you use this studio space for free.' He stopped talking and scribbled down a sum which seemed colossal to Megan. 'What do you think? Will you do the pictures for me for this fee?'

'But … I turned the job down!'

'What's that got to do with anything? One wasn't at the expense of the other. I know I have a bit of a reputation, Megan, but I've never been deliberately cruel.'

She blushed. 'Sorry, Jack, it's just that people don't make offers like that very often.'

Jack smiled. 'That is true – and I'm not being entirely benevolent. I want the pictures before I open.'

'Which is when?'

'Mid to end of August.'

'Oh my God, Jack!'

'Can you do it?'

'I have no idea. I'd have to work non-stop after I've finished at the café, and at weekends.'

'Do you want to give it a try then?'

'Yes.' A smile erupted across Megan's face. 'Yes please. Thank you so much.'

Beaming back at her, Jack felt a glow of well-being rise in his chest. He may not have got the manager he'd hoped for, but seeing the happiness in Megan's eyes at the prospect of being allowed to paint again was worth that disappointment.

'Why don't you go and give Peggy and Scott the good news, and tell them you'll be running their new branch now?'

Megan smiled at him. 'I will. Thank you.'

'Can I ask one favour though?'

'Sure.'

'Don't tell them where my place is yet. I'll tell them myself, tomorrow. I don't think it would be fair for you to take the brunt of Peggy's ire.'

'Thanks, Jack. I wasn't looking forward to that bit of the conversation!'

'I bet!'

Megan felt lightheaded. 'I haven't dreamt this, have I? Have you really just given me the chance to paint again?

'It means a lot to you, doesn't it.'

'It does.' Megan pulled her phone out of her bag, ready to call Nick with her news the second she left the restaurant. 'Until I went to Izzie's I hadn't thought much about all the dreams I used to have about making a career out of painting and drawing. Just working enough to pay the rent was a big enough task.'

'But now you want more?'

'Yes.' She frowned. 'Do you think that's greedy?'

Jack laughed. 'To have dreams and go for them? Of course not. That, Megan, is what life is all about.'

'Like you and this restaurant.'

'Quite.' Jack paused as he looked about him. 'Believe it or not, I would rather this place had been further away from Pickwicks. I didn't decide to set up here so I could cause trouble. It really is the ideal place for what I want to do in the price bracket I can afford, and it provides me with a home as well.'

'I can see that.' Megan ran a hand across the rustic walls. 'It isn't going to be easy persuading Peggy though. Just when they have enough of a steady income to go for a second branch, you come along and provide even more competition.'

'I know.' Jack made a face. 'I bet Kit and Amy will have a few choice words for me as well.'

'I'd put money on it!'

Chapter Sixteen

Friday 17th June

Amy sat down with a sigh so loud it even took her by surprise. Surely she shouldn't be this tired? It hadn't been a particularly challenging day at work, but even the short steps up to her office seemed to take her breath away these days.

'If I'm like this now, what on earth will I be like by mid-August?'

Placing her hands on her bump, she kicked a pile of newspapers off the coffee table and put her feet up, closing her eyes. She knew she was insane to have invited friends around for food after a day at work, but she wanted to host one last dinner party before she got too big to move, or before the house was overtaken by child safety equipment and she could no longer get to the fridge.

Plus there was always the outside chance that Jack would get itchy feet and disappear again. Amy wanted to get all her close friends and their partners together quickly, in case Jack screwed someone else he shouldn't and did another midnight flit.

'Not exactly the best role model for you, is he?' Amy had taken to chatting to her bump, and from the constant tumble dryer-type movements of her fast-growing baby, she was convinced it was listening. 'Perhaps he'll be the godfather whose example is the one you learn *not* to follow. He's very kind though. Mummy loves him very much and he is one of Daddy's best friends, so I hope you'll love him too. Although I should warn you that Uncle Jack is a bit hopeless; you'll probably end up having to look after him!'

Amy glanced at her watch. She had two hours until her guests were due to arrive. Thankful that Paul had talked her out of cooking, and was going to pick up a load of Marks and Spencer's finest pre-prepared food, Amy hauled herself off the comfort of the sofa and waddled – there was no other word adequate to describe how she moved these days – towards the bathroom. A hot shower and a change into her cosiest maternity clothes and she'd feel much livelier.

Rob and his wife Debbie arrived on the doorstep just as Kit and Phil walked up the drive behind them. Amy smiled to see that in both cases, the men carried wine, and the woman held an alternate soft drink so that there was something for Amy to enjoy as well as the non-pregnant members of the group.

The 'crikey, you've grown even more than when I saw you a few days ago,' conversations had only just finished, and jackets were being hung in the hallway, when the doorbell rang again and Jack arrived.

Engulfing Amy is one of his habitual giant hugs, Jack passed her a large cake tin. 'I wasn't sure what you were off eating, or if you were craving anything, so I made these. Bit of a mixture of things to appeal to all tastes.'

Amy undid the lid, her eyes lighting up. 'Thanks, Jack.' She immediately picked out the top tiny cupcake from a mountain of others below. 'What flavour is this one?'

'Light lemon and poppy seed.'

Amy popped into her mouth in one go. 'Oh, wow, Jack! That was heavenly. Do you have a kitchen already, then?'

'I sweet-talked the lady in the hotel kitchen, and she let me bake them in return for favours so far unspecified.'

'You are shameless!'

'This is true. The poor woman is doomed to be disappointed.' Jack rescued the tin from Amy's arms. 'I was sort of thinking these would make a good pudding, or snacks for you over the next few days.' He couldn't help but laugh as Amy grabbed another two cakes and chewed them up. 'You had any weird food cravings then?'

'I'm currently eating an extra-large number of cheese scones, which I've more or less been mainlining for the past month – before that it was pizza. I can't help wonder if I'll ever want to eat either of them ever again after the birth.'

He slapped her hand playfully as she took another cake. 'This pregnancy lark making you peckish then?'

Amy laughed. 'Yep! Thanks, Jack, these are delicious. Do you want to take them through to the kitchen and give them to Paul before I eat them all? He's in charge of the food tonight.'

As the friends sat around Amy and Paul's dining table, the seven of them squashed up against each other as the table wasn't really equal to the task of supporting more than four people, Paul began to serve up the gorgeous-smelling spicy meatballs, potatoes wedges, and various side dishes. 'Not really up to the standards you're used to these days, Jack mate, but I didn't want Amy stood in the kitchen.'

Jack smiled, 'Quite right.' He took a large helping of sour cream from a nearby bowl. 'And anyway, I love this type of food!'

The evening soon relaxed into chatty conversation about the baby, the bookshop, and property renting. The food disappeared quickly, along with a couple of bottles of white wine and a pitcher of iced orange juice. Jack, who'd been gearing himself up to tell them all about his bistro plans but was wary of ruining such a great atmosphere, took a deep breath when, as he was helping Paul carry a jug of coffee, pot of tea, and Jack's tin of mini cupcakes to the table, Phil asked him the inevitable question.

'Come on then, Jack, we can all see why cooking appeals, and having had a sneaky taste of your cakes in the kitchen I can see you have talent in that area, but come clean, mate. Why are you here now? You had a good job in Kent, what happened this time? Running from a bloke by any chance?'

An uncomfortable silence landed on the table until Kit dug her husband in the ribs and Amy and Jack exchanged glances.

'It's OK.' Jack blew out an exhalation of air through his teeth. 'Phil is right. Some of you know already, but yes, it was a bloke. Isn't it always?'

'Look, Jack, I'm sorry, I was only teasing, I didn't mean...'

'It's OK, Phil.' Knocking back the remainder of his glass of wine, Jack said, 'Tell you what, fill up this glass and my coffee cup, and I'll tell you the gory details.'

Soon he had everyone laughing and rolling their eyes at his hopelessness to read the signs when it came to relationships. Sending himself up, Jack quickly slipped back into old habits, and was soon explaining himself in song lyrics. 'Honestly, Deep Purple said it all in "California Jam", when they went on about making mistakes again before you fall. If that isn't me all over!

'I loved working at Kennedy's, but I didn't like working for Gareth much. He was a bit of a bully – just a little more than you'd expect even a chef to be. I only ended up having sex with him out of anger – which I grant you is a crap excuse, but then I've had sex with people for less sensible reasons. You could have knocked me down with a feather when I discovered he'd fancied me all along.'

'What are you like?' Amy shook her head sadly, 'I wish we could find you someone nice to share your life with.'

Jack looked at his friends; they were all indicating their agreement with Amy. 'You are good people, and after all I've put you through in the past, it's remarkable that I'm even here with you now, but believe me, the world is better off with me being single. History has conclusively proven that I can't handle a relationship, and that I am a destructive force in that area. My new life involves a new career, a new home, and no more men – although I'm keeping my old friends!'

Amy, reminded of the mantra 'New job, new home, new life' that she'd played over and over in her head when she'd left her lonely days in Scotland behind her, felt tears gather in her eyes. 'Oh, Jack, that's so sad. You should be with someone.'

Paul passed her a tissue quickly. 'You OK, love?'

Amy smiled through her tears, 'Sorry, my bloody hormones are all over the place, but you should, Jack, you should have someone special.'

Raising a glass to his friend, Jack said, 'The single life is the best thing for me, and besides, I'm going to be far too busy to meet anyone worth meeting for ages.'

'Does that mean you've found somewhere to turn into

"Jack's Bistro"?' Rob passed the cake tin to Debbie, 'Although I assume it won't really be called "Jack's Bistro".'

With butterflies rolling in his stomach, Jack swallowed hard. This was it; the time to come clean. 'I have indeed, but no, it won't be called Jack's Bistro. I haven't got a name sorted for it yet, to be honest.'

'How exciting!' Debbie immediately started firing potential restaurant names at them all. 'Jack's Nosh? The Gorgeous Cupcake Bistro?'

As the influence of the wine they'd all drunk began to take hold, Jack found himself drowning in potential, increasingly silly restaurant names.

'Bistro-mania…'

'Pasta'n'Chips…'

'Delicious Delights…'

His face aching from laughing, Paul refilled Jack's coffee cup. 'So, once you've chosen from that list of most excellent restaurant names, when will your new place be ready to roll? In time for a party to wet our baby's head I hope? Amy said she'd asked you.'

Feeling as though he'd missed his moment to confess where his bistro was, Jack said, 'Well, that all depends when Donahue Junior is due and if I am up and running by then, but as I said to Amy, I would be absolutely delighted!'

'Excellent!' Amy clapped her hands excitedly, 'Sometime early September for a party then.'

'Oh, that's perfect!' Jack began to mentally plan what he might cook for them all. 'I hope to open before the end of August, so I will keep whichever evening you desire free, and we can welcome the newcomer to our crew in style!'

'And', Kit added, 'if all goes according to plan, then we'll be celebrating the twins getting their A level results as well.'

'Oh yes!' Phil added, 'and we should be celebrating your next novel launch, shouldn't we, love?'

Kit went pale. 'Um, hopefully. Yes.'

Not missing Kit's discomfort, Jack broke in, 'Well it looks as if I'll be putting by a couple of magnums of champagne, rather than the odd glass by then!'

'And,' Amy chipped in, 'let's not forget that Peggy has her birthday in August as well!'

At the mention of Peggy, Jack found it was his turn to blanch. 'Well, I think I'd best stop messing about and order in an entire lorry full of the sparkly stuff in.' He peered into his cooling cup of coffee. 'Actually, guys, there is something I should tell you about the restaurant. The thing is...'

Paul, who had been out in the kitchen, suddenly appeared holding a bottle of champagne and tapped the side of his glass theatrically with a spoon.

'As we're talking about celebrating the birth of our baby,' he reached out a held his wife's hand, 'this seems the perfect opportunity for us to ask you all, Kit, Phil, Rob, Debbie, and of course you, Jack, if you'd be godparents to our little bundle when he or she comes along. Unofficial ones of course, as there'll be no actual christening. That'll be his or her choice when they've grown up.'

'All of us?' Rob was beaming.

'Yes!' Amy laughed, 'I know convention states three godparents per child, but since when did any of us stick to convention?'

With a pop of the cork, Paul began to fill some glasses. 'To our child's godparents. May you all lead him or her astray in your own special ways!'

Jack's head hit his pillow hard that night.

'Amy's child's godfather!' He was utterly delighted, but he was also worried. *Will they still want me to be godfather when they find out how close my new place is to Pickwicks?*

Chapter Seventeen

Saturday 18th June

'Oh, let's have a look!'

Megan placed a plate of steaming hot cheese scones on the café table alongside a latte glass full of peppermint tea, and peered over Amy's shoulder at the scan photographs her friend was holding.

'It's incredible.' She tilted her head to try and make out each individual limb of the tiny human on the grey photograph before her. 'It's so weird to think that we're looking at a person. A tiny person who is right now tucked up safe and sound inside you!'

'Tell me about it.' Amy felt the nervous tension which accompanied her almost permanent indigestion swirl alongside her high-kicking baby.

'You looking forward to it?' Megan handed back the scan shot, before smiling. 'Sorry, that was a silly question, of course you are!'

'I am. I'm also nervous.' Amy held her belly protectively. 'I know the evidence is overwhelming, but I can't quite get my head around the fact that this is really happening.'

'I'm not surprised! I'd love children, but the idea of giving birth freaks me out big time. I haven't even got my ears pierced as I don't like pain!'

Amy grinned at the wince Megan made. 'Funnily enough, although I'm obviously concerned about having the baby, it isn't the prospect of the birth that keeps me awake at night.'

'It isn't?'

'No. That's the easy part. It's the being a mum bit that scares the hell out of me!'

'Easy part?' Megan looked incredulous. 'Seriously?'

Amy laughed at the waitress's horrified expression. 'Sure, the birth will be tough, but it'll pass. Bringing up a child lasts *for ever*. And you only know if you've done it wrong when it's too late, and you've already screwed your child up!'

Seeing that Amy was genuinely worried, the waitress gave her a kind smile. 'You'll be amazing. You and Paul were born to have kids.'

'Thanks, although it'll be kid, not kids. It's a miracle we've got this one on the way at our age. I'm pretty sure this little handful will be an only child.'

Megan pointed across the café to where Kit was sitting. 'Or maybe it's twins, like Kit had! You positive there isn't a second little person tucked in behind that one on the ultrasound pic?'

'I feel big enough for triplets, let alone twins, but I'm assured there is only one in there. And thank goodness! No way could I cope with twins.' Amy followed Megan's gaze to where Kit sat in her corner. 'Is Kit OK today? I've not seen her typing this morning. I didn't sit with her on purpose because I thought she was working.'

'Having an imagining day, she said. I guess writers do a lot of that.'

'Well, when you top Kit's coffee up, tell her she's welcome to join me if she needs an imagination break.'

Megan took a few steps towards Kit with her coffee jug in hand, before pivoting on the balls of her feet, and heading straight back to Amy again.

'What's wrong?' Amy frowned when she saw the concern on Megan's face.

'I think you should go and sit with Kit now.'

'Really?'

'Yes, she's crying.'

'Kit?' Amy was already offering tissues before an embarrassed Kit nodded an invitation to sit down. 'Whatever is it?' She took her friend gently by the shoulder. 'This isn't like you.'

Angrily wiping her tears away, Kit shrugged. 'That's just it. I don't feel like me, and I hate it. I *hate* this feeling, and what's

102

worse, I know why I feel like this. I have rationalised it all out in my mind, I know it has to happen, and yet I can't seem to stop the glooms overtaking me every five minutes.'

Although she'd listened carefully, Amy wasn't sure what Kit was talking about. 'So why do you feel like this, if you don't mind me asking?'

Kit smiled at the confused look on Amy's face, 'Sorry, hun. You came in for a rest, and all you've got is a friend surrounded by soggy tissues!'

Relieved her friend had retained her self-deprecating sense of humour, Amy opened her mouth to reply, but instead of sympathy, a gasp of pain escaped her throat as she clutched her stomach.

The writer sat bolt upright. 'Amy? You alright?'

Breathing more easily, Amy sat back in her seat, 'Sorry about that. I've been getting Braxton Hicks contractions for a couple of days now, and some of them are a bit sharp.'

Kit grimaced. 'You poor thing! I remember them hurting big time.'

'I bet they were worse with two babies inside you.'

Kit laughed. 'I've no idea. I only had the twins. I don't know how it feels to have one baby at a time.'

'I hadn't thought of that!' Amy rubbed a hand gently over her bump, soothing away the last traces of the tightness that had swamped her so suddenly. 'Now tell me, what's going on with you then?'

Kit, cross with herself for being so feeble, explained about her writer's block, and how she was as sure as she could be that it was the imminent departure of her children that was at the root of the problem.

'It's so annoying. I hoped that if I could track down the issue that was blocking me I'd be alright, but as I was saying to Jack the other day, the block seems to have become a habit now, and I'll be damned if I can shift it.'

'Frustrating.'

'To say the very least.' Kit swivelled her laptop around so that Amy could see all she'd written that day.

'It's blank.'

'And the annoying thing is that my head *isn't* blank. It is teeming with every single word that is dying to hit the page, but I can't make it happen.' Kit slammed down the screen. 'Enough of that, I'm sure it'll sort itself soon. How are you? Ready for the big day?'

Amy pulled a face. 'I was saying to Megan earlier; the birth bit is daunting, but I'm not nervous about that, it's the…'

'Bringing the child up bit?'

'I knew you'd understand. I am terrified of what lies ahead.'

'Good.'

'Good?' Amy frowned.

'Yes. If you weren't nervous then you wouldn't be normal. You probably wouldn't be such a good parent as I know you will be if you weren't terrified.

Amy smiled gratefully. 'If I had the energy to lumber round to give you a hug, I would! Thanks, Kit!'

The women raised their respective drinks in a toast to each other, as Amy said, 'You know, if you want to beat the empty nest syndrome while the twins are off being trainee grown-ups, I'll always be up for some help with childcare. Donahue Junior here is going to be your godchild after all.'

She suddenly felt a new wave of doubt creep up on her. 'This poor child is going to need all the expert help it can get! I haven't even held a baby before!'

'Neither had I before the twins. Honestly, you'll be great. Instinct will take over, and once the antenatal classes start you'll learn loads in a very short time.'

'Thanks, Kit.' Amy took a sip of peppermint tea. 'I wish the classes started a bit earlier, though. Leaving them until the end of the seventh month seems pushing it awfully fine to me.'

Just then, Helena came in through the front door, ready to start her shift, and waved across at her mum. Waving back, Kit leaned a little closer to Amy, whispering conspiratorially, 'There *is* something else I wanted to talk to you about.'

'Is it Jack?'

'No, although I guess it's sort of connected to him. Here's the thing: Helena has a massive crush on Phil and Rob's new assistant. Trouble is, I'm pretty sure the lad is gay. And Jack agrees with me. You've been there – what do I do?'

'Oh, hello.' Jack didn't like the way his heart contracted when he saw that Rupert was the only one in Reading Nature. Having psyched himself up to talk to Rob about where he was opening the restaurant, Jack felt wrong-footed at his friend's absence. 'Rob not in today?' He asked the question merely for something to say; it was obvious his friend wasn't in.

'He's nipped over to Kew to collect a batch of their new guidebooks to sell. Shouldn't be too long.' Rupert felt awkward, wanting to engage Jack in conversation but not entirely sure what to say – and still feeling wary after hearing so many negative things about the man's past.

'Oh, right.' Feeling oddly tongue-tied, Jack said, 'Do you mind if I browse while I wait?'

'Of course not, it's a bookshop.'

Stupid thing to say. Jack cursed himself. 'You'd think I'd know that, seeing as I used to own this place.'

Keeping his eyes firmly on the computer screen so he didn't spend time admiring the annoyingly handsome back view of Jack's bum-hugging jeans and white cotton shirt, Rupert said, 'It must have been hard giving his place up. Not sure I could.'

'I knew it was going into good hands, and although I do miss it sometimes, I love what I'm doing now even more.'

'I can understand that. I adore cooking – well, being creative generally, really. Although I have to admit I'm not exactly gifted in the culinary department.'

Beginning to relax, Jack said, 'Phil tells me photography's your thing.'

'It is. I love it. Although I'm not as good at that as I'd like to be either.'

Jack smiled. 'Phil said your pictures are outstanding. You're entering some sort of competition, aren't you?'

Rupert blushed, hating that his face always gave him away. 'Well that's very kind of Phil, but I have a long way to go before I'm that good.'

'I'd like to see them sometime – if you're happy with sharing your work, that is. Natural history, as you can tell from

105

the fact I opened this bookshop, is something of a passion of mine.'

Shyly, Rupert gestured to the computer screen. 'You can help me now if you like. I'm narrowing down the photos I've taken at Kew to those that are good enough to turn into postcards – and those that might be potentials for the competition.'

Pushing the shop door open about half an hour later, Rob dumped the box of new books on the counter before he noticed the two men sat at Rupert's computer, deep in conversation.

Catching the amused expression on Rob's face, Jack immediately gave him a glare that told him in no uncertain terms that if he started matchmaking he'd regret it. 'And what time do you call this, Robert? I wouldn't have put up with this tardy timekeeping when I was the boss!'

'When you were the boss, it was anyone's guess if you'd turn up at all!'

Jack gave both men his best impish smile. 'Rupert, would you mind terribly if I borrowed your already-late boss for a little while? I have something I need to talk to him about.'

'No problem.' Rupert picked up a pile of paperwork, 'I have plenty to get on with, and I doubt it'll be busy this morning.'

Intrigued by what Jack might want to talk to him about that he hadn't been able to say last night, Rob followed Jack outside, the shop and into the nearest café.

As they sat down at the café's window seat, Jack jumped into conversation first before Rob could start quizzing him. 'Yes, Rupert is gay. No, I am not interested, so don't waste your breath, mate. Now, can I talk to you about something?'

'You've done what?!' Rob almost choked on his mouthful of iced orange juice as he took in what Jack had just said.

'The old Italian place on Richmond High Street. I've bought it.' Jack was not encouraged. Rob's reaction was exactly the opposite of the one he'd hoped for.

'Talk about stepping on peoples' toes, Jack!'

'Peggy and Scott will be more than a bit put out then?'

Rob stared at his friend in disbelief, 'Are you kidding me, mate? They'll go ballistic.'

Kit stared at the mountain of clothing in the ironing basket. They were all so *big*. No children's clothes sat awaiting the attention of her iron any more. As she slid the hot surface over one of Phil's white shirts, she couldn't stop herself from picturing all the cute little garments that Amy would be folding into drawers soon.

'For goodness' sake, woman! Snap out of it.'

Kit knew she was in danger of tipping into depression if she wasn't careful. If only she could write! It has always been like therapy for her. All her fears and hopes and secrets and worries were always made better when she played them out in a make-believe world on paper.

A noise from above her made her turn the iron off and call up the stairs. 'What's going on up there, Phil?'

'Come and see!'

The bedroom curtains had been drawn even though it was only seven o'clock in the evening. Phil had moved their portable television and DVD player from its usual stand in the corner of the room to a table that he'd temporarily stationed at the foot of the bed.

'I haven't caught you indulging in some private fetish, have I?'

'Much as I miss your erotica days, love, no.' Phil ushered his wife to the bed, where he's already plumped up the pillows so she could comfortably sit down. 'Now you wait there for a minute.'

Sitting back, wondering what on earth her husband was up to, Kit asked, 'Where's Helena?'

'Out with friends.'

'At least she isn't hounding poor Rupert then.' She sighed. 'How the hell are we going to get her to leave him alone?'

'She'll get fed up eventually. Forget about that for now.' Phil passed his wife a glass of wine and, with remote control in hand, climbed up on the bed beside her.

'What's all this?' A smile started to grow across her face as

107

he put his arm around her.

'I know you're struggling, love, and I want to help. You're going to miss the twins, and so will I, but we don't have to forget everything that's gone before. Even though they don't need us all the time any more, they do still need us.'

Kit frowned but, trusting her husband, laid her head on his shoulder.

'Ready?'

'I think so, although I'm not sure what this is yet.'

Phil pressed 'play' in response. Seconds later they were laughing with tears shining in their eyes as the old camcorder recordings he had made of the twins from birth, and throughout their childhoods, burst onto the screen.

'Oh, wow!' Kit couldn't stop the happy tears streaking her face as her husband passed her a box of tissues. 'When did you do this?'

'I converted the old films yesterday. Rupert has a software package that did the trick. Now, let's indulge in some memories and loosen up that writer's block, shall we?'

Chapter Eighteen

Monday 20th June

A nervous smile on her freckled face, Megan, her arms full of art supplies, knocked clumsily on the door of Jack's new restaurant.

Come on, Jack! She glanced over her shoulder, as if she expected to see either Peggy or Scott bearing down on her with accusations of industrial espionage flying from their lips. Jack had told her she could drop off the first of her bits and pieces before work, and had sworn he'd be there. *Come on!*

At last a shadow appeared behind the blind on the main door, and Jack relieved her of a heavy bag of paints and brushes.

'You got enough stuff here?'

Megan, who still wasn't convinced she'd got inside without being spotted, said, 'That isn't even half of it!'

'I know, I was joking. Come and see.' Jack led her up the narrow staircase and ushered her into his converted spare bedroom. She was astonished.

'When did you do this?'

The room had been scrubbed clean from top to bottom. There was a new white chest of drawers, a narrow side table, an anglepoise lamp and a box of daylight bulbs, plus several empty jars and cloths, all waiting to be pressed into artistic service.

'Yesterday. I had fun hitting the junk shops.' Jack didn't mention that he'd needed to keep his brain busy to stop it drifting towards Rupert. 'The only thing I couldn't find was an easel. Do you have one?'

'I do indeed.' She stroked the side of the slim table lovingly. 'Nick will bring that and the canvases over as soon as it's convenient for you.'

'This evening?' Jack was warmed by Megan's enthusiasm, 'I have a feeling I might need some light relief tonight.'

'Oh, why's that then?'

'Because Rob, quite rightly, has told me I have to tell Peggy about this place today. It isn't fair on you to leave it until she finds out by accident.'

'Ahh.'

'Have you told Peggy and Scott about taking the job with them yet?'

'No. I thought I'd see if they knew about your plans before I did that. I wanted to make sure I knew how to gauge what I said. I intended to tell them this morning.'

'I'll come along to Pickwicks with you now then.'

Wary, Megan looked away as she asked, 'You're going to tell them about this place at the same time as I tell them I'm staying?'

'Bad idea?'

She shrugged. 'I honestly don't know, but I do feel a bit like piggy in the middle. Peggy will be upset if she knows I was aware of where you were all along. She may not want me to work for her after all if she finds out.'

'Don't worry, I'll tell her I put you in an impossible position, and that you felt awful having to withhold information, but you were just trying to do the best for everyone.'

Megan snorted. 'Well, that's pretty much the truth anyway!'

'I know.' Jack climbed back down the stairs. 'Right, new plan. I'll give you a half-hour head start while I call the removal firm I have on stand-by in Kent. That will give you time to pass on your good news before I arrive.'

'Thanks, Jack.' Megan felt a nervous fizz well up inside her. 'Call me a coward, but I might choose the moment of your arrival to go to the bank to collect the days float!'

Perspiration gathered on the palms of Megan's hands as she walked into Pickwicks. She knew it was ridiculous to be so nervous. She hadn't done anything wrong, but she still felt she'd let her employers down.

Oh well, here goes. She waved a greeting at Kit, who was already installed in her space in the corner of the room and was looking far happier than she had done lately, although she didn't seem to be actually putting her fingers on the keyboard.

Glad that the rest of the café was currently empty, Megan called to Peggy, 'Can I have a quick word?'

Hope blossomed on Peggy's face. 'Have you made a decision about the job?'

'I have.'

Tilting her head to one side quizzically, Peggy said, 'Should I be worried that you look a bit concerned?'

'Shall we go through and tell Scott as well?'

Following her chief waitress into the kitchen, Peggy had to bite her tongue against the temptation to bombard Megan with questions. Instead she announced to Scott, 'Megan has news.'

Scott looked up; his face was smeared with a dusting of flour. 'So, what's the verdict? Do we get to employ you at Pickwicks number two, or are you off to pastures new?'

Grateful for Scott's calm manner, Megan hung her bag on her coat hook, and put on her apron. 'If you'll still have me, then I'd love to run your second branch. Thank you.'

'We'll definitely have you! Why wouldn't we?' Peggy swept her friend up into a hug.

'Well I shouldn't even have considered Jack's offer, but, well…'

Scott rescued her sentence for her. 'Of course you should! This is your life after all; you have to do what's best for you.'

'Thanks, Scott.' Megan felt choked, especially as she was still feeling disloyal. 'I haven't done too badly out of the arrangement in the end.'

'How do you mean?' Relaxing a little now she knew she didn't have to advertise for a manageress for their new branch, Peggy pulled a piece of paper off their list pad and began to scribble things down on it.

'Jack has commissioned me to do some paintings to hang in his new restaurant. That means that not only can I keep working for you guys, but I can spend time on my art too – something I've been really missing lately.'

111

'Congratulations!' Scott was thrilled, 'that's wonderful!'

Peggy smiled as she added more food to her order list. 'That's great, Megan, honey. I expect that once you and Nick have a place of your own, you'll have more space to get down to some serious drawing again.'

Knowing that she should come completely clean and tell Peggy that she was going to work in Jack's converted room, but not wanting to go down that road until Jack himself had visited, she simply said, 'I'm looking forward to it.' Then, glancing at her watch, she said, 'I'd better get on. Has the till float been sorted yet? I can do that now if you like – be good practice for my new managerial role.'

Jack gritted his teeth as he hung up the phone. The last thing he'd wanted to do was talk to Gareth, but as the removal firm would need access to the bungalow he'd rented from his ex-boss – and Gareth was the only one with a key – he'd had no choice. It had not been the most pleasant of conversations. Now, as Jack readied himself to walk down to Pickwicks to confess to Peggy and Scott, he had a nasty feeling that the day's confrontations were not over yet.

Considering all the problems Kit was having writing, Jack was surprised to see her at her usual table as he walked into the coffee shop. Unsure if it was good that she was there or not, he was torn. Did he speak to Kit first, as he would normally when he had a problem, or did he go straight into the kitchen, where a covert signal from Megan had told him the proprietors were?

His indecision was cured by Kit waving him to her table. Shooting Megan an apologetic look, he headed to her.

'I didn't expect to see you today, Jack. Coffee?'

'I'd love one, but I can't stop this morning, sadly, I've got to crack on with getting adverts for staff sorted and working on my menu, otherwise I'll never be open on time.'

Kit was genuinely shocked. 'I had no idea you were after staff already. When are you going to stop being so mysterious about this bistro of yours? Did you decide on a name for it?'

Jack shook his head. 'Despite all your inventive name suggestions the other night, I am no nearer deciding on a name, but I'll get there.'

'And where is *there* exactly, Jack?' Kit felt a trickle of suspicion. 'How come you're here so early? You said you were staying in a hotel fairly near your new place, didn't you?'

Wishing that Kit hadn't always been able to see straight through him, Jack checked over his shoulder to make sure they weren't being overheard. 'I've been afraid to tell you.'

'Oh, hell, Jack, what have you done now?'

'You sounded like Sharon from Within Temptation then!'

'Jack! Don't you dare start quoting song lyrics at me!'

Noting the warning tone in her voice, Jack swallowed back the lines from "What Have You Done Now?" and began to fiddle with the sugar bowl. 'I was trying not to cause trouble, but of course, as usual, I failed.'

'What are you talking about?'

Lowering his voice, Jack leaned forward a fraction. 'The restaurant. Well, my restaurant now.'

'What about it?'

'It's, umm, it's…'

'Oh, for goodness' sake, Jack, spit it out. I can't think what on earth you have to be so cloak and dagger about.'

'OK. The thing is … well … you know the Italian place that closed down on the main road through Richmond?'

'Yeah.' Kit nodded, 'It's over the road from the lane that leads to here and … Oh my God, Jack, you haven't?'

His silence said far more than any words could have done.

'Oh, Jack! But what about Peggy?'

The coffee pot smacked down onto the table, making Kit jump even higher than Jack did. 'Yes, Jack? What about me? What about my business? What about everything that Scott and I have been working so hard for, for so many years?'

The quiet anger that escaped from Peggy's mouth was far more intimidating than the shouting rage he'd expected.

Kit looked from Jack to Peggy, her mouth open, not sure what to say. Her gaze took in Megan's horrified face.

Oblivious to the waitress's presence behind her, Peggy's voice began to crescendo, 'Not only did you try and poach my best member of staff, are you seriously telling me that you are

113

going to open up in direct competition to Pickwicks?'

Scott, who'd come through on hearing his wife's raised voice, caught sight of Megan, and immediately put a comforting arm around her.

'OK. Stop!' All eyes in the café turned towards the cook. 'What is going on?'

Peggy, reining in her temper as best she could, said, 'Well, the first thing that is going on is that Jack is leaving.'

'We should give Jack the chance to explain, Peggy,' Scott said.

'Explain? He's supposed to be our friend, and he is opening up right opposite us, just when we need Pickwicks to do as well as possible!' Peggy pointed to the door, 'Leave, Mr Brown. You are barred.'

With apologetic looks at Kit and Megan, Jack got to his feet. 'I'm sorry. If you'd let me explain…'

'Out!'

Silence fell as the door of the café closed behind Jack.

Megan had gone so pale that Kit got up, and unsure what to say, and guided the waitress to the chair she'd just vacated.

'Did you know, Megan?' Peggy was trying hard to keep her voice level, but there was no disguising the feeling of betrayal in her eyes.

Sadly, Megan nodded. 'Apart from all the reasons I gave you before, that's why I didn't take the job. I couldn't be part of stealing your customers. I wanted to tell you, but Jack didn't think it was fair that I should take your anger, so he said he'd come and tell you – which is why he was here so early.'

'But he didn't come and tell us, did he? I had to find out by overhearing!'

Kit winced. 'That might be my fault.'

'What? You as well? Do any of my friends have an ounce of loyalty?'

'Oh for goodness' sake, Peggy! Think! The reason you overheard about the bistro in the first place was because Jack was telling me what he'd done. And if you remember, I was in the middle of telling him he was insane!'

Peggy sagged slightly as she sat down. 'Oh. Sorry, Kit. I'm just so bloody cross. We really need this place to do better than ever right now.'

'Why? What's happening?'

Embarrassed, Megan didn't know where to put herself. She felt she should say something, but what? 'I'm so sorry, Peggy, Scott, I didn't want to cause trouble, and Jack said he'd sort it, and…'

Scott gave his waitress a kind smile, 'I know. Tell you what, go and get yourself a drink, wash your hands, take a deep breath, and then go into waitress mode – that sound OK?'

Megan was puzzled. 'You aren't going to sack me, then?'

Peggy shook her head. 'Why would we do that? You're going to be our new manageress.' Peggy gave a reassuring nod. 'Scott, why don't you get that cuppa and take Megan out the back for some air?'

As she watched her husband usher their shell-shocked waitress away, Peggy turned to Kit. 'Time I told you a few things.'

'Have you been holding out on me as well, Peggy?'

'Only because I was scared it would all go wrong.'

'What would go wrong?'

Peggy picked up the coffee that she'd poured for Jack, and began to tell Kit the full story behind their expansion plans and how they hoped it would earn them enough money to be able to retire early to a bungalow.

'I had no idea. Poor Scott, although not surprising after his accident, I suppose.'

'Exactly. That's why we want to save up for a bungalow, so stairs aren't a problem in the future.' Peggy shrugged sadly. 'Suddenly that dream doesn't seem quite so realistic, although Scott's arthritis is becoming as real as it gets.'

'Why didn't you tell me?' Kit was beginning to wonder how many other secrets her friends were harbouring.

'It was all going so right we didn't want to jinx it.' Peggy crashed her cup back into its saucer. 'Well, so much for that!'

JULY

In which the champagne looks as though it might have to go back in the fridge...

...

Chapter Nineteen

Monday 4th July

Jack blew on the tomato sauce he'd scooped from the pan bubbling away on the hob, cooling it before he gave it an exploratory taste. Working it around his taste buds, he decided it was a better blend of ingredients that the previous batch he'd made, but wasn't as good as his initial tomato and basil sauce base.

With a feeling of satisfaction, Jack made a note in his recipe book – a book he fully intended to write up properly and publish one day – and, pouring the remains of the mixture into a lidded pot so he could eat it for his own dinner later, sat down to plan out the next stage of his own spin on pasta sauce.

He was aware of his mobile vibrating in his pocket. It was probably Kit or Amy. They'd been calling almost non-stop since he'd been thrown out of Pickwicks, but as he was expecting Amy to tell him he could no longer be godfather to her child, nor host their naming celebration now he'd upset Peggy, and that Kit would only be calling to tell him off, then he couldn't face answering it. Anyway, he'd convinced himself that perfecting his menu was far more important than anything else right now. If he had no menu, then he would have hurt his friends for nothing, and that would make everything even worse.

On her almost daily visits to the mini art studio upstairs, Megan hadn't said much about life at work. Jack assumed that Pickwicks 2 was going full steam ahead, and that she was still going to be running it, but he didn't dare ask. Instead they kept to safe subjects, like her art, his flat's decor now he'd moved in properly, and the new menu.

He hadn't told anyone, but Jack needed the bistro to work as much as Peggy and Scott needed Pickwicks 2. His inheritance, which had kept him living the easy life for so long, was virtually gone. His grandfather's money had acquired him Reading Nature and a house; both of which he'd sold. He'd travelled a good deal after Amy's wedding, treated his friends, and helped his family, paid to do a horticultural course, invested in Kennedy's – money he knew he'd never see again – and now he'd used the last of it to buy his bistro and the adjoining flat. This was it. This time he had to stick to his plan, and make it work. He knew avoiding his friends and concentrating solely on the bistro would have consequences of its own, but Jack couldn't think of anything else he could do

Even though Rob was still talking to him, Jack was also keeping away from Reading Nature and Kew, taking the frequent walks he needed to clear his head around Richmond Park instead. He told himself this decision was nothing to do with avoiding bumping into Rupert; but he also knew that was a lie.

Groaning through gritted teeth as he brainstormed ideas of dishes to compliment the goat's cheese and chilli bread that had become his signature starter at Kennedy's, Jack found himself thinking about the young photographer. Rupert was creeping into his mind far too often to be ignored. Determined not to complicate things further, Jack tried not to remember how impressed he'd been by Rupert's photographs, and how much in common they had. They even had the same friends.

Or they'd *had* the same friends…

The recent incident at Pickwicks had further underlined for Jack that he never wanted to hurt anyone ever again. It was that feeling that had led him to decide on a name for his bistro. He could only hope that, once the dust had settled, and he'd proved that he wasn't aiming to poach Pickwicks trade, that they'd accept it as a peace offering. In the meantime, he was going to keep his bistro's name a secret.

'You glad you agreed to this then?' Scott's usual toothy smile flashed at Megan as she dipped a sponge into a bucket of water with soda crystals so she could help scrub the walls of the new café.

'Definitely.' Megan paused to wring out her sponge. 'I feel much better now a decision's been made. Jack didn't mind me staying with you guys, you know. I do wish Peggy would calm down and go and see him. I know it seems like he's encroaching on your territory, but I can't see our usual afternoon crowd being swayed by Jack's fancy nouvelle cuisine stuff, not when they like your food so much.'

'I know.' Scott pulled out a tray rack from the oven and carried it to the sink for a thorough scrub before it had a blasting in the dishwasher. 'I can't budge her right now, but she'll come round. And before you ask me again, no, she doesn't blame you. Not for a minute.'

Continuing to work, Megan said, 'I know it would be naive to say it won't make any difference to Pickwicks having another restaurant nearby, but I can't help thinking it might be rather nice to have a place we could all go together after work. Be good to have Jack serve us food rather than Peggy serving him, for a change.'

The image of Jack waiting on them made Scott laugh. 'I doubt he'd leave his kitchen to wait on tables. He seems more addicted to his cooking than I am to mine! I have to admit, I am curious. I'd like to try his menu.'

'Well, if it's anything like as good as the food I've sampled while I've been round there painting, then it is going to be good.'

Scott feigned shock. 'What! Better than my cheese scones?'

'Don't you go fishing for compliments, Mr McIntyre! Your scone and sandwich supremacy is assured!'

'So I should hope!' Scott put the last piece of the oven into the dishwasher, and clicked it into life. 'How goes the art anyway? You enjoying getting back to it?'

'I'm loving it.' Megan's face broke into a happy smile. 'I've been so lucky.'

'You don't regret staying with us, then? I mean, you could have more time for your art if you worked for Jack, couldn't you?'

121

'Not at all. Once Jack assured me that he would buy my artwork with no hard feelings if I stayed with you, my decision was made. That was before I knew where his bistro was, of course. After I found that out I couldn't work for him anyway – but you know about all that.'

Washing his hands, Scott turned to look at his waitress. 'Do you mind me asking, are you much out of pocket because of your loyalty? We know you and Nick are saving up for a place of your own, so Peggy and I were thinking, we'd like to offer you higher wages, but...'

Megan held up her hand to stop the conversation in its tracks. 'You are very kind, but with the money Jack has offered me for my pictures, Nick and I suddenly have the deposit we need for the terrace we want to rent. Now I just need to earn a better wage so we can pay the rent and save for a place to buy in the future.'

'So, Jack's still loaded then?'

'I'm not sure he is any more. He hasn't said anything, but I get the impression he's sinking everything he has into this venture.'

'Has he found anyone for his staff yet?'

'He has an apprentice chef lined up from one of the local catering colleges, but otherwise I don't think so. I know he designed an advert, but I'm not sure if he's done anything with it yet. I haven't liked to ask him.' Stepping back from the clean wall with an air of satisfaction, Megan dried her hands and surveyed her new domain. 'How about us? Have we got a shortlist of staff to interview yet?'

'Three potential waitresses and two lunchtime cooks are in the running at the moment. The advert has another couple of days to run, and then we'll sort the interviews. Will you be alright doing those?'

'What?' Megan blanched. 'Me?'

'Of course, you'll be their manager. Peggy will be with you, and I'll sit in for the cooks, but you'll have the last word. After all, you're the one who'll have to work with them.'

Taking off her wet apron, Megan surveyed the kitchen. 'This is all so grown up!'

'Tell me about it!'

Kit re-read the page she'd managed to force out of her fingertips. This was better. It wasn't very good, but it was a real improvement on the nothing she was producing a fortnight ago.

Over the past few days, she had managed to fulfil her new small goal of completing two hundred words a day, rather than her usual two thousand. It was a far cry from the volume of words she was supposed to be creating, and she was still a month behind in her schedule, but it was something. Phil's patience and kindness, his DVD, his insistence that they make plans for just the two of them, and his constant unconditional love, were more than she thought she deserved, but had really helped.

Yet her frustration at not being able to churn out the words at breakneck speed was still simmering beneath the surface, ready to erupt at any moment. With Megan often over at the new café in Mortlake, Helena was working longer hours in Pickwicks, and Kit suspected one of the reasons she couldn't quite get back to her old levels of efficiency and concentration was because her daughter was around all the time.

Her regular café spot wasn't her retreat anymore, and while she was proud of Helena for sticking at the job and earning herself some money, she couldn't shift the feeling of being checked up on. *Surely it should be Helena that feels like that, not me.*

Deleting a line of text that was far from her usual standard, Kit was sighing quietly as Peggy arrived at her side.

Sitting down with a large black coffee and a cheese scone for her friend, Peggy pulled a wrapped-up object from her large apron pocket.

'What's this?'

Peggy nodded at the parcel. 'It's a present. Open it.'

'But it isn't my birthday or anything.'

'Don't be awkward, open it.'

Kit unwrapped the spotty blue and white paper, puzzlement crossing her face as she pulled out a black biro and a brand new fancy coloured notebook.

'If I remember rightly, these were your implements of choice before you got all successful. Remember?'

Tears filmed over Kit's eyes. She whispered, 'Yes. Yes they were. I wrote everything out in longhand first, didn't I.'

'Well then, hun. My old mum, bless her, used to say if you were stuck in the now you should go back to the then. So back you go. Write some short stories. Just for fun. Just because you enjoy the process. Get the flow back.'

Kit threw her arms around her friend, making Helena look across the café in concern for a second before Peggy shook her head to assure her waitress that her mother was alright.

'Oh, Peggy, thank you.'

'No need to thank me, just remember that you do this job because it's fun.' Peggy straightened herself up. 'Now, you be a good girl and sit there and write me something saucy, woman, I've got tea and cake to serve.'

Chapter Twenty

Thursday 7th July

Amy glanced at the clock on her computer screen for the third time in as many minutes. How could time be moving so slowly? She loved her job, and usually the days flew by. For the last few weeks, however, the hours and minutes dragged at an ever slower pace.

Moving in general was becoming more awkward, and Amy was finding the act of walking to the office physically difficult. The plush leather swivel chair that her co-manager Chris had ordered especially for her, after she'd secured her first international deal for Home Hunters, was no longer comfortable at her increased size, and there didn't seem to be any position she could assume at her desk that was anything other than awkward.

Over the past two weeks, Chris had been working extra hours so Amy could reduce her own to three-quarter time, but as she ended a call with a particularly difficult client, a wave of utter exhaustion overtook her. They really needed to get her some maternity cover sorted. She was beginning to see that her original plan of working right up until the week before the baby was due was optimistic to say the least.

Amy flicked through her emails. There were only two applicants for the job so far. Interviews had been set up for the following week, but having read the applicants' CVs and cover letters, she wasn't hopeful for either of them.

Glancing over at her co-manager, Amy saw Chris was looking almost as tired as she was. Although he was being very understanding, she knew he couldn't carry the business on his own for long. She didn't dare tell Chris that she was already beginning to reconsider her decision to return to work full-time after the baby was born.

Switching back to the spreadsheet of the week's property viewings that still had to be booked, Amy couldn't contain a yawn.

'You alright, boss?'

Amy smiled as Lauren put a fruit tea of unrecognisable flavour in front of her. 'Thank you. Your timing, as ever, is perfect.'

Her PA laughed. 'One of the first things you told me after you hired me was that there was never a bad time to bring you a cup of coffee. I'm assuming that the principle still holds now you're drinking a different beverage?'

'Bless you. That principle will always hold! Although,' Amy shifted in her seat to offset the heartburn that had become her constant companion over the last a couple days, 'the increased trips to the bathroom as a consequence are less welcome.'

Leaning against the wall, her own coffee in hand, Lauren said, 'You can't have that long to go now, can you? I've lost track.'

'Too long for comfort.' She rubbed her bump affectionately. 'This one's due on the twenty-sixth of August.'

'I've been meaning to ask, did your friend find you in the end? The guy who popped in the other week.'

'Jack? Yes, thanks.' Amy grinned at the recollection of her friend's face at seeing her pregnant state. 'It was quite a shock for him. He didn't know I was expecting.'

Lauren smirked. 'He was a bit of alright. Easy on the eye. How come you know him?'

Amy raised her eyebrows playfully. 'Are you implying that it's out of character for me to know good-looking men?'

'Oh, I didn't mean…'

'It's OK, I was teasing, and yes, Jack is very gentle on the vision. It's easy to see why the boys like him so much.'

'Boys? Oh.'

'Afraid so, so I'd save your fantasies in that direction if I was you.'

'Oh, I don't know.' Lauren winked. 'Nothing wrong with a

bit of male-on-male action! Love that in a naughty book.'

'Lauren!' Amy was genuinely shocked, and then realised she shouldn't be. As Kit kept telling her, this was the age of erotica, and anything went.

Thoughtfully she said, 'Tell me, Lauren, why haven't you applied for my job? You'd be perfect for it. You already know my job inside-out, and it would be great experience for you.'

'Me? You think I could?' Lauren looked uncertain as she flicked a stray section of brown fringe from her face, reminding Amy of herself before she'd forced herself to get to grips with her confidence issues.

'I have no doubt at all. I can't imagine why I haven't asked you before, but as you say, we've been so busy. And to be honest, I haven't been thinking terribly straight lately!'

'I'm not sure I'm good enough ... I mean, what if I lost a client? And then there's Chris...'

'What about Chris?'

'Well ...' Lauren shuffled her feet. 'He's a bit daunting, isn't he.'

'Don't you worry about that. Now listen...'

Having been waiting impatiently for his wife's return from work, Paul swung the front door open as Amy reached it.

'You look happy, what's happened?'

Kissing her on the nose, he took her bag and steered her to the sofa. 'That's because I am happy. I've managed to swing an extra two weeks of paternity leave! I'll be able to stay at home and look after you and baby for a whole month. Isn't that the best news?'

'Yes, yes it is! But a month ... are you sure the British Museum can cope for that long without you?'

'Medieval stuff tends to stay the same, you know, even if you leave it unattended for a month!'

'You know what I mean! Your staff, and the exhibitions, and school visits, and tourists and everything?'

Panic had suddenly gripped Amy, although she couldn't explain why. Paul being around to help her for much longer than she'd assumed should have been comforting – but now she was feeling even more anxious than before.

Swallowing back the sensation that she was being swamped by life, Amy shared her own news. 'Looks like we've solved the problem of maternity cover for me too.'

'That's fantastic.' Paul started fussing round, pulling off her shoes and plumping up sofa cushions. 'I can really take care of you now. Do you think I should start my leave before the baby comes, or only once you go into labour?'

'Paul, did you hear what I said?' Amy, who had a premonition that if she didn't stop him fussing around her now she was going to be sick of it by bedtime, let alone by the time their child arrived, spoke firmly. 'Stop dancing around like a demented Mary Poppins and sit down a minute.'

'Sorry, love, I'm just so excited!'

'Me too, but if you wear yourself out now trying to look after me when all I want to do is rest, then you'll have no energy left for baby duty. That's when I'm *really* going to need your help.'

'Can't argue with that.' Paul cuddled up next to his wife. 'Go on then, how have you solved the maternity cover crisis? Weren't the interviews supposed to be next week?'

'The answer was there all the time. Right in the office. It's insane that Chris and I didn't see it before.'

'What answer?'

'Lauren.'

'Your PA?'

'Yes. She's bright, quick-witted, and although she is a bit shy, that'll soon change once she's tackled a few of our more, shall we say, *delicate* customers. She already knows how Home Hunters runs, is used to Chris's little ways, and won't want to hound me out of my job when I go back.'

'And what about the other people who applied? You'll still have to interview them.'

'Yes, but neither of them are up to it on paper. The best candidate of the two could easily do Lauren's current job for a few months instead, though.'

Paul looked at his wife levelly. 'And if, when the baby is here you can't bear the thought of going back to work full-time, you and Lauren might be able to job share?'

'How did you know I was thinking about that?'

'Could be because I'm psychic – or it could be because I have a feeling you won't want to go back at all, not even part-time?'

'You are marvellous!' Amy kissed Paul hard. 'But as we live in London I know that not working at all isn't an option. Part-time though: I'd love that. Anyway, the only advice Kit has given me so far is to keep a tiny toe-hold on adult life, otherwise parenthood overtakes everything. Which she says is great for a while, but boredom is only an inch away if you aren't careful.'

'Kit said that?'

'Yep.'

'That isn't true, is it?' Paul looked shocked.

Amy couldn't help but laugh, 'I expect it is. Nothing but nappies, feeding, and lack of sleep for weeks – it doesn't sound madly stimulating for the brain, however worthwhile it is. Kit may well have a point.'

'Suppose so. But I'll stick to my idea that it will be wonderful from start to finish if that's OK with you.'

'Daft man, you …' Amy inhaled a sharp breath. 'Ouch!'

Paul sat up quickly. 'Are you alright? What is it?'

Amy sat up, and tried to breathe slowly as her stomach briefly went rock solid, and then relaxed again, 'Bloody hell.'

'Amy?'

'Don't worry.' Amy exhaled slowly, and then paled as it happened again.

'God, you're not in labour now, are you? We don't start classes until next week!' Paul had gone nearly as pale as his wife as he held her hand.

Shaking her head firmly, Amy said nothing, but pointed to the pregnancy book on the table.

Picking it up, Paul showed her page after page until she nodded. He read out loud, '*Braxton Hicks are sometimes called practice contractions. They are sporadic uterine contractions that can start early in pregnancy, but are not usually felt until the third trimester; and mostly occur in the final two months of pregnancy*. Hell, you've got those?'

Amy did her best to relax back against the sofa. 'Yes. I've had a couple before, but I didn't want to worry you.'

'That is so fantastic! Means it won't be long.' Paul's reaction, his face a picture of excitement, sent her into a further mini panic.

'But I'm not ready! I haven't got everything I need yet. We haven't had any antenatal lessons, and that was bloody painful! If I can't stand a few of those Braxton things, how on earth will I cope with real labour?'

Chapter Twenty-one

Friday 18th July

Guilty for not having been in touch with Amy to check on how she was, Jack's conscience had finally got the better of him. Determined not to talk about himself – and especially not the bistro – he'd made the call, and was immediately delighted to hear that Amy had managed to reduce her pre-maternity leave working hours.

'That's fantastic news.' He pushed the pile of notes he'd been making away from the edge of the table and rested his bottom against it as he spoke to Amy down the phone. 'So does that mean you can leave work earlier than you planned?'

'Sort of.' Amy gave an encouraging nod across the office to Lauren, who was being shown how to use their database by Chris. 'I will have to keep coming in every day, but I can finish at two each afternoon.'

'That sounds far more manageable.'

'You aren't kidding. It's about three o'clock that I start to flag, so being home by then will be a Godsend.'

'Wasn't Lauren the one I spoke to when I went looking for you?'

Amy laughed as she turned from watching her secretary come to grips with one of the facets of her job, and switched on her PC. 'That's her; the poor girl thought you were hot.'

'Well, if you've got it!'

'Cocky as ever, Mr Brown.'

'Cock something anyway, as I was –'

Amy laughed louder. 'Stop right there, Jack, I'm at work!'

'Oh alright then, I'll behave.' Faking a sulk down the phone, Jack moved away from the table. 'I'd better let you go and be a

131

mega-successful corporate businesswoman then.'

'Before you go and rustle up more for that menu of yours, any news on Helena and Rupert?'

Jack felt a cold shiver, 'How do you mean?' *Surely Rupert hadn't given into her advances? Helena is lovely, stunning, clever – and female.* Jack could see all the potential disasters that faced Rupert lining up inside his head...

Oblivious to the crisis going on in Jack's mind, Amy said, 'Has Rupert managed to convince Helena to back off yet? I can't understand why she won't take her mother's word when Kit says Rupert is gay.'

'Would you have believed anyone if they'd told you I was gay when we were her age?'

Amy was quiet for a second. 'I suppose not. But why doesn't Rupert tell her himself? I don't get it.'

'Because, my darling ex, he isn't ready to know it himself. Even if he is sure, he isn't ready to acknowledge it yet, and that is his prerogative.' Not wanting to go any further with that particular conversation, sure Amy would detect his over-interest if he did, Jack changed the subject. 'Right, I'd better go back to hunting for staff.'

'No luck yet?'

'To be fair, I haven't tried very hard yet. I was sort of hoping I'd encounter someone suitable.'

'You mean you'd pinned all your hopes on Megan and hadn't considered she'd resist your charms?'

'How did you know?' He sighed. 'To be honest, I think she'd have taken the job if Peggy and Scott hadn't decided to expand their own empire at the same time.'

'Most inconsiderate of them.'

'Are you being sarcastic, Mrs Donahue?'

'Yes. Now go and get some job adverts placed. I really do have to go and make hotshot business decisions.'

Jack hung up, a warm glow inside him. Life might not be perfect now he was back in Richmond, what with Peggy continuing hostilities, and his sexual self-denial wasn't proving easy, but being able to chat to Amy and Kit again, not to mention Rob, Paul, and Phil, was definitely worth coming home for.

Reading through his advertising plan, Jack called the first of the local newspapers on his list.

Peggy hung up the phone after talking to the marketing girl at the local paper, having placed a small advert for waitressing staff for their new premises. She glanced at the calendar hanging on the kitchen wall: there wasn't long until the planned opening in August. Suddenly there seemed to be so much to do – including choosing a name for the place, booking a signwriter, and most important of all, finalising the contract. The owner of the café had taken a holiday and, although all was above board and going to plan according to their solicitor, she knew she wouldn't relax until all the dotted lines had signatures on them.

Looking around her small domain, Peggy felt a familiar rush of contentment. Pickwicks was the love of her life, apart from Scott, and had been for so long now that she couldn't help feeling as though she was cheating on it by even considering another branch.

'Silly woman!' she muttered to herself as she wiped the tables, and cast an eye over the flowers, seeing which required replacing and which were in desperate need of water.

Her anger at Jack had evaporated, but she was sure it would do him good to feel out of favour for a while. He'd always been too full of himself in her opinion, and although she couldn't deny that he had a kind streak, he could certainly do with being taken down a peg or two.

She knew that what annoyed her most was the fact that Jack didn't have to open at all during the day – he was wealthy enough not to have to work full stop – but still planned on opening his bistro at three o'clock daily. Rationally, she was sure Megan was right; they wouldn't affect each other's trade. They were too different – plus Pickwicks closed at five anyway, so realistically they could share customers, not steal them from each other.

Even so, Jack's decision to open on their doorstep grated. Thank goodness they'd hung onto Megan. If he'd taken her

133

away, Peggy knew she'd never been able to forgive him.

Putting the phone down, Jack ticked 'call papers' off his incredibly long to-do list, and was about to tackle the next task, when his conversation with Amy began to echo around his head.

Kit had asked him to help with the Helena and Rupert situation, but he hadn't wanted to get involved. Still, he didn't want his goddaughter's heartbroken as badly as her mother's had been – and he certainly didn't want Rupert to have to go through the guilt he'd been through when he'd walked out on both Amy and Kit.

With a vague feeling he was interfering where he shouldn't, Jack called Reading Nature. If Rupert answered the phone, then fate was telling him to help. If Rob or Phil answered, fate was telling him it was time he asked his mates if they'd like to go to the pub later.

Looking up from his coffee cup, Jack allowed himself a glance towards the door before telling himself off for acting like a lovestruck teenager. This meeting was *not* a date. This was a bit of kindly advice for Rupert before his life got out of control. Nonetheless, he felt oddly nervous, and didn't like how the sensation in his stomach reminded him of when he'd first met Toby...

A voice at the back of his head kept prodding him, telling him Rupert wouldn't have agreed to come for a coffee if he hadn't felt something in return. Jack stamped the voice down.

I am not going down that road again. I'm just not.

He had given up watching out of the window of the café near the bookshop, and was reading a newspaper when Rupert finally came through the door, and signalled to the waitress, who knew him from all the take-out coffees he'd ordered for the bookshop, for his usual caramel latte.

'I'm so sorry I'm late. We had a lunchtime rush.'

Smiling up at the younger man, Jack nodded. 'That's good. I remember when we used to go days without any customers at all.'

'We have the odd day like that, but mostly we have a steady trickle of people, and at lunchtime, and post-school, we tend to be borderline busy.'

'Sure you're OK leaving Rob to it then?'

'It's my lunch break.' Rupert, whose insides had been doing backflips ever since Jack had asked if he had time for a quick chat, was determined to keep things casual. The last thing he wanted was any emotional complications. 'It's good to see you, Jack, but to what do I owe the pleasure?'

Stirring the remains of his Americano, Jack decided to dive straight in. 'I'm risking offending you, to be honest. I'm on a mission at the request of Kit, and Amy as well, really. And thinking about it, on my own behalf too. After all, she is my goddaughter…'

Rupert frowned. He suspected he already knew what Jack was about to say, but hoping he was wrong, asked, 'Who is? And what are you talking about?'

'Helena.' Jack pushed the cold coffee dregs away, 'Look, Rupert, I know it is absolutely none of my business, but you are going to have to tell her. I know you aren't ready, I know it won't be easy, and I know you'll hate it because it'll mean upsetting someone – worse, it will mean upsetting your boss's daughter. But if you don't tell her it is going to get one hell of a lot worse.'

Feeling defensive, Rupert's expression clouded. 'And what makes you such an expert?'

'I think I need another cup of coffee before I answer that.'

Rupert watched Jack get up and order, trying not to feel annoyed. He wasn't sure if he was angry that his personal life was being interfered with, or because his choice of when to come out was being taken away from him by events beyond his control.

Sitting back down, Jack sighed. 'Look, I know you're cross. I would be as well, but if you don't come out, at least to Helena, you are going to have to live with one hell of a lot of guilt for a very long time. Especially, if you decide that maybe you'll give it a go with her just because it would be easier than saying no, on the faint chance that you might be straight after all.'

Rupert's voice was barely a murmur. 'How the hell did you know that I was considering that?'

'I think it's time I told you a story. The story of my friends Amy and Kit, and me. Are you sitting comfortably? Then I'll begin…'

Chapter Twenty-two

Saturday 9th July

With Jack's words of warning from the previous day ringing in his ears, Rupert had found he was unable to relax during his morning class at Kew in case Helena popped up again. Now, having been blissfully uninterrupted by any purple-haired young women, he was enjoying an off duty walk around Kew Gardens with his camera.

Skirting the Princess of Wales Conservatory, he decided to take up position and sit quietly where he was until a bird worth photographing came along. And if one didn't come by, then at least he was out of view of anyone who might, possibly, be searching for him.

With his back resting against the trunk of an oak tree, his ears soaking up the chatter of unseen birds, Rupert mulled over everything Jack had told him. At first the story had seemed unbelievable, and yet he knew it was all true – the conversations he'd overheard between Rob and Phil were enough to confirm the truth of the dramas Jack described. There was no doubt that in telling Rupert he needed to come clean with Helena, the man knew what he was talking about.

Rupert had felt increasingly awkward as he'd listened to Jack revealing his personal history. Not just because he always found it difficult to listen to other people's confidences, but because he knew he'd been dangerously close to heading down the same road himself.

The problem, apart from not finding women attractive, was that he was pretty sure he wouldn't fancy Helena even if he *was* straight. She was too confident for him; too full of herself. And yet, the idea that he should try and go out with her, just to see if it could work, had persisted – right up until Jack had met him yesterday.

Suddenly, the thought of being with Helena made him shudder against the tree trunk in a way that made Rupert ashamed of himself. Jack had talked a lot of sense, and although the idea scared him to the bone, it was time for him to man up. Time to be proud of who he was.

Closing his eyes against the ray of sunshine that flickered through the canopy of leaves above, Rupert knew he was lucky. He wouldn't have to explain himself to his workmates or his new friends. In fact, as Jack had already informed him that they'd assumed he was gay from day one, there was no big announcement to make. All Rupert had to do was carry on being himself – except for the problem of Helena. That *had* to be addressed. And so did the other problem...

He fished his mobile out of his pocket. His mother had called again. Deciding to deal with the Helena issue first, he hesitantly stuffed the phone away again.

Making up his mind to go to Pickwicks on his next day off to talk to her, he allowed himself time to ignore the unpleasant task of upsetting someone, and began to indulge in a Jack-fuelled daydream.

'Hello, you.'

Rupert sat up with a start, embarrassingly aware that his daydream had begun to develop definite fantasy qualities, and the way he was sitting could well be showing off this fact far too clearly for his liking. His face bright red, he asked, 'How did you know I was here?'

Leaning against a nearby tree, giving Rupert an excellent view of her legs, Helena said, 'Dad mentioned you were taking more photographs today. I'd love to see them sometime.'

'But this place is huge! You must have been searching for me for absolutely ages.'

'Only a little while. I was sure you'd be tucked away hunting out potential pictures.'

Containing a groan, Rupert saw that his plan of being cruel to be kind was going to have to be brought forward. 'Come on, let's go and have a drink.'

'Thanks.' Helena fiddled with the purple streak at the edge of her fringe in what he suspected she thought was a seductive manner. 'I know it's warm, but I quite fancy a hot chocolate.'

Rupert tried not to notice how she seemed to be walking with an extra wiggle of her hips as he politely answered all her questions on the way to the café, which suddenly seemed miles away.

Finally settling her at a secluded table, he queued up for their drinks, his brain madly deciding how to phrase his let down as nicely as possible.

'Look, Helena,' Rupert put the unseasonably warm drink down in front of her, 'we need to talk.'

Helena smiled brightly. 'You sound like someone in a film.'

'Do I? Well, I suppose ... I mean, what I have to say is hardly original. It's probably been said in lots of films.' Rupert took a drink to stop himself talking rubbish.

Sipping her drink, Helena asked, 'Do you watch a lot of films?'

'No. Yes. Some. I'm quite picky. The thing is, Helena...'

Cupping her mug, making sure that he had a good look at her scarlet fingernails, she interrupted again, 'I *love* going to the cinema. My favourite movie is *When Harry Met Sally*. I know it's old, but it is *soooo* sweet. All that stuff about men and women never truly being able to be friends because the sex bit gets in the way. Inspired storyline! Mum would have killed to have been the first person to write that. That must have been the first time that plot angle was ever used in a film. What do you think?'

Opening his mouth to say that the sex part would never get in the way for them, Rupert was feeling lucky for being given such an easy opening into such tricky subject, when he realised that Helena hadn't actually been expecting him to answer. She was still ploughing on with her film-based monologue.

'That angle has sort of been integral to most chick flicks since then. Mind you, I like a good action movie as well, don't you? My dad was *so* excited about the last Star Wars film. He was like a kid again, waiting to see Han Solo on the screen after so long. Mind you, I have to admit it was better than I thought it would be. The woman playing Rey was fantastic. Do you have any favourite stars? I really like…'

Realising that every question Helena asked was merely rhetorical, Rupert began to let the conversation wash over him like white noise. He was fairly certain she'd worked out that he was going to give her the "we can only ever be friends and no more" speech, and was trying to delay the inevitable. Or maybe she wasn't? He didn't know her well enough to judge.

Eventually, after what like a lifetime, Helena ran out of steam, and Rupert noticed that she was looking at him expectantly, probably waiting for some sort of response to whatever question she'd just asked.

Taking his chance, with no idea of what she was expecting him to say, Rupert grabbed the pause in conversation and launched into the speech he'd been rehearsing in his head while she'd been talking, 'Helena, you're a lovely girl, but I can't be the person you want me to be. Not only are you way too young for me, not to mention my boss's daughter, I simply don't go out with women. I'm sorry.'

Helena's mouth opened and closed once or twice before she said, 'Don't be silly. Of course you do. You haven't found the right girl yet. The right type of woman, if you like. And don't worry. Dad really likes you.'

Even though she was sounding as positive and self-assured as she always did, Rupert could see that Helena's expression had darkened a fraction, and her eyes had a sheen of doubt.

'Helena, beautiful though you are … at the risk of quoting from another film, even if you were the last woman on earth you still wouldn't be my type.'

Rupert wanted to evaporate into thin air. Not only did he feel like the most despicable person on the planet, but he felt as though every single pair of eyes in the busy café was burning into his back, hating him for upsetting the young woman who'd flounced out in an embarrassment of angry tears.

Her accusations of leading her on rang in his ears, but none of Helena's hurt-fuelled retorts had hit him as much as the last that she'll hurled at him. As tears cascaded down her made-up face, making her look like a soggy Bratz doll, she yelled, 'Well, it's your loss! Your loss! If you think Jack bloody Brown will ever fall in love with you, you're very much mistaken. He is bad news, just you ask my mum. Ask Amy!'

The look on his face must have given far more away than Rupert would ever have wished, for Helena, grabbing a handful of serviettes from the tables dispenser to wipe over her face, smearing her make-up further in the process, hissed at a volume that was less than subtle, 'Oh my God, you are, aren't you? You're in love with Jack!'

He didn't turn to watch her storm out.

Rupert sat where he was for a long time. It was bad enough that he'd hurt her. He knew he hadn't led her on, but if she needed to believe that, then so be it, but he wasn't secretly in love with Jack – was he? He just found him attractive – which was perfectly understandable as he was very handsome. And Jack was the only gay man Rupert knew locally, and he got on with him well. They had lots in common, and...

'Oh, no. I can't be. Everyone says Jack is a total nightmare in the relationship department. Even Jack himself says that.'

Rupert stared blankly into his cold coffee.

So much for a peaceful afternoon off.

Chapter Twenty-three

Saturday 9th July

One look at Helena's smudged mascara was enough for Kit to guess what had happened.

Pulling her daughter in for a cuddle, she said nothing, but passed her the box of tissues from her dressing table so she could clean up her face. Then, kissing the top of her head, Kit sat Helena on the edge of the bed, found her daughter's favourite jeans and cosy hoodie, and placed them next to her. 'You get comfortable, and then we're going to go out.'

'What?'

'We are going over to Amy's for cake and champagne.'

'What the hell do I have to celebrate?' Helena angrily scrunched up the soggy tissue in her hands.

'*We* have plenty to celebrate. The most important thing being that you, in about three hours' time, are going to feel like toasting the rest of your life.'

'I am?'

'I promise.'

'But I want to hide. I've been such an *idiot*.' Laying her head on her mum's shoulder, Helena sniffed loudly, 'And I can't go out for champagne in an old hoodie anyway.'

Kit couldn't help but smile at her daughter. Helena might be heartbroken, but she was still worried about her appearance. 'You can wear anything you like. Now, take a deep breath, and I'll be back in thirty seconds.'

Helena felt the tears well back up inside her. She felt so stupid! As her mum came back in, she scrubbed at her eyes crossly with the sleeve of her faded blue top. 'Thanks, Mum.'

'What for?'

'For not saying I told you so.' Helena dissolved into a fresh flood of tears, as she cuddled against her mum in a way she hadn't done since she was ten years old, when her beloved pet rabbit had passed away.

Paul had been ushered out to do the shopping so that Amy, Kit, and Helena could have some girl time. The champagne was on Amy's patio table, her a glass jug of chilled orange juice was ready in, and a giant sugar-frosted lemon cake stood ready to be sliced. As an afterthought, Amy had put out a pretty square box of tissues, just in case the tears hadn't finished flowing before her visitors arrived.

Then, with an encouraging kick from her baby, Amy sat in the sunshine to wait for a ring on the doorbell.

Rupert headed to Reading Nature at top speed. He knew he didn't really have anything to apologise for, but he felt he owed Phil an explanation as to why he could be going home to a very angry, tearful Helena that evening. Fearful that he could be about to lose the only job he'd ever enjoyed because he'd upset the boss's daughter, he knew he couldn't leave things alone, otherwise he'd only worry until he went back to work on Tuesday morning.

Glad that the shop was fairly quiet, Rupert steered his confused boss into the tiny staff kitchen and, with his pulse racing, explained exactly what had just happened at Kew.

'I'm so sorry, Phil. I honestly didn't do anything to encourage her. It's not like I'd ever go out with –'

Phil interrupted Rupert with a patient sigh. 'What is it about the women in my family?'

'Sorry?'

'Thanks for telling me, Rupert. It can't have been easy for you, especially as Helena can be … shall we say single-minded.' Putting the kettle on, Phil told Rupert not to worry and to stay exactly where he was. 'Hide out in here for a while and have a cuppa.'

Heading back into the shop, Phil picked up the phone. 'Jack, mate, I know you're busy, but if you've got a minute, then we could do with you over here.'

Amy ushered Kit and Helena through the house and out into her sunny narrow garden. 'Just what the doctor ordered?'

Helena's bottom lip began to wobble as she saw the effort Amy had gone to for her. Unable to speak for fear of letting out another landslide of emotion, she simply nodded her thanks.

'This is amazing, Amy, thanks.' Kit gently hugged her friend. 'Look at you! Are you sure you still have a month to go?'

'Tell me about it! I'm not going to be able to fit through the front door soon.' Turning her attention to Helena, Amy smiled, 'Right then, Helena. I know we are going to come across like two interfering old women, but please, if you never take any of our advice ever again, trust us now. You have to talk about this *today*. Don't bottle it up. Let it out. We aren't being nosy, we know precisely what damage bottling this stuff up does – and we care for you too much to let you be as stupid as we are!'

Pouring Helena an iced Buck's Fizz, and Kit some of the champagne Paul had bought for after the baby was born, Amy lowered herself back onto her chair.

'Now then,' Amy raised her glass, 'here's to *not* getting mixed up with men who are confused about their sexuality!'

'You did it then?'

Looking up from tweaking the photographs on his laptop, Rupert was surprised to see Jack. He felt colour rise across his face as Helena's accusing words echoed in his ears. 'Hello, Jack. Yes, I did it. But not quite in the way I'd planned.'

'Does it ever go to plan?'

'There speaks the voice of experience.'

'You have no idea!' Jack poured himself a coffee from the jug in the corner of the kitchen. 'That's why I'm off men right now. Well, off relationships, anyway. I never quite manage to get it right. No matter how I try, I always end up hurting the people I care about…'

Feeling oddly as if he was being warned off, Rupert replied, 'I guess I've been living the single life for similar reasons.'

'So then,' Jack stirred his drink slowly, 'tell me.'

Helena's hand shook as she took a sip of the blissfully cold drink. 'It seemed so perfect to start with. I found him at taking photos at Kew. He was on his own, and it was easy to chat and felt so relaxed…'

Rupert pushed away his empty coffee cup, knowing he'd already had enough caffeine that day to give his heart palpitations. 'I'd planned to find Helena on my day off on Monday, to tell her it was hopeless, just like we discussed yesterday. But then she turned up at Kew this lunchtime. I have no idea how she found me. I was tucked away in the trees. It was beginning to feel like I was being stalked. Talk about uncomfortable.'

Amy nudged the tissue box nearer to Helena as the tell-tale shortening of breath became more pronounced and tears began to brew.

'He asked me to go for drink. I thought it was a date. It felt like a date. We chatted all the way to the café, and Rupert got me a hot chocolate. He was so kind and…'

'Honestly, Jack, I know Helena is your goddaughter and everything, and I don't want to cause offence, but my God, she can talk! I didn't get a word in on the whole walk from the wood to the café.'

Jack smiled ruefully. 'You were taking her for a drink to try and soften the blow?'

'*Try* is the right word.'

'Tried and failed?'

'In spectacular style.'

'And then …' The tears were in full flow now, but silently, as if Helena was all sobbed out but her tear ducts hadn't registered it was time to dam the waterfall. 'Then Rupert … Rupert … sat me at this lovely secluded table. I thought it was because he wanted us to be alone, but…'

'I picked the table as far as way from other people as possible, so that if Helena went insane not too many people would notice. I have to work at Kew after all, and most of the café staff know me.'

Jack groaned. 'Let me guess. Helena thought you were being romantic rather than diplomatic?'

'Exactly.'

Blowing her nose with a sound like a foghorn, Helena took another glug of the Buck's Fizz, which was rather stronger than she'd expected, and was definitely making her confide more than she normally would. 'We had this chat about films. I was so sure Rupert was about to ask me out to the cinema, and then…'

'It was awful, Jack. Awful. I'm sure Helena sensed I was going to give her the whole, "I can't go out with you" speech, and she just talked and talked so that I wouldn't be able to get the words I had to say out. She started on about films. It was unbelievable; she just kept talking.'

Jack fought back the instinct to put his hand over Rupert's as it rested on the table. 'But eventually you must have been able to get a word in edgeways?'

Kit nodded encouragingly at her daughter. 'You're so brave. It's so horrid having a broken heart, but not bottling it up and hiding it inside is important. I don't want you to go all bitter like I did, or all sad and lonely like Amy did.'

'Thanks, Kit!' Amy raised her eyebrows at her friends.

'I didn't mean…'

Amy raised her hand, 'I'm joking.' Cutting another massive slice of cake and sliding it across to Helena, she confided, 'I was a mess, hun. A feeble, embarrassing, ashamed, pathetic heap of a person when I lost Jack. And although we'd been together a year, so it was a bit different from what you're suffering now, I made it so much worse for myself by not talking to anyone about it for thirteen lonely years.'

147

'Thirteen *years*?' Helena whispered in shock. 'You didn't even tell your best friend?'

'Jack was my best friend.'

'Oh God, how awful. You poor thing!'

Amy grinned. She patted her stomach, which had started twinging in a way that was extremely inconvenient. 'I think things turned out alright in the end.'

Kit finished the contents of her glass and poured herself a top-up. 'So, what happened next? Come on, you might as well get it all off your chest, then you can make a totally fresh start, and have no emotional hang-ups on your shoulders when you go to university.'

'*If* I get my A levels.'

Shaken by Helena's unusual lack of confidence, Kit inwardly cursed the side effects of unrequited love. 'You will, sweetheart. You will.'

Taking another deep breath, Helena relayed Rupert's statement that he'd never be able to be with her, even though she was beautiful, because she'd never be his type. She sniffed hard. 'He was saying he was gay, wasn't he? Like you guys thought all along. Right?'

'You did it, then? You told her you were gay?'

'Well.' Rupert looked a bit uncomfortable, 'What I actually said was that even if she was the last woman in the world, she wouldn't be my type.'

'Isn't that a line from a film?'

Rupert groaned. 'Don't you start!'

'What?'

'It doesn't matter.' Rupert lowered his eyes to the computer screen which had gone into sleep mode.

Jack's eyes narrowed. 'You've never said it, have you?'

'No. Not yet.' Rupert turned the screen back on, simply for something to do. 'You must think me a terrible coward.'

Oh, sod it. Jack put his hand out and put it over Rupert's as it rested on the mouse he'd attached to his laptop. 'No. I don't think that. Not at all.'

The tears had disappeared in time with the champagne.

'You'll be drunk!' Amy laughed at Kit as she knocked back the remains of her drink.

'Nah, this stuff doesn't do anything for me.' She glanced at her daughter, 'You alright, love?'

'What?' Helena, although far from drunk – as her mother had been putting no more than a token gesture of champagne in her glass after the first properly proportioned Bucks Fizz – was looking very sleepy.

'You OK?'

'I feel like a complete fool. I won't ever be able to look Rupert in the eye again, but surely it's better to find out now, than to go out with him and then discover he was gay, don't you think?'

Amy and Kit looked directly at each other, and toasting her with their full glasses, answered Helena with an emphatic, 'Yes!'

Chapter Twenty-four

Monday 11th July

Kit's face broke into a broad smile. She waited for Peggy to be between customers before beckoning to her with an almost forgotten rush of excitement.

It had been a long time since she'd had an email from an erotica publisher addressed to her old pen name, Katrina Penny, and even longer since she'd had an email which made her smile from ear to ear.

'What's up?' Peggy refilled her friend's coffee cup by way of automatic pilot, and then rested her weary legs for thirty seconds. 'Helena's doing fine. She's a bit quiet, but that's not a problem; and until about ten minutes ago, we've been so busy that she's had plenty to take her mind off things. Which you'd have noticed if you ever lifted your head from your work!'

Kit had called Peggy the evening before to let her know that Helena was suffering from bruised pride, and might need handling with kid gloves today. 'Thanks, hun, that's good to know, but no, that's not it. I wanted to tell you, Peggy McIntyre, that you are a total star!'

'Well of course I am! Why exactly am I of the shiny and pointy persuasion today, though?'

'Because that erotic story you made me write…'

'I hardly *made* you write it. I thought it would be a good way of shaking off the final traces of the writer's block.'

'And a damn good idea it was too. Once I'd done it, I thought I might as well see if I could sell it.'

'It got taken?'

'It did! I'd forgotten what a massive rush getting a short story taken for an anthology gives you!'

'Katrina Penny rides again! If that doesn't deserve a toast then I don't know what does!'

'Thanks, Peggy, although I'd better stick to toasting with coffee today. I rather overdid the champagne at the weekend when Amy and I were trying to cheer up Helena.'

'Hangover?'

'Not so much a hangover as an inability to wake up properly! Caffeine in slow regular injections is very much called for today!'

'No comment!' Peggy winked, 'So, the words are flowing again then?'

'Yes. My editor is delighted. She was beginning to panic, and I can't say I blame her! The novel is churning itself out again, sometimes into the notebook, and sometimes on the laptop.' Kit lifted her coffee cup in salute to her friend. 'Thanks, Peggy. Thanks ever so much.'

'You are more than welcome. Um ... there is *one* price for my assistance, however.'

Kit pulled a stapled set of printed pages from her bag and passed it across to her friend. 'Yes, Peggy, you can have a copy of the story.'

'Young Rupert looks a lot happier,' Rob said to Phil once their colleague had left for Kew, 'but how's Helena doing?'

'Sheepish is the word for my daughter at the moment.' Phil knocked a pile of pound coins together and started counting out another handful from the till. 'I know it sounds a bit harsh, but I think it was a lesson she was overdue learning. I love her to bits, but I am well aware that Helena has always been a bit too confident for her own good.'

'Funny, really, because you and Kit aren't like that.'

'Probably too much reality TV.'

'Probably.'

Phil started stacking a third pile of coins. 'Has our plan worked or not, do you think?'

Rob shrugged. 'I don't know, but Jack was in the kitchen with Rupert a long time.'

'And he came over quickly when I called, didn't he?'

Rob gave Phil a thoughtful look. 'You're convinced those two would be good for each other, aren't you? I mean, why don't you think Jack would screw Rupert up like he has all the rest?'

'Call it a hunch.'

'And...'

'They have heaps in common. They both love nature, art, photography and all that. Plus, Rupert comes from a well-off family, so he'll never be after Jack for his money, and Jack has always been young for his age, whereas Rupert has an old head on young shoulders. They meet in the middle.'

'If I didn't know better, mate, I'd say you were turning into an old romantic!'

'Or I might just want Jack off the market for all our sakes!'

'Good point.' Rob nodded. 'Very wise, just in case your Helena gets another crush, huh?'

Phil threw the receipt book at Rob. 'That is not remotely funny! For that, you can call Debbie and see if you're allowed out for a pint tonight. I thought we should get Paul out for a pub trip. Might be his last chance for a while.'

'You have a deal.'

Megan took the man's rain-soaked jacket. 'Really, it's no problem.'

'I didn't bring an umbrella. The weather was so lovely when I left home this morning.' His grey eyes shone at the waitress as he spoke.

'It was lovely here as well. That summer cloudburst seems to have caught us all on the hop. We have a number of our guests' jackets and jumpers drying out in the yard. I'll just put yours with the others and come back to take your order.'

When Megan returned to the evidently wealthy man – if his designer clothes, genuine Rolex, and confident air were anything to go by – she couldn't stop herself from thinking that the phrase 'silver fox' suited him perfectly. His grey-flecked brown hair was short, his tight short-sleeved shirt revealed him to be fit, and there was more than a little twinkle in his eye. She'd have been making serious George Clooney comparisons if she was into older men.

'What can I get you, sir?'

'A cup of your finest coffee would be great, and a tuna and mature cheddar panini, please. And some local information, if you can?

'I'll do my best.'

'I have an appointment this afternoon at a local restaurant; a new place opening soon. The owner's a Jack Brown. Like an idiot, I've left my iPad with all the info on in my hotel room and my phone absolutely refuses to find a signal. You don't happen to know the place, do you?'

It was only after the George Clooney man had gone, his suave charm disappearing with him, that Megan began to wonder about his story. It was all a bit implausible ... he didn't seem the sort of man to be disorganised enough to ever leave home without his iPad, nor did Megan know of any phone networks that didn't work around here ... *Oh well*, Megan thought to herself, *I don't suppose it'll matter. Jack is hardly going to complain that I've sent a good-looking man to his door. And, anyway, it could all have been true.*

'How the hell did you find me?'

'Come off it, Jack, it wasn't exactly difficult. The removal men you hired to empty the bungalow had a Richmond address on the side of their van.'

'So what? I could simply have been moving my stuff to a friend's place before going travelling again.'

'Don't give me that crap. You have the cooking bug badly, and I already knew that you planned to open your own place one day. You told me – if you remember.'

Groaning inwardly as he recalled their post-coital conversation, Jack merely said, 'More fool me.' He folded his arms over his chest, 'Tell me then, Sherlock, how did you find this place?'

'There aren't many fledgling restaurants in the area. And I asked someone.'

'Asked who?'

'A very sweet thing at Pickwicks, that café you used to go on about.'

Jack went cold. Turning up here was bad enough, but for Gareth to have gone to Pickwicks somehow felt like a personal invasion. 'And I assume you told the young lady in question that you had a legitimate reason to see me?'

'I told her I had an appointment to see you regarding your restaurant.'

'You lied to my friend.'

'Yes. And a very pretty friend she was too. Young, blonde, petite.'

Must have been Megan. Jack didn't say anything for a moment, before walking to the front door, 'I'd like you to leave now, please.' He was trying hard not to shout. He'd be damned if he'd give Gareth the satisfaction of seeing him lose control. 'I'm sorry I couldn't be what you wanted me to be, but you treated me like shit over those last few weeks. When I left, I had no desire to ever set eyes on you again. I would rather that had remained the case.'

Gareth flashed his self-assured smile and stood up. He surveyed the restaurant as he did so. 'This could be a nice place, Jack. I love the artwork. I've been looking for someone to do some new pictures for Kennedy's. I'm giving the whole place a facelift.'

'Goodbye, Gareth.'

'If you feel like passing on the artist's name to me, I'd pay the proper rate.'

'*Goodbye,* Gareth.'

Pushing a card into Jack's hand, Gareth walked away without a backward glance.

It was a business card for Claridges.

Gareth had written his room number on the back.

Chapter Twenty-five

Saturday 16th July

'Jack did say he was coming, didn't he?' Phil placed a fresh round of beer and lager on the small wooden table in between himself Rob and Paul. 'Not like him to be late if alcohol is involved.'

Phil checked his phone. 'He did, and I haven't had a text saying he'd be late. Maybe he's got a date?'

Paul lifted his pint of beer in salute to Phil as thanks for the purchase. 'Amy was so sure he'd settled down a bit. She'd be disappointed if he's given up on his resolution to be a good boy and hit the clubs.'

'Actually, I was thinking that he might be out on a proper date. With a nice bloke for a change.' Phil and Rob exchanged glances.

Paul looked from one friend to another. 'Well, don't keep me in suspense. What have you been up to? Matchmaking, by any chance?'

Jack's concentration had been all over the place since his former boss had disappeared out of the bistro. Gareth hadn't even said what he wanted or what he was doing in London. Was he just passing – or had he come specifically to turn up at the bistro? If the whole point of his visit had been to unsettle Jack, then it had worked.

Standing before the fourth in the series of paintings that Megan had done for him, Jack stared hard. They were exquisite. Fine details of architecture from around the bistro, all in close-up, were alive with flashes of terracotta and yellow. The more he looked, the more he could see a larger spectrum of warm colours, and the more drawn into the details of the art he became. No wonder Gareth had liked them.

Megan had been so nervous when she'd presented Jack with her completed pictures. They were the fastest pieces of art she'd ever produced in her life. She need not have worried though, because Jack had loved them instantly.

He'd been looking forward to showing the artwork, and the bistro in general, to Rupert. He had – he hoped – managed to make the invitation to come and see the place before it opened sound like a friendly gesture rather than a date-like one. Now, with Gareth unexpectedly sniffing around, he wished he'd asked Rupert out on a date there and then. If he was off the market, Gareth might take the hint and bugger off back to Kent.

As soon as he'd had the thought, Jack felt ashamed of himself. Rupert was far too nice a guy to be used like that. If he wanted to go out with him, Jack knew the only way on earth it could work for either of them was to develop a friendship first.

Jack had tried the mutual lust thing before. It never lasted. All of his friends' longstanding relationships, whether straight or gay, were the products of friendship and mutual respect. 'Face it,' Jack spoke to the empty restaurant, 'you're in your forties, and suddenly you want what you're friends have got.'

The spectre of Gareth grew in his head again, and Jack could visualise the two of them together in Kennedy's kitchen, breaking every rule in the health, safety and hygiene book… *Damn!* Jack's body instantly reacted to the memory. *Damn that man.*

Grabbing his coat, the invitation to the pub with his friends wiped from his mind, Jack slammed out into the London night…

Monday 18th July

Jack had got as far as the club door on Saturday night, but he hadn't gone inside. He'd been in the queue for only two minutes when an image of Amy's disapproving face had filled his mind. She'd forgiven him for upsetting Peggy, but if he went back on his resolution to behave better, she'd be so disappointed in him. It wasn't, he knew, as if he was going to the club because he fancied a dance.

Instead he'd gone for a walk, then, suddenly remembering the pub meeting, had texted Rob to apologise, explaining that his ex had turned up and he wasn't in the mood for company. Then, not entirely sure if he was doing the right thing or not, he had called Rupert to rearrange his bistro visit from next week to today.

Now, as he waited for Rupert to arrive, Jack found he was nervous. This was new territory for him. When he'd first begun seeing Toby he'd felt apprehensive, and his body had fizzed with expectation, but he knew now that had been nothing beyond wanting Toby to fancy him as much as he did in return. At no point had it mattered that Toby respected him, or approved of his choices. It had been quite a shock to find it really mattered to him that Rupert liked his bistro. He wanted Rupert to love Megan's art, and approve of his menu choices. He wanted Rupert to feel at home here, to sense that this was a good place to come for a meal – or at least it would be once everything had been finalised.

Having dressed with rather more care than usual, Jack closed the door on Megan's faintly paint-smelling studio, and checked his appearance in the mirror before heading downstairs to get ready for the courier to arrive with a delivery of menu holders, napkins, and heavy-duty table clothes.

Jack was counting a pile of exquisitely made cream linen napkins when there was a tentative knock at the door. His pulse accelerated a fraction as he saw Rupert, looking equally apprehensive, come into his bistro.

Smiling a welcome, he said, 'What do you think?'

'It's fantastic.' Rupert walked straight to the first of Megan's pictures, as though drawn to them by an invisible force. 'Where did you get these? They're stunning.'

As Rupert moved from one painting to the next, Jack explained about Megan's artwork, and how it was her dream to make art her living one day.

Thoughtful, Rupert had to restrain himself from caressing the canvases with his fingertips. 'Don't you find you want to reach out and touch them?'

Swelling with pride for Megan, and relieved beyond description that Rupert liked what he'd seen of his restaurant so far, Jack beamed. 'That is exactly it. They are tangible things, aren't they? Megan is one talented young lady.'

'Does she take commissions?'

'I'm sure she would if you asked her.' Jack felt a twinge of guilt. He'd been wondering if he should have told Megan that Gareth liked her work. Gareth was many things, but he wasn't given to saying he liked something if he didn't. He would never have commented on wanting some art like his if he hadn't meant it, and Jack knew that Megan and Nick could do with the sort of money Gareth could afford to pay.

Rupert shoved his hands in his trouser pockets to prevent himself from touching the canvas before him. 'Has Megan considered setting up an art website? That would make taking commissions much easier. I could help her do that if she'd be interested. I've been considering setting one up for my photos, but my work isn't quite good enough yet.'

'Are you kidding me? Your stuff is totally good enough!' Jack shook his head. 'Maybe you and Megan should set a joint site up – after all, you're as lacking in confidence as each other, at least where your art is concerned. And, frankly, you're both excellent at what you do.'

'Oh,' Rupert blushed, 'um, thanks, Jack.' He looked around the dining room, not daring to meet Jack's eye. 'You know, doing a combined website with Megan could actually work well – if you think we'd get on.'

'I'm sure you would. Would you like me to invite her over to meet you? I'm sure she'd be keen.'

'That would be good, but perhaps don't tell her about the website idea until I've seen if we do get along? Maybe tell her I'm interested in a commission, for the time being.'

'And are you?'

'I might be, actually. My mother would love the detail in these.'

Jack sent a text to Megan, before asking Rupert if he fancied a complete tour of the bistro.

With a pile of sample menus in one hand, and a heap of ideas scribbled in his notebook on the table before them, Jack sat with Rupert on the cosy sofa that he'd placed in the reception area of the restaurant. 'What do you think? Too pretentious or about right?'

He sipped his coffee anxiously as Rupert ran an eye over the first two sample menus. He seemed to be taking for ever to scan the A4 sheets of paper.

'When do you open?'

'Mid-August. I'm planning a critic's launch first, and then I'll open properly.' Jack felt more anxious by the second. Why didn't Rupert just say if he liked the look of the meal choices or not?

'And you have all your staff in place?'

'Almost. I have an interview set up for a front of house manager and receptionist tomorrow. I have some students from the local catering college hired to work in the kitchen, and a waitress booked. I need a pot washer as well; although I've got an idea about who'd be suitable for that job, so as long as the food is OK, then I'm good to go.'

Rupert laid the menus on his lap. 'I'll be honest, Jack, because I can tell how important this is to you.'

Jack felt his heart sink. 'Does that mean I should change the menus?'

'No. It means you should invite me over again very soon and cook me a meal from this list. It's perfect. It's balanced, and provides something for everyone.'

'Really?'

'Really. I have been to a lot of restaurants. Trust me.'

'You have?'

'My father is something of a gourmet. He has been on Michelin star panels in his time.'

'Seriously?'

'Seriously.' Rupert nodded at the menu he held. 'I promise you, Jack, if I didn't think this looked right, I would tell you.'

Fighting the urge to kiss the man sat next to him, Jack simply said, 'Thank you, Rupert. That means a lot to me.'

Asking a more personal question than he normally would, Rupert said, 'I get the impression that this is a more important project to you than any that have gone before. I am right?'

'You are.' Jack met Rupert's eyes for a moment, before dropping his gaze back to his menus. 'I haven't told the others, well, apart from Amy, but I have to run this business properly. In the past I've always had my inheritance to fall back on, but that is no longer possible after paying for all my travels, a chef's course, and buying the bistro outright. This is the biggest gamble I've ever taken.'

'And it will pay off.'

'Will it?' This time Jack did meet Rupert's eyes, and the younger man didn't move away.

'It will.'

Jack could feel his body moving in towards Rupert, even though every part of his brain was telling him he'd only hurt him, and he shouldn't really, he really…

'Honestly, Jack! You shouldn't rob them from the local High School. Especially when you and I have unfinished business!'

Gareth Kennedy stood in the bistro doorway. 'You two kids are so cute. You didn't even hear me knock, did you?'

Furious, Jack stood up. 'That'll be because I'd bet my pension on the fact that you *didn't* bloody knock. What the hell do you want, Gareth?'

'What do I want? Quick bunk-up in the kitchen as usual, if you're offering.'

Rupert, his face ablaze with humiliated embarrassment, got up, grabbed his jacket, and wordlessly strode to the door.

'Rupert, it isn't what you think, it's…'

Jack's words fell on empty space.

Chapter Twenty-six

Tuesday 19th July

Rupert had given up the struggle for sleep by five o'clock that morning, and by seven he was sat at his desk in the corner of Reading Nature.

Twenty-four hours ago he had dared to hope that perhaps he'd found someone was capable of understanding accepting him for who he was. A close friend, if not a potential partner, who'd already faced many of the hurdles associated with not being straight. Someone to confide in.

It felt like a lifetime had passed since then.

Fool.

The close-ups of leaves he had photographed on his last trip to Kew began to merge together on the screen before him as he faced the fact that Jack's reputation was true. How could he have been so stupid as to imagine it would be different with him?

Closing his eyes and counting to ten, Rupert switched the computer off and threw himself into planning the next month's worth of children's natural history lessons. No way was he getting suckered into any games, least of all by someone as notorious as Jack Brown.

Jack couldn't sleep. His head screamed in time with his fast-growing hangover, and he didn't know where he was.

Holding in his cries of self-loathing so he didn't disturb the man who was fast asleep beside him, Jack kept his firmly eyes shut. Whatever he did seemed to upset people. It didn't matter that he never meant to; that even when he was trying hard not to, he still did. *Oh, what's the point!*

Yesterday, when he'd been sat on his new sofa with Rupert talking about Megan and websites and commissions, Jack had felt right. Not just right, but braver somehow. He had even contemplated being the better man and passing on Gareth's contact details to Megan so they could talk potential art projects for Kennedy's. Feeling guilty because he knew he couldn't possibly do that now because Gareth would misinterpret the move as affection, Jack wondered how the hell he always managed to mess things up so spectacularly.

Now, more than ever before, Jack saw that his determination not to have any sort of relationship had been the right thing to do. If he needed proof of that, the last twenty-four hours had given him just that. The instant he'd relaxed with Rupert everything had gone wrong. In a fit of self-pity and frustration, after he'd tried calling Rupert a few times and found his mobile switched off, Jack had chucked in the towel on his recently acquired principles and gone clubbing.

At first it had been a sobering experience. Walking into Heaven, after an absence of a few years, he found he was much older than the majority. But that hadn't been a problem for long. Within ten minutes Jack had found himself under the unflinching scrutiny of a twentysomething blond called Andy, who had even more confidence with the boys than he did.

Than he *used* to have.

Now, as Jack lay next to Andy in his uncomfortable double futon, the sheets between them twisted and neglected, Jack found himself face to sleeping face with himself from twenty years ago. The thought made his headache thump twice as hard.

He'd have to go and apologise to Rupert in person, and fast, before word got back to Kit and Amy via Rob and Phil. *Idiot!* Jack mentally listed the hundreds of things he ought to do that day to get the bistro ready for its opening. Not to mention the preparations he wanted to make for the job interview he was conducting that afternoon.

Taking a last look at the sleeping Adonis next to him, Jack, with a stealth developed from years of experience, crept out of bed, scooped up his clothes, dressed, and escaped into early morning London without a backward glance.

'Who told you?'

'No one. But Rob called Paul and Paul called me, to tell me that Rupert hasn't spoken a word all morning and that Phil suspected you had something to do with his black mood.'

'Oh, great!'

'Are you going to let me in, Jack?' Amy rubbed her back as she stood on the bistro doorstep. 'Us pregnant women types need a sit down every ten minutes you know, especially after a hard day at work. Time for a chat, perhaps?'

'I didn't mean to cause trouble, you know. I never do. It just seems to happen.'

'So you keep saying.' Amy tilted her head to one side and looked at her ex carefully. She had never seen him so defeated. 'Come on, Mr Brown, tell me all about it.'

Having thought better of turning up at Reading Nature dressed in the clothes another man had taken off him only a few hours before, Jack had gone straight home. After taking the longest shower ever, he had tried – and failed – to call Rupert twice more.

Deciding that if Rupert didn't want to talk to him, and acknowledging that wasting time he didn't have crossing London to set the record straight wouldn't change anything, Jack had done the sensible thing. After sending a text saying that he could explain about Gareth – but not mentioning his clubbing experience – Jack had prepared for the front of house manager interview, submitted the first three months' worth of menus to the printers, and made a start on a press release for the bistro's grand opening. He'd been about to get himself some coffee before the interview candidate arrived at five o'clock, when Amy had knocked at the door.

Herbal tea now to hand, Amy stretched her legs out on the reception sofa, and having listened to all the gory details of Jack's most recent adventure said, 'What does this Gareth guy actually want, then?'

'I have no idea.' Jack shrugged. 'To stir things up for me. Make trouble. He said something about looking for art, but I

165

don't buy that for a minute.'

'Could he be worried about the competition? Work-wise I mean, not personally?'

'I can't see why. Kennedy's is in another part of the country, for goodness' sake. Anyway, his restaurant is excellent; it has a great reputation, plus the food he serves is quite different from what I intend to do. And arrogant though I can be, I honestly don't think he has come all this way because he can't get enough of my body.'

'You're growing up at last, aren't you.'

'Cheeky!' Jack smiled for a second before the gloom re-descended.

'So … Rupert then?'

'What?'

'OK, no need to be so defensive! I've heard nice things about him.'

'Even from Helena?'

'That's a rather different situation.'

'He was very grateful to you and Kit. I heard all about it via Phil. Helena hardly gave Rupert the chance to speak. He couldn't get a word in edgeways to explain her misunderstanding.'

'I can imagine.' Amy put her empty cup down and swung her legs off the sofa. 'What are you going to do then, Jack?'

Jack looked at his watch, 'I have an interview with a bloke called Mike in half an hour for the front of house job, and then I need to make a list of all the last minute things I have to sort before I open. I can't believe how close that is now!'

'Tell me about it.' Amy patted her bump, and immediately wished she hadn't as it tightened uncomfortably. 'Actually, I meant what are you going to do about Gareth and Rupert?'

'Nothing.' Jack knocked his cup back onto its saucer. 'Until Gareth tells me what he's up to I shall ignore him. I'm not interested in playing games with him. As to Rupert, well … I've thought about it, and he's better off without me. He's a lovely guy. He deserves better than someone who shags anyone that happens to be passing whenever the going gets tough.'

Amy tilted her head to one side. 'I'm never seen you so

ashamed of your actions before. Not like this. You're seriously cross with yourself about last night, aren't you?'

'Yes.'

Picking up her bag, Amy said, 'I'd better let you get ready for Mike to arrive. Fingers crossed he's the perfect chap for the job. I want to pop in and see how Peggy and Scott are getting on with their own plans for world domination before I run out of steam.'

Jack hugged her. 'Thanks for coming over. Can I ask you something before you go?'

'Of course.'

'How's Megan doing setting up Pickwicks 2?'

'OK, I think. It's not long until that opens either.'

'Do they have a name for it yet, or is it really going to be called Pickwicks 2?'

'Not that I know of. Have you got a name for this place yet?'

'Yep, but for now I'm keeping my lips sealed.'

'Fair enough! Right then, I must go, or I'll end up being on your interview panel.'

'One more question?' Jack spoke quietly, and Amy instantly worried about what he was going to say.

'Sure.'

'Do you still want me to be godfather? I would totally understand if you'd changed your mind. I'm hardly good example material, am I?'

Amy stared at Jack and shook her head. 'Oh, you silly little gay person!' She kissed him hard on his designer-stubbled cheek. 'You were top of the list from the start. Now, get on with doing what needs doing today, then text Rupert again. Invite him for a taster meal session like you discussed with him yesterday. Ignore this Gareth guy, and get this place ready for my baby's naming party at the start of September. Yes?'

Jack couldn't speak, but his expression flooded with gratitude.

'Now, I have a question for you before I go.'

'Anything, Amy. Anything.'

'Please can I use your bathroom?'

Chapter Twenty-Seven

Tuesday 19th July

Amy arrived at Pickwicks in time to let the last customer out of the door. She found Peggy behind the counter packing supplies for the new café.

'Hi, Amy, great timing! Could you be an angel and close up for me?' Peggy gestured to the unaccustomed muddle in front of her. 'As you can see I'm a bit up to my eyes in it.'

Flipping the 'Open' sign to 'Closed' and bolting the door, Amy asked, 'Can I help? I'm no good at heavy lifting right now, but I can do everything else. Tables need a wipe?'

'Don't worry, Megan's about to do that. She's stacking the dishwasher. Kit's in the kitchen, she'll be out in a minute. You could help me wrap these spare plates in bubble wrap so they don't break on the way to the new place.'

'No problem. How come they weren't delivered straight there?'

'These are just extras we don't need here. Saving a few pennies here and there.'

'Sounds sensible. So, is it all systems go with Pickwicks 2 now? Is that its name, by the way?'

'The new cook has been chosen. Scott is in the kitchen with Kit. He's getting her to read through the formal job offer letter he's written, checking for spelling mistakes and such.'

'Fantastic. And the name?'

'We're torn between Little Nell's Café and Fezziwig's.'

Amy nodded approvingly. 'Keeping up the Dickensian theme then.'

'Yep, which do you prefer?'

'Little Nell's, I think. When do you need to decide by?'

'Soon-ish, as we have to order a sign, and I'd like to put the name at the top of the menus, get some business cards printed and all that.'

As usual, the fact that the café was closed didn't mean that the hard work was over. The excitement of helping her friends prepare for the new opening was precisely what Amy needed to take her mind off her increasing anxiety about forthcoming parenthood. The next day's order of milk, bread, and perishables had been placed, and the endless round of filling the dishwasher, lifting the chairs, and cleaning the floor was being tackled by Megan.

It was a long time since Amy had worked at the café, and although she loved her current job she missed the camaraderie of Pickwicks sometimes. Placing the last spare plate in a box, Amy listened as Megan sat next to her and read through the list of things she would have to do after Peggy and Scott signed the final piece of paperwork the next day.

The kitchen door swung open. Kit held the draft letter in her hand. 'This is fine now, Scott. Just type in those few minor changes and it's good to go.' Her gaze fell on Amy, and her face broke into a bigger smile, 'Hello there, Mrs Donahue! What are you doing in these parts when you should be snoozing at home?'

'I figure I'll have plenty of time to get bored on the sofa when I'm on maternity leave. I went to see Jack, and I wanted to come and see how it was going here. I must admit, I didn't expect to walk in and be given jobs to do.'

'Just like old times!'

'I'm rather enjoying it, to be honest.' Amy adjusted her position on the chair. 'How's everything with you now then?'

Once Kit had brought her up to date, she revealed what Jack had said about his crush on Rupert – a fact that made Kit groan.

'That is exactly what Helena predicted would happen, albeit out of spite. I'm not sure she really believed it.'

'Well, from what the boys tell me, it sounds as though the crush is mutual.'

Kit sighed. 'Poor Helena! She's very much happier, but she's still a bit bruised on the pride front. I can see the attraction for Jack this time, though. Rupert is a very nice bloke. You've not met him yet?'

'Not so far. I'm sure I'll encounter him once the baby is born. Kew will be on my pushing-the-pram route once I get to that stage.'

'Do you have a pram yet?'

'Not yet. We thought we'd get one this weekend. I fancy one of those pushchairs with a car seat attached. They look much easier to push around shops than a bulky pram.'

'I'm sure they are. I had one of those massive double buggies. It was a nightmare doing anything that involved doorways.'

The phone ringing in the background didn't interrupt Amy or Kit's conversation, nor did Scott's conversation when he picked up – not until they heard his usually placid voice snap, 'What!' down the line.

One look at Scott's expression was enough to tell the women around him that something was wrong. Very wrong. It was so unusual seeing anything other than positivity in his expression. The effect of seeing him scowling was unnerving.

'Oh my God!' Peggy's face drained of colour. 'What's happened?' Memories of the day she'd had a phone call telling her that her husband had been involved in a car crash came back to her. Rushing across the café, she grabbed his hand. 'What? Is everything OK?'

Scott held Peggy tightly as he closed the call with, 'Thank you for letting us know so quickly. I will be back in touch as soon as I've spoken to our solicitor.'

'Solicitor?' Amy, Kit, and Megan exchanged worried glances as Peggy slumped down onto the nearest seat.

'Scott, please. Tell me what's happened.'

Sitting next to his wife, taking both her hands in his, he said, 'No point in making those changes to the chef's letter now. We've lost our second Pickwicks. The landlord has changed his mind.'

'What?' Peggy's reply came out as a barely comprehensible whisper.

Scott beckoned to the others. 'Megan, make us some strong

171

coffee and I'll tell you everything.' He raked his hand through his short black hair. 'It affects us all in one way or another.'

The coffee was poured, and the Pickwicks staff, past and present, sat around a table, Scott explained, 'The landlord no longer wants to rent out the premises in Mortlake. He wants to sell it outright so he can buy a place he's seen while he was abroad. We can't afford to buy it, therefore we've lost it.'

'But we signed the papers, and ...' Peggy stammered, but got no further.

'The only way we can buy it, love, is if we use all the money we've saved for our retirement, and thanks to my stupid legs, we really need to plan that sooner rather than later. I'm so sorry, Peggy.'

'It's not your fault.' Peggy tried not to cry.

Not sure if she should say anything or not, but suddenly seeing her own career disappearing in front of her eyes, Megan said, 'But there was a contract?'

Scott grimaced. 'There was a clause in it that said the landlord had the right to change his mind up until the day before exchange – which is today. Or rather, *was* today.'

'But that's so unfair!' Amy's eyes came to rest on the boxes of equipment ready to head to Mortlake. 'Will they compensate you for the money you've already spent on getting the place ready?'

'I'll call our solicitor in a moment and see what he can do about getting some inconvenience costs, but I'm not holding out a great deal of hope.'

No one knew what to say. The gloom that had invaded the room cloaked the place like a blanket.

Kit was the first to break the silence. 'Right; we should give you two some space. When are you going to see the solicitor, Scott?'

Shaken out of his introspection by Kit's question, Scott got up. 'I'll call now. Hopefully we can get an appointment as soon as possible.'

While Scott disappeared upstairs to make the call in private, Kit turned to a shocked-looking Megan. 'Come on, hun; let's get all that stuff out the back. Staring at it will just make

172

everything feel worse.'

Amy put her hand out to Peggy. 'Scott might be able to sort something out. Don't give up yet.'

Peggy smiled bravely at her friend, but there was no hiding the devastation in her eyes. 'You're very kind, Amy, but I doubt it.' Forcing a happy expression on her face, Peggy looked around her, 'It did feel a bit like cheating on this place, maybe it was never meant to be.'

'You OK, Megan?' Kit didn't like the pallor to the waitress's face.

'What? Oh, yes, I just feel so sorry for Peggy and Scott. How awful for them.'

'And for you.' Kit spoke gently. 'Will you have to look for a new job now? I know you and Nick are trying to save for that place of your own.'

Megan sighed. 'Maybe. I earned a fair bit for Jack's pictures, but that won't last long. I'll keep working here until something else comes along.'

'You won't go and work for Jack now then?'

'Too late. He was interviewing for the front of house job today. If I'm going to be an ordinary waitress, I'd rather do that here. The hours are more social for a start, even if the wages are marginally lower. Anyway, I couldn't leave Peggy now! She and Scott must be in pieces.'

Leaving Megan in the storeroom at the back of the kitchen, Kit returned to the main café to see Scott pacing the floor.

'Any news?'

'We have an appointment with the solicitor at nine o'clock tomorrow morning. He couldn't say much over the phone as he doesn't know all the details yet, but he'll get in touch with the estate agent right away and we'll get an idea of what we can do tomorrow. He did say, however, that the landlord was within his rights to change his mind. There is no way that we'll get to keep the new branch.' He turned to Peggy. 'Sorry, love.'

'So it's all about damage limitation?' Peggy said as she stood up, brushing her apron down with her usual determination.

173

'That's about it.'

'Then we'd better go over that contract tonight with a fine toothcomb, and make a list of every penny we have invested in that place so we can show the solicitor tomorrow.'

'That's my girl.' Scott embraced his wife.

Proud of her friends' determination, Kit offered to come in early and help run Pickwicks with Megan the following morning so Peggy and Scott could go and see the solicitor without worrying about the café.

'The question I'm dying to ask,' said Amy as she returned from yet another trip to the bathroom, 'is … will you be looking for another venue?'

Peggy's frown returned. 'I honestly don't know. Things would be a lot easier if we didn't have to worry about the extra competitor Pickwicks suddenly has, thanks to bloody Jack! What the hell was he thinking, getting a place so near to Pickwicks? He doesn't need the money.'

Shocked by Peggy's outburst, Amy and Kit exchanged glances, before Amy said, 'He does, actually.'

'But he's loaded! Isn't he?' Peggy's expression lost some of its hostility.

'Not anymore.' Kit smiled encouragingly at Amy, as if telling her it was alright to explain.

'Jack's sunk almost all of his remaining money into the bistro, so he needs his enterprise to work every bit as much as you needed yours to. I promise you, Peggy, he didn't pick that bistro to annoy you, it just happens to be the best place he could afford. I'm sure if you went for a visit you'd be reassured.'

Chapter Twenty-eight

Wednesday 20th July

Jack turned his mobile phone off and on again in the hope that his lack of texts or calls was merely due to a technological issue, and not because Rupert didn't want to talk to him.

On the plus side, he hadn't heard anything from Gareth either, and he'd begun to dare hope that his ex-employer had done whatever it was he wanted to do in London and gone back to Kent.

Sat at his desk, scanning his eyes down the list of emails that demanded his attention, Jack was disheartened to see that there had been no further applicants for the job as front of house manager. The interview he'd had with Mike had been good fun. The guy had been friendly and had some experience, but something about him had told Jack he wasn't right for the job. He was neither charismatic nor engaging enough, and the first point of contact in his bistro needed to be both of those things.

So, with the opening day fast approaching, Jack still had no house manager and no kitchen hand, although he had an idea about the latter. Deciding that he might as well tackle that issue now, and co-inside it with a long overdue attempt at being a grown up, and go and explain and apologise to Rupert about Gareth, he shut down his PC and headed towards his old bookshop.

Rob looked up from where he was bagging up a collection of books for a customer, and nodded a greeting to his friend. Only when the young mum and her enthusiastic offspring had departed from the shop did he talk to Jack.

'We wondered when you'd turn up.' Rob shook his head.

'Phil and Rupert are out running a children's course at Kew. They'll be back in about an hour if you'd like to wait.'

To Rob's surprise, Jack looked uneasy. 'Do you think I should?'

'What exactly have you done this time?'

'You mean you don't know?' Jack sounded mockingly defensive. 'Usually you guys have all my problems aired and sorted before I even get here!'

'Don't be like that! We worry about you.'

'Sorry,' Jack dropped his defences a fraction, 'but you know what I mean.'

'Guilty as charged, but it's only because we want you to be happy, mate. Anyway, in this instance you're safe. Rupert keeps his business to himself, and although Phil tells me that you've spoken to Kit and Amy, the girls' lips are sealed.' Rob's eyes twinkled playfully. 'Honestly, what is a boy to do for gossip these days?'

Jack felt his defences collapse completely, and the hint of a smile started at the corner of his lips, 'Rupert hasn't said anything at all?'

'Not a thing. It was only speculation on our behalf that you were involved until you spoke to Amy, and all she and Kit would say is that you hadn't done anything wrong, and that it was all a misunderstanding.'

Hope dared to flicker in Jack's chest. 'Did you pass that on to Rupert?'

'No way, mate! Rupert is the most private person in the world, and I respect that totally. He's obviously down, but that could as easily be because of Helena and his fear that her crush could cost him his job than anything to do with your charms.'

'Right.' Jack couldn't decide if that was good or not. He was relieved that Rupert was, as he'd suspected, a guy that kept his private life private. After almost two decades of his personal dealings being open for discussion – largely through his own indiscretions – he found this refreshing.

'Sadly I can't wait around, although I probably should.' Jack glanced towards the door, half hoping that Rupert would walk through it early. 'I have a hell of a lot to do.'

'Bistro ready to roll then?'

'Nearly. I'm missing two main members of staff, but otherwise, I am getting there.' Which reminds me, I came over to talk to Phil as well. Can I leave Phil a note? Maybe I should leave one for Rupert…'

Rob tilted his head to one side, 'Are you talking to me or yourself now?'

Jack shrugged. 'Um, both, I think.'

'You want a coffee while you wait, or have you really come all this way across London just to disappear again?'

'When you put it like that, I guess it would be a waste of time not to hang on a bit.'

'Exactly, anyway, it's coffee time. Could you pop into the kitchen and stick the kettle on while I sort out the post?'

Passing Rob his coffee, and pulling out one of the stalls behind the desk that he used to sit on when he owned the bookshop, Jack concentrated on not letting his gaze stray to the front door too often. 'This place doing alright then?'

'It is. I never thought I'd see the day when we were employing extra staff, especially after how hard we had to struggle to keep the place open during the recession. Rupert has been a boon. His postcards have been a massive hit at Kew, and the teaching is proving far more popular than I could ever have imagined.'

'Was that your idea? It's fab.'

'Can't take credit for that one. That was Phil.'

'Well, I'm pleased for you all. My grandfather would have been thrilled to see his inheritance lead to so much great stuff. He loved the great outdoors as much as I do.'

'And as much as Rupert does?'

Jack shook his head with a knowing grin. 'You can stop fishing right there, Robert. There is nothing to tell. We had a misunderstanding. I came over here hoping to put it right. End of story.'

'Message received and understood.' Rob took a sip of coffee. 'So, what do you think of this business at Pickwicks then?'

'I know Peggy wouldn't believe me, but I really do wish

them well. They work so hard, a second branch is a fantastic idea.'

Rob put his mug down with a frown. 'You mean you haven't heard?'

'Heard what?'

'They lost the new café. The landlord bailed on them.'

'What?' Jack slopped some of his coffee over the side of his mug, burning his hand. As he sucked it better, he mumbled, 'Seriously? You aren't joking?'

'Of course I'm not. Peggy and Scott are gutted.'

'I bet they are. And what about Megan? She had a promotion tied up with the new place.'

'She'll have to go back to being the chief waitress rather than co-runner.'

'But they must have invested so much in the new place. New crockery, menus … everything?'

'They did. According to Phil, Kit is looking after Pickwicks this morning so Scott and Peggy can see their solicitor and see what they can recoup from the mess.'

'Do you think they'll try for another place?'

'I have no idea, mate. It'll depend on if anything else they can afford is going, I suppose. They may not want to try again. Kit said they were very downhearted.'

'I bet. I'd have been devastated if I was them.' Getting off his stall, Jack pushed his coffee away, 'I have to go. Do you have a piece of paper?'

Frowning, Rob pushed a notebook and a pen towards Jack. 'Aren't you going to wait for Phil and Rupert?'

'I was. But if Kit is at Pickwicks I can talk to her instead of Phil, and hopefully, if Rupert is half the man I hope he is, he'll understand.'

Dear Rupert,

I don't blame you at all for not answering my calls, but I would like to explain. I have no idea what Gareth wants. He's my old boss, and is very much in the past. Sorry I missed you this morning, but I have to go and make sure my friends at

178

*Pickwicks are alright. If you can face trying my menu after all,
then give me a call.*
Your friend,
Jack

Folding the piece of paper in half, Jack handed it to Rob. 'I'm
trusting you not to read this.'

Rob immediately placed the unopened note on Rupert's
desk. 'As if I would!'

Jack rolled his eyes. 'As if!'

Running towards the Underground station, Jack thought fast. If
there wasn't going to be a second Pickwicks, then Megan would
be available to work for him. He stopped in his tracks. *You
can't swoop in like a vulture and steal Megan now they are
disappointed. Think, man, think...*

By the time Jack had arrived at Richmond station, a plan had
begun to form in his mind. A plan which could, should Peggy
and Scott agree to it, solve all their problems in one go. Jack
just hoped Peggy would let him cross the threshold of
Pickwicks for long enough to be able to explain his idea.

'It's amazing. You're so clever!'

'Thanks, Kit.' Megan hid the portrait of Peggy and Scott in
its protected spot in Scott's kitchen cupboard, 'It's beginning to
come together. I don't have much time to work on it at the
moment, but it should be ready before Peggy's birthday.'

'Seems incredible that Peggy is going to be fifty-five. She
doesn't look old enough! I hope the solicitor is giving them
good news this morning. It won't be much of a birthday for her
if they have to put their retirement plans on hold.'

Megan put her apron on, ready to face the first coffee
drinkers of the day, 'They won't retire yet though, will they? I
know Scott has to take it easy sometimes because of his legs
and back, but they are so full of life. I can't imagine this place
without them.'

'I know. Pickwicks *is* them, isn't it? But I am fairly sure
Scott finds the days a lot harder than he lets on sometimes. The

179

fact he can walk at all is such a miracle. The plan is for them to retire early enough for them to be able to do all the things they want to do before Scott ends up in a wheelchair.'

Megan's pale face grew even more pallid. 'Is that the ultimate prognosis then? Will Scott end up in a chair?'

'The more active he is now, the better for later – but yes. That's what the consultant told him would most likely happen in the end. Which is why they want – well, need – a bungalow.'

'And they are rare and expensive around here.'

'Precisely.' Kit put on one of the spare aprons. 'Come on then, let's open the café for them. I'll help until Helena gets here at ten. If it goes quiet then, I'll write. Otherwise I'll keep going until Peggy and Scott get back.'

Chapter Twenty-nine

Thursday 21st July – 10.30 a.m.

As Peggy and Scott pushed open the door to their hot drinks-and-scones empire, Pickwicks was brimming with visitors. Exchanging glances, the café owners gave each other brave smiles as they watched Kit, Megan, and Helena engaging busily with their clients.

With an encouraging squeeze of his wife's hand, Scott went into the kitchen as Peggy headed to the counter. Washing her hands, she plastered her very best customer service smile onto her face, then threw herself into the fray.

Politely excusing herself from the pensioner who was eagerly telling her, in fits of pink-cheeked giggles, about the latest sexy romance she'd been reading, Kit went to join Peggy at the counter. 'And?'

'I'll tell you everything properly later, but the potted version is that we can't claim back any of the money we have spent on stuff for the new place, though we have had our deposit returned as well as a small payment to cover the cost of the redecorating we did.'

Kit began to polish the coffee machine. 'Is that good or not?'

'Well it isn't terrible, but it means we have nearly two thousand pounds worth of equipment we don't need.'

'Will you look for someone else? A different Pickwicks 2, I mean?'

'I think we'll have to, otherwise it's all such a waste of money – not to mention plates, cutlery, and everything – but there's very little is available in our price range right now. Not unless we're prepared to travel right across London. And, to be honest, I'm not sure I can face doing all the preparation again and then potentially lose another place.'

The words of support that Kit had been about to give Peggy were lost with the arrival of a large group of young mums and toddler-filled pushchairs. The writer moved to serve the new arrivals.

Peggy looked confused. 'Don't you want to get back to work, now we're back?'

'After I've helped you deal with this lot! Anyway,' Kit gave her friend a wink, 'I'm writing about a café in my current novel. I can use this as research!'

'Seriously? You're writing a novel set in a café?'

'Can you think of a better place to set a story about life, friends, love, and everything in between?'

12 p.m.

Not totally sure that Peggy would even let him into Pickwicks, Jack took a deep breath as he marched along the alleyway that led to the café.

As he'd travelled along on the Tube the solution had all seemed blindingly obvious. His idea was straight-forward and sensible, but he had no idea if Peggy and Scott would see it that way. It could be the very last thing they'd want to do. 'Still,' Jack said to himself, 'I owe it to my friends to try.'

Peering through the window, Jack saw how busy it was inside. He hesitated. He could see that Kit was still there, which meant that either Peggy and Scott weren't back from their meeting, or that it was so busy, they needed every available hand, and she'd been wrenched up off her writers' seat to pitch in.

As he watched, Helena came out of the kitchen, her hands full with plates of paninis and chips. He hadn't considered that she'd be working today, and suddenly Jack wondered if he should return later. When Helena wasn't there. Not that he'd done anything to upset his goddaughter directly – but if there was even a remote possibility of something happening with

Rupert, then Jack suspected Helena wouldn't exactly be thrilled with him.

Checking his watch, his common sense took hold. *Of course they're busy, you idiot, it's lunchtime.* Backing away, hoping none of his friends had spotted him loitering outside, Jack returned to the bistro to think things through more rationally. Maybe he'd make a few notes. A proper business plan, perhaps...

Kit had just collapsed onto her seat in the corner of the café when her phone rang.

'Oh, hi, Amy ... no, no real news as such. Peggy's going to fill us in at closing time. Looks as if it'll be a case of having to find a new place so they don't lose the money they've spent on new equipment ... How are you, anyway?'

Midway through reassuring Amy that her insides feeling like a tumble dryer on full cycle was perfectly normal at that stage of pregnancy, Kit saw the door to the café open a fraction and Jack poke his head around it.

'Amy, I have to go. Jack's here ... yes, Jack! I'm pretty sure he is still barred ... yes, I'll call as soon as I know what's happening.'

Not sure if Peggy had noticed Jack's tentative arrival or not, Kit scooted to the door. 'Jack, what are you doing here? This isn't the best day to appeal to Peggy's better nature.'

'I heard.' Jack glanced towards the kitchen door. 'Rob told me. He assumed I already knew. Why didn't you tell me?'

'Because Peggy already thinks you're out to steal her trade – or at least she did until Amy spoke to her – but if you knew about Pickwicks 2 falling through you might have asked Megan to work for you again, and that would *not* have gone down well.'

'I'm not that mean!'

'I know, Jack, but as I said, things aren't going too well for Peggy and Scott right now. Logic doesn't come into it.'

Keeping an eye on the kitchen door, bracing himself for Peggy to spot him, Jack said, 'Hang on, what do you mean Amy spoke to Peggy?'

'Oh, don't get on your high horse, Amy was defending you.'

'OK, OK … I know it might cause fireworks, but I am here to help. Do you think that Peggy and Scott will talk to me? I have an idea that might solve their problem and bring an end to hostilities.'

'You do?'

'I hope so … let's just say it's worth a shot.'

Kit was dying to ask more questions, but instead she looked behind her. 'This place is closing in half an hour. Peggy was going to tell us all about the meeting this morning. I can go and ask her if you can come in if you like, but until then I'd wait outside. Respect for Peggy and Scott and all that.'

'Absolutely. Thanks, Kit.' Jack slid back outside and leaned against the wall of the small shop opposite. It had been a while since he'd looked properly at the café that formed the home and working life of so many of his friend's lives.

He was surprised how nervous he felt. Peggy didn't frighten him, but he found he desperately wanted her forgiveness, for their friends' sakes as much as his own. It wouldn't be comfortable raising a glass of champagne to his future godchild if Peggy and Scott wouldn't even speak to him at Amy and Paul's baby's party.

The door to the café opened, and Scott came out. 'Hi, Jack, how's tricks?'

'Up and down – but I suspect not as crap as they've been for you guys over the last twenty-four hours.'

'Fair comment.' Scott looked curiously at his visitor. 'You have a proposal for us?'

'Yes. It may not appeal, and if not, that's fine – but if it does, then it could make everyone happy.'

'You'd better come in then. I should warn you, Jack, if this turns out to be an elaborate plot to steal Megan, then Peggy may go for your balls with the kitchen scissors.'

Jack nodded. 'Noted.'

Following Scott inside, he saw that Peggy was talking to the last two customers of the day, Kit was back in her writing corner, and Helena was collecting up dirty cups and saucers, which meant that Megan, presumably, had to be in the kitchen.

Jack sat at the large table indicated by Scott and waited. He wished that Rupert would phone. Even a text telling him to get lost would be better than silence. The not knowing was in danger of driving him to distraction. His daydreams about Rupert had even extended into the quiet of his sleep.

As the final coffee drinkers left, Peggy locked the door after them and, with an expression of uncompromising determination on her face, pulled out a seat opposite Jack. Then, without acknowledging his existence, Peggy called to her colleagues, 'Alright, everyone, it's explanation time. Let's hear what Jack has to say for himself. Then Scott and I will fill you in on events.'

Feeling decidedly uneasy as Peggy crossed her arms over her ample bosom, Jack exchanged glances with Kit, who nodded at him encouragingly.

'Right then. First of all, I should underline that I am not here to poach Megan. And I should also say that I'm truly sorry that your expansion plans have fallen through.'

'Get to the point, Jack,' Peggy said.

'Right. OK then. Forgive me if I've misunderstood the situation, but as I see it, you have been cheated out of your second premises, and –'

'Not exactly cheated. The landlord was within in his rights, and –' Scott abruptly stopped when his wife dug him in the ribs and signalled to Jack to keep talking.

'And you've been left with a load of equipment you don't need. So, and I should emphasise that I don't expect an immediate answer unless you totally hate the idea, and you have no obligation or anything, and –'

'Jack! Get on with it!' Kit felt she was about to burst with the suspense.

'Sorry. So, I am opening a restaurant nearby. I'm having trouble securing a front of house manager. You two are having trouble finding convenient premises, or at least you will do if you haven't started looking yet, because I spent a few hours this afternoon hunting for you, and there's nothing within a five-mile radius that's worth investing in.'

Studying the suddenly rapt expressions of his quiet audience, he ploughed on. 'I'm going to have my work cut out cooking for the evenings, let alone the afternoons, but as I believe Amy told you, I'm not playing at being a restaurant owner. This *has* to be a viable business.

'How about you, Peggy and Scott, run my bistro in the afternoons? There's a different clientele from your Pickwicks regulars to be targeted, and if you do lose some of your customers to me for a while, fifty per cent of the takings from that would be yours to keep anyway.'

Scott and Megan exchanged glances, before looking at Peggy, who said, 'Keep talking.'

'My proposition is that we should jointly run my place between the hours of three and six o'clock, from Monday to Saturday. After six, the bistro would take over. That way the opening times between the bistro and this place would only overlap by a couple of hours. Let's face it: we'd have a different client base at my place than at Pickwicks, which mostly has morning and lunch diners. I'm going for the post-work crowd. If it worked, and we wanted to extend the hours to cover lunch later on, then so be it.

'So, to simplify things: Peggy and Scott could run the late afternoon coffee business until six, and then the business would revert to me. I know it sounds complicated, but it's possible. What do you think?'

Scott and Peggy stared at each other in shock, before Scott asked, 'Are you serious, Jack? You'd share your premises just so we don't lose the money on the equipment we've purchased?'

'Yes. I haven't ordered as much stuff as I need yet, as I was saving on costs where I could, but I always envisaged different sets of crockery for the day and night customers.'

'And would you expect any financial investment?'

'Not at first, Scott. If it worked well, then in a year we might have a rethink, but in the first instance I would simply require half the takings. I know half sounds a lot, but I'd be paying half the wages as well during that time, and providing all of the electricity, water, and so on.'

Megan stared at her hands. She didn't want Peggy or Scott

to see her expression, in case they saw the fervent hope that they'd say yes written all over her face. This was too important a decision for her to influence just because she could see a way of getting the job she'd wanted all along.

'There are a great deal of things to discuss, Jack, but right now,' Scott held out his hand, 'Peggy and I need to have a talk on our own.'

'Totally understandable.' Jack got to his feet. 'I'll leave you all in peace. You have my number. Call me when you're ready.'

Leaving a tableful of thoughtful faces behind him, Jack had reached the café door when a figure appeared on the other side. 'Oh, for God's sake! What the hell do you want, Gareth? This is bordering on stalking now!'

Gareth gave him an infuriating grin. 'No need to get your knickers in a twist, Jack. I tried the bistro, but you weren't there.'

Jack was aware of all the eyes in the café boring into his back, trying to get a good look at the man he was talking to. 'I said what do you want? And, more to the point, when are you going home again?'

'I told you, I'm in London looking for new art for Kennedy's. I'm sure your inflated ego would like to think that I'm after your body, but trust me, it isn't worth the train fare.'

Not rising to the taunt, Jack locked eyes with Gareth, and echoed Peggy's earlier demand. 'Get to the point.'

'I want you to tell me who did those paintings for you. They are the best pieces I've seen since I arrived in the city.'

Chapter Thirty

Thursday 21st July

Jack couldn't decide if he'd done Megan a favour, or made her life more difficult, by introducing her to Gareth. He was sure he'd hear soon enough though. Knowing Gareth, at that very moment he'd be telling the assembled masses at Pickwicks all about Jack's time at Kennedy's.

In spite of his ex-employer's unexpected arrival, Jack felt pleased. Even if Peggy and Scott didn't go for his plan, they hadn't thrown him out, nor had they turned his idea down flat. The more he thought about it, the more Jack was sure it would help them out, at least in the short term.

The sound of his mobile phone buzzing into life, alerting Jack to the arrival of a text message as he reached the bistro, sent a shot of excited anxiety down his spine. Assuming it would either be Megan asking him about Gareth or Peggy asking him about the café share scheme, he was surprised to see that it was Rupert's number flashing on the small screen before him.

Your place, seven o'clock tonight? Tell me the whole story. The truth please.

Jack showered fast, changed, and waited apprehensively, torn between cooking and offering to take Rupert out for dinner, if he showed signs of staying for more than a ten-minute chat. Trying to distract himself from the worst-case scenario – Rupert not believing a word he said about Gareth – and debating if he should mention his recent one-night stand or not, Jack stood in the doorway of Megan's studio. How would it feel if she worked on a commission for Gareth here?

His pondering was interrupted by a loud knock on the front door. Glancing at his watch, he saw it was only half past six. Either Rupert was early, or he was about to run the gauntlet with Gareth again.

He was wrong on both fronts.

Jack opened the door to a glowing Megan, who threw her arms around him. 'Thank you so much, Jack! I can't believe what you've done for me. Especially as you obviously can't stand Mr Kennedy.'

Hugging Megan back, Jack asked, 'Did he offer you a commission then?'

'He did! I've just been talking to Nick on the phone. He was virtually dancing down the line!'

'Gareth offered you a *big* commission then?'

'Huge! Four small canvases and two giant ones. I honestly thought my days of working on six-foot canvases were over.'

Smiling in the face of his friend's excitement, Jack said, 'Well, I hope you're extracting a super-huge pay cheque from him. Charge him London rates.'

'I will!' Megan felt her excitement die down. 'Umm, Jack, I know you don't like him. I must admit, I didn't like to the way he spoke about you.'

'My time with Gareth wasn't my finest hour. I probably deserved it. '

'The thing is … can I still use your room as a studio if I'm working for him? I'd be able to pay rent for it now, of course.'

'Of course you can!' Jack smiled, 'But I'm not sure you'll get the big canvases up and down the stairs too easily.'

'I wondered about that. I might even have to do them in situ. I'm going to do the smaller pieces first. Mr Kennedy is sending me close-up photographs of details from the restaurant to interpret.'

Jack beamed. 'I'm pleased for you, Megan. That's great. Umm, do you mind me asking – and I don't want to put you on the spot or anything – but has Peggy said anything about my café idea?'

'Not a word. She and Scott disappeared upstairs while I spoke to Mr Kennedy.' She shuffled her feet. 'I hope they say yes. If they do, do you think that…'

'You'll get the manager post? I hope so, Megan. I really do. If you could leave Pickwicks and work here from three in the afternoon until ten in the evening, then you'll be able to paint in the mornings. Although we'll have to fit an air filter or something in up there so the paint fumes don't reach downstairs!'

Megan held up her hands, showing Jack that her fingers were well and truly crossed.

'You'll have to set up a website or something to advertise your art now. My friend Rupert was only talking about setting up a site for his photography the other day, and maybe collaborating with you, to make it a joint venture. He'll be here soon, if you'd like me to ask him about it?'

Megan noticed for the first time that Jack was dressed up for a date. 'Yes, please. That would be awesome, but I'd better go. You look like you have plans, and I want to go and tell Nick everything all over again in person.'

'Will you be able to put down a rental deposit on a house with Gareth's money?'

'Absolutely; in fact with that and the money you've paid us, we have enough for the first few months' rent as well! I can't quite get my head around the last forty-eight hours. It's been one hell of a rollercoaster ride.'

'Tell me about it.' Jack smiled, 'Well, you know how the song goes. "Life is a Rollercoaster"!'

Megan groaned. 'You didn't really quote Ronan Keating at me, did you, Jack?'

'Um … I might have done. But for goodness' sake, don't tell Kit!'

Rupert hooked his laptop bag higher onto his shoulder. He was determined that his meeting with Jack wasn't going to be interpreted as a date on any level. This was merely a convenient opportunity for Jack to set the record straight. If that went well, then Rupert would show him the three photographs he found himself unable to choose between for the forthcoming photo competition.

Swallowing his misgivings, he knocked on the bistro door.

Jack, looking inconveniently attractive in a crisp white shirt and grey denims, offered his hand in welcome as Rupert walked in, 'Thanks for getting in touch. I am so sorry.'

'So you said.'

Noting the businesslike tone of Rupert's voice, Jack felt the tiny amount of hope he'd harboured die down. 'Would you like a drink while I explain?'

'I think that would be a very good idea.'

With two glasses of white wine sitting between them on one of the restaurant's virgin tables, Jack started from the beginning.

'I've told you about my initial relationships with Kit and Amy. I'm far from proud of how I treated them, but I am also overwhelmingly glad I had them in my lives back then – and more miraculously, that they still are now.'

Rupert said nothing as he listened, playing the stem of his wine glass between his fingertips as he waited for Jack to go on.

'Anyway, more recently, although it's also ancient history now, I met a man called Toby. He was a waiter in a café I stumbled across by accident, on the other side of London. I fell for him big time. He helped me come out to my father. However, my trust was misplaced. Not that long after I'd confessed to my family I discovered that Toby wasn't so much interested in me as my inheritance. I also found out he wasn't the monogamous type. I may not be the most stable bet, but I was always loyal to the one I was with – even if I wasn't with them for long.

'I haven't really talked about Toby much since we split up. I was with him for nearly three years; longer than I've ever been with anyone.'

Jack was aware that every now and again he was repeating himself; that he was fast losing track of what he'd told Rupert the last time they'd met. Carrying on in the face of his silent companion, he said, 'That's when I decided enough was enough. No more relationships, no more one-night stands; no more hurt for me and no more hurting other people. Something I held firm on until, as you are aware, I buckled prior to leaving

Kent.'

'Gareth?'

'Gareth.' Jack risked making eye contact for a split second, and his heart began to thump faster in this chest. 'He was my boss. I never particularly liked him as a person, but I have a great deal of respect for his culinary expertise. He took a gamble taking me straight from college when I was a good twenty years older than my fellow trainee chefs. He taught me a lot.'

'So you slept with him because you thought you owed him?'

Trying not to hear the disapproval in Rupert's voice, Jack took a long sip of the chilled wine. 'No. We had a one-off shared incident of insanity after a very heated exchange. Things got physical in anger before they got … well … To say I was ashamed of myself doesn't cover it.'

'You saw it as a one-off, he didn't. Is that what you're telling me?'

'Pretty much. I had no idea he liked me in that way. I always suspected he liked all the sweets in the shop, as it were, but as he'd only just started dating a particularly hot blonde with the correct girlie bumps in all the right places, I was caught somewhat off-guard when he declared his undying devotion.'

'He did?'

'Sadly, yes.' Jack took another gulp of wine. 'I had to leave. I'd dreamt about opening my place one day, but events hurried things a little.'

'Why is he here, Jack?'

'Art.'

'I'm sorry?'

'Gareth is in London to buy new decor for Kennedy's.'

'Then why come here?'

'To annoy me? To make himself feel better? To check out the restaurant? I honestly don't know. Either way, his visit has done some unexpected good.'

'It has?'

'He saw Megan's paintings.' Jack pointed to the nearest canvas. 'He loved them, and has commissioned her to do six for his place. She's going to charge him a mint, I'm pleased to say.'

Rupert, who had been struggling to keep the impassive expression on his face, gave up the fight. 'That's fantastic! I love these.' He stood up and re-examined the pictures he'd seen on his last visit. Without turning to face Jack, he said, 'You aren't interested in seeing Gareth again then?'

'No. No I'm not.' Jack held his breath.

'And is there anything else I should know?'

'Yes.'

Rupert, who had expected the answer to be no, twisted around at the waist, 'Go on then. Tell me the worst. Might as well get all the skeletons out of the cupboard in one go.'

'I'm not sure I want to.'

'Why not?'

'Because I don't want you to walk out of that door again. I want to take you out to dinner and get to know you better. If I tell you, then you'll leave; and I wouldn't blame you one bit.'

Rupert sat back down. 'Tell me, Jack. I am making no promises, but I will let you speak without interruption.'

With his eyes fixed unwaveringly on the top of his wine glass, his hands clenched on each of his knees, Jack began to explain about his trip to Heaven, the frustration and sense of failure that had sent him there. And then how he'd felt the following morning, waking up in a stranger's bed on the other side of the city. Again.

The silence across the table lasted a long time. Jack couldn't bear to look up. He didn't want the last image of Rupert stored in his memory to be that of him leaving the bistro, never to return.

At last, the younger man spoke. 'I'm hungry. Curry? I saw a nice-looking place as I walked from the Tube.'

Jack hadn't expected to get much sleep, knowing that Rupert was only a wall away on the sofa bed in the living room, but in fact he'd been out like a light. The previous evening had progressed from the early unease of his confession, to a gorgeous Indian meal, and a conversation about each other's lives that had never faltered, going from the arrival of the complementary poppadoms to the after-meal tea and beyond, to them sitting on Jack's sofa until the early hours of the morning.

It had felt the most natural thing in the world to ask Rupert to stay, and although he would have been lying if he'd said he didn't want to share a bed with his guest, this was something he didn't want to ruin by rushing, and so he'd said nothing.

Now, over coffee, orange juice, and Jack's homemade croissants, Rupert switched on his laptop. 'Can you help me pick out the best photo, then? As I said last night, I can't narrow it down, and I can only enter one shot.'

'Sure.' Moving around the table so he was sat next to Rupert, Jack couldn't stop the smile on his face. 'These are breathtaking. I'm not surprised you can't narrow your choice down.'

As Jack studied each photograph in turn, Rupert said, 'You know Phil and Rob will never believe I slept in the spare room, don't you?'

'True. Although it's none of their business that you're even here, and I wasn't planning on telling them. I'm not ashamed or anything; I just want to keep this safe for a while. Does that sound soppy?'

'No. It sounds good.' Rupert placed a tentative hand on Jack's. 'I don't want to tell anyone either. Not yet.'

Chapter Thirty-one

Tuesday 26th July

'Will you stop being so over-excited! Your demented puppy routine is making me more nervous than I am already.'

Paul couldn't stop smiling. He was positively bouncing as they walked along. 'There's nothing to be nervous of, love. This is where we find out all the nitty-gritty bits.'

'Exactly!' Amy felt as though she was heading further out of her depth with every step along the clinic's corridor towards the antenatal classroom. 'I'm scared enough as it is without being told about the nitty gritty. I was perfectly happy in denial, thank you very much.'

Paul shook his head lovingly. 'But you wanted the parenting classes to start last week. You said so?'

Seeing that her husband was in his element, Amy tried harder to hide the fact that she was terrified. 'But what if I can't do it?'

'Which bit?'

'All of it.' Amy took Paul's hand, partly to slow him down and partly for courage. 'I can't begin to imagine how it's going to feel to be a parent, even though I've known it will happen, all being well, for months now. I can feel our child moving inside me, and it is wonderful, miraculous, and one hundred per cent terrifying!' She stopped her slow wobbly walk and looked at her husband. 'Aren't you even a little bit worried?'

Paul cupped her chin. 'Of course I am. A million things worry me. I'm frightened of not being able to care for you both, or provide for you, or be a good dad. Scared of not being strong enough for you during the birth – or worse, being held up and not getting to you in time. But I'm not as scared as I am excited about doing exactly those same things.'

Amy threw her arms around Paul. 'Thank you. I'm just having a panic. It's probably because we're finally here. It seems to have taken so long to get to the antenatal stage. Makes it all very real.'

Paul patted his wife's baby bump affectionately, 'More real than this?'

'Oddly, yes.'

Taking a deep breath, Amy followed Paul into the stiflingly warm antenatal room, which had two pink walls and two blue ones. Amy couldn't help speculating if those who knew they were having girls would be sent to sit on the pink side, those with boys due on the blue one, and those who didn't know yet, like her and Paul, would be given chairs in the middle of the room.

Amy was about to share her colour theory with Paul when they were descended upon by a broadly smiling woman in her late forties. 'Hi, you must be Mr and Mrs Donahue?'

'Amy and Paul.' Paul shook her hand as Amy nervously looked at the woman's practical short-sleeved shirt, jeans, and sensible shoes.

'I'm Jean, and I'll be taking care of you from now until b-day!'

'B-day?' Amy couldn't help but like Jean straight away. She exuded a very welcoming quiet confidence.

'Baby day.' Jean indicated two empty chairs at the side of the room. 'Come and say hello to your fellow almost-parents.'

Five minutes later, Amy and Paul had been introduced to three other couples and two unaccompanied women, who, much to her relief, seemed as apprehensive as she was.

Once everyone was kitted out with fruit tea, water, or orange juice, Jean dived into her introductions, the plan for the next few classes, and a rally of reassurances that Amy knew the midwife must have spoken a thousand times before, but somehow seemed to work.

Half an hour later, after everyone had introduced themselves, declared if they were having a boy, girl, or didn't know, and what their biggest fear was, as well as the thing they were looking forward to the most, Amy felt more comfortable, and much less alone. As every woman there was expecting their first baby; there wasn't a future mother in the place who wasn't a heap of anxious excitement.

After teaching them some calming exercises with a gust of exuberance, Jean announced, 'Right, everyone, that's all for today. Obviously this is just the introduction session. You all have four to eight weeks left to go, and in that time we'll go through pain relief techniques, baby care, looking after yourselves once baby has arrived, feeding your child and so on. In the meantime, before we meet here again on Friday, I'd like you all, if you haven't already designed one, to put together a birth plan and pack your bag ready for the hospital. If you are planning a home birth, still pack a bag – hopefully you won't need it, but birth isn't an exact science, and if you have to go into hospital at the eleventh hour, the last thing you want to do is start hunting for clean nightshirts and nappies as the ambulance pulls up on the drive!'

Amy felt her nerves begin to swirl again as Jean walked between her comrades, handing out sheets of paper.

'These are examples of various birthing plans. They are not the law and the prophets. You're at liberty to change them to suit you. Remember, this is your baby and your body, which makes it your choice – as far as Mother Nature will allow, of course! There is also a list of everything you'll need for the hospital printed on the back of the leaflet. If I was you, I'd add "a good book" to the bottom of the list, as there is one heck of a lot of hanging around on b-day, and it can get a bit dull.'

'Between the blasts of pain, you mean?' Amy smiled at the comment from the young woman sat on her own in the front row, as she voiced her own thoughts precisely.

Jean laughed. 'To begin with the moments of pain will be few and far between, and hanging round in a hospital room is truly dull. Clara, I promise I'll go through all of that with you on Friday.'

The young woman gave Jean a thankful smile, and Amy was relieved at how the midwife had made her reply sound genuine and not patronising.

'So, troops,' Jean waved her arms, 'my phone number is on the top piece of paper I've given you. Any worries, you call me. I'll be here for another twenty minutes if you want to ask me anything in private today, otherwise I look forward to seeing you at the end of the week.'

Leaving Paul chatting to another future father, Amy decided to be brave, and went to talk to Jean.

'Hi, Amy,' Jean smiled. 'How can I help?'

Feeling suddenly shy, Amy almost whispered, 'It's probably nothing but, well, I'm getting a lot of indigestion which the usual cures don't seem to touch, and my stomach seems to be tightening more and more every day. I'm being paranoid, I expect, but, well...'

'You want to know if that's normal.'

'Well, yes.'

'Oh, I'm getting that as well.' Amy hadn't noticed Clara follow her to the front of the room. 'The indigestion, I mean, although I haven't had any belly tightening, should I have been?'

Jean nodded kindly. 'This is exactly why I'm here. There is no such thing as normal in pregnancy. Some of you will get horrific indigestion, some will experience Braxton Hicks tightening, some will get ordinary occasional stomach tightening, and some will get none of the above. It doesn't mean anything bad is happening.'

Having given her advice for coping with indigestion, Jean sent Clara, who still had two months to go, on her way. 'Amy, you have only four weeks before you're due, yes?'

'Yes.'

'Does the tightening keep you awake?'

'Sometimes.'

'It does sound like Braxton Hicks. It's not unusual, but if it would put your mind at rest, I can book you in for a check-up tomorrow if you like?'

'I don't want to put you to any trouble, especially as I suspect I'm being over anxious.'

'Not at all. My job is to look after you. That means helping with your private worries as well as your baby. Now then,' Jean opened her diary, '3.30 OK for you?'

'Perfect, thank you. Sorry to be a pain!'

Jean shook her head. 'You're not a pain – in fact, you're the bravest person here. I'm sure that every almost-mum in this room wanted to ask a question, but you were the only one who dared. So good for you!'

'I'm really proud of you.' Echoing Jean's sentiments, Paul kissed Amy's check as he delivered her back to her office. 'I'm so glad you asked Jean for help.'

'I've been driving myself mad worrying about the skin-tightening thing.'

'You should have said!'

'Probably, but you only know what I know, which is what it says in the book, and as Jean said, the books are only general guides. They can't be right for everyone, can they.'

Paul hugged her. 'Well, just be safe this afternoon, you must be tired. I'll see you tonight.'

Climbing up the stairs to the Home Hunters office, Amy tried to ignore the feeling of nausea that had started to swim in her stomach alongside the indigestion. Cursing herself for getting into such a nervous state before the class, Amy sat at her desk with a relieved sigh, and not caring that she was at work, kicked off her shoes.

Lauren arrived like magic with a cup of mint tea and a big smile. 'You alright, boss?'

'This flipping indigestion is driving me mad.' Taking the tea, Amy tapped the seat next to her, 'Come on then, Lauren, let me show you the bits of my job that don't come with a handbook.'

Lauren frowned. 'Such as?'

'Such as which clients need at least two pairs of kid gloves when you're dealing with them, which ones will always try and wangle a discount out of you that is far greater than we are able to give, and which ones will try and swap two weeks in their Marbella villas for a fortnight in London. Preferably with you in residence wearing a scanty bikini!'

The afternoon passed quickly, and as Amy taught Lauren all

the tricks she'd learnt in dealing with the more challenging clients on the Home Hunters books, the heartburn and nausea diminished, leaving her wondering if she needed her appointment with Jean the following day after all.

Chapter Thirty-two

Tuesday 26th July – 3 p.m.

'Hello there.'

Amy was surprised to see Jack appear by her Home Hunters desk as the clock ticked around to three o'clock.

'I had some work this side of town, so I thought I'd walk you home. It was your first parenting class today, wasn't it?'

'It was, and I am very ready to go home!' Amy slipped her shoes back on and picked up her bag. 'Luckily the class wasn't as scary as I thought it would be. I have a lovely midwife called Jean, who has put my mind at rest about a few things.'

'That's great.' Jack helped lever Amy out of her chair, and with a flirty wave at Lauren which made Amy raise her eyes to heaven and back, he escorted her to the door.

As they hit the fresh air, Amy's stomach tightened, making her catch her breath for a split second before the sensation passed. Glad that Jack hadn't noticed, she said, 'You have news.' It wasn't a question, but a statement. She could see that Jack was bursting with something to tell her.

'I have indeed. I assume Kit told you that Peggy and Scott lost the second Pickwicks?'

'I was there at the time helping them get ready for the opening. What a nightmare for them! Have they found anywhere new yet? I had to go and see Chris about a difficult client, so couldn't hang around to see what happened next. I meant to call Peggy and see how she is, but by the time I get home all I'm fit for is crashing out on the sofa. I'm ashamed to say I tend to fall asleep pretty fast. I've got hardly any energy left for anything, even phoning my friends.'

Pleased that Kit hadn't told Amy about his offer to Peggy

and Scott yet, Jack filled her in on the plan.

'I can't believe Kit didn't tell me! I can't believe you didn't tell me!' Amy felt put out.

'Kit probably thought you had enough to worry about, and I haven't told anyone. I have no idea if they'll accept my proposition or not.'

'Fair enough. I guess I'll have to get used to being out of the loop once the baby is here and takes over my life!' Amy stopped walking, a fresh sharp pain making her gasp.

Jack paled slightly. 'You alright?'

'Just this bloody heartburn. It sort of gets trapped behind my ribs, and there isn't much room in there right now. I'm fine.'

Looking unconvinced, Jack steadied his pace so they were walking slower. 'I hate indigestion, must be horrid when your belly is permanently full.'

'You have no idea! It's been making me feel rough on and off all afternoon.'

Jack's eyes narrowed. 'On and off, you say?'

'Yes.' Amy caught his expression. 'Don't panic, Jack, I'm not in labour. I have a month to go yet. Apparently this is normal. I'm tired and fed up of being massive though. So, tell me, what else is happening? Sorted things with Rupert yet?'

Remembering his promise to Rupert to keep things between them low-key for now, Jack simply said, 'He accepted my explanation about Gareth. Even better, Rupert has agreed to set up a website for Megan to advertise her art. They might even do a joint site, so he can sell his photographs as well.'

'Now that is fabulous.' Amy took hold of Jack's arm, more for companionship she told herself, rather than because she was beginning to feel dizzy. 'Kit did tell me about Megan having a new commission. She was thrilled apparently because although she wasn't going to have a wage increase as a waitress, she now had this big sum coming in from her art. Who was it from? Do you know?'

'From Gareth.'

'Gareth from Kent? That Gareth? Your sort-of-ex Gareth?'

'The very same.'

'How do you feel about that? It must be strange to think that

Megan will … ouch!' Amy gripped Jack's arm and clutched her bump in shock for a second before carrying on as if nothing had happened, 'be drawing pictures for the bloke that you left the job you loved to get away from?'

Jack stared at Amy. 'Sod Gareth! You said *ouch*. Pregnant women saying ouch is not normal.'

Amy laughed despite her fast growing nausea. 'Saying ouch, and a lot more besides, is fairly common at certain stages of pregnancy.'

'Exactly! At one *very* certain stage!'

'Oh Jack, stop overreacting.' Trying to ignore her fast-growing anxiety, Amy said, 'I'm fine.'

'Fine?'

'Well, I'm a bit queasy. Trust me to get sickness at the end of pregnancy as well as the beginning!'

'At least you didn't get it all the way through. My sister threw up for the whole nine months. It was horrible.'

'I bet it was! Can we talk about something else? I'm sure I'm just really tired.'

Unconvinced, Jack agreed, 'Well, one of the things I was going to tell you about was the opening menus I've designed for my bistro. I'm pleased with them, but a bit nervous about them as well. It's so important to get the first menu right. Sets the tone of the place and all that.'

Amy listened as Jack began to list all the delicious sounding meals he was planning. His exuberance and excitement at what lay ahead for his new life was contagious. 'I can't believe we're starting such major new ventures in our lives at the same time. Isn't it amazing how far we've come!'

Jack smiled. 'It is. It's …' He stopped talking as he caught the expression, 'are you sure you're alright?'

Amy's face had become pallid. 'I feel a bit odd, actually. I've gone all dizzy. Sit down. Must sit down.'

Trying to stay calm, Jack lowered his friend onto a blessedly handy bench at the side of the path. 'I'm going to call Paul.'

'Thanks.' Amy began to breathe harder. 'Oh, God … Jack, I think … but it can't be coming now. It just can't! There is so long to go … aww, hell's teeth!'

'Damn, Paul isn't answering.'

'Ohhhhh.'

'That's it, I'm calling an ambulance.'

'But I haven't even packed my hospital bag or anything or…'

Jack held Amy's hand as he spoke into his mobile. 'Ambulance please, yes … I'm Jack Brown and I'm with my friend Mrs Amy Donahue on a bench at the corner of Paradise Road and Church Road … yes, she eight months pregnant, and I'm as sure as I can be that she's gone into labour … Yes, dizzy and nauseous with stomach pains every few minutes … Well yes, I suppose they are contractions … No, I haven't timed them, it's caught us on the hop … yes … Thank you … yes … bye.'

'Jack?' Amy couldn't stop herself from panicking, 'My baby can't be coming! I've only had one antenatal class. I don't know what to do!'

'I'm not sure the baby knows that!'

'I want Paul. Can you try him again?'

Jack redialled his friend's number, holding Amy close. 'I'm already on it, Amy. Already on it. You concentrate on breathing slowly and keeping calm.'

'Calm? Seriously?'

Jack felt her hand grip his harder as he muttered under his breath, 'Come on, Paul, answer the damn phone!'

'If he isn't answering then call Jean.'

'Jean?'

'Midwife. Number on paper in bag.' Amy found she could either concentrate on talking or not being sick, but not both. The ambulance seemed to be taking forever.

Rifling through Amy's bag for the midwife's number, Jack did his best to sound positive, swallowing his own fears for his friend. 'No such thing as a standard pregnancy.'

Amy laughed through a weird snorting breath, 'You sound like Jean.'

'Got it!' Jack fished the paper from Amy's bag and hammered in the phone number, inwardly praying that she answered quickly. 'Hello? Is that Jean? I'm with Amy

Donahue; you met her this morning … yes, that's her. I'm waiting for an ambulance with her, looks like the baby is making an early guest appearance … yes, thank you.'

Jack passed the phone to Amy.

'Jean? Help!'

The moment they arrived at the hospital, Jack leapt out of the ambulance, and promising Amy he wouldn't stray far from her side, tried to call Paul again. 'Come on, come on…'

Running into the hospital's reception, Jack said, 'I'm sorry, Amy, I can't get him to answer. What was he doing this afternoon?'

'Giving a tour.'

As the receptionist signed her in, Amy was relieved to spy Jean coming towards her at a satisfyingly fast pace. 'Boy, am I glad to see you!'

'You couldn't wait for the check-up tomorrow then!' Jean smiled, 'Come on, let's get you more comfortable. You must be Jack?'

'Hello, yes, I've been trying to get hold of Paul, but his phone is off.'

Tears welled up in Amy's eyes. 'I really want him here.' Suddenly she felt as if she'd been brave all on her own for ages, and although she was glad Jack was there, Amy knew Paul would never forgive himself if he missed the birth. 'I'm frightened.'

'Let's tackle one thing at a time, shall we?' She soothed Amy into a wheelchair. 'You wait here while I show Jack where he can go to make a phone call.'

Drawing Jack to one side, out of earshot of Amy, Jean said, 'If you follow us into the examination room now, then you'll know where to find us after you've been back outside to call Paul a few more times. I suggest you ring every single person he knows and set people hunting him down, then get back in here. Amy is going to need a friend.'

'She is OK, isn't she?'

'The baby is rather early, but she's strong. I'm going to examine her with a doctor to establish if she's in labour, or if something else is going on.'

'Something else?'

'Make those calls and then come into the exam room. No need to knock or anything. Just come and hold her hand. Oh, and while you're on the phone, does Amy have a girlfriend she trusts?'

'Kit.'

'Call her. Amy's going to need things for the hospital – nightwear, books, and nice things to help her along. Would Kit know the sort of things Amy would want?'

'Definitely.'

'Then call her first.'

'First?'

'First.'

'Have you made a decision yet?'

Megan had been putting off asking Peggy any questions about Jack's proposal to share the afternoon session at his bistro, but as the days ticked by she was getting more anxious to know what her bosses had decided.

Peggy put down the cloth she was using to wipe the tables. 'To tell you the truth, we've been back and forth. I'm sorry to keep you hanging like this.'

'Not at all, I was just curious.'

'Part of me thinks it is a great idea, but another part of me isn't sure if I can trust Jack. Is he responsible enough to risk going into business with? It's a big decision.'

'Jack has grown up a lot lately.'

'If we did go for it, would you run it for us? The part of the bistro that would be ours, I mean.'

'If you wanted me to, but that would be your choice. I'd be happy either here or there.'

'You are very loyal, Megan, but this is your future as much as ours that we're deciding here.' Peggy was going to expand further when the phone rang.

'Oh, hello, Jack, I'm afraid we are still thinking about … Oh, oh hell, no, Kit isn't here, she left half an hour ago. She's probably on the Tube if she isn't answering; you know there's no signal down there.'

Picking up on her boss's tone, Megan came closer to the phone as Peggy kept talking, 'OK, Jack, keep calm. Leave it to me. You get back to Amy, I'll call Kit, and Megan will keep trying Paul until we find him. We'll sort this. Now off you go. Send Amy our love.'

Chapter Thirty-three

Tuesday 26th July

'How do you know Jack then?' Jean pulled a seat close to where Amy's head rested on a pillow and took her hand as a doctor attended to what she'd referred to as "the business end of things."

Amy couldn't help but smile at the absurdity of being asked about her ex-boyfriend while having her husband's baby, but was glad that Jean was working to keep her overactive imagination occupied – and off the doctor, who was adding to her discomfort big time. 'Now that's a story and a half!'

'He's obviously very fond of you.'

'Jack is my dearest friend … he is going to be …' Suddenly Amy started to cry. She'd been trying so hard not to let more than the occasional tear roll down her cheek, but abruptly she couldn't hold back the flow.

'Come on, Amy, what is Jack going to be?'

'Godfather to my baby. My baby … is alright, isn't it?'

Jean opened her mouth to reply, but the doctor beat her to it, reassuring Amy in his calming Scottish burr, 'I can't see why not, hen. I think it's just a case of your bairn being in a hurry to join its mum.'

'Oh, thank you!' Amy's tears came even faster, but now they were as much in relief as in fear.

The door opened and Jack rushed to her side. 'What's happening? Amy?' Jack looked at the midwife for an explanation as to why Amy was crying, not actually sure he wanted to hear the answer.

'It's OK. I'm OK, or should I say, we're OK. I'm just early.'

Jack shook his head, laughing in relief. 'Now why doesn't

that surprise me!? Like mother, like child.'

'Paul?'

'I've left Peggy and Megan tracking him down.'

'He still isn't answering then?

'No, and nor is the museum switchboard, but then it is the height of the tourist season, so they'll be beyond busy. Don't worry, if I know Peggy she'll have called Rob and Phil and got them hunting him down. Meanwhile, Kit is getting all your supplies.'

'But Kit won't know what to bring me.'

'Amy, love, Kit *is* the mother of twins.'

Amy smiled. 'Of course. Sorry. Thanks, Jack. Thanks for being here for me.'

As the doctor departed, and Jean left to make sure there was a delivery suite ready for Amy, she told them that, although things had moved fast at first, they'd slowed down a lot now. Amy still had a little while to go, and that if they wanted to go for a walk or something, they could as long as they stayed on this hospital floor.

Alone with Amy in the sterile room, Jack felt surprisingly calm. 'So your indigestion wasn't indigestion, then.'

'I think it was to start with, but it sort of developed!' Amy reached out and held Jack's hand again. 'Do you think Paul's going to get here in time?'

Jack – who'd been privately wondering if Paul would ever forgive him for being the one who was there for the birth if he didn't make it in time – said, 'He'll be here.'

Nodding silently, Amy suddenly half sat up, 'I haven't told Chris! He'll be expecting me at work tomorrow.'

Smoothing her hair from her forehead, Jack said, 'Why don't you concentrate on what you're doing? Paul can make all your phone calls when he gets here. Shall we have a walk or something? I seem to remember my sister telling me she'd walked up and down the hospital corridors right up until the birth itself. She swore gravity helped.'

'Good idea, I'm getting stiff stuck here.' Amy pulled herself up. 'Can I hold onto you though? I feel a bit weird.'

'We could hobble and wobble towards the café if there is

one. I'm gagging for a cup of coffee, and I bet you must be hungry. You'll need energy for what lies ahead.'

'I'm not that hungry, but you're probably right. Maybe we could hunt down a packet of biscuits or something I could nibble on.'

As they ambled slowly to the door, Amy stopped dead. 'I haven't phoned my parents. My mum will be gutted that she didn't know I was in labour until it was all over.'

'Amy, you are priceless! Stop worrying about letting other people down and concentrate on yourself, please.'

'OK.' Pausing to catch her breath before finally making it into the corridor, Amy asked, 'Did I thank you for being here, Jack?'

'A lot. I was hardly going to run away and leave you to have a baby at the side of the road, was I?'

'I know, but you could have got me here and then gone home. You must have so much to do before opening the bistro. I would have understood.'

'Amy Donahue, you just listen to me for a minute. That is my godchild in there.' Jack's expression cracked as they stopped to let a trolley push past them. He had been determined not to cry, but now tears snuck out of his eyes regardless. 'Not only that, but you are the only woman I have ever loved – so don't even think about putting the opening of a *restaurant* higher on my priority list than your welfare. Got it!'

Amy mumbled, 'Yes, Jack,' as the sign for the café loomed into view.

'Once Paul arrives I'll leave you to it. Until then, I stay. Enough said. Right then, I need coffee.'

Amy caught a glance of her ex's dark brown eyes, and saw clearly what she had always known. Jack would have loved kids of his own, and for a while he, like her, had thought that they would have them together.

But that had been then.

Half an hour later Amy was back in the examination room, wandering round in circles munching her way through a packet of chocolate digestives at a speed that Jack would never have believed possible if he hadn't witnessed it.

'I'm going to have to serve chocolate digestives at your baby's naming party.'

Amy laughed. 'They'd go well with the champagne!'

'I have no doubt about that. I could start a new trend!'

They'd got into routine now. Every now and then Amy would stop moving and Jack would rub her back hard as she breathed deeply, before they carried along with their conversation as if nothing had happened.

'Now that your youngster is making an early guest appearance, I will have to bring your party forward. Are you and Paul planning an actual christening or just a party?'

'Just the party. If he or she wants to be baptised when they're older then that's their choice to make, not ours.'

'It isn't that long until Peggy's birthday either, is it?'

'Do you think she'll want a party?'

'I have no idea. At least she is talking to me now.'

'Kit's twins' exam results will be out soon as well, won't they. That's three reasons for a party already. We could have a joint do; it'll be much more fun that way. What do you think? You up for a bigger party? Get in crates of champagne rather than a few bottles?'

'Not to mention the digestive biscuits.'

'Essential.'

Amy stopped suddenly and gasped, 'Fuckin' hell…'

Her un-Amy-like bad language was interrupted by the opening of the examination room door. Jean was back, carrying a tray complete with a jug of iced water and two glasses.

'Hi, guys. You must be getting to the hot and bothered stage by now.'

'Some cold water would be wonderful. Thanks, Jean.' Amy caught her breath again and sat down on the side of the bed.

'No problem. If you lie down a minute, Amy love, I'll see how you're progressing.'

Jack sat next to Amy's head and took hold of her hand. 'We've been walking up and down a bit, it seems to be helping.'

'Excellent. Now then, let's take a peep.'

214

Amy increased her grip on Jack's hand as Jean checked her.

'Blimey, Amy! I don't envy Paul holding your hand during the actual birth if you're gripping me this hard now!'

'Oops, sorry.' Amy relaxed her hold a bit, but she didn't let go of Jack's hand as she spoke to Jean, 'Please don't tell me I've got hours left to go. I'm already worn out!'

The midwife laughed. 'Not at all, it seems you're ready to go along to the delivery room.'

'What? But I can't! Paul isn't here yet!'

'Sorry, Amy, for a first birth this is happening fast. Let's hope that bodes well for a trouble-free swift labour.'

'But Paul isn't here!'

'No, but you have some friends outside who tell me that he's on the way. Daddy has time to get there.'

On hearing the word 'Daddy', Jack and Amy simultaneously dropped hands.

'Who's here?' Amy silently willed Paul to move faster through whatever traffic he was stuck in.

'I think they said Kit and Peggy, does that sound right?'

'Yes.'

'They have your things, but if you don't feel up to seeing them then I can just bring in your stuff and send them away.'

'I'd like to see them. Is there time?'

'I think so, but only for ten minutes, then I'm going to take you down to the delivery suite, OK?'

'But Paul…'

Jack put his arm around Amy's shoulders. 'He will make it, and you won't be alone for a single second until he does. I promise.'

'I love you, Jack Brown.'

Jack kissed her nose. 'And I love you, now just wait there. I'll fetch the others.'

Jean waited until Jack was outside before saying, 'You have a good friend there. Does he have children?'

'He's one of the best, but sadly no, I don't think children are going to happen for him.'

'Shame, he'd make a great dad.'

Amy was spared further comment by the arrival of her

215

friends with a multitude of bulging carrier bags.

Kit engulfed her friend, 'Can't you wait for anything, woman!'

'That's what Jack said!' Her eyes fell on the shopping, 'Thanks so much for all that, Kit, what have you got? Looks as though you cleaned out the baby shop!'

Peggy flexed her arms theatrically. 'It feels like she brought you weightlifting stuff!'

'Take no notice of Peggy! She has an even better gift for you.'

'You do?'

'Paul. He'll be here really soon now. His phone cut out in the museum basement, and he's not long been up in the main office.'

'Is he OK?'

'I think panicked would cover it.'

'I bet!' Jack took a step back from Amy, pleased that Paul was going to be on time, but aware of a feeling of disappointment that he was a little ashamed of, and would never ever admit to.

Amy clenched her teeth. 'Contraction …'

Kit winced on her behalf. 'How you finding them so far? Gas and air or painkillers come your way yet?'

Shaking her head by way of reply, Jack spoke for Amy. 'She's been incredible: nothing so far, but of course, we're only just beginning.'

'We?' Peggy smiled at Jack.

'I meant Amy. I've just been an admiring witness.'

Her powers of speech back, Amy said, 'I think the time for a little something is fast approaching though!'

Barely was her breath back, when another contraction hit the back of the last, 'Oh, shiii …'

Kit and Peggy exchanged looks as Kit said, 'Time to get that midwife back in here.'

They had no sooner spoken than the door flew open, and a red-faced, breathless Paul ran across the room, looking almost as exhausted as his wife.

Chapter Thirty-four

Tuesday 26th July

The moment Paul arrived, Jean gently ushered Kit and Peggy outside the room before taking Jack to one side.

'You've been incredible. Amy will never forget today, and I don't imagine you will either. Will you be alright?'

Feeling far from alright, Jack said, 'Amy, Paul, and the baby are all that matters. Look after them, won't you?'

Jean said nothing more, but nodded with a kind smile as, unnoticed by Amy and Paul, Jack left the room, and joined his friends on the other side of the door.

'You want a drink, Jack?' Kit pointed to the sign for the café. 'Peggy and I are heading that way. You must be gagging for a coffee.'

Jack shrugged. 'Thanks, but I'm going to head home. Fancy being on my own for a bit.'

'Sure, no problem.'

Kit exchanged glances with Peggy as they watched Jack disappear towards the exit.

'I've never seen him so subdued.' Peggy looked back over her shoulder. 'That boy has grown up. Megan told me he had.'

Kit, who had a good idea how Jack would be feeling, said, 'He has. And not before time.'

Jack hadn't got far from the hospital when he found himself pulling his mobile phone from his pocket and, without thinking about what he was doing, he called Rupert's number.

'I don't suppose you fancy a drink or a meal or something tonight, do you? I feel a bit weird. A bit flat maybe, I'm not sure ...'

217

It had only taken one sip before Kit and Peggy had mutually declared their coffee undrinkable, and had set off back to Pickwicks to find an anxious Megan and Scott waiting for news, glasses of champagne already in hand.

Catching the significance of his wife's raised eyebrows, Scott beamed his familiar white-toothed smile and poured out two more glasses of bubbly. 'Well, it's never too early to wet the baby's head, is it!'

Megan raised her glass. 'Don't keep us in suspense then: what news? Has Amy had the baby? Did Paul make it in time? I've been ringing you both, but there's been no answer.'

'No baby yet, and yes, Paul is there. Although it was all nick of time stuff.' Kit pulled her mobile from her bag, noting the list of missed calls and messages. 'Sorry, guys, I turned my phone off in the hospital and forgot to put it back on.'

Peggy's hand dived into her pocket! 'Whoops, so did I. Sorry!'

Scott was amazed. 'But you two never forget to have your phones on!'

The women shrugged as Kit said, 'Must have been the excitement of it all. Honestly, I've never shopped for things so quickly in my life – and speaking as a fervent anti-shopper, that's saying something. I hope I got Amy the right stuff.'

'I'm sure you did.' Peggy smiled, 'Amy was tired but doing well. It shouldn't be much longer now.'

Scott took hold of Peggy's hand. 'And what's your excuse for not reconnecting with the modern world?'

His wife smiled. 'It could possibly have been the shock of witnessing Jack being responsible and sensible.'

Rupert was waiting for Jack outside the Tube. 'So, why do you feel weird and a bit flat then?'

'For that conversation, I am going to need at *least* two pints, and quite possibly a large plate of chips.'

'We'd better go the nearest ghastly gastropub then. Come on.'

Letting himself be led along the road into the nearest pub, Jack felt semi-dazed. So much had happened in the last few hours. He craved time alone to let it all sink in, and yet, at the same time, he was afraid to be on his own in case his growing melancholy took root.

Sensing his friend was trapped under some heavy thoughts, Rupert sat Jack down at one of the only free tables, and then went to the bar and ordered two plates of fish and chips and a couple of pints of beer. It was good to be the one taking charge for a change, rather than being the one who needed help and advice.

Collecting some cutlery, he placed the tray of drinks down before sitting opposite Jack.

'Are you ready to tell me why you feel weird, or would you rather I made small talk for a while?'

Warmed by Rupert's consideration, Jack shared his thoughts. 'I feel weird because I have just come from the maternity hospital. Amy has gone into labour. I was with her at the time, so I was the one who had to call the ambulance, go with her, hold her hand, and take care of her while the others tracked Paul down.'

'Blimey.' Rupert took a small sip of beer. 'And once Paul arrived, even though you'd been looking after Amy until that point, you were no longer required. Were made to feel in the way, even?'

'That's it. I know it wasn't personal, and that Amy and Paul need each other now more than ever, but ...' Jack let his sentence trail off, and took solace in a deep draught of beer. 'Odd to think that while we're here all comfortable, about to eat chips, Amy is in the middle of having a baby. It feels right and wrong at the same time.'

Taking another mouthful of his beer for Dutch courage, Rupert said, 'Tell me to mind my own business, but would I be correct in assuming that once upon a time, you thought that if you were ever with Amy in a delivery suite, you'd be the one expecting the baby with her?'

Jack sighed. 'I can't argue with that. Even though I know how ridiculous and indeed how selfish it is, not to mention how long ago Amy and I were together ...' Jack trailed off his sentence and shook his head at himself.

'I hope they're all alright. Everything was happening at such speed, I'm sure they must have had the baby by now.' He glanced at the phone he'd left on the table between them. 'No news yet though.'

Without passing judgement on Jack's confused feelings, Rupert concentrated on the positives, and raised his glass. 'To Amy, Paul, and their new arrival. Here's to a happy and healthy start to life.'

'I ought to go home.' Megan's watch told her that it was already seven o'clock. 'Nick and I are supposed to be going out later. Are you sure there are no messages on your phones yet, guys?'

Kit and Peggy simultaneously checked their mobiles again and shook their heads.

'Promise you'll call me as soon as you hear from Paul. Any time. Promise?'

Rupert chewed his first chip thoughtfully, as if trying to decide whether to tell Jack something or not.

'What is it?' Jack noticed the considered expression on his companion's face. 'You look trapped in indecision.'

'I was.' Rupert laid down his fork. 'I was wondering if I ought to tell you about my father.'

'And? Are you going to, or are you already wishing you hadn't mentioned it?'

Rupert couldn't help but laugh. 'It's frightening how well you know me already!'

Jack held his tongue and tried not to let his eyes kept drifting to the phone in the hope of news from Amy, as Rupert began to explain.

'You told me, when we had dinner the other day, about your ex, Toby. About how you went over to Spain to come out to your dad together. Was your dad really as calm about it as you said he was?'

Cradling his glass, Jack said, 'I was very lucky. Dad and his girlfriend Jane were so kind. I wish I'd told Mum before she died, although Dad said she'd worked it out years before. They

220

were respecting my right to come out to them when I was ready.'

'And you had no idea that they knew, or had at least suspected?'

'Not a clue,' Jack scowled at his former self, 'but I was so full of myself back then, I probably wouldn't have noticed even if I'd lived with them. I'm not sure I'll ever forgive myself for not talking to Mum about my life before it was too late.'

Quiet for a moment, Rupert said, 'It sounds as though she would have understood your decision not to say anything until you were ready, though.'

'She would have. We were really close.' Jack took another sustaining drink, 'Ironically, I was on my way to tell her and Dad everything the day Mum told me about her cancer. Naturally, I kept my news to myself. It suddenly all seemed so trivial.' Jack looked up. 'Anyway, we were going to talk about your folks, not mine.'

Rupert frowned. 'My family, sadly, aren't quite as easy-going.'

'They have no idea you're gay?'

'I'm sure my mother has her suspicions. She's never said anything though. She wouldn't dare.'

Jack's eyes narrowed. 'How do you mean?'

'My father.'

'He'd take it badly?'

Rupert laid down his knife and fork so he wasn't tempted to stab his meal as the frustration he felt about his father threatened to spill over. Steadying himself as he caught Jack's concerned expression, Rupert said, '"Victorian" sums up most aspects of my father.'

'Ahhh. I see.'

'You do?'

'You told me last time that he had made his money in the City. That he goes to a Club, and that he lives in his own rarefied atmosphere of what he considers to be *proper*. Plus, you're his only child. The only boy of parents who had children later in life.'

With a sad nod of his head, Rupert said, 'You've got it. It

wouldn't be so bad if he was an easy person to stand up to, but he's one of those men who can't conceive of the idea that he could ever be wrong. The rest of the world should come into line with his way of thinking and not the other way around ... I haven't even told my parents about my current job, Jack! I love it, it's the best job I've ever had as far as I'm concerned, but to my father ... Let's just say it doesn't have the required executive status.'

'I see.' Jack cut some batter from his fish. 'And how about your mum?'

'Mother – I *have* to call them Mother and Father, not Mum and Dad – is lovely. When it's the two of us on our own we get on fine, and the tension that tends to linger whenever Father's around isn't there.'

'But?'

'But ... I suspect she's a tiny bit afraid of my father, so I don't tell her things that could make her life more difficult. No way would she stick up for me if my father decided to ban me from the house or...'

Jack looked doubtful as Rupert's sentence tailed off. 'Are you sure about that? I mean, she is your mother. Mothers as a rule tend to side with their children before their husbands – as far as I can tell, anyway. I mean, can you imagine Kit or Debbie siding with their husbands against their children?'

'No, but then Rob and Phil are a far cry from my father.' To deflect the conversation, Rupert picked up Jack's mobile. 'Still no word from Amy.'

Jack, despite his worry at the lack of communication from the hospital, wasn't willing to let Rupert drop the subject. 'I can't imagine Amy siding with Paul over her child either, can you?'

'I don't know Amy, but no, from what you've told me, I can't.' Rupert pushed his food around the oval plate. 'Maybe it isn't that Mother is afraid of him, just in awe of him. I don't know.' Shoving his dinner away, he groaned. 'You must think me rather pathetic.'

'No. I think you're a decent man trying to do his best by his family. But you're losing out on having someone in your life in the meantime, and I suspect you're beginning to resent that, aren't you?'

Suddenly the atmosphere across the table subtly changed. Rupert could feel the words he wanted to say on the tip of his tongue, but wasn't sure he dared. But, if he didn't say them now, would he have another chance?

'OK, so here's the thing.' Rupert swallowed hard. 'Yes, I've been holding back from having a relationship because each time I go to my parents' place my father expects me to arrive with a future wife in tow so we can hurry up and give him a new heir.

'He's pinning his hopes on having a grandson to pass everything on to and skip my generation. I'm sure he sees me as something of a glitch. Of course, it won't have occurred to him that I might give him a granddaughter and not a grandson.'

Jack smiled ruefully. 'You mean, when your mother was pregnant he decided she should have a son, and so she did. Therefore wanting a son is a case of mind over matter. If you gave him a granddaughter he'd have assumed you can't have been trying hard enough, in true Henry VIII style?'

'That's about it. Biology lessons weren't very comprehensive when he was at school.' Rupert sighed. 'It hardly matters, does it? There will be no grandchildren, and no one to pass their mausoleum of a house onto bar me.'

Silence descended across the table, until Jack reached out and took hold of Rupert's hand. 'I always wanted kids one day, but, well … as you say, the situation is academic. I am very lucky though, I have two godchildren, and I'm about to have a third. Plus, my sister has given me a niece and nephew.'

Feeling an unaccustomed sensation of being safe, Rupert cast an anxious eye around the nearby tables, but no one was paying them any attention at all.

Seeing his uncertainty, Jack gave Rupert's hand a reassuring pat and then let go. 'I could come with you. If you like?'

'Come with me where?'

'To visit your parents.'

Rupert almost choked on a chip. 'You want to meet them? Why?'

'Because until you tell them who you are, you'll never truly be at peace with yourself, and you and I will never really get started. You could tell them about your new job, and we could see what happens from that point onwards.'

Looking directly into Jack's deep chocolate-coloured eyes, Rupert saw he was right. A shy smile crossing his face as he nodded at his companion.

The silence of apprehensive happiness was broken by the buzz of Jack's phone. Snapping it up, Jack read the text quickly.

'Is it about Amy?' This time Rupert took Jack's hand without worrying about what anyone else might think.

'No, it's Kit asking if I've heard anything yet. Surely my next godchild should be here by now? I hope Amy's alright.'

Chapter Thirty-five

Wednesday 27th July

Kit woke up, rolled over, and immediately reached for her mobile phone, fully expecting to see a message awaiting her. But there was no news from Amy.

Jack woke up smiling. Despite his doubts about the wisdom of meeting Rupert's father so soon, he was convinced it was the right thing to do. Pulling himself out of bed, Jack thought back to the small yet memorable kiss Rupert had placed on his lips before, without a backward glance, he'd dashed home to his flat in Kew.

Reaching for his phone, Jack opened the text waiting for him. He grinned to see that Rupert had sent him an early morning *Hello*, but his pleasure was soon replaced with concern. There were no other texts. There was no news from Amy.

Scott turned from the sink where he was washing the flour from his early morning scone-baking off his fingers, 'Any news from the hospital?'

'Not a word.' Peggy stared at her mobile expectantly, but there were no missed texts or messages. There was no news from Amy.

Amy didn't think she would ever stop crying. Fatigue had wrapped her in a blanket of the most complicated and conflicting emotions she'd ever experienced.

Fear, joy, bewilderment, unending worry, and a total overriding love filled her heart as she gazed in awe at the tiny bundle she cradled in her arms. No words came to her lips as she locked eyes with Paul. Sat next to his wife on the narrow delivery room bed, Paul cried silent tears as he stroked a finger lightly over his child's head, ruffling the fine covering of downy hair.

Resting her head on the pillows, Amy closed her eyes. She could feel her baby wriggle slightly in her arms as a new wave of exhausted happiness swamped her.

Paul looked from his shattered wife to his sleeping child with an incomprehension he couldn't define. He couldn't see how Amy had done that. The birth, which had started so quickly, had slowed right down, and then, some hours later, had become difficult when the baby had raised its arm at just the wrong moment and become stuck. Several frightening minutes had passed while Jean, as unflappable as ever, had explained to them that they'd need to use a ventouse to help deliver the baby.

Watching Amy in so much pain, not being able to do anything but hold her hand and pass her the gas and air when she asked, had been the most frustratingly difficult thing Paul had ever done in his life.

Once the emergency delivery equipment, which looked to Paul like a mini vacuum cleaner with a weird suction cap attachment, had been correctly placed, the birth had happened with an acceleration of speed and activity that was every bit as frightening as the complication it was putting right.

That had been two hours ago now, but it felt as if years had passed as, watching his wife finally slip into some much-needed kip, Paul gently picked his child off Amy's lap.

'Hello, little one.' He looked into the small, round face, marvelling at its perfection as he rubbed the baby's tiny nose softly against his larger one, and the silent tears of happy disbelief began again. He whispered softly, scared of waking Amy, 'I can't believe we have you. We never thought …' He took a slow inhalation of air as he sat down, tucking his baby against his chest. 'We never thought we'd be this lucky.'

Overcome with the events of the past twenty-four hours, Paul looked lovingly at his wife. He couldn't wait to tell everyone. So far, only the new grandparents had been informed, to cries of joy and promises to visit very soon, but no one else knew. As much as they wanted to tell all their friends, at the same time they wanted to treasure this time on their own, until they'd all three had some rest.

The door to the delivery room opened very quietly. Jean came in, whispering, 'How are we doing then?'

Paul just smiled.

'I think that look tells me all I need to know.' Jean, who was clearly pretty exhausted herself, said, 'I'm about to go off duty, but there will be a nurse along soon. I'm afraid she'll have to wake Amy and move her so we can use this room for someone else, and she'll also tell you to get off home.'

'Home?' Paul looked down at his child. 'I can't possibly leave!'

'I know it's hard, Paul, but that's how it works. Dad goes home, gets some kip and a change of clothes, then comes back this afternoon all fresh and ready to relieve Mum of her duties for a while.'

'I guess that makes sense. Going to be tough leaving them though.'

'I know, but you'll be in a better position to help Amy after a couple of hours sleep and a shower.'

'Oh, thank God!'

'What is it?' Peggy shot to Kit's table as the writer gestured in her direction. 'Amy?'

'Sort of. It's Jack. Hang on … Sorry, Jack, we've all been going mad with worry over here at the café … Really? Oh wow … nothing at all? Well, OK then. I'll tell the others, we'll see you at five. Thanks, Jack.'

By the time Kit had hung up, Peggy and Megan were crowded around the table.

'Amy is alright. Baby was born at eight thirty this morning.'

'Eight thirty this morning? Not last night?! Oh hell, that was ages since she went into labour.' Megan looked horror struck.

'Little mite got its arm stuck on departure, apparently.'

'Hang on,' Peggy was almost bouncing at the good news, 'what flavour was it?'

Kit laughed. 'Flavour?'

'Yes. A raspberry or a blueberry?'

'I've never heard of babies coming in flavours before! I don't know.'

'Was Jack being all mysterious or something?'

'Apparently Paul called him on his way out of the hospital. Paul will be here, at Pickwicks, at five o'clock with all the details and some photos. Amy is too tired for visitors today, but we can go and see her tomorrow.'

Megan dashed off to serve some new customers, calling over her shoulder, 'I bet she's totally wiped out.'

'Shame we don't know the flavour though, I was going to nip out and get a card.'

'We can do that tomorrow.' Kit glanced up from her novel manuscript, 'So exciting. I didn't think I'd get to cuddle a baby again until either Helena or Thomas had kids. I can't wait!'

Peggy laughed, 'Don't tell me you're all broody, Mrs Lambert?'

'Not at all!' Kit thought back over her recent worries about the twins leaving home, and knew that wanting more children had never factored in her feelings of displacement. 'I've done all that, and although I miss it, I have new things ahead of me; but grandchildren might be nice one day.'

'Good job it is Helena's day off. She'd have freaked out if she'd heard that.'

'And they aren't saying if it's a boy or a girl?'

'Not a word.' Jack was enjoying being the purveyor of the good news, and as he told Rupert that Amy and her child were safe and sound, he felt warmth fill him. 'Paul called me a little while ago. He was so kind. Thanked me for looking after Amy. I have to admit I'm a bit relieved about that.'

'You didn't think he'd hold it against you, did you? That you were there at the start and he wasn't?'

'It crossed my mind.'

Rupert paused, before saying, 'Are you OK then?'

He didn't have to say more for Jack to understand what he was really asking. 'Yes, thanks. And thanks for listening to my self-pity last night.'

'Likewise.' Rupert paused again, fiddling with the scroll button on his mouse as he did so. 'Were you serious? You know, about meeting my parents?'

'Yes. Providing you'd like me to. If it would make things more difficult for you, then obviously I won't. But if you want morale support next time you go, then I'm happy to come along.'

'Well, actually … I've been asked to go for lunch this coming Saturday. Mother said I was welcome to bring a friend.'

'You mean a date – as in a future wife?'

'I suspect that is what she meant.'

'I'll come on two conditions.'

'Which are?'

'You tell your mother in advance that the friend you are bringing is a colleague from work. That way, me being a bloke won't be too much of a surprise. And when you talk about work I think we should use your official title of *Educational Liaison to Kew Gardens*, rather than saying you're a shop assistant!'

'Agreed. And second?'

'Second, you pass on the baby news to Rob, assuming Kit hasn't beaten us to it, and then shut the shop early and come to Pickwicks with me at five o'clock to hear Paul's news.'

Rupert suddenly felt unsure. 'But I'm not part of the group, Jack. I mean, I ought to keep the shop going while Rob comes over.'

Jack felt an odd constriction in his heart when he realised that Rupert might not be there to hear about his new godchild for the first time. 'Rupert.'

'Yes?'

'You're with me, so you *are* part of the group. I need you to be there when I find out if I have a godson or a goddaughter. I'm not sure why it matters to me, but it does.'

Rupert's cheeks glowed as a blush started to form. 'I'll be there.'

'Are you sure you're alright about me doing this without you?'

Amy smiled at Paul as he handed their baby into her open

229

arms. 'Of course I am. They have to know, they've been very patient waiting for news. I bet Jack's getting worried!'

'But you should be there as well.'

'I'll be there the first time they meet our beautiful baby – and anyway, I'm done in, and so are you! Go to Pickwicks, show off the photos, fill them in on our news, then get some food and go home. You've only had two hours' sleep since yesterday. You'll need to be full of life when we come home the day after tomorrow.'

Kissing his wife and his child, Paul picked up his tablet, which had about a world record number of photographs on it, and with lots of backward glances and waves, left the two of them behind him.

'You're very quiet, mate, are you alright?'

Rob looked anxiously at Rupert as they walked along Richmond's main street on the way to Pickwicks.

'Fine. I'm just not very good at meeting people I don't know.'

'You know Kit and Phil, they'll both be there, and Jack of course. Megan, Peggy, and Scott are lovely. In fact, it's a miracle you've been working at Reading Nature for so long without coming across them before.'

Footsteps running up behind them made them turn to see Jack racing to catch them up.

'Hi, guys, good timing!'

Rob said nothing about the glance that Rupert and Jack exchanged, saving it to tell Debbie about later. 'You honestly don't know if it's a boy or a girl, Jack?'

'Not a clue. Amy told Paul she wanted us all told at the same time. Beyond knowing that everyone is fit and healthy, I'm as much in the dark as everyone else.'

Pushing the door to Pickwicks open, the boys found Kit, Peggy, Scott, and Megan sat with cups of coffee, and Phil cradling his eternal pot of tea, all looking expectantly at the door.

Kit smiled. 'Any sign of Paul out there?'

'Didn't see him,' Jack glanced at his watch, 'but we're a few minutes early, and I bet it was difficult for him to leave Amy and the baby in the hospital.

Rob and Phil nodded at the same time, as Phil said, 'I hated leaving Kit and the twins, but the blokes get more or less booted out of the door after the birth. Or they did when we had our two.'

Noticing that Rupert was looking a bit awkward, Jack began to introduce him to the Pickwicks team members he hadn't met before just as the door opened, and a tired but beaming Paul came in.

'I don't suppose there is another cup of tea in that pot, Philip?'

Immediately Paul was ushered into an empty seat, tea was poured, and when no one could stand it any longer, Kit blurted, 'Well, come on? Boy or girl? Is Amy OK?'

Paul reached into his rucksack, and placed his tablet on the table. Opening an album of photographs, he announced, 'Ladies and gentlemen, let me introduce you to my daughter: five pounds in weight exactly, blonde-haired, blue-eyed, a month early but fit and healthy in every way. This magnificent mini miracle is Poppy Rose Donahue.'

Chapter Thirty-six

Thursday 28th July

Jack, a bunch of flowers in one hand and a lemon yellow teddy bear in the other, walked into the hospital's postnatal ward, and searched along the row of beds for Amy. At last he spotted her, baby Poppy discreetly feeding under the copious folds of her mum's oversized shirt.

'Amy? Can I come in?'

Looking up from her child, Amy's face broke into a wide grin. 'Of course – but aren't you already in?'

'You know what I mean! I didn't want to disturb you mid-feed. That looks as if it needs concentration.'

'You aren't kidding! This is one of those things that you definitely need to practise beforehand, but simply can't. Luckily, Poppy seems to know what to do.'

Jack drew up a chair and sat down. 'Does it hurt?'

'It does a bit. Everything is tender right now, as you'd imagine. It's OK though.' Amy smiled towards the gifts Jack was carrying. 'Which is for me and which is for Poppy?'

'Well, the bear is obviously for you.'

'As I thought.' Amy laughed. 'They're lovely flowers, thanks, Jack. And while we're about it, thanks for everything you did for me on Tuesday. Seems a lifetime ago, but I couldn't have managed without you.'

'Yes you could. You've always been the strong one, but thanks anyway. I'm glad I was there for you.'

Amy laughed again. 'Strong one? Hardly! Hang on; this little miss has fallen asleep on the job.' A few deft moves later, Poppy had been lifted away and Amy's dignity was intact under a re-buttoned shirt. Holding her baby out to Jack, she said,

'Fancy being the first person apart from Paul, myself, and the nurses to give your latest goddaughter a cuddle?'

Jack, who'd been looking forward to a cuddle since he'd woken up that morning, said, 'You sure it's OK? I mean, she's only just eaten.'

'She may well puke down your back, but then she could do that anytime. Don't tell me you aren't dying to have a snuggle, because I won't believe you. I happen to know you love babies.'

Taking the offered bundle with extreme care, Jack swallowed back the emotion lodged in his throat as Amy tucked the yellow bear into the cot next to her bed. 'Doesn't he look cosy? Poppy will be able to cuddle up with him at bedtime.'

'Him?'

'Poppy's my daughter, isn't she? The chances of her giving any of her teddies a female name, when the time comes for her to make such big decisions, are remote.'

'True.' Jack couldn't stop looking at Poppy. Her fine blonde hair was so soft, and as he held her, a tiny hand escaped from the blanket she was wrapped in and gripped his finger with a strength that could have broken a lesser man. 'Did you manage to get any sleep last night?'

'Some, which is better than the "none" most of the mums in here got last night, so I'm not complaining. I've been pretty much napping along with Poppy.'

'You could doze now if you want. We're OK here, aren't we, tiny one.' Jack settled back with Poppy resting on his chest.

Amy's heart constricted for him. 'You look so comfortable.'

'We are, aren't we, Pops?'

'Pops?'

'Yes. Don't tell me you haven't shortened her name to Pop already. You always shorten names. I've always been stunned you don't call me Ja.'

Amy laughed. 'Yes, I'm already calling her Pop sometimes.'

'When are you going home?'

'Tomorrow.'

'But you've only just given birth! They can't ship you out that fast, can they?'

'I'm doing OK. Poppy is eating well and she's putting weight on, so they don't need to keep me here. It isn't like the old days, Jack. They don't keep you in for the full week after the birth unless you aren't well. And to be honest, although I won't get that much rest once I'm home, I'd like to get no sleep in my own bed rather than no sleep in this one. It is so uncomfortable!'

'Really? We aren't uncomfortable, are we, Pops?' Jack waved Poppy's hand towards her mum as the baby opened her eyes and seemed to looked directly into his, her blue gaze meeting his brown one.

His whisper of 'Oh!' was almost unnoticeable, but Amy heard it.

'You alright?'

Full of wonder, Jack murmured, 'Your daughter has your eyes. Sorry, Poppy caught me by surprise. She is so like you.'

'I know – but she's also very long, so she'll probably be tall like her dad.'

Quiet again, Jack sat up straighter now Poppy was awake, cradling her on his arm. 'When is Paul coming in? I thought he'd be here.'

'Not for an hour or so. He's filling the house with food and stuff. Pop's early arrival caught us out a bit. We didn't even have a car seat until last night.'

'Anything I can get for you? The flowers and bear were just treats. I'd like to get you a proper present.'

'You don't have to do that! It's not like a birthday or a wedding or anything.'

'It's exactly like a birthday!'

Amy giggled. 'So it is. Told you I was tired! Lack of sleep is making me stupid.' She looked around the busy ward at all the other mothers, their visitors and the collection of quiet, crying, or grizzling babies, 'Lots of birthdays. But honestly, Jack, you're doing enough right now. How is the restaurant coming on? I'm sorry I won't be around to help as much as I'd have liked.'

Kissing the top of his goddaughter's head, Jack smiled. 'You're forgiven in the circumstances. It is all coming together

235

nicely at last. The sign for the front is arriving this week, the menus are in place, I've secured the local food suppliers I wanted, and a local warehouse has a standing order for the alcohol now that the licensing bench has agreed my drinks and entertainment licence.'

Taking a cup of fruit tea for herself and a coffee for Jack from the ever-happy orderly, who was pushing her drinks trolley through the packed ward, Amy inclined her head toward her friend's beverage. 'I can't wait to get back to that stuff.'

'You still off the liquid black gold?'

'A bit. I love the smell of coffee again already, but I can't quite face drinking it yet. I'm sure I will want one desperately the second I push Pops into Pickwicks and get hit with the aroma of Peggy's coffee.'

'I don't doubt it.' Jack gazed lovingly at Poppy, who'd gone back to sleep in his arms. 'This little angel is going to be fussed to bits the second you walk through the café door.'

'We won't be short of babysitters.' Amy rested her head on her propped up pillows, 'Anyway, you were telling me about the restaurant. Are you going to let me know the name yet?'

'Nope. Not until our welcome to the world party for Poppy – which will also be my launch party now she's made an early appearance.'

'Are you sure you want us to crash your pre-launch party?'

'One hundred per cent sure. The actual critic's launch will be terrifying! If I get bad reviews for my food I'm doomed. Well, not doomed, but the better that first week goes the better for me long term. It'll be good to have a lighter event to look forward to.'

'I'll talk to Paul, but I'm sure he'll be up for it. Thanks, Jack. So,' Amy twinkled her eyes at her friend, 'enough of the small talk, what's the current situation with Rupert then?'

Rupert knew he should have called his mother earlier. A lot earlier. He'd lost count of the number of missed calls and texts she'd sent him over the past few weeks.

With mixed feelings of guilt and foreboding, he took advantage of being the only person in the bookshop, and called her number. Leaning against the counter, Rupert half hoped the phone would go to voicemail, but he knew it wouldn't. His mother always answered the phone, because his mother was always free.

'Rupert!'

The joy in her voice instantly added to Rupert's guilt. 'Hello, Mother, how are you?'

'All the better for hearing your voice. How are you? Busy, I assume, as it's been so long since we saw you.'

Not for the first time, Rupert found himself wishing his mother would be less accepting about his lack of calls, and maybe even a bit cross with him. He knew that years of saying the right thing had become second nature to her; and that no matter how much she minded the neglect from her only child, she'd never mention it. Sometimes, Rupert hated himself for having inherited some of his father's characteristics.

'I have been busy. Actually, I wondered if I could come over to see you. You mentioned a meal on Saturday in your last message. Is that offer still open?'

'Of course it is. This is your home!'

'I know, but ... Look Mother, I'm sorry. I know I haven't been in touch as much as I should have been. As much as I'd have liked to have been, even, but the thing is…'

Rupert's mother, as if sensing something was about to be said that might cause trouble, cut across him, 'It's alright, dear. I know how it is. You're young and have a busy life. Are you working at the moment?'

'Yes. I have a job I love.'

'That's good. Well, you can tell us all about it at the weekend. Your father will be pleased to see you.'

'Will he?'

'Of course.'

'Right.' Rupert willed a book buyer to come through the door so he could legitimately say he had to go. 'Umm ... would it be OK to bring a friend along?'

'A girlfriend?'

'Sorry.' The hopeful pleasure in his mother's question cut Rupert to the quick, but determined not to show it, he calmly replied, 'Jack is just a good friend.'

'A good friend?'

Rupert ignored the uncertainty in his mother's question, 'He used to own the business I work for, but now he's moved on to pastures new.'

'Not for any unsavoury reason, I hope?'

'Not at all. Jack came into an inheritance and decided to travel for a while.' Rupert winced at his need to please. He'd only mentioned Jack's inheritance because he knew it would lift his status from a friend to a worthwhile acquaintance in his father's eyes, when his mother reported back on their conversation.

'Well, I look forward to meeting Jack. What's his proper name? You know your father will ask.'

'Jack Brown.'

'Brown? Not related to the Hampshire Browns, I suppose?'

'Not to my knowledge.' Rupert sighed. 'I know that isn't a grand enough name for Father, but if it helps you can tell him that Jack is wealthy, works hard, is the owner of an excellent restaurant, and is generally strong in wind and limb.'

'No need to be sarcastic, Rupert.'

'Sorry.'

'We'll say no more about it for now.'

Mercifully, the bookshop door swung open, and a collection of young children and two parents came in. 'I'm sorry, I'm needed. Shall we say 1.30 on Saturday?'

'Come at one. We can chat while lunch is cooking.'

Hanging up the phone, Rupert found that his palms were sweating. God knows what they'd make of Jack.

He didn't have time to think about it for long though, as one of the children was tugging a man towards the counter. 'That's him, Dad, that's the nice man who talks about naughty squirrels at Kew Gardens!'

Chapter Thirty-seven

Saturday 30th July

'Sorry to turn up so soon after you've got home. I can disappear again if you like?' Kit had arrived on Amy and Paul's doorstep at nine o'clock in the morning, weighed down by carrier bags.

'Not at all.' Paul pointed to Kit's luggage, 'But if you're planning on moving in, I have to warn you, we're about to become packed to the rafters. We're expecting Amy's parents any moment.'

Kit laughed. 'Don't worry; I won't disturb you for long if you are on in-law alert.' Holding up the bags, she said, 'This lot was Helena's. You may not want any of it, but it's all yours if you do.'

'Blimey. There's loads in these! Are you sure you don't want to keep any of it?'

'I've been having a grand clear-out. There's a bulging suitcase of all the baby clothes I'm too sentimental to part with still at home.'

Taking the bags from Kit, Paul gestured towards the living room door. 'Amy and Poppy are in there. Go on through, they'll be pleased to see you.'

Kit pushed open the door and peeked in, moving quietly in case the girls were asleep.

Amy had been lying on the sofa, her eyes closed, as Poppy dozed in a wicker Moses basket, but she snapped to attention as her friend walked into the room. 'Kit! How wonderful. I've been dying to introduce you to Poppy. Come on in.'

'Don't get up! I didn't mean to wake you.'

'You didn't. I was only resting my eyes while madam there was spark out.'

Tiptoeing across the carpet, Kit looked down at the tiny form, snug in a pale yellow romper suit, her hand clutching the leg of a matching coloured teddy bear. 'Oh, Amy, she's adorable!'

A happy smile crossed Amy's face. 'Thanks. She is, isn't she?'

'Keeping you up?' Kit assessed Amy more carefully, noting the dark circles under her eyes and the washed-out pallor to her already pale face.

'She's only three days old. We aren't really in a routine yet.'

Kit nodded. The sensation of non-stop demands, all of which resulted in her being worn out, from when the twins were babies was a feeling she would never forget.

She sat next to her friend. 'It'll get easier, I promise.'

'You sure?' Amy stared at her hands. All the worries that kept her company in the middle of the night came racing to her lips, as unexpected tears appeared at the corners of her eyes. 'What if I'm doing it wrong? What if I'm feeding her when she has tummy ache, or winding her when she wants to sleep or … I don't know. What if I don't understand what my own child needs?'

'Come here.' Kit wrapped an arm around Amy. 'Have a good cry, hun. You need to let go of it. Nothing you are saying is any different to what every other new mother says a couple of days in.'

'Promise?' Amy sniffed, unable to prevent the tears she'd been given permission to flow. 'I love her so much. What if I'm letting her down?'

'Spoken like a true parent.' Kit reached for the tissue box on the coffee table. 'Here you go. Have a good blow. Take a deep breath, wipe the sleep from your eyes, and then take a proper look at your little girl. Go on.'

Amy frowned at Kit, not sure why she was being told to look at Poppy now, when that was all she'd been doing for the last two days. But as she watched her daughter, happy, comfortable, and relaxed in sleep, her grip still latched onto Jack's teddy bear, Amy beamed.

'She's OK, isn't she?'

'Yes, love. She's a knockout, and you are doing a great job. I guarantee that when the health visitor comes to check on you both, she will say exactly the same thing.'

Amy hugged Kit just as Paul pushed open the door with a tray of drinks in his hands and two full carrier bags hanging off his fingers below.

'Oh good grief, what's that lot?' Amy looked from Paul to Kit.

'I forgot to say, in my eagerness to see my goddaughter; Phil and I have been having a sort-out. It seemed a good time to lay a few of my own ghosts to rest and tackle the twins' baby clothes at the same time. We've been generally clearing and tidying out all the stuff I've never been strong enough to throw away. I wondered if there was anything here that you'd find useful. Anything you don't want can go to charity.'

Amy opened the first bag and pulled out a delightful pair of tiny cream tights and a flowery soft blue dress wrapped together in white tissue paper. 'These are gorgeous. Are you sure you don't want to keep them?'

'Slim though Helena is, I can't see her squeezing into those again.'

'You know what I mean!'

'I know. I was saying to Paul just now, I've got a suitcase packed to the brim with the clothes I'm keeping for sentimental reasons. These are the extras; they're too good to throw away.'

Amy laid the tiny dress on her lap. 'I can't imagine Helena ever having been that small.'

'The twins were early like Poppy, so they were pretty dinky. There are premature sizes in this bag. The other one is a mix of newborn and nought-to-three months clothes.'

The ring of the doorbell sent Paul to his feet again. As he disappeared, Amy leaned towards Kit and speaking quietly, asked, 'You sure about this, Kit? Are you OK now? I know you haven't been having a great time yourself lately.'

Kit's gaze fell on the form of Poppy, who was beginning to wriggle in a way that made it clear she'd be waking up very soon. 'I'm fine. Back to my old *take on the world* self. Phil has been amazing. Really understanding about my empty nest thing.

And with you and Peggy onside, how could I not be alright? Thanks for bearing with me on this, Amy. I was worried my sadness at leaving the life you're just beginning would ruin it for you. I'd hate to have done that.'

'You couldn't ruin this for me. Look at her!'

'The problem with my two children being exactly the same age is that they arrived together and will leave together. I went from a house of two to a house of four literally overnight. Now the reverse is about to happen, it feels very odd.'

'I bet it does.'

'It's only six weeks now until Thomas leaves for Exeter and Helena heads to Bath; assuming they get their A levels.'

'Which they will, because they are every bit as clever as their parents.'

'Well, they're certainly as clever as their parents used to be!' Kit laughed, not allowing herself to dwell on the twins' forthcoming departure. 'Do you mind if I take a few pics of Poppy to show Peggy and Megan? They'll kill me if I don't bring them a full progress report. It looks as though she's stirring anyway, so it won't wake her.'

'No problem.'

The buzz of excited voices came from the hallway, as Kit put her phone in her pocket and stood to leave. 'Sounds as if your parents have arrived. I'll leave you to it.'

Amy's grin widened further. 'Thanks for these, Kit. I'll have a good sort through later, but I can't imagine I'll waste any of it. You don't have to rush off. My folks would love to meet you.'

'And I'd love to meet them, but this is their big grandparent moment. Anyway, Thomas gets home from his travels tomorrow. I can't wait to see him. I'm even looking forward to tackling the pile of washing that he'll be bringing with him. So I've got a fair bit to do at home once I've written today's word quota.' Kit watched Amy scoop a restless Poppy from the crib.

'Come and see us at Pickwicks soon. The others are dying to see you and Poppy, and there is so much news for you to catch up on. I'll go out of the back door so you can meet your folks in peace.'

'Thanks, Kit.' Amy hadn't finished waving to Kit's

retreating figure when the door burst open and her parents rushed in, engulfing their daughter and granddaughter in an effusively emotional cuddle.

'Mum, Dad, I'm so glad you're here!' Amy burst into more happy tears as Paul rescued his daughter from the crush, before officially holding Poppy up to show her off.

'Pippa, Frank, meet your granddaughter. This is Poppy Rose.'

The second Kit walked across the threshold of Pickwicks she was more or less mugged by Peggy and Megan for the baby photos she'd promised to bring with her.

After they'd all declared Poppy utterly gorgeous, and that they couldn't wait for Amy to bring her over, Kit settled at her writing table and found herself on the receiving end of one of Peggy's extra-large cups of black coffee.

'You seem much happier today, Peggy. Would I be correct in assuming you have come to a decision about the second café?'

'We have.' Peggy glanced over her shoulder to make sure Megan could manage on her own for a moment, before sitting down. 'I haven't had the chance to talk to Jack or Megan yet, so this goes no further for now, but we've decided to take up Jack's offer of the bistro share.'

'Oh, I'm so pleased!' Kit was delighted, 'It's such a perfect solution, and far less hassle for you and Scott. But, if you don't mind me asking, what made you change your mind? I know you guys get on fine most of the time, but you've never been Jack's number one fan.'

'It was seeing him looking after Amy at the hospital. We all know their history well enough to suspect that can't have been easy for him, and yet he did everything for her. Just for her. There was nothing in the situation for him at all. He was acting from pure love and kindness. I know you tell me he's like that, but I'd never seen that side of him before.'

'Yes you have!' Kit felt indignant on Jack's behalf. 'He was brilliant when Scott was injured after the accident. Jack was here all the time keeping this place going.'

Peggy was solemn. 'That's what Scott said, and of course you're both right, but there is no denying Jack could have done that merely to get closer to Amy again. He had a lot of ground to make up with her at the time. I know you'll think I'm being harsh, but this is our future. It's our retirement plan. I absolutely had to keep emotion out of the decision.'

'And yet it was emotion that finally decided you?' Kit frowned.

'Not emotion. It was a respect for Jack that I didn't have before.'

Unconvinced, but glad that Peggy's decision had been made, Kit said, 'Well, however you got there, I'm glad you're going in with him. Let me know when it's official and I'll shout yippee out loud rather than just on the inside.'

'Thanks, Kit. Scott is delighted. We've done a load of sums – all very dull – and it looks like the dream of buying a bungalow to retire, while not as close as we'd hoped, is a little nearer than it was yesterday.'

Lifting her coffee cup, Kit smiled. 'I'll drink to that.'

Chapter Thirty-eight

Saturday 30th July

Jack had been covertly watching Rupert out of the corner of his eye since they'd climbed aboard the first-class compartment of the train. As they whizzed across the English countryside to Cambridge, Jack thought his friend looked almost as tired as Amy had when he'd visited her in the maternity ward.

'Are you ready for this?'

'As I'll ever be.' Rupert kept his eyes glued on the scenery outside the window, without really seeing it at all. 'I'm not going to come out today, Jack. All I'm planning to do is to introduce you, and tell them about my new job. That's enough in one go, believe me. You'll understand that when you meet them.'

'I didn't expect you to come out. You'll know when the time is right, and that is your decision to make, not mine.' Getting up, Jack picked up their train tickets. 'Time I waved these in the buffet cart and fetched our complementary coffee. You look like you need a caffeine fix.'

Returning with two thick paper cups, Jack sat back down. 'I know I've forced your hand, but I only meant to get you to contact your parents. To break the barriers down a bit. I'm sorry if I've made you lose sleep over this. Losing Mum … it made me see that sometimes the tomorrow you think you'll always have to sort things out doesn't come.'

'I know,' Rupert smiled at his companion, 'I wasn't blaming you for my sleepless night. I blame myself. I got so fed up with my father's digs and gibes about not doing a "proper job" that, rather than face him head on, I've hidden away. Doing nothing felt better than doing something else that was bound to disappoint him.'

'I'm sorry.' Jack placed a comforting hand lightly on Rupert's thigh. 'Maybe you should regard this as simply a trip to see your mother, and if you manage to get some sort of approval from your father that'll be an added bonus.'

Snorting through his resignation, Rupert placed his hand over Jack's. 'I'm looking forward to seeing my mother, but where my father is concerned we should be aiming for a more realistic goal. Let's go for him not sighing and shaking his head theatrically in my direction more than twice.'

Jack took a sip of his grainy coffee, 'I have a feeling your father and I may not get on.'

'I can guarantee it, but I'm sure my mother will like you – privately, at least.'

'Oh my God, Rupert!'

'What?'

Jack stared out of the taxi window as they pulled onto a wide gravel driveway. 'You never told me your parents lived in a mansion!'

'It's only a house Jack; it's not a stately home or anything.'

'Rupert, it's a bloody *huge* house with grounds! That makes it a mansion in my book.'

As the taxi came to a halt beside the front door, Jack half expected a butler to appear and magically open it for them.

'I suppose it's a little mansion-like. But that's just it, you see. It's a house. It isn't a home.' Paying the cab driver, Rupert stalked across the gravel. 'Come on, I always use the back door.'

They were almost at the rear of the house, which gave way to a tiered garden which was obviously a labour of love for someone, when Rupert stopped moving, and pulled Jack into the privacy of an ivy-clad nook in the wall.

'You OK, Rupert?'

'Nervous as hell, to be honest.' Rupert whispered, keeping alert for signs of life. 'I know I said I wasn't coming out to them today, but … well…'

'Well what?'

'Just seeing us together; won't it be obvious?'

A flutter of hope darted around Jack's chest, and he couldn't help but smile. 'You think so? You think we look like a couple?'

Rupert suddenly felt awkward. 'Maybe.'

'Good.' Jack backtracked, trying to keep the pleasure from his face, 'Although perhaps not good here and now.'

Taking a quick glance around to make sure there was no one about, he leaned forward and kissed Rupert lightly on the lips. 'Being so close to you on the train and not kissing you was driving me nuts. Anyway, you needed that for luck.'

Slightly flushed, Rupert said, 'Well, now they'll definitely guess, which I suppose will prevent me from having to actually tell them.'

Jack shook his head kindly. 'More likely they'll think you've just dragged along your mate from the office along to say hello.'

'Perhaps.' Sounding far from convinced, Rupert moved towards the back door. 'They'll be in the drawing room.'

'Once more into the breach…' Jack tapped Rupert backside as they moved towards the house. 'One quick question before we go in?'

'Yes?'

'Why don't you wear jeans? Your bum would look so good in denim.'

Rupert cheeks went a little pink as he said, 'How about I tell you that on the way home?'

'Home to my place?'

'Oh yes. I'm going to need a cuddle or two after this.' Rupert took a deep breath as he opened the backdoor. 'Here goes nothing then.'

'Rupert, darling!'

A slim, middle-aged woman in a floral summer dress, with rich auburn hair, swooped down upon her son with a smile so wide that Jack thought that Rupert must have been overplaying the under-the-thumb wife card. His mother was so like him. Similar build, hair colour, and now that Jack found himself faced with her neat outstretched, freckled arm, so he could shake her hand, he noticed that Rupert, just like baby Poppy, had inherited his mother's eyes.

'I'm very pleased to meet you, Mrs Ashton.' Jack found himself smiling easily at the woman, whose grip gave away that she was much stronger than she appeared. He couldn't help wondering if that applied to all parts of her personality too.

'And you, Jack was it?'

'Jack Brown, Mrs Ashton.'

Rupert's mother indicated a sofa opposite the armchair upon which she now perched, in the room where they'd found her. Far too posh to be merely a living room, this had to be the drawing room that Rupert had referred to.

Following the unspoken instruction, Jack sat down as Rupert offered to make tea, and disappeared, presumably into the kitchen. Eager not to let any opportunities for awkward silences occur, Jack pointed to two watercolours over the fireplace. 'What beautiful artwork. Did you paint those, Mrs Ashton?'

'Yes. Thank you.' Rather taken aback at the compliment, Mrs Ashton added, 'I created those many years ago now, just after Rupert left for school.'

'That must have been hard for you. I imagine he was great company as a child. Always into everything.'

Mrs Ashton frowned. 'Er, yes, yes he was. How did you know that?'

'Rupert is so passionate about his work, about imparting knowledge to others. He seems interested in everything. Keenness and a zest for life like that is often inherited.'

'Oh.' At a loss for what to say, she said, 'So, you work with Rupert then?'

'I used to own the business where he works. I've been good friends with the current owners for many years.' Not wanting to go too far down the road of how well he knew Rupert while he wasn't in the room to speak for himself, Jack pointed again to the two watercolours. 'May I take a closer look?'

'Yes. But please be kind. I haven't examined them properly in years. They may not be very good up close.'

The paintings were of a matching pair of kingfishers. The one on the left of the fireplace dived one way, the one on the right in the opposite direction. The detail was intricate and accurate; the play of the light on the water, the reflection, and the shadow were, as far as Jack could see, perfect. He knew in an instant that these weren't just good, they were excellent. Megan would love them.

'Do you sell your work, Mrs Ashton? These are exquisite!'

'Are they?'

'They are.' Jack stepped away. 'Thank you for letting me enjoy them.'

'I ... it's my pleasure.' Mrs Ashton smiled a little wider as the door was pushed open and Rupert came through with a tray of tea and coffee.

'Mrs Daniels says dinner will be in an hour, Mother. I have to say it smells delicious.'

Jack contained his surprise at the family having a cook, turning his attention instead to the fact that there were only three cups on the tray, which had to mean Rupert's father was not expected to join them. He said nothing however, as Rupert perched next to him on the sofa, looking decidedly uneasy.

'Have you two been getting on alright?'

'Very well.' Mrs Ashton arranged the cups onto their saucers. 'Jack likes my paintings.'

'I've always loved kingfishers.' Jack said, 'When I was young my grandad used to take me out for long walks along the river. If we were lucky, we'd see them dive. So graceful – and so fast! I think that's when I first fell in love with the countryside.'

Pouring two cups of tea, and a coffee for Jack, Rupert felt a new wave of affection for his friend, who had already endeared himself to Rupert's mother. 'I got my love of nature from you, Mother. Do you remember? We used to go on long walks too, didn't we?'

'We did.' The light in Mrs Ashton's eyes dimmed a fraction. To Jack it seemed as if Rupert's mother had suddenly mentally collected herself, and felt she'd lapsed in her responsibilities in some way by being so welcoming. 'So, you know the men my son works for, Mr Brown? What manner of business would that be exactly?'

Mr Brown? Jack wasn't sure what he'd done to deserve the relegation back to his surname, but determined to remain friendly, said, 'It involves working with nature, actually.'

Rupert spoke with exasperation. 'Father isn't listening behind the door, Mother. Mrs Daniels says he has been delayed. You are free to be friendly to us for at least another twenty minutes.'

Jack was aghast, and yet the small sag of Mrs Ashton's shoulders showed she had relaxed back into her previous state of welcome.

'I apologise, Jack. Perhaps Rupert has told you, my husband is rather proper. He would not like me to use your Christian name until he has also met your acquaintance.'

'And deemed if you're suitable company for me or not.' Rupert grumbled as he picked up his tea. 'Honestly, Mother, why do you put up with his strange rules?'

Not answering her son's question, possibly because she couldn't, Mrs Ashton turned her attention back to his friend. 'I've always liked the name Jack. Did you know that it derives from the English names Jackin or Jankin, and is a diminutive of the name John? It was such a popular name during medieval times that the word Jack was used as a slang term for "man".'

Jack looked so impressed that Rupert laughed. 'My mother is full of general knowledge like that. She could be the queen of any quiz team – if she was allowed to do anything fun or ordinary.'

'I knew that the name was English, but I didn't know the rest. That's fascinating.'

Smiling at Jack, Mrs Ashton added, 'The original meaning is "gracious", the same as John. And in Scotland, the name for John is Ian. I do love facts like that.'

Jack spoke eagerly. 'So do I. When I was at university my girlfriend was studying archaeology and history. She was always coming out with stuff like that. I suspect you already know that the surname Ashton comes from a town that is entered via a row of ash trees?'

'I did,' Rupert's mother looked pleased, 'but I'm thrilled you know as well.'

250

Rupert sipped his tea quietly, not sure if his mother was thrilled about Jack's interest in nature and trivia, or if it was the fact he'd mentioned he'd had a girlfriend that had restored her smile.

Chapter Thirty-nine

Saturday 30th July

The door to the drawing room opened, and with that one movement, despite the heat of early afternoon sunshine streaming through the window, the temperature dropped.

Jack didn't miss the exchange of wary glances between mother and son as Mr Ashton strode into the room. Seconds earlier Mrs Ashton had been relaxed in her chair, eagerly answering Jack's questions about her charming garden; a place she'd referred to as her sanctuary. Now she sat bolt upright, her shoulders braced, and although she wasn't actually gripping the arms of her chair, Jack suspected she was having to force herself not to. *Surely Rupert would have said if his father was violent?*

The air of unease continued to sweep across the room as Mr Ashton, overdressed in suit, waistcoat, and silk tie, clasped his hands behind his back and, completely ignoring Jack, stood in front of his son, who'd already jumped to his feet.

'Well, young man, what have we done to deserve this honour?'

Jack felt himself bristling on Rupert's behalf. If his father had said those words, they'd have come out with laughter and a wry smile. Mr Ashton spoke every word as if they were loaded with reproach.

Holding his father's stare for far longer than he'd normally dare, Rupert said, 'I thought you and Mother would like to know about my new job. I also thought you might like to meet one of my friends.' Determined not to let his father stonewall Jack, Rupert gestured towards his friend, who immediately stood up and held out his hand. 'This is Mr Jack Brown.'

'I'm very pleased to meet you, Mr Ashton. You have a delightful home.'

Staring at Jack's hand as if it might be contagious, Mr Ashton eventually shook it. Then taking his palm away as quickly as possible, and giving it a none too subtle wipe down his suit front, he plunged both hands into his pockets, his eyes not leaving Jack as he asked, 'So tell me, how do you know my son?'

'I used to own the business Rupert works for. Obviously I continue to keep an eye on the place, and I'm good friends with the new management. Rupert and I hit it off straight away. We have many mutual interests.'

'Is that so?'

Mr Ashton's appraising stare was beginning to get on Jack's nerves. He was about to expand on his statement about the bookshop when Rupert beat him to it, his usual non-combative demeanour gone.

'Yes, Father, it is. Why do you have to make the fact Jack and I have things in common sound so sinister? It's what happens when you are friends with someone.'

Mrs Ashton was as astonished as her husband that Rupert had spoken so sharply. 'There's no need to accuse your father, Rupert, he's worried about you.'

'No he isn't, Mother; he's worried that news of my latest employment will not be good enough to share with his peers at that antiquated Gentleman's Club he spends so much time in.'

'Rupert!' Mr Ashton's bark was far harsher than his son's, and for a short time Jack didn't know where to look. Determined not to show his unease, Jack was about to attempt to steer the conversation onto less thorny ground when, mercifully, Mrs Daniels announced that lunch was served.

The fact that the household had someone to cook and serve their food underlined for Jack exactly how far up the social scale Mr Ashton saw himself to be. His pride in the employment of Mrs Daniels showed itself as he directed the seating of the table.

Jack, who had been placed between Mr and Mrs Ashton, but at such an angle around the large oval table that he was unable to easily catch the eye of Rupert, gave his host ten out of ten for tactics. Mr Ashton was clearly a successful businessman for a reason.

Once the expressionless Mrs Daniels had departed the room, a silence descended on the diners. All that could be heard was the crunching of the delicious paté on toast. In a friendlier climate, Jack would have enquired about the paté recipe.

After three painfully quiet minutes had passed, he couldn't stand the atmosphere any longer.

'Rupert tells me that you are an eminent figure in the City, Mr Ashton?'

Mr Ashton's eyes widened. 'He did, did he?'

'Yes.' Without waiting for Mr Ashton's tongue to catch up with his raised eyebrows, Jack added, 'My family also worked in the stock market, I wonder if you're acquainted with them, sir?'

Mr Ashton's hectoring tone quelled to a begrudging mumble. 'It's possible, but I doubt it.'

Avoiding looking at Rupert, in case his expression was one of bewilderment as this unexpected revelation, the chef said, 'Of course, you may be too young to remember my grandfather, but he was something of a high-flyer in his day.'

'Really?'

Seeing that his father was either too stubborn or too proud to ask who Jack's grandfather was, just in case he hadn't heard of him, and he really did turn out to be important, Rupert said, 'I had no idea you had family in the City as well. What was your grandfather's name?'

'Edward Barnard-Cooper. My mother's father. He was the best man I've ever known.'

If he hadn't been looking for it, Jack would have missed the mild flicker of interest that crossed Mr Ashton's face.

Rupert's mother, who'd been playing with the food on her plate rather than eating it, looked at Jack with renewed interest, amusement edging into her eyes. 'I know that name from when I worked in London myself. He was an expert on the Exchange, if I remember rightly?'

Jack beamed. 'So the stories say, although I didn't know the business side of him. He kept all that very separate from real life.' Hoping this last sentence had hit home with Rupert's father, Jack addressed Mrs Ashton alone, 'I hadn't realised you were in the City as well. Did you enjoy it?'

'I was one of the secretaries. I gave it up when I got married; but yes ... yes, I loved my work. It was an exhilarating environment to work in.'

Feeling that the thaw in hostilities was in danger of freezing up again, Jack kept talking, 'I imagine giving up work was what was expected to executives wives back then. I always think it's sad when talent goes to waste though, but of course you have another talent. Two others, in fact.'

'I do?' Two high points of colour appeared on her cheeks as she adjusted to the fact she was receiving an unexpected compliment.

'From what I saw of your garden, the workmanship looked fantastic, and clearly you have a skilled eye as a watercolourist.'

Rupert risked a glance at his father. He looked as though he'd been sucking on a lemon. 'I'm sure Jack would love a tour of the garden after lunch, Mother. He has qualifications in horticulture.'

Before Mrs Ashton could respond, her husband jumped in. 'Horticulture? I can't imagine that your grandfather would have been very impressed by that.'

Jack spoke firmly, his eyes resting directly on those of Mr Ashton, 'Edward Barnard-Cooper evidently wasn't of your acquaintance then, sir? If he was, you'd have known he was a member of the Royal Horticultural Society, an avid lover of the natural world, and encouraged his children and grandchildren to follow their passions, whatever they might be. He hoped that they'd always have something in their lives that lay beyond the remit of work. A pastime for when they needed to leave everyday stresses behind them.'

Turning to Mrs Ashton, Jack added, 'Forgive me if I sound blunt, I meant no disrespect after you kindly invited me to your home. My grandfather felt very strongly about the importance of having time outside of work.'

Swallowing carefully, Mrs Ashton nodded, and as though

256

giving into an internal struggle, said, 'I think your grandfather and I would have got along extremely well, Jack. If you'd like a walk around my garden after lunch I'd be delighted to show you. Please, call me Angela.'

Rupert watched from the drawing room window as the man he hoped he could think of as his boyfriend talked in animated fashion to his mother amongst the terraced flowerbeds. He couldn't remember the last time he'd seen her so relaxed, and the fact she had invited Jack to use her Christian name in front of his father was unprecedented.

Cradling a glass of port, Rupert was surprised at how little tension had settled in his shoulders. Normally when he was summoned to have port with his father, Rupert was on tenterhooks, bracing himself for the latest round of disappointment-laden questions about his future.

During the remainder of Mrs Daniels' first-class roast beef and a massive helping of Baked Alaska, there had been a two-way conversation between Jack and his mother about the benefits of various soil types over others, and the walks Jack and his grandfather had taken at every opportunity. His father hadn't had the chance to get any early digs in about Rupert's lack of girlfriend and high-flying career. *Although*, Rupert thought, *he's probably saved up all the barbed comments for now*. He was also sure he would have a landslide of disapproval against Jack to put up with as well, but somehow his father's bluster had lost its sting. He merely seemed cantankerous and a bit sad. Rupert began to wonder if his father knew how much his antiquated attitude had caused him to miss out on over the years.

The door opened behind him, and Rupert took a sustaining sip of alcohol before greeting his father with a positive comment, hoping it would pave the way for a more friendly conversation than usual. 'An excellent meal. Mrs Daniels continues to serve you well.'

His hope went unfounded.

'Don't try and divert me away from the subject, young man. Who the hell is he?'

'If you are referring to our guest, his name is Jack Brown, as I have already said. His grandfather on his mother's side was Edward Barnard-Cooper. This same grandfather left Jack and his sister an inheritance that allowed them to follow their passions – as you'd know if you were listening over dinner.'

'All I read from the mealtime conversation was that *Mr* Brown was given a heap of money which meant he has been able to waltz around wasting time for years. I don't suppose he even managed to get a decent education.'

'Or perhaps, he got a first degree at university, set up a company he loved, nurtured it, made it work, and then sold it on as a successful going concern before moving on to a new challenge.'

Sitting down in the wing-backed armchair that had its back to the window, Rupert's father caressed the bowl of his glass, looked unconvinced as he asked, 'And this new challenge?'

'A bistro in Richmond. Jack is a qualified chef.'

'Richmond?'

'You find it hard to accept Jack has premises in such a sort after location, and yet you know nothing about him. You'd already written him off before you set eyes on him. Is that because he my friend and therefore must be no good? Is it because he made Mother laugh? Or perhaps it's because he has disappointed you by coming from a successful family when you'd already decided he was going to be a no-hoper?'

Sucking in his cheeks, Rupert's father spoke as though spitting acid, 'And when on earth did coming from a successful background make anyone a successful child? I mean, look at you!'

Rupert's insides froze. He returned his gaze to the garden while he fought to control the rage that suddenly burnt inside him. Jack and his mother had moved further back amongst the flowerbeds, but he could see they were happily engaged in a discussion which, judging by his mother's gesticulating, was going well.

Without diverting his eyes from the activity outside the window, Rupert took a deep breath. 'I'm sorry I have been such a let-down to you, Father. I did try to be who you wanted me to

258

be, but it made me unhappy. And I wouldn't have been a very good lawyer anyway. I had a horror of doing something dreadful by mistake and bringing shame on you and mother. I don't imagine it ever occurred to you that I was trying to *save* you from embarrassment by giving up my legal career, did it?'

The stunned silence from his father answered Rupert's question. 'I assumed not. And now, if you don't mind, I'm going to join Mother and Jack. At least they look as though they are having a good afternoon.'

Placing his empty glass on the table he stood before his father, 'And, in case there is any part of you that cares about what I'm doing with *my* life, I am the Educational Liaison Officer for Kew Gardens and Reading Nature. That's the company Jack set up just outside of Kew Gardens with his grandfather's money. I love my job, and have at last found something that I *am* good at.'

With his pulse racing through his body, perspiration breaking out on his palms, Rupert strode towards the door. He wasn't sure what made him hesitate and turn to face his father for the final time that day; but with his adrenalin pumping in his veins, Rupert kept talking to the man in the chair, who was looking suddenly far older than his sixty-one years.

'And while I have your attention, I think it's time I put you out of your misery. There will be no wife, and therefore no heir. I'm sorry, Father, but that's how it is.'

'You mean you're … your mother said you were, but I couldn't comprehend that a son of mine could be…'

'Could be happy?' Rupert cut across his father's sentence before he could go any further. 'Well, I am happy. Very happy. Are you happy, Father?'

Chapter Forty

Saturday 30th July

'Rupert?'

Angela Ashton frowned as she saw the speed at which her son, red-faced and hunched around the shoulders, shot out of the back door and came to rest next to Jack. 'Whatever is it, Rupert? Are you alright?'

'I'm sorry, Mother.'

'Sorry for what?'

Jack, who'd been studying Rupert's expression, had already worked out what must have happened. 'You told him everything, didn't you?'

Although he hadn't run far, Rupert was out of breath. His angry frustration made his chest feel constricted and tight. 'I didn't mean to. He made me so cross, and suddenly I didn't see why I should put up with his belittling anymore. Why shouldn't I be who I really am within my childhood home?'

'How did he take it?'

'I didn't hang around to find out. But as Father isn't chasing me across the lawn I guess he's either too shocked to move, or is in his study rewriting his will, leaving everything to that bloody Club instead of me.'

Nodding slowly, the colour beginning to return to Angela's face as she comprehended what her son had finally admitted to her husband. 'I told your father years ago, Rupert, but he didn't believe me.'

'You knew?'

'Of course I knew. I'm your mother.' Angela smiled at Jack. 'I suspect your mother knew before you told her as well.'

'She died before I had the chance to speak to her, but my

dad said she did.' Jack held out his hand to Rupert. 'Are you alright?'

With a silent look to his mother to make sure it was OK, Rupert took Jack's hand. 'I am now.' He squeezed his boyfriend's palm before dropping it and hugging his mother with more affection than he'd shown her in years. 'I'm sorry I've kept away so much. It wasn't you.'

'I know, dear.' Angela felt tears stream down her face as she held her son. 'I've never minded you being gay. Not for one minute. But I don't have to tell you that your father's not an easy man to live with, and if he doesn't want to see something he is quite capable of being blind to it.'

'Are you sure you're alright with it, Mother?'

Smiling through her tears of relief, Angela looked at Jack. 'You've always had good taste, Rupert. You have a good man here, don't mess it up.' Keeping her son close for a few more seconds, Angela stepped back, 'Now, boys, if you'll excuse me, I have to go and sort out your father. It's about time I stood up to him myself. If you can do it, Rupert, so can I.'

'Do you want me to come with you?'

'It's OK. You two get back to the station or you'll miss your train. Best to let your father simmer for a minute, but don't worry, he'll come around.'

'You think so?'

'Well, maybe not – but I can hope!' Stretching out a hand to Jack, Angela shook it warmly. 'Thank you for coming today, Jack, you've proved to be the breath of fresh air I badly needed. I will certainly be implementing a few of your suggestions in the garden.'

'And painting a few of the flowers, I hope.' Jack returned her smile. 'Thank you for making me so welcome. Oh, and don't forget about the restaurant launch, will you? I'll post an invite. We'd love you to be there – and Mr Ashton as well, if he'll come.'

A contentment he hadn't felt since he was a small child swept over Rupert as the train carried him and Jack back to London.

'You're very quiet. You OK?'

Rupert nodded. 'Very OK. Thank you for being so lovely to my mother.'

'That was hardly a chore, she's delightful. We have a lot in common. I think she would have got on with my mum like a house on fire.' Jack tried to push down the feeling of regret that his mother had missed out on meeting Angela. 'I hope you didn't mind me inviting her to the restaurant opening? We got chatting about the bistro, and she was so enthusiastic, and gave me so many great ideas for meal combinations, it seemed the natural thing to do.'

'I don't mind at all. I doubt my father will come though.'

'Probably not.' Jack twisted in his seat so he could see Rupert's face properly. 'Your mother will be alright, won't she? He won't harm her?'

'Father's a control freak, but not a thug. And I have a feeling that now she's been proved right about the lack of white weddings and grandsons – not to mention after he has digested the news that I gave up legal work precisely so I *didn't* embarrass him – he'll be grumpy but resigned.'

'I suspect your mother is a lot stronger than he is.'

Rupert rested his head on Jack's shoulder. 'I'm glad you liked her. She obviously thinks you a suitable boyfriend for me.'

'Which is lucky, because I'd rather been hoping that's how you saw me.'

Travelling along in happy silence, they watched the fields of Cambridgeshire merge into the suburbs of London. Comfortable, with Rupert cuddled up next to him, Jack was beginning to fall asleep when his mobile began to vibrate in his pocket.

'Oh, hello, Megan. Everything alright?'

'Slow down!'

Rupert was almost out of puff as he ran behind Jack along the street towards Pickwicks. 'Peggy won't have changed her mind before you get there.'

His eyes gleaming with joy, Jack laughed as he slowed to a walk. 'I'm sorry, but I want to hear it directly from Peggy and

Scott. I won't allow myself to truly believe what Megan said until I hear Peggy say it myself.'

Rupert grabbed Jack's elbow as they turned into the lane that led to Pickwicks. 'Megan wouldn't have called if there was even a chance that Peggy was going to change her mind.'

'You're probably right, but, well … Look, today has already been very good to me. I'm not known for having a lot of luck.' He held Rupert's hand. 'Although I must confess, dragging you to Pickwicks as soon as we got off the train wasn't top of my list of interesting things to do on our return to London.'

Blushing, Rupert said, 'Well, nor mine, but this is so exciting!' He glanced at his watch. 'The café will be closed now though, won't it? It's almost six o'clock.'

'Everyone will still be there cleaning up though, and hopefully, if she got my text, Amy will be there as well.'

'You invited Amy?'

'The more witnesses the better!'

Stopping abruptly, Rupert decided not to mention that he was quite nervous about meeting Amy, considering how much Jack obviously adored her, but said, 'Hang on … what if Helena is there? I haven't seen her since she and I … um … you know.'

'Trust me, if Helena is there she'll act as though nothing ever happened. Pride and all that. But it's late, I'm pretty sure she won't be around.'

Pickwicks was at a standstill. The tables were littered with used cups and teapots, and there was a stack of dirty glasses gathered on a tray, which had been abandoned on the counter. The reason for this hiatus in the usual post-customer industry was obvious to Jack and Rupert as soon as they knocked on the locked café door.

Amy had brought Poppy for her very first trip to Pickwicks, and Peggy and Megan were queuing alongside Kit for a cuddle. To Rupert's relief, there was no sign of Helena.

Leaving Poppy in Kit's capable hands, Amy escaped from the cooing and ahhhing and let Jack and Rupert in.

'I'm so pleased you came! How's my little girl?'

'Do you mean me or Poppy?' Amy smiled at Jack, knowing

264

full well he meant Poppy as she put out her hand to Rupert, 'I'm so pleased to meet you. I assume you are Rupert?'

'And you have to be Amy, I've heard so much about you.'

'I dread to think!'

'It's all been good, I promise.' Rupert found he liked Amy already. He could see instantly why Jack cared for her so much, and the sense of relief he felt shocked him. It wasn't until he'd set eyes on her that Rupert realised how badly he'd wanted to like Amy, and for her to like him in return.

Letting go of Amy, Jack pointed across the café. 'I assume I'm going to have to break through that scrum to get a cuddle of my goddaughter?'

'You'll have to wrestle Peggy out of the way for sure. She's made it clear she's next in line for a snuggle when Kit gives Poppy up.'

'Then I'd better wait patiently. I don't want to annoy Peggy today!'

Amy laughed, 'Now she and Scott have decided they want in at the bistro, they won't change their minds.'

Rupert smiled. 'That's what I keep saying.'

'I know you're both right, but I need to chat to them properly. There's a lot to discuss. We need to arrange meetings, the legal stuff and all that. I also want to see if they are OK with Megan running the show, and to see if Megan still wants to, for that matter.' Jack looked around; he could see Kit, Megan, and Peggy with Poppy by her pram. 'Where is Scott anyway?'

'Hiding in the kitchen.' Amy started to walk towards the counter, and called out, 'Shall I make us all a cuppa?'

Kit gave a very obliging Poppy a tiny kiss, before passing her to Peggy, 'No you don't, Amy Donahue, I'll make it! Am I right in thinking this will be the first coffee you've drunk since you started getting morning sickness?'

Peggy, who'd just got Poppy comfortable on her lap, said, 'You're joking! Is it really, Amy?'

'It is! I'm only just back to fancying coffee again, and I wanted my first cup to be a Pickwicks special.'

'In that case,' Peggy stroked a finger across Poppy's soft cheek as she spoke, 'Kit, stand away from the coffee machine!

Megan, could you make Amy a cup of coffee please?'

Kit laughed, 'Are you casting aspirations on my coffee-making skills, Peggy?'

'Yes. No offence, honey; you may be an expert coffee drinker, but your coffee *making* most certainly needs work!'

Jack, who'd been watching the activity around him with a feeling of love for the women in his life, added, 'And while you're there, Megan…'

'Yes, I know, I'll make a full round of coffees! But only if I get the next Poppy cuddle.'

'It's a deal.' Amy took the chance to sit down, and patted the chair next to her for Jack to sit down as Rupert went to help Megan with the drinks and to chat to her about their combined website.

'Tell me,' Amy spoke quietly. 'Did the meal go well? Is Rupert officially with you now?'

'Ish.' Jack was trying to be vague, but he was given away by his smile.

'Ish?'

'We're going slowly, but it feels good like this. His father's a nightmare, but his mother is lovely. I'm hoping she'll come to the bistro opening. I think you'd really like her.'

Amy clapped her hands. 'I'm chuffed for you, Jack. He looks like a nice man. Why don't you bring Rupert over for a takeaway soon so he can meet Paul as well? I'd say I'd cook, but mealtimes are something of a fractured affair in our house now we have Poppy.'

'Takeaway sounds great. I'd love to bring Rupert round, thanks.' Jack looked over to where his boyfriend was handing out coffee cups to Kit and Peggy. 'Where is Paul, anyway?'

'He took Mum and Dad into London for a shopping trip this afternoon. I suspect they may be in the process of spoiling their first granddaughter rotten.'

As Amy's coffee cup made its way to her table, Poppy decided she'd had enough of being handed around like a gift in a game of pass the parcel, and began to cry.

With a groan of resignation at her baby's ability to always need her when she was about to relax, Amy stood up, but

Rupert halted her progress and passed her a cup of coffee. 'I'll take her, you drink your coffee.'

Taking the baby from Peggy, Rupert started to murmur to Poppy softly as he walked her up and down the café. Almost instantly the crying morphed into gurgles of contentment.

Delighted, Amy smiled. 'Rupert, you're a natural, thank you so much. You aren't on hire for midnight call-outs, are you?'

'Only in dire emergencies!'

While Peggy went to drag Scott away from cleaning the kitchen, Amy asked, 'Do you like children, Rupert?'

'Very much. I'd happily babysit your daughter from time to time … if you'd like me to, of course.'

'You have a deal!' Amy turned to look at Jack. His smile widened as the look in his ex-girlfriend's eyes told him very clearly that, at last, he had found a good man.

AUGUST

In which many champagne bottles are put on ice...

Chapter Forty-one

Monday 8th August

'And so the party, or naming ceremony as Jack keeps calling it, will be held at the bistro on the eighteenth of August.' Amy pushed the pram handle back and forth as she chatted to Kit across the café table in the sunshine of Kew Gardens.

'Well, it is Poppy's naming ceremony, isn't it, everything else that's going on is just extra.' Kit smiled down at her sleeping goddaughter. 'Any gifts you'd like for her? If this was a christening there'd be presents.'

'We don't expect presents. Mum suggested that if people want to give Poppy something, then we should open a bank account for her and tell people they can donate some money to her future.'

'That's an excellent idea. We'll do that.'

'Does that sound mercenary?'

'Not at all. Anyway, it'll prevent you from drowning in hundreds of items of clothing you can't stand, mountains of bibs, and a whole host of pewter mugs and spoons neither you nor Poppy will ever know what to do with.'

'There speaks the voice of experience.' Amy took a sip of coffee as she rested back in the sunshine and watched the tourists go by. 'I still don't think the party should be just thought of as being for Poppy though. We all have is so much to celebrate. The bistro opening, Megan's new job and her blossoming art career, Peggy's birthday is only two days after the opening, and your novel has *finally* been drafted.'

'Less of the *finally,* thank you very much – although I grant you the deadline was cut to the wire!' Kit watched the sleeping baby wriggle against the mattress. 'I'll be exactly the same empty nest wise when Poppy leaves home. Mind you, right now I can't imagine waving her off to school, let alone university.' Amy looked at her daughter. 'It seems unreal that she's virtually two weeks old already.'

'It'll go faster than you can ever imagine.'

Noting the wistful tone to her friend's voice, Amy said, 'I bet it's great to have Thomas back. Did he have a good time?'

'Adventure of a lifetime by the sound of it! And yes, it's great to have him back. We all went out for a meal last night and listened to his tales. Although I think some of the information I could have done without knowing!'

Amy laughed. 'I can imagine. He's a good-looking boy! So, how are you doing with the whole life after the twins have left bit?'

Kit squinted into the sunshine. 'We won't know for sure that they're going until their results come out on the eighteenth. Helena's like a cat on hot bricks. The sooner we find out if she's got the grades she needs, the better.'

'I'm assuming Thomas is chilled about it.'

'Yes, my son is very much of the "what will be, will be" persuasion. How they can be twins when they're so different beats me.'

A gurgling from the pram alerted the friends to the fact that the baby was now awake and grinning happily at the shadows being cast over her by the tree leaves she was shaded beneath.

Slowing the rocking of the pram to a halt, Amy said, 'But assuming they get the grades they want, when do they go?'

'Helena starts at Bath on the twentieth of September, and Thomas will be off to Exeter two days later. Such a relief they start on different days! Makes the logistics of getting them where they need to be so much easier.'

'Just as well Jack is planning to line up the champagne bottles at the naming ceremony. It's been a hell of a long time since we had so much to celebrate. In fact, we haven't had a party all together since that one after Scott's accident.'

'What about your wedding? I seem to remember dancing for Britain at the party after that – although I grant you I was a touch worse for wear after a fair bit of Pinot!'

'True. It was great – but Jack wasn't there, was he?'

'Ah, yes, so he wasn't. And this time we'll have Rupert with us as well.' Kit took a final sip from her coffee cup, 'What do you think of young Mr Ashton then?'

Amy put down her own cup and scooped up Poppy to check her nappy didn't need changing before they took a walk around the grounds. 'He's lovely. Perfect for Jack. You?'

'I couldn't agree more.'

'And is Helena OK with it?'

'Helena has said nothing about it at all, which pretty much means she is embarrassed by the whole episode and is pretending it never happened. Frankly, that's the best thing for all of us!'

'So that's settled then?' Peggy smiled as Jack and Scott shook hands over the freshly signed paperwork.

Sitting back down, Jack raised a cup of Peggy's finest coffee in his new colleagues' direction. 'I can't tell you how delighted I am that you're doing this with me. I have to admit, the afternoon coffee and cake side of the enterprise was daunting me the most.'

Scott pulled his notebook towards him. 'I find that surprising. The idea of serving full meals for a non-stop run of demanding diners would surely be the most difficult thing?'

'Well, it isn't easy, but it is exciting! I love the nightly challenge. It's a bit like spinning plates, and knowing that if you drop just one the whole display will be ruined.'

Peggy laughed. 'I can well imagine! Which is why we're quite happy to leave all that to you!' She slid the contract they'd signed into an envelope ready to hand to their solicitors, 'So, let's go through this one more time then.'

Scott rolled his eyes. 'Peggy, love, we've signed now. It's all agreed.'

'I know, but I want to triple check we haven't left anything off the list.'

'Good plan.' Jack picked up a pen, and flipped his own notebook back open. 'The contract between the three of us will officially begin on the twenty-seventh of August, which is the second Saturday after Poppy's naming ceremony. I'll talk to Megan properly tomorrow, but she already knows that she'll be my right-hand girl, spending the first few days setting up your side of the proceedings, making sure the coffee machine works, helping me with the last-minute adverts, and training up the evening waiting staff. They're all from the local silver service college course, so they pretty much know the drill anyway.'

Peggy scribbled a note on her notepad. 'And when does Thomas start in the kitchen?'

Jack, who had taken Kit's son on as kitchen hand for a month, until a local student could take over the job, said, 'The day before the launch. Which will be...' he checked his diary, 'the fifteenth. His job will largely be washing up, loading and unloading the dishwater, and fetching and carrying. He won't need much training.'

'And Thomas is happy to serve at the naming ceremony party as well, rather than being at the party as a guest?'

'Yes. He and Helena, along with your new girl for Pickwicks ... what's her name again?'

'Teresa,' Peggy looked at her notes, 'Teresa Parkin.'

'Right, all three of them will do the drinks and help serve the food, but then they can join in with the celebrations after the meal. It's a party, after all. It'll be a good chance for Teresa to get to know everyone.'

Peggy read a menu sheet Jack had given her earlier. 'And you're set on this as the menu? I have to admit, it sounds delicious.'

'That's the meal I'll be serving for the critics at the private launch as well. I am unbelievably nervous about that!'

Delivering one of his brilliant smiles, Scott said, 'You'll be fine, mate. I'm looking forward to both events. Did all the people you invited for the critics' meal accept? The newspaper and food magazine people, as well as us local business folk?'

'They did. The place will be packed. Fingers crossed it goes to plan!'

'I have all the afternoon food items listed here. I'm going to steer away from the type of food we serve at Pickwicks, as agreed. Are you alright with helping cook if life gets too hectic,

274

Jack?'

'No problem, mate, as long as I can leave you to it from six in the evening so I can sort the prep for the evening. Don't forget, I'll have Craig from the catering college doing most of that for me from five o'clock.'

The three friends looked at each other. 'We really have got this sorted, haven't we?'

'I think so.' Jack got up and fished his bag from where he'd left it by the counter, grabbed three glasses from the counter, and passed them to Scott and Peggy. 'I'm sure we'll find things we've missed as we go along, but in the meantime, we should toast our new venture.'

Pouring out the champagne, Jack stood up and said, 'Here's to The Olive Branch!'

'I do love that name, Jack.' Peggy smiled, 'It's perfect for the bistro.'

'Well, I thought it was high time I offered you an olive branch, Peggy, especially after you thought I was poaching your staff. I can't tell you how glad I am you accepted it.'

Megan couldn't stop re-reading the email on the computer screen before her. Not only had Gareth Kennedy sent a glowing response after receiving the first of the pictures he'd commissioned, but he'd asked for business cards and website details to pass on to guests who'd already enquired about her work. He had also hinted heavily that there could be future commissions for Kennedy's in the offing.

For Megan, her new working hours couldn't come fast enough. And although she knew that her managerial role would be demanding she was really looking forward to both the challenge, and to being free in the mornings to paint, which was what she really longed to do.

As she read the email for the fifth time, her mind drifted back to the small terraced house she and Nick had viewed the night before. If Gareth did pass more work her way, and other commissions followed, then maybe their dreams of eventually buying a small place together rather than renting could come true.

Glancing at her watch, she saw she had ten minutes left before she had to get back to work. Taking a chance, she called Rupert.

'Hi, it's Megan. Is this a good time?'

'Sure, I was in the middle of sorting some new stock. How's it going in coffee and cake land?'

'Great, but it's even better in art land. I've just heard from Gareth Kennedy, apparently there's been interest in my first piece. He was asking about a website and business cards.'

Rupert put down the pile of books he'd been holding. 'If you're still up for sharing one, I'm happy to set us up a site.'

'I was hoping you'd say that! Thanks, Rupert, I wouldn't know where to start on my own.'

'Once the initial setup is done, it's quite simple. I'll talk you through it. Are you still painting in Jack's spare room?'

'I am, but not for much longer. Jack was going to fit a vent to get rid of the paint fumes, but we ran out of time, and I don't want the smell of paint ruining his opening night so I'm looking for a new studio.'

'There's always my place, I'm hardly there these days. It's only tiny, but you can use it if you like. Why don't we discuss that as well when we meet to talk about the site? Tomorrow night any good? Say about seven at the bistro?'

'Perfect. I'll be there finishing off the portrait of Peggy and Scott.' Megan felt her spirits rise even higher. 'Any news on the photography competition?'

'No. The closing date has passed now so I don't imagine I made the cut. Never mind, it was great fun having a go.' The bell in the shop rang, alerting Rupert to the presence of a customer. 'Sorry, Megan, I have to go. I'll see you tomorrow. Bring Nick; that way maybe Jack will stop working long enough to join us for a chat and a takeaway.'

Chapter Forty-two

Monday 15th August

Megan crept out of bed as quietly as possible, trying not to wake Nick. It was only six o'clock in the morning, but she'd been lying awake for hours, mentally listing everything she had to do that day.

Incredibly nervous though she was about her first evening managing at The Olive Branch, Megan couldn't begin to imagine how Jack must be feeling. Despite the early hour, she was sure he'd be awake too.

Deciding to give up trying to doze, Megan got up, leaving Nick a note on the small kitchen table he shared with the other lodgers, saying she'd see him later. Picking up the pre-packed bag of clothes she was intending to wear that evening, she slipped out into the bustle of commuting Londoners.

Rupert turned over, expecting to find Jack's sleeping form next to him, but the space was empty – and by the chill of the sheets, had been for some time.

Pulling on his clothes, he headed downstairs into the bistro. He discovered Jack at the nearest table, scribbling at speed, a mountain of paperwork in front of him, the remnants of several cups of coffee cluttered around him.

Pouring two fresh cups from the machine behind the counter, Rupert sat opposite his boyfriend. 'How many hours have you been up?'

Jack grimaced. 'One or two.' He held up a handful of pieces of paper from the clutter of different menus before him. All of them had been altered in some way from their original state. 'I want this to be perfect, you know.'

'I know.' Rupert picked up the nearest menu, which until yesterday had been a neatly printed cream sheet of mouth-watering food choices. Now it was covered with ballpoint pen annotations and scribbles, signs of an insecurity in Jack that he hadn't seen before.

'Put your pen down, Jack.'

'But…'

'No excuses. Put down the pen and pick up the coffee cup.'

Jack looked at Rupert properly, and felt a smile start at the corner of his lips. 'You sounded like your father then. All stern and sensible.'

'I'm choosing to take that as a compliment!'

'Indeed!' Jack took a sip of coffee, and waved a hand over the mess in front of him. 'I have to do this, Rupert. If this evening doesn't go well then all my hard work will have been for nothing and –'

'And it *will* be amazing.' Cutting across Jack, Rupert laid a reassuring hand over his. 'You and Megan have worked your socks off. Thomas has practised getting everything you and Craig need to prepare the meals to your work stations in record time all week. The students from the college are briefed and ready to be here at six o'clock. Every single thing that could go wrong has been discussed and contingency plans laid. The necessary food is in the fridges, and the fresh food delivery will be here at ten, so you can prepare *this* menu. So, why have you drawn over it? It *is* perfect; you know it is.'

'But what if it isn't? What if the balance isn't right? Don't you think I should offer two fish choices and not just one, and is the beef too heavy with the cranberry pie side dish? Shouldn't I have more than one dessert choice? I know that's my signature dish and I want everyone to try it, but what if people don't like it?'

Jack had been talking so fast that Rupert hadn't had a chance to calm his boyfriend's growing panic. Gathering up the menus that littered the table and stacking them decisively into one pile, he said, 'Jack, this is just nerves. You've practised and practised the dishes on this menu.' He brandished the one that was destined for the tables that evening. 'You've been over it until you were blue in the face and Thomas has had steam coming out of his trainers! You'd be mad to change it now and risk a dish going wrong.'

Jack exhaled slowly. 'But what if I've got it all wrong?'

'You haven't.' Rupert stood up and gestured to the restaurant. 'Look around you. The decor is spot on, the art is fantastic, the menus are well-presented and professional, and the whole feel of the place is welcoming and stylish without being imposing or invasive.'

'What you're saying is that I should stop panicking and get on with it?'

'That is exactly what I'm saying. But first, I'm saying get in the kitchen and warm up those pots and pans by making us a hearty breakfast. It's going to be a long day, and there's no way you'll get through it without some food inside you.'

'Oh, I do like it when you're all dominant.' Jack winked at Rupert. 'And what will you be doing while I rustle up two servings of eggs and bacon?'

'Clearing up this mess, having a shower, and then I'm going to do whatever you need me to help with today. Now go cook some breakfast, Mr Chef Man.'

Jack stuck his tongue out and started to sing 'How Do Y'Like Your Eggs in the Morning?'

Rupert laughed. 'You really are old, aren't you? Singing a Dean Martin song first thing in the morning!'

'Cheek! Do I need to point out that you recognised it, and therefore must be old as well?'

Jack was about to disappear into the kitchen when Rupert said, 'Well, I hope I get my kiss with those eggs!'

Megan arrived at The Olive Branch in time to find Jack and Rupert finishing their breakfasts.

'Morning, boys. I'm impressed, Jack, I was way too nervous to eat properly this morning!'

Rupert pointed to the seat next to him. 'I'll grab you a coffee. This could be the only chance you get to sit down today.'

Jack passed the menu he'd been playing with over to Megan.

'What do you think?'

'Why have you changed this? You aren't really going to alter the menu at the eleventh hour, are you?'

Rupert smiled at Megan. 'I'm glad you said that. I've been telling him he'd be mad to change anything after all the work that's gone into getting tonight ready.'

Jack held up his hands in defeat. 'I was only asking what Megan thought of the menu in general, I didn't mean for tonight. You've convinced me to stick to how things are already.'

'Thank God for that!' Megan took a sustaining sip of coffee. 'Umm, actually, Jack … the smell of bacon is making me hungry. I don't suppose there's any left?'

Rupert passed the list of guests to Megan as she finished laying out the last set of crockery. 'I've double-checked all the bookings, and everyone who said they'd be here is definitely coming.'

'Fantastic.' Megan ran her eyes down the mix of local business owners, newspaper and magazine food critics, and Rupert's parents. 'How come Jack's dad isn't on the list?'

'He and Jane are in New Zealand and couldn't get a flight back. They're planning to come over in a month or so, though. I have to admit I'm a bit nervous about meeting them.'

'I'm sure they'll love you.' Megan studied the layout of the room carefully. 'I'm trying to work out which the best tables are, so we can sit the most important critics at them.'

'Good plan, although thanks to the great lighting the majority of the seats are good. Perhaps Peggy and Scott could go over by the kitchen door, and maybe I'll sit with my parents in the far corner. Neither are bad spots, but they're the tables with the least space, comparatively speaking.'

'That's a good idea. They won't mind, will they?'

'Scott and Peggy won't,' Rupert ran a hand through his hair, 'and my mother won't care. My father might, though. On the other hand, as he's pretty much decided Jack is a waste of space, and that I'm a disappointment to the family name, he wouldn't be happy even if the food came on solid gold plates served by the Queen.'

'He won't ruin it for Jack, will he?'

'No, he doesn't work like that. He'll save his grievances up to fire at me later on – or possibly hiss them at me under his breath across the table, depending what mood he's in.'

'Jack said he was a bit difficult.'

'Jack was being kind.'

Thomas flexed his tired shoulder muscles as he walked around the kitchen, examining each work station in turn. He didn't think he could possibly make them any cleaner if he tried. Every dish, spoon, knife, fork, herb, spice, and pan was laid out precisely as Jack and Craig had dictated. The dishwasher was empty, the sinks were shining so brightly they could double as mirrors, and the aprons were spotless and folded ready for instant use.

Looking at his watch, he stood back up, and went into the restaurant, where he found Jack, Rupert, and Megan deep in conversation about the order of service for the evening ahead.

'Sorry to interrupt, guys, but I've got everything I can do this early in the day, done.'

Jack smiled. 'Thanks, mate. Why don't you head to Pickwicks, get some food, and take a break for an hour? You're going to need all your energy later.'

'You're not going to start effing and blinding at me like Gordon Ramsay, are you?'

'Maybe not as bad as Mr Ramsay, but I can't promise I won't get a bit hot under the collar as the stress levels rise.'

Thomas grinned. 'Forewarned is forearmed, as Mum always says. I'll go and grab some food. Why don't you guys come? You've been at it non-stop for hours. You need a break or you'll be too exhausted to do well tonight.'

'He's right, Jack,' Megan said. 'If you don't take a rest you won't have enough energy left to shout at us later!'

Without letting Jack open his mouth to protest, she pushed the boys out of the door before following and locking the bistro door behind them.

Four hours later, Megan nodded approvingly at Jack in his smart new chef's whites. Craig looked neat and efficient, and Thomas was freshly aproned and waiting to start the first dash to the fridge for the supplies required. The air in the kitchen was electric with anticipation.

Dressed in her best suit, her stomach awash with nerves, her customer greeting expression firmly in place, Megan said, 'Good luck, Jack.'

'And to you. Everything ready out there?'

'Yes. The girls from the college are excellent, and very confident.'

'Good.' Jack examined his workforce then, his blood racing, said, 'Let's do this!'

Rupert embraced his mother as she got out of the taxi. 'It's so good of you both to come. I hope you found a nice hotel for the night.'

'We did. Just up the road. Even if we hadn't, I wouldn't have missed this for the world.' Angela Ashton studied her son. 'Is Jack alright? Not too nervous, I hope?'

'He's doing wonderfully. I can't tell you how important this evening is to him.'

'I can imagine.'

Rupert turned to his father, who was studying the front of the bistro as if it might explode. 'Shall we go in?'

'This had better be worth the trip. I won't be backwards at giving my opinion if it isn't up to standard.'

Keeping his expression neutral, Rupert said, 'As long as you spread the word widely when you see how good Jack's food is, then I'll settle for that.'

Angela put a restraining arm on her husband's arm, and much to Rupert's amazement said, 'Richard, if you ruin this for Rupert and Jack, I will never forgive you. Now, come on, the smell from the kitchen is incredible. I'm dying to tuck in.'

Jack wasn't sure which part of him was more sore: his feet from the rigours of the day, or his throat from all the talking. The time between plating out the first serving of beef and the last helping of dessert seemed to have been only seconds. And no sooner had he passed Thomas the final serving spoon to put in the dishwasher than came the first of many knocks on the kitchen door.

Everyone wanted to talk to Jack. Each journalist had questions to ask, the local radio critic had booked an appointment for a future interview, and Angela, who hadn't been able to resist coming to see behind the scenes, had given him a hug and ordered him out into the restaurant to meet his satisfied customers.

The moment he'd walked into the bistro, the place had erupted into peals of applause, and Jack had found himself taking a bow, and embraced by a glowing Megan as he thanked everyone for their kindness and support in return.

While Megan went to fetch Thomas and Craig from the kitchen so they could receive the thanks they also deserved, Peggy, Scott, and Rupert smothered Jack in a wave of congratulations that he would never forget. Nor would he forget the relieved look on Peggy's face when Scott whispered to her, 'See, I told you he'd be a good cook.'

Now, all the guests had finally gone, Nick had taken a worn out Megan home, and only Rupert and his parents remained.

Angela was effusive. 'Thank you, Jack. That was outstanding. And that pudding! Rupert said it was something special, and he wasn't kidding. You will be doing that at the party, won't you?'

'You are very kind, and yes, I'll be doing the same dessert on Friday.' Jack, knowing he was taking a risk even asking, turned to Rupert's father, 'I'm so glad you came, sir. Did you enjoy the evening?'

Rupert held his breath, and looked at his father. 'Well, Father, did you like it?'

Mr Ashton dug his hands deep into his suit pockets. 'It was better than I expected. You'll do as a chef, Mr Brown; just make sure you keep hold of that manageress. She was superb. Worth two of you.'

Chapter Forty-three

Wednesday 17th August

Megan had just finished washing down the restaurant tables when the phone rang for the fifth time that morning.

'Good morning, The Olive Branch. How may I help you?'

Pulling the diary towards her, Megan pencilled in another booking for the twenty-seventh of August. *At this rate*, she thought to herself as she recorded the client's phone number, *we'll be fully booked for the whole first week.*

Returning to the tables, which had been moved into a loose circle, so everyone could sit as close together during the naming party meal as the layout of the bistro would allow, Megan flicked the first of the navy table clothes in place. Then she lay out the mats, cutlery, and a napkin at each setting. Unlike for the critics' launch, Megan didn't put the menus on the table. Amy had forbidden Jack to cook more than one choice, as it would be too much work when he was supposed to enjoy the party as well.

Megan was happily putting an extra shine onto the wine glasses, reflecting on how well the critic's meal had gone, when Rupert burst through the front door, brandishing an envelope.

'Blimey, Rupert, you gave me a fright, I almost dropped this glass.'

'Sorry Megan! Is Jack here?'

'He's in the kitchen showing Thomas and Craig what's needed for tomorrow night.' Noting Rupert's excitement, Megan said, 'What is it, what's happened?'

Calling over his shoulder as he disappeared into the kitchen, Rupert said, 'Something that's going to make our website look even better!'

Before Megan could find out what he meant, Rupert came back into the dining area with Jack in hot pursuit.

'Tell me!' Jack was staring at the envelope. 'What is it?'

'I did it.'

'Did what?' Megan and Jack spoke in unison.

'My photo has reached the final of the competition. You know; the one you picked, Jack. The bumblebee collecting nectar.'

Jack, tea towel in his hands, hugged his boyfriend. 'That's fantastic! I'm so proud of you.'

Taking her turn to congratulate Rupert, Megan said, 'I can see why you said it was good news for the website! Putting *National Photography Competition Finalist* on the home page isn't going to do us any harm.'

Sitting on the sofa in reception, Rupert passed the letter to Jack.

As Jack read, Rupert explained to Megan, 'I assumed I was out of the running because I hadn't received an email from them, but it seems they do things the old-fashioned way – which I love, because it means I can keep this letter for ever.'

'We should frame it!'

Rupert laughed. 'And hang it in the bathroom?'

'No! In the restaurant reception.'

'I was joking. The winner is announced at a ceremony at the Randolph Hotel in Oxford in a month. Will you come with me?'

'I certainly will.'

Megan was thrilled for Rupert, but felt she had to ask. 'Is it an evening do, Rupert? If it is, and I'm sorry to be a wet blanket here, but unless it's a Monday night when we're closed, Jack is going to have to be here cooking.'

Rupert suddenly felt deflated. 'Ah, of course. I was so excited, I hadn't stopped to think. It's on a Friday night.'

'Oh hell,' Jack looked disappointed, 'I'm so sorry, Megan's right. I won't be able to leave the restaurant, not so soon after we've launched. Damn it.'

'It's alright. I'd have loved you to have come, obviously, but I understand. I could ask my mother.' Once Rupert had had the

286

idea, he began to smile. 'Actually, that could be a lot of fun! Now she and I are back in regular contact, it would be great to spend more than just the occasional hour together.'

'You could stay over at the Randolph. Why don't you give her a quick call?'

'You sure you don't mind, Jack?'

'Of course I don't. Angela will be as proud of you as I am.' The chef beamed. 'We'll have something else to celebrate tomorrow!'

'Thanks.' Rupert couldn't stop smiling. 'Although, let's keep it between ourselves for a minute. We'll celebrate with the others if I actually win. I don't really like being the centre of attention, let's leave that role to Poppy.'

Peggy and her companion stopped next to Kit's table. 'And the writer sat here is Kit. Kit is something of a permanent fixture at Pickwicks, and once you get to know her I'm sure she'll tell you all about her colourful past.'

Kit looked up from her work and stuck her tongue out at Peggy, before smiling at the young woman next to her. 'You must be Teresa. I'm pleased to meet you. How are you finding Pickwicks?'

The young woman had a nervous smile. 'There's lots to remember, but I'm enjoying it so far.'

'Has the coffee machine fought back at you yet?'

Peggy tutted. 'Take no notice. Kit here is bitter because I told her she doesn't make good coffee! You'll be fine.'

Before Kit could respond, Peggy and Teresa disappeared to serve some new guests. Watching the new waitress, Kit was reminded of both Amy and Megan when they first started working at Pickwicks. Keen and happy, but not quite confident enough to take the lead from Peggy just yet, Kit had a feeling that Teresa, who she judged must be fresh out of university, would fit in perfectly.

It already felt strange without Megan around. Kit sighed quietly into her cup of coffee. It would be stranger still when Helena was gone too. The regulars had taken a shine to her, even though she hadn't been there long, and though she hadn't really wanted Helena working there in the first place, she was still going to miss having her daughter around at work as well as home.

Kit looked at the clock in the corner of her computer screen. It was four o'clock in the afternoon. In less than twenty-four hours her children would know if they were going to their chosen universities, or if they were facing the university sorting system in the hunt for an emergency plan if their grades weren't good enough for their first choices.

The mere idea of them not getting what they'd set their hearts on sent butterflies whizzing around Kit's stomach. Knowing all she could do was offer tea and sympathy if things didn't go to plan made her feel rather useless, and yet Kit knew there was nothing she could do. Her children weren't children anymore. This letting go lark, even though she'd come to terms with the fact it had to happen, wasn't getting any easier.

Maybe after tomorrow ... maybe once I know for sure they've got the results they need and that they're really going...

Amy hung up the telephone. She'd spent the past ten minutes assuring her mum that they wouldn't let the naming ceremony at tomorrow's party start without her or her dad, should they get stuck in the summer holiday traffic on the way into London.

Looking at the tiny white outfit laid out on her bed, Amy felt a pang of emotion. She stroked the soft cotton, and smiled. Despite all the sleepless nights, the constant demands on her to feed, wash, change, and cuddle her child; there were still times when she couldn't quite get over the fact that she was mother to such a gorgeous little girl.

Poppy was out with Paul and his overjoyed parents, who'd arrived the night before to see their grandchild for the first time. Although they'd invited her to go with them, Amy had taken the chance to grab some peace and quiet, and get ready for the party. She knew this might be the only chance she'd get to sort out what she and Paul would wear, before all her focus returned to Poppy.

Taking a summer dress out of the wardrobe, which Paul had bought her last year and which Amy was delighted to be able to get back into so soon after pregnancy, she hung it on the outside of the door, alongside a smart pair of summer trousers and shirt for Paul. Then, sitting back on the bed, telling herself she simply didn't have time to fall asleep, she phoned Jack.

'How goes the chaos? Anything I can do this end?'

'Amy! Thanks for calling. I was going to give you a shout later.'

'I can call back if this is a bad time? I just had a rare moment to myself.'

'You've not sent Poppy out to work already, have you?'

Amy chuckled into her mobile. 'Not yet! I thought I'd wait until she was at least on solids before I got Peggy to give her a weekend job at Pickwicks.'

Jack laughed. 'I wouldn't mind betting she ends up working there eventually!'

'You're probably right! Paul and his parents have gone for a walk with Poppy in the hope she'll have a nap.'

'Well, we're on schedule here. Megan has played a blinder getting the restaurant ready, as much food prep as I can do beforehand has been done, Rupert has got in extra champagne and wine, Scott is making a cake the size of Manhattan, and Thomas is up to speed with the dishwasher.'

'Sounds great. Are you sure I can't bring anything?'

'Just yourself, your husband, assorted parents, and my goddaughter.'

'Thanks, Jack, you're the best. Twenty years ago I would never have believed you'd be doing this for me.'

'Twenty years ago I was a total git.' Jack gave a self-deprecating laugh. 'Now for goodness' sake, stop talking to me and take the chance to have a nap. I'll see you at one o'clock tomorrow afternoon for the best meal of your life!'

Putting down the phone, Amy closed her eyes. 'I won't sleep, I'll have a quick relax for a few minutes, and then I'll go and start cooking tonight's meal.'

Two hours later, she was quietly rocked awake by an apologetic Paul, who had a large glass of orange juice for her in one hand and a hungry baby in the other.

Chapter Forty-four

Thursday 18th August

Amy rubbed her eyes and looked at the bedside clock. She groaned. It was only three o'clock in the morning. 'Oh, Poppy! You can't possibly be hungry again.'

Hauling herself out of bed for the third time that night, she picked up her crying child. 'Alright, alright.' As she headed to the bedroom door, she was vaguely aware that Paul was mumbling in his half-woken state, asking if she was OK.

Knowing he'd go back to sleep quicker if she left him alone, Amy vowed that, assuming she wasn't so tired that she slept through the whole thing, that afternoon's naming ceremony would be the perfect time to introduce Poppy to a bottle. 'Bottles your Daddy can hold!'

As soon as she'd settled herself into an armchair, and Poppy was feeding as though it had been days rather than only two hours since she'd last feasted, Amy felt bad. It wasn't Paul's fault he couldn't feed his daughter. He'd been amazing during his paternity leave. Everything he could do, he did – bath time had quickly become 'Daddy time', and during daylight hours Paul had changed far more nappies than she had.

Resting her head against the chair back, Amy tried not to worry about how she was going to cope when he went back to work. Stroking Poppy's hair softly, she murmured, 'Now you will go back to sleep for me properly after this, won't you, sweetheart, or Mummy is going to be a ratty monster for your party this afternoon.'

Four hours later Paul scooped his daughter off his wife's lap before covering a sleeping Amy with a blanket. Then, taking a wide-awake Poppy upstairs to be fussed over by his parents, he crept into the kitchen to put the kettle on.

His attempts not too make too much noise as he put tea and coffee into their respective mugs, fell flat as Amy, hugging the blanket around her shoulders, came to join him.

'I was trying not to wake you.'

'I know, it's OK,' Amy picked up the nearest mug of coffee and cradled it in her palms. 'Thanks for the blanket. Is Poppy alright?'

'She's busy being doted on by Mum and Dad upstairs. I assume asking if you had a bad night would be a silly question?'

'It wasn't so much fractured as splintered. I was up three times. I meant to come back to bed, but clearly my body had other ideas.'

'I'm not surprised.' Paul pulled Amy into his side for a cuddle. 'I'm sorry, love. I'd get up for you if I could.'

'I know. Poppy is very much making up for the fact she was born early and needs to put a bit of weight on.' Amy kissed her husband lightly. 'I was wondering if we should try her with a bottle for the first time this afternoon, otherwise I have a horrible feeling that Poppy's unerring sense of timing will mean I'll miss the whole thing while I'm feeding her.'

'That's a great idea. I'm quite keen to feed her, actually, and I know my mum is dying to.'

Amy laughed. 'So is mine, actually. They'll be ready to grab a bottle and pounce on Poppy the minute she's hungry. It'll be a race to her mouth!'

Paul, who was already getting the brand new bottles and breast pump out of the cupboard so he could sterilise them before Amy used them, said, 'You're probably right. Although I wouldn't mind betting that Jack is first in the queue to feed Poppy when the time actually comes!'

Megan felt unusually content as she turned over and lay against her boyfriend's sleeping side. Being able to stay in bed past seven o'clock in the morning was a luxury she was already appreciating, and was proving to be the best perk about her new job.

The news that she and Nick had been waiting for had come through yesterday afternoon. They had been accepted as the tenants of the small terraced house, positioned almost exactly midway between their two places of work. In only one month's time they would finally have a place to live together.

The bottle of wine they'd drunk to celebrate was making Megan's dehydrated throat cry out for water, and her need for hydration was fighting the rest of her body's need to remain under the cosy duvet. Sensing her restlessness, Nick turned over and kissed the end of her nose.

'Cup of tea, babe?'

Megan beamed. 'Oh yes, please. You'd better be careful, or I'll be expecting a cuppa in bed every morning when we're tucked up in our own home.'

'Well, if you are a very good girl, you might just get one.'

Phil and Rob looked up as Rupert, fresh from his morning session teaching at Kew Gardens, came through the shop door. It wasn't lost on the two friends that their assistant had a great deal more bounce in his step these days, not to mention more confidence.

Rob took the box of pamphlets Rupert had brought with him from Kew. 'Lesson go well this morning?'

'Yes. Just a small class, but very enthusiastic. All good here?'

'Quiet.' Phil passed Rupert a cup of coffee. 'Which is for the best, perhaps, as I'm on edge waiting for Kit to call me.'

'What for?'

'Twins get their exams results this morning. Honestly, the atmosphere at breakfast could be cut with a knife.'

'What with that and the party tonight, Phil and I were discussing the benefits of closing early,' Rob added. 'It would be great not to have to rush before we head to Jack's place. Is he ready for tonight? I know he's had the critics' launch, but *this* is the big one!'

Rupert laughed. 'Bigger than all the restaurant critics coming?'

'Absolutely! It's much easier to impress strangers than it is to please friends. Especially Kit and Amy.'

'Come off it, Rob, Kit and Amy are the easiest-going women I've ever met.'

Phil laughed this time. 'Well, far be it for me to cast aspersions on my lovely wife, but when it comes to Jack, she'll always tell him the truth. Especially now she has her oomph back! So if it isn't up to scratch, she'll be letting him know.'

Rob nodded. 'Amy's the same. They care for him too much to fob him off with pleasantries if the place isn't going to cut it.'

Rupert took the weight off his feet. 'And I thought the critics were a tough gig!'

Phil winked. 'We're only joking! It'll go brilliantly. The girls already know he's a fab cook. Peggy and Megan have been full of how wonderful the meal was at the launch. Kit's hardly shut up about it, and I think Amy has more to worry about than if Jack's signature dessert is up to it. What is this secret pudding of his anyway?'

'Sworn to secrecy, I'm afraid,' Rupert grinned. 'I promise it'll be worth waiting for. Jack is one of hell of a chef.'

'Oh go on!' Rob fluttered his eyelashes at Rupert. 'Pretty please? I won't tell him you told us, promise.'

'Yeah, right!' Rupert shook his head, but his smile stayed in place as his phone rang. 'Oh excuse me, that's my mother.'

Disappearing in to the back room to take the call, Rupert could hear Phil's phone burst into life behind him, leaving Rob to help the customer who'd chosen that precise moment to walk through the door.

Phil's insides did a backflip as he listened to what his wife was saying down the line. 'I'm on my way, love. Hang on.'

Rob glanced up from the till. 'Everything OK?'

'I'm not sure. Kit says she needs me at home now. She sounded upset and wasn't making a lot of sense. Must be one of the kids not getting their grades. I'm sorry, mate, I have to go.'

'Sure, go, go…'

Rob had no sooner ushered Phil out of the door towards his wife and children, than Rupert came out of the storeroom looking as if he'd had a nasty shock too.

'Not you as well?'

'What?' Rupert frowned.

'Well, Phil's dashed off. Some crisis with the twins' exam results. God, I hope neither of them has failed!'

'Failed what?'

'Their A levels, of course – you know, like we were talking about a few seconds ago?' Rob examined his assistant more carefully. 'You look like you've seen a ghost. What's happened?'

Rupert glanced around the shop, which was empty again, 'Could you man the shop on your own for a while, Rob? I'm really sorry, but I have to go.'

'It's not Jack, is it? The party is still on?'

'What? Oh, yes, the party's on, but I'm not sure I'll be there.'

'Why not?'

'Because I've got to see my mother. She's just walked out on my father!'

Rupert tried to remain rational. There was no way he was going to have time to catch the train to Cambridge, find his mother, sort things out, and get back in time for the party and to see Jack be officially named as one of Poppy's godparents.

He tried to call Jack again, but his mobile was never on in the kitchen. It was too early for Megan to be in the restaurant, so although he'd tried the landline number, Rupert wasn't surprised when no one picked the call up.

It was all his fault. If he hadn't turned up at his parents' home with Jack, he was sure, this wouldn't have happened. He should have kept things as they were. That way, although he would still have been on his own, his mother and father would be together. Rupert's heart constricted. Would the price of reuniting his parents be giving Jack up? *Could I do that?* He felt sick at the mere idea. *And what about Mother? Am I being cruel wanting her to stay with such an antiquated man just because I don't want divorced parents?*

As he arrived at the station, Rupert made a beeline for the departure boards. He was checking the time of the next train from Marylebone to Cambridge when his phone rang. He

295

couldn't decide if he was pleased or disappointed it wasn't Jack when he realised it was his mother's number flashing on the screen.

'Mum? Are you alright? I'm on my way.'

Angela Ashton spoke softly so she didn't make her son jump. 'So I see.'

Rupert spun around to see his mother, talking to him through the phone, but also standing only a few feet away. His confusion was overtaken by relief that she was, physically at least, fine.

'What's going on? Are you OK?'

'Better than I've been for years, Rupert. But are you?' Angela frowned as she scrutinised her son's panicked expression. 'You called me Mum. You never call me Mum. Although I think I prefer it. Mother is a bit stuffy, don't you think?'

Rupert opened his mouth, but it was a few seconds before he could find the words. 'Well … yes, I always though Mum and Dad would be nicer than Mother and Father, but Father wouldn't wear it, and it sort of stuck.'

'And yet you called me Mum just now.'

'Feels more right now, somehow. Not sure why.'

Rupert looked at his mother properly for the first time in years. More relaxed than he'd ever seen her, her hair was shiny, and her expression, which was usually one of indecision as to whether she should look pleased or not, was serene. Her eyes looked clear and bright. Her shoulders were back, her hunched, tense air gone. She looked stunning in her summer dress and sandals.

Rupert glanced at the small suitcase on wheels by her feet. 'You really have left him, haven't you?'

'Long overdue.' Sensing what her son was going to say next, Angela held her hand up to stop him. 'And no, it is not your fault. It isn't Jack's fault either. It's my fault.'

'What do you mean?'

'Come on, we need a cup of coffee. I'll tell you all about it.'

Allowing her to steer him towards the nearest café, Rupert sat deep in thought, before texting Jack to apologise for not being there to help prepare for the party, as his mum returned with the drinks.

'The short version is that when we got back to the hotel after the launch, your father had one too many whiskeys, and his opinions about gay people rather clashed with my own. Simply put, I've had enough of his bigotry and stuck-in-the-past attitude. And I've had enough of being squashed. That's how it's felt, Rupert; that I've been squashed for years. I want to paint again, to explore the world a bit, to work in a stately home garden, to do something other than being the businessman's wife.'

'Did you say all that to Father?'

Angela pulled a face. 'You can imagine his response.'

Rupert shook his head sadly, 'I'm sorry, Mum. I know you've done the right thing, but I'm still sorry.'

Taking her son's hand, Angela said, 'I do love him, Rupert, but I'm tired of being taken for granted. I haven't quite given up hope of opening his eyes to the twentieth century. We'll see if he realises what he's lost before I get too into being footloose and fancy-free, shall we?'

Rupert couldn't help but smile. 'You think he'll fight to get you back?'

'I hope so, but if he doesn't then it's his loss.'

'You're remarkable!' Rupert stood up. 'Come on, Mum, if we get a move on, we can get back to the bistro in time for the start of the party. You can drop your stuff at my place on the way, there's plenty of room. I'm basically living at Jack's now, so Megan's using it as her temporary studio.'

'Thanks, Rupert.'

His mum was smothering him in a cuddle when Rupert said, 'Hang on, did you say it was time to drag Father into the twentieth century? Surely you mean the twenty-first?'

'One step at a time!' Angela laughed. 'Now, enough of your father. I want to hear all about this photography competition. I am so proud of you!'

Chapter Forty-five

Thursday 18th August

Sweat ran down the back of Phil's shirt. By the time he finally pushed open the front door after sprinting from the Tube to his home, he was a mass of anxiety – not to mention absolutely roasting.

During the journey, he had gone from imagining Kit with a miserable and disappointed twin by her side, who was having to go through the clearing process to get a place on a different course, to thinking they'd both failed everything and their mum didn't know who to comfort first. It had been like that when the twins were babies. One pair of hands hadn't been enough when they'd been hungry, tired, or needed their nappies changing at exactly the same time.

Kit was on the sofa, box of tissues in hand, eyes streaming, a carbon copy of how he'd found her sitting only a few weeks before.

'What is it, love? What's wrong? Where are the kids?'

'Out. Celebrating.'

Phil frowned. 'Celebrating? Then why…?'

'They got the grades. They're going, Phil. They're really going. They arrived together, and now they're going together, all at once.'

Phil felt torn between finding the twins to tell them how incredibly proud he was of them, yelling at Kit for making him panic, and biting his tongue while he held his wife tightly. She clearly hadn't got as far past the empty nest syndrome as she'd made out. Trying not to make it obvious that he was looking at his watch to see how long they had before getting ready for the party, he crouched before her.

'Come on, love, wipe your eyes. We should be thrilled for the kids. They've worked so hard for this.'

'I know.' Kit sniffed, 'I feel like the biggest cow for crying. I am so proud of them. And I'm excited for them, really I am. But it means they're going to leave home next month, doesn't it?'

Pushing Kit's fringe from her teary eyes, Phil spoke softly. 'It means they are going to have an incredible adventure. To make their own mistakes, have their own successes, and stand on their own two feet. You wouldn't begrudge them that, would you?'

'Of course not. I want them to go; I want them to have everything they want. It's just…'

'Come on, love, we've been through all this. You are allowed to miss them, you know!'

'I know. I'm sorry.' Kit leaned forward and hugged her endlessly understanding husband, 'What would I do without you?'

'I dread to think.' He winked at her. 'Now, I want to see the twins. Where are they? What grades did they get exactly?'

'I promised I wouldn't say. They want to tell you themselves.' Taking a long ragged breath, Kit cleared her eyes with a decisive wipe, 'They're grabbing a drink with their mates in the pub on the corner before heading to Jack's.'

'Well, come on then, we'll join them.'

'They won't want us cramping their style!'

Phil shook his head. 'First you don't want them to go, then you don't want to go and see them. What are you like, woman?'

'Oh, you know what I mean!'

'Yes I do, but on this occasion the kids will have to put up with it!' Phil spoke decisively. 'Go and lose all trace of those tears. We'll nip to the pub so I can find out what they got, and then we'll come home and get ready. We can't be too long or we'll be late for Poppy's do.'

Taking her kindly mother-in-law's advice, Amy applied an extra layer of foundation to the dark circles under her eyes. She didn't think she'd ever felt so exhausted in her life. Although

300

she had tried to get back to sleep after breakfast, she hadn't been able to switch off. Now, as she peered down at Poppy, who smiled up from her crib, Amy mentally crossed her fingers that her daughter wouldn't get her cream dress grubby before the naming ceremony, and that she might manage not to be hungry again until after the meal.

Amy had been so looking forward to today; to seeing all her friends and showing off her daughter, but now the time to get ready had arrived, she wasn't sure she even had the energy to stand up.

As her gaze landed on the dress hanging on her wardrobe door, Amy couldn't help but remember the last party when they'd all been together. Before she was married; before Jack had run away. She hadn't been sure she wanted to go to that party either, although for very different reasons.

A gurgle from the crib made Amy smile through her fatigue. 'Alright, Pop, I hear you. You're ready to party with Uncle Jack and Auntie Kit. Tell you what: I'll do you a deal. You let me have a rest, and enjoy the afternoon, and then I'll take you to the soft play area in the park the very second you are old enough to go!'

Thomas and Helena, flushed from their recent successes, were getting their respective instructions from Jack and Megan. Teresa was looking nervous but happy as Peggy helped her get to grips with Jack's coffee machine, Scott was putting out cups and saucers, and Craig was bustling around The Olive Branch's kitchen, making sure every plate was laid out ready to be filled with the food he and Jack had been preparing since eleven that morning.

Everything was ready.

Jack looked at the clock on the wall. It was half past twelve. 'Where the hell is Rupert?'

Megan shrugged. 'Amy isn't here yet either, but then babies always have last minute feeds, nappy changes and stuff. I assumed Rupert, Kit, and Phil would be here early though.'

'Rupert has sent a few texts, so I know he and Angela are on their way.'

'Not his father?' Megan straightened a tablemat that didn't need straightening.

'If the garbled message he left on my voicemail is anything to go by, then Angela has walked out on him.'

'Seriously? Oh my goodness.'

Jack frowned. 'I have a horrible feeling it might be my fault.'

'How on earth can it be your fault?'

Megan didn't have time to hear Jack's reply, for the first of many knocks on the bistro door came as Nick, closely followed by Lauren and Chris from Home Hunters and Rob, Debbie, and their three girls, arrived.

No sooner had they been provided with drinks when Phil and a rather pink Kit arrived. Megan raised her eyebrows playfully. 'You wouldn't be a touch worse for drink, would you, Mrs Lambert?'

'As if!' Kit grinned. 'We might have had a drink or two to congratulate the twins.'

Megan's hand flew to her mouth. 'Their exams. I forgot to ask them. I'm so sorry.'

Phil looked surprised. 'Didn't they tell you?'

'Not a word, although to be honest, as soon as they crossed the threshold they were press-ganged into work. There hasn't been time for talking. How did they do?'

'Brilliantly!' Kit hiccupped. 'Oh dear, I think I'd better start with a very strong coffee!'

'Teresa is manning the coffee machine,' Megan laughed, communicating to Peggy and her new waitress that the need for caffeine in her vicinity was suddenly urgent. 'So, how did they do?'

Kit opened her mouth to share the news, but Phil butted in. 'We should let the twins tell everyone after the meal.'

Nodding profusely, Kit thanked Teresa for the coffee, before asking Megan where Amy was.

'Not here yet, nor is Rupert or …' Megan turned as the door opened, 'I stand corrected. Here they are.'

Amy, and Paul with baby Poppy in his arms, came in together with both sets of parents, laden with changing bags and

302

a crib, closely followed by Rupert and Angela. Covertly beckoning to Megan while Jack wasn't looking, Rupert passed her a bag that he'd been hiding behind his back.

Peering inside the carrier bag, Megan asked, 'Are these what I think they are?'

Rupert put a finger to his lips. 'They are. Not a word, OK?'

Megan's heart rate increased as she slipped the carrier bag behind the bar. Then, picking up the nearest bottle of champagne and hoping that she could open it without spilling too much, she popped the first cork of the evening.

Chapter Forty-six

Thursday 18th August

Scott, resplendent in a dashing suit and bow tie, stood with Amy, Paul, and baby Poppy.

'We are here to welcome the beautiful Poppy Rose Donahue into the caring arms of her family, her godparents, and her friends.'

Happiness swelled in Amy's chest, her exhaustion forgotten as they she listened to Scott welcome her child to the world.

'Poppy, daughter of Amy and Paul, has already endeared herself to us all. On this day of many celebrations, we formally introduce Poppy to her appointed honorary godparents, those adults who she will be able to turn to for help through the course of her life. Please come forward, Kit, Phil, Debbie, Rob, and Jack.'

His face shining with joy, Rupert watched as Jack took his place next to Debbie. He knew his boyfriend had never thought this day would come; that there had been a time when the idea Jack and Amy could even be friends had been laughable.

Rupert caught his mother's eye. She looked free somehow, and yet as he observed her watching Kit take Poppy from Paul, and promise before them all to care for her for ever, Rupert knew his mother was quietly coming to terms with the huge changes that were suddenly entering her own life.

Kit passed an obliging Poppy to Phil, who repeated the same promise his wife had just made. Then, at last, it was Jack's turn. Scott inclined his head to his new business partner. 'And finally, Jack, do you also willingly take on the responsibility of caring for Poppy whenever she needs you, to help guide her along the mixed pathways of life?'

Holding his newest goddaughter close, Jack was in danger of being overcome with emotion. Here he was in his new business, being watched by a man he knew he'd fallen in love with, surrounded by his best friends, and cradling a tiny version of Amy, who was staring up at him with wide, unblinking blue eyes that he was sure weren't ever going to miss a thing. Jack's mutter of, 'Oh, yes,' was almost lost as his voice choked up, while a miniature hand gripped his thumb as though it was never going to let go.

Scott was still talking, wrapping up the simple ceremony, but Jack didn't hear him. He was too busy struggling with the rapid realisation that, after years of messing up, years of travelling and trying to find himself, what he'd been searching for had been here all along. He had a real chance of happiness. And this time, he was determined he wasn't going to cock it up.

Sending up a silent prayer of thanks that her daughter had neither cried over, nor been sick down, the front of any of her godparents, Amy settled a sleeping Poppy into the crib which Paul had installed in Jack's bedroom, switched on the baby monitor, and returned to her friends.

Sinking onto a chair with Paul on one side and Jack on the other, Amy let out a sigh of relief just as Helena and Teresa came out of the kitchen, their arms carefully balancing dinner plates.

Once the food was served, and the waiting staff had joined them at the table, Paul got to his feet, and holding up his glass of champagne, said, 'Ladies and gentlemen, I'd like you to join me in a toast to Jack, Debbie, Rob, Kit, and Phil for agreeing to be there for Poppy – and to Scott for being such a gifted non-vicar!'

The brief round of applause was halted by Jack, who got to his feet, tapping a spoon against his glass to capture everyone's attention. 'Don't worry, I'm not about to give a load of speeches. I just wanted to quickly thank you all for your support in getting The Olive Branch off the ground. Especially to Peggy, Scott, and Megan. Now, enough of that – let's eat!'

As appreciative noises about the food, the restaurant, and

general chatter filled the bistro, Jack sat back in his seat and allowed himself a moment of calm. He thought the launch had gone well, but only when the papers and magazines reported their opinions would he know if he was destined to be just another chef, or one who could try for a Michelin star; an ambition he hadn't even shared with Rupert yet.

Yet, as he watched his friends, who'd already demolished the starters and were now polishing off the main course with a fervour that told him, for them at least, his culinary skills were not in question, Jack knew that running a standard family restaurant wouldn't be the end of the world.

As Helena got up to collect the empty plates, and Thomas did the rounds with refilling glasses with more champagne, Jack got back to his feet. 'As you are well aware, today's party is to celebrate the birth of Poppy Rose, but it is also a good excuse for a long overdue get together, and to congratulate a few other people.'

Megan, knowing this was her cue, got up and with a nod to Nick, who silently dashed upstairs, cleared her throat and said, 'I would like you all to join me in wishing my dear friend and co-boss, Peggy, a very happy fifty-fifth birthday for two days' time.'

Reappearing, Nick passed a carefully wrapped gift to a laughing Peggy.

'Should I save this until the day before I open it?'

The cries of 'Open it now!' echoed so loudly around the table that Amy glanced anxiously at the baby monitor, half expecting Poppy to wake up.

As Peggy ripped open the paper with the enthusiasm of someone a tenth her age, Megan said, 'This is from Scott, not me.'

Lifting the canvas up, Peggy was speechless as she saw an image of herself and Scott looking straight back at her; forever smiling in pencil and pastel.

'Do you like it?' Megan asked nervously. Peggy's unaccustomed silence was unnerving her.

'Oh, yes!' Peggy turned the picture around so all her friends could see it. 'I love it! Scott, did you really commission this?'

307

'I did. Megan has done an exceptional job.'

'I absolutely love it.' Peggy didn't know who to hug first, her husband or her friend, so she put the picture down and grabbed them both at once, while Jack, mindful of the fact that Craig would be in the kitchen plating up the desserts, pulled the gathering back to order.

'We have one more announcement before pudding!' Jack gestured to Thomas and Helena, who both blushed as they got to their feet.

Helena, who even smiled at Rupert, as she stood with her twin brother, said, 'Today we got our A level results. Thomas and I have got into the universities we wanted! I'm off to Bath, and Thomas is going to Exeter, heaven help them!'

Digging his sister playfully in the ribs, Thomas shouted, over the 'Well dones' of the adults, 'I got two As and a B, while my clever clogs sister here got three As!'

Jack joined in the applause, and was about to say something else, when Rupert called out, 'Oh, forget all the speeches, Jack, we want to try your dessert!'

To calls of 'Too right,' and 'Pudding, pudding, pudding!' Thomas, Helena, and Teresa dashed into the kitchen to collect Jack's special final course.

'Time to put us out of our misery, Jack,' Rob called across the table, 'what is this dessert you've been keeping secret?'

Peggy laughed. 'It's a bit special! I've been looking forward to having it again since I had my last mouthful at the critics' launch.'

Jack smiled. 'OK, OK, you've been patient for long enough. I hope you all like it! If you don't, please say and I'll dig you out some of my homemade apple pie and custard instead.'

'Oh for heaven's sake, Jack,' Phil shook his head, 'what is it?'

But Jack didn't have to answer, for Teresa and the twins were back, their arms full of plates of dark chocolate chilli mousse with luscious homemade vanilla ice cream.

As the cries of 'delicious' and 'that was unbelievable' died away, and the last pudding dish was cleared from the table, Phil, Rob, and Nick pushed the tables to the side of the restaurant. Rupert turned up the music that had been faintly playing in the background, picked up the closest bottle of champagne and began to top up any empty glasses.

Paul, who had been up to check on Poppy, returned to the party with his daughter in his arms, clearly ready for her next meal.

Amy automatically sat down, and put her arms out to take her daughter, when Paul said, 'Why don't I have a try?'

'Oh, yes!' Amy smiled, 'Jack, could we have a jug of water to warm a bottle?'

'Bottle? Yes! Oh, can I feed her?'

Paul laughed, 'I knew you'd say that, and you can later, but if you don't mind, I'd like to do this one. It's her very first bottle after all.'

'Of course.' Jack got up to fetch the hot water, before remembering something his sister had once told him, 'Amy, I know you'll want to see if Poppy will take your milk from a bottle, but if you're nearby she may not do it.'

Amy frowned. 'How do you mean?'

'Susan told me that her two would only take bottles if they couldn't see her, as they preferred milk direct from source – if you see what I mean!'

Amy's mum, who had also spotted the bottle being taken from the bag, agreed. 'Jack is quite right, sweetheart. Poppy will sense your milk, and chances are you'll leak like hell while she's drinking the bottle if you're too near.'

'Ugh, really?'

'I'm afraid so.'

Partly reluctant, partly relieved that she could sit down in peace, Amy and Jack went to join Kit and her family over the other side of the restaurant just as Megan passed the freshly warmed bottle of milk to Paul.

'I hope she takes it.' Amy welcomed the large coffee Rupert presented to her.

Jack smiled, 'I'm she will. Now why don't you have some of these with your coffee?'

'You remembered!'Amy laughed as he magically produced a packet of chocolate digestives. 'Not quite chocolate biscuits and champagne, but close!'

'Coffee, champagne, same thing to you, isn't it!' Jack winked. 'Hmmm, I wonder if Poppy would rather have a drop of coffee than milk? She is your daughter after all!'

Amy stuck her tongue out playfully. 'She may turn out to be a tea drinker like her father!'

Jack laughed. 'Can't see it myself.'

Helena shook her head. 'Did we take coffee from the bottle then, Mum? You drink even more of the stuff than Amy does.'

Thomas screwed up his nose, 'I bet you did. That'll be why I can't stand the stuff.'

Kit shook her head. 'I never did understand you, Thomas!'

'You'll be glad to be shot of the pair of us.'

Kit held her hands out to her children. 'I'm going to miss you like you wouldn't believe.'

'Even all the washing?'

'Even that.'

'Cool!' Thomas and Helena exchanged a high five. 'We were chatting about that. We reckon it'll be easier for us to save all the dirty washing and bring it home once a month for you. Cheaper than the laundrette.'

Kit rolled her eyes at her children as Rupert joined them, and they watched Paul feed a happy Poppy.

Rupert slipped his hand into Jack's. 'I want one.' He kept his gaze fixed straight ahead of him. 'How about you?'

Jack's eyes widened as he saw the direction of his boyfriend's line of sight lay on Poppy. A smile hit every part of his face, warming his heart as he saw the tiny mutual nods of approval from Kit and Amy as he softly asked Rupert, 'You want to try and adopt one day?'

'I'd love to.'

'But that means we'd have to get married and stuff?'

'Yes.' Rupert turned to face Jack. 'What do you think about that idea? One day, I mean.'

Jack opened his mouth to reply, but as he was about to speak, Paul arrived with a full-bellied Poppy, and deposited her in Jack's open arms. 'I don't suppose you fancy taking on some godfather duties and having a go at burping her while I get a drink?'

Holding Poppy close, rubbing her back soothingly, Jack whispered, 'Yes, Rupert. Yes, I think that's a very good idea.'

Epilogue

Jack hadn't said much for the rest of the evening; instead he'd quietly observed his friends enjoying themselves while his mind raced, desperate for the moment when he could talk to Rupert alone.

Now, the party over, sat on the edge of the bed, his heart hammered in his chest as he watched Rupert change out of his suit into old clothes so he could help tidy up. Almost too scared to ask what he desperately needed to know, Jack said, 'Did you mean it? What you said downstairs about adopting and stuff?'

Pulling a polo shirt over his head, Rupert smiled. 'All of it.'

Exhaling a rush of tension, Jack was about to declare his happiness when Rupert put a finger to his boyfriend's lips and fished a carrier bag from under the bed.

Taking out the two newspapers that had been hidden inside, Rupert threw them on the bed. Jack frowned at them for a split second before he realised what he was looking at. 'Is it in both of them?'

Rupert's eyes shone. 'Read them.'

Jack found his hands were shaking, 'Should I have a strong coffee first? Have you read them already?'

'Megan had them hidden behind the bar for me, so I skimmed them while I was fetching the champagne earlier.' Sitting next to Jack, Rupert turned each paper to their dedicated Food and Drink pages for him. 'Just read them. Then I'll get us some coffee.'

Jack's pulse suddenly thumped very loud in his ears as he picked up the *Metro*.

Not quite sure he could trust what he was reading as he digested each word of the lead article, he glanced at Rupert, whose grin widened. Passing Jack the local paper, he said, 'Keep reading. The *Metro* review is great, but this one is even better.'

Jack scanned the proffered page. 'This is staggering! *"Despite this being the opening evening at Richmond's brand new eatery, The Olive Branch – a friendly bistro on the High Street – is already running like a well-oiled machine. Courteous service, an excellent choice of food and wine, and a pleasant ambience paved the way to an evening of beautifully presented flavoursome food..."*'

'The word is spreading. Can you imagine how great the later reviews will be if the early ones are this good?' Rupert kissed his stunned boyfriend's cheek. 'I don't think I've ever seen you gobsmacked before. Surely you knew you'd done well at the opening? Even my father liked the food, although I doubt he'll ever admit it.'

Jack raised his eyebrows. 'You don't say! All that we need now is for you to win that photography competition, and all our dreams will have come true!'

'We'll have to wait and see about that, won't we,' Rupert laughed. 'Although getting to the final is more than I could have hoped for. I'm sure there must be other dreams we could make come true first!'

'Like me getting to see you wearing a pair of jeans?' Jack winked.

Shaking his head, Rupert smiled as he walked to the bedroom door. 'Not a chance! So, future husband of mine, do I fetch us a cup of The Olive Branch's finest coffee to celebrate with, or is it time for another glass of champagne?'

The End

For more information about **Jenny Kane**

and other **Accent Press** titles

please visit

www.accentpress.co.uk

Jenny Kane

Abi's House

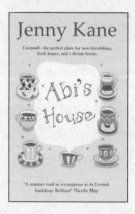

Newly widowed at barely thirty, Abi Carter is desperate to escape the Stepford Wives lifestyle that Luke, her late husband, had been so keen for her to live.

Abi decides to fulfil a lifelong dream. As a child on holiday in a Cornwall she fell in love with a cottage – the prophetically named Abbey's House. Now she is going to see if she can find the place again, relive the happy memories … maybe even buy a place of her own nearby?

On impulse Abi sets off to Cornwall, where a chance meeting in a village pub brings new friends Beth and Max into her life. Beth, like Abi, has a life-changing decision to make. Max, Beth's best mate, soon helps Abi track down the house of her dreams … but things aren't quite that simple. There's the complicated life Abi left behind, including her late husband's brother, Simon – a man with more than friendship on his mind …

Will Abi's house remain a dream, or will the bricks and mortar become a reality?

Kristen Bailey

Souper Mum

Monday morning can't get any worse for harassed mum-of-four Jools Campbell when, after a frantic school run, she's cornered in the supermarket by pompous celebrity chef Tommy McCoy, who starts criticising the contents of her trolley. Apparently the fact that she doesn't make her own bread or buy organic is tantamount to child abuse. In a hurry and short of patience, she berates McCoy for judging her when she hasn't the time or the money to feed her family in line with his elitist ideals.

Unbeknownst to Jools, her rant has been filmed and immediately goes viral on YouTube, making her a reluctant celebrity overnight. With McCoy determined to discredit her by delving into her personal life, Jools decides it's time to fight her corner in the name of all the fraught mums out there who are fed up with being made to feel bad by food snobs like him. Armed with some fish fingers and her limited cooking repertoire, Jools must negotiate the unfamiliar world of celebrity while staying true to her instincts as a mum.

Jo Bartlett

Somebody Else's Boy

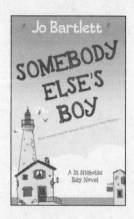

Will Nancy and Jack be allowed to embrace the future, or will their histories forever bind them to the past?

Drama teacher Nancy O'Brien puts her ambitions on hold to support her family, and returns to her idyllic seaside home town, St Nicholas Bay. Jack has his own reasons for heading to the Bay; a young widower desperate to come to terms with his loss, he hopes setting up home there with baby son, Toby, might just enable him to survive the future.

As Nancy and Jack become closer, not everyone is thrilled, in particular Toby's grandmother, who can't bear to see her late daughter 'replaced'. When Spencer – the only man Nancy's ever really loved – reappears, her living arrangements with Jack seem set for disaster.

Karen King

I do? - Or do I?

Local journalist Cassie is getting married to hot-shot, reliable Timothy and his mother Sylvia nicknamed 'Monster-in-Law' wants to plan the entire wedding. When Sylvia books the exclusive ID Images to take photographs of the extravagant do, Cassie has no idea what she's walking into.

The elusive JM, ID Images' newest photographer, just so happens to be Jared, Cassie's first love and ex-fiancé, who broke off their engagement to travel and take photos of far-reaching wonders. He's back to pay for his next wild adventure.

Cassie decides it's best to pretend not to know him, but when she's asked to write an article for her newspaper, she's tasked with a column surrounding all things wedding related. When Cassie jokingly writes a column meant for herself depicting her situation, a co-worker submits it in place of the real article and it's soon making headlines, with readers asking the age old question - Who Will She Choose?

Rosie Orr

Something Blue

Anna has a grown-up son, an ex-husband somewhere in Australia, and a feckless married lover. Sporting new scarlet underwear, and not much else, she is horrified to open her door one afternoon not to lover Jack but to son Sam and his girlfriend. They have come to announce their engagement – and to tell her that their wedding is only weeks away!

Anna is soon in the throes of preparations for a traditional Irish wedding: keeping at bay the Versace-wearing mother of the bride, dealing with the return of her ex-husband, and wondering whether Jack will ever have the gumption to leave his wife. And then the big day arrives, bringing hotel cats, destroyed crème brûlée and a surprisingly attractive photographer…

Debby Holt

The Soulmate

A novel about love, loss and starting again.

Widower Henry Drummond is marking time, drifting towards retirement, until he accidentally saves a life.

His daughter Maddie is at a wedding with the love of her life. But he is the groom and she is not the bride.

They both decide they need to change their lives, preferably with a soulmate by their sides. But as Henry's mother tells him, 'Love is a complicated business and it is not for the easily discouraged.' Strange encounters, humiliations and excitements come along and romance keeps eluding them. Soon family crises get in the way. But their quest has taken on a life of its own, with surprising consequences for all concerned.